Why Another Intermediate Microeco[...]

A Note to Our Colleagues

Microeconomics is the closest thing economics has to a canon. It comprises the essential base of knowledge for all the various forms and extensions of the discipline. Our mission in writing a textbook for the intermediate course: to help a student grow from someone who has learned some economic principles to someone who can use economics as an economist does, applying the tools of economic analysis to any circumstance. When done the right way, economics is extremely useful: useful for business, useful for policy, useful for life. We have strived to write a book of useful economics.

We looked at the major intermediate microeconomics texts and wanted something different. We felt these books, while often well done, have not fully kept up with the dramatic rise of empirical work in the applied microeconomics research. We think undergraduates and business school students will find a microeconomics text compelling if it explains the theory, demonstrates how to use it, and provides real-world data to back it up. Our goal has been to combine an accessible and clear writing style with current, vivid, and occasionally quirky examples to help all readers see the beauty, power, utility, and practicality of economic thinking.

Ultimately, any text is only a tool and a complement to what students learn in the classroom and from one another. We hope that this text will help you to start them on that journey to using economics.

Austan Goolsbee   **Steven Levitt**   **Chad Syverson**

Annotated Contents for the Complete *Microeconomics*

The preferences of consumers (demand) combine with the decisions of firms (supply) to determine the quantity sold and price of goods. The benefits of market transactions at this price are split between consumers and producers. Many factors and policies can alter market outcomes.

How do consumers decide which goods, and how much of each, to consume, in the face of an enormous set of goods and services from which they can purchase?

How do companies decide which combination of inputs to use in production, and how does this decision affect their costs of production? Cost curves show how costs change with a firm's output level and are crucial in determining what a market's supply side looks like.

In perfect competition, all firms take the market price as given, and industry supply reflects the aggregation of the cost curves of individual firms. Industry supply combines with market demand to determine price and quantity movements in the short and long term.

In a monopoly, a firm has the ability to choose at what price it sells its product and this ability implies that the monopolist chooses to produce less than the competitive industry does. Pricing power can be exerted on the market in many ways, including schemes that charge higher prices to consumers with a greater willingness to pay.

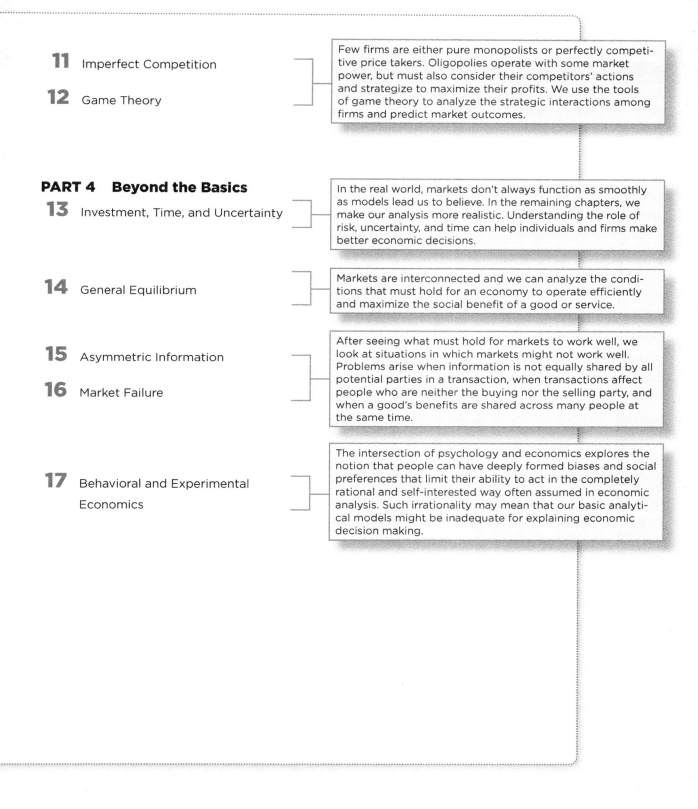

Examples and Applications
for Chapters 1–11

The empirical and applied approach to teaching and learning in Goolsbee, Levitt, and Syverson's *Microeconomics* is shown in this listing of features.

10 Market Power and Pricing Strategies

11 Imperfect Competition

Using *Microeconomics*

Intermediate microeconomics is the course that decides majors and introduces the tools that are fundamental to effective decision making in business, government, and everyday life. *Microeconomics* bridges the gap between the theory and practice of microeconomics. In a course that is too often overwhelmingly theoretical, *Microeconomics* provides an empirical dimension that will make the course immediately relevant and useful to students. *Microeconomics* provides examples that offer unusual perspective on the seemingly ordinary. With carefully crafted features, the text moves students from understanding the basics of economic principles to applying the powerful and revelatory tools of economic analysis. See below and the pages following for examples of these features, as well as readers' reactions to them.

theory and data

Theory and Data discussions summarize research and provide an empirical dimension, revealing how economic theory relates to real-world data.

Golfers' Backward-Bending Labor Supply Curves

Tiger Woods is perhaps the most recognizable face in professional golf. He's won 71 PGA tour events and picked up 14 Majors. He's lent his name to campaigns for Nike and Titleist—and taken home a cool $40 million and $20 million, respectively, for the work. But it's not just his athletic skill that separates him from the average American laborer: He's probably one of the few people facing wages on the backward-bending portion of his labor supply curve. In other words, as his wages increase, he actually decreases the number of tournaments in which he plays.

PGA rules allow each golfer to elect which and how many events to play in, meaning the athlete considers the labor–leisure tradeoff separately for each tournament event. With tournament payoffs in the millions of dollars for just four rounds of golf, you probably think it a no-brainer to play. Indeed, for most golfers, it is. Generally, around 100 players sign up for any given event. This doesn't even include the over 1,000 hopefuls who play in brutal qualifying rounds, vying for just 25 spots on the PGA Tour.

Given the opportunity, these hopefuls would gladly play every tournament, but as economists Otis Gilley and Marc Chopin discovered, players like Tiger Woods don't.* In a 2000 paper, Gilley and Chopin looked at how low- and middle-income PGA players in the 1990s responded to increases in their wages and compared this result to the effects of wage increases on high-income players. Whereas low-level players entered more events as their event winnings increased, golfers at the top of their game decreased their tournament play as their wages increased. Top golfers were actually operating on the backward-bending portion of their labor supply curve! In particular, for every $1,000 increase in expected per-event winnings, the number of tournaments entered in a season by high-income players decreases by 0.05 to 0.1. For these select players, the income effect dominated the substitution effect, and faced with the leisure–labor tradeoff, they elected to consume more leisure.

Workers in other fields—including many economists—often spend their leisure time on the golf course. But for a professional golfer, a day on the green is work, not leisure. So just what does a PGA player do on his day off? Gilley and Chopin found that married golfers took more days off than did single golfers. Drawing on their own experiences as family men, the two hard-working economists concluded that golfers must be taking off work to spend more quality time with their wives and kids. The example of Tiger Woods, however, shows that the predictions of economic theory don't always hold up in the real world.

---

* Otis W. Gilley and Marc C. Chopin, "Professional Golf: Labor or Leisure." *Managerial Finance* 26, no. 7 (2000): 33–45.

"Students often complain about the abstractness of course material. Theory and Data examples will convince students of the relevance of the subject matter and show students how theory translates into the real world."

—*Marie Rekkas, Simon Fraser University*

"[T]he authors have done an exceptional job in general of finding current and interesting research related to the topics discussed in the chapters."

—*Paul Hettler, California University of Pennsylvania*

(see page 5-25)

Goolsbee   Levitt   Syverson

application

The Cost of the Black-Liquor Loophole

A recent example of an (accidental) subsidy gone awry is the so-called black-liquor loophole in the law that gave companies tax credits for using alternative fuels. The tax credit is given to businesses that combine alternative fuels with traditional fossil fuels used in their operations, with the idea of encouraging companies to reduce their fossil fuel use in doing so.

It turns out that there is a chemical by-product of paper making called "black liquor" that paper companies have traditionally recycled to use as fuel in their plants. The government determined that this chemical qualified as an alternative fuel under the definition in the law. However, the paper companies couldn't qualify for the tax credit unless they *combined* the alternative fuel with a fossil fuel. So they started adding a bit of diesel fuel—a fossil fuel they weren't using at all before—to the black liquor before burning it. This led to two results. First, paper companies used more diesel than they did before, even though the point of the tax credit was to encourage movement away from use of fossil fuels. Second, paper companies got paid (in the form of tax credits) to burn the black liquor they were already using without payment. They got paid a lot too: This tax credit, originally projected to cost the government $61 million, ended up costing an estimated $6 to $8 *billion* in tax credits in 2009, almost all of it going to paper companies.

How does our analysis in this section explain what happened? The tax credit became, in practice, a diesel subsidy for the paper industry. By tying the credit to the use of blended fuels, it lowered the effective price of diesel that the paper companies faced. Before, when they had to pay the market price, their quantity demanded for diesel to fuel their plants was zero—they had a plentiful and cheap alternative in the black liquor. But now every gallon of diesel they bought came with a big tax credit attached—meaning they faced a downward-shifted supply curve for diesel. The quantity of diesel they demanded at these lower supply prices became positive.

As a result of this policy, the paper companies and the diesel sellers are better off because of the subsidy. (The former very much so in this case.) But the costs are large. First, there is deadweight loss: An industry that wasn't using diesel before because it had a superior alternative now demands it, even though the industry values it at less than the cost of supplying it. Second, the government has to pay the subsidy. And as noted above, that's a really big number. So big, in fact, that Congress closed the loophole in 2010 because they decided that we couldn't afford it. ∎

(see page 3-42)

freakonomics

Even Animals Like Sales

If you think the laws of economics only apply to humans, think again. Monkeys, and even rats, behave in ways that would make you think they've taken intermediate micro.

Some of the most intensive testing of the economic behavior of animals was carried out by Yale economist Keith Chen and his co-authors on a group of Capuchin monkeys. As a first step, Chen introduced the monkeys to the concept of money. He gave them "money" in the form of metal washers that they could exchange for various types of foods including Jell-O, grapes, and Marshmallow Fluff (Capuchin monkeys *love* sweet foods).

After about six exasperating months, these monkeys finally figured out that the washers had value. Chen observed that individual monkeys tended to have stable preferences: Some liked grapes the best, others were fans of Jell-O. How did he learn this? He would give a particular monkey a coin and then offer that monkey a choice between a bowl of three Jell-O cubes and a bowl of six grapes and see which one the monkey chose.

Next, Chen did what any good economist would do: He subjected the monkeys to price changes! Instead of getting three Jell-O cubes for one washer, he would offer the monkey, say, the choice between a single Jell-O cube per washer and a bowl of six grapes per washer. Thus, the relative price of Jell-O became three times as high. The monkeys responded exactly the way economic theory would predict, shifting their consumption away from the goods whose prices had risen.[*]

Perhaps it is not that surprising that monkeys, one of our closest relatives in the animal kingdom, would be sophisticated consumers. But there is no way rats understand supply and demand, is there? It seems they do. Economists Raymond Battalio and John Kagel equipped rats' cages with two levers, each of which dispensed a different beverage.[†] One of these levers gave the rat a refreshing burst of root beer. Rats, it turns out, love root beer. The other lever released quinine water. Quinine is a bitter-tasting substance initially used to treat malaria, and now used primarily to give vodka tonics their distinctive flavor. Rats are far less fond of quinine than they are of root beer, and they made that quite clear to the researchers by pressing the root beer lever far more often. Battalio and Kagel, like Chen, then explored changes in "prices" (how much liquid came out per press of the lever) and in the rats' budget constraint (how many times they could press the levers each day). Like monkeys (and humans), the rats consumed less of a drink when its relative price increased. Even more interesting is that when the rats were made very poor (i.e., they got very few lever presses each day), they shifted their consumption away from root beer toward quinine water. The researchers found that root beer is a luxury good for rats, and quinine water is an inferior good! Wonder what rats would make of a vodka tonic. . . .

Just Like Us?

Courtesy M. Keith Chen

[*] That wasn't the only human-like behavior these monkeys exhibited when exposed to money — for the whole amusingly sordid story, see the epilogue to *SuperFreakonomics*.

[†] A description of the work by Battalio and Kagel may be found in: Tim Harford, *The Logic of Life: The Rational Economics of an Irrational World* (New York: Random House, 2008), pp. 18–21.

(see page 5-12)

2.1 figure it out

Suppose that the demand and supply curves for a monthly cell phone plan with unlimited texts can be represented by

$$Q^D = 50 - 0.5P$$
$$Q^S = -25 + P$$

The current price of these plans in the market is $40 per month. Is this market in equilibrium? Would you expect the price to rise or fall? If so, by how much? Explain.

Solution:

There are two ways to solve the first question about whether the price will rise or fall. The first is to calculate the quantity demanded and quantity supplied at the current market price of $40 to see how they compare:

$$Q^D = 50 - 0.5P = 50 - 0.5(40) = 50 - 20 = 30$$
$$Q^S = -25 + P = -25 + 40 = 15$$

Because quantity demanded is greater than quantity supplied, we can tell that there is excess demand (a shortage) in the market. Many people are trying to get texting plans, but are finding them sold out because few suppliers want to sell at that price. Prices will rise to equalize quantity supplied and quantity demanded, moving the market to equilibrium.

Alternatively, we could start by solving for the market equilibrium price:

$$Q^D = Q^S$$
$$50 - 0.5P = -25 + P$$
$$1.5P = 75$$
$$P = \$50$$

The current market price, $40, is below the market equilibrium price of $50. (This is why there is excess demand in the market.) Therefore, we would expect the price to rise by $10. When the market reaches equilibrium at a price of $50, all buyers can find sellers and all sellers can find buyers. The price will then remain at $50 unless the market changes and the demand curve or supply curve shifts.

"This feature is extremely important in my opinion. I would definitely use it in class and assign similar problems for homework."

—*Nara Mijid,*
Central Connecticut State
University

"Love the Figure It Out! I think that this is a great addition to the text. The problems are also not so easy that the students [wouldn't] need help on them."

—*Jennifer VanGilder,*
Ursinus University

(see page 2-16)

make the grade

Does quantity supplied equal quantity demanded in equilibrium?

Solving for the market equilibrium as we just did is one of the most common exam questions in intermediate microeconomics classes. The basic idea is always the same: Take the equations for the demand curve and the supply curve, solve for the equilibrium price, and then plug that equilibrium price back into either the supply curve or the demand curve (it does not matter which) to determine the equilibrium quantity. It is simple, but it is easy to make math errors under the time pressure of an exam, especially if the demand and supply curves take on more complicated forms than the basic examples we deal with here.

A simple trick will ensure that you have the right answer, and it only takes a few seconds. Take the equilibrium price that you obtain and plug it into *both* the demand and supply curves. If you don't get the same answer when you substitute the equilibrium price into the supply and demand equations, you know you made a math error along the way because the quantity demanded must equal the quantity supplied in equilibrium.

(see page 2-14)

An Intuitive and Optional Presentation of Calculus

For instructors who wish to present key concepts with calculus, the text offers calculus appendices to accompany five chapters:

Chapter 4: The Calculus of Utility Maximization and Expenditure Minimization

Chapter 5: The Calculus of Income and Substitution Effects

Chapter 6: The Calculus of Cost Minimization

Chapter 7: The Calculus of a Firm's Cost Structure

Chapter 9: The Calculus of Profit Maximization

There are also additional appendices available online. For a list, please visit iLikeiMic.com.

All the calculus appendices employ the same conversational tone and intuitive approach as the text, helping students familiar with calculus take their understanding of microeconomics further. Each appendix includes examples and Figure It Out problems, often the same as those used in the chapter. To give students an opportunity to practice what they have learned, each appendix includes additional problems that require the use of calculus.

5.A figure it out

A sample problem will make breaking down the total effect of a price change into the substitution and income effects even clearer. Let's return to Figure It Out 4.4, which featured Antonio, a consumer who purchases burgers and fries. Antonio has a utility function $U(B,F) = B^{0.5}F^{0.5}$ and income of $20. Initially, the prices of burgers and fries are $5 and $2, respectively.

a. What is Antonio's optimal consumption bundle and utility at the original prices?

b. The price of burgers increases to $10 per burger, and the price of fries stays constant at $2. What does Antonio consume at the optimum at these new prices? Decompose this change into the total, substitution, and income effects.

Solution:

a. We solved this question in the Chapter 4 Appendix, but the answer will be crucial to solving for the total, substitution, and income effects in part (b). When a burger costs $5 and fries cost $2, Antonio's original constrained optimization problem is

$$\max_{B,F} B^{0.5}F^{0.5} \ s.t. 20 = 5B + 2F$$

We found that Antonio consumes 2 burgers and 5 orders of fries, and his utility for this bundle is $B^{0.5}F^{0.5} = 5^{0.5}2^{0.5} = 10^{0.5}$.

b. When the price of hamburgers doubles to $10 each, Antonio faces a new budget constraint: $20 = 10B + 2F$. Antonio's new utility-maximization problem is

$$\max_{B,F} B^{0.5}F^{0.5} \ s.t. 20 = 10B + 2F$$

Therefore, we should write his constrained optimization problem as a Lagrangian and solve for his new optimal bundle at the higher burger price:

$$\max_{B,F,\lambda} \mathcal{L} = B^{0.5}F^{0.5} + \lambda(20 = 10B + 2F)$$

$$\frac{\partial \mathcal{L}}{\partial B} = 0.5B^{-0.5}F^{0.5} - 10\lambda = 0$$

$$\frac{\partial \mathcal{L}}{\partial F} = 0.5B^{0.5}F^{-0.5} - 2\lambda = 0$$

$$\frac{\partial \mathcal{L}}{\partial \lambda} = 20 - 10B - 2F = 0$$

Then we use the first two conditions to solve for λ and then solve for F as a function of B:

$$\lambda = 0.05B^{-0.5}F^{0.5} = 0.25B^{0.5}F^{-0.5}$$

$$F^{0.5}F^{0.5} = 20(0.25)B^{0.5}B^{0.5}$$

$$F = 5B$$

microeconomics

Austan Goolsbee
The University of Chicago Booth School of Business

Steven Levitt
The University of Chicago

Chad Syverson
The University of Chicago Booth School of Business

Worth Publishers

Senior Vice President, Editorial and Production: Catherine Woods
Publisher: Charles Linsmeier
Senior Acquisitions Editor: Sarah Dorger
Media and Supplements Editors: Jaclyn Ferry, Lukia Kliossis
Developmental Editors: Jane Tufts, Bruce Kaplan
Consulting Faculty Editor: Linda Ghent
Assistant Editor: Mary Melis
Marketing Manager: Scott Guile
Market Development Manager: Steven Rigolosi
Associate Market Development Manager: Kerri Russini
Marketing Assistant: Julie Tompkins, Lindsay Neff
Art Directors: Babs Reingold, Kevin Kall
Interior Designer: Amanda Kavanagh
Photo Editor: Ted Szczepanski
Director of Development for Print and Digital Products: Tracey Kuehn
Associate Managing Editor: Lisa Kinne
Project Editor: Robert Errera
Production Manager: Barbara Seixas
Composition: TSI Graphics
Printing and Binding: RR Donnelley

Library of Congress Control Number: 2012940039

ISBN-13: 978-1-4641-2901-8 (DocuTech)
ISBN-10: 1-4641-2901-0 (DocuTech)
ISBN-13: 978-1-4641-0689-7 (CourseSmart)
ISBN-10: 1-4641-0689-4 (CourseSmart)

Printed in the United States of America

First printing 2012

Worth Publishers
41 Madison Avenue
New York, NY 10010
www.worthpublishers.com

about the authors

This breakthrough text revitalizes the intermediate microeconomics course by focusing on the tools people need to make better decisions in business and in their lives. The authors make the core concepts underlying the field real and relevant, answering the question, "How could you actually use this for something?" with the latest empirical work and memorable, meaningful examples.

The Authors

Austan Goolsbee is the Robert P. Gwinn Professor of Economics at the University of Chicago Booth School of Business. He earned a bachelor's and a master's degree from Yale University and a PhD in economics from the Massachusetts Institute of Technology. Goolsbee's work focuses on the new economy, government policy, taxes, and technology. He was appointed chairman of the Council of Economic Advisers in 2010, returning to the University of Chicago in August 2011. Goolsbee serves as a member of the U.S. Census Advisory Committee and as a research fellow for the American Bar Foundation.

Steven Levitt is the William B. Ogden Distinguished Service Professor of Economics at the University of Chicago, where he directs the Becker Center on Chicago Price Theory. He earned a bachelor's degree from Harvard University and his PhD from Massachusetts Institute of Technology. He has taught at the University of Chicago since 1997. In 2004, Levitt was awarded the John Bates Clark Medal, and in 2006, he was named one of *Time* magazine's "100 People Who Shape Our World." He co-authored *Freakonomics* and *SuperFreakonomics*, and he is also the co-author of the popular *Freakonomics* blog.

Chad Syverson is Professor of Economics at the University of Chicago Booth School of Business. His research spans several topics, with a particular focus on the interactions of firm structure, market structure, and productivity. His work has earned multiple National Science Foundation awards. He serves on the editorial boards of several economics and business journals and is a research associate of the National Bureau of Economic Research. He earned bachelor's degrees in economics and mechanical engineering from the University of North Dakota and a PhD in economics from the University of Maryland. Syverson joined the Chicago faculty in 2001.

brief contents

This volume contains chapters 1–11 only of *Microeconomics* by Goolsbee, Levitt, and Syverson.

contents

contents

contents

contents

contents

contents

contents

contents

contents

contents

contents

Adventures in Microeconomics

It is morning in Peru's Selva Alta hills, and the sun has been up for a few hours. Rosa Valencia looks admiringly at the coffee plants she's grown. The coffee plants' fruits, called *cherries* because of the red hue they take on when ripe, are ready for harvest. Rosa's workers handpick the fruit and carry it to the outbuilding where it is processed. There, other workers sort the cherries, then remove the fruits' flesh to expose the two seeds—the coffee beans—inside. The beans are washed and prepared for drying and roasting.

That same morning, about 4,000 miles away in Toronto, Lauren Russell struggles with a physics problem. She's at her favorite coffee shop, a block off campus, for her mid-morning break. Sitting on the table next to her book is her usual, a skinny cappuccino. Every few moments, between calculations, Lauren takes a sip and savors the deep, rich flavor of the coffee.

Lauren and Rosa have never met each other, nor are they ever likely to. Yet, their morning routines are connected to one another because the two women are part of the same market, the market for coffee. Lauren's preferences for her study break beverage connect her to Rosa, who provides a critical input to that drink. Both women benefit from this connection: Rosa profits from growing coffee and Lauren gets a cappuccino at a price she is willing to pay. This is microeconomics at work.

1.1 Microeconomics (and What It Can Teach Us about Rosa and Lauren)

Lauren and Rosa's connection is the consequence of almost innumerable decisions and transactions that combine to make Rosa believe that growing coffee is worth her time and effort and to deliver Lauren's cappuccino at a price she is willing to pay. This book is about investigating those many decisions and transactions, and how they interact in markets.

Before we delve deeper into this book's topics, we need to be very clear about how we're going to approach the study of markets. We will be looking at these decisions through the framework of *micro*economics. **Microeconomics** is the branch of economics that studies the specific choices made by individuals (like Lauren) and firms (like Rosa's coffee plantation). In contrast, *macro*economics looks at the world through a wider lens and is a description of the larger, complex system in which consumers and firms operate. Macroeconomics takes hundreds of millions of individuals like Rosa and Lauren, and tries to describe and predict the aggregation of their individual decisions. In this book, we steer clear of the macroeconomic questions.

microeconomics
The branch of economics that studies the specific choices made by individuals and firms.

Learning the Tools of Microeconomics

Microeconomics can't address every question about the economy, but it does provide the tools necessary to answer a dazzling number of questions about the choices individuals and firms make. The set of tools microeconomics gives you can be used to solve almost any economic problem an individual person or firm faces.

What sorts of tools will we be learning to use as we explore the study of microeconomics? We always start with *theories* and *models*, explanations of how things work that help us understand and predict how and why economic entities (consumers, producers, industries, governments, etc.) behave as they do. To learn the intricacies of the theories and models, we use the tools of graphs and mathematics.

Then we use theories and models to look at how people and firms actually behave in a huge variety of economic (and some seemingly noneconomic) situations. Studying the interaction between microeconomic theory and the events, decisions, and empirical data from the real world involves an additional set of tools in the study of microeconomics. Each chapter includes the following sections that illustrate this interaction:

■ *Application* sections help us understand theory at work by showing how microeconomics can be used to inform economic decision making in a variety of interesting, real-world situations. Want to know how members of OPEC decide how much oil to produce? Or, how the NBA sets contracts for rookie players? Or, how and why consumers and producers act as they do in the markets for housing, movies, electricity generation, corn, satellite radio, music, and concrete? *Applications* delve into the specifics of how consumers and producers act in real life.

■ *Theory and Data* sections look at current microeconomic research to see how the data gathered by microeconomists inform and test the predictions of theory across a wide range of topics such as golf tournaments, phone service, cigarette smoking among college graduates, the use of gym memberships, the relation between hospital input choices and Medicare, and determining the market for a new (legal) drug.

■ *Freakonomics* essays reveal the surprising ways in which economic analysis provides a unique perspective for exploring a huge variety of phenomena in the world around us. These essays look at topics as diverse as a homemade toaster, White House photography, football stadiums, Indian fishermen's cell phones, cheating, blackmail, the illegal drug industry, and Victoria's Secret pricing. Such stories give us a framework for thinking about the economic phenomena that surround us.

freakonomics

Thomas Thwaites's Toaster

Thomas Thwaites must really like toast.

Not content simply to buy a toaster to make his toast, in 2009 Thwaites set out on a mission to make a toaster from scratch. He started with the raw materials, gathering copper, mica, nickel, and oil (to make plastic), some of which he extracted himself from abandoned mines in the English countryside. He even figured out a way to turn his microwave into a smelter in order to forge the iron parts needed for the toaster's grill and spring. In the end, his homemade contraption was indeed capable of making toast about as well as the cheapest toaster you can buy at Walmart for under $20. If you factor in time, effort, and money spent, Thwaites' toaster cost thousands of times more to make than the store-bought version.

A very expensive custom-built toaster.

Courtesy Thomas Thwaites

It should not have come as a surprise to Thwaites that making a toaster from scratch would be hard work, at least not if he knows anything about economics. Think about the goods and services you've consumed so far just *today,* and all the different materials, technology, workmanship, and coordination that went into making them. The modern economy is nothing short of miraculous. All of us—Thwaites included—have become completely dependent on the market's amazing ability to deliver a nearly infinite variety of products to us at a tiny fraction of the cost and effort it would cost us to produce them ourselves.

Compared to other things we use as consumers, a toaster is fairly simple. Imagine trying to build a computer or an automobile completely from scratch, starting from the rawest materials. Even making your own dinner, if you had to grow the food, would be life-consuming.

No doubt Thomas Thwaites' toaster experiment taught him—the hard way—about the modern economy. If his goal is to learn economics, we suggest a different approach the next time he gets a craving, say, for ice cream. Rather than raising cows, growing sugar cane, and hand-harvesting vanilla beans, we suggest he visit his local convenience store and enjoy some store-bought ice cream while he finishes reading Chapter 2 of this book.

Using the Tools of Microeconomics

Here's a very old joke: One day, a tourist in New York City asked a passer-by: "How do you get to Carnegie Hall?" and the New Yorker replied, "Practice, practice, practice."

That's how you excel in your microeconomics course too: practice, practice, practice. You need plenty of experience with wielding the tools of microeconomics to become good at it, and there's plenty of help on this front as you go through each chapter.

- In each chapter, you will find several worked out problems titled *Figure It Out*. These problems are typical of the problems you will encounter in your homework sets, quizzes, and exams, and they appear throughout the chapters to illustrate how to translate your understanding of theory, graphs, and mathematics into successful problem-solving skills. Each Figure It Out shows, step-by-step, how to understand what, exactly, a problem is asking you to do, and then how, exactly, to solve it using the tools you've just learned.

- At the end of each chapter, you will find a set of *Problems* to solve. The variety of problems will prepare you well for excelling at applying the tools you've learned to new situations, scenarios, and dilemmas.

- In many chapters, you will find a *Make the Grade* box with hints and explanations about how to successfully navigate the sometimes-confusing pathways through microeconomic theory, application, and practice.

1.2 This Book (and How Rosa and Lauren Would See It)

We begin our investigation of microeconomics with an overview of how the preferences of consumers like Lauren (the demand side of a market) combine with the decisions of firms like Rosa's coffee plantation (the supply side) to determine the quantity sold and price of goods such as coffee. We explore, for example, why consumers' and suppliers' responses to price changes differ, and how these differences affect what happens when consumer preferences or production technologies change. And we see how the benefits of a market transaction, such as buying a cappuccino, are split between consumers (like Lauren) and producers (like the coffee shop and Rosa).

Consumers' and Producers' Decisions

After this overview, the next section of the book digs a lot deeper into each side of the market, starting with consumers' decisions. Lauren could have had some drink other than coffee that morning—tea, milk, juice, or a smoothie—or she could have done something completely different with her time and money, such as go to McDonald's for an Egg McMuffin or download a few songs from iTunes. What determines how often she has coffee instead of tea, or how often she goes to a coffeehouse instead of somewhere else? If Lauren becomes richer, will her choices change? We answer the question of how consumers decide which goods, and how much of each, to consume, in the face of the enormous numbers of goods and services they are offered. Then we see how adding up these decisions across all consumers gives us the total market demand curve.

After investigating consumer behavior in detail, we explore questions dealing with producers' decisions. For example, how do companies like Rosa's plantation decide which combination of inputs such as agricultural machinery (capital), hired hands (labor), and fertilizer (materials) to use in production? As we see, it turns out that those types of decisions for firms are similar in many respects to the decisions consumers make when deciding what products to buy.

Once we've described firms' input mix choices, we look at how these affect their costs of production. We pay particular attention to how these costs change with a firm's output level, as embodied in firms' cost curves. If Rosa doubles her production, for example, will her total costs double, more than double, or less than double? We focus on cost movements as a firm's output changes because they are crucial in determining what a market's supply side looks like.

Market Supply Structures

Speaking of supply sides, the book's next section will compare many possible configurations of market supply. We start with the canonical case of perfect competition. In a perfectly competitive market, all firms take the market price as given (they don't have any ability to choose the price they can sell their products at) and decide how much they want to produce. This is close to Rosa's case. The international coffee market is large and decentralized, so how much coffee she decides to put on the market is not going to noticeably move its market price. We see how in this situation industry supply reflects the aggregation of the cost curves of Rosa and every other coffee plantation, and how industry supply combines with market demand to determine price and quantity movements over both the short and long runs.

After perfect competition, we move to the other extreme: monopoly. When only one firm is selling to a market, the situation differs in several ways from perfect competition. The key distinction is that the firm now has the ability to choose what price it sells its products at. We see that this ability implies that if Rosa were a monopolist selling to the world's coffee consumers, she would choose to produce less than the competitive industry does—even if she had the capacity necessary to do so. This is because doing so would raise the price she could sell her coffee at. We see why governments might want to (and sometimes do) step into such situations using antitrust laws. Next, we discuss other ways monopolists use their pricing power. This includes schemes that charge higher prices to consumers with a greater willingness to pay, or combining products together and selling them as a single bundle to consumers.

In the book's final look at market supply-side structures, we investigate oligopolies. Oligopolies exist when multiple firms interact strategically in the same market. In such markets, firms have some ability to choose their prices, but their fortunes are determined, in part, by the actions of the other firms in the market. (They dish it out as well as they take it, though: Their own actions impact other firms as well.) These sorts of situations are common; few firms are either pure monopolists or perfectly competitive price takers. Strategic interactions among firms raise all sorts of interesting questions that we can analyze using the tools of game theory. For example, how might we expect a firm like Lauren's favorite coffee shop to respond to a price cut by a competing shop down the street? Or, how would it react if a new coffeehouse were considering opening across the street?

Beyond the Basics

After these detailed looks at the basics of markets' supply and demand sides, we study several specific subjects in the final section of the book. The economic concepts covered here are present in many markets. In some applications, these concepts deepen our understanding of markets by supplementing the basic analytical structure we introduce in the first parts of the book. In other cases, the basic structure may be inadequate to grasp all the necessary elements of economic interactions, so these concepts will be absolutely necessary to understand the behavior of particular markets.

The first specific topic we explore is the combined role of risk, uncertainty, and time in economic decision making. These features are especially prominent in investment decisions—choices that typically involve paying an upfront cost with the hope of earning a future return—so these decisions are a focus of our exploration. Understanding risk, uncertainty, and time's interactions in investment choices helps us answer questions such as whether Rosa should invest in a new bean-drying facility, or whether Lauren should go to graduate school.

Next, we explore how markets are interconnected. Changes in the supply or demand of one good can lead indirectly to similar or opposite shifts in other markets. After studying this interconnectedness, we can see how a supply disruption in China's tea-growing areas can raise the price at which Rosa can sell her coffee and the price that Lauren must pay for her cappuccino. Once we're able to tie markets together, we can analyze the conditions that must hold for an economy to operate efficiently. For example, are producers supplying the "right" mix of coffee and tea, and doing so at the lowest possible cost? Being able to answer such questions allows us to determine whether markets are working to maximize the social benefit of a good or service.

After seeing what must hold for markets to work well, we look in detail at a series of situations in which markets might *not* work well. One set of situations involves markets in which information about tastes, costs, or product quality is not equally shared by all potential parties in a transaction. For example, if Rosa wants to buy a used tractor for the plantation, she wouldn't know with 100% accuracy how well the tractor works before buying it, and she might be especially concerned that the current owner was selling the tractor precisely *because* it didn't operate up to par. How does this lack of accurate information affect her decision? Or, if Lauren wants to convince a potential employer she would be a hard-working employee before she gets the job, how might she do it?

A second set of situations in which markets may not operate efficiently includes transactions that affect people who are neither the buying nor the selling party, or markets in which a good's benefits are shared across many people at the same time. An example would be Rosa's decision whether or not to apply pesticides to her crop. Doing so would not only affect the economics of her own operation, but would also have spillover effects on others. A neighboring coffee plantation might benefit from facing a smaller population of local insects, for instance. On the other hand, other neighbors, workers, and maybe coffee consumers could be harmed by the chemical pollution that pesticide use involves. What makes these situations interesting—and what causes markets to have difficulty delivering the socially optimal outcome—is that Rosa is likely to take into account the pesticide's impact on her own production when deciding whether to use it or not, but is less likely to consider its effects on neighboring farms, the local population, and coffee drinkers in Toronto.

The book concludes with an exploration of behavioral economics. This study of the intersection of psychology and economics has become an increasingly prominent part of economic research. People often have deeply formed biases and social preferences that limit their ability to act in the completely rational, self-interested way that we often assume in economic analysis. If this is true, then our basic analytical structure—even when supplemented with knowledge of the deeper concepts discussed above—may be inadequate for explaining economic decision making.

Focus on Data

All of these topics provide you with microeconomic tools to study the world around you. Over the past fifty years, this set of tools has expanded and changed. Microeconomics has evolved into a more empirical discipline, that is, one that uses much more data analysis and experiments, and not just abstract theory, to explore economic phenomena. In the 1960s, if you wanted to analyze data, a slide rule (a two-piece sliding ruler used primarily for multiplication and division) was your weapon. The computing revolution changed this. As you'll learn in this book, when the price of a good (like computing) decreases, the quantity consumed of that good increases. Much more of modern-day economists' effort toward understanding the economy centers on data and measurement than before. In fact, go see your microeconomic professor during his office hours today, and you'll most likely find him typing away at his desktop computer, completing empirical research.

Let the Fun Begin!

By the end of your microeconomics course, you will have the resources necessary to examine the world as an economist does. We've already used microeconomic tools to broadly describe a very specific economic exchange between coffee producer Rosa and university student Lauren. But what's so powerful about microeconomics is that it can be applied to any market, not just to a market like the one inhabited by Rosa and Lauren. You can use microeconomics to think rationally about any of the dozens of choices (economic and noneconomic) you face each day. By the end of your study of intermediate microeconomics, you'll not only *be able to* think like an economist—you'll see *how useful it is* to think like an economist.

Supply and Demand

The pursuit of gold has driven people to extremes for centuries. Much of the initial exploration of the Americas was funded with the hope of acquiring gold. Centuries later, the discovery of gold at Sutter's Mill in Coloma, California, in 1848 triggered a gold rush that led 300,000 men, women, and children to migrate to California, turning San Francisco from a sleepy hamlet to a thriving city.

In recent years, the search for gold has taken on a decidedly modern flavor. It might surprise you to know that as many as 400,000 Chinese workers currently spend their days mining for gold. But they aren't panning for gold in a stream or working in a gold mine. Rather, they are seated in front of computer screens, logged onto online games like *World of Warcraft,* using virtual picks and axes to mine virtual gold that they sell on eBay to players willing to pay real money for the virtual gold that serves as the game's currency.

Whether the gold is real or virtual, the economic forces at work that determine its price and how much of it is "mined" are the same. In this chapter, we explore these forces, the two most powerful forces in economics: supply and demand.

Armed with an understanding of supply and demand, we can begin to tackle some of the fundamental questions in economics: How do consumers and producers interact in the market for a good or service to determine how much is sold and at what price? What happens to the market if tastes change, new technologies are invented, the government intervenes, or any one of a wide range of other forces changes?

This chapter outlines the basics of the supply and demand model. We first introduce the concept of the demand curve, which embodies consumers' desires for goods, and then move on to the supply curve, which embodies producers' willingness to make those goods available. We explain why these concepts are so useful in describing and analyzing markets, especially when we combine them to understand the concept of market equilibrium. We then analyze how equilibrium prices and quantities are influenced by the variety of forces that affect markets: consumer tastes, input prices, overall economic activity, new goods that can be substituted for an existing good, innovations that make a product easier to produce, and so on. Finally, we dig deeper and look at how quantities demanded and supplied respond to price changes, and discuss how this responsiveness affects market equilibrium.

2.1 Markets and Models

Modern economies are amazingly complex. Producers from all over the world offer a nearly unlimited number and variety of goods and services from which consumers can choose. A large supermarket will have more than 100 different kinds of cold cereal on the shelf. There are thousands of degree-granting colleges and universities. On any given day, millions of items are on sale on Amazon or eBay. With over 6 billion people in the world, each of them with different tastes and incomes, and 10s of millions of businesses that supply goods and services to these people, how do consumers decide what products, and how much of each, to buy? And how do producers know what products to produce? And who decides at what price the products sell?

Answering these questions might seem like a hopelessly complex task. Indeed, if we tried to tackle them all at once, it *would* be hopeless. Instead, we follow the economist's standard approach to complexity: Simplify the problem until it becomes manageable.

The supply and demand model represents the economist's best attempt to capture many of the key elements of real-world markets in a simple enough way to be easily analyzed. We start exploring that model by first defining what we mean by a market, and then discussing the model's most important assumptions. As you will see, the simplifying assumptions underlying the model are fairly strong. While actual markets don't often conform to all of these assumptions, the supply and demand model has proven to be remarkably useful for thinking about how an economy functions. We'll see the broad usefulness of the supply and demand model once we assemble it and put it to work.

What Is a Market?

The idea of a market is central to economics. What do we mean when we use the term "market"? In the strictest sense, a market is defined by the specific product being bought and sold (e.g., oranges or gold), a particular location (a mall, a city, or maybe the Internet), and a point in time (January 2012, maybe, or even 8:13 P.M. on January 4, 2012). In principle, the buyers in a market should be able to find the sellers in that market, and vice versa, although it might take some work (what economists call "search costs") to make that connection.

In practice, the kinds of markets we talk about tend to be much more broadly defined than these examples. They might be broader in terms of the product (e.g., fruit or groceries rather than oranges), the location (often we consider all of North America or even the world as the geographic market), or the time period (the year 2012 rather than a specific day). These broader markets often have more general interest and more data to analyze, but as we will see, defining markets this broadly makes the assumptions of the supply and demand model less likely to hold. Thus, we face a tradeoff between studying small, less consequential markets that closely match the underlying assumptions and broader, more important markets that do not match our assumptions well.

Now that we have defined a market, we are ready to tackle the key assumptions underlying the supply and demand model.

Key Assumptions of the Supply and Demand Model

There are four basic assumptions that underpin our development of the supply and demand model. Table 2.1 summarizes these assumptions. You will notice that the assumptions of the supply and demand model are in many cases very unrealistic, and few of the markets you participate in satisfy all these assumptions. It turns out, however, that a strength of this model is that when some (or even most) of the specific assumptions of the model fail, it still manages to provide a good description of how markets work in the real world. No model is perfect, but the supply and demand model has survived the test of time and is the workhorse of economics because of its flexibility and broad applicability. Developing a deep understanding of the basic supply and demand model is one of the most important tools you can have as an economist, even if the model does not perfectly fit every market. Plus, economics isn't completely wedded to the most stringent form of the model. Much of the rest of this book, and the field of economics more generally, are devoted to examining how changing the model's assumptions influences its predictions about market outcomes.

1. **We restrict our focus to supply and demand in a single market.** The first simplifying assumption we make is that rather than trying to tackle all markets at once, we look at how **supply** (the combined amount of a good that all producers in a market are willing to sell) and **demand** (the combined amount of a good that all consumers are willing to buy) interact in just one market to determine how much of a good or service is sold and at what price it is sold. In focusing on one market, we won't ignore other markets completely—indeed, the interaction between the markets for different kinds of products is fundamental to supply and demand. (We'll focus extensively on these interactions in Chapter 14.) For now, however, we only worry about other markets to the extent that they influence the market we're studying. In particular, we ignore the possibility that changes in the market we're studying might have spillover effects on other markets.

supply
The combined amount of a good that all producers in a market are willing to sell.

demand
The combined amount of a good that all consumers are willing to buy.

2. **All goods bought and sold in the market are identical.** We assume that all the goods bought and sold in the market are homogeneous, meaning that a consumer is just as happy with any one unit of the good (e.g., an ounce of gold or a tomato) as any other unit.[1] If we use the supply and demand model to analyze the market for "cars," it is only really a crude approximation to

Table 2.1	**The Four Key Assumptions Underlying the Supply and Demand Model**
1.	We focus on supply and demand in a single market.
2.	All goods sold in the market are identical.
3.	All goods sold in the market sell for the same price, and everyone has the same information.
4.	There are many producers and consumers in the market.

---

[1] Throughout this book, we often use the word "good" to mean both tangible goods, like trucks, computers, jewelry, and so on, and services, like haircuts, dog walking, financial planning, and so on. In this usage, anything a consumer values—tangible or not, concrete or abstract—is a good.

automobile markets in the real world. There are many different types of cars in reality, and consumers do not view them as identical. Most consumers would not be as happy with a Kia as they would be with a Ferrari sold at the same price. In the strictest sense, cars of the same make and model might not even be considered a single market. For instance, if a consumer wants only a silver Toyota Prius, then the market relevant to her is the market for silver Toyota Prii. To simplify our analyses, we often ignore such detail and treat groups of goods as though they were identical.

commodities
Products traded in markets in which consumers view different varieties of the good as essentially interchangeable.

The kinds of products that best reflect this assumption are **commodities,** which are traded in markets where consumers view different varieties of the good as essentially interchangeable. Goods such as wheat, soybeans, crude oil, nails, gold, or #2 pencils are commodities. Custom-made jewelry, the different offerings on a restaurant's menu, and wedding dresses are unlikely to be commodities; the consumer typically cares a lot about specific varieties of these goods.

3. **All goods sold in the market sell for the same price and everyone has the same information about prices, the quality of the goods being sold, and so on.** This assumption is a natural extension of the identical-goods assumption above, but it also implies that there are no special deals for particular buyers and no quantity discounts. In addition, everyone knows what everyone else is paying.

4. **There are many buyers and sellers in the market.** This assumption means that no particular consumer or producer has a noticeable impact on anything that occurs in the market and on the price level in particular. This assumption tends to be more easily justified for consumers than for producers. Think about your own consumption of bananas, for instance. If you were to stop eating bananas altogether, your decision would have almost no impact on the banana market as a whole. Likewise, if you thought you were potassium-deprived and increased your banana consumption fourfold, your effect on the market quantity and price of bananas would still be negligible. On the producer side, however, most bananas (and many other products) are produced by a few big companies. It is more likely that decisions by these firms about how much to produce or what markets to enter will substantially affect market prices and quantities. We're going to ignore that possibility for now and stick with the case of many sellers. Starting in Chapter 9, we analyze what happens in markets with one or a few sellers.

Having made these assumptions, let's see how they help us understand how markets work, looking first at demand and then at supply.

2.2 Demand

Pike Place Market, one of the best known public markets in the world, spans several blocks in the northwest corner of downtown Seattle. It has operated continually since 1907, and on any given day hosts hundreds of vendors selling everything from fish and meat to produce and flowers to crafts and antiques. The market sees approximately 10 million visitors per year.

Factors That Influence Demand

Tomatoes are a popular item for shoppers at farmers' markets like Pike Place Market. All sorts of factors influence how many tomatoes consumers purchase at the market. Let's discuss the most important.

Price   The price of tomatoes is probably the most important consideration. Few consumers would pay $40 per pound for tomatoes. At $1 a pound, however, there would be many interested customers.

The Number of Consumers   All else equal, the more people there are in a market, the greater the quantity of the good desired. If there are a lot of people visiting the market on a given day, a relatively large amount of tomatoes will be sought for purchase.

Consumer Income or Wealth   As a consumer becomes richer, he will buy more of most goods. Tomatoes (and clothes and cars and jewelry and porterhouse steaks) probably fall in that category for most people. Sometimes, however, when a consumer becomes richer, he buys less of a good. For example, he might buy a car and stop taking public transportation and might stay in nice hotels instead of youth hostels. The consumption of these goods still responds to income or wealth, but in a different direction.

Consumer Tastes   A change in consumer preferences or tastes for tomatoes (given the consumer's income and tomato prices) will change the amount of tomatoes the consumer wants to purchase. Taste changes can be driven by all sorts of forces. For example, news about the health benefits of eating tomatoes would make many consumers want to eat more of them. On the other hand, news about salmonella being found in some tomato crops will make consumers reluctant to purchase them. For other products, taste changes might arise due to a really popular advertising campaign, fads, changes in demographics, and so on.

Prices of Other Goods   Produce vendors at Pike Place Market sell other goods such as onions and peppers that consumers can use to make their salads or top their burgers. Goods that can be used in place of another good are called **substitutes.** When the price of a substitute good falls, consumers will want to buy more of it and less of the initial good. The lower the prices of onions and peppers relative to the price of tomatoes, the fewer tomatoes consumers will want to buy. We can also think of tomatoes in some other market (say, at another location, like a consumer's neighborhood grocery store) as substitutes for tomatoes at Pike Place Market. If grocery store tomatoes become cheaper, shoppers at Pike Place are going to want to buy fewer tomatoes there.

substitute
A good that can be used in place of another good.

Vendors at Pike Place Market also sell goods that consumers like to use with tomatoes. Goods that are often purchased and used in combination with a certain good are called **complements.** When the price of a complement falls, consumers will want to buy more of it and more of the initial good. There are some goods that people like to consume with tomatoes—basil, for instance, or mozzarella cheese or lettuce. If basil prices fall, consumers are likely to want to buy *more* tomatoes as a result.

complement
A good that is purchased and used in combination with another good.

The prices of substitutes and complements both affect how much of a good consumers want to buy, but they have opposite effects. A price decrease in a good's substitute will cause consumers to want less of the good; a price decrease in a good's complement will cause consumers to want more of the good.

Demand Curves

In economics, "demand" is a catch-all word that captures the many different factors that influence the willingness of consumers to purchase a good. With so many factors influencing demand, it is difficult to wrap our minds around what would happen if all those various factors changed at the same time. We simplify the problem by considering what happens to the amount consumers demand when only a good's price changes, while everything else that determines consumer demand stays the same. (Later in the chapter, we look at how changes in all the other factors that influence demand affect the quantity of a good consumers demand.)

demand curve

The relationship between the quantity of a good that consumers demand and the good's price, holding all other factors constant.

Graphical Representation of the Demand Curve   The result of this simplifying assumption is a **demand curve**. Figure 2.1 depicts a demand curve for tomatoes at the Pike Place Market. The curve shows how the quantity of tomatoes that consumers want varies with the price of tomatoes. Price is on the vertical axis and quantity demanded is on the horizontal axis. This demand curve shows that when the price of tomatoes is $5 per pound, no tomatoes are desired. At a price of $4 per pound, consumers are willing to buy 200 pounds of tomatoes. At prices of $3, $2, and $1, the quantities of tomatoes demanded rise to 400, 600, and 800 pounds, respectively.

The point about demand curves holding all factors other than price constant is so important that it is worth saying it again: A demand curve is drawn with the assumption that there is no change in *any* of the other factors—such as consumers' incomes, tastes, or the prices of other goods—that might also affect how much of a good consumers buy. This means the demand curve in Figure 2.1 embodies the results of the following thought experiment (demand curves for other goods reflect similar thought experiments specific to their own contexts). We show up at Pike Place market some weekend and observe both the price of tomatoes and the total amount that consumers buy. Imagine that we have magical powers that allow us to go back in time. We use those powers to replace the price tags on tomatoes at the market, lowering their price by $1 per pound. Then we let the weekend happen all over again—the same weather, the same visitors to the market, the same set of items on display, and so on; the only difference is that tomatoes are $1 per pound cheaper. We then count up the total amount of tomatoes consumers buy at this new price. We continue using our magic powers to keep reversing time over and over, adjusting tomato prices up and down and by a different amount each time. When we connect all of the price and quantity combinations we have collected in this way, we have a demand curve.

The demand curve in Figure 2.1 exhibits a fundamental characteristic of demand curves: They slope downward.[2] This is another way of saying that, all else equal, the lower the price of a good, the more of it consumers will buy.

Figure 2.1 : **Demand for Tomatoes**

The demand curve D_1 for tomatoes at Pike Place Market shows how the quantity of tomatoes demanded varies with the price. As the price of tomatoes decreases, consumers demand greater quantities of tomatoes, creating a downward-sloping demand curve. At a price of $5 per pound, consumers demand no tomatoes; at $4, $3, $2, and $1, consumers are willing to purchase 200, 400, 600, and 800 pounds of tomatoes, respectively.

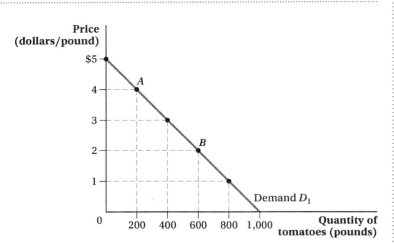

---

[2] An interesting but unusual exception to this is a Giffen good, which has an upward-sloping demand curve. We will discuss such goods in Chapter 5. Demand curves for regular (non-Giffen) goods can also sometimes be flat, as we discuss in the next section. We explore the deeper reasoning behind why demand curves usually slope down in Chapters 4 and 5.

Mathematical Representation of the Demand Curve   The demand curve in Figure 2.1 can also be represented mathematically by the equation

$$Q = 1{,}000 - 200P$$

where Q is the quantity demanded (in pounds) and P is the price (in dollars per pound). This equation implies that every \$1 per pound increase in price leads to a 200-pound decline in the quantity of tomatoes demanded.

Because of the odd condition in economics of plotting price on the vertical axis and quantity on the horizontal axis, and because it is easier to work with in certain contexts, economists often write demand curve equations in the form of the price as a function of quantity. This approach results in an **inverse demand curve**. The inverse demand curve simply rearranges the demand curve to put price in terms of quantity rather than the other way around.

We can find the inverse demand curve by solving for P:

$$Q = 1{,}000 - 200P$$

$$200P + Q = 1{,}000$$

$$200P = 1{,}000 - Q$$

$$P = 5 - 0.005Q$$

One thing this inverse demand curve makes clear is that no consumer will be willing to buy tomatoes at a price greater than \$5 per pound, because the vertical intercept of the inverse demand curve (i.e., the price when the quantity demanded Q equals zero) is \$5 per pound. This level is also called the **demand choke price.**

Shifts in Demand Curves

A given demand curve such as D_1 in Figure 2.1 illustrates how the quantity demanded of a good changes as its price, and only its price, changes. When one of the other (nonprice) factors that affect demand changes, the change can affect the quantity of tomatoes consumers want to buy at every price. For example, if there is an outbreak of salmonella poisoning, and public health officials believe that tomatoes may be the source of the outbreak, consumers' tastes will change. They will want fewer tomatoes at any given price than they did before and the demand curve will shift down and to the left to D_2, as shown in Figure 2.2. Mathematically, the demand curve D_2 corresponds to $Q = 500 - 200P$.

inverse demand curve
A demand curve written in the form of price as a function of quantity demanded.

demand choke price
The price at which no consumer is willing to buy a good and quantity demanded is zero; the vertical intercept of the inverse demand curve.

Figure 2.2   Shifts in the Demand Curve

The demand curve D_1 shifts with a change in any nonprice factor that affects demand. If tomatoes are suspected to be a source of salmonella, consumers will demand fewer tomatoes at any given price and the demand for tomatoes will shift inward, from D_1 to D_2. In contrast, if tomatoes are found to have cancer-fighting properties, the demand for tomatoes will shift outward, from D_1 to D_3.

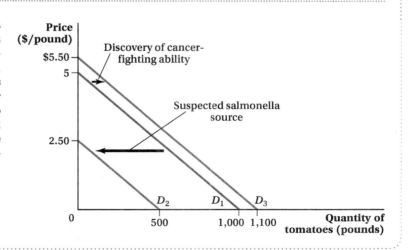

Similarly, if scientists discover that tomatoes help prevent cancer, consumers who wanted to buy 200 pounds of tomatoes at $4 per pound may now want to buy 300 pounds at $4. Those who wanted to buy 600 pounds at $2 per pound will now want to buy 700 pounds, and so on. Because consumers demand a higher quantity of tomatoes at any given price, the whole demand curve for tomatoes will shift out to the right from D_1 to D_3, illustrated in Figure 2.2. Mathematically, the new demand curve D_3 is described by the equation $Q = 1,100 - 200P$. Note that we are shifting the demand curves in the simplest way—sliding them over with the same slope. In real markets, this doesn't need to be true. The new curve can change steepness too, if demand becomes more or less sensitive to price.

The changes in the quantity demanded at every price that occur when any nonprice factor changes illustrate an essential distinction. When a good's price changes but nothing else does, this change creates a movement *along* a fixed demand curve. Changes in any of the other factors that influence demand create *shifts* in the demand curve. To clarify this distinction, economists distinguish **changes in quantity demanded,** which happen when a change in a good's price creates movement along a given demand curve (e.g., the move from point A to point B in Figure 2.1), from **changes in demand,** which happen when a good's entire demand curve shifts (e.g., the shifts from D_1 to D_2 and D_3 in Figure 2.2).

Quantity demanded is a single number, expressed in units of the good: 400 pounds of tomatoes, 30 cars, or 20 movie downloads, for example. Different prices imply different quantities demanded; the combination of all such price–quantity combinations is represented by the demand curve. Shifts in consumers' desired quantities caused by changes in any (or all) other factors move this entire combination of prices and quantities demanded—that is, they shift the demand curve.[3]

We motivated the shifts from D_1 to D_2 and D_3 in Figure 2.2 as changes in consumer tastes. But similar pictures occur for a change in any other nonprice factor that affects consumers' quantity demanded. The increase in demand reflected by the shift to D_3 would also occur if beautiful weather leads to higher attendance at the market. Of course, had the weather been cold and rainy, the number of customers at the market would fall, and the demand curve would have shifted inward to, perhaps, D_2.

change in quantity demanded
A movement *along* the demand curve that occurs as a result of a change in the good's price.

change in demand
A shift of the entire demand curve caused by a change in a determinant of demand other than the good's own price.

theory and data

Changes in Taste and the Demand for Cigarettes

If you were a cigarette company executive in 1960, you had to feel optimistic. Between 1940 and 1957, the share of Americans over the age of 25 who smoked had risen from 38% to 46%. Affluent people were more likely to smoke than the poor, so with people getting richer over time, the demand for cigarettes was likely to skyrocket.

But things didn't turn out as the executives planned. Today, only about 20% of the adult population smokes. Moreover, among those who currently do smoke, the number of cigarettes smoked per day is smaller than it was for the average smoker 50 years ago.

Why has the quantity demanded for cigarettes shrunk so much? One factor that no doubt has contributed to the decline is a rising price. In 1960 a pack of cigarettes cost around 30 cents. Adjusting for inflation, that's equivalent to $2.20 in 2010 dollars. But the

[3] Economists often draw demand curves as straight lines, and we do so as well throughout much of this book. This is really just for convenience. As their name suggests, demand curves in reality can be, and probably quite often are, *curves*. Also, when we use the word "shift," this includes not only parallel shifts of the demand curve as shown in Figure 2.2, but also rotations (which change the steepness or slope of a demand curve). We'll later discuss in further detail what economic forces affect the slopes of demand curves.

average price for a pack of cigarettes today is $4.80, more than twice as high. Much of that price increase is the result of heavy taxation—taxes that now account for more than half of the price of cigarettes. Price changes are unlikely to be the whole story, however. Based on economists' measurements of smokers' sensitivity to price changes, a price increase of this size explains only about half the drop in quantity demanded. Looking at changes in who smokes further reinforces the idea that price increases are not the whole story: Currently, fewer than 15% of Americans with college degrees smoke, compared to more than 25% of people with less education. That is the reverse of the pattern in the 1950s. In general, we expect high-income people to be *less* sensitive to price changes than the poor, so it is unlikely that rising prices would lead cigarette consumption to shift sharply toward those with low education. Clearly, something else happened.

One major "something" was the realization on the part of consumers that smoking is dangerous. The 1964 Surgeon General's Report, considered one of the top news stories that year, broadly disseminated information on the link between lung cancer and cigarette smoking that had been steadily growing in the academic community. In 1970 the addition of the ubiquitous Surgeon General's Warning to all cigarette packages sold in the United States furthered the spread of this information. Knowledge of the health risks associated with smoking led the demand curve for cigarettes to shift inward. What does it mean for a demand curve to shift inward? It means that *holding price constant,* the quantity demanded is lower.

Thus, the observed decline in demand for cigarettes reflects both movements along the demand curve (the rising price) and shifts in the demand curve (awareness that smoking is dangerous), as shown in Figure 2.3. Economist Damien de Walque studied whether these types of shifts in the demand curve are also related to the fact that the highly educated smoked more in the 1950s, but smoke much less today.[*] There is a growing body of evidence suggesting that more education pays off not just in the labor market, but in many other activities as well. (The benefits are especially great when you study economics—well, at least that's what economists will tell you.) People with more education have better access to information and are better prepared to properly interpret the information they receive, so it makes sense that the highly educated would react more to information about the risks of smoking than would the less educated. That is exactly what de Walque found in his study.

Figure 2.3   **Prevalence of Smoking by Education Category in the United States, Age 25 and Older, 1940–2000**

Prior to the mid-1960s, smoking prevalence was high across all educational groups, ranging from approximately 40 to 45% of the population. After the Surgeon General's Warning in 1964, the percentage of smokers declined more among the highly educated than among those with a high school education or below. In 2000 approximately 30% of people with a high school education or below smoked, while only around 15% of people with more than a college degree were smokers.

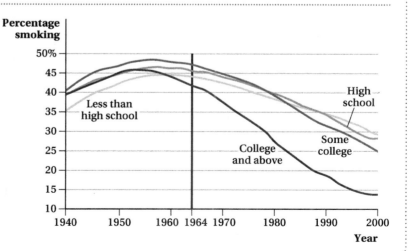

[*] Damien de Walque, "Education, Information, and Smoking Decisions: Evidence from Smoking Histories in the United States, 1940–2000," *Journal of Human Resources* 45, no. 3 (2010): 682–717.

Why Is Price Treated Differently from the Other Factors That Affect Demand?

Why do prices get special treatment relative to the other determinants of demand? After all, nothing prevents us from putting, say, income on the vertical axis in Figure 2.1 instead of price.

There are at least three reasons why economists focus on the effects of a change in a good's price. First, price is typically one of the most important factors that influence demand. Second, prices can usually be changed frequently and easily. Therefore, when we contemplate how markets respond to changes or "shocks," price fluctuations are likely to be a common response. Third, and most important, of all the factors that influence demand, price is the only one that also exerts a large, direct influence on the other side of the market—on the quantity of the good that producers are willing to supply. Price therefore serves as the critical element that ties together demand and supply. Let's turn to that other side of the market now.

2.3 Supply

We have one half of the demand and supply model assembled. In this section, we present the supply half. By supply we mean the combined amount of a good that all producers in a market are willing to sell.

Factors That Influence Supply

Just as there are many factors that determine demand, so too with supply. Let's discuss these again in the context of our Pike Place Market tomatoes example.

Price   Just as it does with demand, price plays an important role in supply decisions. If farmers expect to be able to sell tomatoes at $40 a pound at Pike Place Market, the market will be loaded with them. The farmers will grow more tomatoes and choose to sell them at Pike Place rather than other outlets. If they expect the price to be only $1 per pound, there will be a much smaller quantity available for sale.

Suppliers' Costs of Production   Suppliers' production costs will change when input prices and production technology change. There are many inputs a supplier must use to produce tomatoes and bring them to market, including land, tomato seeds, fertilizer, harvesting equipment, booth rental prices at markets like Pike Place, and the gasoline needed to ship tomatoes to markets, to name just a few. If the prices of these inputs change, the suppliers' costs will change and will influence the quantity of tomatoes supplied to the market.

production technology
The processes used to make, distribute, and sell a good.

Similarly, changes in **production technology,** the processes used to make, distribute, and sell a good such as tomatoes, will change the costs of production. The more efficient these processes are, the lower the costs to sellers of providing tomatoes for sale. Lower costs will raise sellers' willingness to supply tomatoes.

The Number of Sellers   More farmers bringing tomatoes to Pike Place will raise the available supply.

Sellers' Outside Options   Farmers who are busy selling tomatoes at Pike Place Market aren't selling some other product or selling tomatoes at some other place. A change in farmers' prospects for doing business in markets for other goods or in other markets for tomatoes can affect their willingness to supply tomatoes at Pike Place Market. These prospects depend on factors such as the prices of other goods the farmers might be growing and selling (radishes, peppers, or green beans) or tomato prices at markets other than Pike Place.

Supply Curves

Just as we introduced demand curves as a way to think in a more focused way about demand, we can do the same thing for supply. Supply curves, like demand curves, capture the idea that factors that influence supply can be divided into two sets: price and everything else. Supply curves isolate the relationship between price and quantity supplied.

Graphical Representation of the Supply Curve   Figure 2.4 depicts a supply curve for tomatoes at the Pike Place Market. The vertical axis reflects the price of the good, and the horizontal axis is the quantity supplied. The curve indicates that, for example, if the price of tomatoes is $2 per pound, 200 pounds of tomatoes will be offered for sale. If the price is $5 per pound, the quantity supplied will be 800 pounds.

The **supply curve** in the figure slopes upward: Holding everything else equal, producers are willing to supply more of a good as price rises.[4] The simple intuition behind the upward slope of most supply curves is that, given their costs of production and other nonprice factors, firms want to supply a greater quantity to the market when prices are high. For example, many firms experience increasing costs of production as their output rises. When this is the case, they need to earn a higher price in the market in order to induce them to produce more output.

supply curve
The relationship between the quantity supplied of a good and the good's price, holding all other factors constant.

Mathematical Representation of the Supply Curve   The supply curve in Figure 2.4 is expressed mathematically as

$$Q = 200P - 200$$

where Q is the quantity supplied (in pounds of tomatoes) and P is the price in dollars per pound. This indicates that holding everything else constant, for every dollar increase in price, the quantity supplied of tomatoes increases by 200 pounds.

Figure 2.4   :   **Supply of Tomatoes**

The supply curve S_1 for tomatoes at Pike Place Market shows how the quantity of tomatoes supplied varies with the price. As the price of tomatoes increases, producers supply greater quantities of tomatoes, creating an upward-sloping supply curve. At a price of $1 per pound, producers supply no tomatoes; at $2, $3, $4, and $5, respectively, producers supply 200, 400, 600, and 800 pounds of tomatoes.

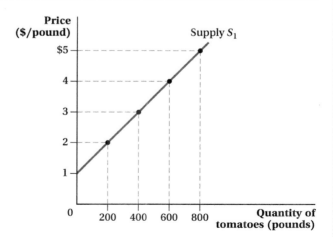

---

[4] We typically expect that supply curves slope upward, although in some cases (especially in the long run), they may be horizontal, and in others they might be perfectly vertical. We will discuss these special cases later.

inverse supply curve
A supply curve written in the form of price as a function of quantity supplied.

Just as it is common to write demand curves as inverse demand curves (price as a function of quantity demanded), economists often use **inverse supply curves** as well:

$$Q = 200P - 200$$

$$200P = Q + 200$$

$$P = 0.005Q + 1$$

The inverse supply curve makes clear that no firm will be willing to supply tomatoes at a price of $1 per pound (or less), because the vertical intercept of the supply is $1 per pound (i.e., the price at which the quantity supplied Q equals zero). This is often called the **supply choke price.**

supply choke price
The price at which no firm is willing to produce a good and quantity supplied is zero; the vertical intercept of the inverse supply curve.

Shifts in the Supply Curve

A given supply curve such as S_1 in Figure 2.4 illustrates how the quantity supplied of a good changes as its price, and only its price, changes.

When one of the other (nonprice) factors that affect supply changes, the change affects the quantity of tomatoes that suppliers want to sell at every price. For example, if someone invents a machine that can harvest tomatoes faster and at lower cost, producers who wanted to produce 600 pounds of tomatoes at $4 per pound will now be willing to supply 800 pounds of tomatoes at $4. Those who were willing to supply 200 pounds at $2 will now be willing to supply 400 at $2, and so on. Because producers supply more tomatoes at every price, the whole supply curve will shift out to the right from S_1 to S_2, as shown in Figure 2.5. The way we've drawn it, that additional quantity is the 200 pounds at any price, though there's nothing that says all supply shifts must exhibit this pattern.[5] Mathematically, the supply curve S_2 is described by the equation $Q = 200P$.

change in quantity supplied
A movement *along* the supply curve that occurs as a result of a change in the good's price.

Similarly, if there is a drought, it will cost producers more to irrigate their fields. They will want to supply fewer tomatoes at any given price than they did before and the supply will shift up and to the left, to S_3. Mathematically, the supply curve S_3 corresponds to $Q = 200P - 600$.

Analogous to demand curves, the changes in a good's price when everything else stays constant lead to **changes in quantity supplied,** movements *along* a supply

---

Figure 2.5   Shifts in the Supply Curve

The supply curve S_1 shifts when any nonprice factor that affects supply changes. If a faster harvesting method is developed, the supply of tomatoes will shift outward, from S_1 to S_2. In contrast, if there is a drought, the supply of tomatoes will shift inward, from S_1 to S_3.

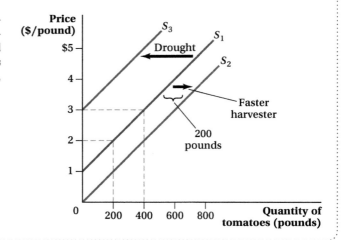

---

[5] Note that, just like demand curves, there's no requirement that supply curves be linear. We just draw them as such for simplicity.

curve. Changes in any other factors that influence supply change the quantity supplied at any given price and create *shifts* in the supply, which is called a **change in supply.**

Quantity supplied is a single number, such as 600 pounds of tomatoes, 100 iPads, or 40 haircuts, and different prices imply different quantities supplied. Supply curves show all possible price–quantity combinations producers would supply. Changes in any (or all) other factors move the entire combination of prices and quantities supplied—that is, they shift the supply curve.

change in supply
A shift of the entire supply curve caused by a change in a determinant of supply other than the good's own price.

Why Is Price Also Treated Differently for Supply?

Supply curves isolate the effect of prices on supply just as demand curves isolate price effects on demand. We mentioned one of the big reasons for this focus on price in the demand curve is that price is the only factor that has a direct influence on both demand and supply. Price is the critical element that ties together the two sides of a market. Price's roles in both the demand and supply sides of a market mean that prices can adjust freely to make the quantity demanded by consumers equal to the quantity supplied by producers. When this happens, we have a market in which everyone who wants to buy at the current price can do so, and everyone who wants to sell at the current market price can do so as well.

As we see in the next section, we can also use the supply and demand model to predict how changes in nonprice factors affect market outcomes. To get to the point where we *can* do that, however, we need to identify an initial market price and quantity sold. Treating price as special allows us to do that.

2.4 Market Equilibrium

The true power of the demand and supply model emerges when we combine demand and supply curves. Both relate quantities and prices, so we can draw them on the same graph, with price on the vertical axis and quantity on the horizontal axis. Figure 2.6 overlays the original demand and supply curves for tomatoes at Seattle's Pike Place Market. As a reminder, expressed as equations, the demand curve is $Q = 1{,}000 - 200P$ (with an equivalent inverse demand curve $P = 5 - 0.005Q$), and the supply curve is $Q = 200P - 200$ (with an inverse supply curve of $P = 1 + 0.005Q$).

The point where the supply and demand curves cross is the **market equilibrium.** The equilibrium is labeled as point E on Figure 2.6, and the price and quantity

market equilibrium
The point at which the quantity demanded by consumers exactly equals the quantity supplied by producers.

Figure 2.6   Market Equilibrium

The intersection of the supply curve S_1 and the demand curve D_1 at point E represents the market equilibrium. The equilibrium price and quantity of tomatoes are $3 per pound and 400 pounds, respectively.

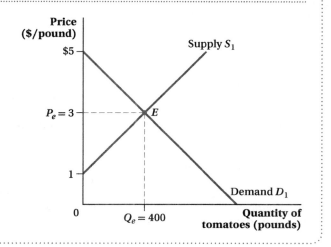

equilibrium price
The only price at which
quantity supplied equals
quantity demanded.

associated with this point are labeled P_e and Q_e. The **equilibrium price** P_e is the *only* price at which quantity supplied equals quantity demanded.

The Mathematics of Equilibrium

So what is the market equilibrium for our Pike Place tomatoes example? We can read off Figure 2.6 that the equilibrium price P_e is $3 per pound, and the equilibrium quantity Q_e is 400 pounds. But we can also determine these mathematically by using the equations for the demand and supply curves. Quantity demanded is given by $Q^D = 1,000 - 100P$ (we've added the superscript "D" to quantity just to remind us that equation is the demand curve), and quantity supplied is $Q^S = 200P - 200$ (again, we've added a superscript). We know that at market equilibrium, quantity demanded equals quantity supplied; that is, $Q_e = Q^D = Q^S$. Using the equations above, we have

$$Q^D = Q^S$$

$$1,000 - 200P = 200P - 200$$

$$1,200 = 400P$$

$$P_e = 3$$

At a price P of $3 per pound, quantity demanded Q^D equals quantity supplied Q^S, so the equilibrium price P_e is $3, as we see in Figure 2.6. To find the equilibrium quantity Q_e, we plug this value of P_e back into the equation for *either* the demand or supply curve, because both quantity demanded and quantity supplied will be the same at the equilibrium price:

$$Q_e = 1,000 - 200P_e = 1,000 - 200(3) = 1,000 - 600 = 400$$

We just solved for the equilibrium price and quantity by using the fact that the quantity demanded equals the quantity supplied in equilibrium, and substituting the demand and supply curve equations into this equality. We could have obtained the same answer by instead using the fact that the price given by the *inverse* demand and supply curves is the same at the market equilibrium quantity. That is,

$$5 - 0.005Q_e = 1 + 0.005Q_e$$

Solving this equation gives $Q_e = 400$ pounds, just as before. Plugging $Q_e = 400$ back into either the inverse demand or supply equation indicates that the market price P_e is $3 per pound, as expected.

make the grade

Does quantity supplied equal quantity demanded in equilibrium?

Solving for the market equilibrium as we just did is one of the most common exam questions in intermediate microeconomics classes. The basic idea is always the same: Take the equations for the demand curve and the supply curve, solve for the equilibrium price, and then plug that equilibrium price back into either the supply curve or the demand curve (it does not matter which) to determine the equilibrium quantity. It is simple, but it is easy to make math errors under the time pressure of an exam, especially if the demand and supply curves take on more complicated forms than the basic examples we deal with here.

A simple trick will ensure that you have the right answer, and it takes only a few seconds. Take the equilibrium price that you obtain and plug it into *both* the demand and supply curves. If you don't get the same answer when you substitute the equilibrium price into the supply and demand equations, you know you made a math error along the way because the quantity demanded must equal the quantity supplied in equilibrium.

Why Markets Move toward Equilibrium

When a market is in equilibrium, the quantity demanded by consumers and the quantity supplied by producers are equal at the current market price. To see why equilibrium is a stable situation, let's look at what happens when price is at a non-equilibrium level. If the current price is higher than the equilibrium price, there will be excess supply. If the price is lower, there will be excess demand.

Excess Supply   Suppose the price in a market were higher than the equilibrium price, say, at P_{high} instead of P_e, as shown in Figure 2.7a. At that price, the quantity supplied, Q^S_{high}, is greater than the quantity demanded, Q^D_{high}. Producers come out of the woodwork wanting to sell at this high price, but not all producers can find willing buyers at that price. The excess quantity for sale equals $Q^S_{high} - Q^D_{high}$, the horizontal distance between the supply and demand curves at P_{high}. This excess quantity supplied is known as a **surplus**. To eliminate this surplus, producers need to attract more buyers, and to do this, sellers must lower their prices. As price falls, quantity demanded rises and quantity supplied falls until the market reaches equilibrium at point E.

Excess Demand   The opposite situation exists in Figure 2.7b. At price P_{low}, consumers demand more of the good (Q^D_{low}) than producers are willing to supply (Q^S_{low}). Buyers want a lot of tomatoes if they are this cheap, but not many producers will deliver them at such a low price. At the low price, the quantity demanded Q^D_{low} is greater than the quantity supplied Q^S_{low}, and a **shortage** exists. To eliminate this shortage, buyers who cannot find the good available for sale will bid up the price and enterprising producers will be more than willing to raise their prices. As price rises,

surplus
The amount by which quantity supplied exceeds quantity demanded when market price is higher than the equilibrium price.

shortage
The amount by which quantity demanded exceeds quantity supplied when market price is lower than the equilibrium price.

Figure 2.7 : **Why P_e Is the Equilibrium Price**

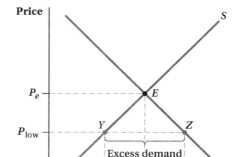

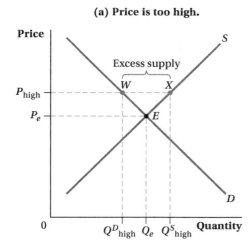

(a) Price is too high.

(b) Price is too low.

(a) At the price P_{high} above the equilibrium price P_e, producers supply the quantity Q^S_{high}, while consumers demand only Q^D_{high}. This results in a surplus of the good, as represented by the distance between points W and X. Over time, price will fall and the market will move toward equilibrium at point E.

(b) At the price P_{low} below the equilibrium price P_e, producers supply the quantity Q^S_{low}, while consumers demand Q^D_{low}. This results in a shortage for the good, as represented by the distance between points Y and Z. Over time, price will rise and the market will move toward equilibrium at point E.

quantity demanded falls and quantity supplied rises until the market equals equilibrium at point E.[6]

Adjusting to Equilibrium   It is important to note that in the real world an equilibrium can be mysterious. In our stylized model, we're acting as if all the producers and consumers gather in one spot and report to a sort of auctioneer how much they want to produce or consume at each price. The auctioneer combines all this information, computes and announces the market-clearing price, and only then do all the sellers and buyers make their deals at the announced market-clearing price. But few markets work this way in the real world. Real markets must rely on what the great eighteenth-century Scottish economist Adam Smith called the "invisible hand." Producers independently decide how much to produce of their products given what price they expect to be able to sell them at, and consumers show up at stores, gas stations, or Web sites to buy the good. Sometimes producers might supply too much or too little in the short run, but through the market, these mistakes tend to be corrected. Economists typically assume that the market reaches equilibrium one way or another, without being too specific about the process.

2.1 figure it out

Suppose that the demand and supply curves for a monthly cell phone plan with unlimited texts can be represented by

$$Q^D = 50 - 0.5P$$
$$Q^S = -25 + P$$

The current price of these plans in the market is $40 per month. Is this market in equilibrium? Would you expect the price to rise or fall? If so, by how much? Explain.

Solution:

There are two ways to solve the first question about whether the price will rise or fall. The first is to calculate the quantity demanded and quantity supplied at the current market price of $40 to see how they compare:

$$Q^D = 50 - 0.5P = 50 - 0.5(40) = 50 - 20 = 30$$
$$Q^S = -25 + P = -25 + 40 = 15$$

Because quantity demanded is greater than quantity supplied, we can tell that there is excess demand (a shortage) in the market. Many people are trying to get texting plans, but are finding them sold out because few suppliers want to sell at that price. Prices will rise to equalize quantity supplied and quantity demanded, moving the market to equilibrium.

Alternatively, we could start by solving for the market equilibrium price:

$$Q^D = Q^S$$
$$50 - 0.5P = -25 + P$$
$$1.5P = 75$$
$$P = \$50$$

The current market price, $40, is below the market equilibrium price of $50. (This is why there is excess demand in the market.) Therefore, we would expect the price to rise by $10. When the market reaches equilibrium at a price of $50, all buyers can find sellers and all sellers can find buyers. The price will then remain at $50 unless the market changes and the demand curve or supply curve shifts.

---

[6] Prices can sometimes remain at levels other than their equilibrium value for extended periods of time, especially if there are policy-based interventions in the market, such as price ceilings (maximum prices allowed by law) or price floors (minimum prices prescribed by law). We discuss these sorts of situations in Chapter 3.

The Effects of Demand Shifts

As we have learned, demand and supply curves hold constant everything else besides price that might affect quantities demanded and supplied. Therefore, the market equilibrium depicted in Figure 2.6 will hold only as long as none of these other factors change. If any other factor changes, there will be a new market equilibrium because either the demand or supply curve will have shifted.

Suppose the demand for tomatoes falls when, as in our example on the previous pages, a news story reports that tomatoes are suspected of being the source of a salmonella outbreak. The resulting change in consumer tastes causes the demand curve to shift in (i.e., to the left), as Figure 2.8 shows, from D_1 to D_2.

How does the market equilibrium change after this demand shift? The equilibrium price and quantity both fall. The equilibrium quantity falls from Q_1 to Q_2, and the equilibrium price drops from P_1 to P_2. The reason for these movements is that if prices stayed at P_1 after the fall in demand, tomato farmers would be supplying a much greater quantity than consumers were demanding. The market price must fall to get farmers to rein in their quantity supplied until it matches the new, lower level of demand.

We can solve for the new equilibrium price and quantity using the same approach we used earlier, but using the equation for the new demand curve D_2, which is $Q = 500 - 200P$. (The supply curve stays the same.)

$$Q^D = Q^S$$

$$500 - 200P_2 = 200P_2 - 200$$

$$400P_2 = 700$$

$$P_2 = 1.75$$

So the new equilibrium price is $1.75 per pound, compared to $3 per pound from before the demand shift. Plugging this into the new demand curve (or the supply curve) gives the new equilibrium quantity:

$$Q_2 = 500 - 200(1.75) = 150$$

The new equilibrium quantity is 150 pounds, less than half of what it was before the negative demand shift.

Figure 2.8   Effects of a Fall in the Demand for Tomatoes

After a salmonella outbreak, the demand for tomatoes decreases, causing a leftward shift of the demand curve from D_1 to D_2. This fall in demand results in a new equilibrium point E_2 lower than the initial equilibrium point E_1. The equilibrium quantity falls from Q_1 (400 pounds) to Q_2 (150 pounds), and the equilibrium price falls from P_1 ($3) to P_2 ($1.75).

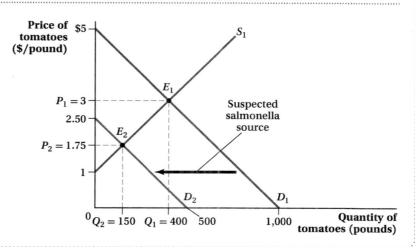

We could have just as easily worked through an example in which demand increases and the demand curve shifts out. Perhaps tastes change and people want to drink their vegetables by downing several cans of tomato juice a day or incomes rise or substitute produce items become more expensive. In the face of a stable supply curve, this increase in demand would shift the curve up to the right and cause both the equilibrium price and quantity to rise. At the initial (pre-shift) market price, the post-shift quantity demanded would outstrip sellers' willingness to supply. The price would have to rise, causing a movement along the supply curve until the quantities supplied and demanded are equal.

Shifts in Curves versus Movement along a Curve   This analysis highlights the importance of distinguishing between shifts in a demand or supply curve and movements along those curves. This distinction can sometimes seem confusing, but understanding it is critical to much of the analysis that follows in this book. We saw in Figure 2.8 what happens to a market when there is a change in consumers' tastes that make them view a product more negatively. That change in tastes made consumers want to buy less of the product at any given price—that is, caused an inward *shift* in the demand curve. Remember, anything that changes how much consumers want to buy of a good at any particular price must shift the demand curve. At the same time, this change in tastes had no effect on how much producers wish to sell at any given price. It doesn't affect their costs of producing or their outside options. So supply does not change, and the supply curve doesn't shift. However, the *quantity supplied* does change. It falls in response to the reduced demand. This change in quantity supplied is a movement *along* the supply curve. The only reason that the quantity supplied falls in this example is because the shift in the demand curve has made the equilibrium price lower, and at a lower price, suppliers produce less of the good. Therefore, a *shift* in the demand curve causes a movement *along* the supply curve to the new equilibrium.

2.2 figure it out

Draw a supply and demand diagram of the market for paperback books in a small coastal town.

a. Suppose that a hurricane knocks out electrical power for an extended period of time. Unable to watch television or use a computer, people must resort to reading books for entertainment. What will happen to the equilibrium price and quantity of paperback books?

b. Does this change reflect a change in demand or a change in quantity demanded?

Solution:

a. Books are a substitute good for television shows and computer entertainment. Because there is no power for televisions or computers (effectively raising the price of these substitutes), the demand for books will rise, and the demand curve will shift out to the right. As the figure shows, this shift will result in a

higher equilibrium price and quantity of books purchased.

b. Because the hurricane changes the availability (and therefore the effective price) of substitute goods, this shifts the amount of books demanded at any given price. This is a change in the demand for paperback books.

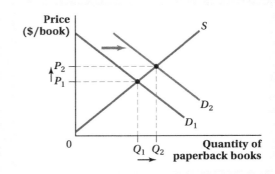

freakonomics

The Price of Fame: President Obama and the Paparazzi

Being president of the United States has its perks—you are the most powerful person in the world, people wait on you hand and foot, and you get to live in a pretty nice house rent-free. But being the president also has its downsides. For instance, every step you and your family take is in the public spotlight. Media coverage of the Obama family has been intense, even by White House standards. The president was particularly troubled by the toll on his daughters Sasha and Malia, so he asked his staff to come up with some solutions to the paparazzi problem.

The White House provided the media with this photo of Malia and Sasha Obama leaving for their first day of school in 2010.

The Obama-Biden Transition Project

Their solution shows that someone in the Obama administration knows some economics. White House staff recognized that the number of paparazzi photos represents a market equilibrium. Because of the public's strong demand for pictures of the Obama family, media outlets are willing to fork over large sums of money for high-quality photos. At those prices, many photographers are willing to devote a lot of time to stalking the First Family and supply the market with a huge number of photographs. A hypothetical initial equilibrium in the market for photographs of the Obama family is illustrated in Figure A.

Figure A

One way to reduce the number of paparazzi taking photos to supply the equilibrium quantity would be to decrease the demand for the photos and shift the demand curve inward. If that were to happen, both the price and quantity of paparazzi photos would decline. How could the White House reduce the demand for paparazzi photos? One thing we know from economics is that if two goods are substitutes, the demand for one good will fall if the price for the other good decreases because consumers will shift away from buying the first good and toward buying the second, cheaper good. So the administration needed a substitute for paparazzi pictures. The answer? Staged photos taken by White House photographers, given to media outlets for free.

Each White House–approved picture of Sasha and Malia hunting for Easter eggs or of the First Dog Bo running around the lawn lowered the demand for paparazzi photos, leading to a decrease in the price unauthorized paparazzi photos could command. As a result, fewer paparazzi spent their days milling around the White House lawn, and the number of unauthorized photos being published de-creased, as shown in Figure B. Perhaps most impor-tant to President and Mrs. Obama, it meant that Sasha and Malia could go to their first day of school like nor-mal kids — or, at least, like normal kids who happen to have several secret servicemen, the D.C. police, and the White House photographer with them.

After seeing the initial success of this photo proj-ect, the administration ventured into the world of so-cial media and created Facebook and Flickr accounts with photo albums depicting everything from staff meetings in the Oval Office to the president instigat-ing a snowball fight on the White House lawn. Up next for the White House presidential photo project? Given the current budget deficit, perhaps they should consider selling the pictures — just as long as they keep the price below the market equilibrium price!

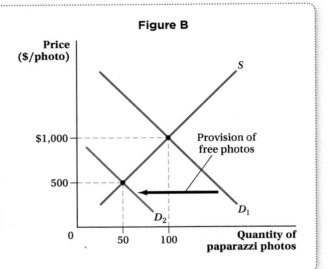

Figure B

The Effects of Supply Shifts

Now let's think about what happens when the supply curve shifts, but the demand curve does not. Figure 2.9 shows the case in which the supply of tomatoes rises, shifting the sup-ply curve out from S_1 to S_2. This shift implies that, at any given price, farmers are willing to sell a larger quantity of tomatoes than before. Such a shift would result from a reduc-tion in farmers' input costs—for example, if fertilizer prices fell. The logic of why a cost reduction increases quantity supplied at any given price is straightforward: If the farmers can make an average profit of (say) $1 per pound when the price is $3 per pound, then a $1 decrease in cost (which increases their profit) will lead farmers to offer more for sale. Note, however, that this cost change has no direct impact on the demand curve. Holding price fixed, consumers are no more or less willing to buy tomatoes than they were before.

Figure 2.9 shows how the equilibrium changes. The supply curve has shifted from its original position S_1 (given by the equation $Q = 200P - 200$) to S_2 (given by the equation

---

Figure 2.9   Effects of an Increase in the Supply of Tomatoes

With cheaper fertilizer, farmers supply more to-matoes at every given price and the supply curve shifts outward from S_1 to S_2. The equilibrium quantity increases from Q_1 (400 pounds) at E_1 to Q_2 (600 pounds) at E_2, while the equilibrium price falls from P_1 ($3/pound) to P_2 ($2/pound).

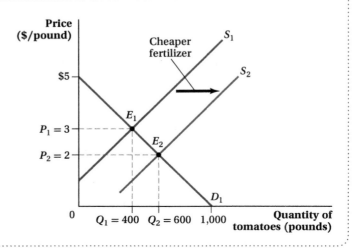

$Q = 200P + 200$). If the price stayed at the original equilibrium price P_1 after the supply shift, the amount of tomatoes that sellers would be willing to supply would exceed consumers' quantity demanded. Therefore, the equilibrium price must fall, as seen in the figure. This drop in price causes an increase in quantity demanded along the demand curve. The price drops until the quantity demanded once again equals the quantity supplied. The new equilibrium price is P_2, and the new equilibrium quantity is Q_2.

We can solve for the new equilibrium price and quantity using the equations for the original demand curve and the new supply curve:

$$Q^D = Q^S$$

$$1,000 - 200P_2 = 200P_2 + 200$$

$$400P_2 = 800$$

$$P_2 = 2$$

The cost drop and the resulting increase in supply lead to a fall in the equilibrium price from $3 to $2 per pound. This is intuitive: Lower farmers' costs end up being reflected in lower market prices. We can plug this price into either the demand or new supply equation to find the new equilibrium quantity:

$$Q_2 = 1,000 - 200(2) = 600$$

$$Q_2 = 200(2) + 200 = 600$$

The equilibrium quantity of tomatoes increases from 400 to 600 pounds in response to the increase in supply and the fall in the equilibrium price.

Again, we could go through the same steps for a decrease in supply. The supply curve would shift up to the left. This decline in supply would increase the equilibrium price and decrease the equilibrium quantity.

2.3 figure it out

Suppose that the supply of lemonade is represented by $Q^S = 40P$, where Q is measured in pints and P is measured in cents per pint.

a. If the demand for lemonade is $Q^D = 5,000 - 10P$, what are the current equilibrium price and quantity?

b. Suppose that a severe frost in Florida raises the price of lemons and thus the cost of making lemonade. In response to the increase in cost, producers reduce the quantity supplied of lemonade by 400 pints at every price. What is the new equation for the supply of lemonade?

c. After the frost, what will be the equilibrium price and quantity of lemonade?

Solution:

a. To solve for the equilibrium price, we need to equate the quantity demanded and quantity supplied:

$$Q^D = Q^S$$

$$5,000 - 10P = 40P$$

$$50P = 5,000$$

$$P = 100 \text{ cents}$$

To solve for the equilibrium quantity, we want to substitute the equilibrium price into either the demand curve or the supply curve (or both!):

$$Q^D = 5{,}000 - 10(100) = 5{,}000 - 1{,}000 = 4{,}000 \text{ pints}$$
$$Q^S = 40(100) = 4{,}000 \text{ pints}$$

b. If the quantity supplied of lemonade falls by 400 pints at every price, then the supply curve is shifting left (in a parallel fashion) by a quantity of 400 at each price:

$$Q^S{}_2 = Q^S - 400 = 40P - 400$$

The new supply curve can be represented by $Q^S{}_2 = 40P - 400$.

c. To solve for the new equilibrium, we would set $Q^D = Q^S{}_2$:

$$Q^D = Q^S{}_2$$
$$5{,}000 - 10P_2 = 40P_2 - 400$$
$$50P_2 = 5{,}400$$
$$P_2 = 108 \text{ cents}$$

Solving for equilibrium quantity can be done by substituting the equilibrium price into either the demand or supply equation:

$$Q^D = 5{,}000 - 10(108) = 5{,}000 - 1{,}080 = 3{,}920 \text{ pints}$$
$$Q^S = 40(108) - 400 = 4{,}320 - 400 = 3{,}920 \text{ pints}$$

As we would expect (see Table 2.2 below), the equilibrium price rises and the equilibrium quantity falls.

Summary of Effects

Table 2.2 summarizes the changes in equilibrium price and quantity that result when either the demand or supply curve shifts while the other curve remains in the same position. When the demand curve shifts, price and quantity move in the same direction. An increase in demand leads consumers to want to purchase more of the good than producers are willing to supply at the old equilibrium price. This will tend to drive prices up, which in turn induces producers to supply more of the good. The producers' response is captured by movement along the supply curve.

When the supply curve shifts, price and quantity move in opposite directions. If supply increases, the supply curve shifts out, and producers want to sell more of the good at the old equilibrium price than consumers want to buy. This will force prices down, giving consumers an incentive to buy more of the good. Similarly, if supply shifts in, the equilibrium price has to rise to reduce the quantity demanded. These movements along the demand curve involve price and quantity changes in opposite directions because demand curves are downward-sloping.

Table 2.2 — **Effect of Shifts in Demand and Supply Curves in Isolation**

Curve that Shifts	Direction of Shift	Impact on Equilibrium Price	Quantity
Demand Curve	Out (increase in D)	↑	↑
	In (decrease in D)	↓	↓
Supply Curve	Out (increase in S)	↓	↑
	In (decrease in S)	↑	↓

application

Supply Shifts and the Video Game Crash of 1983

People love video games. About two-thirds of households in the United States have at least one game-playing member. Sales of video game consoles and software were around $15.5 billion in the United States in 2010. To put that number in perspective, it is almost 50% more than 2010's total domestic box office haul of $10.5 billion, and about the same size as the total combined U.S. sales of McDonald's and Burger King restaurants that year.

Seeing these numbers, you'd never know that in the industry's early days, there was a point when many people declared video games a passing fad and a business in which it was impossible to make a profit. Why did they say this? The problem wasn't demand. Early video games, from *Pong* to *Space Invaders* and consoles like the Atari 2600, were a huge hit and cultural touchstones. The problem was supply—way too much of it. In 1983 a set of factors combined to lead to a massive supply shift for the industry in North America that ended up crippling it for years.

Two primary factors led to the supply shift. Home video consoles, led by the Atari 2600 but also including popular machines from Mattel and Coleco, had taken off in the early 1980s. At this early point in the industry, console producers hadn't yet learned the best way to handle licensing arrangements with third-party games producers. As a result, just about anyone could write a game title for a console if they wanted to. And just about everyone did. Even Quaker Oats had a video games division! The pet food company Purina contracted with a software developer to create a game that would publicize its Chuck Wagon brand dog food. (The game, *Chase the Chuck Wagon*, involved a dog chasing a chuck wagon through a maze.) In essence, there was a gold rush: Too many producers, each hoping to capture just a part of the fast-growing market, all entered at the same time, leading to a much larger total supply than any producer expected individually beforehand. The same phenomenon occurred in console production as well. Several companies made clones of Atari's market-leading console, and others produced their own machines and lines of games.

The leading console makers didn't help themselves any with their own game-production decisions either. The most infamous failures were Atari's self-produced games *Pac-Man* and *E.T. the Extra-Terrestrial*. Atari management expected unprecedented sales for both, due to the extreme popularity of the arcade version of the former and the movie tied to the latter. In fact, Atari produced 12 million copies of *Pac-Man* even though there were only 10 million consoles in existence at the time, presuming that not only would just about every owner of a console buy the game, but also millions of others would buy a console just to play the game. Both were rushed through production to take advantage of the holiday shopping seasons. The games were a mess, and quantity supplied well exceeded quantity demanded even at the depressed prices in the market.

The sudden rush of producers to put product on the market created an outward shift in the supply curve—producers' behavior made clear that they were willing to produce more at any given price in early 1983 than they were just a couple years earlier, in early 1981. And while the demand for home video games had been trending upward as the technology diffused through households, the rush to produce new titles and consoles probably didn't have much of an effect on the demand curve. (In fact, because of the poor quality of the new games, it may have even shifted the demand curve inward.) It's reasonable to assume, then, that the demand curve was unmoved by the producer gold rush. The supply and demand model predicts the consequences of this supply shift on the market. A shift out in the supply curve in the face of constant demand will lead to an increase in quantity and a drop in prices, as shown in Figure 2.10. (These days, video game companies take more care in rolling out new games.)

That's exactly what happened in the video game industry. Price changes, in particular, were precipitous. Games that had been selling a year earlier at list prices of $35–$50 were being sold for $5 or even $1. Console prices fell by double-digit percentages as well. With games going at these rates, quantities increased somewhat, but nowhere near enough to

---

Figure 2.10   Effects of an Increase in the Supply of Video Games

In 1983 a sudden increase in the number of video game producers shifted the supply curve from S_{1981} to S_{1983}. At the equilibrium, the price of video games dropped from P_1 ($35) to P_2 ($5), while the quantity increased from Q_1 to Q_2.

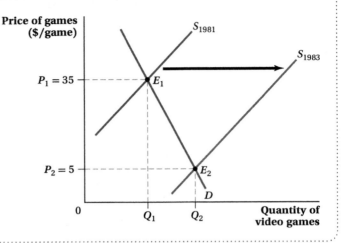

---

make them profitable for their producers. Dozens of firms—console and games makers alike—went out of business. Atari, which until then had been a cash cow, was sold by its parent Warner Communications and never recovered. The carnage was so total that some retailers, figuring the market was hopeless, refused to stock games anymore. It essentially wiped out producers from the market for three to four years, an eternity in this fast-moving industry where technological races are seemingly never-ending. Things finally turned around when a company known as Nintendo managed to convince retailers that its all-new 8-bit Nintendo Entertainment System would revitalize the moribund industry. ∎

2.4 figure it out

Last month, you noticed the price of asparagus rising, and you also noted that there was less asparagus being sold than in the prior month. What inferences can you draw about the behavior of the supply and demand for asparagus?

Solution:

We need to work backwards to determine what could have happened to either supply or demand to lead to the change described in this question. Let's start with the change in price. The equilibrium price of asparagus is *rising*. This must mean one of two things: Either the demand for asparagus rose or the supply of asparagus fell. (If you have trouble seeing this, draw a couple of quick figures.)

We also know that the equilibrium quantity of asparagus fell. A drop in the equilibrium quantity can only have two causes: either a decrease in the

demand for asparagus or a fall in the supply of asparagus. (Again, you may want to draw these out to see such results.)

Which shift leads to both a rise in equilibrium price and a fall in equilibrium quantity? It must be a decrease in the supply of asparagus, as shown in the figure.

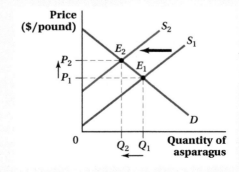

Did the curve shift, or was it just a movement along the curve?

A common type of exam question on demand and supply will involve one or more "shocks" to a market—changes in factors that influence demand or supply. Your job will be to sort out how those shocks affect demand and supply, and by extension, the equilibrium price and quantity in the market. Generally, the trickiest part of questions like these is figuring out whether changes in price and quantity are the result of moving along a given demand or supply curve, or whether the curves are shifting.

If you follow a few simple steps, this type of question need not be too difficult.

1. **Figure out what the shock is in any particular problem.** It is the change that causes a shift in either the supply curve, the demand curve, or both. There is a nearly infinite variety of shocks. A pandemic could wipe out a large number of consumers, a new invention might make it cheaper to make a good, a different good that consumers like better might be introduced, or inclement weather may damage or kill off a large portion of a certain crop.

   Importantly, though, a change in either the price or the quantity of the good *in the market being studied* cannot be the shock. The changes in price and quantity in this market are the *result* of the shock, not the shock itself. Be careful, however: Changes in prices or quantities in some *other* market can serve as a shock to this market. If the price of chunky peanut butter falls, for example, that could be a shock to the market for grape jelly or the market for creamy peanut butter.

2. **Determine whether the shock shifts the demand or supply curve.**

   a. *To figure out whether a shock shifts the demand curve and how it shifts it,* ask yourself the following question: If the price of this good didn't change, would consumers want to buy more, less, or the same amount of the good after the shock? If consumers want more of the good at the same price after the shock, then the shock increases the quantity demanded at every price and shifts the demand curve out (to the right). If consumers want less of the good at the same price after the shock, then the shock decreases demand and the demand curve shifts in. If consumers want the same amount of the good at the same price, then the demand curve doesn't move at all, and it's probably a supply shock.

   Let's go back to the grape jelly example. Our shock was a decline in the price of peanut butter. Do consumers want more or less grape jelly (holding the price constant) when peanut butter gets cheaper? The answer to this question is probably "more." Cheap peanut butter means consumers will buy more peanut butter, and since people tend to eat peanut butter and jelly together, consumers will probably want more jelly even if the price of jelly stays the same. Therefore, the decline in peanut butter's price shifts the demand for grape jelly out.

   b. *To figure out whether a shock shifts the supply curve and how it shifts it,* ask yourself the following question: If the price of this good didn't change, would suppliers want to produce more, less, or the same amount of the good after the shock? In the jelly example, a change in the price of peanut butter doesn't affect the costs of making jelly—it's not an input into jelly production. So it's not a supply shock. An increase in the price of grapes, however, would be a supply shock in the market for grape jelly.

3. **Draw the market's supply and demand curves before and after the shocks.** In the jelly example, we would draw the original demand and supply curves, and then add the new demand curve (to the right of the initial demand curve) that results from the increase in the demand for jelly because of lower peanut butter prices. From this, it's easy to execute the final step, interpreting what impact the shock has on equilibrium price and quantity. For grape jelly, the increase in demand will result in a higher equilibrium price and quantity for jelly because the demand shift creates movement up and to the right along the jelly supply curve.

Practice in following this recipe will make manipulating supply and demand curves second nature.

What Determines the Size of Price and Quantity Changes?

Thus far, the analysis in the chapter (summarized in Table 2.2) tells us about the *direction* in which equilibrium price and quantity move when demand and supply curves shift. But we don't know the size of these changes. In this section, we discuss the factors that determine how large the price and quantity changes are.

Size of the Shift   One obvious and direct influence on the sizes of the equilibrium price and quantity changes is the size of the demand or supply curve shift itself. The larger the shift, the larger the change in equilibrium price or quantity.

Figure 2.11   Size of Equilibrium Price and Quantity Changes, and the Slopes of the Supply and Demand Curves

(a) Demand curve shift with flatter supply curve

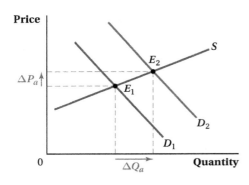

(b) Demand curve shift with steeper supply curve

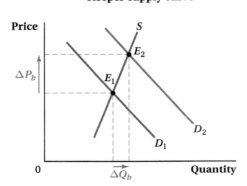

(c) Supply curve shift with flatter demand curve

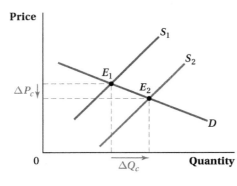

(d) Supply curve shift with steeper demand curve

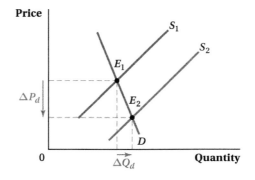

(a) With a relatively flat supply curve, a shift in demand from D_1 to D_2 will result in a relatively small increase in equilibrium price ΔP_a and a relatively large increase in equilibrium quantity ΔQ_a.
(b) With a relatively steep supply curve, a shift in demand from D_1 to D_2 will result in a relatively large increase in equilibrium price ΔP_b and a relatively small increase in equilibrium quantity ΔQ_b.

(c) With a relatively flat demand curve, a shift in supply from S_1 to S_2 will result in a relatively small decrease in equilibrium price ΔP_c and a relatively large increase in equilibrium quantity ΔQ_c.
(d) With a relatively steep demand curve, a shift in supply from S_1 to S_2 will result in a relatively large decrease in equilibrium price ΔP_d and a relatively small increase in equilibrium quantity ΔQ_d.

Slopes of the Curves   Even for a fixed-size demand or supply curve shift, the magnitudes of the resulting equilibrium price and quantity changes can vary. Specifically, the *relative* sizes of the price and quantity changes depend on the steepness of the demand and supply curves. If the demand curve shifts, then the slope of the supply curve determines whether the shift leads to a relatively large equilibrium price change and a relatively small equilibrium quantity change, or vice versa. If the supply curve shifts, it's the slope of the demand curve that matters.

Figure 2.11 demonstrates this. Panels a and b show the same shift in the demand curve, from D_1 to D_2. In panel a, the supply curve is relatively flat, while in panel b, it's relatively steep. When the demand curve shifts, if the supply curve is flat, the change in the equilibrium quantity (ΔQ_a) will be relatively large but the change in price (ΔP_a) will be small. When the supply curve is steep (panel b), the price change (ΔP_b) is large and the quantity change (ΔQ_b) small. Similarly, panels c and d show the same supply curve shift, but with differently sloped demand curves. The same results hold for shifts in the supply curve—flatter (steeper) demand curves result in larger (smaller) changes in quantity relative to price changes.

This analysis raises an obvious question: What affects the slope of demand and supply curves? We discuss the economic forces that determine the steepness or flatness of demand or supply curves next.

 application

The Supply Curve of Housing and Housing Prices: A Tale of Two Cities

From panels a and b of Figure 2.11, we can see that, when the demand curve shifts, the slope of the supply curve determines the relative size of the change in equilibrium price and quantity. Data for housing prices provide a good application of this idea. Specifically, we can look at how urban housing prices respond to an increase in the demand for housing caused by population growth.

Consider housing in the cities of New York City and Houston. New York is incredibly dense. Because the metropolitan area is so built up, it is expensive for developers to build additional housing. As a result, developers' costs rise so quickly with the amount of housing they build, the quantity of housing supplied doesn't respond much to price differences. There's only so much the developers can do. This means the supply curve of housing in New York is steep—the quantity supplied isn't very responsive to changes in price. Equivalently, it would take a very large increase in housing prices to induce housing suppliers to be willing to increase the quantity of housing they build. (We'll talk more in the next section about the factors that determine the price sensitivity of quantity supplied and quantity demanded.)

New York City.

Houston, on the other hand, is much less dense. It is surrounded by farm and ranch land, and there is still a lot of space to expand within the metro area. This means developers can build new housing without driving up their unit costs very much; they can just buy another farm and build housing on it if the price is right. For this reason, the quantity of housing supplied in Houston is quite responsive to changes in housing prices. That is, the housing supply curve in Houston is fairly flat.

Theory predicts that in response to an outward shift in the demand for housing in the two cities, New York (with its steep supply curve) should see a relatively large increase in the equilibrium price and very little change in the equilibrium quantity of housing. Houston, on the other hand, with the flatter supply curve, should see a relatively small increase in price and a large increase in quantity for an equal-size shift in demand.

Houston, Texas.

Figure 2.12   Population Indices for New York and Houston, 1977–2009

Between 1977 and 2009, the population in New York grew by about 15%, while the population in Houston more than doubled.

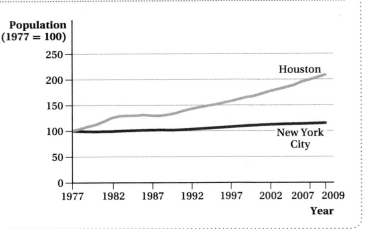

So let's look at some data. Look first at Figure 2.12, which shows how the populations of the New York and Houston metro areas changed from 1977 to 2009. (The figure shows the population index for each metro area, giving the city's population as a percentage of its 1977 value.) Population in both cities rose over these 32 years. New York metro area's population grew about 15%, while Houston's population saw a far greater rise, more than doubling.

We can think of these population influxes as being tied to outward shifts in the demand curve for housing in each city. Again, the prediction of the supply and demand model is that the equilibrium price response to a given-sized shift in demand should be larger in New York, where the supply curve of housing is steep (like that in Figure 2.11b), than in Houston, with its flatter supply curve (as in Figure 2.11a).

Looking at Figure 2.13, it's clear this prediction holds. The figure depicts a housing price index for both the New York and Houston metro areas, showing the price of housing in the cities (again, as an index based on their 1977 values). Despite having a considerably smaller increase in population, New York saw a tenfold rise in average housing

Figure 2.13   Housing Price Indices for New York and Houston, 1977–2009

From 1977 to 2009, housing prices in New York rose at a much faster rate than those in Houston.

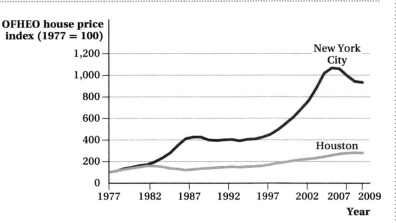

prices over the past 30 years. House prices went up in Houston too, as you would expect in a city that more than doubles in population, but by only a fraction of the increase seen in New York. In comparing these two cities, we see a clear pattern that the price effects of demand shifts in a market depend on the shape of the supply curve. ■

Changes in Market Equilibrium When Both Curves Shift

Sometimes, we are faced with situations in which supply and demand curves move simultaneously. For example, Figure 2.14 combines two shifts: decreases (inward shifts) in both supply and demand. Let's return to the tomato market at Pike Place Market and suppose that there is a big increase in oil prices. This increase drives up the cost of production because harvesting and distribution costs rise for sellers. Increased oil prices also decrease the demand for tomatoes. Because driving to the market gets more expensive for consumers, there are fewer people buying at any given price. The original equilibrium occurred at the intersection of D_1 and S_1, point E_1. The new equilibrium is at point E_2, the intersection of D_2 and S_2.

In this particular case, the simultaneous inward shifts in supply and demand have led to a substantial reduction in the equilibrium quantity and a slight increase in price. The reduction in quantity should be intuitive. The inward shift in the demand curve means that consumers want to buy less at any given price. The inward shift in the supply curve means that at any given price, producers want to supply less. Because both producers and consumers want less quantity, equilibrium quantity falls unambiguously, from Q_1 to Q_2.

The effect on equilibrium price is not as clear, however. An inward shift in demand with a fixed supply curve will tend to reduce prices, but an inward shift in supply with a fixed demand curve will tend to raise prices. Because both curves are moving simultaneously, it is unclear which effect will dominate, and therefore whether equilibrium price rises or falls. We have drawn the curves in Figure 2.14 so that equilibrium price rises slightly, from P_1 to P_2. But had the supply and demand curves shifted by different amounts (or had they been flatter or steeper), the dual inward shift might have led to a decrease in the equilibrium price, or no change in the price at all.

As a general rule, when both curves shift at the same time, we will know with certainty the direction of change of either the equilibrium price or quantity, but never both. This result can be seen by a closer inspection of Table 2.2. If the demand

---

Figure 2.14   **Example of a Simultaneous Shift in Demand and Supply**

An inward shift of both the supply and demand curves results in a new equilibrium point E_2 at the intersection between S_2 and D_2. At E_2, the price has increased slightly from P_1 to P_2, and the quantity has decreased from Q_1 to Q_2.

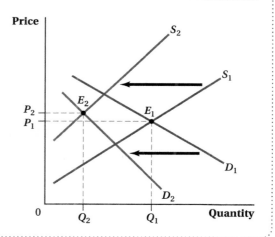

Figure 2.15   **When Both Curves Shift, the Direction of Either Price or Quantity Will Be Ambiguous**

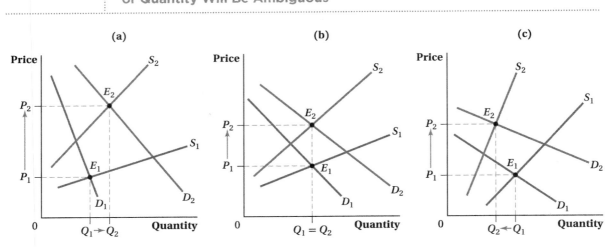

(a) In all three panels, there is an outward shift in demand $(D_1$ to $D_2)$ and an inward shift in supply $(S_1$ to $S_2)$. Here, both equilibrium price $(P_1$ to $P_2)$ and quantity $(Q_1$ to $Q_2)$ increase as a result.

(b) Equilibrium price increases from P_1 to P_2, while equilibrium quantity stays the same $(Q_1 = Q_2)$.

(c) Equilibrium price increases from P_1 to P_2, while equilibrium quantity decreases from Q_1 to Q_2.

and supply curve shifts are both pushing price in the same direction, which would be the case if (1) the demand curve shifted out and the supply curve shifted in or (2) the demand curve shifted in and the supply curve shifted out, then the same shifts 1 or 2 will push quantities in opposite directions. Likewise, if the shifts in both curves serve to move quantity in the same direction—either (3) demand and supply both shift out or (4) demand and supply both shift in—the shifts 3 and 4 have opposing effects on equilibrium prices. The example we just looked at in Figure 2.14 involved a case of form 4.

This ambiguity is also apparent in the example in Figure 2.15. The directions of the shifts in the demand and supply curves are the same in each panel of the figure: Supply shifts inward from S_1 to S_2, and demand shifts outward from D_1 to D_2. Both of these shifts will lead to higher prices, and this is reflected in the change in the equilibrium (from point E_1 to E_2). But as can be seen, whether the equilibrium quantity rises, falls, or stays the same depends on the relative size of the shifts and the slopes of the curves. The figure's three panels show examples of each possible case. When examining a situation in which both supply and demand shift, you might find it helpful to draw each shift in isolation first, note the changes in equilibrium quantity and price implied by each shift, and then combine these pieces of information to obtain your answer.

2.5 Elasticity

Mathematically, the slopes of demand and supply curves relate changes in price to changes in quantity demanded or quantity supplied. Steeper curves mean that price changes are correlated with relatively small quantity changes. When demand curves are steep, this implies that consumers are not very price-sensitive and won't change their quantity demanded much in response to price changes. Similarly, steep supply curves mean that producers' quantities supplied are not particularly sensitive to price changes.

Flatter demand or supply curves, on the other hand, imply that price changes are associated with large quantity changes. Markets with flat demand curves have consumers whose quantities demanded change a lot as price varies. Markets with flat supply curves will see big movements in quantity supplied as prices change.

The concept of elasticity expresses the responsiveness of one value to changes in another (and here specifically, the responsiveness of quantities to prices). An **elasticity** relates the percentage change in one value to the percentage change in another. So, for example, when we talk about the sensitivity of consumers' quantity demanded to price, we refer to the **price elasticity of demand:** the percentage change in quantity demanded resulting from a given percentage change in price.

Slope and Elasticity Are Not the Same

You might be thinking that the price elasticity of demand sounds a lot like the slope of the demand curve: how much quantity demanded changes when price does. While elasticity and slope are certainly related, they're not the same.

The slope relates a change in one level (prices) to another level (quantity). The demand curve we introduced in the tomato example was $Q = 1,000 - 200P$. The slope of this demand curve is -200; that is, quantity demanded falls by 200 pounds for every dollar per pound increase in price.

There are two big problems with using just the slopes of demand and supply curves to measure price responsiveness. First, slopes depend completely on the units of measurement we choose. Suppose we measured tomato prices P in cents per pound rather than dollars. Now the demand curve would be $Q = 1,000 - 2P$, because the quantity of tomatoes demanded would fall by 2 pounds for every 1 cent increase in price. But the fact that the coefficient on P is now 2 instead of 200 doesn't mean that consumers are 1/100th as price-sensitive as before. Nothing has changed about consumers' price responsiveness in this market: The quantity demanded still falls by 200 pounds for each $1 increase in price. The change in the slope simply reflects a change in the units of P. The second problem with slopes is that you can't compare them across different products. Suppose we were studying consumers' grocery shopping patterns, and wanted to compare consumers' price sensitivity for tomatoes in the market at Pike Place Market to their price sensitivity for celery hearts, for instance. Does the fact that consumers demand 100 fewer celery hearts for every 10 cent per celery heart increase in price mean that consumers are more or less price elastic in the celery market than in the tomato market? The slope of the celery demand curve implied by these numbers is -100 (if we measure quantity demanded in hearts and price in cents per celery heart). How could we ever compare this slope to the -200 slope for tomatoes?

Using elasticities to express responsiveness avoids these tricky issues, because everything is expressed in relative percentage changes. That eliminates the units problem (a 10% change is a 10% change regardless of what units the thing changing is measured in) and makes magnitudes comparable across markets.

The Price Elasticities of Demand and Supply

The price elasticity of demand is the ratio of the percentage change in quantity demanded to an associated percentage change in price. Mathematically, its formula is

Price elasticity of demand = (% change in quantity demanded)/(% change in price)

The price elasticity of supply is exactly analogous:

Price elasticity of supply = (% change in quantity supplied)/(% change in price)

To keep the equations simpler from now on, we'll use some shorthand notation. E^D will denote the price elasticity of demand, E^S the price elasticity of supply, $\%\Delta Q^D$ and

elasticity
The ratio of the percentage change in one value to the percentage change in another.

price elasticity of demand
The percentage change in quantity demanded resulting from a 1% change in price.

$\%\Delta Q^S$ the percentage change in quantities demanded and supplied, respectively, and $\%\Delta P$ the percentage change in price. In this shorthand, the two equations above become

$$E^D = \frac{\%\Delta Q^D}{\%\Delta P} \text{ and}$$

$$E^S = \frac{\%\Delta Q^S}{\%\Delta P}$$

So, for example, if the quantity demanded of a good falls by 10% in response to a 4% price increase, the good's price elasticity of demand is $E^D = -10\%/4\% = -2.5$. There are a couple of things to note about this example. First, because demand curves slope downward, the price elasticity of demand is always negative (or more precisely, always nonpositive; in special cases that we will discuss below, it can be zero). Second, because it is a ratio, a price elasticity can also be thought of as the percentage change in quantity demanded for a 1% increase in price. That is, for this good, a 1% increase in price leads to a −2.5% change in quantity demanded.

The price elasticity of supply works exactly the same way. If producers' quantity supplied increases by 25% in response to a 50% increase in price, for example, the price elasticity of supply is $E^S = 25\%/50\% = 0.5$. The price elasticity of supply is always positive (or again more precisely, always nonnegative) because quantity supplied increases when a good's price rises. And just as with demand elasticities, supply elasticities can be thought of as the percentage change in quantity in response to a 1% increase in price.

Price Elasticities and Price Responsiveness

Now that we've defined elasticities, let's use them to think about how responsive quantities demanded and supplied are to price changes.

When demand (supply) is very price-sensitive, a small change in price will lead to large changes in quantities demanded (supplied). That means the numerator of the elasticity expression, the percentage change in quantity, will be very large in magnitude compared to the percentage change in price in the denominator. For price elasticity of demand, the change in quantity will have the opposite sign as the price change, and the elasticity will be negative. But its magnitude (its absolute value) will be large if consumers are very responsive to price changes.

Examples of markets with large-magnitude price elasticities of demand would be those where consumers have a lot of ability to substitute away from or toward the good in question. (We also saw above how substitute products can lead to shifts in the demand curve. Substitutes are therefore an example of a force that can rotate demand curves as they shift.) The demand for apples at the grocery store is probably fairly price-responsive because consumers have an array of other fruits they could buy instead if apple prices are high; if apple prices are low, they will buy apples instead of other fruits. The price elasticity of demand for apples might be something like −4: for every 1% increase in price, consumers' quantity demanded would fall 4%.

Markets with less price-responsive demand have elasticities that are small in magnitude. The demand for candy at the circus (certainly for the parents of small children) probably has a fairly small price elasticity of demand. In this case, the price elasticity of demand might be something like −0.3: for every 1% increase in price, quantity demanded would fall by 0.3%. (If you prefer, you could also express this as saying for every 10% price increase, quantity demanded would drop by 3%.)

Markets with large price elasticities of supply—where the quantity supplied is sensitive to price differences—would be those where it was easy for suppliers to vary their amount of production as price changes. Perhaps they have a cost structure that allows them to make as many units as they'd like without driving up their per-unit costs too much. In the market for software, for example, if a program is wildly popular and drawing a high price, it's fairly easy for the game's producer to print more DVDs or make additional copies available for download. So, the elasticity of supply might be quite large in this market, something like 12 (a 1% increase in price leads to a 12% increase in quantity supplied).

Markets with low price elasticities of supply have quantities supplied that are fairly unresponsive to price changes. This would occur in markets where it is costly for producers to vary their production levels, or it is difficult for producers to enter or exit the market. The supply curve for tickets to the Super Bowl might have a very low price elasticity of supply because there are only so many seats in the stadium. If the ticket price rises today, the stadium owners can't really put in additional seats. The supply elasticity in this market might be close to zero. It's probably slightly positive, however, because the owners could open some obstructed-view seats or make other temporary seating arrangements.

 **application**

Demand Elasticities and the Availability of Substitutes

We discussed how the availability of substitutes can affect the price elasticity of demand. When consumers can easily switch to other products or markets, they will be more responsive to changes in price of a particular good. This means that, for any small rise in price, there will be a large decline in quantity demanded and the price elasticity of demand will be relatively large (in absolute value).

Economists Glenn and Sara Ellison found an extreme example of the effect of substitution possibilities and extreme demand elasticities to match.[7] They look at the markets for different CPUs and memory chips on a price search engine Web site. The Web site collects price quotes for well-defined chips and chipsets from hardware suppliers and then groups the quotes together (ranked by price) with links to the corresponding suppliers. While Ellison and Ellison show that suppliers make heroic efforts to frustrate the search engine, it still makes it extremely easy to compare multiple suppliers' prices for certain products. Because the product in this case is so standardized, little distinguishes one chip from another. As a result, consumers are able and willing to respond strongly to any price differences across the suppliers of the chips.

This easy ability for consumers to substitute across suppliers means the demand curve for any given supplier's CPUs and memory chips is extremely elastic. If a supplier's price is even a slight bit higher than that of its competitors, consumers can easily buy from someone else. Ellison and Ellison, using data collected from the Web site, estimated the price elasticity of demand for any single chip to be on the order of −25. In other words, if the supplier raises its price just 1% higher than that of its competitors (which works out to a dollar or two for the chips listed on the Web site), it can expect sales to fall by 25%! This is a huge price response, and it's due to the many substitution possibilities the search engine makes available to consumers. Thus, the availability of substitutes is one of the key determinants of the price elasticity of demand. ∎

Elasticities and Time Horizons   Often, a key factor determining the flexibility consumers and producers have to respond to price differences, and therefore the price elasticity of their quantities demanded and supplied, is the time horizon.

In the short run, consumers are often limited in their ability to change their consumption patterns, but given more time, they can make adjustments that give them greater flexibility. The classic example of this is in the market for gasoline. If there is a sudden price spike, many consumers are essentially stuck having to consume roughly the same quantity of gas as they did before the price spike. After all, they have the same car, the same commute, and the same schedule as before. Maybe they can double up on a few trips, or carpool more often, but their ability to respond to prices is limited. For

[7] Glenn Ellison and Sara Ellison, "Search, Obfuscation, and Price Elasticities on the Internet," *Econometrica* 77, no. 2 (2009): 427–452.

this reason, the short-run price elasticity of gasoline demand is relatively low; empirical estimates by economists that specialize in the market suggest it is around −0.2. That is, for a 1% change in the price of gas, the quantity demanded changes by only −0.2% in the direction opposite the price changes. Over longer horizons, however, individuals have greater scope to adjust their consumption. If the gas spike is permanent, or at least persistent, they can set up a permanent ride-sharing arrangement, buy a more efficient car, or even shorten their commute by moving closer to where they work. The long-run price elasticity of demand for gasoline is therefore much larger in magnitude; empirical studies typically find it is something like −0.8. This means that in the long run, consumers can make four times the quantity adjustment to price changes they can make in the short run.

The same logic holds for producers and supply elasticities. The longer the horizon, the more scope they have to adjust output to price changes. Manufacturers already producing at capacity might not be able to increase their output much in the short run if prices increase, even though they would like to. If prices stay high, however, they can hire more workers, build larger factories, and new firms can set up their own production operations and enter the market.

For these reasons, the price elasticities of demand and supply for most products are larger in magnitude (i.e., more negative for demand and more positive for supply) in the long run than in the short run. As we see in the next section, larger-magnitude elasticities imply flatter demand and supply curves. As a result, long-run demand and supply curves tend to be flatter than their short-run versions.

Terms for Elasticities by Magnitude   Economists have special terms for elasticities of particular magnitudes. Elasticities with magnitudes (absolute values) greater than 1 are referred to as **elastic.** In the above examples, apples have elastic demand and software has elastic supply. Elasticities with magnitudes less than 1 are referred to as **inelastic.** The demand for circus candy and the supply of previous wine vintages are inelastic. If the price elasticity of demand is exactly −1, or the price elasticity of supply is exactly 1, this is referred to as **unit elastic.** If price elasticities are zero—that is, there is no response in quantity to price changes, the associated goods are called **perfectly inelastic.** Finally, if price elasticities are infinite in magnitude (−∞ for demand, +∞ for supply)—the quantity demanded or supplied changes infinitely in response to any price change—this is referred to as **perfectly elastic.**

Elasticities and Linear Demand and Supply Curves

As we discussed above, economists often use linear (straight-line) demand and supply curves, mostly for the sake of convenience. Because they are so common, it's worth discussing how elasticities are related to linear curves. Even more important, drawing this connection shows exactly how curves' slopes and elasticities, the two measures of price responsiveness we've been using, are related but still different.

We can rewrite the elasticity formula in a way that makes it easier to see the relationship between elasticity and the slope of a demand or supply curve. A percentage change in quantity ($\%\Delta Q$) is the change in quantity (ΔQ) divided by the original quantity level Q. That is, $\%\Delta Q = \Delta Q/Q$. Similarly, the percentage change in price is $\%\Delta P = \Delta P/P$. Substituting these into the elasticity expression from above, we have

$$E = \frac{\%\Delta Q}{\%\Delta P} = \frac{\Delta Q/Q}{\Delta P/P}$$

where E is a demand or supply elasticity, depending on whether Q denotes quantity demanded or supplied.

elastic
A price elasticity with an absolute value greater than 1.

inelastic
A price elasticity with an absolute value less than 1.

unit elastic
A price elasticity with an absolute value equal to 1.

perfectly inelastic
A price elasticity that is equal to zero; there is no change in quantity demanded or supplied for any change in price.

perfectly elastic
A price elasticity that is infinite; any change in price leads to an infinite change in quantity demanded or supplied.

Rearranging terms yields

$$E = \frac{\Delta Q/Q}{\Delta P/P} = \frac{\Delta Q}{\Delta P} \cdot \frac{P}{Q}$$

or

$$E = \frac{1}{\text{slope}} \cdot \frac{P}{Q}$$

Elasticity of a Linear Demand Curve   Suppose we're dealing with the demand curve in Figure 2.16. Its slope is −2, but its elasticity varies as we move along it because P/Q does. Think first about the point A, where it intercepts the vertical axis. At $Q = 0$, P/Q is infinite because P is positive ($20) and Q is zero. This, combined with the fact that the curve's (constant) slope is negative, means the price elasticity of demand is $-\infty$ at this point. The logic behind this is that consumers don't demand any units of the good at A when its price is $20, but if price falls at all, their quantity demanded will become positive, if still small. Even though this change in quantity demanded is small in numbers of units of the good, the *percentage* change in consumption is infinite, because it's rising from zero.

As we move down along the demand curve, the P/Q ratio falls, reducing the magnitude of the price elasticity of demand. (Remember, the slope isn't changing, so that part of the elasticity stays the same.) It will remain elastic—that is, have a magnitude larger than 1—for some distance. Eventually, the absolute value of the elasticity will fall to 1, and at that point the demand curve is unit elastic. For the curve in Figure 2.16, this happens to be when $P = 10$ and $Q = 5$, because $E^D = -(1/2) \times (10/5) = -1$. This is labeled point B in the figure.[8] As we continue down and to the right along the demand curve, the magnitude of the elasticity will fall further and demand will become inelastic. At the point where the demand curve hits the horizontal axis (point C in the figure), price is zero, so $P/Q = 0$, and the price elasticity of demand is zero.

Figure 2.16   :   **Elasticity of a Linear Demand Curve**

The ratio between price and quantity (P/Q) and the magnitude of the elasticity of a demand curve decrease as we move down the curve. At point A, $Q = 0$, $P/Q = \infty$, and the price elasticity of demand is $-\infty$. Between points A and B, the demand curve is elastic with a price elasticity of demand less than -1. At point B, the demand curve is unit elastic, or the price elasticity of demand equals -1. Between points B and C, the demand curve is inelastic with a price elasticity of demand greater than -1. At point C, $P = 0$, $P/Q = 0$, and the price elasticity of demand equals zero.

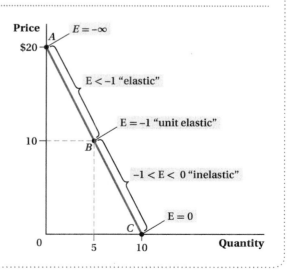

---

[8] For a linear demand curve that intersects both the price and quantity axes, the point where the demand curve is unit-elastic is always the midpoint. The curve's slope equals the price where it crosses the vertical axis (call this P_Y) divided by the quantity where it crosses the horizontal axis (call this Q_X), so 1 over the slope equals $-Q_X/P_Y$. The price-to-quantity ratio at the midpoint equals $(P_Y/2)/(Q_X/2)$, or simply P_Y/Q_X. The elasticity, which is the product of these two ratios, must therefore equal -1.

Figure 2.17   :   **Elasticity of a Linear Supply Curve**

The ratio between price and quantity (P/Q) and the magnitude of the elasticity of a supply curve decrease as we move up the curve. At point A, $Q = 0$, $P/Q = \infty$, and the price elasticity of supply is ∞. From B to C to D, the decrease in P/Q is reflected in the decrease of the slopes of the rays from these points to the origin. Unlike the demand curve, the price elasticity of supply will never reach zero because the supply curve never intercepts the quantity axis.

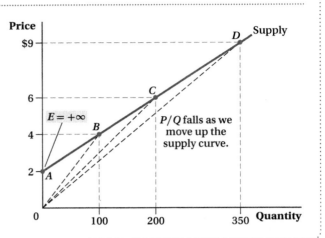

To recap, the price elasticity of demand of changes from $-\infty$ to zero as we move down and to the right along a linear demand curve.

Elasticity of a Linear Supply Curve   A somewhat similar effect is seen as we move along a linear supply curve, like the one in Figure 2.17. Again, because the slope of the curve is constant, the changes in elasticity along the curve are driven by the price-to-quantity ratio. At point A, where the supply curve intercepts the vertical axis, $Q = 0$ and P/Q is infinite. The price elasticity of supply is $+\infty$ at this point. The same logic holds as with the demand curve: For the smallest increase in price, the quantity supplied rises from zero to a positive number, an infinite percentage change in quantity supplied.

As we move up along the supply curve, the P/Q ratio falls. While it's probably obvious to you that it must fall from infinity, you might wonder whether it keeps falling, because both P and Q are rising. It turns out that, yes, it must keep falling. The way to see this is to recognize that the P/Q ratio at any point on the supply curve equals the slope of a ray from the origin to that point. (The rise of the ray is the price P, and its run is the quantity Q. Because slope is rise over run, the ray's slope is P/Q.) We've drawn some examples of such rays for different locations on the supply curve in Figure 2.17. It's clear from the figure that as we move up and to the right along the supply curve, the slopes of these rays from the origin continue to fall.

Unlike with the demand curve, however, the P/Q ratio never falls to zero because the supply curve will never intercept the horizontal axis. Therefore, the price elasticity of supply won't drop to zero. In fact, while the P/Q ratio is always falling as we move up along the supply curve, you can see from the figure that it will never drop below the slope of the supply curve itself. Some linear supply curves like the one in Figure 2.17 intercept the vertical axis at a positive price, indicating that the price has to be at least as high as the intercept for producers to be willing to supply any positive quantity. Because the price elasticity of supply equals $(1/\text{slope}) \times (P/Q)$, such supply curves approach becoming unit elastic at high prices and quantities supplied, but never quite get there. Also, because P/Q never falls to zero, the only way a supply curve can have an elasticity of zero is if its inverse slope is zero—that is, if it is vertical. We discuss cases like this below.

The demand for gym memberships in a small rural community is $Q = 360 - 2P$, where Q is the number of monthly members and P is the monthly membership rate.

a. Calculate the price elasticity of demand for gym memberships when the price is $50 per month.

b. Calculate the price elasticity of demand for gym memberships when the price is $100 per month.

c. Based on your answers to (a) and (b), what can you tell about the relationship between price and the price elasticity of demand along a linear demand curve?

Solution:

a. The price elasticity of demand is calculated as

$$E = \frac{\Delta Q/Q}{\Delta P/P} = \frac{\Delta Q}{\Delta P} \cdot \frac{P}{Q}$$

Let's first calculate the slope of the demand curve. The easiest way to do this is to rearrange the equation in terms of P to find the inverse demand curve:

$$Q = 360 - 2P$$
$$2P = 360 - Q$$
$$P = 180 - 0.5Q$$

We can see that the slope of this demand curve is -0.5. We know this because every time Q rises by 1, P falls by 0.5.

So we know the slope and the price. To compute the elasticity, we need to know the quantity demanded at a price of $50. To find this, we plug $50 into the demand equation for P:

$$Q = 360 - 2P = 360 - 2(50) = 360 - 100 = 260$$

Now we are ready to compute the elasticity:

$$E = \frac{1}{-0.5} \cdot \frac{50}{260} = \frac{50}{-130} = \text{-}0.385$$

b. When the price is $100 per month, the quantity demanded is

$$Q = 360 - 2P = 360 - 2(100) = 360 - 200 = 160$$

Plugging into the elasticity formula, we get

$$E = \frac{1}{-0.5} \cdot \frac{100}{160} = \frac{100}{-80} = -1.25$$

c. From (a) and (b), we can see that as the price rises along a linear demand curve, demand moves from being inelastic ($0.385 < 1$) to elastic ($1.25 > 1$).

Perfectly Inelastic and Perfectly Elastic Demand and Supply

The formula relating elasticities to slopes also sheds some light on what demand and supply curves look like in two special but often discussed cases: perfectly inelastic and perfectly elastic demand and supply.

Perfect Inelasticity   We discussed above that when the price elasticity is zero, demand and supply are said to be perfectly inelastic. When would this be the case? We just saw that this will be true for any linear demand at the point where it intercepts the horizontal (quantity) axis. But what would a demand curve look like that is perfectly inelastic everywhere? A linear demand curve with a slope of $-\infty$ would drive the price elasticity of demand to zero due to the inverse relationship between elasticity and slope. Because a curve with an infinite slope is vertical, a perfectly inelastic demand curve is vertical. An example of such a curve is shown in Figure 2.18a. This makes intuitive sense: A vertical demand curve indicates that the quantity demanded by consumers is completely unchanged regardless of the price. Any percentage change in price will induce a 0% change in quantity demanded. In other words, the price elasticity of demand is zero.

While perfectly inelastic demand curves are uncommon (after all, there are almost always possibilities for consumers and producers to substitute toward or away from a good as prices hit either extreme of zero or infinity), we might see some approximations to this case. For example, diabetics might have very inelastic demand for insulin. Their demand curve will be almost vertical.

The same logic holds for supply: A vertical supply curve indicates perfectly inelastic supply and no response of quantity supplied to price differences. The supply of tickets for a particular concert or sporting event might also be close to perfectly inelastic, with a near-vertical supply curve, due to capacity constraints of the arena.

One implication of perfect inelasticity is that any shift in the market's demand or supply curve will result in a change only in the market equilibrium price, not the quantity. That's because there is absolutely no scope for quantity to change in the movement along a perfectly inelastic demand curve from the old to the new equilibrium. Likewise, for perfectly inelastic supply, if there is a demand curve shift, all equilibrium movement is in price, not quantity.

Perfect Elasticity   When demand or supply is perfectly elastic, on the other hand, the price elasticity is infinite. This will be the case for linear demand or supply curves that have slopes of zero—those that are horizontal. An example of such a curve is shown in Figure 2.18b. This shape makes intuitive sense, too. As flat demand or supply curves imply large quantity responses to price differences, *perfectly* flat curves imply infinitely large quantity changes to price differences. If price is just above a horizontal demand curve, the quantity demanded will be zero. But if price fell just a bit, to below the demand curve, the quantity demanded would be infinite. Similarly, a small price change from above to below a horizontal supply curve would shift producers' quantity supplied from infinite to zero.

Figure 2.18   Perfectly Inelastic and Perfectly Elastic Demand Curves

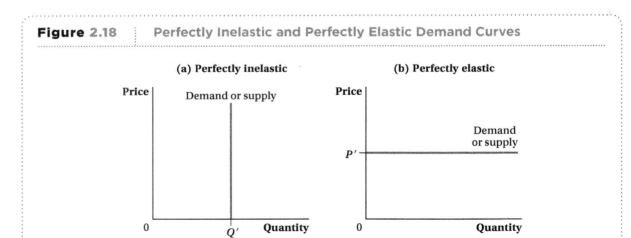

(a) Perfectly inelastic

(b) Perfectly elastic

(a) When a demand or supply curve is vertical, its slope is infinite and it is perfectly inelastic. In other words, any change in price will result in a 0% change in quantity demanded or supplied.

(b) When a demand or supply curve is horizontal, its slope is zero and it is perfectly elastic. In other words, any change in price will result in an infinitely large change in quantity demanded or supplied.

When might we see perfectly elastic demand or supply curves? Small producers of commodity goods probably face demand curves for their products that are approximately horizontal. (We'll discuss this more in Chapter 8.) For instance, a small corn farmer can probably sell as many bushels of corn as she wants at the fixed price offered by the local grain elevator. While the elevator couldn't really handle an infinite amount of corn, it has the capacity to buy much more corn than the farmer could ever practically sell. So from the farmer's perspective, the quantity demanded at the offered price can grow as large as would ever matter for her. At the same time, if the farmer decided that the elevator's price was too low and insisted that she be paid more than the going rate, the elevator would likely refuse to buy any corn from the farmer. Effectively, then, it is as if the farmer faces an infinite quantity demanded for her corn at the going price (or below it, if for some reason she's willing to sell for less) but zero quantity demanded of her corn above that price. In other words, she faces a flat demand curve at the going market price.

Supply curves are close to perfectly elastic in competitive industries in which producers all have roughly the same costs, and entry and exit is very easy. (We'll also discuss this point more in Chapter 8.) These conditions mean that competition will drive prices toward the (common) level of costs, and differences in quantities supplied will be soaked up by the entry and exit of firms from the industry. Because of the strictures of competition in the market, no firm will be able to sell at a price above costs, and obviously no firm will be willing to supply at a price below costs. Therefore, the industry's supply curve is essentially flat at the producers' cost level.

As opposed to the perfectly inelastic case, shifts in supply in a market with perfectly elastic demand will only move equilibrium quantity, not price. There's no way for the equilibrium price to change when the demand curve is flat. Similarly, for markets with perfectly elastic supply, demand curve shifts move only equilibrium quantities and not prices.

The Price Elasticity of Demand, Expenditures, and Revenue

There's an interesting and useful relationship between consumers' expenditures on a good and the price elasticity of demand. Namely, expenditures rise with prices if demand is inelastic, but decrease with prices if demand is inelastic. If demand is unit elastic, a change in price has no impact on expenditures. This same relationship holds between firm revenue and the price elasticity of demand.

To see why this is the case, recognize that expenditures and revenue are the products of price and quantity:

$$\text{Total expenditure} = \text{Total revenue} = P \cdot Q$$

Now think about how expenditure will change when price rises. (In the rest of this section, we examine what happens to expenditure when price changes, but we could instead focus on how prices change revenue and get the same result.) Obviously, the direct impact of the price increase will tend to raise expenditures. However, the higher price will also reduce quantity demanded, which tends to reduce expenditures. Which of these opposing effects is stronger depends on the price elasticity of demand.

We can be more specific. The percentage change in a product of two numbers is approximately equal to the sum of the percentage changes in the product's components. That means the percentage change in total expenditure due to a price change equals the percentage change in price plus the percentage change in quantity demanded that results. Of course, since price and quantity demanded move in opposite directions, when one of these changes is positive, the other change will be negative. For example, suppose that price rises. If the percentage increase in price is larger than the percentage drop in quantity demanded, expenditures will increase as a result of the price hike.

Expenditures will decrease if the opposite holds true and the percentage drop in quantity demanded is larger than the price change.

To see this more explicitly, remember the formula for the price elasticity of demand:

$$E^D = \frac{\%\Delta Q^D}{\%\Delta P}$$

If demand is inelastic (the elasticity is smaller than 1 in absolute value, or between −1 and zero if you prefer), then the percentage drop in quantity (the numerator) will be smaller than the percentage increase in price (the denominator). This means the direct effect of price outweighs the quantity effect, and expenditures rise. If demand is elastic (the elasticity is greater than 1 in absolute value) on the other hand, then the percentage drop in quantity (the numerator) will be larger than the percentage increase in price (the denominator). In this case, the indirect effect of the price increase is larger than the direct effect, and total expenditures fall. For unit elastic demand (an elasticity of −1), the percentage increase in price exactly equals the percentage decrease in quantity demanded, so expenditure doesn't change.

For a downward-sloping linear demand curve like the one shown in Figure 2.16 this property means that total expenditures will follow a particular pattern as we move along the demand curve. Let's start at the curve's intercept with the horizontal axis, point C. There, price is zero, so implied expenditure is also zero. Easy enough. Now let's start increasing the price, so we're moving up and to the left along the demand curve. As we know from our previous discussion, along the portion of the demand curve closest to the horizontal intercept, the demand is inelastic. Therefore, the percentage increase in price from moving up the demand curve is larger than the percentage decrease in quantity demanded, meaning expenditures must rise. As we keep increasing price and moving up the demand curve, demand will continue to be inelastic and expenditures will continue to rise until point B, where demand becomes unit elastic. At that point, we know that expenditures will not change when price increases. However, as we keep increasing price and moving further up the demand curve, demand becomes price elastic. This means that the percentage drop in quantity demanded is larger than the percentage increase in price, and expenditure starts to fall. This drop in expenditures continues as we keep raising price and moving up the demand curve. Eventually, we reach point A. There, quantity falls to zero and therefore so do implied expenditures.

If we plot these changes in expenditure along the demand curve versus the price, we get Figure 2.19. When price is zero at point C, so are expenditures (we've labeled the

---

Figure 2.19   :   **Expenditures along a Linear Demand Curve**

At point C, price and expenditures are zero along the demand curve. Between points C and B, the demand curve is inelastic, and expenditures increase with the increase in price along the demand curve. Point B is the maximum expenditures point; at B, the demand curve is unit elastic, and expenditures neither rise nor fall. Between points B and A, the demand curve is elastic, and expenditures decrease with the increase in price along the demand curve.

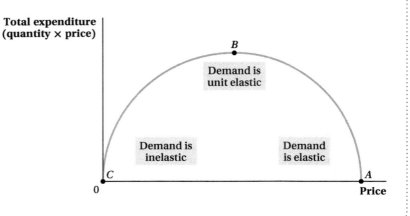

expenditure plot with points on the demand curve in Figure 2.16 to which they correspond). As price rises through the inelastic part of the demand curve, so do expenditures. When price hits the level at B, demand is unit elastic and expenditures are neither rising nor falling. At higher price levels, expenditure falls as price rises until finally hitting zero again at point A. Notice how expenditure is maximized at point B, where demand is unit elastic. This is because at lower prices demand is inelastic and expenditures rise with price, but at higher prices demand is elastic and expenditures fall in price.

Income Elasticity of Demand

We've been focusing on price elasticities to this point, and with good reason: They are a key determinant of demand and supply behavior and play an important role in helping us understand how markets work. However, they are not the only elasticities that matter in demand and supply analysis. Remember how we divided up all the factors that affected demand or supply into two categories: price and everything else? Well, each of those other factors that went into "everything else" has an influence on demand or supply that can be measured with an elasticity.

The most commonly used of these elasticities measure the impact of two other factors on quantity demanded. These are the income elasticity of demand and the cross-price elasticity of demand.

The **income elasticity of demand** is the ratio of the percentage change in quantity demanded to the corresponding percentage change in consumer income (I):

$$E^D_I = \frac{\%\Delta Q^D}{\%\Delta I} = \frac{\Delta Q^D}{\Delta I} \cdot \frac{I}{Q^D}$$

income elasticity of demand
The percentage change in quantity demanded associated with a 1% change in consumer income.

(Equivalently, it is the percentage change in quantity demanded associated with a 1% increase in consumer income.)

Income elasticities describe how responsive demand is to income changes. Goods are sometimes categorized by the sign and size of their income elasticity. Goods that have an income elasticity that is negative, meaning consumers demand a lower quantity of the good when their income rises, are called **inferior goods.** This name isn't a comment on their inherent quality; it just describes how their consumption changes with people's incomes. (Note, however, that low-quality versions of many product categories are inferior goods by the economic definition.) Examples of likely inferior goods are bus tickets, youth hostels, and hot dogs.

inferior good
A good for which quantity demanded decreases when income rises.

Goods with positive income elasticities (consumers' quantity demanded rises with their income) are called **normal goods.** As the name indicates, most goods fit into this category.

The subcategory of normal goods with income elasticities above 1 is sometimes called **luxury goods.** Having an income elasticity that is greater than 1 means the quantity demanded of these products rises at a faster rate than income. As a consequence, the share of a consumer's budget that is spent on a luxury good becomes larger as the consumer's income rises. (To keep a good's share of the budget constant, quantity consumed would have to rise at the same rate as income. Because luxury goods' quantities rise faster, their share increases with income.) Yachts, butlers, and fine art are all luxury goods.

normal good
A good for which quantity demanded rises when income rises.

luxury good
A good with an income elasticity greater than 1.

We will dig deeper into the relationship between incomes and consumer demand in Chapters 4 and 5.

Cross-Price Elasticity of Demand

The **cross-price elasticity of demand** is the ratio of the percentage change in one good's quantity demanded (say, good X) to the percentage change in price of *another* good Y:

$$E^D_{XY} = \frac{\%\Delta Q^D_X}{\%\Delta P_Y} = \frac{\Delta Q^D_X}{\Delta P_Y} \cdot \frac{P_Y}{Q^D_X}$$

cross-price elasticity of demand
The percentage change in the quantity demanded of one good associated with a 1% change in the price of another good.

(To avoid confusion, sometimes the price elasticities we discussed above, which are concerned with the percentage change in quantity demanded to the percentage change in the price of the *same* good, are referred to as **own-price elasticities of demand.**)

own-price elasticities of demand

The percentage change in quantity demanded for a good resulting from a percentage change in the price of that good.

When a good has a positive cross-price elasticity with another good, that means consumers demand a higher quantity of it when the other good's price rises. In other words, the good is a substitute for the other good: Consumers switch to the good when the other one becomes more expensive. Many pairs of goods are substitutes for one another—different brands of cereal, meals at restaurants versus dinners at home, colleges, and so on. Economist Aviv Nevo measured the substitutability of different cereals. He found that Froot Loops, for example, is a substitute for other kids' cereals, like Frosted Flakes and Cap'n Crunch ($E^D_{XY} = 0.131$ and 0.149, respectively). However, it is much less of a substitute for the more adult Shredded Wheat, which had a cross-price elasticity of only 0.020.[9]

When a good has a negative cross-price elasticity with another good, consumers demand less of it when the other good's price increases. This indicates that the goods are complements. Complements tend to be goods that are consumed together. If either of the goods within each pair were to become more expensive, consumers would buy not just less of that good itself, but of the other good in the pair as well. Milk and cookies are complements, as are tennis rackets and tennis balls, and computers and software.

2.6 figure it out

Suppose that the price elasticity of demand for cereal is −0.75 and the cross-price elasticity of demand between cereal and the price of milk is −0.9. If the price of milk rises by 10%, what would have to happen to the price of cereal to exactly offset the rise in the price of milk and leave the quantity of cereal demanded unchanged?

Solution:

The first step will be to see what happens to the quantity of cereal demanded when the price of milk rises by 10%. We can use the cross-price elasticity to help us with this. The cross-price elasticity for cereal with respect to the price of milk is equal to $\dfrac{\%\Delta Q_{cereal}}{\%\Delta P_{milk}} = -0.9$. Using the equation, we know that the denominator is 10 since the price of milk rose by 10%, so we get

$$\frac{\%\Delta Q_{cereal}}{\%\Delta P_{milk}} = \frac{\%\Delta Q_{cereal}}{10} = -0.9$$

$$\%\Delta Q_{cereal} = -9$$

Thus, when the price of milk rises by 10%, the quantity demanded of cereal falls by 9%.

Now we must consider how to offset this decline in the quantity of cereal demanded with a change in the price of cereal. In other words, what must happen to the price of cereal to cause the quantity of cereal demanded to *rise* by 9%? It is clear that the price of cereal must fall because the law of demand suggests that there is an inverse relationship between price and quantity demanded. However, because we know the price elasticity of demand, we can actually determine how far the price of cereal needs to fall.

The price elasticity of demand for cereal is $\dfrac{\%\Delta Q}{\%\Delta P} = -0.75$. To offset the decline in cereal consumption caused by the rise in the price of milk, we need the percentage change in quantity demanded to be +9%. Therefore, we can plug 9% into the numerator of the ratio and solve for the denominator:

$$\frac{\%\Delta Q}{\%\Delta P} = -0.75$$

$$\frac{9}{\%\Delta P} = -0.75$$

$$\%\Delta P = \frac{9}{-0.75} = -12$$

The price of cereal would have to fall by 12% to exactly offset the effect of a rise in the price of milk on the quantity of cereal consumed.

---

[9] Aviv Nevo, "Measuring Market Power in the Ready-to-Eat Cereal Industry," *Econometrica* 69, no. 2 (2001): 307–342.

2.6 Conclusion

This chapter introduced the concepts of supply and demand, two of the most important ideas in economics. Using the simplified supply and demand framework, we examined a variety of topics, including equilibrium price and quantity, the effects of shocks to supply and demand, and elasticities.

But, the various cases we looked at in this chapter are, for the most part, simplified and very abstract. In reality, measuring a market's demand and supply curves and determining the equilibrium price and quantity can be more challenging and complex. For example, firms hoping to make production decisions based on the types of analysis we've done here need to observe a wide range of data—prices, elasticities, demand curves, and so on—that are often not known exactly in the real world. As a result, producers might rely on more trial-and-error practices than allowed for in our simplified model. Indeed, our own experience with firms is that the people making the production decisions don't always approach and analyze them as economists would. If they did, firms might see more financial success. Beginning with Chapter 6 and continuing through Part 3, we talk more about situations that producers face in the real world, and the production decisions they have to make, such as how much of a product to produce, how to produce it, and whether they should enter a particular market at all. And we see how these decisions are reflected in a firm's supply curve. In the meantime, the simplified supply and demand framework we've developed here provides a valuable structure for delving into a deeper analysis of markets and equilibrium price and quantity in upcoming chapters.

Summary

1. Economists use models to analyze markets. Models employ simplifying assumptions to reduce the incredible complexity of the real world so that general insights can be learned. The **supply** and **demand** model is one of the most used analytical frameworks in economics. This model makes several assumptions about the market that is being analyzed, including that all goods bought and sold in the market are identical, they are all sold for the same price, and there are many producers and consumers in the market. [**Section 2.1**]

2. Demand describes the willingness of consumers to purchase a product. There are many factors that affect demand, including price, income, quality, tastes, and availability of **substitutes.** Economists commonly use the concept of a **demand curve,** which essentially divides these factors into two groups: price and everything else. A demand curve relates consumers' quantity demanded to the price of the good while holding every other factor affecting demand constant. A change in a good's price results in a movement along a given demand curve. If nonprice factors change, the quantity demanded at every price changes and the whole demand curve shifts. [**Section 2.2**]

3. Supply describes the willingness of producers to make and sell a product. Factors that affect supply include price, available **production technologies,** input prices, and producers' outside options. **Supply curves** isolate the relationship between quantity supplied and price, holding all other supply factors constant. A change in a good's price results in a movement along a given supply curve. If nonprice factors change, the quantity supplied at every price changes and the whole supply curve shifts. [**Section 2.3**]

4. Combining demand and supply curves lets us determine the **market equilibrium** price, which is where quantity demanded equals quantity supplied. This equilibrium can be determined because demand and supply curves isolate the relationships between quantities and the one factor that affects both demand and supply: price. At the equilibrium, every consumer who wants to buy at the going price can, and every producer who wants to sell at the current market price can as well. [**Section 2.4**]

5. Changes in the factors (other than price) that affect demand or supply will change the market equilibrium price and quantity. Changes that increase demand and shift out the demand curve

will raise **equilibrium price** and quantity in the absence of supply shifts; when the changes decrease demand and shift the demand curve in, price and quantity will fall. Changes that increase supply and shift out the supply curve, assuming no change in the demand curve, will increase equilibrium quantity and reduce price. Changes that decrease supply and shift in the supply curve decrease quantity and raise price. [**Section 2.4**]

6. If both supply and demand shift, either the effect on equilibrium price or the effect on equilibrium quantity will be ambiguous. If demand and supply move in the same direction, equilibrium quantity will follow, but the impact on price is unknown. On the other hand, if demand and supply move in opposite directions, equilibrium price will move in the same direction as demand (increase when demand rises, fall when demand decreases) but we cannot say with certainty what the effect on equilibrium quantity will be. [**Section 2.4**]

7. Economists typically express the sensitivity of demand and supply to various factors, but especially price, in terms of elasticities. An **elasticity** is the ratio of the percentage changes in two variables. The **price elasticity of demand** is the percentage change in quantity demanded for a 1% change in price, and the price elasticity of supply is the percentage change in quantity supplied for a 1% price change. [**Section 2.5**]

8. Total expenditure and total revenue are both equal to price times quantity demanded. When demand is **elastic** ($|E^D| > 1$), an increase in price will lead to a fall in expenditures (revenue), while a decrease in price will lead expenditures (revenue) to increase. When demand is **inelastic** ($|E^D| < 1$), expenditure (revenue) rises when price rises and falls when price falls. When demand is **unit elastic** ($|E^D| = 1$), a change in price has no effect on total expenditure (revenue). [**Section 2.5**]

9. Other common demand elasticities measure the responsiveness of quantity demanded to changes in income and the prices of other goods. The **income elasticity of demand** is positive for **normal goods** and negative for **inferior goods.** The **cross-price elasticity of demand** is positive for substitutes and negative for complements. [**Section 2.5**]

Review Questions

1. There are four key assumptions underlying the supply and demand model. Name these assumptions.
2. Complements and substitutes of a given good affect the demand for that good. Define complements and substitutes.
3. What simplifying assumption do we make to build a demand curve? Why is the demand curve downward-sloping?
4. What is the difference between a change in quantity demanded and a change in demand?
5. Why is the supply curve upward-sloping?
6. What is an inverse supply curve? Why do economists often represent supply using the inverse supply curve?
7. What is the difference between a change in quantity supplied and a change in supply?
8. Define market equilibrium. What is true of the quantity supplied and demanded at the market equilibrium?
9. What happens when price is below the equilibrium price? Why?
10. In what direction will price and quantity move as a result of a demand shift?
11. In what direction will price and quantity move as a result of a supply shift?
12. Why is the direction of change of *either* price *or* quantity unknown when both supply and demand shift?
13. What happens to equilibrium price when demand and supply shift in the same direction? What happens to equilibrium quantity in the same situation?
14. What is the difference between an elasticity and slope?
15. We learned that economists have special terms for elasticities of particular magnitudes. Name the magnitudes for the following: inelastic, elastic, unit elastic, perfectly elastic, and perfectly inelastic.
16. What is total expenditure? Total revenue?
17. Why must you know the price elasticity of demand to be able to predict the effect of a change in price on total expenditure?
18. Using the concept of income elasticity of demand, describe normal, luxury, and inferior goods.
19. Using the concept of cross-price elasticity of demand, describe substitutes and complements.

Problems

1. Is there a difference between movements along a demand curve and shifts in a demand curve? How would you explain this difference to a friend who is taking this course and is confused about the issue?

2. The demand for organic carrots is given by the following equation:

$$Q^D_O = 75 - 5P_O + P_C + 2I$$

where P_O is the price of organic carrots, P_C is the price of conventional carrots, and I is the average consumer income. Notice how this isn't a standard demand curve that just relates the quantity of organic carrots demanded to the price of organic carrots. This demand function also describes how other factors affect demand—namely, the price of another good (conventional carrots) and income.

   a. Draw the demand curve for organic carrots when $P_C = 5$ and $I = 10$.
   b. Using the demand curve drawn in (a), what is the quantity demanded of organic carrots when $P_O = 10$?
   c. Using the demand curve drawn in (a), what is the quantity demanded of organic carrots when $P_O = 5$?
   d. Now, suppose $P_O = 10$ and $P_C = 15$ (I remains at 10). What is the quantity demanded of organic carrots? Compared with your answer in (b), has there been a change in demand or quantity demanded? Demonstrate using a graph.
   e. What happens to the demand for organic carrots when the price of conventional carrots increases? Are organic and conventional carrots complements or substitutes?
   f. What happens to the demand for organic carrots when the average consumer income increases? Are carrots a normal or an inferior good?

3. Out of the following events, which are likely to cause the demand for coffee to increase? Explain your answers.
   a. An increase in the price of tea
   b. An increase in the price of doughnuts
   c. A decrease in the price of coffee
   d. The Surgeon General's announcement that drinking coffee lowers the risk of heart disease
   e. Heavy rains causing a record-low coffee harvest in Colombia

4. How is each of the following events likely to shift the supply curve or the demand curve for fast-food hamburgers in the United States? Make sure you indicate which curve (curves) is affected and if it shifts out or in.
   a. The price of beef triples.
   b. The price of chicken falls by half.
   c. The number of teenagers in the economy falls due to population aging.
   d. Mad cow disease, a rare but fatal medical condition caused by eating tainted beef, becomes common in the United States.
   e. The Food and Drug Administration publishes a report stating that a certain weight-loss diet, which encourages the intake of large amounts of meat, is dangerous to one's health.
   f. An inexpensive new grill for home use that makes delicious hamburgers is heavily advertised on television.
   g. The dollar rises relative to foreign currencies, so that it becomes expensive for foreign tourists to travel to the United States on vacation.
   h. The minimum wage rises.

5. Your roommate remarks that it is strange that a flight from New York to Chicago costs more than a flight from New York to Orlando, since New York and Chicago are closer than New York and Orlando. What is your roommate assuming about the relationship between distance and price? How do you explain these prices?

6. Suppose that a hard freeze destroys a large portion of the Florida orange crop. At the same time, the *Journal of the American Medical Association* releases the results of a new study showing that drinking large quantities of orange juice substantially reduces one's risks of both heart disease and cancer. What is the likely effect of these two events on the price of orange juice? On the quantity of orange juice sold?

7. Suppose that you have been collecting vintage lightning rods for the past 30 years. When you began, finding lightning rods for sale meant drifting from town to town and antique store to antique store hoping that you would find a lightning rod for sale. The availability made possible by the Internet now means that you can easily find hundreds of lightning rods for sale at any given time.
   a. Draw a diagram showing how the invention and popularization of the Internet have caused the demand curve for lightning rods to shift.
   b. Suppose that the only change in the market for lightning rods is the change you described in (a). How would that change affect the equilibrium price of lightning rods and the equilibrium quantity of lightning rods sold?

8. In March 2002 the retail price of gasoline was $1.19 per gallon—exactly the same as it was in August 1990. Yet, total gasoline production and consumption rose from 6.6 million barrels per week in 1990 to 8.7 million barrels per week in 2002. Using the graph below, draw the appropriate shifts in the demand and supply curves to explain these two phenomena.

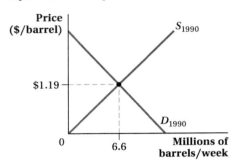

9. When the demand for toilet paper increases, the equilibrium quantity sold increases. Consumers are buying more, and producers are producing more.
   a. How do producers receive the signal that they need to increase production to meet the new demand?
   b. Does the increased production reflect an increase in supply, or an increase in the quantity supplied? Explain your answer, referring to (a).

10. Suppose the demand for towels is given by $Q^D = 100 - 5P$, and the supply of towels is given by $Q^S = 10P$.
    a. Derive and graph the inverse supply and inverse demand curves.
    b. Solve for the equilibrium price and quantity.
    c. Suppose that supply changes so that at each price, 20 fewer towels are offered for sale. Derive and graph the new inverse supply curve.
    d. Solve for the new equilibrium price and quantity.

11. Your university has an honors program that accepts exactly 40 freshmen each year. Every year before soliciting applications, students are informed of the standards for program participation. The admissions staff observed that whenever the difficulty of the program requirements increased (decreased), they received fewer (more) applicants than in the previous year and have since begun to adjust requirements for each incoming group of students in an attempt to equate the number of applicants with the number of spots in the program. Though the system is not perfect, the administrators are able to estimate their applicant pool relatively accurately.
    a. In this situation, what is the "price" that determines how many students will apply to the honors program? Also, assume that the people who run the honors program do not plan to expand or contract it. Depict the demand and supply curves that represent this situation.
    b. How does the way "price" is determined in this situation differ from the way we normally think about the determination of equilibrium price?
    c. Assume that applicants to the honors program are usually the most qualified students at the university. If the university began offering merit scholarships to incoming students, how would we expect the difficulty of the program to change over the next few years? Demonstrate your answer with a graph.
    d. The president of the university became so impressed with the rigor of the first honors program that she decides to double its size. Assuming that the larger program accepts applicants in the same way, what will likely happen to the standards of the expanded honors program? Demonstrate your answer with a graph.
    e. Instead of expanding the first honors program, the faculty recommends introducing a whole new one. Suppose the first was an honors program in science. How would standards change for the science honors program if the new honors program were in math? How about art history? Explain your answers.

12. Consider the market for van Gogh paintings and assume no forgeries are possible.
    a. Is the supply of van Gogh paintings somewhat elastic, somewhat inelastic, perfectly elastic, or perfectly inelastic? Why?
    b. Draw the supply curve for van Gogh paintings.
    c. Suppose there are only 10 van Gogh paintings in the world, and the demand curve is $Q = 50 - 0.5P$. What is the equilibrium price?
    d. A tragic fire destroys five of the paintings. What is the new equilibrium price?

13. Suppose the demand for down pillows is given by $Q^D = 100 - P$, and that the supply of down pillows is given by $Q^S = -20 + 2P$.
    a. Solve for the equilibrium price.
    b. Plug the equilibrium price back into the demand equation and solve for the equilibrium quantity.
    c. Double-check your work by plugging the equilibrium price back into the supply equation and solving for the equilibrium quantity. Does your answer agree with what you got in (b)?
    d. Solve for the elasticities of demand and supply at the equilibrium point. Which is more elastic, demand or supply?
    e. Invert the demand and supply functions (in other words, solve each for P) and graph them. Do the equilibrium point and relative elasticities shown in the graph appear to coincide with your answers?

14. Suppose that budding economist Buck measures the inverse demand curve for toffee as $P = \$100 - Q^D$, and the inverse supply curve as $P = Q^S$. Buck's economist friend Penny likes to measure everything in cents. She measures the inverse demand for toffee as $P = 10,000 - 100Q^D$, and the inverse supply curve as $P = 100Q^S$.

   a. Find the slope of the inverse demand curve, and compute the price elasticity of demand at the market equilibrium using Buck's measurements.

   b. Find the slope of the inverse demand curve, and compute the price elasticity of demand at the market equilibrium using Penny's measurements. Is the slope the same as Buck calculated? How about the price elasticity of demand?

15. Suppose that innovations in agriculture lower the cost of producing lettuce by 10%. This cost reduction effectively shifts the inverse supply curve downward by 10% at every quantity.

   a. Assume that the price of lettuce is determined by the forces of demand and supply. Graph the market for lettuce initially, and then illustrate the effects of the technological innovation.

   b. Will lettuce growers be able to capture the cost savings provided by the new technology, or will they end up passing the savings along to consumers? Explain, using your graph.

   c. How does your answer depend on the price elasticity of demand for lettuce? Explain, using two graphs to illustrate your point.

16. Some policy makers have claimed that the U.S. government should purchase illegal drugs, such as cocaine, to increase the price that drug users will face. Does this idea have any merit? Illustrate this logic in a simple supply and demand framework. How does the elasticity of demand for illegal drugs relate to the efficacy of this policy? Are you more or less willing to favor this policy if you are told demand is inelastic?

17. Consider the following problems on elasticity:

   a. When bottlers increased the price of canned soda from vending machines by 10%, sales dropped by 2.5%. Calculate the elasticity of demand for canned soda.

   b. Refer to part (a). The total revenue received by bottlers from their sales of canned soda is equal to the price of canned soda times the number of cans sold ($TR = P_{\text{soda}} \times Q_{\text{soda}}$). In approximate percentage terms, what was the impact of the bottlers' price change on total revenue?

   c. Sal the Sail Salesman's boss has just told him that if he fails to increase the volume of his sail sales by 8%, he'll be fired. In order to meet his goal, Sal is considering putting his sails on sale. If the price elasticity of demand for sales is −2.66, how much should Sal lower his price in order to meet his goal?

   d. Yogi eats a sizable quantity of pizza by the slice, and generally pays $5 per slice at a vending cart outside his office. When a new vendor on the block begins offering pizza at $3 per slice, Yogi finds that his monthly total expenditures on pizza rise. What can we say about Yogi's elasticity of demand for pizza?

18. Suppose that a typical consumer has an inverse demand for frog's legs given by the following: $P = \dfrac{3}{Q^D}$. A graph of that inverse demand curve is given below:

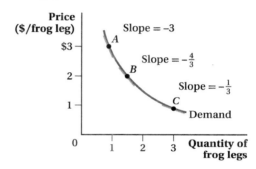

   a. Show that the demand curve is unit-elastic.

   b. If this customer came into your restaurant and asked for frog's legs, would you be better off charging a high price or a low price?

19. One type of elasticity that economists often use is the cross-price elasticity, which is measured as the percentage change in the quantity of a good when the price of a different good changes by 1%.

   a. What sign might you expect the cross-price elasticity to have if the two goods are shampoo and hair conditioner? Why?

   b. What sign might you expect the cross-price elasticity to have if the two goods are gasoline and ethanol? Why?

   c. What sign might you expect the cross-price elasticity to have if the two goods are coffee and shoes? Why?

20. One type of elasticity that economists often use is the income elasticity, which is measured as the percentage change in the quantity of a good when the income of consumers changes by 1%.

   a. What sign might you expect the income elasticity to have if the good in question is Swedish massages?

   b. What sign might you expect the income elasticity to have if the good in question is Ramen noodles?

   c. What sign might you expect the income elasticity to have if the good in question is table salt?

Using Supply and Demand to Analyze Markets

In Chapter 2, we introduced the tools of supply and demand analysis. We learned about the economic decisions that supply and demand curves embody, and defined what it means for a market to be in equilibrium. In this chapter, we put those tools to work to take a deeper look at how markets operate. We study how to measure the total benefits that consumers and producers gain in any given market, and how these benefits change when demand or supply shifts. We also see how various government interventions into markets affect the well-being of consumers and producers.

Governments often enact policies that affect how markets work. The purpose of these policies can be to serve a particular constituency, to raise necessary tax revenue, or (as we'll see in Chapter 16) to correct a market failure. For example, every time gas prices rise above the public's tolerance, some politicians predictably call for a top limit on gas prices (called a *price ceiling*). Judging from the opinion polls that are usually taken at such times, this policy strikes many people as being a good idea. Are they right? Whether changes in market conditions are the result of government market interventions or changes in any of the many factors that affect supply, demand, or both, we can use supply and demand analysis to figure out not only what happens to price and quantity, but also who benefits, who loses, and by how much.

3.1 Consumer and Producer Surplus: Who Benefits in a Market?

To begin to understand the market impact of any policy, we need a way to measure the benefit consumers and producers obtain from buying and selling goods and services in a market. Economists measure these benefits using the concepts of consumer and producer surplus.

Consumer Surplus

Consumer surplus is the difference between the price consumers would be willing to pay for a good (as measured by the height of their demand curves) and the price they actually have to pay. Consumer surplus is usually measured as an amount of money.

To see why we define consumer surplus this way, let's think like an economist. Say a person is lost in the desert with no water, is getting extremely thirsty, and has $1,000 in his pocket. He stumbles upon a convenience store in this desert where he sees a bottle of Dr Pepper for sale. What is he willing to pay for the drink? Quite likely, his entire $1,000. Applying the concept of elasticity from Chapter 2, we can say this guy's demand for something to drink is almost perfectly inelastic: He will demand the one bottle of Dr Pepper almost regardless of its price. Let's say the store is asking $1 for the bottle of Dr Pepper. Mr. Thirsty was willing to pay $1,000 for the Dr Pepper but only had to pay the $1 market price. After the transaction, he has his drink *and* $999 left in his pocket. That $999—the difference between what he was willing to pay and what he actually paid—is his consumer surplus.

We can take this one-person example and extend the consumer surplus to the demand curve for an entire market. For example, let's return to Pike Place Market but now consider the market for apples. The market demand curve in Figure 3.1 tells us how many pounds of apples consumers are willing to buy at any given price. Let's assume that the market price of apples is $3.50 per pound.

If every point along the market demand curve represents a different person's willingness to pay for a pound of apples, we can measure each person's consumer surplus just as we did for Mr. Thirsty. The person at point A on the demand curve is willing to pay up to $5 for a pound of apples. If the price is $3.50 per pound, she will buy the apples and also keep $1.50 of consumer surplus. Person B is willing to pay $4.50 per pound and receives $1 of consumer surplus, while Person C receives $0.50 of consumer surplus. The person at point D is willing to pay $3.50 for a pound of apples and must pay the market price of $3.50 a pound. Thus, there is no consumer surplus for this individual.[1] Person E will not buy any apples; he is willing to pay only $3 per pound, which is below the market price. If you want to know the total consumer surplus for the entire market, add up all of the gains for each individual who buys apples—person A, person B, and so on.

After adding up all the gains, you will find that the total consumer surplus in the entire Pike Place apple market is the area under the demand curve and above the price, the area of the shaded triangle CS in Figure 3.1. The base of the consumer surplus triangle is the quantity sold. The height of the triangle is the difference between the

---

consumer surplus
The difference between the amount consumers would be willing to pay for a good or service and the amount they actually have to pay.

---

[1] Some years ago, there was an economist who was hired away by another university. As part of the deal to lure him, the new school gave him a big raise. When he arrived at the new university in the fall, his new dean said that the school was happy he had decided to come. The economist responded that if they really were happy, then he hadn't asked for enough money. He wanted to leave them with no consumer surplus.

market price ($3.50) and the **demand choke price** ($5.50 per pound), the price at which quantity demanded is reduced to zero.[2]

In this example, the demand curve represented a collection of consumers, each with a different willingness to pay for a unit of the good. Those with a high willingness to pay are located at the upper left portion of the curve; those with a lower willingness to pay are down and to the right along the curve. The same logic also applies to an individual's demand curve, which reflects his declining willingness to pay for each additional unit of the good. For instance, an apple buyer might be willing to pay $5 for the first pound of apples he buys, but only $4 for the second pound and $3.50 for the third pound (maybe he has limited ability to store them, or just plain gets a bit tired of eating apples after a while). If the market price is $3.50 per pound, he will buy 3 pounds of apples. His consumer surplus will be $1.50 for the first pound, $0.50 for the second, and zero for the third, a total of $2. Doing this calculation for all apple buyers and adding up their consumer surpluses will give a total consumer surplus of the same type shown in the triangular area in Figure 3.1.

demand choke price
The price at which quantity demanded is reduced to zero.

Producer Surplus

Just as consumers gain surplus from engaging in market transactions, so do producers. **Producer surplus** is the difference between the price producers are willing to sell their goods for (measured by the height of the supply curve) and the price

producer surplus
The difference between the price at which producers are willing to sell their good or service and the price they actually receive.

Figure 3.1   Defining Consumer Surplus

Consumer surplus is the difference between the amount consumers are willing to pay and the amount they actually have to pay. The market demand curve shows how many pounds of apples consumers are willing to buy at a given price. The consumer at point A is willing to pay $5 for 1 pound of apples; at a market price of $3.50, this person has a consumer surplus of $1.50. Similarly, at the market price of $3.50, consumers at points B, C, and D have consumer surpluses of $1, $0.50, and $0, respectively. The consumer at point E does not purchase any apples. The total consumer surplus is the area under the demand curve and above the price, represented by the area of the shaded triangle CS, with the base of the triangle the total quantity sold and the height the difference between the market price and the demand choke price.

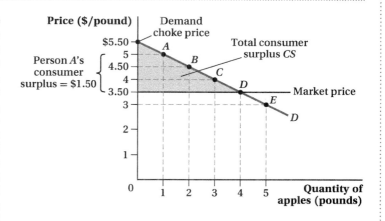

---

[2] There are two technicalities about this kind of calculation you should be aware of if you want to be completely precise. First, this area is a triangle only if the demand curve is a straight line. We use straight-line demand curves here because they are easy, but demand curves in real life are often curved. Second, calculating the total consumer surplus in dollars is only accurate if the marginal utility of income is constant. We discuss the idea of utility in Chapter 4. If a dollar of income is worth a lot more when income is low than when income is high, then we can't say for sure that all dollars of consumer surplus have the same impact on people's happiness.

they actually receive for the good. The supply curve in the Pike Place apple market (Figure 3.2) tells us how many pounds of apples producers are willing to sell at any given price. If we think of every point on the supply curve as representing a different apple seller, we see that Firm V would be willing to supply apples at a price of $2 per pound. Because it can sell apples at the market price of $3.50, however, it receives a producer surplus of $1.50.[3] Firm W is willing to sell apples for $2.50 per pound, and so receives $1 of producer surplus, while Firm X receives $0.50 of producer surplus. Firm Y, which is only willing to sell a pound of apples for $3.50, receives no surplus. Firm Z is shut out of the market; the market price of $3.50 per pound is less than its willingness to sell ($4). The total producer surplus for the entire market is the sum of producer surplus for every seller along the supply curve. This sum equals the triangle above the supply curve and below the price, the area of the shaded triangle PS in Figure 3.2. The base of the triangle is the quantity sold. The height of the triangle is the difference between the market price ($3.50) and the **supply choke price** ($1.50 per pound), the price at which quantity supplied equals zero. Here, that's $1.50 per pound; no seller is willing to sell apples below that price.

supply choke price
The price at which quantity supplied equals zero.

This particular supply curve represents a collection of producers that differ in their willingness to sell. The same logic applies to an individual producer's supply curve in cases where the firm's cost of producing additional output rises with its total output. In these cases, the firm must be paid more to sell additional units.[4] The firm's producer surplus is the sum of the differences between the market price and the minimum price the firm would need to receive to be willing to sell each unit.

Figure 3.2   **Defining Producer Surplus**

Producer surplus is the difference between the price at which producers are willing to sell their goods and the price they actually receive. The market supply curve shows how many pounds of apples sellers are willing to supply at a given price. The seller at point V is willing to sell his apples at a price of $2 per pound; at a market price of $3.50, this person receives a $1.50 producer surplus. Similarly, at the market price of $3.50, sellers at points W, X, and Y receive producer surpluses of $1, $0.50, and $0, respectively. The seller at point Z does not sell any apples. The total producer surplus is the area above the supply curve and below the price, represented by the area of the shaded triangle PS, with the base of the triangle the total quantity sold and the height the difference between the market price and the supply choke price.

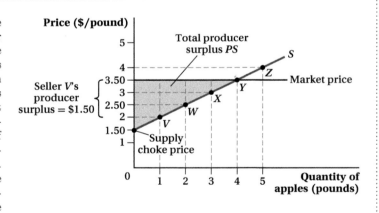

---

[3] Resist the temptation to call producer surplus "profit." While it seems natural to do this here, we will see in later chapters that the term "profit" has a precise meaning in economics, and it's not exactly this.

[4] We're also assuming here that the firm takes the market price as given. We'll discuss firms' supply behavior in this and the alternative case where a firm has price-setting power in Chapters 8 and 9.

3.1 figure it out

The demand and supply curves for newspapers in a Midwestern city are given by

$$Q^D = 152 - 20P$$
$$Q^S = 188P - 4$$

where Q is measured in thousands of newspapers per day and P in dollars per newspaper.

a. Find the equilibrium price and quantity.

b. Calculate the consumer and producer surplus at the equilibrium price.

Solution:

a. Equilibrium occurs where $Q^D = Q^S$. Therefore, we can solve for equilibrium by equating the demand and supply curves:

$$Q^D = Q^S$$
$$152 - 20P = 188P - 4$$
$$156 = 208P$$
$$P = \$0.75$$

Therefore, the equilibrium price of a paper is $0.75. To find the equilibrium quantity, we need to plug the equilibrium price into either the demand or supply curve:

$$Q^D = 152 - 20P \qquad\qquad Q^S = 188P - 4$$
$$= 152 - 20(0.75) \qquad\qquad = 188(0.75) - 4$$
$$= 152 - 15 \qquad\qquad = 141 - 4$$
$$= 137 \qquad\qquad = 137$$

Remember that Q is measured in terms of thousands of papers each day, so the equilibrium quantity is 137,000 papers each day.

b. To calculate consumer and producer surplus, it is easiest to use a graph. First, we need to plot the demand and supply curves. For each curve, we can identify two points. The first point is the equilibrium, given by the combination of equilibrium price ($0.75) and equilibrium quantity (137). The second point we can identify is the choke price for demand and supply. These can be determined by setting Q^D and Q^S equal to zero and solving for P:

$$Q^D = 152 - 20P \qquad\qquad Q^S = 188P - 4$$
$$0 = 152 - 20P \qquad\qquad 0 = 188P - 4$$
$$20P = 152 \qquad\qquad 4 = 188P$$
$$P = 7.6 \qquad\qquad P = 0.02$$

So the demand choke price is $7.60 and the supply choke price is $0.02.

The demand and supply curves are graphed in the figure on the next page. Consumer surplus is the area below demand and above the price (area A). Its area can be calculated as

$$CS = \text{area } A = \frac{1}{2} \times \text{base} \times \text{height} = (0.5) \times (137{,}000 - 0) \times (\$7.60 - \$0.75)$$
$$= (0.5) \times 137{,}000 \times \$6.85 = \$469{,}225$$

Producer surplus is the area below price and above supply (area B):

$$PS = \text{area } B = \frac{1}{2} \times \text{base} \times \text{height} = (0.5) \times (137{,}000 - 0) \times (\$0.75 - \$0.02)$$
$$= 0.5 \times 137{,}000 \times \$0.73 = \$50{,}005$$

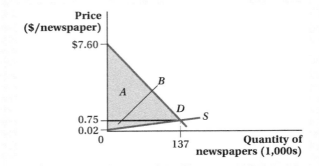

application

The Value of Innovation

Equipped with the concepts of consumer and producer surplus, we can do a quick analysis of one of the most important issues in economics—the introduction of new products. Economists emphasize the importance of innovation and new goods in raising a society's standard of living. In any discussion of the value of innovation, we need a way to compute how much benefit a new product gives to consumers.

A simple suggestion for valuing a new product would be to just add up what people paid for it. However, that approach would not be correct because, in reality, many consumers value the product at much more than the price they paid to get it. Consumer surplus, however, *does* measure the full benefit of the new product because it tells us how much consumers value the product *over and above* the price they pay.

A key factor in determining the amount of potential consumer surplus in a market for a new good is the steepness of the demand curve: All else equal, the steeper it is, the bigger the consumer surplus. That's because steep demand curves mean that at least some consumers (those accounting for the upper-left-hand side of the demand curve) have very high willingness to pay for the good. (You can see this on a price-quantity demand curve diagram. First, draw a horizontal line representing an equilibrium market price. Next, draw various demand curves with different slopes that intersect this price at the same point—i.e., so that the equilibrium quantity demanded is the same. You will see that the consumer surplus triangles will be larger for steeper demand curves.)

Let's look at eyeglasses as an example. Economist Joel Mokyr explained in his book *The Lever of Riches* that the invention of eyeglasses around the year 1280 allowed craftsmen to do detailed work for decades longer than they could before. If we think of glasses as a "new technology" circa 1280, we can visualize what the demand curve for glasses might have looked like. Because many people in 1280 would be quite blind without glasses, the demand curve was probably very steep—there was a set of individuals with a very high willingness to pay for glasses. This would also imply that demand wasn't particularly sensitive to prices. This steepness of the demand curve probably remained stable for the next 700 years, until the first commercially available contact lenses came on the market in the latter half of the twentieth century.

In Chapter 2, we learned that readily available substitute goods are likely to make demand more elastic. This is true of glasses, too: When contact lenses became available, the demand for glasses became more price elastic. How would this change in elasticity affect the consumer surplus people get from the existence of eyeglasses? Figure 3.3 illustrates the answer. Consumer surplus in 1950 is large because the demand for glasses D_1 is inelastic—if you want to see better, glasses are the only game in town. The consumer surplus is the area above the price and below D_1, or area $A + B$. Many people would be willing to buy glasses even if the price were much higher than P. (That's what having an inelastic demand means.)

When contact lenses become available, the demand for glasses becomes much more elastic, as shown by curve D_2. Even if just as many people buy glasses at the equilibrium price as before, a sharp rise in the price of glasses would cause many people to stop buying them because now they have an alternative. The figure shows that the consumer surplus from glasses declines after contacts come on the market. The area below the new, flatter demand curve and above the price is only area B.

After contacts are available, glasses are not worth as much to consumers because there are now other ways in which they can improve their eyesight. If glasses are the only way to fix your eyesight, you might be willing to pay thousands of dollars for them. Once you can buy contacts for $300, however, there is a limit to how much you would pay for glasses. You might still buy the glasses for $200, but you would certainly not be willing to pay $1,000 for them, and the change in consumer surplus reflects that change. Glasses are a miracle invention if they are the only way to correct one's vision (so they yield a higher consumer surplus). Remember that consumer surplus depends on the *most* that people would be willing to pay for the product. That maximum price goes down if alternatives are available. When alternative methods of vision correction are available, however, glasses are just another option rather than a virtual necessity, and the consumer surplus associated with them falls.

If you're concerned these examples imply that innovation destroys surplus, remember that the substitute goods create surpluses of their own. They have their own demand curves, and the areas under those curves and above the substitute goods' prices are also consumer surplus. For example, while the invention of contact lenses does reduce the consumer surplus provided by glasses, it creates a lot of surplus in the new contact lens market. ■

Figure 3.3   Consumer Surplus and the Elasticity of Demand

D_1 represents the demand for glasses in 1950 before a popular substitute good, contact lenses, were available. D_1 is relatively inelastic, and the total consumer surplus, $A + B$, is large. D_2 represents the demand for glasses after contact lenses were put on the market. D_2 is now relatively elastic, and the total consumer surplus B is relatively small.

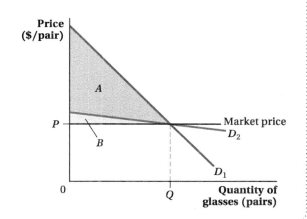

application

What is LASIK Eye Surgery Worth to Patients?

Laser-assisted in situ keratomileusis, commonly known as LASIK surgery, gives some people with vision problems an alternative to glasses and contact lenses. In the procedure, doctors use a laser to change the shape of the cornea to improve vision, usually to a point where patients can get rid of their corrective lenses.

Suppose we wanted to know how valuable LASIK surgery is to the patients who receive it. According to a market study commissioned by AllAboutVision.com, in 2010, the procedure cost about $2,150 per eye when performed by a reputable doctor. There were an estimated 800,000 LASIK procedures in 2010. A simple estimate for the value of this new procedure would be the number of surgeries times the cost (800,000 times $2,150, or about $1.7 billion). By now, however, you should realize that this measure of value is not a correct measure of the procedure's benefit to consumers because many people value the procedure at more than the price they paid. To determine the full benefit, we need to compute the consumer surplus—the benefit people receive from LASIK above and beyond what they have to pay for it.

To begin this computation, we need a demand curve for LASIK surgery. Because glasses and contacts are substitutes for LASIK, the demand curve will be flatter than if there were no substitutes. If LASIK were the only way to correct vision problems, then the nearly 70 million people now using corrective lenses in the United States would be willing to pay a lot for it. Because alternatives exist, however, if the price of LASIK goes up too much, many people will not opt for it, implying that LASIK's demand curve isn't very steep.

A hypothetical but realistic demand curve for LASIK procedures in 2010 is

$$Q_{LASIK} = 2{,}400{,}000 - 750 P_{LASIK}$$

where Q_{LASIK} is the quantity of LASIK procedures demanded and P_{LASIK} is the price per eye of the procedure. Plugging in a price of $2,150 per eye gives a quantity demanded of 787,500 procedures, right around the 2010 estimate. This demand curve is graphed in Figure 3.4. We can use this demand curve to determine the consumer surplus from LASIK.

We know the consumer surplus is the area of the triangle that is under the demand curve but above the price:

$$CS = \frac{1}{2} \times \text{base} \times \text{height}$$

$$= \frac{1}{2} \times (\text{quantity sold}) \times (\text{demand choke price} - \text{actual price})$$

Note that, for this demand curve, the demand choke price (P_{DChoke}) occurs where Q_{LASIK} is equal to zero, or

$$Q_{LASIK} = 0 = 2{,}400{,}000 - 750 P_{DChoke}$$

$$750 P_{DChoke} = 2{,}400{,}000$$

$$P_{DChoke} = 2{,}400{,}000/750 = 3{,}200$$

So the consumer surplus from LASIK is

$$CS = \frac{1}{2}(\text{quantity sold})(P_{DChoke} - \text{actual price})$$

$$= \frac{1}{2}(787{,}500)(\$3{,}200 - \$2{,}150)$$

$$= \frac{1}{2}(787{,}500)(\$1{,}050)$$

$$= \$413 \text{ million}$$

Figure 3.4   Valuing LASIK Eye Surgery

The demand curve for LASIK is shown by the equation $Q = 2,400,000 - 750P$. The shaded triangle represents the consumer surplus in the LASIK market. We can use the actual price ($2,150), the choke price ($3,200), and the equilibrium quantity sold (787,500) to calculate the triangle's height (demand choke price − actual price) and base (quantity sold). The equation for the total consumer surplus thus becomes $CS = \frac{1}{2} \times$ (quantity sold) × (demand choke price − actual price), yielding a consumer surplus of approximately $413 million.

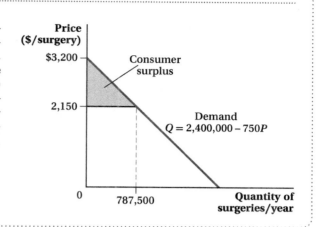

This calculation suggests that the people who got LASIK surgery in 2010 valued the surgery by about $413 million above and beyond what they paid for it. They paid about $1.7 billion for the surgery, but would have been willing to pay as much as 25% more. Because LASIK didn't exist as a product a couple of decades ago, that value was only created once the procedure was invented and a market established for it. This example suggests how important new goods can be for making consumers better off and raising the standard of living.

We can do the same sorts of calculations to compute the amount of producer surplus in a market. You'll see such an example in the next section. ◼

The Distribution of Gains and Losses from Changes in Market Conditions

One nice thing about our definitions of producer and consumer surpluses is that we can analyze the impact of any changes on either side of a market in a way that builds on the analysis we started in Chapter 2. There, we learned how shocks to supply and demand affect prices, quantity demanded, and quantity supplied. Now we can show how these shocks affect the benefits producers and consumers receive from participating in a market.

Figure 3.5 shows the initial supply and demand in the market for donuts. We see that at the market price P_1, the donut buyers' benefit from buying donuts is greater than the price they pay for the donuts (reflected in the consumer surplus area $A + B + C + D$). Similarly, the donut makers' benefit from making the donuts is greater than the price at which they sell the donuts (reflected in the producer surplus area $E + F + G$).

Now let's suppose that a shock hits the donut market. Because of a poor berry harvest, the price of jelly filling goes up. (We're assuming that the filling the bakers use actually has some real fruit in it!) When this shock hits, the cost of making donuts rises, and suppliers are no longer willing to supply as many donuts at any given price. The supply of donuts falls, as reflected in the inward shift of the donut supply curve from S_1 to S_2. In response to the jelly shock, the equilibrium price of donuts rises to P_2, and the quantity of donuts bought and sold in the donut market falls to Q_2.

These changes affect both consumer and producer surplus. The higher equilibrium price and lower equilibrium quantity both act to reduce consumer surplus. Compared

Figure 3.5   :   **Changes in Surplus from a Supply Shift**

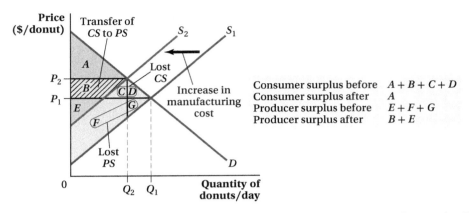

Consumer surplus before   *A + B + C + D*
Consumer surplus after   *A*
Producer surplus before   *E + F + G*
Producer surplus after   *B + E*

S_1 and D are the initial supply and demand for donuts. At market price P_1, consumer surplus is the area $A + B + C + D$, and producer surplus is the area $E + F + G$.

An increase in the manufacturing costs of donuts causes the supply curve to shift leftward from S_1 to S_2. At the new equilibrium price (P_2) and quantity (Q_2), consumer surplus has been reduced to the area A. The new producer surplus is shown by $B + E$. The effect of a supply shift on producer surplus is ambiguous. This ambiguity results because the lower equilibrium quantity acts to reduce producer surplus (by area $F + G$), while the higher equilibrium price increases producer surplus (by area B).

to triangle $A + B + C + D$ in Figure 3.5, triangle A is much smaller. While these price and quantity effects imply that inward supply shifts must reduce consumer surplus, there is no general rule for their impact on producer surplus. The lower equilibrium quantity that results from the supply shift reduces producer surplus, but the higher price increases it. These opposing effects can be seen in Figure 3.5. Some of the producer surplus before the shift—specifically, the space $G + F$ between the old and new supply curve and below the demand curve—is lost. But the price increase shifts some of what was consumer surplus before to producer surplus. This shifted surplus is area B. These effects on consumer and producer surplus are reversed for outward supply shifts.

We can also do a similar analysis for the effects of demand shifts. An inward shift in demand leads to a lower equilibrium price and quantity, both of which reduce *producer* surplus. The impact on consumer surplus, however, is ambiguous. Having a smaller equilibrium quantity reduces consumer surplus, but this reduction is counteracted by the drop in price. Similar to the supply shift case above (but in the opposite direction), the inward demand shift transfers to consumers part of what was producer surplus before. We see these effects in the application that follows.

 **application**

How Much Did 9/11 Hurt the Airline Industry?

After terrorists attacked the United States on September 11, 2001, the demand for air travel fell substantially, bringing the airline industry to its knees. Many congressional leaders wanted to compensate the airlines for the losses they suffered as a result, but there was a great debate over how much money was at stake. Using supply and demand industry analysis and our consumer and producer surplus tools, we can estimate the reduction in producer surplus that the airlines suffered after 9/11.

Statistics from the U.S. Department of Transportation (DOT) show that in the fourth quarter (October through December) of 2000, there were about 148.9 million enplanements (an enplanement is defined as one passenger getting on a plane).[5] In the fourth quarter of 2001, the first full quarter after the attack, there were only 123.6 million enplanements, a drop of 17% from the previous year. According to the DOT data, the average ticket price that airlines received per enplanement in the fourth quarter of 2000 was $122.22. In the fourth quarter of 2001, this average revenue had fallen to $104.82. This change in average revenue measures the price change over the period.

To figure out the damage to the industry, we need to compute the change to producer surplus.[6] Let's think of September 11th as creating a negative shift of the demand curve and assume no changes to the supply curve to make it easy: At every price, consumers demanded a lower quantity of plane travel. This shift is illustrated in Figure 3.6. Prices and quantities decreased in response to this event—just as the model suggests.

Figure 3.6 shows that the producer surplus fell when the demand curve shifted. Before the attack, producer surplus was the area above the supply curve and below the price, or $A + B + C$. After the attack, price and quantity fell and producer surplus fell to just area C. The loss to the airlines, then, was the area $A + B$.

Figure 3.6   Airlines and September 11

After September 11, the demand curve for air travel shifted inward, from D_{2000} to D_{2001}. In 2000 the equilibrium price and quantity were $122.22 and 148.9 million enplanements, respectively, and the producer surplus was the total shaded area, $A + B + C$. After September 11, the equilibrium price and quantity fell to $104.82 and 123.6 million enplanements, respectively, and the producer surplus was reduced to the area C. The area $A + B$ represents the loss in producer surplus to the airlines and was over $2.3 billion.

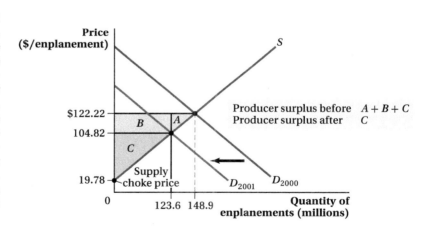

[5] Enplanements is one of many standard airline measures of quantity. If you fly a non-stop round-trip flight from Los Angeles to Chicago, for example, that would count as two enplanements because you got onto the airplane two times in your trip. We could have used a different measure of quantity such as revenue passenger miles (the number of miles that paying customers flew), and the answer would be very similar.

[6] We simplify our analysis by ignoring the modest supply effects of increases in costs from increased security requirements that the government did not pay for directly.

To calculate the producer surplus in this market, we need to know the equation for the supply curve. If we assume the supply curve is linear, we can use the data from our two equilibrium points to derive the equation for our inverse supply curve. The slope of the supply curve is the ratio of the change in equilibrium prices over the change in equilibrium quantities:

$$\text{slope} = \frac{P_2 - P_1}{Q_2 - Q_1} = \frac{\$122.22 - \$104.82}{148.9 - 123.6} = 0.688$$

Now that we have the slope, we can use either (or even better both!) equilibrium points to determine the supply choke price (the vertical intercept of the supply curve):

$$122.22 = P_{S\text{Choke}} + 0.688(148.9) \qquad \text{or} \qquad 104.82 = P_{S\text{Choke}} + 0.688(123.6)$$

$$P_{S\text{Choke}} = 122.22 - 102.44 \qquad\qquad\qquad P_{S\text{Choke}} = 104.82 - 85.04$$

$$= \$19.78 \qquad\qquad\qquad\qquad\qquad = \$19.78$$

So now we know that the industry's inverse supply curve is $P = 19.78 + 0.688Q$. Using the inverse supply equation allows us to match up the equation with the diagram in Figure 3.6.

With this inverse supply curve equation in hand, we can now calculate producer surplus before and after 9/11. Before 9/11, producer surplus is the area below the equilibrium price of $122.22 per enplanement and above the supply curve, for the entire quantity of 148.9 million enplanements. This would be areas $A + B + C$ in the graph. Since these three areas combine to form a triangle, we can calculate producer surplus before 9/11 as

$$\text{producer surplus} = \frac{1}{2} \times \text{base} \times \text{height} = \frac{1}{2}(148.9)(\$122.22 - \$19.78) = \$7,626.66$$

(The units of this producer surplus value are millions of dollars, because the quantity number is in millions of enplanements and the price is in dollars per enplanement.)

After 9/11, the equilibrium price fell to $104.82 per enplanement and the equilibrium quantity fell to 123.6 million enplanements. This means that producer surplus became only area C after 9/11, which was equal to

$$\frac{1}{2} \times \text{base} \times \text{height} = \frac{1}{2}(123.6)(\$104.82 - \$19.78) = \$5,255.47$$

These calculations indicate that the producer surplus in the airline industry fell by $2,371.19 million, or over $2.3 billion, as a result of the terrorist attack on 9/11.

One interesting thing to note about this calculation is that even after the 9/11 attack, the producer surplus is a big number. Comparing the $5.255 billion of producer surplus in 2001 Q4 to that quarter's reported (in the Air Carrier Financial Statistics) operating profit of −$3.4 billion (i.e., a $3.4 billion *loss*) for the industry leaves a puzzle. How can there be such a large producer surplus if the airlines had such a large loss? In reality, the puzzle is not so puzzling because producer surplus and profit are distinct concepts. The key distinction is the fixed costs firms pay—the expenses each must incur even if it doesn't produce a thing. Those costs aren't reflected in the supply curve, so they don't count against producer surplus. But they do come out of the firm's profits (and airlines have a lot of fixed costs). We learn more about fixed costs, the nature of the supply curve, and the connection between producer surplus and profit in Chapters 7 and 8.

By the way, if all we cared about was the drop in producer surplus after 9/11, there was another way to do the calculation we just did. We could have computed the size of areas A and B directly without actually solving for the supply curve. Rather than computing $A + B + C$ and subtracting C, we could have computed the size of rectangle B and triangle A using just the quantity and price data. This calculation would have given us the same answer for the *change* in producer surplus, but it would not have let us compute the *overall size* of the producer surplus before and after 9/11. ■

3.2 figure it out

A local tire market is represented by the following equations and in the diagram on the next page:

$$Q^D = 3,200 - 25P$$
$$Q^S = 15P - 800$$

where Q is the number of tires sold weekly and P is the price per tire. The equilibrium price is $100 per tire, and 700 tires are sold each week.

Suppose an improvement in the technology of tire production makes them cheaper to produce so that sellers are willing to sell more tires at every price. Specifically, suppose that quantity supplied rises by 200 at each price.

a. What is the new supply curve?

b. What are the new equilibrium price and quantity?

c. What happens to consumer and producer surplus as a result of this change?

Solution:

a. Quantity supplied rises by 200 units at every price, so we simply add 200 to the equation for Q^S:

$$Q^S_2 = 15P - 800 + 200 = 15P - 600$$

b. The new equilibrium occurs where $Q^D = Q^S_2$:

$$3,200 - 25P = 15P - 600$$
$$3,800 = 40P$$
$$P = \$95$$

We can find the equilibrium quantity by substituting the equilibrium price into either the supply or demand equation (or both):

$$Q^D = 3,200 - 25(95) \qquad\qquad Q^S_2 = 15(95) - 600$$
$$= 3,200 - 2,375 \qquad\qquad\qquad = 1,425 - 600$$
$$= 825 \qquad\qquad\qquad\qquad\quad = 825$$

The new equilibrium quantity is 825 tires per week. Notice that because supply increased, the equilibrium price fell and the equilibrium quantity rose just as we would predict.

c. The easiest way to determine the changes in consumer and producer surplus is to use a graph such as the one on the next page. To calculate all of the areas involved, we need to make sure we calculate the demand choke price and the supply choke prices before and after the increase in supply.

The demand choke price is the price at which quantity demanded is zero:

$$Q^D = 0 = 3,200 - 25P$$
$$25P = 3,200$$
$$P = \$128$$

The demand choke price is $128.

The supply choke price is the price at which quantity supplied is zero. Because supply is shifting, we need to calculate the supply choke price for each supply curve:

$$Q_1^S = 0 = 15P - 800$$
$$15P = 800$$
$$P = \$53.33$$
$$Q_2^S = 0 = 15P - 600$$
$$15P = 600$$
$$P = \$40$$

The initial supply choke price is \$53.33 but falls to \$40 when supply increases.

With the choke prices and the two equilibrium price and quantity combinations, we can draw the supply and demand diagram.

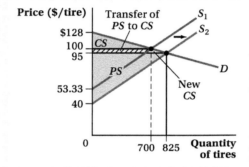

Consumer surplus: The initial consumer surplus is the area of the triangle below the demand curve but above the initial equilibrium price (\$100):

$$CS_{initial} = \frac{1}{2} \times base \times height$$
$$= \frac{1}{2} \times (700 - 0) \times (\$128 - \$100) = (0.5)(700)(\$28) = \$9,800$$

The new consumer surplus is the area of the triangle below the demand curve and above the new equilibrium price (\$95):

$$CS_{new} = \frac{1}{2} \times base \times height$$
$$= \frac{1}{2} \times (825 - 0) \times (\$128 - \$95) = (0.5)(825)(\$33) = \$13,612.50$$

So, after the outward shift in supply, consumer surplus rises by \$3,812.50.

Producer surplus: The initial producer surplus is the area of the triangle below the initial equilibrium price and above the initial supply curve (S_1):

$$PS_{initial} = \frac{1}{2} \times base \times height$$
$$= \frac{1}{2} \times (700 - 0) \times (\$100 - \$53.33) = (0.5)(700)(\$46.67) = \$16,334.50$$

The new producer surplus is the area of the triangle below the new equilibrium price and above the new supply curve (S_2):

$$PS_{new} = \frac{1}{2} \times base \times height$$
$$= \frac{1}{2} \times (825 - 0) \times (\$95 - \$40) = (0.5)(825)(\$55) = \$22,687.50$$

The increase in supply also led to a rise in producer surplus by \$6,353.

3.2 Price Regulations

Politicians call regularly for price ceilings on products whose prices have risen a lot. In this section, we explore the effects of direct government interventions in market pricing. We look both at regulations that set maximum prices (like a gas price ceiling) and minimum prices (price floors like a minimum wage).

Price Ceilings

A **price ceiling** establishes the highest price that can be paid legally for a good or service. Price ceilings get passed all the time. At various times, there have been price ceilings for cable television, auto insurance, flood insurance, electricity, telephone rates, gasoline, prescription drugs, apartments, food products, and many other goods.

To look at the impact of a price ceiling, let's suppose the city council of a college town passes a pizza price control regulation. With the intent of helping out the college's financially strapped students, the city council says no pizzeria can charge more than $8 for a pizza. Let's say the demand curve for pizzas in a month during the school year is described by the equation $Q^D = 20{,}000 - 1{,}000P$. The cheaper pizzas get, the more students will eat them, so the demand curve slopes downward as usual. If the price were zero, 20,000 pizzas would be sold per month (it's not that big a college, and there are only so many meals one can eat). The demand choke price is $20 per pizza—if the price were $20 per pizza, no pizzas would be sold.

Let's say the supply of pizzas is given by $Q^S = 2{,}000P - 10{,}000$. Supply slopes upward because when prices are higher, the pizzerias will make more pizzas. If the price is below $5, they make no pizzas. For each $1 increase in the price of a pizza after that, an additional 2,000 pizzas per month would be supplied.

Figure 3.7 graphs the supply and demand curves described by these two equations. It shows that the free-market equilibrium is at point w; that is, before price controls the equilibrium price for a pizza is $10, and at that price, 10,000 pizzas are supplied and demanded. Given these baseline market conditions, we can study the impact of the price ceiling using the graph or the equations. Let's start with the graph.

price ceiling
A price regulation that sets the highest price that can be paid legally for a good or service.

Figure 3.7   The Effects of a Price Ceiling

A price ceiling affects both producer and consumer surpluses. Before price controls in the pizza market, consumers pay $10 per pizza, and producers supply 10,000 pizzas per week at the equilibrium point w. Consumer surplus is the triangle $A + B + C$, and producer surplus is $D + E + F$. When a price ceiling of $8 is put in place, pizzerias supply only 6,000 pizzas (point x), but consumers demand 12,000 pizzas (point y), creating a shortage of 6,000 pizzas. Because pizzerias are now selling fewer pizzas at a lower price, producer surplus is reduced to area F. The new consumer surplus is the area $A + B + D$, and the net gain to consumers is $D - C$. The shaded area $C + E$ is the deadweight loss created by the price ceiling.

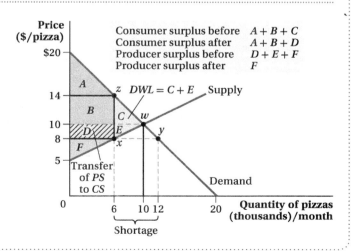

Consumer surplus before $A + B + C$
Consumer surplus after $A + B + D$
Producer surplus before $D + E + F$
Producer surplus after F

$DWL = C + E$

Graphical Analysis   Before any price controls, the consumer surplus for pizza-eating students is given by the area below the demand curve and above the $10 free-market price, $A + B + C$. The producer surplus is the area above the supply curve but below the price, $D + E + F$.

When the city council implements the price control regulation, the highest price the pizzerias can charge is $8 per pizza, which is less than the market-clearing price of $10. At $8, students demand a total of 12,000 pizzas (point y). This quantity demanded is larger than the 10,000 pizzas demanded at the free-market equilibrium because the price ceiling price is lower than the free-market price. At an $8 price, however, pizzerias are only willing to supply 6,000 pizzas. Because the quantity demanded exceeds the quantity supplied at that price, there is a shortage of 6,000 pizzas (sometimes this condition is also referred to as excess demand). Because the actual quantity of pizzas is limited to the number that suppliers are willing to sell, we end up with 6,000 pizzas sold at $8, and a large number of students frustrated that they cannot buy the additional 6,000 pizzas they would like to even though they are willing to pay the $8 per pie price.

Now let's consider the consumer and producer surplus to figure out how much better or worse off the two groups are as a result of the price controls. It's clear that the pizzerias are worse off. In the free market, they would have sold more pizzas (10,000 versus 6,000) at a higher price ($10 versus $8). The producer surplus after the price control law is everything below the capped price and above the supply curve; producer surplus shrinks from area $D + E + F$ to area F.

The law was passed to benefit students by lowering pizza prices. But we can't actually say for sure whether they are better off as a result. The new consumer surplus is the area below the demand curve and above the price, area $A + B + D$. The consumer surplus now includes area D because the price is lower. We call area D a **transfer** from producers to consumers, because imposing price controls shifted that area from being part of producer surplus to being part of consumer surplus. However, fewer pizzas are bought after the price cap law, resulting in consumers losing area C. Therefore, the net impact of the price cap on consumers depends on the relative sizes of the surplus transferred from the producers (area D) and loss reflected in area C. For those students who are able to buy the 6,000 pizzas in a month at a price that is $2 lower than they did before the law was enacted, life is good. They are the ones to whom area D is transferred. But for the students who would have enjoyed 4,000 more pizzas in the free market that they can no longer buy, life is a hungry proposition.

The producer surplus and consumer surplus represented by areas $C + E$ have disappeared because of the price ceiling. No one receives these surpluses anymore. Their combined areas are known as a **deadweight loss (DWL).** Deadweight loss is the difference between the maximum total surplus that consumers and producers could gain from a market and the combined gains they actually reap after a price regulation, and it reflects the inefficiency of the price ceiling. It's called a deadweight loss because it represents a set of surplus-generating transactions (pizza purchases, in this case) that would have occurred in an unregulated market with a customer who was willing to buy and a producer who was willing to sell at the market price. Area C is the deadweight loss suffered by consumers; area E is lost by producers.

Why is there a loss in consumer surplus if the students get to keep the money that they're not spending on pizza? Remember, the students missing out on the 4,000 pizzas after the price control law don't want to save the $10—they want the pizza! The reason there is a loss of consumer surplus is that the pizzas those students would have gotten in a market without a price control would be worth *more* than $10 to them. People who buy are on the part of the demand curve that is above the market price (except that individual right *at* the market price); their willingness to pay is greater than the price they have to pay. The price control results in their losing that difference.

Some producer surplus also becomes deadweight loss as a result of the price ceiling. There are pizzerias that would be willing to sell pizzas for more than $8 but less than

transfer
Surplus that moves from producer to consumer, or vice versa, as a result of a price regulation.

deadweight loss (DWL)
The reduction in total surplus that occurs as a result of a market inefficiency.

the $10 equilibrium price. Once the $8 price ceiling is in place, pizzerias will pull 4,000 pizzas off the market because $8 is not enough to cover their costs of making those extra pizzas. So both students and pizzerias were benefiting from transactions that took place before the price control; once the price ceiling is imposed, however, those transactions no longer take place and these benefits are lost.

Analysis Using Equations Now let's compare the free and regulated markets for pizzas using the supply and demand equations we described earlier. To determine the free-market equilibrium using the equations, we set quantity supplied equal to quantity demanded and solve for the market clearing price P:

$$Q^S = Q^D$$
$$2{,}000P - 10{,}000 = 20{,}000 - 1{,}000P$$
$$3{,}000P = 30{,}000$$
$$P = \$10$$

Plugging that price back into either the supply or demand equation gives an equilibrium quantity of 10,000 pizzas:

$$
\begin{array}{ll}
Q^S = 2{,}000P - 10{,}000 \qquad \text{or} & Q^D = 20{,}000 - 1{,}000P \\
\quad = 2{,}000(10) - 10{,}000 & \quad = 20{,}000 - 1{,}000(10) \\
\quad = 20{,}000 - 10{,}000 & \quad = 20{,}000 - 10{,}000 \\
\quad = 10{,}000 & \quad = 10{,}000
\end{array}
$$

The consumer surplus in the free market is the triangle $A + B + C$. The area of that triangle is

$$CS = \frac{1}{2} \times (\text{base}) \times (\text{height})$$
$$= \frac{1}{2} \times (\text{quantity sold}) \times (\text{demand choke price} - \text{market price})$$

The demand choke price is the price at which $Q^D = 0$. In this case,

$$0 = 20{,}000 - 1{,}000(P_{D\text{Choke}})$$
$$1{,}000(P_{D\text{Choke}}) = 20{,}000$$
$$(P_{D\text{Choke}}) = \$20$$

The consumer surplus triangle is

$$CS = \frac{1}{2} \times (\text{quantity sold}) \times (P_{D\text{Choke}} - \text{market price})$$
$$= \frac{1}{2}(10{,}000)(\$20 - \$10)$$
$$= (5{,}000)(\$10) = \$50{,}000 \text{ per month}$$

(Remember that quantities are measured in pizzas per month, so the consumer surplus is measured in dollars per month.)

The producer surplus is the triangle $D + E + F$ in the graph. The area of that triangle is $PS = \frac{1}{2} \times (\text{quantity sold}) \times (\text{market price} - \text{supply choke price})$.

The supply choke price is the price at which quantity supplied is zero:

$$Q^S = 2{,}000P - 10{,}000$$
$$0 = 2{,}000(P_{S\text{Choke}}) - 10{,}000$$
$$P_{S\text{Choke}} = 10{,}000/2{,}000 = \$5$$

Plugging this price into the equation for producer surplus, we find

$$PS = \frac{1}{2}(\text{quantity sold}) \times (\text{market price} - P_{S\text{Choke}})$$
$$= \frac{1}{2}(10{,}000)(\$10 - \$5)$$
$$= (5{,}000)(\$5)$$
$$= \$25{,}000 \text{ per month}$$

Now let's consider the impact of the price ceiling. The price of a pizza cannot rise to $10 as it did in the free market. The highest it can go is $8. We saw in the graphical analysis that this policy led to a shortage. The shortage is the difference between the quantity demanded and the quantity supplied at the price ceiling (P_c):

$$Q_{pc}^{D} = 20{,}000 - 1{,}000P_c$$
$$= 20{,}000 - 1{,}000(8)$$
$$= 12{,}000$$
$$Q_{pc}^{S} = 2{,}000P_c - 10{,}000$$
$$= 2{,}000(8) - 10{,}000$$
$$= 6{,}000$$

The shortage is 12,000 − 6,000 or 6,000 pizzas per month. This means that there are students ringing pizzerias' phones off the hook trying to order 6,000 more pizzas, but whose orders the pizzerias won't be willing to fill at the new market price.

Next, we compute the consumer and producer surpluses after the price control is imposed. Producer surplus is area F.

$$PS_c = \frac{1}{2}(Q_{pc}^{S}) \times (P_c - P_{S\text{Choke}})$$
$$= \frac{1}{2}(6{,}000)(\$8 - \$5)$$
$$= (3{,}000)(\$3) = \$9{,}000 \text{ per month}$$

which is just over one-third of the $25,000 of producer surplus pizzerias were making before the price ceiling. It is no wonder that producers fight against laws like this one.

The consumer surplus is now areas $A + B + D$. An easy way to figure the value for this surplus is to add the area of triangle A to the area of the rectangles B and D. Triangle A has an area of

$$\text{Area of } A = \frac{1}{2}(Q_{pc}^{S}) \times (P_{D\text{Choke}} - \text{price at point } z)$$

where the price at point z is the price at which quantity demanded equals the new quantity supplied of 6,000 pizzas. To figure out this price, set $Q^D = Q_{pc}^{S}$ and solve for the price:

$$Q^D = 20{,}000 - 1{,}000P_z = Q_{pc}^{S}$$
$$20{,}000 - 1{,}000P_z = 6{,}000$$
$$20{,}000 - 6{,}000 = 1{,}000P_z$$
$$P_z = 14{,}000/1{,}000 = \$14$$

This means that, if the price of a pizza were actually $14, exactly 6,000 pizzas would be demanded. With this value for the price at point z, we can now calculate:

$$\text{Area of } A = \frac{1}{2}(Q_{pc}^{S}) \times (P_{D\text{Choke}} - P_z)$$
$$= \frac{1}{2}(6{,}000)(\$20 - \$14)$$
$$= (3{,}000)(\$6)$$
$$= \$18{,}000 \text{ per month}$$

The area of rectangle B is

$$B = Q_{pc}^S \times (P_z - \text{free-market price})$$

$$= (6,000)(\$14 - \$10)$$

$$= \$24,000 \text{ per month}$$

and the rectangle D is

$$D = Q_{pc}^S \times (\text{free-market price} - P_c)$$

$$= (6,000)(\$10 - \$8)$$

$$= \$12,000 \text{ per month}$$

Adding these three areas, we find that total consumer surplus after the pizza price ceiling is $A + B + D = \$54,000$ per month.

Therefore, consumers *as a group* are better off than they were under the free market: They have \$4,000 more of consumer surplus per month. However, this outcome hides a big discrepancy. Those students lucky enough to get in on the 6,000 pizzas for \$8 rather than \$10 are better off, but there are 4,000 pizzas that would have been available in the free market that are no longer being supplied. Students who would have consumed those missing pizzas are worse off than they were before.

What is the deadweight loss from the inefficiency of the price-controlled market outcome? The full DWL is the area of triangle $C + E$ in the figure, so

$$\text{DWL} = \frac{1}{2} \times (\text{free-market quantity} - Q_{pc}^S) \times (P_z - P_c)$$

$$= \frac{1}{2}(10,000 - 6,000)(\$14 - \$8)$$

$$= \frac{1}{2}(4,000)(\$6)$$

$$= \$12,000 \text{ per month}$$

The Problem of Deadweight Loss   As we have seen, a price ceiling creates a deadweight loss. This deadweight loss is just that: lost. It's surplus that was formerly earned by consumers (C) or producers (E) that neither gets when there is a price ceiling. This analysis has shown that price ceilings and other mandates and regulations can come with a cost, even if they don't involve any direct payments from consumers or producers (as taxes do).

A natural way to think about the size of the deadweight loss is as a share of the transfer D. Because the price control was designed to transfer surplus from pizzerias to students, the deadweight loss tells us how much money gets burned up in the process of transferring surplus through this regulation. In this case, the deadweight loss (\$12,000) is just as large as the transfer. In other words, in the process of transferring income from pizzerias to students through the price ceiling, one dollar of surplus is destroyed for every dollar transferred.

This example illustrates the dilemma of using regulations to transfer income. If somehow the city council could get the producers to directly pay the consumers the amount $D - C$ without changing the price, the consumers would be just as happy as with the price control, because that's all they net in the deal after losing the deadweight loss. The producers would be better off as well. Rather than being left with just F, they would have their free-market producer surplus of $D + E + F$ minus their payment of $D - C$. The areas D in these two values cancel, leaving the pizzerias $E + F + C$, which is larger than the F in producer surplus they get under the price ceiling law. Deadweight loss occurs because the price-control regulation transfers income by changing prices, and price changes affect incentives and lead to inefficiency. Practically speaking, though, it's difficult to figure out how to organize the payment of $D - C$ without changing the price. A per pizza subsidy paid by pizzerias to students, for example, would have the same result as reducing the price and would thus have its own deadweight loss as we describe in Section 3.5.

Importance of Price Elasticities   The elasticities of supply and demand are the keys to the relative sizes of the deadweight loss and the transfer. Consider two different pizza markets in Figure 3.8. In panel a, the curves are relatively inelastic and show little price sensitivity. In panel b, the relatively elastic supply and demand curves reflect a greater amount of price sensitivity. It's clear from the figure that if the same price control rule is applied to both markets, the deadweight loss will be larger as a share of the transfer in the market with more elastic supply and demand.

The intuition behind this result is that the price ceiling's deadweight loss comes about because it keeps a set of sellers and buyers who would be willing to trade in the market at the free-market price from doing so. If the number of people in this set is small (in other words, the quantity after the regulation is close to the quantity before), then the deadweight distortion is small. How large that number of people is depends on how sensitive demand and supply are to prices. If demand and supply are relatively inelastic, the number of people and firms changing their quantity demanded or supplied will be small, and the DWL will be small. If demand and supply are relatively elastic, the number of people and firms who change their quantity demanded or supplied will be large.

Nonbinding Price Ceilings   In the pizza example, the price ceiling was below the free-market equilibrium price. What if a ceiling were set above the equilibrium price? Suppose the city council passed a law that limited the price of pizzas to $12 instead of $8, for example.

Figure 3.8   Deadweight Loss and Elasticities

(a)

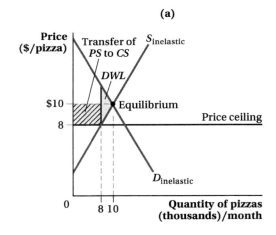

(b)

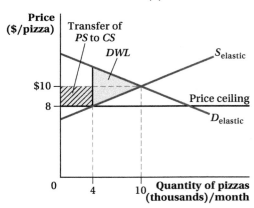

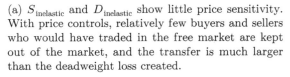

(a) $S_{inelastic}$ and $D_{inelastic}$ show little price sensitivity. With price controls, relatively few buyers and sellers who would have traded in the free market are kept out of the market, and the transfer is much larger than the deadweight loss created.

(b) In a market with a more elastic supply and demand curve, $S_{elastic}$ and $D_{elastic}$, a relatively large group of buyers and sellers who would have traded in the free market are kept out of the market, and the deadweight loss created by the price control is much larger than the transfer.

In such cases, the price ceiling has no effect. Because it is set at a level above where the market would clear anyway ($10 in the pizza case), it won't distort market outcomes. There will be no impact on price, no excess demand, and no deadweight loss. Price ceilings at levels above the equilibrium price are said to be **nonbinding,** because they do not bind or keep the market from arriving at its free-market outcome.

nonbinding price ceiling
A price ceiling set at a level above equilibrium price.

If conditions in the market change, however, a price ceiling that was once nonbinding could become binding. Suppose, for example, that enrollment increases at the college, and as a result, the demand for pizzas shifts out to a point at which the equilibrium price would be $13. If this shift were to occur, a $12 price ceiling would start to bind, leading to excess demand and deadweight loss in the market. (A large inward shift in the supply curve from the original equilibrium could also make a formerly nonbinding ceiling start to bind.)

Price Floors

The other major type of price regulation is a **price floor** (sometimes called a **price support**), a limit on how low a product's price can go. Lawmakers around the world use price floors to prop up the prices of all sorts of goods and services. Agricultural products are a favorite, especially in wealthier countries. As early as the 1930s, the United States federal government began setting price supports for agricultural goods such as milk, corn, wheat, tobacco, and peanuts. The goal was to guarantee farmers a minimum price for their crops to protect them from fluctuating prices. Many of these price supports remain today. We will use the tools of consumer and producer surplus to analyze price floors just as we used them for price ceilings.

price floor (or price support)
A price regulation that sets the lowest price that can be paid legally for a good or service.

Let's look at the market for peanuts. The unregulated market for peanuts is shown in Figure 3.9. The equilibrium quantity of peanuts is 20 million tons, and the equilibrium price of peanuts is $500 per ton. The government decides that farmers should be getting more than $500 per ton for their peanuts, so it passes a regulation that peanuts must sell for no less than $1,000 per ton.

Immediately, we know there is going to be a problem. At the higher price, peanut farmers want to sell a whole lot of peanuts—30 million tons. But at that price, quantity demanded is much lower—only 10 million tons. (Peanut butter sandwiches are just too

---

Figure 3.9   The Effects of a Price Floor

A price floor affects both producer and consumer surpluses. Before price controls in the peanut market, consumers pay $500 per ton, and producers supply 20 million tons of peanuts. Consumer surplus is the triangle $A + B + C$, and producer surplus is $D + E + F$. When a price floor of $1,000 per ton is put in place, peanut farmers supply 30 million tons of peanuts (point y), but consumers demand only 10 million tons of peanuts (point x), creating an excess supply of 20 million tons of peanuts. Consumer surplus is reduced to A. Producer surplus is now $B + D + F$, and the net gain to producers is $B - E$. The deadweight loss is $C + E$.

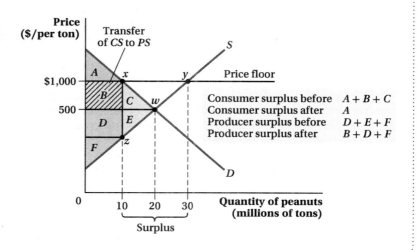

Consumer surplus before	$A + B + C$
Consumer surplus after	A
Producer surplus before	$D + E + F$
Producer surplus after	$B + D + F$

expensive when peanuts cost $1,000 per ton.) This imbalance leads to excess supply in the market: Sellers want to sell more of the product at that price than buyers want to buy. This is indicated in the figure by the 20-million-ton difference between the quantity of peanuts supplied and the quantity demanded at the price floor.

The goal of the price floor policy is to help farmers, so we need to look at the producer surplus to know how well the policy accomplishes its goal. Before the regulation, producer surplus was the area $D + E + F$. After the regulation, prices go up for all the peanut farmers who are still able to find buyers, so producers gain area B as a transfer from consumers. The farmers sell 10 million tons of peanuts and receive $500 per ton more than they were receiving in the free market. But peanut growers lose some of their market. The reduction in quantity demanded from 20 million to 10 million tons knocks out producers who used to sell peanuts at market prices and made a small amount of producer surplus from it. This area E then becomes the producers' part of the deadweight loss (DWL) from the regulation.

Overall, the producers gain surplus of $B - E$. If supply and demand are sufficiently elastic (i.e., if both curves are flat enough), producers could actually be made *worse off* from the price floor that was put in place to help them. This is because area E—the producers' share of the DWL—may be larger than the transfer from consumers, area B. This outcome is another application of our discussion above about how the deadweight loss grows as the supply and demand curves become more elastic.

How do consumers fare when the price floor is enacted? You can probably guess: Consumer surplus falls from $A + B + C$ to A. Area B is the surplus transferred from consumers to producers and area C is the consumer part of the DWL.

The price floor policy therefore transfers income from consumers to peanut farmers, but only by burning $C + E$ (the DWL) to do it. Again, if there were some way for the consumers to directly pay the peanut farmers a set amount equal to area B, the farmers would obtain more surplus than they get with the regulation (producer surplus of B versus $B - E$), and the consumers would be better off too (consumer surplus of $A + C$ instead of A). By changing the actual price of peanuts instead of making a transfer unrelated to quantity, the price support distorts people's incentives and leads to inefficiency as reflected by the DWL of $C + E$.

This analysis also illustrates the everlasting dilemma of price supports. The quantity supplied at the price floor is greater than the quantity demanded. So what happens to the extra peanuts? They accumulate in containers rather than being sold on the market. To avoid this outcome, a government will often pay the producers who can't sell their output in the regulated market to *stop* producing the extra output (20 million extra tons of peanuts in our example). The United States Department of Agriculture, for example, oversees various programs to reduce the surplus of price-supported crops on the market. One such program, the Conservation Reserve Program (CRP), paid farmers $1.85 billion in 2010 (an average of about $55 per acre) for holding land out of production. The program does have environmental benefits that mitigate some of the losses, but it also serves to reduce the quantity of subsidized crops that is grown, effectively by replacing those subsidies with CRP payments. There are also a number of programs that distribute millions of dollars annually ($871 million in 2010) of commodity foods—like peanut butter!—to school lunch programs and needy individuals on the condition that the foods will not be resold. Again, these programs serve to take surplus crops off the market.

Another example of a price support is a minimum wage. Here, the "product" is labor and the "price" is the wage, but the analysis is the same. If the government tries to help college students save tuition money by mandating that all summer internships pay at least $40 an hour, the quantity of labor supplied for internships will be much greater than the quantity demanded. As a result, there will be a lot of unemployed intern-hopefuls who would have been working at the equilibrium wage.

Just as with our earlier examples, how many people a minimum wage adds to the number of unemployed (the excess quantity supplied in the price floor figure), the amount of income transferred to workers (the change in producer surplus), and the size of the deadweight loss all depend on the elasticity of labor supply and labor demand. The price floor's deadweight loss arises because a set of sellers and buyers who would be willing to trade in the market at the free-market price will not do so at the regulated price. When suppliers and demanders are relatively insensitive to price, the number of transactions that the price floor prevents from happening is relatively small, and therefore so is the deadweight loss. Large price elasticities imply a large number of destroyed transactions and a large deadweight loss.

Nonbinding Price Floors   If a price floor is set below the free-market equilibrium price, it will have no effect on the market. **Nonbinding price floors** have no effect on price and do not create excess supply or deadweight loss. Just as with nonbinding price ceilings, however, conditions in a market may change to make a price floor that was once unbinding start to bind. Suppose the peanut price floor had been set at $400, below the equilibrium price of $500. If there is a sufficiently large outward shift in supply or inward shift in demand, the free-market equilibrium price may fall below $400, causing the price floor to start to affect the market.

nonbinding price floor
A price floor set at a level below equilibrium price.

3.3 Quantity Regulations

Sometimes, rather than regulating prices, governments impose quantity regulations. We discuss some of these regulations and analyze their effects on market outcomes in this section.

Quotas

A **quota** is a regulation mandating that a certain quantity of a good or service be provided. Quotas are occasionally used to force firms to produce a certain amount of a good (say, a vaccine in preparation for a flu epidemic or armaments during a war), but most often they are used to limit the amount of a good that is produced.

quota
A regulation that sets the quantity of a good or service provided.

For example, countries wanting to limit imports but not wanting to publicly announce tariffs (taxes on imports) can limit imports by establishing a quota. The U.S. government imposes quotas on the amount of sugar that can be imported from various countries, for example.[7] In other circumstances, a government may limit the amount of fish people can catch or the production of milk or oil.[8] The nation of Bhutan has a quota on the number of foreign tourists that can visit in a given year. France limits the amount of U.S. television shows that can be broadcast on TV. Singapore limits the number of cars that people can buy. London's Heathrow Airport limits the number of direct flights from U.S. airports. Taxis need medallions to operate, and doctors need licenses to practice.

Zoning laws impose another type of quota. Most towns and cities have zoning laws that limit the amount or type of construction that can go on in a certain area. A common zoning restriction limits the number of certain businesses considered by some to be unsavory, such as pawn shops or tattoo parlors. Such restrictions can be thought of as quotas on the amount of services these stores can provide in a local market. Let's consider as an example the impact of a quota on the amount of tattoo services that can be provided in the fictional town of River City.

---

[7] Legally, the current sugar quotas aren't completely binding. If a country goes over its quota allocation, it can still export sugar to the United States, but it must pay an additional tariff to do so. In practice, however, this tariff is so high that it all but eliminates shipments beyond the quota allocation.

[8] As we will see in Chapter 16 when we discuss externalities, there may be reasons for governments to limit the production of certain goods. For now, we just want to know what effects quotas have in a standard market situation.

Suppose the city's demand curve for tattoos is $Q_d = 2{,}500 - 20P$, and the supply curve is $Q_s = 100P - 3{,}500$, where the quantities demanded and supplied are both measured in the number of tattoos per year. We can analyze the effects of a quota on price and quantity by using graphs and equations.

Graphical Analysis In the free market, the equilibrium quantity of tattoos supplied and demanded for tattoos in River City is 1,500 tattoos per year and a price of $50 per tattoo (Figure 3.10). The consumer surplus in this market is $A + B + C$ and the producer surplus is $D + E + F$.

Suppose that River City's mayor becomes convinced that tattoo shops are a blight on society and rules that no more than 500 tattoos can be purchased per year in the city. He enforces this quota by requiring everyone who wants a tattoo to buy a tattoo permit before getting inked.

The quota creates a regulatory bend in the supply curve so that it becomes vertical at the quantity of 500. In other words, no matter what the price of tattoos is, parlors cannot supply more than 500. When this happens, the supply curve becomes perfectly inelastic at 500, making the new supply curve S_2 look like the red line in Figure 3.10. Now the demand curve intersects supply at point z rather than at point x, and the price rises from $50 to $100. Consumer surplus falls from area $A + B + C$ to area A, which is the only area that is below the demand curve and above the post-quota price P_{quota}. The post-quota producer surplus is above the supply curve and below the new price. This area $B + D + F$ includes a surplus transfer B from consumers to producers. The area $C + E$ is the deadweight loss.

Analysis Using Equations The equilibrium price is the price that exists when quantity supplied equals quantity demanded:

$$Q^D = Q^S$$

$$2{,}500 - 20P = 100P - 3{,}500$$

Solving for P and Q, we find

$$P = 50 \text{ and}$$

$$Q^D = 2{,}500 - 20(50) = 1{,}500 \qquad \text{or} \qquad Q^S = 100(50) - 3{,}500 = 1{,}500$$

Figure 3.10   **The Effects of a Quota**

In the free market for tattoos in River City, producers supply 1,500 tattoos per year at a price of $50 per tattoo at the equilibrium (point x). Consumer surplus is $A + B + C$, and producer surplus is $D + E + F$. After the mayor of River City enacts a law requiring a permit to get a tattoo, the supply for tattoos becomes vertical at the quantity of 500 tattoos. At the new equilibrium (point z), producers supply 500 tattoos at the increased price of $100 per tattoo. Consumer surplus is reduced to A. Producer surplus is $B + D + F$, and the net gain to producers is $B - E$. The deadweight loss is $C + E$.

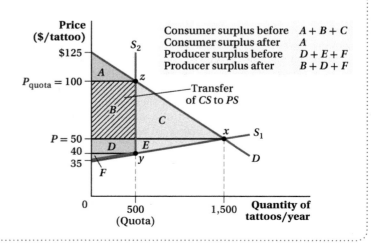

Consumer surplus before	$A + B + C$
Consumer surplus after	A
Producer surplus before	$D + E + F$
Producer surplus after	$B + D + F$

At the free-market equilibrium price and quantity, the consumer surplus is

$$CS = \frac{1}{2} \times (\text{base}) \times (\text{height})$$

$$= \frac{1}{2} \times Q \times (P_{DChoke} - P)$$

The demand choke price P_{DChoke} is the price at which $Q^D = 0$, which in this case is

$$Q^D = 2{,}500 - 20(P_{DChoke}) = 0$$

$$20P_{DChoke} = 2{,}500$$

$$P_{DChoke} = \$125$$

Consumer surplus is therefore

$$CS = \frac{1}{2} \times Q \times (P_{DChoke} - P)$$

$$= (\tfrac{1}{2})(1{,}500)(\$125 - \$50)$$

$$= (750)(\$75) = \$56{,}250$$

The producer surplus is the triangle $D + E + F$ in the graph. That triangle's area is

$$PS = \frac{1}{2} \times Q \times (P - P_{SChoke})$$

The supply choke price P_{SChoke} is the price at which quantity supplied is zero:

$$Q^S = 100 \times P_{SChoke} - 3{,}500 = 0$$

$$P_{SChoke} = 3{,}500/100 = \$35$$

Producer surplus in the unregulated tattoo market is then

$$PS = \frac{1}{2} \times Q \times (P - P_{SChoke})$$

$$= \frac{1}{2} \times 1{,}500 \times (\$50 - \$35)$$

$$= (750)(\$15) = \$11{,}250$$

After the 500-tattoo quota is implemented, the supply curve is the same up to $Q_S = 500$, at which point it becomes perfectly inelastic (point y). The equilibrium price will be

$$Q^S = Q^D$$

$$500 = 2{,}500 - 20P_{quota}$$

$$P_{quota} = \$100$$

At this price, the consumer surplus is the area A:

$$CS = \frac{1}{2} \times Q_{quota} \times (P_{DChoke} - P_{quota})$$

$$= (\tfrac{1}{2})(500)(\$125 - \$100)$$

$$= (250)(\$25) = \$6{,}250$$

This is dramatically reduced from the free-market surplus of \$56,250. Sorry, River City tattoo fans.

The producer surplus is measured by the areas $B + D + F$. We can break out each of these areas separately:

$$\text{Area } F = \frac{1}{2} \times Q_{quota} \times (\text{price at point } y - P_{SChoke})$$

The price at point y is the price at which the quantity supplied is equal to the quota.

It can be determined by setting $Q^S = 500$ and solving for P:

$$Q^S = 100(\text{price at point } y) - 3{,}500 = 500$$

$$100(\text{price at point } y) = 4{,}000$$

$$\text{price at point } y = 4{,}000/100 = \$40$$

So this means

$$\text{Area } F = \frac{1}{2} \times 500 \times (\$40 - \$35) = \$1{,}250$$

The rectangle B is

$$\text{Area } B = Q_{\text{quota}} \times (P_{\text{quota}} - P)$$

$$= 500(\$100 - \$50) = \$25{,}000$$

and the rectangle D is

$$\text{Area } D = Q_{\text{quota}} \times (P - \text{price at } y)$$

$$= 500(\$50 - \$40) = \$5{,}000$$

Thus, the total producer surplus equals $F + B + D = \$31{,}250$.

Let's compare the quota outcomes to those of the free, unregulated River City tattoo market. Consumers are much worse off after the quota because their surplus has fallen from \$56,250 to only \$6,250. This decrease reflects, in part, the losses of the additional 1,000 people who would be willing to get a tattoo in River City in a free market but cannot with the quota in place. But the loss in consumer surplus also reflects the fact that the quota increases the price of tattoos even for those people who get one. This price increase shrinks the gap between what they are willing to pay for the tattoo and the price they actually have to pay.

On the supply side, the tattoo parlors do just fine. They lose the producer surplus in area E when the quota is imposed, but the quantity restriction leads to much higher prices for their output—they get a huge transfer from consumers (area B), which makes their total producer surplus \$31,250 under the quota instead of \$11,250 without it. This gain could explain why the tattoo parlors may not complain about an ordinance that would reduce the total number of tattoos they could sell, although a noneconomist might expect they would.

The quantity-restricting quota drives up the price of tattoos. In doing this, the quota transfers a bunch of surplus from tattoo buyers to tattoo parlors and creates a significant amount of deadweight loss (area $C + E$, which based on our calculations above totals \$25,000 + \$5,000 = \$30,000).

Government Provision of Goods and Services

The quota example we just discussed set a maximum quantity for the tattoo market. What if a government wanted to mandate a *minimum* amount of a good or service instead? For legal reasons, it can be difficult for a government to actually force companies to provide a certain quantity of a product that they do not want to produce. However, governments can and sometimes do produce goods themselves. In the market for higher education, for example, states run public colleges and universities that directly compete with private colleges and universities. In the insurance market, the government provides flood insurance. Research and development (R&D) conducted by private firms competes with R&D funded by the federal government through institutions like the National Institutes of Health or the National Science Foundation. Weather forecasting from the National Weather Service competes against Accuweather, The Weather Channel, and others. The U.S. Postal Service competes with UPS and Federal Express in package delivery.

To understand the effects of direct government provision of goods and services, let's use the supply and demand model to analyze the college education market. The price

---

Figure 3.11   The Effects of Government Provision of Education

In a market with only private colleges, supply would be S_{priv}, demand would be D, and the equilibrium price and quantity would be P_1, Q_1. When the government opens a new university, there is an outward shift in the supply curve equal to the number of credit hours provided by the government, the quantity Q_{gov}. At the equilibrium, the price decreases to P_{tot}, and the quantity increases to $Q_{tot} = Q_{gov} + Q_{priv}$. Because the increase in the equilibrium quantity is less than Q_{gov}, the quantity supplied by private universities must have been crowded out.

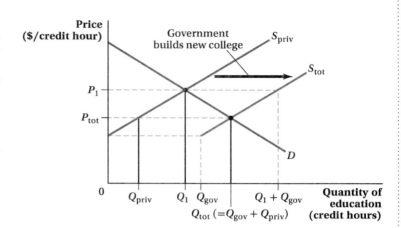

in this market is tuition per credit hour, and the quantity is the total number of credit hours taken.[9] In Figure 3.11, we start with the equilibrium that would exist in the market if higher education were provided only by private schools. The demand curve for education is D and the supply curve is S_{priv}. The equilibrium price and quantity are P_1 and Q_1.

If the government decides that getting more people to attend college is important, it can do so in many ways. It could help pay part of students' costs of attending a private school. (We analyze the impact of such payments, called subsidies, in Section 3.5.) Alternatively, the government could impose a price ceiling on college tuition so that more students could afford it. This price ceiling would have the disadvantage we learned about earlier in this chapter: There would be a shortage of education because more students would want a college education and fewer colleges would be willing to offer this education. Finally, the government could start a public university to directly enable more students to attend college. That's the case we'll look at here.

Let's say the government provides Q_{gov} credit hours at the new state-run university. This increase in credit hours shifts the supply curve from S_{priv} to S_{tot}. Notice that because the government's additional quantity supplied doesn't depend on price, this leads to a parallel outward shift in the supply curve by an amount Q_{gov}.

With this shift in supply, the market tuition falls from P_1 to P_{tot} per credit hour. However—and this is key—the number of credit hours taken will rise less than Q_{gov}, the amount provided by the government. We can see this in Figure 3.11. As we just noted, the horizontal distance between S_{priv} and S_{tot} is Q_{gov}. For the equilibrium quantity of credit hours to rise by an amount equal to Q_{gov}, the equilibrium price would have to remain at P_1, making the quantity of credit hours equal to $Q_1 + Q_{gov}$. The price doesn't stay at P_1, though, because the demand for credit hours is downward-sloping. The equilibrium price instead falls to P_{tot}, and the quantity rises by an amount less than Q_{gov}, to Q_{tot}. Because the total quantity of credit hours increases by less than the amount the government provides, private schools must now supply a number of credit hours (call this Q_{priv}) that is less than Q_1, the quantity they supplied before the government stepped in.

---

[9] In using the supply and demand model here, we are assuming that all colleges, private and public, offer identical educations.

crowding out
A reduction in private economic activity created by greater government presence in a market.

This decline in the quantity supplied by the private schools is known as **crowding out,** a reduction in private economic activity created by greater government presence in a market. Here, crowding out is the equivalent of the deadweight loss seen in our earlier examples. The government pays to provide Q_{gov} credit hours, but it increases the total number of credit hours in the market by less than this amount. Some credit hours formerly offered by private schools and willingly purchased by students are no longer produced. The larger the number of these lost credit hours—that is, the smaller the increase in the equilibrium quantity of credit hours relative to the government-provided quantity—the greater is the inefficiency from crowding out.

The intuition behind why crowding out occurs lies in the fact, seen in the example above, that the equilibrium quantity rises less than the quantity the government produces because demand is downward-sloping. By stepping in and increasing output, the government drives down the market price. This reduces the quantity supplied by private producers. At the original equilibrium price, private producers were willing to supply a certain quantity. At the lower, post-government market price, however, the private producers find it is no longer worth supplying their initial amount.

The same intuition explains how large crowding out will be in a market. When demand is relatively elastic, the increase in supply due to the government won't reduce the equilibrium price much. As a result, private producers won't cut back production a lot, and crowding out will be small. In the extreme case, when demand is perfectly elastic (i.e., if the demand curve were flat), government production won't change the equilibrium price at all. As we just discussed, in this case, the equilibrium quantity will rise by exactly the amount the government produces. On the other hand, if demand is relatively inelastic, government supply will reduce the equilibrium price a great deal. This will lead to large cutbacks in private production and a lot of crowding out. In the extreme case of perfectly inelastic (vertical) demand, crowding out is complete: Price falls and private firms cut back on production one-for-one for each unit the government produces. This makes sense: If quantity demanded is fixed at some specific amount regardless of price, any government provision will only serve to replace private production.

theory and data

Does Public Health Insurance Crowd Out Private Insurance?

The role of the government in providing health insurance is constantly debated in countries where coverage is provided by both private and public payers. The United States is a country with a heavy mix of the two. In 2010 about 150 million Americans were covered by private insurers, but another 50 or so million people were on Medicare, the government-provided health insurance for seniors, and just under 60 million were enrolled in Medicaid, government-provided insurance for low-income individuals and families. Another 50 million were uninsured.

In mixed-payer countries, government-provided coverage is often targeted at population segments like the elderly and poor that many believe would have a difficult time obtaining private coverage. Many policy makers and economists nevertheless believe that public coverage and private coverage might be close enough substitutes to cause expansion of public coverage to crowd out private coverage. In other words, if the government tries to expand coverage in order to reduce the number of uninsured, some of the increased enrollees will be individuals who would have still been covered by private insurance otherwise.

> ### Figure 3.12 : Government Provision of Health Insurance
>
> In a market with only private health insurance, supply would be S_{priv}, demand would be D, and the equilibrium price and quantity would be P_e, Q_e. When the government offers health insurance (in the form of Medicaid), the supply curve shifts out to S_{tot}. At the equilibrium, the price decreases to P_1, and the quantity increases to $Q_1 = Q_{priv} + Q_{gov}$. The quantity supplied by private insurers is crowded out since the total rise in the quantity of insurance coverage falls short of Q_{gov}.
>
>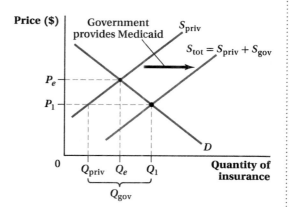

In a well-known study, health economists David Cutler and Jonathan Gruber measured the amount of crowding out that occurred during significant expansions of Medicaid.[*] Specifically, they used law changes that occurred in the late 1980s and early 1990s that greatly expanded the number of women and children eligible for Medicaid coverage. They measured crowding out by looking at the period of this large shift in the quantity of publicly provided insurance and determining if there were any corresponding drops in private insurance among the same population. In terms of Figure 3.12, they compared Q_{gov} (here, the amount of additional Medicaid coverage) to the difference between Q_e and Q_{priv} (respectively, the amount of private coverage before and after the Medicaid expansion).

Using this approach, Cutler and Gruber found evidence of substantial crowding out. For example, the expansion of coverage eligibility led to an additional 1.5 million children obtaining Medicaid coverage. Thus $Q_{gov} = 1.5$ million in Figure 3.12. However, they estimated about 600,000 of these new enrollees had been covered by private insurance beforehand; that is, $Q_e - Q_{priv} = 0.6$ million. Therefore the net change in children covered by medical insurance, $Q_1 - Q_{gov}$, was only about 900,000. This implies a crowd-out rate of 40 percent—for every 10 additional Medicare enrollees, 4 were simply exchanging their private insurance for public insurance. Another way to quantify this is in terms of the changes in uninsured children due to the policy. Before the expansion of coverage there were about 8.6 million uninsured children. Had all of the 1.5 million new enrollees come from this group, it would have cut the number of uninsured children by about 17 percent. But crowding out meant it reduced the number of uninsured by only 10 percent.

This result raises an interesting question about what the mechanism was through which the reduction in private insurance occurred. One possibility is that newly Medicaid-eligible individuals were less likely to pay for private coverage available to them through their employers or other channels. Another possible mechanism is that employers, knowing additional public coverage has been made available, reduced the quality or raised the price of the insurance plans they offered their employees. Cutler and Gruber found some evidence that employers did pare back their plans, but most of the crowding out appeared to have arisen because individuals who were newly eligible for Medicaid avoided using their employer-provided insurance options.

[*] David M. Cutler and Jonathan Gruber, "Does Public Insurance Crowd Out Private Insurance?" *Quarterly Journal of Economics* 111, no. 2 (1996): 391–430.

Just as with deadweight loss, the relative size of crowding out inefficiencies depends on elasticities. But there is a difference. While both supply and demand elasticities determine the amount of deadweight loss, only the demand elasticity matters for crowding out. This is because we've assumed the quantity supplied by the government doesn't depend on the price. As a result, for a given demand curve, the drop in equilibrium price after the government enters the market depends only on how much supply shifts (i.e., how much the government produces), not on the slope of the private supply curve.[10]

3.4 Taxes

Governments at all levels (local, state, federal) tax all kinds of things, and they do it in different ways. Sometimes, suppliers are legally required to remit the tax. Stores in the United States collect sales taxes and send them to state revenue agencies, for example, just as producers in Canada and Europe collect and remit value-added tax (VAT). Sometimes the legal burden falls on consumers, like "use taxes" that states levy on purchases their residents make in other states. In still other cases, the legal burden is shared. For instance, half of the U.S. federal payroll tax (which funds the Social Security and Medicare programs) is paid by employers before workers get their wages, and the other half is paid by workers through a deduction from their wages.

In this section, we use the supply and demand model to show one of the most striking findings in economics: In a competitive market, it doesn't matter whether the buyer or the seller is required by law to actually sign the check and remit the tax to the government; the impact on consumers and producers is always the same. That is, we could change the law so that consumers paid sales tax instead of sellers, or employers have to pay the entire payroll tax, and market outcomes would not change. The total impact of a tax on consumers and sellers depends only on the steepness of the supply and demand curves, not on the identity of the payer. Before we can understand why this is true, however, we first need to look at how taxes affect a market.

Tax Effects on Markets

We start with a no-tax market that is in equilibrium, the market for movie tickets in Boston, Massachusetts (Figure 3.13). The equilibrium is at point x, with a price of P_1, and the quantity of movie tickets sold is Q_1. In 2003 the mayor of Boston, Tom Menino, proposed adding a 50 cent tax to movie tickets to help balance a budget deficit. Many thought Menino proposed the tax because a large number of movie-goers in Boston are college students who live in the Greater Boston area but are not Boston voters. Regardless of his motivation, the tax was defeated by the state legislature.

If it had been enacted, the tax would have required theater owners to pay 50 cents per ticket to the government. Let's look at how such a change would affect the market for movie tickets. The tax is much like a 50 cent per ticket increase in the theaters' costs. We know from Chapter 2 that increases in production costs cause suppliers to supply a smaller quantity at any given price. Therefore, in response to the tax, the supply curve shifts up by the amount of the tax (50 cents) to S_2, and the equilibrium quantity of movie tickets sold falls to Q_2.[11]

But taxes do something different from a typical supply shift: They drive a wedge between the price buyers pay (the market price) and the price that producers actually

---

[10] If, for some reason, the government's quantity supplied *is* sensitive to price, then the elasticity of the supply curve (both the private and government components) will affect the amount of crowding out, just as the demand elasticity does.

[11] A tax expressed in percentage terms, such as a sales tax of 6%, is called an *ad valorem* tax (as opposed to a *specific tax* that is a set dollar amount, like the 50 cents per ticket here). An ad valorem tax version of this tax would shift the supply curve, but not by a fixed amount at every point. Instead, it would rotate the curve by a fixed percent around the point at which quantity supplied is zero.

Figure 3.13   Effect of a Tax on Boston Movie Tickets

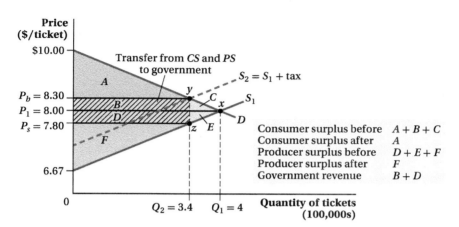

The figure shows the effect of a $0.50 movie tax on the market for Boston movie tickets. In the pre-tax market, supply S_1 and demand D intersect at the equilibrium price of $8 and the equilibrium quantity of 400,000 movie tickets. The consumer surplus is $A + B + C$, and the producer surplus is $D + E + F$. The addition of the $0.50 tax per movie ticket results in an inward shift of the supply curve from S_1 to S_2 by the amount of the tax and decreases the equilibrium quantity to 340,000 tickets. The resulting tax wedge creates two prices: $8.30, the price the buyer faces, and $7.80, the price the seller actually receives. The new consumer surplus is A, and the producer surplus is F. Area $B + D$ is government tax revenue, while area $C + E$ is the deadweight loss.

receive (the market price minus the tax). With a normal supply curve, the price at any point on the supply curve is the price a producer receives for selling its product. With a tax, the product sells for the price P_b (we denote the price the buyers pay with a "b"), but the sellers only receive P_s (we denote the price the seller receives with an "s"). This is the buyers' price minus the tax: $P_s = P_b - \text{tax}$. In other words, the buyers have to pay 50 cents more for any quantity, but the movie theaters don't get to keep the extra money—they receive only the higher price minus the tax.

Because of this wedge, the new equilibrium in the Boston movie market involves *two* prices. The first, point y, is the price ($8.30) that the buyers pay at the theater that includes the 50 cent tax. Thus, $8.30 is the market price. The second, point z, is the price ($7.80) that the suppliers receive after taking the 50 cents out of the higher market price and sending it to the government.

There are two key characteristics to note about the post-tax market equilibrium. First, the price of movie tickets increases, but not by the full 50 cents of the tax. This can be seen in Figure 3.13. The size of the tax is reflected in the vertical distance between P_b ($8.30) and P_s ($7.80). The rise in the price of movie tickets, however, is the distance between $8.30 and the equilibrium price with no tax, $8.00. The reason for this discrepancy is that the tax wedge drives some of the highest-cost theaters out of the market: Once the tax is added to the price, these theaters would have to sell their tickets at a price that is too high for buyers. The second characteristic to note is that the government generates revenue from the tax. The total revenue equals the 50 cent tax times Q_2, the new quantity of tickets sold.

We can apply all the familiar concepts from consumer and producer surplus analysis to this new equilibrium. We just need to remember that the tax creates a second supply curve that we have to keep track of, rather than moving a single supply curve as before. The supply curve that the theater owner cares about is S_1, the initial supply curve. The number of tickets that theaters are willing to supply at any particular price is still given by this curve, even after the tax is imposed, because the level of S_1 reflects the after-tax dollars theater owners take home from selling tickets. But the supply curve actually facing the buyers is S_2. It has been shifted up by the amount of the tax, because that is the price that moviegoers have to pay for a particular quantity supplied.

To make things clearer, let's work through this example in more detail. In Figure 3.13, the demand curve for movie tickets in Boston is $Q^D = 20 - 2P$ and the supply of movie tickets is $Q^S = 3P - 20$, where both quantities demanded and supplied in these curves are measured in hundreds of thousands of tickets. If the legislature passes the tax, all theater owners will be required to remit to the city 50 cents per ticket sold. We can analyze the tax's effect on the market using graphs or equations.

Graphical Analysis   With no taxes, solving the model our usual way gives a free-market equilibrium price P_1 and quantity Q_1 and the resulting consumer and producer surpluses (Figure 3.13).

The tax means buyers now face a new supply curve S_2, equal to S_1 shifted up by $0.50, the amount of the tax. This reduces the number of movie tickets bought in the market from 400,000 to 340,000. At that quantity, the price the buyers are paying rises from $8.00 to $8.30. Because the law requires suppliers (the theater owners) to pay the government a 50 cent tax for every ticket they sell, the suppliers don't get to keep $8.30; they get to keep only $7.80 = $8.30 - 0.50.

What happens to consumer and producer surplus in the post-tax market? The new consumer surplus is smaller than before. In the no-tax market, consumer surplus was $A + B + C$. Now it is only A, the area below the demand curve but above the price that the buyers have to pay, $8.30.

The new producer surplus is also smaller than before. Before the tax, it was $D + E + F$. After the tax, it is only F, the area above the supply curve and below the price that the suppliers receive after they pay the tax, $7.80.

Imposing the tax reduces total producer and consumer surplus from area $(A + B + C) + (D + E + F)$ to just area $A + F$. Where has the surplus in areas B, C, D, and E gone? The area $B + D$ is no longer consumer or producer surplus; it is government tax revenue, the tax times the quantity sold after the tax is implemented. With a tax, there is no surplus transfer between producers and consumers, as we saw in earlier examples. Instead, both producers and consumers transfer some of their surpluses to the government. This tax revenue is then "returned" to consumers and producers in the form of government services, so it is not lost.

Areas C and E are the deadweight loss from the tax. They are surplus that moviegoers and theater owners formerly got from buying and selling tickets at the competitive price. This surplus is gone now because consumers buy fewer tickets at the higher post-tax price and sellers supply fewer tickets at their lower post-tax price.

Just as in the price regulation cases, a natural way to look at the size of the deadweight loss is as a fraction of the surplus transfer. Before, that transfer was from producers to consumers (for a price ceiling) or from consumers to producers (for a price floor). Now, it's from both to the government. The ratio in this case is the area $C + E$ to the area $B + D$, which is the DWL as a share of revenue.

Analysis Using Equations   The no-tax market equilibrium equates quantity demanded and quantity supplied:

$$Q^D = Q^S$$

$$20 - 2P = 3P - 20$$

$$5P = 40$$

$$P_1 = 40/5 = \$8 \text{ per ticket}$$

$$Q^D = 20 - 2(\$8) = 4 \quad \text{or} \quad Q^S = 3(\$8) - 20 = 4$$

Therefore, before the tax, the equilibrium price is $8 and 400,000 tickets are sold.

The pre-tax consumer surplus is the triangle above the price and below the demand curve, as shown in Figure 3.13:

$$CS = \frac{1}{2} \times Q \times (P_{DChoke} - P_1)$$

Again, the choke price is found by determining the price that pushes the quantity demanded to zero:

$$Q^D = 20 - 2P_{DChoke} = 0$$

$$P_{DChoke} = \$10$$

In other words, this demand curve says that if tickets cost $10, no one will go to theaters in the city of Boston (perhaps because theaters in the suburbs are an attractive alternative). Plugging the demand choke price into the CS formula gives a consumer surplus of

$$CS = \frac{1}{2}(400,000)(\$10 - \$8)$$

$$= \$400,000$$

The producer surplus is the triangle above the supply curve and below the price:

$$PS = \frac{1}{2} \times Q \times (P_1 - P_{SChoke})$$

The supply choke price is the price that moves quantity supplied to zero:

$$Q^S = 3P_{SChoke} - 20 = 0$$

$$P_{SChoke} = \$6.67$$

That is, at any price below $6.67 a ticket, no theaters would operate in Boston. Plugging this supply choke price into the PS formula gives a producer surplus of

$$PS = \frac{1}{2}(400,000)(\$8 - \$6.67)$$

$$= \$266,667$$

What happens to consumer and producer surplus when Mayor Menino applies his 50 cent tax? Theaters must pay the state for each ticket they sell. This creates a dual-supply-curve situation. The supply curve for the theater owners is the same as the initial supply curve. The theater is still willing to supply whatever number of tickets the supply curve says at the market price. But now, the supply curve facing buyers is shifted up by the amount of the tax: At each price, the tickets supplied to consumers now cost $0.50 more. The difference between the supply curve that the buyers face and the supply curve that the sellers face is the amount of the tax. In words, the theaters' supply curve says they would be willing to sell 400,000 tickets if they receive $8 per ticket (after the tax gets paid), but for theaters to get $8 per ticket, buyers would actually have to pay $8.50 per ticket because $0.50 of tax needs to be paid out of the price received by the theaters. The prices that result for both the buyer and the seller are summed up in the equation $P_b = P_s + \$0.50$.

To solve for the post-tax quantity and prices, we substitute this expression, which links the two supply prices into our supply and demand equations:

$$Q^D = Q^S$$

$$20 - 2P_b = 3P_s - 20$$

$$20 - 2(P_s + 0.50) = 3P_s - 20$$

$$20 - 2P_s - 1 = 3P_s - 20$$

$$5P_s = 39$$

$$P_s = 39/5 = \$7.80$$

Therefore, the buyers face the following price:

$$P_b = P_s + 0.50 = \$7.80 + 0.50 = \$8.30$$

Now if we plug the buyer price into the demand curve equation and the supplier price into the supply curve equation, they will both give the same after-tax market quantity:

$$Q_2 = 20 - 2(8.30) = 3.4 \qquad \text{or} \qquad Q_2 = 3(7.80) - 20 = 3.4$$

Only 340,000 tickets will be sold once the tax is put into place.

The consumer surplus after a tax is the area below the demand curve but above the price that the buyer pays:

$$CS = \frac{1}{2}(340{,}000)(\$10.00 - \$8.30)$$

$$= \$289{,}000$$

The producer surplus is the area above the supply curve and below the price that the suppliers receive:

$$PS = \frac{1}{2}(340{,}000)(\$7.80 - \$6.67)$$

$$= \$192{,}667$$

So the tax makes consumer surplus fall by \$111,000 and producer surplus fall by \$74,000 from their values in the no-tax market equilibrium. Some of that \$185,000 in lost surplus flows to the government in the form of revenue from the tax, however. That revenue is equal to \$0.50 per ticket times the number of tickets sold after the tax, or

$$\text{Revenue} = 0.50Q_2$$

$$= \$0.50(340{,}000) = \$170{,}000$$

Notice that the total amount of the lost surplus, \$185,000, is more than the amount of revenue that the government generated, \$170,000. The difference of \$15,000 is the deadweight loss of the tax.

A different way to calculate DWL is to compute the area of the triangle whose base is the change in quantity and whose height is the amount of the tax:

$$\text{DWL} = \frac{1}{2} \times (Q_1 - Q_2) \times (P_b - P_s) = \frac{1}{2} \times (Q_1 - Q_2) \times \text{tax}$$

$$= \frac{1}{2}(400{,}000 - 340{,}000)(\$0.50) = \$15{,}000$$

That's about 9% of the revenue generated by the tax. In other words, this tax burns up about \$1 of surplus in DWL for every \$11 of revenue it generates.

Why Taxes Create a Deadweight Loss

Just as we showed in the case of price and quantity regulations, the main determinant of the DWL from a tax as a share of revenue is how much the quantity changes when the tax is added. The size of that change depends, in turn, on how sensitive supply and demand are to prices. The deadweight loss from pizza price controls, for example, came about because there were consumers and suppliers who would like to trade at market prices and would have earned surplus from doing so but were prevented from engaging in these transactions by the price ceiling. With taxes, there are no forbidden transactions. The source of the loss is the same, however. There are people who would have bought tickets at the market price without a tax and would have gained some surplus from doing so. Once the government adds a tax, the after-tax price rises enough so that these consumers no longer want to buy tickets. They get to keep their money, but they were previously able to buy something with it that gave them surplus. Likewise, movie houses lose surplus because some would have shown movies at the pre-tax market price but find the after-tax price too low to justify operating. These lost surpluses are the DWL of the tax.

Why a Big Tax Is Much Worse Than a Small Tax

An interesting result of our analysis is that it implies the inefficiency represented by the size of the deadweight loss gets much bigger as the size of a tax becomes larger. In the movie ticket tax example (Figure 3.13), we saw that the DWL from the tax was area $C + E$ and that the revenue generated was $B + D$. What would happen if Mayor Menino decided to *increase* the ticket tax? How much more revenue and how much more DWL would this large tax increase create?

Figure 3.14 illustrates the outcome for a general case. The larger tax reduces the quantity even further, from Q_2 to Q_3. The DWL under the larger tax is area $C + E + F + H$ (remember that it was only area F with the smaller tax). Government revenue, which was area $D + E$ with a smaller tax, is now area $B + D + G$. That is, the government gains areas B and G because the people who still buy tickets are paying more in taxes. However, the government loses area E, because some people stop buying movie tickets after the tax is raised. If we look at the DWL as a share of the revenue generated, it is clear that the *incremental* revenue generated by increasing this tax causes more inefficiency than the smaller tax did. Initially, the DWL was F, with a revenue gain of $D + E$. But the incremental DWL here is $C + E + H$, while the revenue gain is only $B + G - E$. In fact, if taxes are high enough, the increase in revenue per ticket from the tax will be more than offset by the reduction in the quantity of tickets sold, and there will be no revenue gain at all!

A general rule of thumb is that the DWL of a tax rises with the square of the tax rate.[12] That is, doubling the tax rate quadruples the DWL. That's why economists tend

---

Figure 3.14   **The Effect of a Larger Tax on Boston Movie Tickets**

After an increase in the tax on movie tickets in Boston from t_1 to t_2, the tax wedge between the price consumers pay and the price movie theaters receive increases, while the quantity of movie tickets at the equilibrium (Q_3) decreases. The tax revenue is now $B + D + G$. Area E, a part of the government's tax revenues under the lower tax, is a part of the deadweight loss, $C + E + F + H$. Since the incremental DWL is $C + E + H$ and the revenue gain is only $B + G - E$, the incremental revenue created by the second larger tax is more inefficient than that of the first smaller tax.

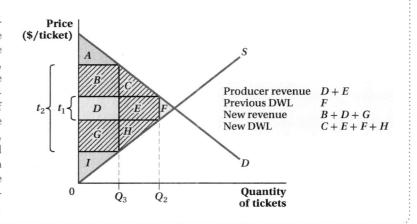

Producer revenue	$D + E$
Previous DWL	F
New revenue	$B + D + G$
New DWL	$C + E + F + H$

---

[12] To see where this intuition comes from, notice that with linear supply and demand curves, the DWL from a tax is a triangle with a height equal to the quantity reduction caused by the tax and a base equal to the tax. Because the supply and demand curves are linear, the quantity reduction is proportional to the tax. Specifically, it will be $\Delta Q = A * t$, where A is some number that depends on the slope of the demand and supply curves. Therefore, the area of the DWL triangle is $\frac{1}{2} * A * t * t = \frac{1}{2} * A * t^2$. This area is proportional to the square of the tax. For nonlinear demand and supply curves, this formula is only an approximation, but if they aren't too nonlinear, the intuition remains the same.

to favor tax policies that exhibit what is called "low rates and broad bases." That is just a way of saying that, all else equal, taxing ten things at a low rate is better than taxing five things at zero and five things at a high rate. Because DWL rises with the square of the tax rate, the overall DWL will be larger with the five high rates than with the ten low rates.

The Incidence of Taxation: The Payer Doesn't Matter

An important thing to note about the movie ticket example is that although we supposed that it would be the theater owners who were legally obligated to remit the 50 cents per ticket tax to the City of Boston, they don't bear the complete burden of the tax. Before the tax came in, the theater owners received $8 per ticket and moviegoers paid $8 a ticket. After the $0.50 tax, moviegoers pay $8.30 a ticket. After they send in the tax, however, the theaters only end up with $7.80 per ticket. Therefore, of the 50 cents going to the government, 30 cents (60%) of it is coming out of consumers' pockets because their price went up by 30 cents. Movie theaters send the tax check to the government, but they are able to pass on much of the tax to consumers through higher prices. This means that the price realized by the suppliers goes down by only 20 cents. Who *really* bears the burden of a tax is called **tax incidence**. The incidence of this tax is 60% on the buyers and 40% on the suppliers.

tax incidence
Who actually pays a tax.

Now let's say Boston changed the rule for who pays the tax to the government. Instead of the theater sending the tax payment to the government, moviegoers would pay the tax by, after buying their ticket at whatever price the theater charges, dropping two quarters in a "Menino Box" as they enter the theater (silly, yes, but this is just to make a point).

Figure 3.15 | Tax Incidence

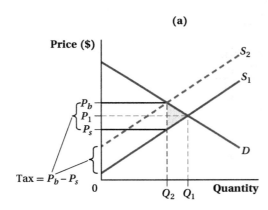
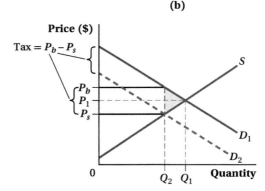

(a) The tax incidence is unaffected by whether the seller or buyer pays the tax. When the seller pays the tax, the supply curve shifts inward by the amount of the tax, $P_b - P_s$, from S_1 to S_2. The equilibrium quantity decreases from Q_1 to Q_2. The seller now faces price P_s at the equilibrium, while the buyer pays price P_b.

(b) When the buyer pays the tax, the demand curve shifts inward by the amount of the tax, $P_b - P_s$, from D_1 to D_2. The equilibrium quantity decreases from Q_1 to Q_2. As in panel a, the seller now faces price P_s at the equilibrium, while the buyer pays price P_b.

Does this change alter the tax incidence? It does not. The equations below show that the tax formula doesn't matter whether you subtract the tax from what the supplier receives or add the tax to what the buyer pays.

$$P_s = P_b - \text{tax}$$

is the same as

$$P_s + \text{tax} = P_b$$

This can also be seen graphically. The original case where the theater remits the tax is shown in Figure 3.15a. When the tax is instead paid by buyers, their quantity demanded depends on the price including the tax. But the price suppliers receive at this quantity demanded is only the price without the tax. To account for this difference, we shift down the demand curve by the amount of the tax, from D_1 to D_2 in Figure 3.15b. But the result hasn't changed: Quantity demanded is still Q_2 and the difference between the buyer's price and the seller's price still equals the amount of the tax. Thus, the incidence of a tax does not depend on who is legally bound to pay it.

That's why a helpful way to picture taxes on a graph is to just forget about whether the tax is moving the supply curve up or the demand curve down. Instead, start from the initial no-tax equilibrium point and move left until the vertical space between the supply and demand curves is the amount of the tax. This gives you the right answer regardless of whether the tax is being legally applied to suppliers or buyers.

This point about tax incidence is fundamental. If you have ever had a job, you probably know that the government takes many taxes out of your pay. Some of these are payroll taxes that appear on your pay stub as FICA (Federal Insurance Contributions Act). They are collected to pay for Social Security and Medicare. In the United States, payroll taxes are legally split evenly between workers and employers. In other words, if you earn wages of $1,000, you have to pay 7.65% of that in payroll taxes and the employer has to pay another 7.65% on its own.[13] Would U.S. workers be better or worse off if the law changed so that the company paid 15.3% and workers paid nothing, or if it instead made the employee pay 15.3% and his or her employers paid nothing? The analyses we've just completed suggest that such changes wouldn't make any difference. In a competitive market, the wage would adjust to the same level regardless of which side of the market actually pays the tax.

make the grade

Did I measure deadweight loss correctly?

A few simple tricks will help you nail problems involving deadweight loss. First, whenever the quantity consumed falls as a result of a government policy, a deadweight loss occurs. (This isn't *exactly* correct; if externalities are present, government policies can actually improve market outcomes. We learn more about externalities in Chapter 16.) If the quantity doesn't get distorted, no deadweight loss occurs. Second, the deadweight loss almost always takes the shape of a triangle, and moreover, that triangle points at the efficient market equilibrium with no market distortion. Why? Because deadweight loss measures the consumer and producer surplus destroyed. As we have seen, this loss in surplus grows as we move further and further away from the efficient equilibrium. The growing distance between the sides of the triangle reflects this fact.

---

[13] FICA taxes apply only to "earned" income like wages and salaries. In 2011 the Social Security tax applied to the first $106,800 of wages per person. After that, only the Medicare part of the tax applied (that rate is 2.9%). The limit is subject to increases from year-to-year, typically at a rate tied to inflation. Also in 2011, Congress temporarily reduced the Social Security rate workers were responsible for, making workers' legal share of the tax less than half.

It turns out that the only thing that matters about the economic effects of this tax is how elastic the supply and the demand for labor are. To see why, let's consider the two extremes.

Elastic Demand with Inelastic Supply   In a market characterized by an elastic demand and an inelastic supply, buyers are very sensitive to price and the suppliers are not. Most labor economists tend to think of the labor market in this way, so that the 15.3% FICA tax (the combined tax rate on the two sides) applies to a market in which labor supply is fairly inelastic (people work a similar amount even if their wage goes up or down) and firms' demand for labor is fairly elastic. This market is illustrated in Figure 3.16a.

Applying the methods we've used throughout this section, we see that the tax is borne almost entirely by the suppliers—here, workers supplying labor. With a tax, employers have to pay wages W_b that are a bit higher than wages without the tax, W_1. But after taxes, the workers receive a wage W_s that is much less than W_1. Therefore, workers are a lot worse off after the tax than employers. And we know from the discussion that we just had on tax incidence that even if the government switched the payroll tax rules so that employers paid the entire amount, workers would not do any better. Their wages would fall almost as much as the employers' tax went up.

Inelastic Demand with Elastic Supply   Figure 3.16b shows a market characterized by inelastic demand (buyers are not sensitive to price) and elastic supply (suppliers

---

Figure 3.16 | Tax Incidence and Elasticities

(a)

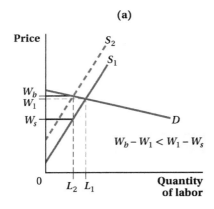

(b)

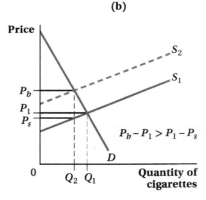

(a) In a labor market where demand is elastic and supply inelastic, we begin with supply curve S_1, demand D, and equilibrium price and quantity (W_1, L_1). The implementation of the tax $W_b - W_s$ shifts the supply curve inward from S_1 to S_2 and decreases the equilibrium quantity of labor from L_1 to L_2. Because laborers in this market are not very sensitive to price and employers are, the effect of the tax on the wages laborers receive is much larger than its effect on the wage employers pay, $W_b - W_1 < W_1 - W_s$.

(b) In the market for cigarettes where demand is inelastic and supply elastic, we begin with supply curve S_1, demand D, and equilibrium price and quantity (P_1, Q_1). The implementation of the tax $P_b - P_s$ shifts the supply curve inward from S_1 to S_2 and decreases the equilibrium quantity of cigarettes from Q_1 to Q_2. Because smokers in this market are not very sensitive to price and cigarette companies are, the effect of the tax on the price consumers pay is much larger than its effect on the price companies receive, $P_b - P_1 > P_1 - P_s$.

are very sensitive to price). In the market for cigarettes, for instance, many buyers are addicted and tend to buy a similar amount no matter how much the price goes up. Cigarette supply is more elastic. You can see in the figure that in this case, consumers bear the brunt of the tax. A tax on cigarettes causes the buyers' price to rise from P_1 to P_b, almost the entire amount of the tax. Suppliers are only a bit worse off than they were before, because they can pass on the higher costs to the inelastic consumers.

We could do this entire analysis using equations, as we did in the movie ticket example. It turns out that there is a general formula that will approximate the share of the tax that is borne by the consumer and the share borne by the producer. Not surprisingly given what we've just discussed, these shares depend on elasticities:

$$\text{Share borne by consumer} = \frac{E^S}{E^S + |E^D|}$$

$$\text{Share borne by producer} = \frac{|E^D|}{E^S + |E^D|}$$

If the price elasticity of supply (E^S) is infinite, the consumers' share is equal to 1; that is, consumers bear the whole burden when supply is perfectly elastic. If the absolute value of the price elasticity of demand $(|E^D|)$ is infinite, the consumers' share of the tax burden is zero, and suppliers bear the whole burden of the tax.

3.3 figure it out

Consider the demand and supply for cola in a market represented by the following equations:

$$Q^D = 15 - 10P$$
$$Q^S = 40P - 50$$

where Q is millions of bottles per year and P measures dollars per bottle. The equilibrium price of cola is $1.30 per bottle, and 2 million bottles are sold each year.

a. Calculate the price elasticity of demand and the price elasticity of supply at the equilibrium price and quantity.

b. Calculate the share of a tax that would be borne by consumers and the share borne by producers.

c. If a tax of $0.15 per bottle is created, what would be the expected price buyers will have to pay? What price will sellers receive after the tax?

Solution:

a. The formula for price elasticity of demand is

$$E^D = \frac{\Delta Q^D}{\Delta P} \times \frac{P}{Q^D}$$

From the demand curve, we can calculate $\frac{\Delta Q^D}{\Delta P}$. Each time P changes by one unit, Q^D falls by 10. Therefore,

$$\frac{\Delta Q^D}{\Delta P} = -10$$

Substituting into the formula for elasticity, we get

$$E^D = \frac{\Delta Q}{\Delta P} \times \frac{P}{Q} = -10 \times \frac{1.3}{2} = \frac{-13}{2} = -6.25$$

The formula for price elasticity of supply is

$$E^S = \frac{\Delta Q^S}{\Delta P} \times \frac{P}{Q^S}$$

From the supply curve, we can see that $\frac{\Delta Q^S}{\Delta P} = 40$. Note that each time P increases by one unit, Q^S rises by 40.

Thus, the price elasticity of supply is

$$E^S = \frac{\Delta Q^S}{\Delta P} \times \frac{P}{Q^S} = 40 \times \frac{1.3}{2} = \frac{52}{2} = 26$$

b. The proportion of the tax borne by buyers will be

$$\frac{E^S}{E^S + |E^D|} = \frac{26}{26 + |-6.5|} = \frac{26}{32.5} = 0.8$$

The proportion of the tax borne by sellers will be

$$\frac{|E^D|}{E^S + |E^D|} = \frac{|-6.5|}{26 + |-6.5|} = \frac{6.5}{32.5} = 0.2$$

So buyers will bear 80% of the tax and sellers will bear only 20% of the tax.

c. If there is a tax of $0.15 per bottle, buyers will bear 80% of the tax:

$$\text{Increase in } P_b = (0.80)(\$0.15) = \$0.12$$

The price buyers pay will rise from $1.30 per bottle (the original equilibrium price) to $1.42.

Sellers will bear the other 20% of the tax:

$$\text{Decrease in } P_s = (0.2)(\$0.15) = \$0.03$$

The price sellers receive will fall from $1.30 per bottle to $1.27.

3.5 Subsidies

subsidy
A payment by the government to a buyer or seller of a good or service.

A **subsidy** is a payment by the government to a buyer or seller of a good or service. It is, in essence, the exact opposite of a tax. In fact, when we analyze the effects of subsidies on markets, we can treat the subsidy as a negative tax. Thus, the price the buyer pays is *lower* than the price the supplier receives after the subsidy. If the government subsidizes gasoline by $1 per gallon, for example, then buyers might pay $3.50 per gallon at the pump, but gas stations receive $4.50 per gallon because they get to add the government dollar to the $3.50. This relationship is

$$P_b + \text{subsidy} = P_s$$

where P_b is the price the buyer pays (the market price) and P_s is the price the seller receives after the subsidy is paid.

Governments tax a lot, but they also subsidize the production of many different goods and services. Let's look at the effects of the U.S. government subsidy for the domestic production of ethanol, a corn-based fuel additive that can be mixed with gasoline. (A common rationale given for the subsidy is to reduce the dependence of the United States on imported oil, though not coincidentally politicians from large corn-producing states have been vocal backers of the policy.) Let's say the government gives fuel producers $1 for every gallon of gas-ethanol mix they sell. This means that if the original supply curve S_1 is what suppliers receive, the supply curve that buyers face will be *shifted down* by the amount of the subsidy, to S_2 (Figure 3.17). The supply curve that buyers face is lower because the amount people pay to fill their tank is less than the amount the gas station receives, since the government is footing part of the bill (the effects of a tax are just the opposite).

Before the subsidy was in place, consumer surplus was everything below the demand curve and above the price that consumers pay (P_1), area $A + B + C$ in Figure 3.17. After the subsidy, consumer surplus will change. But it will not get smaller, as in the case of a tax. It will get larger. The new consumer surplus is the area below the demand curve and above the price that the consumers have to pay (the new lower price, P_b). This is the old consumer surplus $A + B + C$ *plus* the new part $F + G + H$. This additional surplus comes from the lower price and the additional sales at that price.

Before the subsidy, the producer surplus was everything above the supply curve but below the price the suppliers received (P_1), area $F + G + J$. After the subsidy, producer surplus gets bigger, too. The area above the producers' own supply curve S_1 and below the price that the suppliers receive (P_s) is now $F + G + J$ plus $B + C + D$. (We calculate producer surplus using the *producers'* supply curve (S_1) to compute producer surplus because this is the supply curve that embodies the suppliers' costs of production.)

Note that parts of the consumer and producer surplus areas overlap in this case (areas $B + C + F + G$) because both sides are getting more surplus than before. The only way this is possible, however, is if someone else foots the bill. In this case, it's the government. The subsidy costs money. The cost of the subsidy is the subsidy

---

Figure 3.17   :   **The Impact of a Producer Subsidy**

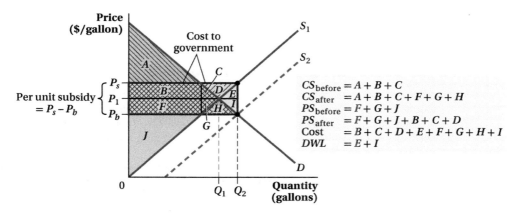

In the pre-subsidy market for gasoline, the supply curve S_1 intersects with the demand curve D at the equilibrium price P_1 and equilibrium quantity Q_1. The consumer surplus is $A + B + C$, and the producer surplus is $F + G + J$. After a government subsidy is put in place, the supply curve shifts down by the amount of the subsidy, $P_s - P_b$, to S_2. At the equilibrium, the quantity increases to Q_2, the price facing suppliers is P_s, and the price facing buyers is P_b. Consumer surplus is now $A + B + C + F + G + H$, and producer surplus is $F + G + J + B + C + D$. The cost of the subsidy is $B + C + D + E + F + G + H + I$, and the deadweight loss is $E + I$. Therefore, the costs associated with the subsidy are larger than the sum of the benefits to producers and consumers.

amount times the quantity produced, $Q_1 \times (P_s - P_b)$, which amounts to the rectangle $B + C + D + E + F + G + H + I$.

This isn't the only cost of the subsidy, however. Like any other price regulation, a subsidy also creates deadweight loss. It might seem odd at first that there would be DWL when both consumers *and* producers are better off after the subsidy. The key is to compare how much their surplus goes up to how much the subsidy costs the government. While consumer surplus went up by $F + G + H$ and producer surplus by $B + C + D$, total government outlays for the subsidy were $(F + G + H) + (B + C + D) + (E + I)$. Therefore, the subsidy's DWL is $E + I$. Society as a whole pays more for the subsidy than the added benefit it gave to consumers and producers. If somehow the government could just turn over the subsidy revenue to consumers without changing the price, society would be better off. By changing the price, it gets some extra people to buy gasoline (with ethanol added) who really were not interested in buying before.

When we looked at the market interventions earlier in this chapter, the DWL derived from the surplus lost by people who would have bought if there were no tax or regulation, but do not buy when the tax is in place and the price is too high. Here, it is the other way around. The DWL comes from people who would *not* have made a purchase in a competitive market. They only make a purchase because the subsidy lowers the price. The amount they value the extra quantity is less than it costs the government to move them to buy it.

A different way to see how this deadweight loss occurs is to think about people giving presents to each other. Economist Joel Waldfogel asked microeconomics students who received Christmas presents how much they thought the gifts they received cost the people who bought them.[14] Then he asked the students how much the gifts were worth to them, apart from the sentimental value. The students valued the presents they got by about 15% less than the cost of the presents. This 15% DWL from Christmas presents is just like the DWL from a subsidy. When the government subsidizes a product, it gives consumers a gift: The consumers value the gift (as measured by the consumer surplus) less than it costs the government to buy it (as measured by the revenue cost).

 application

The Cost of the Black-Liquor Loophole

A recent example of an (accidental) subsidy gone awry is the so-called black-liquor loophole in the law that gave companies tax credits for using alternative fuels. The tax credit is given to businesses that combine alternative fuels with traditional fossil fuels used in their operations, with the idea of encouraging companies to reduce their fossil fuel use in doing so.

It turns out that there is a chemical by-product of paper making called "black liquor" that paper companies have traditionally recycled to use as fuel in their plants. The government determined that this chemical qualified as an alternative fuel under the definition in the law. However, the paper companies couldn't qualify for the tax credit unless they *combined* the alternative fuel with a fossil fuel. So they started adding a bit of diesel fuel—a fossil fuel they weren't using at all before—to the black liquor before burning it. This led to two results. First, paper companies used more diesel than they

---

[14] Joel Waldfogel, "The Deadweight Loss of Christmas," *American Economic Review* 83, no. 5 (1993): 1328–1336. Leave it to an economist to point out the deadweight loss of Christmas!

did before, even though the point of the tax credit was to encourage movement away from use of fossil fuels. Second, paper companies got paid (in the form of tax credits) to burn the black liquor they were already using without payment. They got paid a lot too: This tax credit, originally projected to cost the government $61 million, ended up costing an estimated $6 to $8 *billion* in tax credits in 2009, almost all of it going to paper companies.

How does our analysis in this section explain what happened? The tax credit became, in practice, a diesel subsidy for the paper industry. By tying the credit to the use of blended fuels, it lowered the effective price of diesel that the paper companies faced. Before, when they had to pay the market price, their quantity demanded for diesel to fuel their plants was zero—they had a plentiful and cheap alternative in the black liquor. But now every gallon of diesel they bought came with a big tax credit attached—meaning they faced a downward-shifted supply curve for diesel. The quantity of diesel they demanded at these lower supply prices became positive.

As a result of this policy, the paper companies and the diesel sellers are better off because of the subsidy. (The former very much so in this case.) But the costs are large. First, there is deadweight loss: An industry that wasn't using diesel before because it had a superior alternative now demands it, even though the industry values it at less than the cost of supplying it. Second, the government has to pay the subsidy. And as noted above, that's a really big number. So big, in fact, that Congress closed the loophole in 2010 because they decided that we couldn't afford it. ■

3.4 figure it out

Suppose the demand for and supply of ethanol in a small town are as follows:

$$Q^D = 9{,}000 - 1{,}000P$$
$$Q^S = 2{,}000P - 3{,}000$$

where Q measures gallons per day and P represents price per gallon. The current equilibrium price is $4, and the current equilibrium quantity is 5,000 gallons per day.

Now suppose that the government wants to create a subsidy of $0.375 per gallon to encourage the use of ethanol.

a. What will happen to the price buyers pay per gallon, the price sellers receive per gallon, and the number of gallons consumed each day?

b. How much will this subsidy cost the government (and ultimately taxpayers)?

Solution:

a. Determining the prices that buyers and sellers face under a subsidy is done in a way similar to how we determined the prices for buyers and sellers in the presence of a tax. However, there is one big difference. Now, the price sellers receive is actually larger than the price paid by buyers (due to the subsidy):

$$P_s = P_b + \text{subsidy}$$

So now we know that in our problem

$$P_s = P_b + 0.375$$

Remember that we need to start with the supply and demand equations in the following form:

$$Q^D = 9{,}000 - 1{,}000P_b$$
$$Q^S = 2{,}000P_s - 3{,}000$$

Once we have these, we can substitute for P_s in the supply equation so that it becomes

$$Q^S = 2{,}000P_s - 3{,}000$$
$$Q^S = 2{,}000(P_b + 0.375) - 3{,}000 = 2{,}000P_b + 750 - 3{,}000 = 2{,}000P_b - 2{,}250$$

Now, we can equate Q^D and Q^S to solve for P_b

$$9{,}000 - 1{,}000P_b = 2{,}000P_b - 2{,}250$$
$$3{,}000P_b = 11{,}250$$
$$P_b = 3.75$$
$$P_s = P_b + 0.375$$
$$P_s = 4.125$$

To solve for the quantity of ethanol sold after the subsidy is put in place, we can substitute P_b into the demand equation or substitute P_s into the supply equation. (It is a good idea to do both to check your work.)

$$Q^D = 9{,}000 - 1{,}000P_b = 9{,}000 - 1{,}000(3.75) = 9{,}000 - 3{,}750 = 5{,}250$$
$$Q^S = 2{,}000P_s - 3{,}000 = 2{,}000(4.125) - 3{,}000 = 8{,}250 - 3{,}000 = 5{,}250$$

So, buyers will pay $3.75 per gallon, sellers will receive $4.125 per gallon, and 5,250 gallons will be sold each day. This can be seen in the figure below.

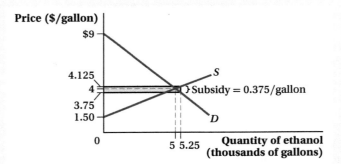

b. The cost of the subsidy will be the subsidy per gallon multiplied by the number of gallons sold:

Cost of subsidy = ($0.375)(5,250) = $1,968.75 per day

freakonomics

Can Economic Incentives Get You Pregnant?

In many countries around the world, the number of babies being born has declined dramatically. In places like China, which instituted a one child per family policy in 1978, the government wanted fewer babies to control the size of the population. In many other parts of the world, especially Europe and Japan, declining fertility poses a problem for governments. Fewer babies mean an aging population. In the next 20 years, the number of retired people worldwide who depend on government pensions will skyrocket, but there will be fewer people of working age to pay the taxes that fund these pensions.

What can governments do about this? One approach would be for governments to run budget surpluses now to cover potential shortfalls in the future. But that sort of austerity is not very popular among elected officials: They would pay the political price of high taxes today but wouldn't be in office 20 years from now to reap the benefits. Another approach would be to encourage additional immigration of working-age individuals. This is another tough sell politically in many countries. Instead, some countries such as France and Sweden are now considering adopting a different economic solution: paying cash to people who have babies.

Can government subsidies encourage the production of babies? You may think this is preposterous—that a couple's decision to become parents is completely unconnected to economics. If so, it just means you don't yet think like an economist. (It is only Chapter 3, though, so there is plenty of time to fix that.) The data suggest that the demand curve for babies slopes downward; that is, when the "price" of having a baby falls, people have more babies. In Israel, which has paid parents to have kids since 1959, economists Alma Cohen, Rajeev Dehejia, and Dmitri Romanov found sizable impacts of government subsidies on fertility.[*] In fact, they estimate that a 2003 reduction in the subsidy offered to new parents decreased the number of children born in 2004 by 12%. Given Israel's population, that amounts to approximately 5,400 babies who would have been born had the old, higher subsidy remained in effect. This pricing effect was seen across all ethnicities and religious groups too, with payouts affecting the family planning of Orthodox Jews as well as Arab Muslims in the country.

Countries of the former Soviet bloc didn't explicitly pay for children, but they encouraged baby-making in other ways. During the Communist reign, many of these countries such as Czechoslovakia and East Germany offered free child care, giving mothers the opportunity to quickly return to work. The allocation of housing was often tied to children; in Prague, for example, a couple had to be married with a child to be eligible for a government apartment.

The despotic ruler of Romania, Nicolae Ceausescu, used a different approach: In 1966, without warning, he banned abortion, which was the primary form of birth control in Romania at the time. The number of children born skyrocketed in the short run, with the fertility rate nearly doubling from 1.9 children per woman in 1966 to 3.7 children per woman, on average, in 1967. The large number of births accomplished Ceausescu's goal of having more boys who could eventually serve in his army. The problem with suddenly banning abortion, however, was that the babies who were born were not wanted or planned for by their parents. This outcome made the parents angry and led to unwanted children who faced much more difficult lives than the typical Romanian child born prior to 1966. Compared to Romanian children born just a year earlier, the cohorts of children born after the abortion ban would do worse in every measurable way: They would test lower in school, they would have less success in the labor market, and they would also prove much more likely to become criminals. Eventually, young protesters born after the abortion ban would overthrow Ceausescu in 1989, and he would be executed.

If Ceausescu had been a better economist, he would have realized that changing prices (in this case, by offering subsidies for babies) can be a more efficient way of incentivizing behavior than outright prohibition. In other words, economics might even have saved Ceausescu's life.

[*]Alma Cohen, Rajeev Dehejia, and Dmitri Romanov, "Do Financial Incentives Affect Fertility?" *NBER Working Paper,* 2007.

3.6 Conclusion

In this chapter, we took the supply and demand hammer and pounded every nail in sight. We saw how you can compute the consumer and producer surplus generated by transactions in a market, learned how to value new goods, and learned what deadweight loss is. We learned to use supply, demand, and total surplus to analyze industries and the ways in which they change in response to changes in the market, particularly to price and quantity regulations, taxes, and subsidies. Being able to do so much with such a simple model makes supply and demand the workhorse of microeconomics.

Summary

1. **Consumer surplus** is the value that consumers receive from participating in market transactions. It is the difference between the most they would pay for something and the price they actually have to pay for it. On a supply and demand graph, consumer surplus is measured by the area under the demand curve and above the price. **Producer surplus** is the benefit that producers receive from participating in market transactions. It is the difference between what they sell their product for and the least they would be willing to receive to sell their product. On a supply and demand graph, producer surplus is measured by the area above the supply curve and below the price. [**Section 3.1**]

2. Using consumer and producer surplus, we can compute how shifts in supply and demand affect the well-being of customers and of companies. An inward shift in supply will cause consumer surplus to fall because both the increase in the equilibrium price and the decrease in the equilibrium quantity this shift causes act to reduce consumer surplus. An outward shift in supply, on the other hand, raises consumer surplus. An inward shift in demand leads to a drop in producer surplus because it decreases both the equilibrium price and quantity. Outward demand shifts have the opposite effect. [**Section 3.1**]

3. If the government imposes a price regulation—either a maximum price or **price ceiling** like rent control or a minimum price or **price floor** like the minimum wage—the quantities supplied and demanded will differ at the market price, resulting in either excess demand or excess supply of the good. Such regulations also create a **deadweight loss** that arises because some of the surplus-creating transactions that took place before the regulation was enacted do not take place in the regulated environment. A direct transfer of income from one side to the other without changing the price would be a more efficient way to help consumers and suppliers. Deadweight losses are largest when supply and demand are most elastic. [**Section 3.2**]

4. If the government imposes a cap on output (a **quota**) or provides output itself, this action will change the market and create a deadweight loss, just as a price regulation does. These actions do not create excess demand or supply, though, because prices are able to adjust and clear the market. [**Section 3.3**]

5. Taxes reduce output and raise price. In doing so, they reduce consumer and producer surplus but generate tax revenue. The revenue they generate is less than the damage they do to surplus, and the difference is the deadweight loss of the tax. The concept of **tax incidence** tells us who really bears the burden of a tax: It does not matter who actually pays a tax by law. All that matters is the elasticities of demand and supply. The more elastic side of the market will bear less of the burden because it can more easily shift away from the taxed good. [**Section 3.4**]

6. **Subsidies** increase both consumer and producer surplus relative to the free-market equilibrium. They still create a deadweight loss, though, because the outlay cost of the subsidy exceeds the amount by which it increases the surplus of the two groups. [**Section 3.5**]

Review Questions

1. Define consumer and producer surplus.
2. What is the demand choke price? How does this price relate to consumer surplus?
3. What is the supply choke price? How does this price relate to producer surplus?
4. How does a supply shift affect consumer and producer surplus in a given market? Consider both inward and outward shifts of the supply curve.
5. How does a demand shift affect consumer and producer surplus in a given market? Consider both inward and outward shifts of the demand curve.
6. What is a price ceiling? Why does a price ceiling create excess demand for (shortage of) a good?
7. What is a price floor? Why does a price floor create an excess supply of (surplus of) a good?
8. What is a deadweight loss? If the price elasticity of a good is large, would you expect the deadweight loss to be large or small?
9. When is a price ceiling nonbinding? When is a price floor nonbinding?
10. What is a quota? How does it differ from a price ceiling or a price floor?
11. What is crowding out? Why does it occur?
12. Why is the relative size of crowding out inefficiencies dependent only on the elasticity of demand and not on the elasticity of supply?
13. What happens to the equilibrium price and quantity of a good when a tax is imposed on the good? Why does a tax create a wedge between the price the consumer pays and the price the producer receives?
14. How does a tax affect consumer and producer surplus? Why does a tax create a deadweight loss?
15. What is the tax incidence? What factors determine the tax incidence?
16. What is a subsidy?
17. How does a subsidy affect consumer and producer surplus?
18. Why does a subsidy create a deadweight loss?

Problems

1. If the supply curve for snowboards in the United States is described by the equation $Q^S = 400P - 8,000$ (where Q is the number of snowboards and P is in dollars per snowboard), compute the producer surplus at a price of $120. What happens to producer surplus if the price falls to $100?
2. The demand for air travel is summarized in the equation $Q^D = 800 - 2P$, where quantity is in millions of enplanements per quarter and price is in dollars per enplanement. How much would consumer surplus change if the rising cost of fuel led airlines to raise the price from $150 to $200?
3. Consider the demand for broadband Internet service, given as follows: $Q^D = 224 - 4P$, where Q is the number of subscribers in a given area (in hundreds) and P is the price in dollars per month. This demand relationship is illustrated in the diagram on the right. Assume that the price of broadband service is $25 per month. Determine the following, paying particular attention to the units in which quantity is denominated:
   a. The total number of subscribers at that price
   b. The total amount paid by subscribers for broadband service, area B
   c. The consumer surplus received by subscribers, area A
   d. The total value to consumers of the broadband service they received, areas A and B

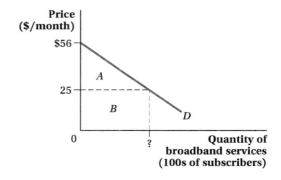

4. Consider the diagram on the next page, which depicts the supply of broadband Internet service. The supply of broadband service is given by $Q^S = 12.5P - 150$, where Q is the quantity of services (in hundreds) and P is the price per month. Assume that the price of broadband service is $25 per month. Determine the following, paying particular attention to the units in which quantity is denominated:
   a. The total number of services providers will supply at that price
   b. The total amount received by producers for that service, areas D and E
   c. The producer surplus received by suppliers, area D

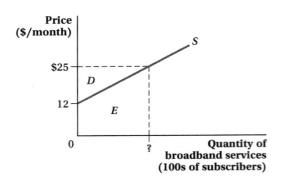

5. Combine the graphs and equations from questions 3 and 4 and determine the following:
   a. The equilibrium price of broadband Internet service
   b. The equilibrium quantity of broadband Internet service
   c. Consumer surplus
   d. Producer surplus
   e. The total surplus received by producers and consumers together
6. Holding price and quantity constant, why does the consumer surplus from a product decline if the demand curve becomes more elastic?
7. Neco Marine in the Republic of Palau estimates that the demand for its scuba diving services is given by $Q^D = 6{,}000 - 20P$, where Q is the number of divers served each year and P is the price of a two-tank dive. The supply of Neco's diving services is given by $Q^S = 30P - 2{,}000$.
   a. Solve for the equilibrium price and quantity.
   b. Find the value of the consumer surplus received by Neco divers. (*Hint*: It may help to draw a graph.)
   c. Find the value of Neco Marine's producer surplus. (*Hint*: It may help to draw a graph.)
   d. Suppose that the demand for scuba diving services increases, and that the new demand is given by $Q^D = 7{,}000 - 20P$. Calculate the impact of this change in demand on the values you calculated in parts (a) through (c).
   e. Are consumers better off or worse off as a result of the demand increase?
8. Is it possible that a regulation like the minimum wage, which is specifically designed to help low-income people, could actually reduce their income? If so, under what supply and demand conditions might this happen?
9. Low-skilled workers operate in a competitive market. The labor supply is $Q^S = 10W$ (where W is the price of labor measured by the hourly wage) and the demand for labor is $Q^D = 240 - 20W$. Q measures the quantity of labor hired (in thousands of hours).

   a. What is the equilibrium wage and quantity of low-skilled labor working in equilibrium?
   b. If the government passes a minimum wage of $10 per hour, what will be the new quantity of labor hired? Will there be a shortage or surplus of labor? How large?
   c. What is the deadweight loss of this price floor?
   d. How much better off are low-skilled workers in this case (in other words, how much does producer surplus change) and how much worse off are employers?
10. The diagram below illustrates the market for beef. Suppose that the government has instituted a price support program for beef by placing a price floor at $4.00 per pound. Under the program, any unsold beef will be purchased by the government and placed in long-term storage.

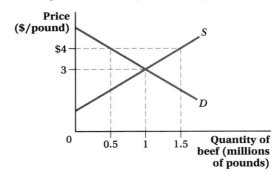

   a. What is the cost to consumers in lost surplus?
   b. What is the cost to taxpayers to purchase the unsold beef?
   c. How much producer surplus do sellers of beef gain?
   d. What is the loss to society of the beef program?
   e. The president of the National Cattleman's Association makes the following semi-extortionary offer to consumers: "Pay us $2.2 million per month forever and we'll lobby our congressmen to abandon the price support program." Should consumers pay the Cattleman's Association? Why or why not?
11. Draw a graph illustrating the impact of imposing a quota on production in a market, where the quota is less than the current equilibrium quantity. What happens to the price of the good, producer surplus, and consumer surplus? Show the deadweight loss from the quota.
12. For decades, the mob ran a "numbers game" in which participants who matched three numbers chosen at random would win a prize. In the 1970s, state governments began authorizing state lottery commissions; those commissions typically offered games similar in structure to the numbers game. Using supply and demand analysis:

a. Predict the effect of the creation of state lotteries on the number of people playing numbers-type games.

b. Predict the effect of the creation of state lotteries on the number of people playing mob-run numbers games.

c. Predict the effect of the creation of state lotteries on the price of playing a numbers-type game.

d. Numbers games are unusual in that tickets don't typically vary in their nominal price—most tickets sell for exactly $1. Given that the nominal price is fixed, how might the price change you indicated in (c) be achieved?

13. Why do taxes create a deadweight loss the same way that regulations do? If a tax and a quota raise prices by the same amount, which causes more deadweight loss? Explain.

14. Consider the market for Cheese Puff Snacks (Q is in bags of Cheese Puffs). The demand for Cheese Puff Snacks is $Q^D = 30 - P$ and the supply is $Q^S = 3P - 10$. To pay for classes about healthy snacking, the government imposes a $4 per bag tax on Cheese Puffs.

a. What are the price paid by buyers, price received by sellers, and the number of bags of Cheese Puffs sold both before and after the tax?

b. What are the deadweight loss and revenue generated from this tax?

c. If the government decides to expand the healthy snacking program and raises the tax by $8 per bag (to the $12 total), what is the *additional* DWL and revenue from increasing taxes by this amount (that is in addition to the DWL and revenue that resulted from the $4 tax)?

15. The demand for ice cream is given by $Q^D = 20 - 2P$, measured in gallons of ice cream. The supply of ice cream is given by $Q^S = 4P - 10$.

a. Graph the supply and demand curves, and find the equilibrium price and quantity of ice cream.

b. Suppose that the government legislates a $1 tax on a gallon of ice cream, to be collected from the buyer. Plot the new demand curve on your graph. Does demand increase or decrease as a result of the tax?

c. As a result of the tax, what happens to the price paid by buyers? What happens to the price received by sellers? How many gallons of ice cream are sold?

d. Who bears the greater burden of the tax? Can you explain why this is so?

e. Calculate consumer surplus both before and after the tax.

f. Calculate producer surplus both before and after the tax.

g. How much tax revenue did the government raise?

h. How much deadweight loss does the tax create?

16. Social Security taxes are taxes on the sale of labor services. Half of Social Security taxes are generally collected from the employer and half from the employee. Does this seem like a good way to structure the tax collection? Can the government dictate who bears what share of the burden of a tax? Explain.

17. Draw a graph for a competitive market with a relatively elastic demand curve and inelastic supply curve. Illustrate on the graph the impact of imposing a per unit tax on the suppliers of the good in terms of consumer and producer surplus, prices and quantities, as well as how much deadweight loss the tax creates and the revenue it generates for the government. Who bears the larger burden of this tax?

18. The U.S. Senate is considering a bill that would tax the sale of laptop computers in order to fund a computer education program for presidential hopefuls. The Congressional Budget Office (CBO) estimates that if it implements a low tax of $12 per laptop, revenue should be sufficient to exactly fund the program. The CBO also estimates that a high tax of $230 per laptop will exactly fund the program.

a. How can a low tax and a high tax raise exactly enough money to fund the program? Illustrate your answer using a graph.

b. Suppose that you are an economic advisor to the Senate Finance Committee, tasked with analyzing the economic impact of the tax proposals. Which proposal do you recommend, and why?

19. Consider the following fiscal scheme designed to directly transfer welfare from coffee drinkers to coffee vendors: The government will impose a $1.00 tax, collected from buyers, for each cup of coffee sold. The government will then subsidize coffee vendors $1.00 for each cup of coffee sold.

a. What will happen to the equilibrium price of coffee?

b. What will happen to the equilibrium quantity of coffee?

c. How will the outcome of this scheme differ from one in which the government collects a $1.00 tax for each cup of coffee sold, and divides the total tax collections equally among all coffee vendors? (It is safe to assume that all coffee vendors are identical.)

Consumer Behavior 4

This chapter is about one key question: Given the seemingly unlimited array of products and services that consumers can buy, how do they decide which ones (and how much of each) to consume? In addition to serving as the building block for the demand curve in the basic supply and demand model, understanding the answer to this simple question is incredibly powerful and its potential applications are enormous.

■ Suppose you're Jeff Bezos at Amazon in 2006, trying to develop the Kindle for introduction to the market the following year. What features do you want to include in this device to maximize profitability? Much of the answer to that question depends on consumers' preferences: what they like to read, where they read, their willingness to pay for screen size, and their distaste for carrying heavy objects, just to name a few examples. Your profitability will also depend on consumers' ability to pay—their income. If you can figure out how all those forces interact, Mr. Bezos, you can build an attractive, desirable digital text display device that could make you bazillions. (You must have figured well: Kindle books now outsell print books on

Amazon, and while Amazon doesn't release figures on the number of devices it sells, some estimate that 8 million units sold in 2010, and Amazon's Kindle-generated revenue including both the devices and the books approached $5 billion a year.)

■   Suppose you manage a grocery store. Pepsi offers to cut your wholesale price if you run a promotion over the coming week. If you drop Pepsi prices by 20%, how much more shelf space should you give to Pepsi instead of Coke? How many customers will switch from buying Coke to Pepsi? How many customers who wouldn't have bought any soft drinks before the promotion will buy them now? Deciding how to handle this situation is another case in which understanding how consumers behave can help someone make the right decision and earn some profit by doing so.

■   Suppose you're an economic analyst working for a development nongovernmental organization (NGO) that needs projections of how a country's consumption patterns will change as its citizens become wealthier. Such projections will help the organization plan and create the infrastructure to move new goods to the country's growing markets. Again, a key part of the answer lies in understanding how consumers make their choices.

■   Suppose you are trying to decide whether to buy a ticket to see your favorite performer live or pay a share to rent a beach house with 10 friends for spring break. How do you make *all* your choices about what to spend your money on? Is your method of making such decisions "right," or could you do better? In this chapter, we examine some simple rules about how you (and other consumers) make choices. You might find that your decision-making methods violate these rules. If so, changing your behavior to take them into account will probably help you make decisions that improve your day-to-day well-being and happiness.

In addition to preparing you to analyze specific applications like these examples, this chapter illustrates a broader point about the study of economics. Like so many problems in economics (and life), the consumer's decision is a *constrained optimization* problem. Consumers try to do the best they can (they try to *optimize*) given that they are limited or *constrained* by the amount of money they have to spend. They have to make tradeoffs but do it in the smartest way they can. The set of techniques and ways of thinking we use to analyze consumers' constrained optimization problems will reappear over and over, in slightly modified ways and different settings, throughout this book and in any economics courses you may take in the future. If you become adept at solving the kind of constrained optimization problem we solve in this chapter, you will have gone a long way toward being able to answer *any* constrained optimization problem.

We begin the chapter by discussing the nature of consumers' preferences (what they like and don't like) and how economists use the concepts of utility—a measure of a consumer's well-being—and utility functions to summarize consumers' preferences. Consumers maximize their utility by trading off the purchase of one good against the purchase of others in a way that makes them the happiest. We'll see how such tradeoffs depend on a consumer's preferences, the amount of income the consumer has to spend, and the prices of the goods. Once we have these concepts in hand, we can combine them to analyze how real-world consumers behave, for example, why people buy less of something when its price rises (i.e., why demand curves slope down), and why they might consume not just more but different things as they become wealthier.

4.1 The Consumer's Preferences and the Concept of Utility

Consumers' preferences underlie every decision they make. Economists think of consumers as making rational choices about what they like best, given the constraints that they face when they make their choices.

Assumptions about Consumer Preferences

Consumers make many choices every day about what to buy and what not to buy. These choices involve many different goods: Buy a giant bag of Twizzlers and walk home, or buy a bus ticket and leave a sweet tooth unsatisfied? Buy a new video game or buy a new water pump for the car? Buy a ticket to the ball game or go to a bar for drinks with friends and watch the game on TV? To make it possible to understand how consumers form their preferences for thousands of goods and services, we need to make some simplifying assumptions. Specifically, we assume that all consumers' decisions about what to buy share four properties and that these properties help consumers determine their preferences over all the combinations of goods and services they might consume.

1. **Completeness and rankability.** This assumption implies consumers can make comparisons across all sets of goods that they consider. Economists use the term **consumption bundle** (or just *bundle*) to describe any collection of these goods. The assumption means that, given any two bundles, a consumer can determine whether she prefers the first bundle to the second bundle, the second to the first, or is indifferent between the two (i.e., views them equally). This assumption is important because it means that we can apply economic theory to any bundle of goods we want to discuss. Whether the bundle includes sapphires and SUVs; movies, motorcycles, modern art, and marshmallows; or iPods, Ikea furniture, and iceberg lettuce, the consumer can decide which bundle she likes better. This assumption does not, however, tell us what kinds of bundles the consumer will like more than others. It just implies she is able to determine if one is better than the other.

   consumption bundle
   A set of goods or services a consumer considers purchasing.

2. **For most goods, more is better than less (or at least more is no worse than less).** In general, we think that more of a good thing is good. If we like a car that is safe in a crash, we would like that car even better if it were even safer.[1] We also assume that consumers can discard unwanted goods at no cost, a concept economists call "free disposal." If you can get rid of things for free, then having more of something will never hurt you, even if it does not make you better off. The free disposal assumption may not always be strictly true in the real world, but it is a useful simplification in our basic economic model of consumer behavior.

3. **Transitivity.** For any three bundles of goods (call them A, B, and C), if a consumer prefers A to B and also prefers B to C, then the consumer must also prefer A to C. For example, if Claire prefers an apple to an orange, and prefers an orange to a banana, then transitivity implies that Claire must also prefer an apple to a banana. Note that, as always, we are holding everything else constant when making these comparisons. Transitivity does *not* mean that Claire has to prefer apples to bananas in all situations, but rather that at a given moment, she prefers apples to bananas. Transitivity imposes a logical consistency on the consumer.

4. **The more a consumer has of a particular good, the less she is willing to give up of something else to get even more of that good.** The idea behind this assumption is that consumers like variety. If you like birthday cake and haven't had cake lately, you might be willing to give up a lot for some cake. You might pay a high price for a cake, take the afternoon to bake a cake, or trade away your last carton of milk for some cake. On the other hand, if you've just polished off two-thirds of a cake, you are unlikely to be willing to pay much money for more, and you may very well want to trade the rest of the cake to get back some of that carton of milk. Like free disposal, it is possible to think of special cases in which the assumption of consumers liking variety will be violated

---

[1] There may come a point at which more of a good thing stops being better. Economists call this a *satiation point*. For instance, the first jelly bean may make us happy, but the 1,437th jelly bean might actually make us sick if we ate it, making us worse off than had we eaten only 1,436. However, because people can sometimes save extra jelly beans for later, trade them to someone else for something they want, or just give them away, satiation points tend not to be very important in practice.

(e.g., most people would prefer having either two water skis or two snow skis to having one of each). Nonetheless, we will almost always adopt this assumption because it holds true in a large number of situations and greatly simplifies our analysis.

The Concept of Utility

Given these assumptions about utility, we could create a list of a consumer's preferences between any bundles she might consume. The problem is that such a list would be a very long and unwieldy one. If we try to analyze a consumer's choices based on millions of pairwise comparisons over these bundles, we would get hopelessly lost.

Economists use the concept of utility and a mathematical relationship called a utility function to describe preferences more concisely. **Utility** describes how satisfied a consumer is. For practical purposes, you can think of utility as being a fancy word for happiness or well-being. It is important to realize that utility is *not* a measure of how rich a consumer is. Income may affect utility, but it is just one of many factors that do so.

A **utility function** summarizes the relationship between what consumers consume and their level of well-being. A function is a mathematical relationship that links a set of inputs to an output. For instance, if you combine the inputs eggs, flour, sugar, vanilla, butter, frosting, and candles in just the right way, you end up with the output of a birthday cake. In consumer behavior, the inputs to a utility function are the different things that can give a person utility. Examples of inputs to the utility function include traditional goods and services like cars, candy bars, health club memberships, and airplane rides. But there are many other types of inputs to utility as well, including scenic views, a good night's sleep, spending time with friends, and the pleasure that comes from giving to charity. The output of the utility function is the consumer's utility level. By providing a mapping between the bundles a consumer considers and a measure of the consumer's level of well-being—this bundle provides so much utility, that bundle provides so much utility, and so on—a utility function gives us a concise way to rank bundles.

Utility functions can take a variety of mathematical forms. Let's look at the utility someone enjoys from consuming Junior Mints and Milk Duds. Generically, we can write this utility level as $U = U(J, M)$, where $U(J, M)$ is the utility function and J and M are, respectively, the number of Junior Mints and Milk Duds the consumer eats. An example of a specific utility function for this consumer is $U = J \times M$. In this case, utility equals the product of the number of Junior Mints and Milk Duds she eats. But it could instead be that the consumer's (or maybe another consumer's) utility equals the total number of Junior Mints and Milk Duds eaten. In that case, the utility function is $U = J + M$. Yet another possibility is that the consumer's utility is given by $U = J^{0.7}M^{0.3}$. Because the exponent on Junior Mints (0.7) is larger than that on Milk Duds (0.3), this utility function implies that a given percentage increase in Junior Mints consumed will raise utility more than the same percentage increase in Milk Duds.

These are just a few examples from the large variety of possible utility functions we could imagine consumers having for these or any other combination of goods. At this point in our analysis of consumer behavior, we don't have to be too restrictive about the form any particular utility function takes. Because utility functions are used to represent preferences, however, they have to conform to our four assumptions about preferences (rankability and completeness, more is better, transitivity, and variety is important).

Marginal Utility

One of the most important concepts related to utility functions is **marginal utility,** the extra utility the consumer receives from a one-unit increase in consumption.[2] Each

---

utility
A measure of how satisfied a consumer is.

utility function
A mathematical function that describes the relationship between what consumers actually consume and their level of well-being.

marginal utility
The additional utility a consumer receives from an additional unit of a good or service.

---

[2] Marginal utility can be calculated for any given utility function.

good in a utility function has its own marginal utility. Using the Junior Mints and Milk Duds utility function, for example, the marginal utility of Junior Mints, MU_J, would be

$$MU_J = \frac{\Delta U(J, M)}{\Delta J}$$

where ΔJ is the small (one-unit) change in the number of Junior Mints the consumer eats and $\Delta U(J, M)$ is the change in utility she gets from doing so. Likewise, the marginal utility of consuming Milk Duds is given by

$$MU_M = \frac{\Delta U(J, M)}{\Delta M}$$

Later in this chapter, we see that marginal utility is the key to understanding the consumption choices a person makes.

Utility and Comparisons

One important but subtle point about the four preference assumptions is that they allow us to rank all bundles of goods for a particular consumer, but they do not allow us to determine how much more a consumer likes one bundle than another. In mathematical terms, we have an *ordinal* ranking of bundles (we can line them up from best to worst), but not a *cardinal* ranking (which would allow us to say exactly how much one bundle was preferred to another). The reason for this is that the units in which we measure utility are essentially arbitrary.

An example will make this clearer. Let's say we define a unit of measurement for utility that we call a "util." And let's say we have three bundles: A, B, and C, and a consumer who likes bundle A the most and bundle C the least. We might then assign these three bundles values of 8, 7, and 6 utils, respectively. The difficulty is that we just as easily could have assigned the bundles values of 8, 7, and 2 utils (or 19, 17, and 16 utils; or 67, 64, and 62 utils, etc.) and this would still perfectly describe the situation. Because there is no real-world unit of measure like dollars, grams, or inches with which to measure utility, we can shift, stretch, or squeeze a utility function without altering any of its observable implications, as long as we don't change the ordering of preferences over bundles.[3]

Does it matter that we have only an ordinal ranking of utility, rather than a cardinal ranking? For the most part, not really. We can still provide answers to the important questions about how individual consumers behave, and how this behavior results in a downward-sloping demand curve.

The one set of questions we will not be able to answer so easily is how to make *interpersonal comparisons*, that is, comparisons of one consumer's utility and another's. Based on utility functions alone, it's impossible to determine which consumer values, say, a set of concert tickets more, or whether society as a whole will be made better off if we take the tickets away from one consumer and give them to another. (We can determine, however, that if one person prefers, say, tickets to Concert A over tickets to Concert B, and the other person prefers Concert B to Concert A, then both consumers

---

[3] In mathematical parlance, these order-preserving shifts, squeezes, or stretches of a utility function are called *monotonic* transformations. Any monotonic transformation of a utility function will imply exactly the same preferences for the consumer as the original utility function. Consider our first example of a utility function from consuming Junior Mints and Milk Duds, $U = J \times M$. Suppose that it were $U = 8J \times M + 12$ instead. For any possible bundle of Junior Mints and Milk Duds, this new utility function will imply the same ordering of the consumer's utility levels as would the old function. (You can put in a few specific numbers to test this.) Because the consumer's relative preferences don't change, she will make the same decisions on how much of each good to consume with either utility function.

welfare economics
The area of economics concerned with the economic well-being of society as a whole.

will be better off if we give the tickets to Concert A to the first person and the tickets to Concert B to the second.) These important questions are addressed in the area known as **welfare economics,** which we discuss in several places in the book. For now, however, we focus on one consumer at a time.

Just as important as the assumptions we make regarding utility functions are the assumptions that we *do not* make. For one, we do not impose particular preferences on consumers. An individual is free to prefer dogs or ferrets as pets, just as long as the four preference assumptions are not violated. Moreover, we typically don't make value judgments about what consumers should or shouldn't prefer. It isn't "right" or "wrong" to like bluegrass music instead of R&B or classical; it is just a description of how a person feels. We also don't require that preferences remain constant over time. Someone may prefer sleeping to seeing a movie tonight, but tomorrow, the opposite may be true.

The concepts of utility and utility functions are general enough to let us account for a consumer's preferences over any number of goods and the various bundles into which they can be combined. As we proceed in building our model of consumer behavior, though, we focus on a simple model in which a consumer buys a bundle with only two goods. This approach is an easy way to see how things work, but the basic model works with more complicated situations, too. In the rare situations in which this is not the case, we will point out how and why things change once there are more than two goods.

4.2 Indifference Curves

As we discussed in the previous section, the right way to think about utility is in relative terms; that is, in terms of whether one bundle of goods provides more or less utility to a consumer than another bundle. An especially good way of understanding utility is to take the special case in which a consumer is **indifferent** between bundles of goods. In other words, each bundle provides her with the same level of utility.

indifferent
The special case in which a consumer derives the same utility level from each of two or more consumption bundles.

Consider the simple case in which there are only two goods to choose between, say, square feet in an apartment and the number of friends living in the same building. Michaela wants a large apartment, but also wants to be able to easily see her friends. First, Michaela looks at a 750-square-foot apartment in a building where 5 of her friends live. Next, she looks at an apartment that has only 500 square feet. For Michaela to be as happy in the smaller apartment as she would be in the larger apartment, there will have to be more friends (say, 10) in the building. Because she gets the same utility from both size/friend combinations, Michaela is indifferent between the two apartments. On the other hand, if her apartment were a more generous 1,000 square feet, Michaela would be willing to make do with (say) only 3 friends living in her building and feel no worse off.

Figure 4.1a graphs these three bundles. The square footage of the apartment is on the horizontal axis and number of friends is on the vertical axis. These are not the only three bundles that give Michaela the same level of utility; there are many different bundles that accomplish that goal—an infinite number of bundles, in fact, if we ignore that it might not make sense to have a fraction of a friend (or maybe it does!).

indifference curve
A mathematical representation of the combination of all the different consumption bundles that provide a consumer with the same utility.

The combination of all the different bundles of goods that give a consumer the same utility is called an **indifference curve.** In Figure 4.1b, we draw Michaela's indifference curve, which includes the three points shown in Figure 4.1a. Notice that it contains not just the three bundles we discussed, but many other combinations of square footage and friends in the building. Also notice that it always slopes down: Every time we take away a friend from Michaela, we need to give her more square footage to leave her indifferent. (Equivalently, we could say every time we take away apartment space, we need to give her more friends in the building to keep her equally as well off.)

Figure 4.1 | **Building an Indifference Curve**

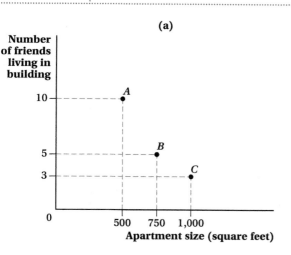

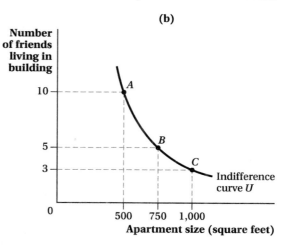

(a) Because Michaela receives utility from both the number of friends in her apartment building and the square footage of her apartment, she is equally happy with 10 friends in her building and a 500-square-foot apartment or 5 friends in her building and a 750-square-foot apartment. Likewise, she is willing to trade off 2 more friends in her building (leaving her with 3) to have a 1,000-square-foot apartment. These are three of many combinations of friends in her building and apartment size that make her equally happy.

(b) An indifference curve connects all bundles of goods that provide a consumer with the same level of utility. Bundles A, B, and C provide the same satisfaction for Michaela. Thus, the indifference curve represents Michaela's willingness to trade off between friends in her apartment building and the square footage of her apartment.

For each level of utility, there is a different indifference curve. Figure 4.2 shows two of Michaela's indifference curves. Which corresponds to the higher level of utility? The easiest way to figure this out is to think as a consumer would. One of the points on the indifference curve U_1 represents the utility Michaela would get if she had 5 friends

Figure 4.2 | **A Consumer's Indifference Curves**

Each level of utility has a separate indifference curve. Because we assume that more is preferred to less, an indifference curve lying to the right and above another indifference curve reflects a higher level of utility. In this graph, the combinations along curve U_2 provide Michaela with a higher level of utility than the combinations along curve U_1. Michaela will be happier with a 1,000-square-foot apartment than a 500-square-foot apartment, holding the number of friends living in her building equal at 5.

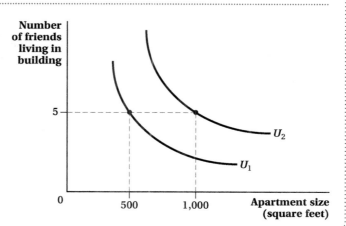

in her building and a 500-square-foot apartment. Curve U_2 includes a bundle with the same number of friends and a 1,000-square-foot apartment. By our "more is better" assumption, indifference curve U_2 must make Michaela better off. We could have instead held the apartment's square footage constant and asked which indifference curve had more friends in the building, and we would have found the same answer. Still another way of capturing the same idea is to draw a ray from the origin—zero units of both goods—through the two indifference curves. The first indifference curve the ray hits has bundles that give lower utility. Remember that by the definition of an indifference curve, utility is the same at every point on any given indifference curve, so we don't even need to check any other points on the two curves to know Michaela's utility is higher at every point on U_2 than at any point on U_1.

Characteristics of Indifference Curves

Generally speaking, the positions and shapes of indifference curves can tell us a lot about a consumer's behavior and decisions. However, our four assumptions about utility functions put some restrictions on the shapes that indifference curves can take.

1.   **We can draw indifference curves.** The first assumption, completeness and rankability, means that we can always draw indifference curves: All bundles have a utility level, and we can rank them.

2.   **We can figure out which indifference curves have higher utility levels and why they slope downward.** The "more is better" assumption implies that we can look at a set of indifference curves and figure out which ones represent higher utility levels. This can be done by holding the quantity of one good fixed and seeing which curves have larger quantities of the other good. This is exactly what we did when we looked at Figure 4.2. The assumption also implies that indifference curves never slope up. If they did slope up, this would mean that a consumer would be indifferent between a particular bundle and another bundle with more of *both* goods. There's no way this can be true if more is always better.

3.   **Indifference curves never cross.** The transitivity property implies that indifference curves for a given consumer can never cross. To see why, suppose our apartment-hunter Michaela's hypothetical indifference curves intersect with one another, as shown in Figure 4.3. The "more is better" assumption implies she prefers bundle E to bundle D, because E offers both more square footage and more friends in her building than does D.

Figure 4.3   Indifference Curves Cannot Cross

Indifference curves cannot intersect. Here, Michaela would be indifferent between bundles D and F and also indifferent between bundles E and F. The transitivity property would therefore imply that she must also be indifferent between bundles D and E. But this can't be true, because more is preferred to less, and bundle E contains more of both goods (more friends in her building and a larger apartment) than D.

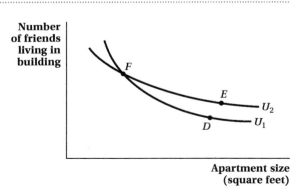

Now, because E and F are on the same indifference curve U_2, Michaela's utility from consuming either bundle must be the same by definition. And because bundles F and D are on the same indifference curve U_1, she must also be indifferent between *those* two bundles. But here's the problem: Putting this all together means she's indifferent between E and D, because each makes her just as well off as F. We know that can't be true. After all, she must like E more than D because it has more of both goods. Something has gone wrong. What went wrong is that we violated the transitivity property by allowing the indifference curves to cross. Intersecting indifference curves imply that the same bundle (the one located at the intersection) offers two different utility levels, which can't be the case.

4. **Indifference curves are convex to the origin.** The fourth assumption of utility—the more you have of a particular good, the less you are willing to give up of something else to get even more of that good—implies something about the way indifference curves are curved. Specifically, it implies they will be convex to the origin; that is, they will bend in toward the origin as if it is tugging on the indifference curve, trying to pull it in.

To see what this curvature means in terms of a consumer's behavior, let's think about what the slope of an indifference curve embodies. Again, we'll use Michaela as an example.

make the grade

Draw some indifference curves to really understand the concept

Indifference curves, like many abstract economic concepts, are often confusing to students when they are first introduced. But one nice thing about indifference curves is that preferences are the only thing necessary to draw your own indifference curves, and everybody has preferences! If you take just the few minutes of introspection necessary to draw your own indifference curves, the concept starts to make sense.

Start by selecting two goods that you like to consume—maybe your favorite candy bar, pizza, hours on Facebook, or trips to the movies. It doesn't matter much what goods you choose (this is one of the nice things about economic models—they are designed to be very general). Next, draw a graph that has one good on the vertical axis and the other good on the horizontal axis (again, it doesn't matter which one goes where). The distance along the axis from the origin will measure the units of the good consumed (candy bars, slices of pizza, hours on Facebook, etc.).

The next step is to pick some bundle of these two goods that has a moderate amount of both goods, for instance, 12 pieces of candy and 3 slices of pizza. Put a dot at that point in your graph. Now carry out the following thought experiment. First, imagine taking a few pieces of candy out of the bundle and ask yourself how many additional slices of pizza you would need to leave you as well off as you are with 12 pieces of candy and 3 slices of pizza. Put a dot at that bundle. Then, suppose a couple more candy pieces are taken away, and figure out how much more pizza you would need to be "made whole." Put another dot there. Next, imagine taking away some pizza from the original 12-piece, 3-slice bundle, and determine how many extra candy pieces you would have to be given to be as well off as with the original bundle. That new bundle is another point. All those points are on the same indifference curve. Connect the dots, and you've drawn an indifference curve.

Now try starting with a different initial bundle, say, one with twice as many of both goods as the first bundle you chose. Redo the same thought experiment of figuring out the tradeoffs of some of one good for a certain number of units of the other good, and you will have traced out a second indifference curve. You can start with still other bundles, either with more or less of both goods, figure out the same types of tradeoffs, and draw additional indifference curves.

There is no "right" answer as to exactly what your indifference curves will look like. It depends on your preferences. However, their shapes should have the basic properties that we have discussed: downward-sloping, never crossing, and convex to the origin.

Figure 4.4   Tradeoffs Along an Indifference Curve

At point *A*, Michaela is willing to give up a lot of friends to get just a few more square feet, because she already has a lot of friends in the building but little space. At point *C*, Michaela has a large apartment but few friends around, so she now would require a large amount of space in return for a small reduction in friends to be left equally satisfied.

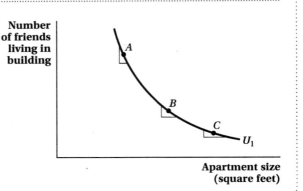

If the indifference curve is steep, as it is at point *A* in Figure 4.4, Michaela is willing to give up a lot of friends to get just a few more square feet of apartment space. It isn't just coincidence that she's willing to make this tradeoff at a point where she already has a lot of friends in the building but a very small apartment. Because she already has a lot of one good (friends in the building), she is less willing to give up the other good (apartment size) to have yet another friend. On the other hand, where the indifference curve is relatively flat, as it is at point *C* of Figure 4.4, the tradeoff between friends and apartment size is reversed. At *C*, the apartment is already big, but Michaela has few friends around, so she now needs to receive a great deal of extra space in return for a small reduction in friends to be left as well off.

Because tradeoffs between goods generally depend on how much of each good a consumer would have in a bundle, indifference curves are convex to the origin. Virtually every indifference curve we draw will have this shape. As we discuss later, however, there are some special cases in which either curvature disappears and indifference curves become straight lines, or where they become so curved that they have right angles.

The Marginal Rate of Substitution

Indifference curves are all about tradeoffs: how much of one good a consumer will give up to get a little bit more of another good. The slope of the indifference curve captures this tradeoff idea exactly. Figure 4.5 shows two points on an indifference curve that reflects Sarah's preferences for t-shirts and socks. At point *A*, the indifference curve is very steep, meaning Sarah will give up multiple t-shirts to get one more pair of socks. The reverse is true at point *B*. At that point, Sarah will trade multiple pairs of socks for just one more t-shirt. As a result of this change in Sarah's willingness to trade as we move along the indifference curve, the indifference curve is convex to the origin.

This shift in the willingness to substitute one good for another along an indifference curve might be a little confusing to you initially. You might be more familiar with thinking about the slope of a straight line (which is constant) than the slope of a curve (which varies at different points along the curve). Also, you might find it odd that preferences differ along an indifference curve. After all, a consumer isn't supposed to prefer one point on an indifference curve over another, but now we're saying the consumer's relative tradeoffs between the two goods change as one moves along the curve. Let's address each of these issues in turn.

Figure 4.5 | The Slope of an Indifference Curve Is the Marginal Rate of Substitution

The marginal rate of substitution measures the willingness of a consumer to trade one good for the other. It is measured as the negative of the slope of the indifference curve at any point. At point *A*, the slope of the curve is −2, meaning that the *MRS* is 2. This implies that, for that given bundle, Sarah is willing to trade 2 t-shirts to receive 1 more pair of socks. At point *B*, the slope is −0.5 and the *MRS* is 0.5. At this point, Sarah is only willing to give up 0.5 t-shirt to get another pair of socks.

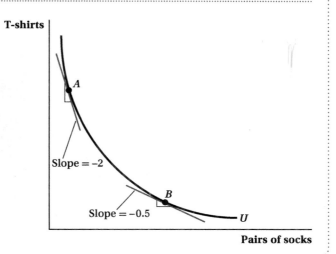

First, the slope of a curve, unlike a straight line, depends on where on the curve you are measuring the slope. To measure the slope of a curve at any point, draw a straight line that just touches the curve (but does not pass through it) at that point but nowhere else. This point where the line (called a tangent) touches the curve is called a tangency point. The slope of the line is the slope of the curve at the tangency point. The tangents that have points *A* and *B* as tangency points are shown in Figure 4.5. The slopes of those tangents are the slopes of the indifference curve at those points. At point *A*, the slope is −2, indicating that at this point Sarah would require 2 more t-shirts to give up 1 pair of socks. At point *B*, the slope is −0.5, indicating that at this point Sarah would require only half of a t-shirt to give up a pair of socks.

Second, although it's true that a consumer is indifferent between any two points on an indifference curve, that doesn't mean her relative preference for one good versus another is constant along the line. As we discussed above, Sarah's relative preference changes with the number of units of each good she already has.

Economists have a particular name for the slope of an indifference curve: the **marginal rate of substitution of *X* for *Y* (MRS_{XY})**. This is the rate at which a consumer is willing to trade off or substitute one good (the good on the horizontal axis) for another (the good on the vertical axis) and still be left equally well off:

$$MRS_{XY} = -\frac{\Delta Y}{\Delta X}$$

(A technical note: Because the slopes of indifference curves are negative, economists use the negative of the slope to make the MRS_{XY} a positive number.) The word "marginal" indicates that we are talking about the tradeoffs associated with small changes in the composition of the bundle of goods—that is, changes at the margin. It makes sense to focus on marginal changes because the willingness to substitute between two goods depends on where the consumer is located on her indifference curve.

Despite the intimidating name, the marginal rate of substitution is an intuitive concept. It tells us the relative value that a consumer places on obtaining a little more of the good on the horizontal axis, in terms of the good on the vertical axis. You make this kind of decision all the time. Whenever you order something off a menu at a restaurant, choose whether to ride a bicycle or drive, or decide on what brand of jeans to buy, you're evaluating relative values. As we see later in this chapter, when

marginal rate of substitution of *X* for *Y* (MRS_{XY})
The rate at which a consumer is willing to trade off one good (the good on the horizontal axis *X*) for another (the good on the vertical axis *Y*) and still be left equally well off.

freakonomics

Do Minnesotans Bleed Purple?

People from Minnesota *love* their football team, the Minnesota Vikings. You can't go anywhere in the state without seeing people dressed in purple and yellow, especially during football season. If there is ever a lull in a conversation with a Minnesotan, just bring up the Vikings and you can be certain the conversation will spring to life. What are the Vikings "worth" to their fans? The answer to that question is obvious: The Vikings are price-less. Or are they?

There has often been discussion that the Vikings would leave the state because the owners

AP Photo/Paul Spinelli

were unhappy with the existing stadium. Two economists carried out a study to try to measure how much Minnesota residents cared about the Vikings.[*] The authors looked at the results of a survey that asked hundreds of Minnesotans how much their household would be willing to pay in extra taxes for a new stadium for the team. Every extra tax dollar for the stadium would be one less the household could spend on other goods, so the survey was in essence asking for the households' marginal rate of substitution of all other goods (as a composite unit) for a new Vikings stadium. Because it was widely perceived that there was a realistic chance the Vikings would leave Minnesota if they didn't get a taxpayer-funded stadium, these answers were also viewed as being informative about Minnesotans' marginal rate of substitution between all other goods and the Minnesota Vikings.[†]

It turns out that fan loyalty does know some limits. The average household in Minnesota was willing to pay $571.60 to keep the Vikings in Minnesota. Multiplying that value by the roughly 1.3 million households in Minnesota gives a total marginal value of about $750 million. In other words, Minnesotans were estimated to be willing to give up $750 million of consumption of other goods in order to keep the Vikings. That's a lot of money—imagine how much people might pay if the Vikings could actually win a Super Bowl.

Alas, stadiums aren't cheap. Officials estimate that a new stadium will cost about $1 billion. That might explain why a law passed by the state legislature in 2012 finally gave the Vikings the stadium they wanted but only agreed to provide $500 million of funding, with the team responsible for providing the remaining money.

The Los Angeles Vikings? Don't even bring up this possibility in conversation with a Minnesotan, unless, of course, you have a check for $571.60 that you're ready to hand over.

---

[*] John R. Crooker and Aju J. Fenn, "Estimating Local Welfare Generated by an NFL Team under Credible Threat of Relocation," *Southern Economic Journal* 76, no. 1 (2009): 198–223.

[†] An interesting feature of this study is that it measures consumers' utility functions using data on hypothetical rather than actual purchases. That is, no Minnesotan had had to actually give up consuming something else to keep the Vikings around. They were only answering a question about how much they would pay *if* it came time to actually make that choice. While economists prefer to measure consumers' preferences from their actual choices (believing actual choices to be a more reliable reflection of consumers' preferences), prospective choices are sometimes the only way to measure preferences for certain goods. An example of this is when economists try to measure the value of abstract environmental goods, such as species diversity.

prices are attached to goods, the consumer's decision about what to consume boils down to a comparison of the relative value she places on two goods and the goods' relative prices.

The Marginal Rate of Substitution and Marginal Utility

Consider point A in Figure 4.5. The marginal rate of substitution at point A is equal to 2 because the slope of the indifference curve at that point is -2:

$$MRS_{XY} = -\frac{\Delta Y}{\Delta X} = -\frac{\Delta Q_{\text{t-shirts}}}{\Delta Q_{\text{socks}}} = 2$$

Literally, this means that in return for 1 more pair of socks, Sarah is willing to give up 2 t-shirts. At point B, the marginal rate of substitution is 0.5, which implies that Sarah will sacrifice only half of a t-shirt for 1 more pair of socks (or equivalently, will sacrifice 1 t-shirt for 2 pairs of socks).

This change in the willingness to substitute between goods at the margin occurs because the benefit a consumer gets from another unit of a good tends to fall with the number of units she already has. If you already have all the bananas you can eat and hardly any kiwis, you might be willing to give up more bananas to get one additional kiwi.

Another way to see all this is to think about the change in utility (ΔU) created by starting at some point on an indifference curve and moving just a little bit along it. Suppose we start at point A and then move just a bit down and to the right along the curve. We can write the change in utility created by that move as the marginal utility of socks (the extra utility the consumer gets from a small increase in the number of socks consumed, MU_{socks}) times the increase in the number of socks due to the move (ΔQ_{socks}), plus the marginal utility of t-shirts ($MU_{\text{t-shirts}}$) times the decrease in the number of t-shirts ($\Delta Q_{\text{t-shirts}}$) due to the move. The change in utility is

$$\Delta U = MU_{\text{socks}} \times \Delta Q_{\text{socks}} + MU_{\text{t-shirts}} \times \Delta Q_{\text{t-shirts}}$$

where MU_{socks} and $MU_{\text{t-shirts}}$ are the marginal utilities of socks and t-shirts at point A, respectively. Here's the key: Because we're moving along an indifference curve (along which utility is constant), *the total change in utility from the move must be zero*. If we set the equation equal to zero, we get

$$0 = \Delta U = MU_{\text{socks}} \times \Delta Q_{\text{socks}} + MU_{\text{t-shirts}} \times \Delta Q_{\text{t-shirts}}$$

Rearranging the terms a bit will allow us to see an important relationship:

$$-MU_{\text{t-shirts}} \times \Delta Q_{\text{t-shirts}} = MU_{\text{socks}} \times \Delta Q_{\text{socks}}$$

$$-\frac{\Delta Q_{\text{t-shirts}}}{\Delta Q_{\text{socks}}} = \frac{MU_{\text{socks}}}{MU_{\text{t-shirts}}}$$

Notice that the left-hand side of this equation is equal to the negative of the slope of the indifference curve, or MRS_{XY}. We now can see a very significant connection: *The MRS_{XY} between two goods at any point on an indifference curve equals the inverse ratio of those two goods' marginal utilities*:

$$MRS_{XY} = -\frac{\Delta Q_{\text{t-shirts}}}{\Delta Q_{\text{socks}}} = \frac{MU_{\text{socks}}}{MU_{\text{t-shirts}}}$$

In more basic terms, MRS_{XY} shows the point we emphasized from the beginning: You can tell how much people value something by their choices of what they would be willing to give up to get it. The rate at which they give things up tells you the marginal utility of the goods.

This equation gives us a key insight into understanding why indifference curves are convex to the origin. Let's go back to the example above. At point A in Figure 4.5, $MRS_{XY} = 2$. That means the marginal utility of socks is twice as high as the marginal utility of t-shirts. That's why Sarah is so willing to give up t-shirts for socks at that point—she will gain more utility from receiving a few more socks than she will lose from having fewer t-shirts. At point B, on the other hand, $MRS_{XY} = 0.5$, so the marginal utility of t-shirts is twice as high as that of socks. At this point, she's willing to give up many more socks for a small number of t-shirts.

As we see throughout the rest of this chapter, the marginal rate of substitution and its link to the marginal utilities of the goods play a key role in driving consumer behavior.

The Steepness of Indifference Curves

We've now established the connection between a consumer's preferences for two goods and the slope of her indifference curves (the MRS_{XY}). We have found that the slope of an indifference curve reveals a consumer's willingness to trade one good for another, or each good's relative marginal utility. We can flip this relationship on its head to see what the shapes of indifference curves tell us about consumers' utility functions. In this section, we discuss the two key characteristics of an indifference curve: how steep it is, and how curved it is.

Figure 4.6 presents two sets of indifference curves reflecting two different sets of preferences for concert tickets and MP3s. In panel a, the indifference curves are steep,

---

Figure 4.6   **The Steepness of Indifference Curves**

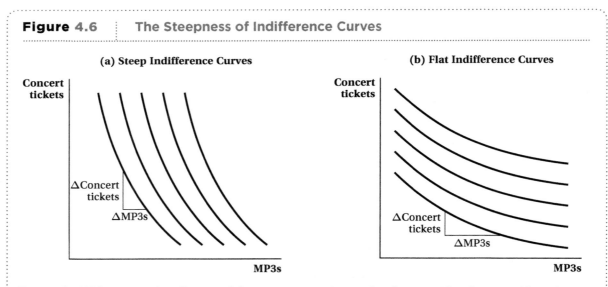

Because the MRS measures the willingness of the consumer to trade one good for another, we can tell a great deal about preferences by examining the shapes of indifference curves. (a) Indifference curves that are relatively steep indicate that the consumer is willing to give up a large quantity of the good on the vertical axis to get another unit of the good on the horizontal axis. Here, the consumer is willing to give up a lot of concert tickets for some additional MP3s. (b) Relatively flat indifference curves imply that the consumer would require a large increase in the good on the horizontal axis to give up a unit of the good on the vertical axis. The consumer with flat indifference curves will give up a lot of MP3s for one additional concert ticket.

while in panel b they are flat. (These two sets of indifference curves have the same degree of curvature so we don't confuse steepness with curvature.)

When indifference curves are steep, consumers are willing to give up a lot of the good on the vertical axis to get a small additional amount of the good on the horizontal axis. So a consumer with the preferences reflected in the steep indifference curve in panel a would part with many concert tickets for some more MP3s. The opposite is true in panel b, which shows flatter indifference curves. A consumer with such preferences would give up a lot of MP3s for one additional concert ticket. These relationships are just another way of restating the concept of the MRS_{XY} that we introduced earlier.

4.1 figure it out

Mariah consumes music downloads (M) and concert tickets (C). Her utility function is given by $U = 0.5M^2 + 2C^2$, where $MU_M = M$ and $MU_C = 4C$.

  a. Write an equation for MRS_{MC}

  b. Would bundles of ($M = 4$ and $C = 1$) and ($M = 2$ and $C = 2$) be on the same indifference curve? How do you know?

  c. Calculate MRS_{MC} when $M = 4$ and $C = 1$ and when $M = 2$ and $C = 2$.

  d. Based on your answers to question b, are Mariah's indifference curves convex? (*Hint*: Does MRS_{MC} fall as M rises?)

Solution:

  a. We know that the marginal rate of substitution MRS_{MC} equals MU_M/MU_C

We are told that $MU_M = M$ and that $MU_C = 4C$. Thus, $MRS_{MC} = \dfrac{MU_M}{MU_C} = \dfrac{M}{4C}$.

  b. For bundles to lie on the same indifference curve, they must provide the same level of utility to the consumer. Therefore we need to calculate Mariah's level of utility for the bundles of ($M = 4$ and $C = 1$) and ($M = 2$ and $C = 2$):

   When $M = 4$ and $C = 1$, $U = 0.5(4)^2 + 2(1)^2 = 0.5(16) + 2(1) = 8 + 2 = 10$

   When $M = 2$ and $C = 2$, $U = 0.5(2)^2 + 2(2)^2 = 0.5(4) + 2(4) = 2 + 8 = 10$

Each bundle provides Mariah with the same level of utility, so they must lie on the same indifference curve.

  c. and d. To determine if Mariah's indifference curve is convex, we need to calculate MRS_{MC} at both bundles. Then we can see if MRS_{MC} falls as we move down along the indifference curve (i.e., as M increases and C decreases).

$$\text{When } M = 2 \text{ and } C = 2, \; MRS_{MC} = \frac{2}{(4)(2)} = \frac{2}{8} = \frac{1}{4} = 0.25$$

$$\text{When } M = 4 \text{ and } C = 1, \; MRS_{MC} = \frac{4}{(4)(1)} = \frac{4}{4} = 1$$

These calculations reveal that, holding utility constant, when music downloads rise from 2 to 4, the MRS_{MC} rises from 0.25 to 1. This means that as Mariah consumes more music downloads and fewer concert tickets, she actually becomes *more* willing to trade concert tickets for additional music downloads! Most consumers would not behave in this way. This means that the indifference curve becomes steeper as M rises, not flatter. In other words, this indifference curve will be concave to the origin rather than convex, violating the fourth characteristic of indifference curves listed above.

theory and data

Indifference Curves of Phone Service Buyers

Harken back to ancient times—1999–2003—when broadband was still a novelty. Most households that wanted to connect to the Internet had to use something known as a dial-up connection. The way it worked was that you hooked your computer up to the phone line in your house, and when you wanted to connect to the Internet, your computer would dial the number of your local Internet service provider (ISP). Then you had to wait, often for a very long time, listening to your computer making a screeching, fingernails-on-a-blackboard sound as it attempted to make the connection. This call to your ISP tied up your phone line (you couldn't talk on the phone while you were connected to the Internet) and was charged just like any other call on your phone bill.

A study by economists Nicholas Economides, Katja Seim, and Brian Viard used data on New York consumers' choices of land-line phone services during 1999–2003 to measure consumer utility functions and indifference curves over two related goods: local and regional phone calls.[*] Their study gives us a clear example of how different types of consumers can have different marginal rates of substitution for the same set of goods. One of their key results is sketched out in the figure shown. The indifference curves of households with Internet access (Figure 4.7a), when drawn with local calls on the horizontal axis and regional calls on the vertical axis, are much steeper than the indifference curves of households without Internet access (Figure 4.7b). For example, they found that a typical household in their data (one of average size and income, owning at least one mobile phone, and making the average number of local and regional calls) had an *MRS* of local for regional calls of about 1.0 if the household had Internet access and 0.5 if it didn't. That means the Internet household would be willing to give up 1 regional call to get another local call and be no worse off. The non-Internet household, on the other hand,

Figure 4.7   New Yorkers' Preferences for Local and Regional Phone Calls, 1999–2003

(a) Households with Internet Service

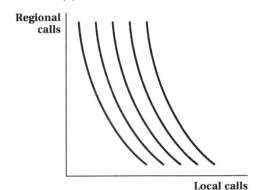

(b) Households without Internet Service

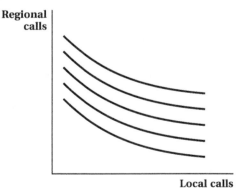

Households with dial-up Internet service (a) have a greater *MRS* (and steeper indifference curves) than households without Internet service (b). Accordingly, households with Internet service are more likely to use local minutes to purchase Internet usage, so they are less willing to trade local minutes for regional minutes.

[*] Nicholas Economides, Katja Seim, and V. Brian Viard, "Quantifying the Benefits of Entry into Local Phone Service," *RAND Journal of Economics* 39, no. 3 (2008): 699–730.

would have to get 2 extra local calls to be no worse off for giving up 1 regional call. (Note that there is nothing special about our choice to put local calls as the good on the horizontal axis and regional calls on the vertical axis. We could have swapped the goods and redrawn the graph.)

Can you guess why having Internet access raised households' *MRS* of local for regional calls? Remember that the *MRS* is the ratio of the household's marginal utility of local calls to the marginal utility of regional calls, or

$$MRS_{LR} = \frac{MU_{local}}{MU_{regional}}$$

If Internet households have higher *MRS* values, their marginal utility of local calls is larger relative to their marginal utility from regional calls. In other words, they obtain greater utility on the margin from consuming local calls than do non-Internet households. This difference in relative marginal utilities most likely reflected that most of these households connected to the Internet using dial-up connections. Every time they went online, they were making a billable local call to their ISP. Their desire to browse the Internet or send e-mails therefore raised the marginal utilities they received from making local calls, which explains the patterns Economides, Seim, and Viard found.

The Curvature of Indifference Curves: Substitutes and Complements

The steepness of an indifference curve tells us the rate at which a consumer is willing to trade one good for another. The curvature of an indifference curves also has a meaning. Suppose indifferences curves are almost straight, as in Figure 4.8a. In this case, a

Figure 4.8 : The Curvature of Indifference Curves

(a) Almost Straight Indifference Curves

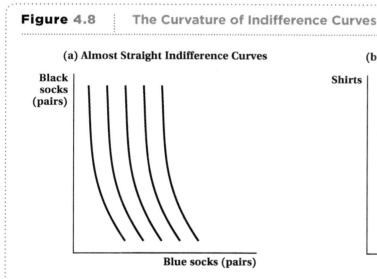

Black socks (pairs)

Blue socks (pairs)

(b) Very Curved Indifference Curves

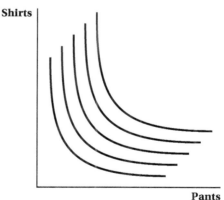

Shirts

Pants

The curvature of indifference curves reflects information about the consumer's preferences between two goods, just as its steepness does. (a) Goods that are highly substitutable (such as pairs of black socks and blue socks) are likely to produce indifference curves that are relatively straight. This means that the *MRS* does not change much as the consumer moves from one point to another along the in-

difference curve. (b) Goods that are complementary will generally have indifference curves with more curvature. For example, if Evan has many shirts and few pants, he will be willing to trade many shirts to get a pair of pants. If a consumer has many pants and few shirts, he will be less willing to trade a shirt for pants.

consumer (let's call him Evan) is willing to trade about the same amount of the first good (in this case, pairs of black socks) to get the same amount of the second good (pairs of blue socks), regardless of whether he has a lot of black socks relative to blue socks or vice versa. Stated in terms of the marginal rates of substitution, the *MRS* of black socks for blue ones doesn't change much as we move along the indifference curve. In practical terms, it means that the two goods are close substitutes for one another in Evan's utility function. That is, the relative value a consumer places on two substitute goods will typically not be very responsive to the amounts he has of one good versus the other. (It's no coincidence that we use in this example two goods, such as socks of two different colors, that many consumers would consider to be close substitutes for one another.)

On the other hand, for goods such as shirts and pants that are poor substitutes (Figure 4.8b) the relative value of one more pair of pants will be much greater when you have 10 shirts and no (or very few) pants than if you have 10 pairs of pants but no (or very few) shirts. In these types of cases, indifference curves are sharply curved, as shown. The *MRS* of shirts for pants is very high on the far left part of the indifference curve (where the consumer has few pants) and very low on the far right (when the consumer is awash in pants).

Perfect Substitutes   The intuition behind the meaning of the curvature of indifference curves may be easier to grasp if we focus on the most extreme cases, **perfect substitutes** and **perfect complements**. Figure 4.9 shows an example of two goods that might be perfect substitutes: 12-ounce bags of potato chips and 3-ounce bags of potato chips. If all the consumer cares about is the total amount of chips, then she is just as well off trading 4 small bags of chips for each large bag, regardless of how many of either she already has. These kinds of preferences produce linear indifference curves, and utility functions for perfect substitutes take on the general form $U = aX + bY$, where a and b are numbers that respectively indicate the marginal utility of consuming one more unit of X and Y. This is precisely the situation shown in Figure 4.9. The indifference curves are straight lines with a constant slope equal to $-1/4$, which means that the MRS_{XY} is also constant and equal to $1/4$. We can't actually say what values a and b take here, only that their ratio is 1 to 4—that is, $a/b = 1/4$. The indifference curves in

Figure 4.9   Indifference Curves for Perfect Substitutes

Two goods that are perfect substitutes have indifference curves that are straight lines. In this case, the consumer is willing to trade one 12-ounce bag of chips for four 3-ounce bags of chips no matter how many of each she currently has and the consumer's preference for chips does not change along the indifference curve. The *MRS* is constant in this case.

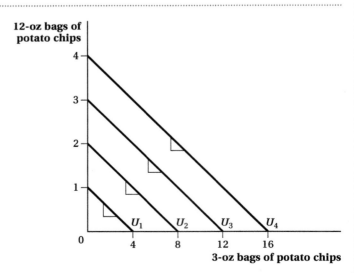

the figure would be the same if $a = 1$ and $b = 4$ or if $a = 40$ and $b = 160$, for instance. This is another demonstration of the point we made above: A transformation of a utility function that does not change the order of which goods the consumer prefers implies the same preference choices.

Different-sized packages of the same good are just one example of why two goods would be perfect substitutes.[4] Another way perfect substitutes might arise is if there are attributes of a product that a particular consumer does not care at all about. For instance, some people might not care about the color of their toothbrush, or whether a bottle of water is branded Aquafina or Dasani. Their indifference curves when comparing red and green toothbrushes or Aquafina and Dasani water would therefore be straight lines. On the other hand, other consumers who *do* care about such features would not view the goods as perfect substitutes, and their indifference curves would be curved.

It is crucial to understand that two goods being perfect substitutes does *not* necessarily imply that the consumer is indifferent between single items of the goods. In our potato chip example above, for instance, the consumer likes a big bag a lot more than a small bag. That's why the consumer would have to be given 4 small bags, not just 1, to be willing to trade away 1 large bag. The idea behind perfect substitutes is only that the tradeoff the consumer is willing to make between the two goods—that is, the marginal rate of substitution—doesn't depend on how much or little she already has of each but is instead constant at every point along an indifference curve.

Perfect Complements   When the utility a consumer receives from a good depends on its being used in fixed proportion with another good, the two goods are perfect complements. Figure 4.10 shows indifference curves for right and left shoes, which are an example of perfect complements (or at least something very close to it). Compare point A (2 right shoes and 2 left shoes) and point B (3 right shoes and 2 left shoes). Although the consumer has one extra shoe at point B, there is no matching shoe for

---

Figure 4.10   Indifference Curves for Perfect Complements

When goods are perfect complements, they have L-shaped indifference curves. For example, at point A, the consumer has 2 left shoes and 2 right shoes. Adding another right shoe while keeping left shoes constant does not increase the consumer's utility, so point B is on the same indifference curve as point A. In like manner, adding another left shoe will not increase the consumer's utility without an additional right shoe, so point C is on the same indifference curve as points A and B. Because shoes are always consumed together, 1 right shoe and 1 left shoe, the consumer's utility rises only when she has more of both goods (a move from point A to point D).

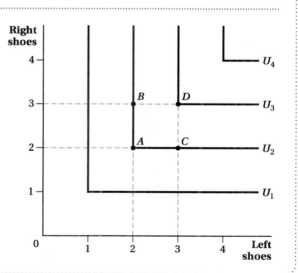

---

[4] You could think of reasons why the different-sized bags might not be perfect substitutes—maybe there's a convenience factor involved with the smaller ones because there's no need to worry about storing open, partially eaten bags. But even allowing for these small differences, they're fairly close to perfect substitutes.

the other foot, so the extra shoe is useless to her. She is therefore indifferent between these two bundles, and the bundles are on the same indifference curve. Similarly, comparing points A and C in the figure, we see that an extra left-footed shoe provides no additional utility if it isn't paired with a right-footed shoe, so A and C must also lie on the same indifference curve. However, if you add an extra left shoe *and* an extra right shoe (point D compared to point A), then the consumer is better off. That's why D is on a higher indifference curve.

Perfect complements lead to distinctive L-shaped indifference curves. Mathematically, this can be represented as $U = \min\{aX,\ bY\}$, where a and b are again numbers reflecting how consuming more units of X and Y affects utility. This mathematical structure means a consumer reaches a given utility level by consuming a minimum amount of each good X and Y. To be on the indifference curve U_2, for instance, the consumer must have *at least* 2 left shoes and 2 right shoes. The kink in the indifference curve is the point at which she is consuming the minimum amount of each good at that utility level.

This L-shape is the most extreme case of curvature of indifference curves. It is at the other extreme from the straight-line indifference curves that arise with perfect substitutes, and its shape produces interesting results for MRS_{XY}. The horizontal part of the indifference curve has MRS_{XY} equal to zero, while on the vertical portion, the marginal rate of substitution is infinite. As we've noted, indifference curves more generally will fall somewhere in between the shapes of the indifference curves for perfect substitutes and perfect complements, with some intermediate amount of curvature.

The proportion in which perfect complements are consumed need not be one-for-one, as in the case of our left- and right-shoe example. Chopsticks and Chinese buffet lunches might be perfect complements for some consumers, for example, but it's likely that they will be consumed in a proportion of 2 chopsticks to 1 buffet. It's hard to eat with just one chopstick.

Different Shapes for a Particular Consumer One final point to make about the curvature of indifference curves is that even for a particular consumer, indifference curves may take on a variety of shapes depending on the utility level. They don't all have to look the same.

For instance, indifference curve U_A in Figure 4.11 is almost a straight line. This means that at low levels of utility, this consumer considers bananas and strawberries

Figure 4.11 | **The Same Consumer Can Have Indifference Curves with Different Shapes**

Indifference curves for a consumer can take on a variety of shapes, depending on the utility level. For example, at low levels of utility, bananas and strawberries may be substitutes and the consumer may just want to buy fruit, not caring whether it is a banana or a strawberry. This means that the indifference curve will be fairly linear, as is the case of U_A. But, at higher levels of utility, the consumer may prefer to have a variety of fruit. This means that she will be willing to give up many bananas for another strawberry when she has a lot of bananas, but is not willing to do so when she only has only a few bananas. Here, the consumer's indifference curve will have more curvature, such as U_B.

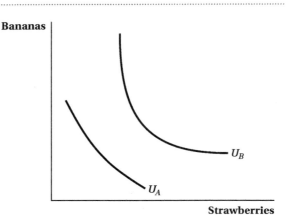

almost perfect substitutes. Her marginal rate of substitution barely changes whether she starts with a relatively high number of bananas to strawberries, or a relatively small number. If all she is worried about is surviving (which might be the case at really low utility levels like that represented by U_A), how something tastes won't matter much to her. She's not going to be picky about the mix of fruit she eats. This leads the indifference curve to be fairly straight, like U_A.

Indifference curve U_B, on the other hand, is very sharply curved. This means that at higher utility levels, the two goods are closer to perfect complements. When this consumer has plenty of fruit, she is more concerned with enjoying variety when she eats. This leads her to prefer some of each fruit rather than a lot of one or the other. If she already has a lot of one good, she will have to be given a very large additional amount of that good to make her willing to give up a unit of the good she has less of. This leads to the more curved indifference curve. Remember, though, that even as the shapes of a consumer's indifference curves vary with her utility levels, the indifference curves will never intersect.

4.2 figure it out

Jasmine can watch hours of baseball (B) or hours of reality shows (R) on TV. Watching more baseball makes Jasmine happier, but she really doesn't care about reality shows—good or bad. Draw a diagram showing a set of Jasmine's indifference curves for hours of baseball and hours of reality shows. (Put reality shows on the horizontal axis.) What is Jasmine's MRS_{RB} when she is consuming one unit of each good?

Solution:

The easiest way to diagram Jasmine's preferences is to consider various bundles of reality shows and baseball and determine whether they lie on the same or different indifference curves. For example, suppose she watches 1 hour of reality TV and 1 hour of baseball. Plot this in Figure A as point A. Now, suppose she watches 1 hour of reality TV and 2 hours of baseball. Plot this as point B. Because watching more hours of baseball makes Jasmine happier, point B must lie on a higher indifference curve than point A.

Now, try another point with 2 hours of reality TV and 1 hour of baseball. Call this point C. Now, compare point A with point C. Point C has the same number of hours of baseball as point A, but provides Jasmine with more reality TV. Jasmine neither likes nor dislikes reality TV, however, so her utility is unchanged by having more reality TV. Points A and C must therefore lie on the same indifference curve.

This would also be true of points D and E. Economists often refer to a good that has no impact on utility as a "neutral good."

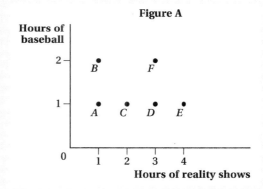

Figure A

Looking at Figure A, we see that there will be an indifference curve that is a horizontal line going through points A, C, D, and E. Will all of the indifference curves be horizontal lines? Let's consider another bundle to make sure. Suppose that Jasmine watches 3 hours of reality TV and 2 hours of baseball, as at point F. It is clear that Jasmine will prefer point F to point D because she gets more baseball. It should also be clear that Jasmine will be equally happy between points B and F; she has the same hours of baseball, and reality shows have no effect on her utility. As shown in Figure B, points B and F lie on the same indifference curve (U_2) and provide a greater level of utility than the bundles on the indifference curve below (U_1).

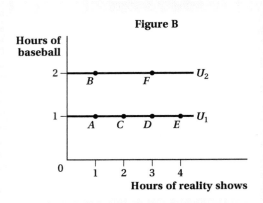

Figure B

Hours of baseball

To calculate the marginal rate of substitution when Jasmine is consuming one unit of each good, we need to calculate the slope of U_1 at point A. Because the indifference curve is a horizontal line, the slope is zero. Therefore, MRS_{RB} is zero. This makes sense; Jasmine is not willing to give up any baseball to watch more reality TV because reality TV has no impact on her utility. Remember that MRS_{RB} equals MU_R/MU_B. Because MU_R is zero, MRS_{RB} will also equal zero.

 application

Indifference Curves for "Bads"

All of the indifference curves we've drawn are for goods that a consumer likes and wants to consume. But sometimes we want to analyze consumer behavior with regard to things that a consumer doesn't want to consume—like air pollution, illness, commute time, or rutabagas. Instead of goods, these things are **bads,** things that would reduce a consumer's utility if she consumed more of them.

> **bad**
> A good or service that provides a consumer with negative utility.

Let's go back to Michaela and her apartment from Figure 4.2 and replace apartment size with distance to work. Greater distance to work is a bad because Michaela's commute time increases. Michaela's indifference curves between commute time (a bad) and the number of friends living in the building (a good) are shown in Figure 4.12.

We see that the result is that indifference curves now slope upward, not downward. Why? Let's first consider bundles A and B, which lie on the same indifference curve, U_1. Notice how bundle B has more commute time than A. Michaela doesn't like to commute, so she has to be given more friends at B to be as well off as she was at point A (in other

---

Figure 4.12   Indifference Curves for a "Bad"

An economic "bad" is a product that reduces a consumer's utility. The consumer's (Michaela's) utility falls as commute time increases. Therefore, to keep Michaela's utility constant, we must provide her with more friends in the building if we increase her commute time. This leads to upward-sloping indifference curves. Indifference curve U_2 provides more utility than U_1, because (holding friends constant) bundle B has more commute time than bundle C, making Michaela worse off. Alternatively, points A and C provide her with a constant amount of commute time, but she has more friends at point C. Thus, Michaela is better off at point C (on U_2) than at point A (on U_1).

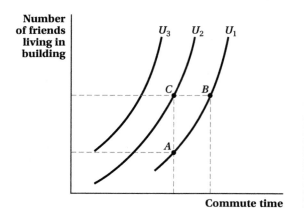

Figure 4.13   Indifference Curves for the Absence of a "Bad"

An economic "bad" can be converted into a "good." By changing the economic bad of "commute time" into the economic good of "saved commute time," we can have two goods that Michaela desires and produce typical downward-sloping, convex indifference curves. Michaela's utility increases with either an increase in the number of friends in the building or an increase in the amount of saved commute time.

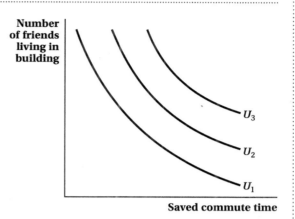

---

words, to keep her on the same indifference curve). Thus, Michaela receives the same level of utility from bundles A and B even though B has more of both products (we use the term "product" loosely). Bundle C has more friends than bundle A but the same commute time, so C must be preferred to A. Indifference curves that lie higher (more friends) and to the left (less commute time) indicate greater levels of utility. So do bads violate our assumption that more is better? Not really. We can keep all of our original assumptions by defining a particular good as an absence or reduction of a bad. In the case of commute time, "saved commute time" is a good. Graphing Michaela's indifference curves in terms of saved commute time—the opposite of a bad—produces the standard, downward-sloping indifference curves we've been working with, as in Figure 4.13. ■

4.3 The Consumer's Income and the Budget Constraint

In the preceding sections, we analyzed how a consumer's preferences can be described by a utility function, why indifference curves are a convenient way to think about utility, and how the slope of the indifference curve—known as the marginal rate of substitution—captures the relative utility that a consumer derives from different goods at the margin. Our ultimate goal in this chapter is to understand how consumers maximize their utility by choosing a bundle of goods to consume. Because consumers do not have an infinite amount of money and because goods are not free, consumers must make tradeoffs when deciding how much of each good to consume. That decision depends not only on the utility consumers get from each good, but also on how much money they have to spend and on the prices of the goods. We have to analyze the interaction among all of these factors.

We start looking at the interactions of utility, income, and prices by making some assumptions. To keep things simple, we continue to focus on a model with only two goods.

1. Each good has a fixed price, and any consumer can buy as much of a good as she wants at that price if she has the income to pay for it. We can make this assumption because each consumer is only a small part of the market for a good, so her consumption decision will not affect the equilibrium market price.

2. The consumer has some fixed amount of income to spend.

3. For now, the consumer cannot save or borrow. Without borrowing, she can't spend more than her income in any given period. With no saving, it means that unspent money is lost forever, so it's use it or lose it.

budget constraint
A curve that describes the entire set of consumption bundles a consumer can purchase when spending all income.

To incorporate prices and the consumer's income into our model of consumer behavior, we use a **budget constraint.** This constraint describes the entire set of consumption bundles that a consumer can purchase by spending all of her money. For instance, let's go back to the example of Sarah and her t-shirts and socks. Suppose Sarah has an income of $50 to spend on t-shirts (which cost $10 each) and socks ($5 a pair). Figure 4.14 shows the budget constraint corresponding to this example. The number of pairs of socks is on the horizontal axis; the number of t-shirts is on the vertical axis. If Sarah spends her whole income on socks, then she can consume 10 pairs (10 pairs at $5 each is $50) and no t-shirts. This combination is point A in the figure. If instead Sarah spends all her money on t-shirts, she can buy 5 shirts and no socks, a combination shown at point B. Sarah can purchase any combination of t-shirts and socks that lies on the straight line connecting these two points. For example, she could buy 3 t-shirts and 4 pairs of socks. This is point C.

The mathematical formula for a budget constraint is

$$\text{Income} = P_X Q_X + P_Y Q_Y$$

where P_X and P_Y are the prices for one unit of goods X and Y (pairs of socks and t-shirts in our example) and Q_X and Q_Y are the quantities of the two goods. The equation simply says that the total expenditure on the two goods (the per-unit price of each good multiplied by the number of units purchased) equals the consumer's total income.

feasible bundle
A bundle that the consumer has the ability to purchase; lies on or below the consumer's budget constraint.

Any combination of goods on or below the budget constraint (i.e., any point between the origin and the budget constraint, including those on the constraint itself) is **feasible,** meaning that the consumer can afford to buy the bundle with her income. Any points above and to the right of the budget line are **infeasible.** These bundles are beyond the reach of the consumer's current income. Figure 4.14 shows the feasible and infeasible bundles for the budget constraint $50 = 5Q_{\text{socks}} + 10Q_{\text{t-shirts}}$.

infeasible bundle
A bundle that the consumer cannot afford to purchase; lies to the right and above a consumer's budget constraint.

The budget constraint in Figure 4.14 is straight, not curved, because we assumed Sarah can buy as much as she wants of a good at a set price per unit. Whether buying the first pair of socks or the tenth, the price is assumed to be the same. As we'll see

---

Figure 4.14   The Budget Constraint

The budget constraint demonstrates the options available to a consumer given her income and the prices of the two goods. The horizontal intercept is the quantity of socks the consumer could afford if she spent all of her income (I) on socks, I/P_{socks}. The vertical intercept is the quantity of her t-shirts she could afford if she spent all of income on t-shirts, $I/P_{\text{t-shirts}}$. Given this, the slope of the budget constraint is the negative of the ratio of the two prices, $-P_{\text{socks}}/P_{\text{t-shirts}}$.

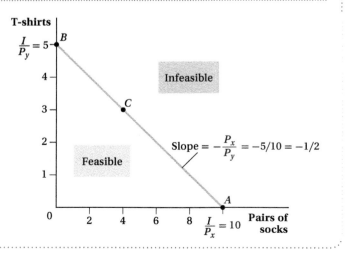

later, if the goods' prices change with the number of units purchased, the budget line will change shape depending on the amount of the goods purchased.

The Slope of the Budget Constraint

The relative prices of the two goods determine the slope of the budget constraint. Because the consumer spends all her money when she is on the budget constraint, if she wants to buy more of one good and stay on the constraint, she has to buy less of the other. Relative prices pin down the rate at which purchases of the two goods can be traded off between one another. If she wants to buy 1 more t-shirt (a cost of $10), for example, she'll have to buy 2 fewer pairs of socks at $5.

We can see the equivalence between relative prices and the slope of the budget constraint by rearranging the budget constraint:

$$\text{Income} = P_X Q_X + P_Y Q_Y$$

$$P_Y Q_Y = \text{Income} - P_X Q_X$$

$$Q_Y = \frac{\text{Income}}{P_Y} - \frac{P_X}{P_Y} Q_X$$

The equation shows if Q_X—the quantity purchased of good X—increases by one unit, the quantity of good Y or Q_Y that can be bought falls by P_X/P_Y. This ratio of the price of good X relative to the price of good Y is the negative of the slope of the budget constraint. It makes sense that this price ratio determines the slope of the constraint. If good X is expensive relative to good Y (i.e., P_X/P_Y is large), then buying additional units of X will mean you must give up a lot of good Y. In this case, the budget constraint will be steep. If on the other hand, good X is relatively inexpensive, you don't have to give up a lot of Y to buy more X, and the constraint will be flat.

We can use the equation for the budget constraint (Income $= P_X Q_X + P_Y Q_Y$) to find its slope and intercepts. Using the budget constraint ($50 = 5Q_{\text{socks}} + 10Q_{\text{t-shirts}}$) shown in Figure 4.14, we get

$$50 = 5Q_X + 10Q_Y$$

$$10Q_Y = 50 - 5Q_X$$

Dividing each side by 10—the price of Q_Y—yields a slope of $-1/2$:

$$Q_Y = 5 - \frac{1}{2}Q_X$$

As we noted earlier, if Sarah spends all her income on socks, she will buy 10 pairs of socks (the x-intercept), while she can purchase 5 t-shirts (the y-intercept) using all of her income. These relative prices and intercepts are shown in Figure 4.14.

As will become clear when we combine indifference curves and budget constraints in the next section, the slope of the budget constraint turns out to play an incredibly important role in determining what consumption bundles maximize consumers' utility levels.

Factors That Affect the Budget Constraint's Position

Because relative prices determine the slope of the budget constraint, changes in relative prices will change its slope. Figure 4.15a demonstrates what happens to our example budget constraint if the price of socks doubles to $10 per pair. The budget constraint rotates clockwise around the vertical axis, becoming twice as steep. That's because P_X/P_Y doubles (because P_X doubles). If Sarah spends all her money on socks, then the doubling of the price of socks means she can buy only half as many with the same income (the 5 pairs shown at A', rather than 10 pairs as before). If, on the other hand, she spends all her money on t-shirts (point B), then the change in socks' prices doesn't affect the bundle she can consume. That's because the price of t-shirts is still the same ($10). Notice that after the price increase, the set of feasible consumption bundles is smaller: There are now fewer combinations of goods that Sarah can afford with her income.

If instead the price of a t-shirt doubles to $20, but pairs of socks remain at their original $5 price (as in Figure 4.15b), then the budget constraint's movement is reversed: The budget constraint rotates counterclockwise around the horizontal axis, becoming half as steep. Someone who wants to buy only socks is unaffected, whereas someone who wants only t-shirts can obtain only half as many (if you could buy a half a t-shirt, that is; we'll assume you can for now), at bundle B'. Notice that this price increase also shrinks the feasible set of bundles just as the socks' price increase did. Always remember that when the price *rises*, the budget constraint rotates toward the origin, and when the price *falls*, it rotates away from the origin.

Now suppose Sarah's income falls by half (to $25) and prices stay at their original levels. With only half the income, Sarah can buy only half as many pairs of socks and t-shirts as she could before. If she spends everything on socks, she can now buy only 5 pairs. If she buys only t-shirts, she can afford 2.5. But because relative prices haven't changed, the tradeoffs between the goods haven't changed. To buy 1 more t-shirt, Sarah still has to give up 2 pairs of socks. Thus, the slope of the budget constraint remains the same. This new budget constraint is shown in Figure 4.15c.

Figure 4.15   The Effects of Price or Income Changes on the Budget Constraint

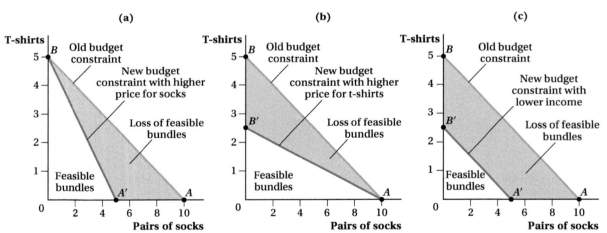

(a) When the price of socks increases, the horizontal intercept (I/P_{socks}) falls, the slope $(-P_{socks}/P_{t\text{-}shirts})$ gets steeper, the budget constraint rotates toward the origin, and the consumer (Sarah) has a smaller set of socks and t-shirt combinations from which to choose. The higher price for socks means that she can buy fewer socks, or if she purchases the same number of socks, she has less money remaining to buy t-shirts.
(b) When the price of t-shirts increases, the vertical intercept $(I/P_{t\text{-}shirts})$ falls, the slope $(-P_{socks}/P_{t\text{-}shirts})$ gets flatter, the budget constraint rotates toward the origin, and again, Sarah has a smaller choice set. The higher price for t-shirts means

that she can buy fewer t-shirts and, for a given purchase of t-shirts, she has less money available to buy socks.
(c) When Sarah's income is reduced, both the horizontal and vertical intercepts fall and the budget constraint shifts in. The horizontal intercept is lower because income I falls; thus, (I/P_{socks}) falls. The same holds for the vertical axis. Because the movement along both axes is caused by the change in income (the reduction in I is the same along both axes), the new budget constraint is parallel to the initial budget constraint. Given a reduction in income, Sarah's choice set is reduced.

Note that had both prices doubled while income stayed the same, the budget constraint would be identical to the new one shown in Figure 4.15c. We can see this more clearly if we plug in $2P_X$ and $2P_Y$ for the prices in the slope-intercept format of the budget constraint:

$$Q_Y = \frac{\text{Income}}{2P_Y} - \frac{2P_X}{2P_Y}Q_X$$

$$Q_Y = \frac{1}{2}\left(\frac{\text{Income}}{P_Y}\right) - \frac{P_X}{P_Y}Q_X$$

In both the figure and the equation, this type of change in prices decreases the purchasing power of the consumer's income, shifting the budget constraint inward. The same set of consumption bundles is feasible in either case. If Sarah's income had increased rather than decreased as in our example (or the prices of both goods had fallen in the same proportion), the budget constraint would have shifted out rather than in. Its slope would remain the same, though, because the relative prices of t-shirts and socks have not changed.

We've now considered what happens to the budget constraint in two situations: when income changes while prices stay constant and when prices change, holding income constant. What happens when prices and income both go up proportionally (e.g., all prices double and income doubles)? The budget constraint doesn't change at all. You have double the money, but because everything costs twice as much, you can only achieve the same bundles you could before the change in price and income. You can see this mathematically in the equation for the budget constraint above: If you multiply all prices and income by whatever positive constant you want (call this constant k), all the k's will cancel out, leaving you with the original equation.

4.3 figure it out

Braden has $20 per week that he can spend on video game rentals (R), priced at $5 per game, and candy bars (C), priced at $1 each.

a. Write an equation for Braden's budget constraint and draw it on a graph that has video game rentals on the horizontal axis. Be sure to show both intercepts and the slope of the budget constraint.

b. Assuming he spends the entire $20, how many candy bars does Braden purchase if he chooses to rent 3 video games?

c. Suppose that the price of a video game rental falls from $5 to $4. Draw Braden's new budget line (indicating intercepts and the slope).

Solution:

a. The budget constraint represents the feasible combinations of video game rentals (R) and candy bars (C) that Braden can purchase given the current prices and his income. The general form of the budget constraint would be Income $= P_R R + P_C C$. Substituting in the actual prices and income, we get $20 = 5R + 1C$.

To diagram the budget constraint (see the next page), first find the horizontal and vertical intercepts. The horizontal intercept is the point on Braden's budget constraint where he spends all of his $20 on video game rentals. The x-intercept is at 4 rentals ($20/$5), point A on his budget constraint. The vertical intercept represents the point where Braden has used his entire budget to purchase candy bars. He could purchase 20 candy bars ($20/$1) as shown at point B. Because the prices of candy bars and video game rentals are the same no matter how many Braden buys, the budget constraint is a straight line that connects these two points.

The slope of the budget constraint can be measured by the rise over the run. Therefore, it is equal to $\frac{\Delta C}{\Delta R} = -\frac{20}{4} = -5$. We can check our work by recalling that the slope of the budget constraint is equal to the negative of the ratio of the two prices or $-\frac{P_R}{P_C} = -\frac{5}{1} = -5$. Remember that the slope of the budget constraint shows the rate at which Braden is able to exchange candy bars for video game rentals.

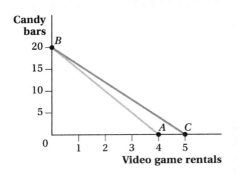

b. If Braden currently purchases 3 video game rentals, that means he spends $15 (= $5 × 3) on them. This leaves $5 (= $20 − $15) for purchasing candy bars. At a price of $1 each, Braden purchases 5 candy bars.

c. When the price of a video game rental falls to $4, the vertical intercept is unaffected. If Braden chooses to spend his $20 on candy bars, at a price of $1, he can still afford to buy 20 of them. Thus, point B will also be on his new budget constraint. However, the horizontal intercept increases from 4 to 5. At a price of $4 per rental, Braden can now afford 5 rentals if he chooses to allocate his entire budget to rentals (point C). His new budget constraint joins points B and C.

The slope of the budget constraint is $\dfrac{\Delta C}{\Delta R} = -\dfrac{20}{5} = -4$. Note that this equals the inverse price ratio of the two goods $\left(-\dfrac{P_R}{P_C} = -\dfrac{4}{1} = -4\right)$.

Nonstandard Budget Constraints

In all the examples so far, the budget constraint has been a straight line. There are some cases in which the budget constraint would be kinked instead.

Quantity Discounts   Suppose Alex spends his $100 income on pizzas and phone calls. A pizza costs $10; if he spends everything on pizzas, he can buy 10. If the price of phone minutes is constant at 10 cents per minute, he can buy as many as 1,000 minutes of phone time. Figure 4.16 portrays this example graphically. The budget constraint in the case where minutes are priced at a constant 10 cents is given by the solid section of the line running from zero minutes and 10 pizzas up to 1,000 minutes and zero pizzas.

Phone plans often offer quantity discounts on goods such as phone minutes. With a quantity discount, the price the consumer pays per unit of the good depends on the number of units purchased. If Alex's calling plan charges 10 cents per minute for the first 600 minutes per month and 5 cents per minute after that, his budget constraint will have a kink. In particular, because phone minutes become cheaper above 600 minutes, the actual budget constraint has a kink at 600 minutes and 4 pizzas. Because the price of the good on the y-axis (phone minutes) becomes relatively cheaper, the constraint rotates clockwise at that quantity, becoming steeper. To find where the budget constraint intercepts the vertical axis, we have to figure out how many minutes Alex can buy if he buys only cell phone time. This total is 1,400 minutes [(600 × $0.10) + (800 × $0.05) = $100]. In Figure 4.16, the resulting budget constraint runs from 10 pizzas and zero minutes to 4 pizzas and 600 minutes (part of the solid line) and then continues up to zero pizzas and 1,400 minutes (the dashed line). It's clear from the figure that the lower price for phone time above the 600-minute threshold means that Alex can afford a set of phone minute and pizza combinations (the triangle above the initial budget constraint and below the dashed line) that he could not afford when phone minutes had a constant price of 10 cents.

Quantity Limits   Another way a budget constraint can be kinked is if there is a limit on how much of one good can be consumed. For example, during World War II in the United States, certain goods like sugar and butter were rationed. Each family could buy only a limited quantity. During the oil price spikes of the 1970s, gas stations

Figure 4.16   Quantity Discounts and the Budget Constraint

When the price of phone minutes is constant at 10 cents per minute, Alex's budget constraint for phone minutes and pizza has a constant slope, as represented by the solid line. If the phone company offers a quantity discount on phone minutes, however, Alex's budget constraint will be kinked. Here, Alex's calling plan charges 10 cents per minute for the first 600 minutes per month and 5 cents per minute after that, resulting in the kink at 600 phone minutes shown by the dashed line. The triangle above the initial budget constraint and below the dashed line represents the set of phone minute and pizza combinations Alex can afford under the new pricing scheme that he could not have purchased at a constant price of 10 cents per minute.

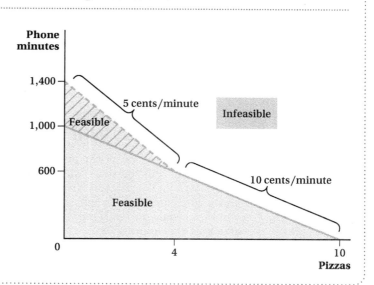

often limited the amount of gasoline people could buy. These limits have the effect of creating a kinked budget constraint.[5]

Suppose that the government (or maybe his parents, if he lives at home) dictates that Alex can talk on the phone for no more than 600 minutes per month. In that case, the part of the budget constraint beyond 600 minutes becomes infeasible, and the constraint becomes horizontal at 600 minutes, as shown by the solid line in Figure 4.17.

Figure 4.17   Quantity Limits and the Budget Constraint

When there is a limit on how much of a good a person can consume, a budget constraint will be kinked. When Alex is limited to 600 minutes on the phone per month, his budget constraint is horizontal at that quantity. The triangle above the horizontal section of the budget constraint and below the dashed line represents the set of phone minutes and pizzas that are now infeasible for Alex to buy. Note that Alex can still afford these sets since his income and the prices have not changed, but the restrictions on how much he can purchase dictate that he cannot buy them.

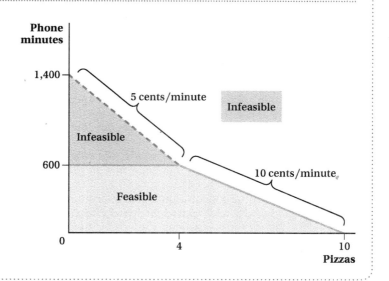

[5] Note that limits on how much a consumer can purchase are a lot like the quotas we learned about in Chapter 3, except now they apply to a single consumer, rather than to the market as a whole.

Note that neither Alex's income nor any prices have changed in this example. He still has enough money to reach any part in the area below the dashed section of the budget constraint that is labeled infeasible. He just isn't allowed to spend it. Consequently, for the flat part of the budget constraint, he will have unspent money left over. As we see in the next section, you will never actually want to consume a bundle on the flat part of the budget constraint. (You might want to see if you can figure out why yourself, before we tell you the answer.)

4.4 Combining Utility, Income, and Prices: What Will the Consumer Consume?

We now have in place all the pieces necessary to determine how much of each good a utility-maximizing consumer will consume. We know the consumer's preferences over all possible bundles of goods from the utility function and its associated indifference curves. The budget constraint shows us which bundles are feasible and which are beyond the consumer's reach given her income and the goods' prices. It's just a matter of combining this information in the right way.

Solving the Consumer's Optimization Problem

As we mentioned in the introduction to this chapter, the choice of how much to consume (like so many economic decisions) is a *constrained optimization* problem. There is something you want to maximize (utility, in this case), and there is something that limits how much of the good thing you can get (the budget constraint, in this case). And as we will see in the next chapter, the constrained optimization problem forms the basis of the demand curve.

Before we try to solve this constrained optimization problem, let's think for a minute about what makes it a tricky problem: It requires us to make comparisons between things (e.g., income and prices) measured in dollars and things (e.g., consumer utility) measured in imaginary units that we can't directly translate into dollars. How can you know whether or not you're willing to pay $3 to get some extra units of utility? Well, you can't, really. What you can figure out, however, is whether spending an extra dollar on, say, golf balls gives you more or less utility than spending an extra dollar on something else, like AAA batteries. It turns out that in figuring out this choice, you and other consumers use your indifference curves and budget constraints in such a way that solving the consumer's optimization problem becomes straightforward.

Maybe you didn't take much note of it earlier when we introduced indifference curves and the budget constraint, but look now at the axes we use to depict these two different concepts. They are the same: The quantity of some good is on the vertical axis, and the quantity of some other good is on the horizontal axis. This arrangement is extremely important, because it means we can display indifference curves and the budget constraint for two goods in the same graph, making the consumer's problem easier to solve.

Figure 4.18 presents an example that shows a combination of indifference curves and a budget constraint. Remember, the consumer wants to get as much utility as possible from consuming the goods, subject to the limits imposed by her budget constraint. What bundle will she choose? The bundle at point *A*. That's the highest indifference curve she can reach given her budget line.

Why is *A* the utility-maximizing consumption bundle? Compare point *A* to another feasible bundle, such as *B*. Point *B* is on the budget constraint, so the consumer can

Figure 4.18   The Consumer's Optimal Choice

The consumer's optimal consumption bundle occurs at the point of tangency between her budget constraint and her indifference curve, shown here at point A. The consumer can afford the consumption bundles represented by points B, C, and D, but these are on a lower indifference curve (U_1) than is point A (U_2). Point E is on a higher indifference curve (U_3), but it lies outside the consumer's budget constraint and is thus infeasible.

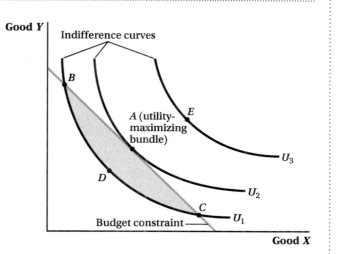

afford it with her income. However, because B is on a lower indifference curve (U_1) than A is (U_2), bundle B provides less utility than A. Bundles C and D are feasible too, but also leave the consumer worse off. The consumer would love to consume a bundle like E because it's on an indifference curve (U_3) that corresponds to a higher utility level than U_2. Unfortunately, the consumer can't afford E: It's outside her budget constraint.

A look at the consumer's optimal consumption bundle A in Figure 4.18 shows that it has a special feature: The indifference curve running through it, U_2, touches the budget constraint once and only once, exactly at A. Mathematically speaking, U_2 and the budget constraint are tangent at point A. As long as the assumptions about utility we established earlier hold, no other indifference curve we can draw will have this feature. Any other indifference curve will not be tangent, and therefore will cross the budget constraint twice or not at all. If you can draw another indifference curve that is tangent, it will cross the indifference curve shown in Figure 4.18, violating the transitivity assumption. (Give it a try—it is a useful exercise.)

This single tangency is not a coincidence. It is, in fact, a requirement of utility maximization. To see why, suppose an indifference curve and the budget constraint never touched. Then no point on the indifference curve is feasible, and by definition, no bundle on that indifference curve can be the way for a consumer to maximize his utility given his income. Now suppose the indifference curve instead crosses the budget constraint twice. This implies there must be a bundle that offers the consumer higher utility than any on this indifference curve and that the consumer can afford. For example, the shaded region between indifference curve U_1 and the budget constraint in Figure 4.18 reflects all of the bundles that are feasible and provide higher utility than bundles B, C, D, or any other point on U_1. That means no bundle on U_1 could be utility-maximizing; there are other bundles that are both affordable and offer higher utility. By similar reasoning, this outcome will be generally true not just for indifference curve U_1, but for any indifference curve that crosses the budget constraint twice.

This means that only at a point of tangency are there no other bundles that are both (1) feasible and (2) offer a higher utility level. This tangency is the utility-maximizing bundle for the consumer.

Mathematically, the tangency of the indifference curve and budget constraint means that they have the same slope at the optimal consumption bundle. This has a very important economic interpretation that is key to understanding why the optimal bundle is where it is. In Section 4.2, we defined the negative of the slope of the indifference curve as the marginal rate of substitution, and we discussed how the MRS_{XY} reflects the ratio of the *marginal utilities* of the two goods. In Section 4.3, we saw that the slope of the budget constraint equals the negative of the ratio of the *prices* of the two goods. Therefore, the fact that the consumer's utility-maximizing bundle is at a tangency between an indifference curve and the budget constraint (and that it's on the budget constraint rather than inside it) gives us this key insight: *When the consumer spends all her income, her optimal consumption bundle is the one at which the ratio of the goods' marginal utilities exactly equals the ratio of their prices.*

This economic idea behind utility maximization can be expressed mathematically. At the point of tangency,

$$\text{Slope of indifference curve} = \text{Slope of budget constraint}$$

$$-MRS_{XY} = -MU_X/MU_Y = -P_X/P_Y$$

$$MU_X/MU_Y = P_X/P_Y$$

Why are the marginal utility and price ratios equal when the consumer maximizes her utility level? If they were not equal, she could do better by shifting consumption from one good to the other. To see why, let's say Meredith is maximizing her utility over bottles of Gatorade and protein bars. Suppose bottles of Gatorade are twice as expensive as protein bars, but she is considering a bundle in which her marginal utilities from the two goods *are not* 2 to 1 as the price ratio is. Say she gets the same amount of utility at the margin from another bottle of Gatorade as from another protein bar, so that the ratio of the goods' marginal utilities is 1. Given the relative prices, she could give up 1 bottle of Gatorade and buy 2 more protein bars and doing so would let her reach a higher utility level. Why? Because those 2 extra protein bars are worth twice as much in utility terms as the lost bottle of Gatorade.

Now suppose that a bottle of Gatorade offers Meredith four times the utility at the margin as a protein bar. In this case, the ratio of Meredith's marginal utilities for Gatorade and protein bars (4 to 1) is higher than the price ratio (2 to 1), so Meredith could buy 2 fewer protein bars in exchange for 1 more bottle of Gatorade. Because the Gatorade delivers twice the utility lost from the 2 protein bars, she will be better off buying fewer protein bars and more Gatorade.

It is often helpful to rewrite this optimization condition in terms of the consumer's marginal utility per dollar spent:

$$\frac{MU_X}{MU_Y} = \frac{P_X}{P_Y} \Rightarrow \frac{MU_X}{P_X} = \frac{MU_Y}{P_Y}$$

Here, the utility-maximation problem can be restated as finding the consumption bundle that gives the consumer the most bang for her buck. This occurs when the marginal utility per dollar spent (MU/P) is equal across all goods. If this is not the case, the consumer is able to adjust her consumption of Good X and Good Y to improve her utility.

Suppose Antonio gets utility from consuming two goods, burgers and fries. His utility function is given by

$$U = \sqrt{BF} = B^{0.5}F^{0.5}$$

where B is the amount of burgers he eats and F the servings of fries. Antonio's marginal utility of a burger $MU_B = 0.5B^{-0.5}F^{0.5}$, and his marginal utility of an order of fries $MU_F = 0.5B^{0.5}F^{-0.5}$. Antonio's income is $20, and the prices of burgers and fries are $5 and $2, respectively. What are Antonio's utility-maximizing quantities of burgers and fries?

Solution:

We know that the optimal solution to the consumer's maximization problem sets the marginal rate of substitution—the ratio of the goods' marginal utilities—equal to the goods' price ratio:

$$MRS_{BF} = \frac{MU_B}{MU_F} = \frac{P_B}{P_F}$$

where MU_B and MU_F are the marginal utilities of burgers and fries, respectively. P_B and P_F are the goods' prices. Therefore, to find the utility-maximizing quantities of burgers and fries, we set the ratio of marginal utilities equal to the goods' price ratio and simplify:

$$\frac{MU_B}{MU_F} = \frac{P_B}{P_F}$$

$$\frac{0.5B^{-0.5}F^{0.5}}{0.5B^{0.5}F^{-0.5}} = \frac{5}{2}$$

$$\frac{0.5F^{0.5}F^{0.5}}{0.5B^{0.5}B^{0.5}} = \frac{5}{2}$$

$$\frac{F}{B} = \frac{5}{2}$$

$$2F = 5B$$

$$F = 2.5B$$

This condition tells us that Antonio maximizes his utility when he consumes fries to burgers at a 5 to 2 ratio. We now know the ratio of the optimal quantities, but do not yet know exactly what quantities Antonio will choose to consume. To figure that out, we can use the budget constraint, which pins down the total amount Antonio can spend, and therefore the total quantities of each good he can consume.

Antonio's budget constraint can be written as

$$\text{Income} = P_F F + P_B B, \text{ or}$$

$$B = \frac{\text{Income}}{P_B} - \frac{P_F}{P_B}F$$

Substituting in the values from the problem gives

$$B = \frac{20}{5} - \frac{2}{5}F$$

$$B = 4 - 0.4F$$

Now, we can substitute the utility-maximization condition $F = 2.5B$ into the budget constraint to find the quantity of burgers Antonio will consume:

$$B = 4 - 0.4F$$

$$B = 4 - 0.4(2.5B)$$

$$B = 4 - B$$

$$B = 2$$

And because $F = 2.5B$, then $F = 5$.

Therefore, given his budget constraint, Antonio maximizes his utility by consuming 2 burgers and 5 servings of fries.

Implications of Utility Maximization

The marginal-utility-ratio-equals-price-ratio result has another implication for the economy as a whole that can initially be quite surprising. Even if two consumers have very different preferences between two goods, they will have the *same* ratio of marginal utilities for the two goods, because utility maximization implies that MRS equals the ratio of the prices.[6]

This might seem odd. If Jack has consumed 9 packs of gum and 1 iTunes download, while Meg consumed 9 downloads and only 1 pack of gum, it seems that Jack likes gum a lot and would therefore be willing to pay more for another pack of gum (and a lot less for iTunes) than Meg. This assertion would be true *if both Jack and Meg had to consume the same bundle*, but they don't have to. They can choose how much of each good they want to consume. Because Jack likes gum a lot, he will consume so much of it that he drives down his marginal utility until, by the time he and Meg both reach their utility-maximizing consumption bundles, they both place the same relative marginal utilities on the two goods. Ultimately, the relative value they place on any two goods (on the margin) is dictated by the relative prices. Because Meg and Jack face the same prices, they have the same marginal values.

This situation is shown in Figure 4.19. To keep things simple, we assume Jack and Meg have the same incomes. Because they also face the same relative prices, their budget constraints are the same. Jack really likes gum relative to iTunes downloads, so his indifference curves tend to be flat: He has to be given a lot of iTunes to make up for any loss of gum. Meg has the opposite tastes. She has to be given a lot of gum to make her no worse off for giving up an iTunes download. Her indifference curves are therefore steep. Nevertheless, both Jack and Meg's utility-maximizing bundles are on the same budget line, and their marginal rates of substitution at those bundles are the same. We've drawn the indifference curves for Jack (U_J) and Meg (U_M) so that they are tangent to the budget line and therefore contain the utility-maximizing bundle.

While they have the same MRS_{XY}, what *is* different is the amount of each good they consume in their respective bundles. Jack, the gum lover, maximizes his utility by choosing a bundle (J) with a lot of gum and not many iTunes. Meg's optimal consumption bundle (M), on the other hand, has a lot of iTunes and little gum. Again, the idea is that the way both consumers end up with the same MRS in their utility-maximizing bundles

---

Figure 4.19   Two Consumers' Optimal Choices

Although they have the same budget constraint, Jack and Meg have different relative preferences and, therefore, different optimal consumption bundles. Because Jack likes gum relative to iTunes downloads, his indifference curve (U_J) is flat and he consumes much more gum than iTunes at his optimal consumption bundle at point J. Meg's indifference curve (U_M) is much steeper and reflects her relative preference for iTunes downloads over gum; her utility-maximizing bundle is shown at point M. Although their consumption bundles are different, the MRS is the same at these points.

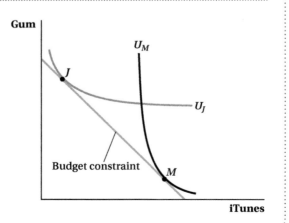

---

[6] Technically, this is true only of consumers who are consuming a positive amount of both goods, or who are at "interior" solutions in economists' lingo. We'll discuss this issue in the next section.

is that each consumes a large amount of the good for which he or she has the stronger preference. By behaving in this way, Jack and Meg drive down the relative marginal utility of the good they prefer until their marginal utility ratio equals the price ratio.

Note that these two indifference curves cross, although earlier we learned that indifference curves can never cross. If a consumer's indifference curves did cross, her preferences wouldn't have the transitivity property, and the bundle located where the indifference curves crossed would supposedly deliver two different utility levels. However, the "no crossing" rule applies only to the indifference curves of one individual. Figure 4.19 shows indifference curves for two different people with different preferences. Transitivity doesn't have to hold across people. If you like gum more than iTunes, and your friend likes iTunes more than, say, coffee, that doesn't imply you have to like gum more than coffee. So the same consumption bundle (say, 3 packs of gum and 5 iTunes downloads) can offer different utility levels to different people.

theory and data

Indifference Curves of Phone Service Buyers Revisited

From the Economides, Seim, and Viard study we discussed earlier, we learned that households with Internet access had higher relative marginal utilities for local phone calls than did non-Internet homes. Because the marginal utilities of regional calls were lower for Internet households, their *MRS* was higher than that for non-Internet households. Using the logic we just discussed, we can see that if the two types of households had the same budget constraint, the outcome would look something like Figure 4.20. Just like Jack and Meg above, consumers with different tastes end up consuming different bundles. Because households with the Internet had steeper indifference curves than those without Internet access, they ended up consuming a larger amount of local calls, shown at bundle *I*. (U_{Internet} is the indifference curve tangent to the budget constraint.) Non-Internet households' phone use was relatively heavy in regional calls instead, as seen in their optimal bundle *NI*. However, because we've assumed all households face the same budget constraint (and therefore the same relative prices), they will all have the same *MRS* at their optimal bundles.

Figure 4.20   Optimal Choices of Internet and Non-Internet Households

Non-Internet households and Internet households have the same budget constraint but different optimal bundles. Non-Internet households consume more regional calls than local calls at their utility-maximizing point (*NI*) because at any given level of local calls, they get higher marginal utility from regional calls. Internet households, on the other hand, consume more local calls than regional calls (point *I*) because they favor local calls on the margin more.

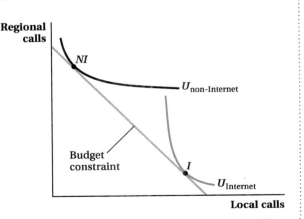

An interesting additional aspect of this market is that households actually have some choice in the relative prices they face. This is because they choose a specific calling plan from the many offered by the various competing phone companies. These menus typically let households trade off higher fixed monthly fees to face lower prices for additional calls on the margin. So, for example, a household could sign up for a billing plan that has a high fixed fee and a low marginal price for local phone service, but a low fixed fee with a high marginal price for regional service. Or vice versa.

How would these sorts of choices show up in our analysis? We know that the impact of different marginal prices would show up as a steeper or shallower budget constraint, depending on whether local or regional calls become relatively more expensive. How would a fixed fee affect the households' choices depicted in the figure drawn? You can think of paying a fixed fee as a reduction in the household's income. It doesn't affect relative prices on the margin, so in and of itself, it doesn't change the slope of the budget constraint. However, it does leave the household with less income to allocate between local and regional calls. Thus, if a household opts to pay a higher fixed fee, its budget constraint shifts in toward the origin.

A household might be willing to pay a higher fee and suffer the related income loss *if* the calling plan significantly lowers the price of the good it expects to consume a lot of. This is because the combination of these income and price changes would both shift (the result of the income change) and rotate (the result of the price change) the budget constraint, so that the household could still reach a higher utility level than before the shift.

An example of this is shown in Figure 4.21. An Internet household's original optimal bundle I from Figure 4.20 is shown (now labeled I_1), along with the original budget constraint (BC_1) and tangent indifference curve (now labeled $U_{Internet,1}$). When the household pays a fee to reduce the price of local calls on the margin, the budget constraint shifts in and rotates counterclockwise, as shown. Notice that the household has suffered a loss in income—it can't even afford its old optimal bundle I_1 anymore; that point is now infeasible. Nevertheless, the new optimal bundle I_2 is on an indifference curve ($U_{Internet,2}$) that corresponds to a higher utility level than the household received before.

By reducing the price of the good it has stronger relative preferences for, the household is actually able to make itself better off by paying a fee and, in effect, reducing its income. (In the next chapter, we spend a lot of time looking at how consumers respond to simultaneous changes in income and relative prices.)

Figure 4.21   :   Paying a Fixed Fee to Reduce the Price of Local Calls

By paying a fee, the Internet household can reduce the price of local calls on the margin, rotating the household's budget constraint from BC_1 to BC_2, due to the now lower relative price for local calls. The household has suffered a loss of income, but the new optimal bundle (I_2) is on an indifference curve ($U_{Internet,2}$) with a higher utility level than the original bundle (I_1 on indifference curve $U_{Internet,1}$).

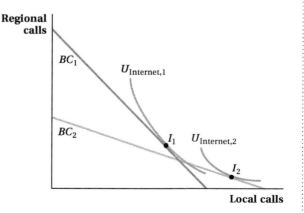

A Special Case: Corner Solutions

Up to this point, we have been analyzing situations in which the consumer optimally consumes some of both goods. This assumption usually makes sense if we think that utility functions have the property that the more you have of a good, the less you are willing to give up of something else to get more. Because the first little bit of a good provides the most marginal utility in this situation, a consumer will typically want at least *some* amount of a good.

Depending on the consumer's preferences and relative prices, however, in some cases a consumer will want to spend all her money on one good. Consuming all of one good and none of the other maximizes a consumer's utility given the budget constraint is called a **corner solution.** (Its name comes from the fact that the optimal consumption bundle is at the "corner" of the budget line, where it meets the axis.) If the utility-maximizing bundle has positive quantities of both goods, like all the cases we've looked at to this point, it is referred to as an **interior solution.**

Figure 4.22 depicts a corner solution. Greg, our consumer, has an income of $240 and is choosing his consumption levels of romance novels and economics textbooks. Let's say a hardcover romance novel costs $20, and an economics text costs $120. Because econ texts are more expensive than romance novels, Greg can afford up to 12 romance novels, but only 2 econ texts. Nonetheless, the highest utility that Greg can obtain given his income is bundle A, where he consumes all economics textbooks and no romance novels.

How do we know A is the optimal bundle? Consider another feasible bundle, such as B. Greg can afford it, but it is on an indifference curve U_1 that corresponds to a lower utility level than U_2. The same logic would apply to bundles on any indifference curve between U_1 and U_2. Furthermore, any bundle that offers higher utility than U_2 (i.e., above and to the right of U_2) isn't feasible given Greg's income. So U_2 must be the highest utility level Greg can achieve, and he can do so only by consuming bundle A, because that's the only bundle he can afford on that indifference curve.

In a corner solution, then, the highest indifference curve touches the budget constraint exactly once, just as with the interior solutions we discussed earlier. The only

corner solution
A utility-maximizing bundle located at the "corner" of the budget constraint where the consumer purchases only one of two goods.

interior solution
A utility-maximizing bundle that contains positive quantities of both goods.

Figure 4.22   A Corner Solution

A corner solution occurs when the consumer spends all his money on one good. Given Greg's income and the relative prices of romance novels and economics textbooks, Greg is going to consume 2 economics textbooks and zero romance novels at his optimal consumption bundle (A). All other feasible consumption bundles, such as point B, correspond to indifference curves with lower utility levels than the indifference curve U_2 at point A. Greg cannot afford consumption bundles at a higher utility level, such as U_3, with his current income.

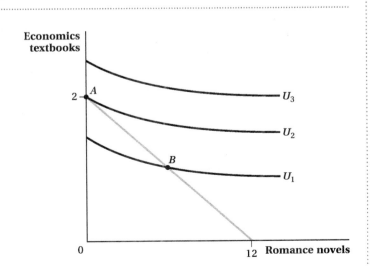

difference with a corner solution is that bundle A is not a point of tangency. The indifference curve is flatter than the budget constraint at that point (and everywhere else). That means Greg's MRS—the ratio of his marginal utility from romance novels relative to his marginal utility from textbooks—is *less* than the price ratio of the two goods rather than equal to it. In other words, even when he's consuming no romance novels, his marginal utility from them is so low, it's not worth paying the price of a novel to be able to consume one. The marginal utility he'd have to give up due to reduced textbook consumption would not be made up for by the fact that he could spend some of his textbook money on novels. In fact, if Greg were allowed to consume a negative quantity of romance novels (that would be kind of like Greg producing some romance novels to sell to other consumers), he would want to.

4.5 figure it out

A pizza chain recently offered the following special promotion: "Buy one pizza at full price and get your next three pizzas for just $5 each!" Assume that the full price of a pizza is $10, your daily income $40, and the price of all other goods $1 per unit.

a. Draw budget constraints for pizza and all other goods that reflect your situations both before and during the special promotion. (Put the quantity of pizzas on the horizontal axis.) Indicate the horizontal and vertical intercepts and the slope of the budget constraint.

b. How is this special offer likely to alter your buying behavior?

c. How might your answer to (b) depend on the shape of your indifference curves?

Solution:

a. To draw your budget constraint, you need to find the combinations of pizza and all other goods that are available to you before and during the promotion. The starting place for drawing your budget constraint is to find its x- and y-intercepts.

Before the promotion, you could afford 4 pizzas a day ($40/$10) if you spent all of your income on pizza. This is the x-intercept (Figure A). Likewise, you could afford 40 units of all other goods per day ($40/$1) if you purchased no pizza. This is the y-intercept. The budget constraint, shown in Figure A, connects these two points and has a slope of $-40/4 = -10$. This slope measures the amount of other goods you must give up to have an

additional pizza. Note that this is also equal to $-P_x/P_y = -\$10/\$1 = -10$.

Once the promotion begins, you can still afford 40 units of all other goods if you buy no pizza. The promotion has an effect only if you buy some pizza. This means the y-intercept of the budget constraint is unchanged by the promotion. Now suppose you buy 1 pizza. In that case, you must pay $10 for the pizza, leaving you $30 for purchasing all other goods. This bundle is point A on the diagram. If you were to buy a second pizza, its price would be only $5. Spending $15 on 2 pizzas would allow you to purchase $25 ($40 − $15) worth of other goods. This corresponds to bundle B. The third and fourth pizzas also cost $5 each. After 3 pizzas, you have $20 left to spend on other goods, and after 4 pizzas, you are left with $15 for other goods. These are points C and D on the diagram.

A fifth pizza will cost you $10 (the full price) because the promotion limits the $5 price to the next 3 pizzas you buy. That means if you choose to buy 5 pizzas, you will spend $35 on pizza and only $5 on other goods, as at bundle E. Now that you have again purchased a pizza at full price, you are eligible to receive the next 3 at the reduced price of $5. Unfortunately, you only have enough income for one more $5 pizza. Therefore, if you would like to spend all of your income on pizza, you can buy 6 pizzas instead of just 4.

As a result of the promotion, then, your x-intercept has moved out to 6, and your budget line has pivoted out (in a somewhat irregular way because of all the relative price changes corresponding to purchasing different numbers of pizzas) to reflect the increase in your purchasing power due to the promotion.

Figure A

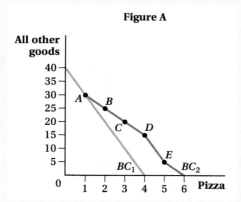

b. It is likely that the promotion will increase how much pizza you consume. Most of the new budget constraint lies to the right of the initial budget constraint, increasing the number of feasible bundles available to you. Because more is preferred to less, it is likely that your optimal consumption bundle will include more pizza than before.

c. If your indifference curves are very flat, you have a strong preference for other goods relative to pizza. For example, look at U_A (Figure B). The slope of this indifference curve is relatively small (in absolute value). This means that the marginal rate of substitution of other goods for pizza is small. If your

indifference curves look like this, you are not very willing to trade other goods for more pizza, and your optimal consumption bundle will likely lie on the section of the new budget constraint that coincides with the initial budget constraint. The promotion would cause no change in your consumption behavior; pizza is not a high priority for you, as indicated by your flat indifference curve.

Figure B

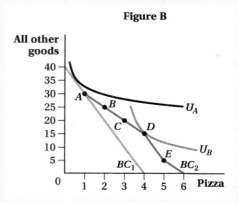

On the other hand, if your indifference curves are steeper, like U_B, your marginal rate of substitution is relatively large, indicating that you are willing to forgo a large amount of other goods to consume an additional pizza. This promotion will more than likely cause you to purchase additional pizzas.

An Alternative Approach to Solving the Consumer's Problem: Expenditure Minimization

Up to this point, our strategy for determining what bundle of goods the consumer will consume has involved maximizing utility subject to the constraint that expenditure cannot exceed the consumer's income. As we discussed above, this is an example of a *constrained maximization* problem.

While this approach is natural and intuitive, any constrained maximization problem can also be solved by reversing the roles played by the constraint and the function being maximized. That is, we can also look at how a consumer decides what bundle to consume as a "constrained minimization" problem: The consumer minimizes expenditure (reflected in the budget constraint) subject to the constraint that she must achieve a given level of utility from this expenditure. Graphically speaking, utility maximization is about finding the highest indifference curve that is tangent to the budget constraint, while expenditure minimization is about finding the lowest budget constraint that is tangent to a given indifference curve.

Economists call this expenditure-minimization setup the "dual" to the utility-maximization problem. They're sort of mathematical mirror images.

Figure 4.23 : Utility Maximization Versus Expenditure Minimization

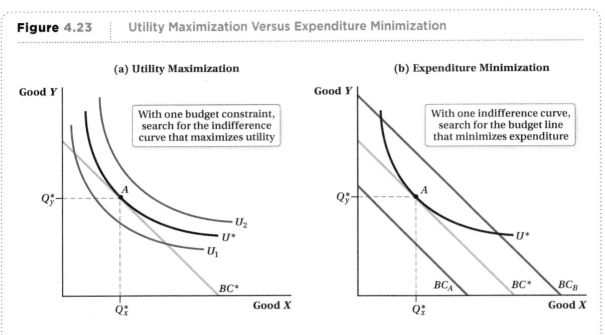

(a) Using the utility-maximization approach, the consumer chooses the bundle with the highest utility level that she can afford given her budget constraint. This occurs at the point of tangency (bundle A) between the indifference curve U^* and the budget constraint BC^*.

(b) Using the expenditure-maximization approach, the consumer begins with an indifference curve of a given utility level, U^*. She then chooses the budget line, BC^*, tangent to U^*. As in panel a, the consumer chooses bundle A, where she consumes quantities Q_x^* and Q_y^*.

Figure 4.23 shows these two approaches graphically. Panel a on the left is an example of the standard utility-maximization approach. The consumer has a fixed income reflected in the budget constraint BC^* and various levels of utility as reflected by the three indifference curves shown. Bundle A, which is at the point of tangency between the budget constraint and the indifference curve labeled U^*, represents the utility-maximizing feasible bundle.

Panel b solves the same problem using the expenditure-minimization approach. In this case, we start with a level of utility that the consumer wants to achieve. Specifically, we start with a given level of utility U^*, which is the same utility level that the consumer has in panel a. Then, we search over different levels of income (or equivalently, expenditure) for the smallest amount of income or expenditure necessary to achieve U^*. Each expenditure level is associated with a different budget line. These budget *lines* are just like the budget *constraints* we have seen earlier—they are straight lines with the slope determined by the relative prices of the two goods. We call them budget *lines* not budget *constraints* because now it is the indifference curve U^* that is the constraint.

In panel b, we've drawn in a few budget lines. We know from before that budget lines further from the origin reflect higher levels of income. Because the consumer wants to achieve his chosen level of utility with the least amount of income/expenditure, he must find the budget line *closest* to the origin that touches U^*. The answer, as in our original approach, boils down to finding the point of tangency between the indifference curve and the budget line. And, as shown in panel b, that point is bundle A, the same bundle from the utility-maximization problem in panel a.

It is no coincidence that the optimal solution in the two panels is the same. The utility-maximization and expenditure-minimization approaches are just two different ways of solving the same problem. Either we fix a budget constraint and try to find the highest indifference curve that is tangent to it (utility maximization), or we fix an indifference curve and try to find the lowest budget line that is tangent to it (expenditure minimization). The reason that the optimal solution in the two panels is the same consumption bundle is that when we set up the utility constraint in panel b's expenditure-minimization problem, we picked the same utility level reached in panel a's utility-maximization problem. If we had chosen any other utility level for our analysis, the minimum-expenditure budget line would be something other than BC^*, and the optimal consumption bundle would not be bundle A.

4.5 Conclusion

This chapter has looked at how consumers decide what to consume. This decision combines two characteristics of consumers, their preferences (embodied in their utility function) and their income, and one characteristic of the market, the goods' prices.

We saw that a consumer will maximize her utility from consumption when she chooses a bundle of goods such that the marginal rate of substitution between the goods equals their relative prices. That is, in this bundle the ratio of the goods' utilities equals their price ratio. Equivalently, the goods' marginal utilities per dollar spent are equal. If this property didn't hold, a consumer could make herself better off by consuming more of the goods with high marginal utilities per dollar and less of the goods with low marginal utilities per dollar.

There is another way to think about the consumer's problem of what and how much to consume. Rather than thinking of consumers as trying to maximize utility subject to a budget constraint, we could think of them as trying to minimize the expenditure necessary for them to reach a given level of utility. This is called the expenditure-minimization problem. We saw how it turns out that this delivers the same rule for optimal consumption behavior: The MRS of the goods should equal their price ratio.

Summary

1. **Utility** is the economic concept of consumers' happiness or well-being, and the **utility function** is the construct that relates the amount of goods consumed (the inputs) to the consumer's utility level (the output). There are properties that we expect almost all utility functions to share: the completeness, rankability, and transitivity of utility bundles, that having more of a good is better than having less, and that the more a consumer has of a particular good, the less willing she is to give up something else to get more of that good. [**Section 4.1**]

2. Consumers' preferences are reflected in their **indifference curves,** which show all the combinations of goods over which a consumer receives equal utility. The set of properties imposed on utility functions imply some restrictions on the shapes of indifference curves. Namely, indifference curves slope downward, never cross for a given individual, and are convex to the origin. [**Section 4.2**]

3. The negative of the slope of the indifference curve is the **marginal rate of substitution of good X for good Y (MRS_{XY}).** The MRS is the ratio of the marginal utilities of the goods in the utility function. [**Section 4.2**]

4. Consumer preferences lead to differences in the steepness and curvature of indifference curves. If a consumer views two goods as **perfect substitutes** or **perfect complements,** their indifference curves will be shaped like straight lines and right angles, respectively. [**Section 4.2**]

5. The consumer's decision about how much of each good to consume depends not only on utility, but also on how much money that person has to spend (her income) and on the prices of the goods. In analyzing the role of income in consumption decisions, we assume the following: Each good has a fixed price, and any consumer can buy as much of a good as she wants at that price if the consumer has sufficient income to pay for it; the consumer has some fixed amount of income to spend; and the consumer cannot save or borrow.

The **budget constraint** captures both a consumer's income and the relative prices of goods. The constraint shows which **consumption bundles** are **feasible** (i.e., affordable given the consumer's income) and which are **infeasible.** The slope of the budget constraint is the negative of the ratio of the prices of the two goods $(-P_X/P_Y)$. [**Section 4.3**]

6. The consumer's decision is a constrained-optimization problem: to maximize utility while staying within her budget constraint. The utility-maximizing solution is generally to consume the bundle of goods located where an indifference curve is tangent to the budget constraint. At this optimal point, the consumer's marginal rate of substitution—the ratio of the consumer's marginal utilities from the goods—equals the goods' relative price ratio.

   A **corner solution**, where the optimal quantity consumed of one good is zero, can occur when a consumer's marginal utility of a good is so low compared to that good's relative price that she is better off not consuming any of that good at all. In such cases, the MRS does not equal the price ratio even though the consumer is at the utility-maximizing consumption bundle. [**Section 4.4**]

7. The consumer's problem of what and how much to consume can be recast as an expenditure-minimization problem. That is, rather than thinking of consumers as trying to maximize utility subject to a budget constraint, we could think of them as trying to minimize the expenditure necessary for them to reach a given level of utility. The optimal choices for both problems result in the same criterion: The MRS of the goods should equal their price ratio. [**Section 4.4**]

Review Questions

1. We make four assumptions about preferences: completeness and rankability, "more is better," transitivity, and consumers want variety. Briefly describe each assumption.

2. What does the term "utility" mean? How does utility relate to a utility function?

3. Define "indifference curve." What does an indifference curve tell us about the consumer?

4. We learned that the slope of the indifference curve is called the marginal rate of substitution of X for Y. What does the MRS_{XY} tell us about a consumer's preferences between two goods?

5. Why does the slope of the indifference curve vary along the curve? What does this variability tell us about consumers' preferences?

6. What does a steep indifference curve indicate about a consumer's preferences? What does a flat indifference curve say?

7. When are two goods perfect substitutes? What does the indifference curve look like, or what is its *curvature*?

8. When are two goods perfect complements? What does the indifference curve look like?

9. In addition to utility, what other factors determine how much of a good to buy?

10. Describe the three assumptions we make when incorporating income into our model of consumer behavior.

11. What is a budget constraint?

12. What determines the slope of a budget constraint? What situation would change the slope of a budget constraint?

13. What do we call the bundle represented by the point of tangency between the consumer's indifference curve and her budget constraint?

14. At the point of tangency, what is true about the ratio of the goods' marginal utilities and the ratio of their prices?

15. What is the difference between these approaches: utility maximization and expenditure minimization?

Problems

1. Which assumption about consumer preferences does each of the following individuals violate?
   a. Randy likes basketball more than football; football more than baseball; and baseball more than basketball.
   b. Paula prefers prune juice to orange juice but cannot decide how she feels about grapefruit juice.
   c. Simon likes superhero comic books but prefers 5 comic books to 10 comic books.

2. By assumption, individual preferences must be transitive so that if A is preferred to B, and B is preferred to C, then A is preferred to C. Suppose that Marsha, Jan, and Cindy individually have transitive preferences over three goods: oranges, apples, and pears. If Marsha, Jan, and Cindy were to vote on whether to name oranges, apples, or pears the "fruit of the month," show that it is possible the preferences for the *group* might *not* be transitive.

3. In Arbitrageville, 1 orange can be exchanged for 4 apples, and 4 apples for 1 orange. The mayor of Arbitrageville likes oranges a lot. He buys 100 oranges and 1 apple at the grocery store. As the mayor piles oranges onto the checkout counter, he tells the clerk, "I just love these oranges. In fact, I think you'd need to offer me three apples to pry one orange from my hands."
   a. Explain why the clerk, a sharp entrepreneur, immediately reaches under the counter and offers the mayor 3 apples.
   b. What should the mayor have said about how many apples the clerk would need to offer him for 1 orange, assuming that the mayor was maximizing his utility? What equation tells us how the mayor's preferences relate to prices?
   c. If the mayor maintained his preferences, how could the clerk wind up with all of the mayor's oranges and the mayor (eventually) without a penny to his name?

4. Draw two indifference curves for each of the following pairs of goods. Put the quantity of the first good on the horizontal axis and the quantity of the second good on the vertical axis.
   a. Paul likes pencils and pens.
   b. Rhonda likes carrots and dislikes broccoli.
   c. Emily likes hip-hop iTunes downloads and doesn't care about heavy metal downloads.
   d. Michael only likes dress shirts and cufflinks in 1 to 2 proportions.

5. Suppose that John is indifferent between consuming bundle A, which consists of 4 apples and 1 peach, and bundle B, which consists of 4 peaches and 1 apple. If John were given the choice between bundle A and bundle C, which contained 3 peaches and 2 apples, which should he pick? (*Hint*: Draw an indifference curve or two.)

6. The table below displays the total utility $U(X)$ that corresponds to the number of units of X consumed by three different consumers (Abe, Barbara, and Chuck), holding everything else constant:

Abe		Barbara		Chuck	
U(X)	*X*	*U(X)*	*X*	*U(X)*	*X*
10	2	10	2	10	2
14	3	10	3	12	3
16	4	10	4	15	4
17	5	9	5	19	5
17.5	6	8	6	24	6

   a. Compute the marginal utility of X for each of the three consumers at each level of X.
   b. Based on the data in the table, can you tell whether any of these consumers are vio-

lating any of the standard assumptions about preferences?
   c. Is it possible that any of these three consumers have the exact same preferences, and that columns for the three consumers differ only because of the arbitrary units that are used to measure utility? Explain.

7. A consumer's utility function is given by $U = XY$, where $MU_X = Y$ and $MU_Y = X$.
   a. What is the utility derived from 1 unit of X and 2 units of Y? What is the utility derived from 2 units of X and 1 unit of Y? What is the utility derived from 5 units of X and 2 units of Y?
   b. How does the consumer rank the following bundles?

Bundle	Quantity of X	Quantity of Y
A	2	2
B	10	0
C	1	5
D	3	2
E	2	3

   c. Graph an indifference curve that shows the bundles of X and Y for which $U = 6$ and $U = 8$. Is the "more is better" assumption satisfied for X and Y?
   d. What are MU_X and MU_Y for the following bundles?

Bundle	Quantity of X	Quantity of Y
F	1	2
G	2	2
H	1	3

   e. Does MU_X diminish, stay constant, or increase as X increases? (*Hint*: You must keep the values of all other variables fixed.)

8. Kelly's utility function is given by $U = 5X + 2Y$, where $MU_X = 5$ and $MU_Y = 2$.
   a. What is MRS_{XY}?
   b. What is MRS_{XY} when $X = 1$ and $Y = 5$? When $X = 2$ and $Y = 2.5$?
   c. Draw a sample indifference curve.

9. Andrea loves to eat burritos with hot sauce. In fact, she cannot enjoy a burrito (B) unless it has three servings of hot sauce (H). She gets no additional enjoyment from more than three servings per burrito. Thus, her utility function is $U = \min\{B, \frac{1}{3}H\}$. Graph Andrea's indifference curves for $U = 1$ and $U = 2$.

10. If Harry considers Cubs tickets a "good" and White Sox tickets a "bad," draw a set of indifference curves for Harry.

11. Josie gets satisfaction from both music and fireworks. Josie's income is $240 per week. Music costs $12 per CD, and fireworks cost $8 per bag.
    a. Graph the budget constraint Josie faces, with music on the vertical axis and fireworks on the horizontal axis.
    b. If Josie spends all her income on music, how much music can she afford? Plot a point that illustrates this scenario.
    c. If Josie spends all her income on fireworks, how many bags of fireworks can she afford? Plot a point that illustrates this scenario.
    d. If Josie spends half her income on fireworks and half her income on music, how much of each can she afford? Plot a point that illustrates this scenario.
    e. Connect the dots to create Josie's budget constraint. What is the slope of the budget constraint?
    f. Divide the price of fireworks by the price of music. Have you seen this number before, and if so, where?
    g. Suppose that a holiday bonus raises Josie's income temporarily to $360. Draw Josie's new budget constraint.
    h. Indicate the new bundles of music and fireworks that are feasible, given Josie's new income.

12. Suppose that only one person in the world sells ice cream. He employs a strange pricing policy: You can buy 1 ice cream cone for $1, but if you buy 2 cones, you have to pay $2 each. If you buy 3, you have to pay $3 each, etc., so that if you buy 10, you have to pay $10 each. You have $100 dollars to spend on ice cream cones and chocolate milk, and chocolate milk costs $1 per unit. Draw your budget constraint. This strange ice cream pricing, where buying more costs you more, is called a quantity surcharge.

13. Matthew is redecorating his apartment. The amount of utility he gets from chairs and couches is listed in the table below, where each number represents how much utility (in utils) he receives from the combination of chairs and couches:

	1 chair	2 chairs	3 chairs	4 chairs
1 couch	5	6	8	20
2 couches	6	7	10	21
3 couches	9	12	16	30

a. What is the marginal utility from buying an additional chair if Matthew has 2 chairs and 2 couches?
b. What is the marginal utility from buying an additional couch if Matthew has 2 chairs and 2 couches?
c. If couches are the same price as chairs, and Matthew wants one more piece of furniture but already has 2 couches and 2 chairs, will he buy a couch or a chair? Explain.

14. Good X sells for $4, and good Y sells for $2. At your current level of consumption, the marginal rate of substitution between X and Y is 4.
    a. Are you maximizing your utility?
    b. If not, are you buying too much X or too much Y? Explain.

15. For Mitzi, shampoo and conditioner are perfect complements. She likes to use 1 squirt of shampoo and 1 squirt of conditioner each time she washes her hair.
    a. Draw a set of indifference curves for Mitzi that illustrate the utility she derives from using shampoo and conditioner.
    b. Assume that shampoo costs $4 and conditioner costs $2. Construct a budget constraint for Mitzi and describe her purchasing habits. What is her optimal bundle likely to look like? (*Hint*: Assume some level of income for Mitzi.)
    c. Suppose that prices change so that shampoo costs $2 and conditioner costs $4. What is likely to happen to Mitzi's optimal bundle as a result? Explain.
    d. How would your answer to (c) change if Mitzi used 2 squirts of shampoo and 1 squirt of conditioner each time she washed her hair?

16. Suppose that there are only two goods, books and coffee. Wally gets utility from both books and coffee, but his indifference curves between them are concave rather than convex to the origin.
    a. Draw a set of indifference curves for Wally.
    b. What do these particular indifference curves tell you about Wally's marginal rate of substitution between books and coffee?
    c. What will Wally's utility-maximizing bundle look like? (*Hint*: Assume some level of income for Wally, and some prices for books and coffee; then draw a budget constraint.)
    d. Compare your answer to (b) to real-world behaviors. Does the comparison shed any light on why economists generally assume convex preferences?

17. Anthony spends his income on fishing lures (L) and guitar picks (G). Lures are priced at $2, while

a package of guitar picks cost $1. Assume that Anthony has $30 to spend and his utility function can be represented as $U(L,G) = L^{0.5}G^{0.5}$. For this utility function, $MU_L = 0.5L^{-0.5}G^{0.5}$ and $MU_G = 0.5L^{0.5}G^{-0.5}$.

a. What is the optimal number of lures and guitar picks for Anthony to purchase? How much utility does this combination bring him?

b. If the price of guitar picks doubles to $2, how much income must Anthony have to maintain the same level of utility?

18. A prominent online movie rental service mails rental DVDs to consumers. The service offers two pricing plans. Under the first plan, consumers face a flat $10 fee each month and can rent as many DVDs as they wish for free. Under the second plan, consumers can rent DVDs for an à la carte price of $2. Assume that a consumer has an income of $20 and uses it to purchase DVD rentals and a "composite good" that costs $1 per unit.

a. Draw a set of indifference curves for a representative consumer, putting DVD rentals on the horizontal axis.

b. Draw the budget constraint for the à la carte movie rental plan, making sure to indicate the horizontal and vertical intercepts. Find the consumer's optimum quantity of movie rentals. Label this point A.

c. Draw the budget constraint for the flat-fee plan, making sure to indicate the horizontal and vertical intercepts. Find the consumer's optimum quantity of movie rentals. Label this point B.

d. Under which plan does the consumer rent more movies?

e. Under which plan does the consumer end up with a lower marginal rate of substitution between movies and the composite good?

f. Under which plan is the consumer more likely to end up viewing *The Perils of Gwendoline in the Land of the Yik Yak*, widely acknowledged to be one of the worst movies of all time?

19. Suppose that doctors' visits cost $20, and the typical consumer has an income of $100. Consumers spend all of their incomes on doctors' visits and a "composite good" that costs $1 per unit.

a. Draw a graph that illustrates the consumer's budget constraint, putting doctor's visits on the horizontal axis. Make sure you indicate the horizontal and vertical intercepts.

Now, suppose the local government is considering two health plans. Under plan A, the government will give out vouchers worth 2 free visits to the doctor. Under plan B, the government will give out four 50% coupons to be used at the doctor's office.

b. Draw the new budget constraint the consumer faces under plan A.

c. Draw the new budget constraint the consumer faces under plan B.

d. For whom is the choice of plan A or plan B not likely to matter—those who are quite well, or those who are quite sick? (*Hint*: Superimpose some indifference curves on your budget constraints.)

e. Which plan would someone who is generally well be likely to choose, if offered a choice?

20. Elaine loves receiving flowers and has a particular fondness for daisies and daffodils. Her relative preferences for the two flowers are illustrated by the set of utility curves in the diagram. The number at the bottom of each indifference curve indicates the amount of happiness she receives from the various combinations of daisies and daffodils on the curve. Elaine's boyfriend Jerry would like to give her enough flowers to provide her with 200 units of happiness, but would like to do so as inexpensively as possible.

a. If daisies sell for $3 and daffodils sell for $6, what is the minimum amount Jerry will have to spend?

b. Suppose that Jerry fails to make it to the flower store on time, so he quickly tucks the money he was planning to spend on flowers [as you determined in part (a)] in a card and gives it to Elaine. If Elaine spends the money on flowers, how much happiness will she receive from her purchase?

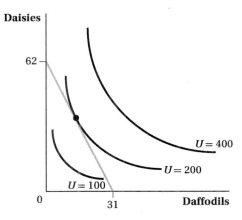

Chapter 4 Appendix:
The Calculus of Utility Maximization and Expenditure Minimization

In the chapters you've read so far, you've probably noticed that we use several different approaches when explaining microeconomic theories and applications. One method is mainly intuitive: Tell a story to illustrate an economic concept or discuss the logic of a model and its implications. This method of economic analysis goes back to Adam Smith and the invisible hand. A second method is the graphical approach. You only have to say "supply and demand" to conjure up a simple but powerful representation of a market. Finally, you've seen some simple mathematical models such as the algebraic representations of supply and demand curves in Chapter 2 and the consumer's budget constraint in Chapter 4. Each of these approaches provides a different window into understanding economic concepts.

Those of you who are familiar with calculus have yet another way to approach microeconomics. The tools of calculus are a natural fit with economics, and most economic models are formally derived using calculus. For some people (especially economists), it's easy to become so caught up in the math that the real economic ideas get lost. We don't want you to fall into that trap. That's why we present the calculus as a supplement to the intuition that we develop in the chapter. The calculus appendices provide an additional set of tools to examine the economic decisions and interactions discussed in the chapter. The logic of the models and the intuition from the chapter are still here in the calculus, only in another form.

So, don't think of the calculus that we explore in the appendices as a substitute for the logic, graphs, and algebra we use to explain microeconomics in the chapters. Instead, think of these techniques and the calculus as complements. As you learn more about microeconomics, you will find that each of these different approaches to understanding microeconomics may be more or less useful depending on the circumstances.

Consumer's Optimization Problem

One of the topics for which calculus provides additional insight is consumer behavior. Let's start by recalling the answer to the consumer's problem that we derived graphically in the chapter before seeing how we can get there using calculus. A consumer maximizes her utility $U(X,Y)$ when

$$MRS_{XY} = \frac{MU_X}{MU_Y} = \frac{P_X}{P_Y}$$

You may have noticed that to solve the optimization problem in the chapter, we just gave you the consumer's marginal utilities of goods X and Y—we didn't actually solve for them. This is because solving for the marginal utilities requires more than just the algebra and geometry we've relied on so far. Calculus allows us to derive the marginal utilities directly from the consumer's utility function. After determining the values of the marginal utilities, we can calculate the marginal rate of substitution. Calculus also provides us with another way to solve the consumer's problem—the Lagrangian—which yields some important insights into utility maximization.

The Marginal Rate of Substitution and Marginal Utility

In the chapter, we develop the connection between the marginal rate of substitution and marginal utility by thinking about how utility from each good changes as the consumer moves a little bit along one of her indifference curves. Here, we work in the opposite direction by starting with utility and seeing how we can use calculus to find the *MRS*. In this way, we examine what happens when we make small changes to the consumption bundle.

Take the consumer who has utility for goods X and Y, $U(X,Y)$. Any of the consumer's indifference curves show how the consumer trades off good X for good Y while keeping utility constant. We can choose any one of these indifference curves and call its level of utility $\overline{U}$:

$$U(X,Y) = \overline{U}$$

We are interested in how the utility from each good changes as we change the quantities of X and Y. So, we will totally differentiate the utility function, setting the total change in utility, dU, equal to zero because we are holding the level of utility constant:

$$dU = \frac{\partial U(X,Y)}{\partial X} dX + \frac{\partial U(X,Y)}{\partial Y} dY = 0$$

$$\frac{\partial U(X,Y)}{\partial X} dX = -\frac{\partial U(X,Y)}{\partial Y} dY$$

$$MU_X dX = -MU_Y dY$$

$$\frac{MU_X}{MU_Y} = -\frac{dY}{dX}$$

The right-hand side of this equation, $-dY/dX$, is the negative of the slope of the indifference curve or the marginal rate of substitution. Therefore,

$$MRS_{XY} = \frac{MU_X}{MU_Y}$$

Utility Maximization

The ratio of the marginal utilities is one piece of the puzzle—the preferences side. To finish the consumer's optimization, we need to relate consumer preferences to the prices of the goods and the consumer's income. Let's start by looking at a consumer whose utility function is the standard Cobb–Douglas functional form, $U(X,Y) = X^\alpha Y^{1-\alpha}$, where $0 < \alpha < 1$, and whose income is $I = P_X X + P_Y Y$. This consumer's utility-maximization problem is written formally as

$$\max_{X,Y} U(X, Y) = X^\alpha Y^{1-\alpha} \text{ subject to (s.t.) } I = P_X X + P_Y Y$$

This is known as a *constrained optimization problem*, in which $U(X,Y)$ is the objective function and $I = P_X X + P_Y Y$ is the constraint. In other words, how much utility the consumer can get is *constrained* by how much income she has to spend. In the chapter, we solved the same constrained optimization problem graphically with the objective of reaching the highest indifference curve while staying on the budget constraint.

If this were an unconstrained maximization problem, finding the optimal combination of variables would be fairly straightforward: Take the partial derivatives of the objective function with respect to each of the variables, set them equal to zero, and solve for the variables. But the presence of the budget constraint complicates the solution of the optimization problem (although without the constraint there wouldn't even be a finite solution to the utility-maximization problem because in an unconstrained world, the consumer consumes infinite amounts of each good).

There are two approaches to solving the consumer's utility-maximization problem using calculus. The first relies on what we already demonstrated in this chapter: At the optimum, the marginal rate of substitution equals the ratio of the two goods' prices. First, take the partial derivatives of the utility function with respect to each of the goods to derive the marginal utilities:

$$MU_X = \frac{\partial U(X,Y)}{\partial X} = \frac{\partial(X^\alpha Y^{1-\alpha})}{\partial X} = \alpha X^{\alpha-1} Y^{1-\alpha}$$

$$MU_Y = \frac{\partial U(X,Y)}{\partial Y} = \frac{\partial(X^\alpha Y^{1-\alpha})}{\partial Y} = (1-\alpha) X^\alpha Y^{-\alpha}$$

Next, use the relationship between the marginal utilities and the marginal rate of substitution to solve for MRS_{XY} and simplify the expression:

$$MRS_{XY} = \frac{MU_X}{MU_Y} = \frac{\alpha X^{\alpha-1} Y^{1-\alpha}}{(1-\alpha) X^\alpha Y^{-\alpha}} = \frac{\alpha}{(1-\alpha)} \frac{Y}{X}$$

Find Y as a function of X by setting MRS_{XY} equal to the ratio of the prices:

$$\frac{\alpha}{(1-\alpha)} \frac{Y}{X} = \frac{P_X}{P_Y}$$

$$Y = \frac{(1-\alpha)P_X}{\alpha P_Y} X, \text{ where } \frac{(1-\alpha)P_X}{\alpha P_Y} \text{ is a constant}$$

Now that we have the optimal relationship between Y and X, substitute the expression for Y into the budget constraint to solve for the optimal consumption bundle:

$$I = P_X X + P_Y \left[\frac{(1-\alpha)P_X}{\alpha P_Y} X \right]$$

$$I = P_X X \left[1 + \frac{(1-\alpha)}{\alpha} \right] = P_X X \left[\frac{\alpha}{\alpha} + \frac{(1-\alpha)}{\alpha} \right] = \frac{P_X}{\alpha} X$$

$$X^* = \frac{\alpha I}{P_X}$$

$$Y^* = \frac{(1-\alpha)P_X}{\alpha P_Y} \left(\frac{\alpha I}{P_X} \right) = \frac{(1-\alpha)I}{P_Y}$$

You can see that the resulting optimal bundle $\left(\frac{\alpha I}{P_X}, \frac{(1-\alpha)I}{P_Y} \right)$ is dependent on all three pieces of the consumer's problem: the consumer's relative preferences $(\alpha, 1-\alpha)$, the consumer's income I, and the goods' prices (P_X, P_Y).

Utility Maximization Using the Lagrangian

The first approach to finding the optimal consumption bundle is precisely the method we used in the chapter; the only difference is that we used calculus to derive the marginal utilities and then solved for the marginal rate of substitution. A second approach introduces something known as the Lagrange multiplier, or λ. The Lagrangian is a technique for transforming a constrained optimization problem into an unconstrained problem by combining the objective function and the constraint into one equation. λ is a variable that multiplies the constraint.

Suppose, for example, that the objective function is $f(x,y)$ and the constraint is $g(x,y) = 0$. The Lagrangian equation is

$$\mathcal{L}(x,y,\lambda) = f(x,y) + \lambda[g(x,y)]$$

Now maximize the equation by taking the partial derivatives of the equation with respect to x, y, and λ, and set them equal to zero. Partial derivatives in this form are known as first-order conditions, or FOC:

$$\frac{\partial \mathcal{L}}{\partial x} = \frac{\partial f(x,y)}{\partial x} - \lambda \frac{\partial g(x,y)}{\partial x} = 0$$

$$\frac{\partial \mathcal{L}}{\partial y} = \frac{\partial f(x,y)}{\partial y} - \lambda \frac{\partial g(x,y)}{\partial y} = 0$$

$$\frac{\partial \mathcal{L}}{\partial \lambda} = g(x,y) = 0$$

So, we have three equations and three unknowns and can solve the system of equations. Note that the third first-order condition is simply the constraint.

Let's see how the Lagrangian can be applied to our consumer facing the utility-maximization problem:

$$\max_{X,Y} U(X,Y) = X^{\alpha} Y^{1-\alpha} \text{ s.t. } I - (P_X X + P_Y Y) = 0$$

(Notice that we wrote the budget constraint so that it is equal to zero—this is important for how we set up the Lagrangian.) This equation can be rewritten in Lagrangian form as

$$\max_{X,Y,\lambda} \mathcal{L} = X^{\alpha} Y^{1-\alpha} + \lambda(I - P_X X - P_Y Y)$$

Take the first-order conditions (FOCs):

$$\frac{\partial \mathcal{L}}{\partial X} = \alpha X^{\alpha-1} Y^{1-\alpha} - \lambda P_X = 0$$

$$\frac{\partial \mathcal{L}}{\partial Y} = (1-\alpha) X^{\alpha} Y^{-\alpha} - \lambda P_Y = 0$$

$$\frac{\partial \mathcal{L}}{\partial \lambda} = I - P_X X - P_Y Y = 0$$

Embedded in these three first-order conditions are the same three pieces of information we've seen before: the marginal utilities of X and Y, the goods' prices, and the consumer's income.

The Lagrange multiplier λ is in the first two first-order conditions. So, solve each of these equations for λ:

$$\lambda = \frac{\alpha X^{\alpha-1} Y^{1-\alpha}}{P_X} = \frac{(1-\alpha) X^{\alpha} Y^{-\alpha}}{P_Y}$$

How can we interpret this Lagrange multiplier? First, recognize that the numerators are the marginal utilities of X and Y. In other words, at the optimum, $\lambda = \frac{MU_X}{P_X} = \frac{MU_Y}{P_Y}$. Therefore, λ is the exchange rate between utility and income—an additional dollar of income allows the consumer to purchase additional goods that generate λ more units of utility. We can also see this in the Lagrangian: If income increases by \$1, maximum utility increases by λ units. In other words, λ measures the marginal utility of income. For example, let's say that λ is 0.5. Then, if you gain \$1 more in income, you'll gain 0.5 units of utility.

Note that this expression for λ is the optimization condition in terms of the consumer's marginal utility per dollar spent that we derived in the chapter. We can rearrange this to get exactly what we showed graphically in the text—that the marginal rate of substitution equals the ratio of the prices:

$$\frac{MU_X}{MU_Y} = MRS_{XY} = \frac{P_X}{P_Y}$$

We can then solve for (X^*, Y^*) exactly as we did in the first approach, starting by finding Y as a function of X using the equality from the first two conditions:

$$\frac{\alpha X^{\alpha - 1} Y^{1 - \alpha}}{P_X} = \frac{(1 - \alpha) X^\alpha Y^{-\alpha}}{P_Y}$$

$$\frac{Y^{1 - \alpha}}{Y^{-\alpha}} = \frac{(1 - \alpha) P_X}{\alpha P_Y} \frac{X^\alpha}{X^{(\alpha - 1)}}$$

$$Y = \frac{(1 - \alpha) P_X}{\alpha P_Y} X$$

Using the last first-order condition, we can plug this value for Y into the budget constraint:

$$I - P_X X - P_Y Y = 0$$

$$I = P_X X + P_Y \frac{(1 - \alpha) P_X}{\alpha P_Y} X$$

$$I = P_X X \left[1 + \frac{(1 - \alpha)}{\alpha} \right]$$

$$I = P_X X \left[\frac{\alpha}{\alpha} + \frac{(1 - \alpha)}{\alpha} \right]$$

$$I = \frac{P_X}{\alpha} X$$

$$X^* = \frac{\alpha I}{P_X}$$

$$Y^* = \frac{(1 - \alpha) P_X}{\alpha P_Y} \left(\frac{\alpha I}{P_X} \right) = \frac{(1 - \alpha) I}{P_Y}$$

4A.1 figure it out

Let's revisit Figure It Out 4.4. Antonio gets utility from burgers (B) and fries (F) in the form

$$U(B, F) = \sqrt{BF} = B^{0.5} F^{0.5}$$

His income is $20, the price of burgers is $5, and the price of fries is $2.

Find Antonio's optimal consumption bundle.

Solution:

To find the optimal consumption bundle, we need to solve the consumer's utility-maximization problem:

$$\max_{B, F} U = B^{0.5} F^{0.5} \text{ s.t. } 20 = 5B + 2F$$

The solution in the chapter uses the approach in which we solve for the MRS_{BF} from the marginal utilities. If instead we use the Lagrangian, we begin by writing Antonio's constrained optimization problem and then solve for the first-order conditions:

$$\max_{B, F, \lambda} \mathcal{L} = B^{0.5} F^{0.5} + \lambda(20 - 5B - 2F)$$

FOC:

$$\frac{\partial \mathcal{L}}{\partial B} = 0.5 B^{-0.5} F^{0.5} - 5\lambda = 0$$

$$\frac{\partial \mathcal{L}}{\partial F} = 0.5 B^{0.5} F^{-0.5} - 2\lambda = 0$$

$$\frac{\partial \mathcal{L}}{\partial \lambda} = 20 - 5B - 2F = 0$$

Use the first two conditions to solve for λ:

$$0.5 B^{-0.5} F^{0.5} = 5\lambda$$

$$\lambda = 0.1 B^{-0.5} F^{0.5}$$

$$0.5 B^{0.5} F^{-0.5} = 2\lambda$$

$$\lambda = 0.25 B^{0.5} F^{-0.5}$$

Set the two expressions for λ equal to each other and solve for F as a function of B:

$$\lambda = 0.1 B^{-0.5} F^{0.5} = 0.25 B^{0.5} F^{-0.5}$$

$$0.1 B^{-0.5} F^{0.5} = 0.25 B^{0.5} F^{-0.5}$$

$$0.1 F^{0.5} F^{0.5} = 0.25 B^{0.5} B^{0.5}$$

$$F = (10)0.25B = 2.5B$$

So, for every order of fries Antonio consumes at the optimum, he will consume 2.5 burgers. Substitute $F = 2.5B$ into the third condition (the consumer's budget constraint) and solve for the optimal bundle (B^*, F^*):

$$20 = 5B + 2F$$
$$20 = 5B + 2(2.5B)$$
$$20 = 10B$$
$$B^* = 2 \text{ burgers}$$
$$F^* = 2.5B = 2.5(2) = 5 \text{ orders of fries}$$

This is where we stopped when we solved Antonio's constrained optimization problem using the first approach we presented in this appendix. But using the Lagrangian, we can also solve for one more variable: the marginal value of Antonio's income, λ, when Antonio is maximizing his utility.

$$\lambda = 0.1B^{-0.5}F^{0.5} = 0.1(2)^{-0.5}5^{0.5} \approx 0.16$$

Therefore, Antonio's utility increases by 0.16 units of utility for every extra dollar of income he has.

Expenditure Minimization

As we saw in the chapter, utility maximization—where you take income as given and find the combination of goods that will give you the greatest utility—is only one way to look at the consumer's optimization problem. Another is expenditure minimization, in which you start with a level of utility and find the cheapest bundle that achieves that utility level. In many ways, expenditure minimization is less intuitive—in real life, you probably do face a set income, but no contract you sign will ever specify your utility. But, ultimately, expenditure minimization leads to the same answer. What is more, the expenditure-minimization technique is extremely useful in the appendices for Chapters 5 and 7. In particular, this technique makes a lot more sense in the context of the producer's cost-minimization problem in Chapter 7.

Let's demonstrate the equivalence of utility maximization and expenditure minimization using Antonio's utility function from the Figure It Out and the Lagrangian method (the first approach is identical to that for utility maximization except that you plug into the utility constraint instead of the budget constraint in the last step). We write out Antonio's expenditure-minimization problem given a constant utility of $\sqrt{10}$ or $10^{0.5}$, the utility at his optimal consumption bundle from the utility-maximization problem above:

$$\min_{B,F} I = 5B + 2F \text{ s.t. } 10^{0.5} = B^{0.5}F^{0.5}$$

or

$$\min_{B,F,\lambda} \mathcal{L} = 5B + 2F + \lambda(10^{0.5} - B^{0.5}F^{0.5})$$

As before, solve for the first-order conditions:

$$\frac{\partial \mathcal{L}}{\partial B} = 5 - \lambda 0.5B^{-0.5}F^{0.5} = 0$$

$$\frac{\partial \mathcal{L}}{\partial F} = 2 - \lambda 0.5B^{0.5}F^{-0.5} = 0$$

$$\frac{\partial \mathcal{L}}{\partial \lambda} = 10^{0.5} - B^{0.5}F^{0.5} = 0$$

Then solve for λ in the first two conditions:

$$\lambda 0.5B^{-0.5}F^{0.5} = 5$$
$$\lambda = 10B^{0.5}F^{-0.5}$$

$$\lambda 0.5B^{0.5}F^{-0.5} = 2$$
$$\lambda = 4B^{-0.5}F^{0.5}$$

Set the two expressions for λ equal to each other and solve for F as a function of B:

$$\lambda = 4B^{-0.5}F^{0.5} = 10B^{0.5}F^{-0.5}$$

$$4F^{0.5}F^{0.5} = 10B^{0.5}B^{0.5}$$

$$F = 2.5B$$

Now substitute F as a function of B into the utility constraint:

$$10^{0.5} = B^{0.5}F^{0.5} = B^{0.5}(2.5B)^{0.5} = (2.5)^{0.5}B^{0.5}B^{0.5}$$

$$B^{*} = \left(\frac{10}{2.5}\right)^{0.5} = 4^{0.5} = 2$$

$$F^{*} = (2.5)2 = 5$$

This optimal bundle of goods costs Antonio

$$5B^{*} + 2F^{*} = 5(2) + 2(5) = \$20$$

the minimum expenditure needed to achieve $10^{0.5}$ units of utility.

Expenditure minimization is a good check of our cost-minimization problem because it should yield the same results. In this case, as with utility maximization, Antonio purchases 2 burgers and 5 orders of fries for a cost of $20 and a total utility of $10^{0.5}$.

Problems

1. For the following utility functions,
   - Find the marginal utility of each good.
   - Determine whether the marginal utility decreases as consumption of each good increases (i.e., does the utility function exhibit diminishing marginal utility in each good?).
   - Find the marginal rate of substitution.
   - Discuss how MRS_{XY} changes as the consumer substitutes X for Y along an indifference curve.
   - Derive the equation for the indifference curve where utility is equal to a value of 100.
   - Graph the indifference curve where utility is equal to a value of 100.
   a. $U(X,Y) = 5X + 2Y$
   b. $U(X,Y) = X^{0.33}Y^{0.67}$
   c. $U(X,Y) = 10X^{0.5} + 5Y$

2. Suppose that Maggie cares only about chai and bagels. Her utility function is $U = CB$, where C is the number of cups of chai she drinks in a day, and B is the number of bagels she eats in a day. The price of chai is $3, and the price of bagels is $1.50. Maggie has $6 to spend per day on chai and bagels.
   a. What is Maggie's objective function?
   b. What is Maggie's constraint?
   c. Write a statement of Maggie's constrained optimization problem.
   d. Solve Maggie's constrained optimization problem using a Lagrangian.

3. Suppose that there are two goods (X and Y). The price of X is $2 per unit, and the price of Y is $1 per unit. There are two consumers (A and B). The utility functions for the consumers are

$$U_A(X,Y) = X^{0.5}Y^{0.5}$$

$$U_B(X,Y) = X^{0.8}Y^{0.2}$$

Consumer A has an income of $100, and Consumer B has an income of $300.
   a. Use Lagrangians to solve the constrained utility-maximization problems for Consumer A and Consumer B.
   b. Calculate the marginal rate of substitution for each consumer at his or her optimal consumption bundles.
   c. Suppose that there is another consumer (let's call her C). You don't know anything about her utility function or her income. All you know is that she consumes both goods. What do you know about C's marginal rate of substitution at her optimal consumption bundle? Why?

4. Katie likes to paint and sit in the sun. Her utility function is $U(P,S) = 3PS + 6P$, where P is the number of paint brushes and S is the number of straw hats. The price of a paint brush is $1 and the price of a straw hat is $5. Katie has $50 to spend on paint brushes and straw hats.

a. Solve Katie's utility-maximization problem using a Lagrangian.
b. How much does Katie's utility increase if she receives an extra dollar to spend on paint brushes and straw hats?

5. Suppose that a consumer's utility function for two goods (X and Y) is

$$U(X,Y) = 10X^{0.5} + 2Y$$

The price of good X is $5 per unit and the price of good Y is $10 per unit. Suppose that the consumer must have 80 units of utility and wants to achieve this level of utility with the lowest possible expenditure.

a. Write a statement of the constrained optimization problem.
b. Use a Lagrangian to solve the expenditure-minimization problem.

Individual and Market Demand

5

n Chapter 4, we learned the basics of how consumers make choices: Preferences (embodied in the consumer's utility function and its associated indifference curves) and income and market prices (both embodied in the consumer's budget constraint) combine to pin down the consumer's utility-maximizing bundle of goods. Variations in preferences are reflected in the shapes of indifference curves, and variations in income and prices are reflected in the location and slope of the budget constraint.

Now that we've built our consumer choice framework, we can show how it forms the basis of the demand curves in Chapters 2 and 3. We'll see exactly where demand curves come from, when they shift, and how to add up individual consumers' demands to get market demand curves.

The importance of a deeper understanding of the determinants of demand is clear: Demand is half the story in any market. Knowing what drives consumer demand is crucial to understanding a number of issues, including:

- why shifts in tastes affect prices,

- the benefits that products offer consumers,

income effect
The change in a consumer's consumption choices that results from a change in the purchasing power of the consumer's income.

■ what happens to purchase patterns as consumers (or even entire countries) become wealthier,

■ how changes in the price of one good affect the demand for other goods, and

■ what factors determine consumers' responses to price changes.

We start this chapter by looking at what happens to a consumer's choices when prices stay fixed and his income goes up or down. This analysis involves finding the consumer's optimal bundle not just once for a particular income level (as we did in Chapter 4), but over and over for every possible amount of income.

Next, we determine how the bundle a given consumer chooses changes as the price of one good in the bundle changes, holding constant income and the price of the other good. Once again, this analysis involves finding the utility-maximizing optimal consumption bundle not just once, but for every possible price of the good in the bundle. By analyzing how the quantity desired of a good changes as the price of that good changes (holding everything else constant), we can map out an individual consumer's demand curve for that good. We'll see that consumers' responses to price changes have two components: the change in relative prices caused by the price change and the change in the purchasing power of the consumer's income caused by the price change.

We then see how changes in the price of *other* goods affect the consumer's decision about how much of a particular good to consume. This effect can increase or decrease the quantity of a good demanded, depending on whether one good is a substitute for the other or if the two goods are consumed together.

After we explore all these features of an *individual's* choices, we show how total *market* demand responds to the same changes. Once this is done, we'll have a full understanding of what determines the same market demand that we took as given in Chapters 2 and 3.

5.1 How Income Changes Affect an Individual's Consumption Choices

In Section 4.3, we learned how changes in income affect the position of a consumer's budget constraint. Lower incomes shift the constraint toward the origin; higher incomes shift it out. In this section, we look at how a change in income affects a consumer's utility-maximizing consumption decisions. This is known as the **income effect**. To isolate this effect, we hold everything else constant during our analysis. Specifically, we assume that the consumer's preferences (reflected in the utility function and its associated indifference curves) and the prices of the goods stay the same.

Figure 5.1 shows the effect of an increase in income on consumption for Evan, a consumer who allocates his income between vacations and fancy gourmet restaurant meals. Initially, Evan's budget constraint is BC_1 and the utility-maximizing consumption bundle is at point A, where indifference curve U_1 is tangent to BC_1. If the prices of vacations and gourmet meals remain unchanged, an increase in Evan's income means that he can afford more of both goods. As a result, the increase in income induces a parallel, outward shift in the budget constraint from BC_1 to BC_2. Note that, because we hold prices fixed, the slope of the budget constraint (the ratio of the goods' prices) remains fixed. The new optimal consumption bundle at this higher income level is B, the point where indifference curve U_2 is tangent to BC_2.

Because U_2 shows bundles of goods that offer a higher utility level than those on U_1, the increase in income allows Evan to achieve a higher utility level. Note that when we analyze the effect of changes in income on consumer behavior, we hold preferences (as well as prices) constant. Thus, indifference curve U_2 does not appear because of some income-driven shift in preferences. U_2 was always there even when Evan's income was lower. At the lower income, however, point B and all other bundles on U_2 (and any other higher indifference curves) were infeasible because Evan could not afford them.

Figure 5.1 | **A Consumer's Response to an Increase in Income When Both Goods Are Normal**

Evan allocates his income between two normal goods, vacations and gourmet restaurant meals. His initial budget constraint BC_1 is tangent to the utility curve U_1 at the optimal consumption bundle A. An increase in Evan's income is represented by the outward parallel shift of BC_1 to BC_2. Since the prices of the goods are unchanged, Evan can now afford to buy more vacations and meals, and his new utility-maximizing bundle is B, where utility curve U_2 is tangent to BC_2. At bundle B, Evan's consumption of vacations and restaurant meals rises from Q_v to Q'_v and Q_m to Q'_m, respectively.

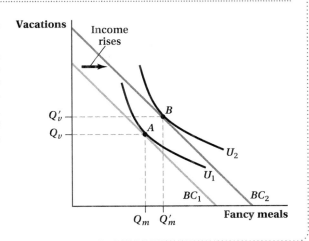

Normal and Inferior Goods

Notice how the new optimum in Figure 5.1 involves higher levels of consumption for both goods. The number of vacations Evan takes rises from Q_v to Q'_v, and the number of gourmet meals increases from Q_m to Q'_m. This result isn't that surprising; Evan was spending money on both vacations and gourmet meals before his income went up, so we might expect that he'd spend some of his extra income on both goods. Economists call a good whose consumption rises when income rises—that is, a good for which the income effect is positive—a **normal good.** Vacations and gourmet meals are normal goods for Evan. As "normal" suggests, most goods have positive income effects.

It is possible that an increase in income can lead to a consumer optimally consuming a smaller quantity of a good. As we indicated in Chapter 2, economists refer to such goods as **inferior goods.** Figure 5.2 presents an example in which one of the goods is

normal good
A good for which consumption rises when income rises.

inferior good
A good for which consumption decreases when income rises.

Figure 5.2 | **A Consumer's Response to an Increase in Income When One Good Is Inferior**

When a good is inferior, an increase in a consumer's income decreases the consumer's consumption of that good. Here, mac and cheese is an inferior good, while steak is a normal good. When the consumer's income increases, shifting the budget constraint outward from BC_1 to BC_2, she consumes less mac and cheese and more steak at the optimal consumption bundle. From initial optimal consumption bundle A to her new optimal consumption bundle B, the quantity of mac and cheese consumed decreases from Q_{mac} to Q'_{mac} while her consumption of the normal good steak increases from Q_s to Q'_s.

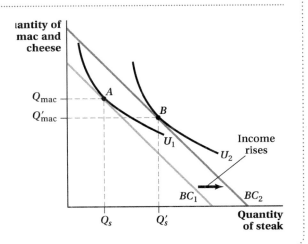

inferior. An increase in the consumer's income from BC_1 to BC_2 leads to more steak being consumed, but less macaroni and cheese. Note that it isn't just that the quantity of mac and cheese *relative to* the quantity of steak falls. This change can happen even when both goods are normal (i.e., they both rise, but steak rises more). Instead, it is the *absolute* quantity of macaroni and cheese consumed that drops in the move from A to B, because Q'_{mac} is less than Q_{mac}. Note also that this drop is optimal from the consumer's perspective—B is her utility-maximizing bundle given her budget constraint BC_2, and this bundle offers a higher utility level than A because indifference curve U_2 represents a higher utility level than U_1. The difference is the shape of the indifference curves for these goods (which comes from the utility function).

What kind of goods tend to be inferior? Usually, they are goods that are perceived to be low-quality or otherwise undesirable. Examples might include generic cereal brands, secondhand clothing, nights spent in youth hostels, and Spam. When we say Spam, we mean the kind you buy in the grocery store, not the kind you get via e-mail. Junk e-mail probably isn't a good at all, but rather a "bad."

We do know that *every* good can't be inferior, however. If a consumer were to consume a smaller quantity of everything when his income rises, he wouldn't be spending all his new, higher income. This outcome would be inconsistent with utility maximization, which states that a consumer always ends up buying a bundle on his budget constraint. (Remember there is no saving in this model.)

Whether the effect of an income change on a good's consumption is positive (consumption increases) or negative (consumption decreases) can often vary with the level of income. (We look at some of these special cases later in the chapter.) For instance, a good such as a used car is likely to be a normal good at low levels of income, and an inferior good at high levels of income. When someone's income is very low, owning a used car is prohibitively expensive and riding a bike or taking public transportation is necessary. As income increases from such low levels, a used car becomes increasingly likely to be purchased, making it a normal good. But once someone becomes rich enough, used cars are supplanted by new cars and his consumption of used cars falls. Over that higher income range, the used car is an inferior good.

Income Elasticities and Types of Goods

income elasticity
The percentage change in the quantity consumed of a good in response to a 1% change in income.

We've discussed how the income effect can be positive (as with normal goods) or negative (as with inferior goods). We can make further distinctions between types of goods by looking not just at the sign of the income effect, but at the **income elasticity** as well, which we discussed in Chapter 2. Remember that the income elasticity measures the *percentage* change in the quantity consumed of a good in response to a given *percentage* change in income. Formally, the income elasticity is

$$E_I^D = \frac{\%\Delta Q}{\%\Delta I} = \frac{\Delta Q/Q}{\Delta I/I} = \frac{\Delta Q}{\Delta I}\frac{I}{Q}$$

where Q is the quantity of the good consumed (ΔQ is the change in quantity), and I is income (ΔI is the change in income). As we noted in our earlier discussion, income elasticity is like the price elasticity of demand, except that we are now considering the responsiveness of consumption to income changes rather than to price changes.

The first ratio in the income elasticity definition is the income effect shown in the equations above: $\Delta Q/\Delta I$, the change in quantity consumed in response to a change in income. Therefore, the sign of the income elasticity is the same as the sign of the income effect. For normal goods, $\Delta Q/\Delta I > 0$, and the income elasticity is positive. For inferior goods, $\Delta Q/\Delta I < 0$, and the income elasticity is negative.

Within the class of normal goods, economists occasionally make a further distinction. The quantities of goods with an income elasticity between zero and 1 (sometimes called **necessity goods**) rise with income, but at a slower rate. Because prices are held constant when measuring income elasticities, the slower-than-income quantity growth implies the *share* of a consumer's budget devoted to the good *falls* as income grows. Many normal goods fit into this category, especially things that just about everyone uses or needs, like toothpaste, salt, socks, and electricity. Someone who earns $1 million a year may well consume more of these goods (or more expensive varieties) than an aspiring artist who earns $10,000 annually, but the millionaire, whose income is 100 times greater than the artist's, is unlikely to spend 100 times more on toothpaste (or salt, or socks . . .) than the artist spends.

necessity good
A normal good for which income elasticity is between zero and 1.

Luxury goods have an income elasticity greater than 1. Because their quantities consumed grow faster than income does, these goods account for an increasing fraction of the consumer's expenditure as income rises. Luxury goods tend to be those that one does not need to live, but that improve the quality of life: first-class airline tickets, jewelry, fancy coffee drinks, beach homes, and so on.

luxury good
A good with an income elasticity greater than 1.

The Income Expansion Path

Imagine repeating the analysis in the previous section for every possible income level. That is, for a given set of prices and a particular set of preferences, we can find the utility-maximizing bundle for every possible budget constraint, where each constraint corresponds to a different income level. Those optimal bundles will be located wherever an indifference curve is tangent to a budget line. In both of the examples above, they'll include bundles A and B.

Figure 5.3 demonstrates an example of such an exercise. In the figure, Meredith allocates her income between bus rides and bottled water. Points A, B, C, D, and E are the optimal consumption bundles at five different income levels that correspond to the budget constraints shown. Point A is Meredith's utility-maximizing bundle for the lowest of the five income levels, point B is the bundle for the second-lowest income, and so on. Note that the indifference curves themselves come from the individual's utility function. We have chosen various shapes here just to illustrate that these points can move around in different ways.

Figure 5.3   The Income Expansion Path

Meredith's income expansion path connects all of the optimal bundles of bottled water and bus rides for each income level. Points A, B, C, D, and E are optimal consumption bundles associated with budget constraints BC_1 through BC_5. Where both bottled water and bus rides are normal goods, the income expansion path is upward-sloping. At incomes higher than that shown at the budget constraint BC_4 and to the right of bundle D, bus rides become inferior goods, and the income expansion path slopes downward.

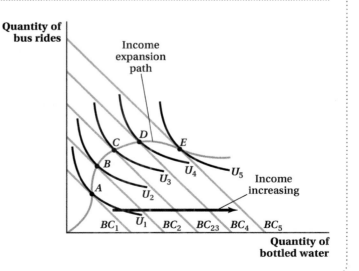

income expansion path
A curve that connects a consumer's optimal bundles at each income level.

If we draw a line connecting all the optimal bundles (the five here plus all the others for budget constraints we don't show in the figure), it would trace out a curve known as the **income expansion path**. This curve always starts at the origin because when income is zero, the consumption of both goods must also be zero. We've drawn in Meredith's income expansion path for bus rides and bottled water in Figure 5.3.

When both goods are normal goods, the income expansion path will be positively sloped because consumption of both goods rises when income does. If the slope of the income expansion path is negative, then the quantity consumed of one of the goods falls with income while the other rises. The good whose quantity falls is therefore inferior. Remember that whether a given good is normal or inferior can depend on the consumer's income level. In the example in Figure 5.3, for example, both bus rides and bottled water are normal goods at incomes up to the level corresponding to the budget constraint containing bundle D. As income rises above that and the budget constraint continues to shift out, the income expansion path begins to curve downward. This outcome means that bus rides become an inferior good as Meredith's income rises beyond that level. We can also see from the income expansion path that bottled water is never inferior, because the path never curves back to the left. When there are only two goods, it's impossible for both goods to be inferior at a given income level. If they were both inferior, an increase in income would actually lead to lower expenditure on both goods, meaning that the consumer wouldn't be spending all of her income.

The Engel Curve

The income expansion path is a useful tool for examining how consumer behavior changes in response to changes in income, but it has two important weaknesses. First, because we have only two axes, we can only look at two goods at a time. Second, although we can easily see the consumption quantities of each good, we can't see directly the income level that a particular point on the curve corresponds to. The income level equals the sum of the quantities consumed of each good (which are easily seen in the figure) multiplied by their respective prices (which aren't easily seen). The basic problem is that when we talk about consumption and income, we care about three numbers—the quantities of each of the two goods and income—but we have only two dimensions on the graph in which to see them.

A better way to see how the quantity consumed of one good varies with income (as opposed to how the relative quantities of the two goods vary) is to take the information conveyed by the income expansion path and plot it on a graph with income on the vertical axis and the quantity of the good in question on the horizontal axis. Panel a of Figure 5.4 illustrates this for the relationship between income and the quantity of bus rides from our example in Figure 5.3. The five points mapped in panel a of Figure 5.4 are the same five consumption bundles represented by points A, B, C, D, and E in Figure 5.3; the only difference between the figures is in the variables measured by the axes.

Engel curve
A curve that shows the relationship between the quantity of a good consumed and a consumer's income.

The lines traced out in Figure 5.4 are known as **Engel curves,** named for the nineteenth-century German economist Ernst Engel who first presented the data in this manner. Engel curves tell you the quantities of goods—bus rides and bottled water, in this case—that are consumed at each income level. If the Engel curve has a positive slope, the good is a normal good at that income level. If the Engel curve has a negative slope, the good is an inferior good at that income. In Figure 5.4a, bus rides are initially a normal good, but become inferior after bundle D, just as we saw in Figure 5.3. In panel b, bottled water is a normal good at all income levels and the Engel curve is always positively sloped.

Whether the income expansion path or Engel curves are more useful for understanding the effect of income on consumption choices depends on the particular question we are trying to answer. If we care about how the relative quantities of the two goods change with income, the income expansion path is more useful because it shows both quantities at the same time. On the other hand, if we want to investigate the impact

Figure 5.4 : An Engel Curve Shows How Consumption Varies with Income

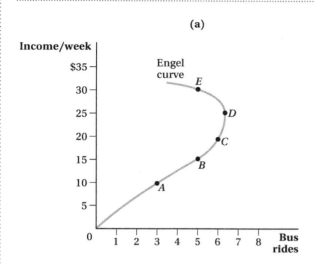

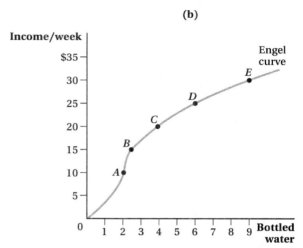

(a) In contrast to an income expansion path, an Engel curve compares the consumption of a single good to the consumer's income. As Meredith's income increases from $10/week to $25/week, her consumption of bus rides increases from 3 to a little over 6 bus rides. At income levels above $25/week, bus rides are inferior goods, and the number of bus rides she takes decreases.

(b) Bottled water is a normal good across all income levels shown here. At an income of $10/week at point A, Meredith consumes 2 bottles of water. At point E, Meredith's income is $30/week, and the number of bottles of water she buys increases to 9 per week.

of income changes on the consumption of one particular good, the Engel curve isolates this relationship more clearly. The most important thing to remember is that the two curves contain the same information displayed in different ways due to the limitations imposed by having only two axes.

 application

Engel Curves and House Sizes

Houses in the United States have been getting larger for several decades. In 1950 newly built houses had an average of about 1,000 square feet (93 square meters) of floor area, a little less than one-fourth the size of a basketball court. By 2008 the average new house was well over twice as large, at 2,519 square feet. Recent debates about "McMansions" and tear-downs, still present even after the housing crash, have highlighted this trend and how it has affected discussions of public policies like zoning laws.

Explanations for this trend vary. Some have suggested homeowners' utility functions have changed in a way that favors more space. But another (not mutually exclusive) possibility is that space is a normal good, so homeowners demand more space as they become wealthier. It isn't necessary for homeowners' utility functions to have changed to see such effects. It could just be that an increase in income has moved them to a different part of their utility function where they demand more space.

The historical patterns are consistent with those that would arise from an income effect at work. Figure 5.5 plots the average size of newly built homes (in square feet) and average inflation-adjusted household income (in thousands of dollars) from 1975 to 2009. Both house

Time & Life Pictures/Getty Images

Then

Brendel/Wikimedia Commons

Now

sizes and income trended upward through this period. The sizes of the changes in these variables were similar too; for every 10% increase in average income, average house size rose by about 11%.[1]

These trends are consistent with income growth driving homeowners to buy larger homes. We should be careful in leaping to this interpretation, though. Many things can trend over time even though they aren't closely related. (For example, population also increased over the period, but it's hard to argue that simply having more people around makes everyone want larger homes.) And even if income effects matter here, other factors that make larger homes more common, such as falling construction costs, could also be changing over time. It would therefore be nice to have additional evidence about the income–house size relationship that doesn't involve simple trends over time.

Such additional evidence does exist. The American Housing Survey (AHS) is conducted every two years and contains information on housing and demographics for thousands of households. Comparing home sizes to income levels across individual households at a given moment in time should complement our analysis of the average trends above.

We fit a curve relating home size and annual household income in the 2007 survey data (a survey containing about 35,000 households) in Figure 5.6. This is very similar to an Engel curve for home size: It shows how much a household's purchases of a good (square feet) varies with its income.[2]

Figure 5.5   **Average New House Size and Household Income in the United States, 1975–2009**

House sizes and income trended upward between 1975 and 2009, increasing at almost the same rate.

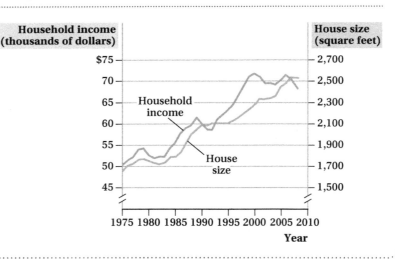

---

[1] These data are collected from various U.S. Census Bureau publications.

[2] It's not exactly an Engel curve for a few reasons. For one, we aren't able to hold constant everything else about households' choices. To read Figure 5.6 as an Engel curve, we're assuming that every household is the same except for its income level. In reality, households might differ in their preferences and size as well as incomes. Furthermore, different households might face various prices for square footage depending on where they live. If these prices are related to income levels (say, because people who live in urban areas both have higher average incomes and face higher house prices per square foot), this could mix up price and income effects. Nevertheless, the relationship in Figure 5.6 is probably close to the true Engel curve for square footage.

Figure 5.6 : An Engel Curve for House Size in the United States

The Engel curve for housing slopes upward, indicating that housing is a normal good. However, for incomes between approximately $175,000 and $250,000 per year, house size does not change much as income grows.

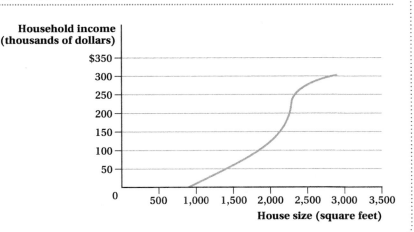

We can see that this Engel curve always slopes up. That is, based on these data, house size is always a normal good. However, there is a considerable income range—from about $175,000 to $250,000 a year—where the size of the income effect is fairly small and home size does not change much as income grows. It's also interesting to compare the average slope of this Engel curve to the size-income correlation we saw in the time trend data. In the time trends in Figure 5.5, 10% income growth was tied to an 11% increase in house size. This relationship is smaller when we look across households in Figure 5.6: People with 10% more income have houses that are around 2% larger. One reason why the relationship across people might be smaller than across time is that the cross section of people includes all houses, not just newly built ones. If home sizes are trending upward over time (which they did from 1950 to 2005), and not just the highest income households are buying new houses, this will reduce the correlation between size and income in the cross section because some higher-income households will be in older, smaller houses. It could also be that factors in addition to income growth (such as preferences) are driving the trends of the past several decades. Nevertheless, it's clear from both sets of data that income changes are strongly related to the demand for house size. ▪

5.1 figure it out

Annika spends all of her income on golf and pancakes. Greens fees at a local golf course are $10 per round. Pancake mix is $2 per box. When Annika's income is $100 per week, she buys 5 boxes of pancake mix and 9 rounds of golf. When Annika's income rises to $120 per week, she buys 10 boxes of pancake mix and 10 rounds of golf. Based on these figures, determine whether each of the following statements is true or false, and briefly explain your reasoning.

a. Golf is a normal good, and pancake mix is an inferior good.

b. Golf is a luxury good.

c. Pancakes are a luxury good.

Solution:

a. A normal good is one of which a consumer buys more when income rises. An inferior good is a good for which consumption falls when income rises. When Annika's income rises, she purchases more pancake mix and more rounds of golf. This means that both goods are normal goods for Annika. Therefore, the statement is *false*.

b. A luxury good has an income elasticity greater than 1. The income elasticity for a good is calculated by dividing the percentage change in quantity demanded by the percentage change in income. Annika's income rises from $100 to $120. Therefore, the percentage change in income is $\frac{\Delta I}{I} \times 100 = \frac{20}{100} \times 100 = 20$. When Annika's income rises, her consumption of golf changes from 9 rounds to 10. Thus, the percentage change in the quantity of rounds demanded is $\frac{\Delta Q}{Q} \times 100 = 100 = \frac{1}{9} \times 100 = 11.1$. To calculate the income elasticity, we divide the percentage change in quantity by the percentage change in price, $\frac{11.1}{20} = 0.555$. Golf cannot be a luxury good for Annika because the elasticity is not greater than 1. Therefore, the statement is *false*.

c. Again, we must calculate the income elasticity, this time for pancake mix. When Annika's income rises from $100 to $120 [a 20% rise as calculated in part (b)], Annika increases her purchases of pancake mix from 5 boxes to 10 boxes. Thus, the percentage change in the quantity of pancake mix demanded is $\frac{\Delta Q}{Q} \times 100 = \frac{5}{5} \times 100 = 100$. This means that the income elasticity of demand is $\frac{\%\Delta Q}{\%\Delta I} = \frac{100}{20} = 5$. Because the income elasticity is greater than 1, pancake mix is a luxury good for Annika. Therefore, the statement is *true*.

5.2 How Price Changes Affect Consumption Choices

In the previous section, we looked at how a consumer's choices change when we vary income, holding prices and preferences constant. In this section, we see what happens when the price of a good changes, holding income, preferences, and the prices of all other goods constant. *This analysis tells us exactly where a demand curve comes from.*

At this point, it is useful to recall exactly what a demand curve is because it has been a few chapters since we discussed the concept. We learned in Chapter 2 that many factors influence the quantity that a consumer demands of a good. The demand curve isolates how one particular factor, a good's own price, affects the quantity demanded while holding everything else constant. Changes in any other factor that influences the quantity demanded (such as income, preferences, or the prices of other goods) shift the location of the demand curve.

Up to this point, we know that demand curves slope downward because diminishing marginal utility implies that consumers' willingness to pay falls as quantities rise. That explanation is correct, but it skips a step. A consumer's demand curve actually comes straight from the consumer's utility maximization. A demand curve answers the following question: As the price of a good changes while holding all else constant, how does the quantity of that good in the utility-maximizing bundle change? This is exactly the question we're going to answer here.

Deriving a Demand Curve

To see how a consumer's utility-maximizing behavior leads to a demand curve, let's look at a specific example. Suppose Caroline is deciding how to spend her income on two goods, 2-liter bottles of Mountain Dew and 1-liter bottles of grape juice, and we want to know her demand curve for grape juice. Caroline's income is $20, and the price of Mountain Dew is $2 per 2-liter bottle. We'll hold these factors (income and price of Mountain Dew) and Caroline's preferences constant throughout our analysis. If we didn't, we would not be mapping out a single demand curve (which, remember, shows the relationship between price of a good and the quantity demanded of that good), but would instead be shifting the demand curve around.

To build the demand curve, we start by figuring out the consumer's utility-maximizing consumption bundle at some price for grape juice. It doesn't actually matter what price we use to start because we will eventually compute the quantity demanded at all prices. Let's start with a price of $1 per liter bottle of grape juice. (It makes the math easy.)

The top half of Figure 5.7a shows Caroline's utility-maximization problem. Her budget constraint reflects the combinations of bottles of Mountain Dew and bottles of grape juice that she can afford at the current prices. With an income of $20, she can buy up to 10 bottles of Mountain Dew at $2 per bottle if that's all she spends her money on, or up to 20 bottles of grape juice at $1 per bottle if she restricts her purchases to grape juice. The slope of the budget constraint equals the negative of the price ratio P_{MD}/P_G, which is −0.5 in this case. Caroline's indifference curve that is tangent to this budget constraint is also shown in the figure. We know that the point of tangency shown is the utility-maximizing bundle. Given her income, her preferences, and the prices of the two juices, Caroline's optimal quantities to consume are 3 bottles of Mountain Dew and 14 bottles of grape juice.

We now have one point on Caroline's demand curve for grape juice: At a price of $1 per liter, her quantity demanded is 14 bottles. The only problem is that the top panel of Figure 5.7a does not have the correct axes for a demand curve. Remember that a

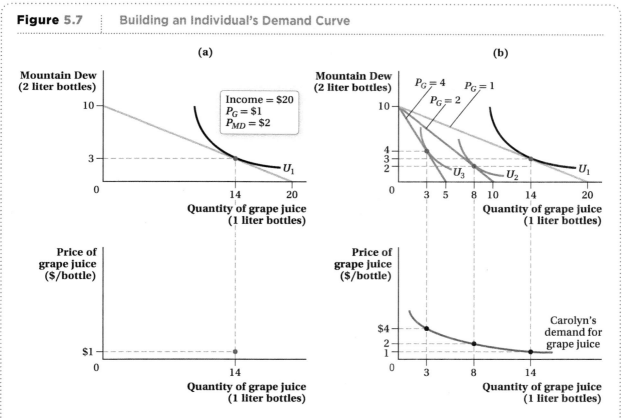

Figure 5.7   Building an Individual's Demand Curve

(a) At her optimal consumption bundle, Caroline purchases 14 bottles of grape juice when the price per bottle is $1 and her income is $20. The bottom panel plots this point on her demand curve, with the price of grape juice on the y-axis and the quantity of grape juice on the x-axis.

(b) A completed demand curve consists of many of these quantity-price points. Here, the optimal quantity of grape juice consumed is plotted for the prices $1, $2, and $4 per bottle. This creates Caroline's demand curve, as shown in the bottom panel.

demand curve for a good is drawn with the good's price on the vertical axis and its quantity demanded on the horizontal axis. When we graphically search for the tangency of indifference curves and budget constraints, however, we put the quantities of the two goods on the axes. So we'll make a new figure, shown in the bottom panel of Figure 5.7a, that plots the same quantity of grape juice as the figure's top panel, but with the price of grape juice on the vertical axis. Because the horizontal axis in the bottom panel is the same as that in the top—the quantity of grape juice—we can vertically transfer that dimension of the figure directly from the top to the bottom panel.

To finish building the demand curve, we need to repeat the process described above again and again for many different grape juice prices. When the price changes, the budget constraint's slope changes, which reflects the relative prices of the two goods. For each new budget constraint, we find the optimal consumption bundle by finding the indifference curve that is tangent to it. Because preferences are constant, the set of indifference curves corresponding to Caroline's utility function remains the same. It's just that the particular indifference curve that is tangent to the budget constraint will depend on where the constraint is. Each time we determine the optimal quantity consumed at a given price of grape juice, we have found another point on the demand curve.

Figure 5.7b shows this exercise for grape juice prices of $1, $2, and $4 per bottle. As the price of grape juice rises (holding fixed the price of Mountain Dew and Caroline's income), the budget constraint gets steeper, and the utility-maximizing quantity of grape juice falls. In our example, Caroline's optimal quantity of grape juice when it costs $2 per bottle is 8 bottles. When the price is $4, she consumes 3 bottles. These combinations of prices and quantities are plotted in the lower panel. These points are all on Caroline's demand curve for grape juice. Repeating this exercise for every possible grape juice price will trace out her whole demand curve, which we've drawn in the figure. Note that Caroline's quantity demanded falls as price rises.

Shifts in the Demand Curve

If a consumer's preferences or income change, or the prices of other goods change, then the demand curve shifts. But the process for tracing out the demand curve under these new conditions is exactly the same: We trace out the utility-maximizing quantity of the good under every possible price. It's just that we do so under the updated circumstances.

Let's look at an example where preferences change. Suppose that Caroline meets a scientist at a party who argues that the purported health benefits of grape juice are overstated and that it stains your teeth red. What happens to Caroline's demand for grape juice? We wouldn't expect the market prices of Mountain Dew or grape juice to change based on this private conversation, nor will Caroline's income be affected by this information. Her preferences toward grape juice will change, however. She'll find it less desirable than before. This will show up as a flattening of Caroline's indifference curves, because now she'll have to be given more grape juice to be indifferent to a loss of Mountain Dew. Another way to think about it is that, because the marginal rate of substitution (MRS) equals $-MU_G/MU_{MD}$, this preference shift shrinks Caroline's marginal utility of grape juice at any quantity, reducing her MRS—that is, flattening her indifference curves.

Figure 5.8 repeats the demand-curve building exercise after the preference change. With the flatter indifference curves (labeled U_1', U_2', and U_3'), Caroline's utility-maximizing consumption bundles have changed. Now her optimal consumption levels of grape juice at prices of $1, $2, and $4 per bottle are 9, 6, and 2 bottles, respectively. The bottom half of Figure 5.8 plots these points on Caroline's new demand curve D_2.

We can see that because Caroline's preferences have changed, she now demands a smaller quantity of grape juice than before at every price. As a result, her demand curve for grape juice has shifted in from D_1 to D_2. This result demonstrates why and how preference changes shift the demand curve. Changes in Caroline's income or in the price

freakonomics

Even Animals Like Sales

If you think the laws of economics only apply to humans, think again. Monkeys, and even rats, behave in ways that would make you think they've taken intermediate micro.

Some of the most intensive testing of the economic behavior of animals was carried out by Yale economist Keith Chen and his co-authors on a group of Capuchin monkeys. As a first step, Chen introduced the monkeys to the concept of money. He gave them "money" in the form of metal washers that they could exchange for various types of foods including Jell-O, grapes, and Marshmallow Fluff (Capuchin monkeys *love* sweet foods).

Just Like Us?

Courtesy M. Keith Chen

After about six exasperating months, these monkeys finally figured out that the washers had value. Chen observed that individual monkeys tended to have stable preferences: Some liked grapes the best, others were fans of Jell-O. How did he learn this? He would give a particular monkey a coin and then offer that monkey a choice between a bowl of three Jell-O cubes and a bowl of six grapes and see which one the monkey chose.

Next, Chen did what any good economist would do: He subjected the monkeys to price changes! Instead of getting three Jell-O cubes for one washer, he would offer the monkey, say, the choice between a single Jell-O cube per washer and a bowl of six grapes per washer. Thus, the relative price of Jell-O became three times as high. The monkeys responded exactly the way economic theory would predict, shifting their consumption away from the goods whose prices had risen.[*]

Perhaps it is not that surprising that monkeys, one of our closest relatives in the animal kingdom, would be sophisticated consumers. But there is no way rats understand supply and demand, is there? It seems they do. Economists Raymond Battalio and John Kagel equipped rats' cages with two levers, each of which dispensed a different beverage.[†] One of these levers gave the rat a refreshing burst of root beer. Rats, it turns out, love root beer. The other lever released quinine water. Quinine is a bitter-tasting substance initially used to treat malaria, and now used primarily to give vodka tonics their distinctive flavor. Rats are far less fond of quinine than they are of root beer, and they made that quite clear to the researchers by pressing the root beer lever far more often. Battalio and Kagel, like Chen, then explored changes in "prices" (how much liquid came out per press of the lever) and in the rats' budget constraint (how many times they could press the levers each day). Like monkeys (and humans), the rats consumed less of a drink when its relative price increased. Even more interesting is that when the rats were made very poor (i.e., they got very few lever presses each day), they shifted their consumption away from root beer toward quinine water. The researchers found that root beer is a luxury good for rats, and quinine water is an inferior good! Wonder what rats would make of a vodka tonic. . . .

---

[*] That wasn't the only human-like behavior these monkeys exhibited when exposed to money—for the whole amusingly sordid story, see the epilogue to *SuperFreakonomics.*

[†] A description of the work by Battalio and Kagel may be found in: Tim Harford, *The Logic of Life: The Rational Economics of an Irrational World.* (New York: Random House, 2008), pp. 18–21.

Figure 5.8 : Preference Changes and Shifts in the Demand Curve

(a) Caroline's indifference curves for grape juice flatten when her preference for grape juice decreases relative to her preference for Mountain Dew. At each price level, she now consumes fewer bottles of grape juice.

(b) Because she purchases fewer bottles of grape juice at each price point, Caroline's demand curve for grape juice shifts inward from D_1 to D_2.

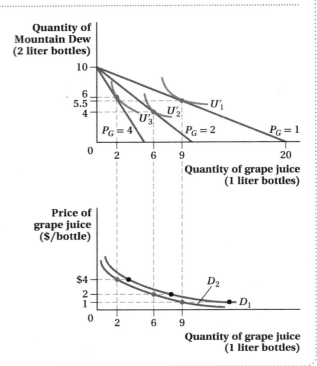

of Mountain Dew also shift her demand curve. (We saw earlier how income shifts affect quantity demanded, and we investigate the effects of price changes in other goods in Section 5.4.) Remember, however, that for any given value of these nonprice influences on demand, the change in the quantity demanded of a good in response to changes in its own price results in a movement along a demand curve, not a shift in the curve.

5.2 figure it out

Cooper allocates $200 of his weekly budget to entertainment. He spends all of this $200 on two goods: theater tickets (which cost $50 each) and movie tickets (which cost $10 each).

a. With theater tickets on the horizontal axis, draw Cooper's budget constraint, making sure to indicate the horizontal and vertical intercepts. What is the slope of the budget constraint?

b. Suppose that Cooper currently purchases 3 theater tickets per week. Indicate this choice on the budget constraint and mark it as point A. Draw an indifference curve tangent to the budget

constraint at point A. How many movie tickets does Cooper buy?

c. Suppose that the price of a theater ticket rises to $80, and Cooper lowers his purchases of theater tickets to 2. Draw Cooper's new budget constraint, indicate his choice with a point B, and draw an indifference curve tangent to the new budget constraint at point B.

d. Once again, the price of a theater ticket rises to $100, and Cooper lowers his purchases of theater tickets to 1 per week. Draw his new budget constraint, show his choice on the budget constraint with a point C, and draw an indifference curve tangent to this new budget constraint at C.

e. Draw a new diagram below your indifference curve diagram. Use your answers to parts (b)–(d) to draw Cooper's demand for theater tickets. Indicate his quantities demanded at $50, $80, and $100. Is there an inverse relationship between price and quantity demanded?

Solution:

a. To start, we need to calculate the horizontal and vertical intercepts for Cooper's budget constraint. The horizontal intercept is the point at which Cooper spends all of his income on theater tickets and purchases no movie tickets. This occurs when he buys $200/$50 = 4 theater tickets (Figure A). The vertical intercept is the point at which Cooper spends his entire income on movie tickets and buys no theater tickets. This means that he is buying $200/$10 = 20 movie tickets. The budget constraint connects these two intercepts. The slope of the budget constraint equals rise/run = −20/4 = −5.

Figure A

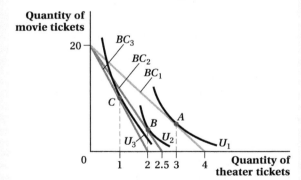

Note that this slope is the negative of the ratio of the two prices $= -\dfrac{P_{\text{theater tickets}}}{P_{\text{movie tickets}}} = -\$50/\$10 = -5$.

b. Maximum utility occurs where the indifference curve is tangent to the budget constraint. Therefore, point A should be the point where this tangency takes place. If Cooper purchases 3 theater tickets a week, he will spend $50 × 3 = $150, leaving him $200 − $150 = $50 to spend on movie tickets. Since movie tickets cost $10 each, he purchases $50/$10 = 5 movie tickets.

c. Cooper's budget constraint will rotate in a clockwise direction. The vertical intercept is not

affected because neither Cooper's income nor the price of movie tickets changes. However, the price of theater tickets has risen to $80, and now if Cooper were to allocate his entire budget to theater tickets, he could afford only $200/$80 = 2.5 of them. This is the new horizontal intercept. If Cooper chooses to buy 2 theater tickets, he will have an indifference curve tangent to this budget constraint at that point (B).

d. The budget constraint will again rotate clockwise and the vertical intercept will remain unchanged. The new horizontal intercept will be $200/$100 = 2. Point C will occur where Cooper's indifference curve is tangent to his new budget constraint at a quantity of 1 theater ticket.

e. The demand curve shows the relationship between the price of theater tickets and Cooper's quantity demanded. We can take the information from our indifference curve diagram to develop three points on Cooper's demand curve:

Point	Price	Quantity of Theater Tickets Demanded
A	$50	3
B	$80	2
C	$100	1

We can then plot points A, B, and C on a diagram with the quantity of theater tickets on the horizontal axis and the price of theater tickets on the vertical axis (Figure B). Connecting these points gives us Cooper's demand curve for theater tickets.

Figure B

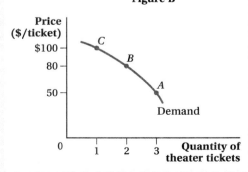

5.3 Decomposing Consumer Responses to Price Changes into Income and Substitution Effects

When the price of a good changes, the demand curve for that good tells us how much consumption will change. This total change in quantity demanded, however, is a result of two distinct forces that affect consumers' decisions: the substitution effect and the income effect. Any change in quantity demanded can be decomposed into these two effects.

1. When the price of one good changes relative to the price of another good, consumers will want to buy more of the good that has become relatively cheaper and less of the good that is now relatively more expensive. Economists call this the **substitution effect**.

2. A price shift changes the purchasing power of consumers' incomes—the amount of goods they can buy with a given dollar-level expenditure. If a good gets cheaper, for example, consumers are effectively richer and can buy more of the cheaper good and other goods. If a good's price increases, the purchasing power of consumers' incomes is reduced, and they can buy fewer goods. Economists refer to consumption changes resulting from this shift in spending power as the **income effect**.

Any change in quantity demanded can be decomposed into these two effects. We introduce them in this book, but we are just scratching the surface. We're going to be upfront with you: The distinction between income and substitution effects is one of the most subtle concepts that you will come across in this entire book. If you go on to take more advanced economics courses, income and substitution effects will come up again and again.[3] There are two reasons why this topic is so difficult. First, we don't separately observe these two effects in the real world, only their combined effects. Their separation is an artificial analytical tool. Put another way, as a consumer you can (and do) figure out how much to consume without knowing or figuring out how much of the change is due to income effects and how much is due to substitution effects. Second, the income effect occurs even when the consumer's income as measured in dollars remains constant. How rich we feel is determined both by how much income we have and how much things cost. If your income stays at $1,000 but the prices of all goods fall by half, you are effectively a lot wealthier. The income effect refers to how rich you feel, not the number of dollar bills in your pocket.

In our overview, we demonstrate income and substitution effects using graphs. The appendix to this chapter describes these effects mathematically.

Figure 5.9 shows how a consumer, Carlos, who spends his income on rounds of golf and restaurant meals, reacts to a fall in the price of restaurant meals. This is just like the analysis we did in Section 5.2. Lower restaurant meal prices lead the budget constraint to rotate outward from BC_1 to BC_2 because Carlos can now purchase more restaurant meals with his income. As a result, the optimal consumption bundle shifts from A (the point of tangency between indifference curve U_1 and budget constraint BC_1) to B (the point of tangency between indifference curve U_2 and budget constraint BC_2). Because of the fall in the price of restaurant meals, the quantity of rounds of golf

substitution effect
The change in a consumer's consumption choices that results from a change in the relative prices of two goods.

income effect
The change in a consumer's consumption choices that results from a change in the purchasing power of the consumer's income.

---

[3] For instance, it is much easier to describe the properties of a demand curve when there is no income effect, only a substitution effect. Demand curves that reflect only substitution effects are known as "Hicksian demand curves" in honor of the economist Sir John Hicks. The demand curves that combine both effects—the kind you're accustomed to working with, and the kind we'll continue to use throughout the text—are called "Marshallian demand curves" after economist Alfred Marshall. Because we stick with this standard demand curve throughout the book, we'll skip the modifier and just keep calling them demand curves.

Figure 5.9   : The Effects of a Fall in the Price of Restaurant Meals

When the price of restaurant meals decreases, Carlos's budget constraint rotates outward from BC_1 to BC_2. The total effect of the price change is shown by the increase in his optimal consumption bundle from point A to point B. In particular, the number of restaurant meals Carlos consumes increases from 3 to 5, and the number of rounds of golf he consumes increases from 5 to 6.

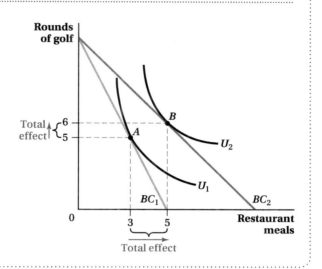

consumed increases from 5 to 6, and the number of restaurant meals Carlos purchases rises from 3 to 5. These overall changes in quantities consumed between bundles A and B are the **total effect** of the price change.

Note that just as in Section 5.2, we figured out the optimal bundle without any reference to income or substitution effects. In the next sections, we decompose the total effect into separate substitution and income effects. That is,

total effect
The total change (substitution effect + income effect) in a consumer's optimal consumption bundle as a result of a price change.

$$\text{Total Effect} = \text{Substitution Effect} + \text{Income Effect}$$

Breaking down the movement from A to B into income and substitution effects helps us understand how much of the total change in Carlos's quantity demanded occurs because Carlos switches what he purchases as a result of the reduction in the relative prices of the two goods (the substitution effect), and how much of the change is driven by the fact that the decrease in the price of restaurant meals gives Carlos more purchasing power (the income effect).

Note that all the examples we work through involve a drop in the price of a good. When the price of a good increases, the effects work in the opposite direction.

Isolating the Substitution Effect

Let's begin by isolating the substitution effect. This part of the change in quantities demanded is due to the change in relative prices, not to the change in Carlos's buying power. To isolate the substitution effect, we need to figure out how many rounds of golf and restaurant meals Carlos would want to consume if, after the price change, there was no income effect, that is, if he had the same purchasing power as before the price change and felt neither richer nor poorer.

For Carlos to feel neither richer nor poorer, *the bundle he consumes after the price change must provide him with the same utility he was receiving before the price change; that is, the new bundle must be on the initial indifference curve U_1.*

So where is this substitution-effect-only bundle on U_1? We know this bundle has to reflect the fact that the goods' relative prices have changed. Those new relative prices are embodied in the slope of the new budget line BC_2. The problem is that there isn't a point of tangency between U_1 and BC_2—as we can see in Figure 5.10. However, there *is* a point of tangency between U_1 and a budget line with the same slope (i.e., the same relative prices) as BC_2. The budget line we're talking about is BC', the dashed line in panel a of Figure 5.10, and the point of tangency is point A'.

Bundle A' is what Carlos would buy if the relative prices of rounds of golf and restaurant meals changed the way they did, but Carlos experienced no change in purchasing power. This is the definition of the substitution effect. Thus, the substitution effect in isolation moves Carlos's demanded bundle from A to A'. To find this effect, we have to shift the post-price-change budget line BC_2 back in parallel (to preserve the new relative prices) until it is tangent to the pre-price-change indifference curve U_1 (to

Figure 5.10 : **Substitution and Income Effects for Two Normal Goods**

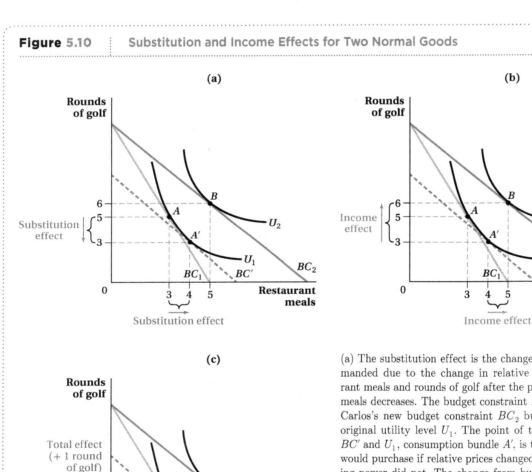

(a) The substitution effect is the change in quantities demanded due to the change in relative prices of restaurant meals and rounds of golf after the price of restaurant meals decreases. The budget constraint BC' is parallel to Carlos's new budget constraint BC_2 but tangent to his original utility level U_1. The point of tangency between BC' and U_1, consumption bundle A', is the bundle Carlos would purchase if relative prices changed but his purchasing power did not. The change from bundle A to bundle A' is the substitution effect.

(b) The income effect is the change in quantities demanded due to the change in the consumer's purchasing power after the change in prices. When the price of restaurant meals decreases, Carlos can afford to purchase a larger bundle than he could before the price change. The change in the quantity of goods consumed from bundle A' to B represents the income effect.

(c) The total effect is the sum of the substitution and income effects. In this case, Carlos consumes 1 more round of golf and 2 more restaurant meals.

keep the original utility level the same). *It's important to recognize that the budget line BC' is hypothetical—Carlos never actually faces it.* Instead, it is a conceptual device that lets us figure out what Carlos would do if he did face it; that is, if relative prices changed in the way they actually did while at the same time any income gains he enjoyed as a result were taken away from him.

There are a few things to notice about the change in quantities due to the substitution effect. First, the quantity of rounds of golf decreases (from 5 to 3), and the quantity of restaurant meals increases (from 3 to 4). The decrease in the quantity of rounds of golf demanded occurs because the price change has caused restaurant meals to become cheaper relative to rounds of golf, so Carlos wants to buy relatively more restaurant meals. Second, while points A and A' are on the same indifference curve (and Carlos therefore gets the same utility from either bundle), it costs Carlos less to buy bundle A' at the new prices than to buy A. We know this because point A is located above BC' and so is infeasible if the budget constraint is BC'. (A', however, being on BC', is feasible with this constraint.)

Carlos therefore responds to the decline in restaurant meal prices by substituting away from rounds of golf and toward restaurant meals. By moving down along U_1, Carlos has effectively made himself better off; he is getting the same utility (he's still on U_1) for less money (bundle A is no longer feasible even though A' is).

Isolating the Income Effect

The income effect is the part of the total change in quantities consumed that is due to the change in Carlos's buying power after the price change. Why is there an income effect even though only the price of a good changed, not the actual number of dollars that Carlos had to spend? The key to understanding this outcome is to recognize that when the price of a good falls, Carlos becomes richer overall. The reduction in a good's price means there's a whole new set of bundles Carlos can now buy that he couldn't afford before because he has more money left over. At the old prices, everything above and to the right of BC_1 was infeasible; at the new prices, only bundles outside BC_2 are infeasible (see panel b of Figure 5.10).

This increase in buying power allows Carlos to achieve a higher level of utility than he did before. The income effect is the change in Carlos's choices driven by this shift in buying power while holding relative prices fixed at their new level. Finding these income-effect consumption changes is fairly easy once we've isolated the substitution

make the grade

Computing substitution and income effects from a price change

There are three basic steps to analyzing substitution and income effects. We start with the consumer at a point of maximum utility (Point *A*) where his indifference curve is tangent to his budget constraint.

1. When prices change, draw the new budget constraint (a price change rotates the budget constraint, altering its slope). Then find the optimal quantity at the point (Point *B*) where this new budget constraint is tangent to a new indifference curve.

2. Draw a new line that is parallel to the new budget constraint from Step 1 and tangent to the

original indifference curve at Point *A'*. The movement along the original indifference curve from Point *A* (the original, pre-price change bundle) to this new tangency (point *A'*) is the substitution effect. This movement shows how quantities change when relative prices change, even when purchasing power of income is constant.

3. The income effect of the price change is seen in the movement from point *A'* to point *B*. Here, relative prices are held constant (the budget lines are parallel) but the purchasing power of income changes.

effect. Remember that to find bundle A', we shifted the new budget constraint back in parallel until it was tangent to the original indifference curve. Doing that shift in reverse reflects the income effect exactly: It is the shift in consumption quantities (from bundle A' to B in panel b of Figure 5.10) due to Carlos's ability to reach a higher indifference curve (U_2 instead of U_1) while holding relative prices fixed (BC_2 and BC' have the same slope).

Therefore, the income effect of the decline in the restaurant meal price is illustrated by the move from the substitution-effect bundle (point A') to the final bundle, point B. Because the decline in restaurant meal prices has, in effect, made Carlos wealthier, he can reach a higher indifference curve U_2 and consume more of both goods. Due to the income effect, his desired quantity of rounds of golf increases by 3 from 3 (at A') to 6 (at B) and his desired quantity of restaurant meals increases by 1 from 4 (at A') to 5 (at B).

In this particular example, the income effect led to increases in the quantities of both rounds of golf and restaurant meals. That means both goods are normal goods. In the next section, we show an example in which one of the goods is inferior.

The Total Effects

The total effects of the decline in restaurant meal prices are shown in panel c of Figure 5.10:

1. The quantity of rounds of golf Carlos desires rises by 1 round of golf from 5 in the initial bundle at point A to 6 in the final bundle at point B. (A decline of 2 caused by the substitution effect is counteracted by a rise of 3 caused by the income effect for a net gain of 1 round of golf.)

2. The quantity of restaurant meals Carlos desires rises by 2 restaurant meals, from 3 in the initial bundle A to 5 in the final bundle B. (A rise of 1 caused by the substitution effect plus a rise of 1 caused by the income effect.)

What Determines the Size of the Substitution and Income Effects?

The size (and as we'll see shortly, sometimes the direction) of the total effect of a price change depends on the relative sizes of its substitution and income effects. So it's important to understand what factors influence how large substitution and income effects are. We discuss some of the more important factors below.

The Size of the Substitution Effect   The size of the substitution effect depends on the degree of curvature of the indifference curves. This can be seen in Figure 5.11. The figure's two panels show the substitution effects of the same change in the relative prices of rounds of golf and restaurant meals for two different indifference curve shapes. (We know it's the same relative price change because the budget constraints experience the same change in slope in both panels.) When indifference curves are highly curved, as in panel a, the MRS changes quickly as one moves along them. This means any given price change won't change consumption choices much, because one doesn't need to move far along the indifference curve to change the MRS to match the new relative prices. Thus, the substitution effect is small. This is unsurprising, because we learned in Chapter 4 that indifference curves have more curvature in cases where the two goods are not highly substitutable. In panel a, the relative price change causes a substitution from A to A', and the consumer moves from purchasing a bundle with 2 restaurant meals and 2 rounds of golf to a bundle containing 3 restaurant meals and 1.25 rounds of golf.

When indifference curves are less curved, as in panel b, the MRS doesn't change much along the curve, so the same relative price change causes a much greater substitution effect. The substitution from A to A' in panel b involves much larger changes in golf and meals consumption than that caused by the same relative price change in

Figure 5.11 | The Shape of Indifference Curves Determines the Size of the Substitution Effect

(a) Curvier Indifference Curve– Smaller Substitution Effect

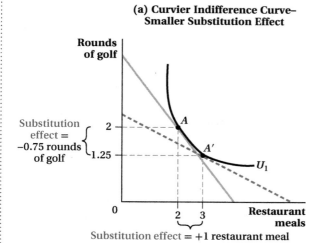

(b) Flatter Indifference Curve– Larger Substitution Effect

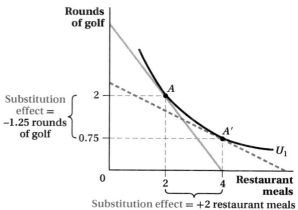

(a) When the indifference curve is highly curved, the *MRS* changes quickly along the curve. Thus, any given price change will not change consumption choices by much. Here, the original consumption bundle *A* is 2 restaurant meals and 2 rounds of golf. After a change in prices, the new optimal consumption bundle is *A′*, and the consumer now demands 1.25 rounds of golf and 3 restaurant meals.

(b) When the indifference curve is less curved, the *MRS* does not change quickly along the curve. Thus, any given price change affects consumption choices more strongly. At the new optimal consumption bundle *A′*, the consumer now demands 0.75 rounds of golf and 4 restaurant meals.

panel a.[4] In panel b, the quantity of restaurant meals purchased grows to 4 (rather than 3) and the quantity of rounds of golf purchased falls to 0.75 (rather than 1.25). Again, we can relate this to what we learned about the curvature of indifference curves in Chapter 4. Indifference curves with little curvature indicate that the two goods are close substitutes. Thus, it makes sense that a price change will lead to a much greater adjustment in the quantities in the consumer's preferred bundle.

The Size of the Income Effect   The size of the income effect is related to the quantity of each good the consumer purchases before the price change. The more the consumer was spending on the good before the price change, the greater the fraction of the consumer's budget affected by the price change. A price drop of a good that the consumer is initially buying a lot of will leave him with more income left over than a price drop of a good with a small budget share (and a price increase will sap a greater share of the consumer's income). For example, consider the effects of a change in the

[4] This logic also explains why perfect substitutes, the special case we discussed in Chapter 4 with per-fectly straight indifference curves, have the largest substitution effects. There, a small relative price change can lead the consumer to shift from one corner solution to another—that is, from consuming all of one good, *A*, and none of the other good, *B*, to consuming only *B* and no *A*. (To see this, sup-pose all a consumer cares about is the number of potato chips he consumes, and he views 3-ounce and 12-ounce bags of chips as perfect substitutes. If the price of 12-ounce bags is less than four times the price of 3-ounce bags, he will only buy 12-ounce bags. But if the price of 12-ounce bags is just a bit more than four times the price of 3-ounce bags, he will only buy 3-ounce bags.) It's also why perfect complements, with their right-angled indifference curves, have no substitution effect; they are always consumed in constant proportion regardless of relative prices.

prices of two goods homeowners deal with: electricity and pest control. A typical consumer spends much more of his budget on electricity. Therefore, a change in the price of electricity will affect his income and alter his purchases by more than a similar change in the price of pest control. (At the extreme, if the consumer currently purchases no pest control, a change in the price of pest control will have no income effect at all.)

5.3 figure it out

Pavlo eats cakes and pies. His income is $20, and when cakes and pies both cost $1, Pavlo consumes 4 cakes and 16 pies (point A in Figure A). But when the price of pies rises to $2, Pavlo consumes 12 cakes and 4 pies (point B).

a. Why does the budget constraint rotate as it does in response to the increase in the price of pies?

b. Trace the diagram on a piece of paper. On your diagram, separate the change in the consumption of pies into the substitution effect and the income effect. Which is larger?

c. Are pies a normal or inferior good? How do you know? Are cakes a normal or inferior good? How do you know?

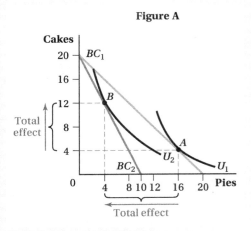

Figure A

Solution:

a. The price of cakes hasn't changed, so Pavlo can still buy 20 cakes if he spends his $20 all on cakes (the y-intercept). However, at $2 per pie, Pavlo can now afford to buy only 10 pies instead of 20.

b. The substitution effect is measured by changing the ratio of the prices of the goods but holding utility constant (Figure B). Therefore, it must be measured along one indifference curve. To determine the substitution effect of a price change in pies, you need to shift the post-price-change budget constraint BC_2 out until it is tangent to Pavlo's initial indifference curve U_1. The easiest way to do this is to draw a new budget line BC' that is parallel to the new budget constraint (thus changing the ratio of the cake and pie prices) but tangent to U_1 (thus holding utility constant). Label the point of tangency A'. Point A' is the bundle Pavlo would buy if the relative prices of cakes and pies changed as they did, but he experienced no change in purchasing power. When the price of pies rises, Pavlo would substitute away from buying pies and buy more cakes.

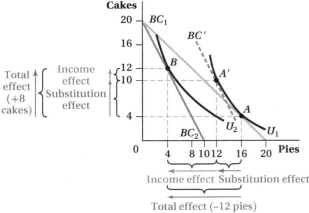

Figure B

The income effect is the part of the total change in quantities consumed that is due to the change in Pavlo's buying power after the price of pies changes. This is reflected in the shift from point A' on budget constraint BC' to point B on budget constraint BC_2. (These budget constraints are parallel because the income effect is measured holding relative prices constant.)

For pies, the income effect is larger than the substitution effect. The substitution effect leads Pavlo to purchase 4 fewer pies (from 16 to 12), while the income effect further reduces his consumption by 8 pies (from 12 to 4).

c. Pies are a normal good because Pavlo purchases fewer pies (4 instead of 12) when the purchasing power of his income falls due to the price increase. However, cakes are an inferior good because the fall in purchasing power actually leads to a rise in cake consumption.

 ## application

Backward-Bending Labor Supply and Income Effects in Leisure

The relative sizes of substitution and income effects can create an interesting phenomenon sometimes observed in individuals' willingness to work. Think for a minute about leisure time (no jokes about skipping class). For just about everyone, leisure is a good, just like rounds of golf, restaurant meals, cakes, pies, electricity, pest control, and all the other examples we have worked with. Consuming more of it raises people's utility.

But if leisure is a good, what is its price? Well, consuming leisure involves using up time. The price of leisure is the value of what one could be doing with that time if she wasn't being leisurely. The main alternative use of leisure time is work. (Economists often consider any time a person spends not working as leisure, whether or not that individual is doing something we might think of as leisurely.) What's the value of working? Aside from any inherent pleasure someone might get from her job, its value is the income she earns from it—or more precisely, the utility she would obtain by consuming goods and services bought with her work income. What this means is that by choosing to take an extra unit of leisure, a person is giving up the income she could have earned had she worked during that period. That lost income equals her wage rate. So that is the price of leisure: a person's wage, and the goods and services that she could have bought with that income.

Based on these ideas, then, we can think of a person's willingness to work as involving a choice between consuming leisure and consuming the goods and services that can be bought with her work income. If we treat those other goods and services as a single good (call it "consumption," with its quantity measured in dollars), the relative price between leisure and consumption is the wage. If a person's wage is $30 per hour, for example, and she chooses to take one more hour of leisure (i.e., work one hour less), she is giving up $30 in consumption.

Economists call the choice of how much to work an individual's labor supply choice, because it involves how much time the person offers to supply to the labor market as a function of the wage level. We can describe the work-leisure choice using the set of tools we've been working with in this chapter: A person has a utility function (with its associated indifference curves) that depends on both the amount of leisure time she spends and the consumption she enjoys from her work income. She maximizes her utility subject to a budget constraint for which the relative price of leisure and consumption equals her wage rate. The only thing that's a bit different in this case is that we aren't taking her income—how much she has to spend on the two goods—as a fixed number, as we usually do. Instead, her income will depend on her choice of how much leisure to take and, therefore, how much work. That would complicate things some, but it turns out we don't need to deal with this explicitly to understand the basic economics underlying how changes in the wage rate affect someone's willingness to work.

Suppose a person's wage goes up. (Maybe she gets a raise.) One consequence of this is that leisure now has a higher price relative to consumption. Choosing to work one less hour has become more expensive in terms of forgone consumption. This change is going to tend to make her choose less leisure (more work) and consume more goods and services. This is a substitution effect applied to these two goods, leisure and consumption.

The substitution effect therefore tends to make people want to work more when their wage rises. (If the wage were to fall instead, it would make leisure relatively cheap and tend to make workers want to work less.) This makes a person's labor supply curve, which shows how much she is willing to work at any given wage level, slope up. That shape is how we usually think of supply curves for anything: The higher the price of the good (the wage here), the higher the quantity of the product (work hours) the producer (worker) is willing to supply.

But there's another effect of an increase in the wage that we hinted at before. For any given level of work—or equivalently, any given level of leisure time—it raises the person's income. This means there is also an income effect of a wage increase, not just a substitution effect. What impact will the income effect have on someone's leisure choice? For most people, leisure is a normal good; they consume more of it as their income rises. If this doesn't seem obvious to you, imagine that you win a $100 million lottery prize, but your job doesn't change. This scenario is a pure income effect: an increase in income without a change in the relative price of leisure, the wage. Would you take more vacation time and work less after winning the lottery? Most people would.

The bottom line of the income effect from an increase in the wage, then, is to make a person want to work less. This is exactly the opposite of the substitution effect. The net effect of a wage change on how much a person is willing to work is the difference between the two. In principle, at least, if the income effect is large enough, a person's labor supply curve will no longer have a positive slope. Instead, there will be a negative relationship between wages and how much an individual is willing to work. An example of this is shown in Figure 5.12. At wages below w^*, the substitution effect dominates; increases in the wage will make the person willing to work more. Above w^*, however, the income effect begins to dominate, and the amount of work the person is willing to supply falls as wages rise. Economists call labor supply curves with this negative slope *backward-bending* labor supply curves.

Economists have found examples of backward-bending labor supply curves in certain markets. In one broad-ranging case, economic historian Dora Costa gathered surveys on the work habits of thousands of U.S. men working in the 1890s.[5] She found that low-wage workers spent more hours per day working than those earning high wages. Specifically, workers in the lowest wage decile (those being paid wages in the lowest 10% of all observed wage rates) averaged 11.1 hours of work per day, but those in the top wage decile (the top 10% of wage rates) only worked 8.9 hours per day. Workers in the highest wage group worked 5% fewer hours than those being paid the median wage, who in turn worked 14% less than those in the lowest wage group. In other words, the daily labor supply curve appeared to exhibit backward-bending patterns.

Figure 5.12 | **Backward-Bending Labor Supply**

When the income effect dominates, laborers choose to consume more leisure and work fewer hours, creating a backward-bending labor supply curve. At wages below w^*, the substitution effect is dominant, and the supply curve is upward-sloping. For any given increase in wages, laborers will choose to work more hours. At wages above w^*, the income effect dominates, and the supply curve is backward-bending. For any given increase in wages, laborers will choose to work fewer hours.

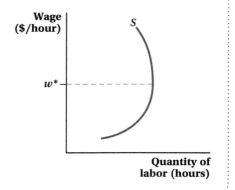

---

[5] Dora Costa, "The Wage and the Length of the Work Day: From the 1890s to 1991," *Journal of Labor Economics* 18, no. 1 (2000): 156–181.

Interestingly, using other data, Costa also showed that the pattern had reversed itself by the 1990s. While workers in that period across the wage scale spent on average less time per day working than a century before, now those at the high end of the scale worked more than those at the low end. Those in the lowest wage decile averaged 7.6 hours per day, and those in the highest averaged 8.5 hours a day. Thus, over the course of the intervening century, the substitution effect became larger relative to the income effect, and eventually started to dominate in magnitude.

It's not clear what factors caused this shift. One possibility is that the overall decline in average daily hours for all workers (which may itself reflect an income effect that affected all workers as the country became wealthier over the twentieth century) meant workers had more free time during the day, reducing their willingness to pay on the margin for another hour of leisure when the wage rose. It might also be that higher-wage workers still want to take more leisure, but this shows up as an earlier retirement age in the later period rather than lower average daily hours. Thus, the income effect is still large in this case, but its effect on day-to-day work choice is smaller relative to its effect over a person's lifetime. ■

theory and data

Golfers' Backward-Bending Labor Supply Curves

Tiger Woods is perhaps the most recognizable face in professional golf. He's won 71 PGA tour events and picked up 14 Majors. He's lent his name to campaigns for Nike and Titleist — and taken home a cool $40 million and $20 million, respectively, for the work. But it's not just his athletic skill that separates him from the average American laborer: He's probably one of the few people facing wages on the backward-bending portion of his labor supply curve. In other words, as his wages increase, he actually decreases the number of tournaments in which he plays.

PGA rules allow each golfer to elect which and how many events to play in, meaning the athlete considers the labor–leisure tradeoff separately for each tournament event. With tournament payoffs in the millions of dollars for just four rounds of golf, you probably think it a no-brainer to play. Indeed, for most golfers, it is. Generally, around 100 players sign up for any given event. This doesn't even include the over 1,000 hopefuls who play in brutal qualifying rounds, vying for just 25 spots on the PGA Tour.

Given the opportunity, these hopefuls would gladly play every tournament, but as economists Otis Gilley and Marc Chopin discovered, players like Tiger Woods don't.* In a 2000 paper, Gilley and Chopin looked at how low- and middle-income PGA players in the 1990s responded to increases in their wages and compared this result to the effects of wage increases on high-income players. Whereas low-level players entered more events as their event winnings increased, golfers at the top of their game decreased their tournament play as their wages increased. Top golfers were actually operating on the backward-bending portion of their labor supply curve! In particular, for every $1,000 increase in expected per-event winnings, the number of tournaments entered in a season by high-income players decreases by 0.05 to 0.1. For these select players, the income effect dominated the substitution effect, and faced with the leisure–labor tradeoff, they elected to consume more leisure.

Workers in other fields — including many economists — often spend their leisure time on the golf course. But for a professional golfer, a day on the green is work, not leisure. So just what does a PGA player do on his day off? Gilley and Chopin found that married golfers took more days off than did single golfers. Drawing on their own experiences as family men, the two hard-working economists concluded that golfers must be taking off work to spend more quality time with their wives and kids. The example of Tiger Woods, however, shows that the predictions of economic theory don't always hold up in the real world.

*Otis W. Gilley and Marc C. Chopin, "Professional Golf: Labor or Leisure." *Managerial Finance* 26, no. 7 (2000): 33–45.

An Example of the Income Effect with an Inferior Good

Figure 5.13 provides another example of decomposing quantity changes into income and substitution effects. Here, however, one of the goods is inferior, at least over the price range explored in the example.

Figure 5.13 shows Judi's utility-maximizing bundles of steak and ramen noodles for two sets of prices. The optimal bundle at the original prices is shown at point A. The price of ramen noodles then drops, rotating the budget constraint outward. With the new budget constraint BC_2, Judi can reach a higher level of utility (U_2) and chooses bundle B to maximize her utility.

To decompose the shift from bundle A to bundle B into its substitution and income effects, we follow the steps we described in the previous section. To find the substitution effect, we shift in the budget constraint after the price change until it is tangent to the original indifference curve U_1. This is shown by the dashed line BC' in panel a of Figure 5.14. The point of tangency between BC' and U_1 is bundle A'. Because this is the bundle that provides the same utility as the original bundle A but with ramen noodles at their new, lower price, the shift from A to A' is the substitution effect. Just as before, the substitution effect leads Judi to consume more of the good that becomes relatively cheaper (ramen noodles) and less of the other good (steak).

The quantity shifts between bundle A' and bundle B, shown in panel b of Figure 5.14, are due to the income effect. As before, this is the change in quantities consumed due to the shift in the budget lines from BC' to BC_2: Judi's increase in buying power while holding relative prices constant. Notice that now the income effect actually *reduces* the quantity of ramen noodles consumed, even though the drop in their price makes Judi richer by expanding the set of bundles she can consume. This means ramen is an inferior good over this income range; an increase in income makes Judi want less of it.

Does the fact that a price drop leads to a reduction in the quantity consumed due to the income effect mean that the demand curve for ramen noodles slopes up? No, because the substitution effect increases the quantity demanded by more than the income effect decreases it. Thus, the quantity of ramen noodles demanded still rises when their price falls even though ramen noodles are an inferior good. We see this outcome in panel c of Figure 5.14 because the total effect on the quantity of ramen noodles is posi-

---

Figure 5.13 : A Fall in the Price of an Inferior Good

When the price of ramen noodles decreases, Judi's budget constraint rotates outward from BC_1 to BC_2. The total effect of this price change is represented by the increase in quantities consumed from the original utility-maximizing bundle A to bundle B. Overall, Judi's consumption of both ramen noodles and steak increases.

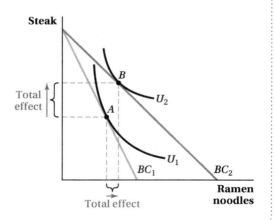

Figure 5.14   Substitution and Income Effects for an Inferior Good

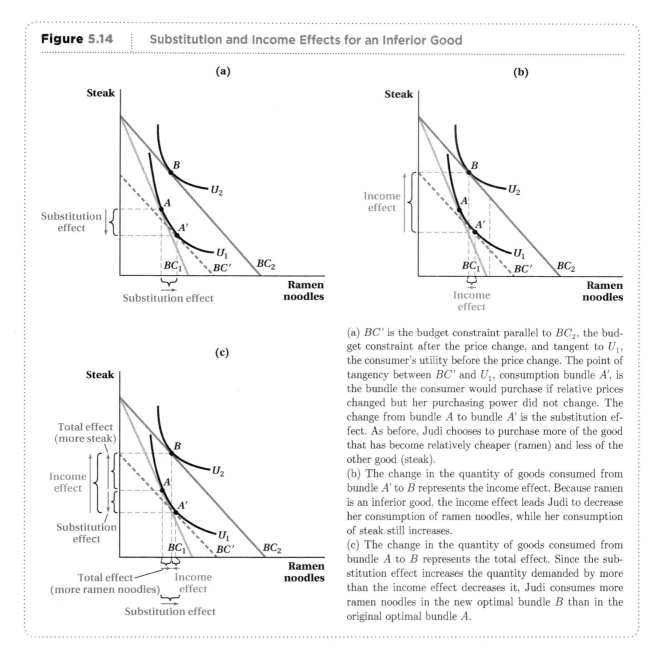

(a) BC' is the budget constraint parallel to BC_2, the budget constraint after the price change, and tangent to U_1, the consumer's utility before the price change. The point of tangency between BC' and U_1, consumption bundle A', is the bundle the consumer would purchase if relative prices changed but her purchasing power did not change. The change from bundle A to bundle A' is the substitution effect. As before, Judi chooses to purchase more of the good that has become relatively cheaper (ramen) and less of the other good (steak).

(b) The change in the quantity of goods consumed from bundle A' to B represents the income effect. Because ramen is an inferior good, the income effect leads Judi to decrease her consumption of ramen noodles, while her consumption of steak still increases.

(c) The change in the quantity of goods consumed from bundle A to B represents the total effect. Since the substitution effect increases the quantity demanded by more than the income effect decreases it, Judi consumes more ramen noodles in the new optimal bundle B than in the original optimal bundle A.

tive: The optimal bundle after ramen noodles become cheaper (bundle B) has a higher quantity of ramen than the optimal bundle before their price fell (bundle A). So the demand curve for ramen does indeed slope down. This is generally the case for inferior goods in the economy—while the income effect will make people want to consume less of them as their price falls, the substitution effect has a larger impact in the opposite direction, leading to a net increase in their consumption.

If the income effect is large enough, however, it is possible that a reduction in the price of an inferior good could actually lead to a net decrease in its consumption. A good that exhibits this trait is called a Giffen good.

Giffen Goods

Giffen good
A good for which price and quantity demanded are positively related.

Giffen goods are goods for which a fall in price leads the consumer to want *less* of the good. That is, an inverse relationship does not exist between price and quantity demanded and the demand curves of Giffen goods slope *up*! The more expensive a Giffen good is, the higher the quantity demanded.

This seemingly paradoxical effect arises because, for Giffen goods, the substitution effect of a price drop, which acts to increase the quantity a consumer demands of the good, is smaller than the reduction in the desired quantity caused by the income effect. Note that this means Giffen goods *must* be inferior goods. The income effect of a price drop can only reduce the desired quantity if the good is inferior; for all normal goods, the income effect of a price drop acts to increase the quantity demanded. Remember, though, that while all Giffen goods are inferior, not all inferior goods are Giffen goods—they are extremely rare. Typically, there will still be a net increase in the quantity demanded when price falls, just as we saw with the ramen noodles example before.

Figure 5.15 shows a graphical example. The two goods are potatoes and meat, and potatoes are the Giffen good. The utility-maximizing bundle at the original prices is shown at point A. When potatoes become cheaper, the budget constraint rotates out from BC_1 to BC_2 and the optimal bundle shifts from A to B. Notice that in this case, the quantity of potatoes consumed at point B is smaller than the quantity consumed at A even though potatoes are now cheaper.

The substitution and income effects underlying this change are shown in panels a and b of Figure 5.16. We isolate the substitution effect the same way as before: shifting the new budget constraint back in parallel until it is tangent to the original indifference curve. This creates changes in the quantity consumed corresponding to the shift from bundle A to bundle A'. As always, the substitution effect increases the quantity of the good that has become relatively cheaper, potatoes, and decreases the quantity of the relatively more expensive good, meat.

The income effect is the change in quantities associated with moving from bundle A' to B. Here, those changes are an increase in meat and a decrease in potatoes. Potatoes are therefore an inferior good, like ramen noodles in the previous example. But here, the negative income effect on potatoes has a larger magnitude than the positive substitution effect, so the net change in potatoes consumed from their drop in price is negative. This is what we saw in the shift from bundle A to B.

Figure 5.15   **A Change in the Price of a Giffen Good**

When the price of a Giffen good falls, the consumer consumes less of that good. Here, when the price of potatoes decreases, the consumer purchases fewer potatoes, as reflected in the change in quantities consumed from bundle A to bundle B.

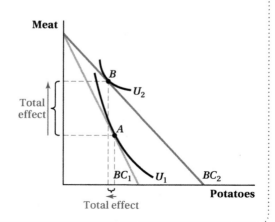

Figure 5.16   Substitution and Income Effects of a Giffen Good

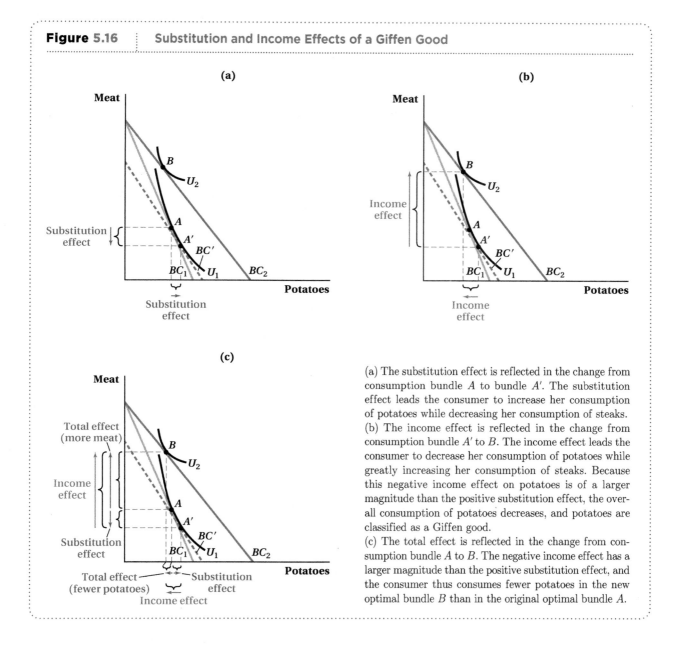

(a) The substitution effect is reflected in the change from consumption bundle A to bundle A'. The substitution effect leads the consumer to increase her consumption of potatoes while decreasing her consumption of steaks.
(b) The income effect is reflected in the change from consumption bundle A' to B. The income effect leads the consumer to decrease her consumption of potatoes while greatly increasing her consumption of steaks. Because this negative income effect on potatoes is of a larger magnitude than the positive substitution effect, the overall consumption of potatoes decreases, and potatoes are classified as a Giffen good.
(c) The total effect is reflected in the change from consumption bundle A to B. The negative income effect has a larger magnitude than the positive substitution effect, and the consumer thus consumes fewer potatoes in the new optimal bundle B than in the original optimal bundle A.

We discussed before that for a good to be a Giffen good, it must be an inferior good, and consumers' preferences for it must have an income effect that is larger in size than the substitution effect. When would we expect this? First, Giffen goods would have to have limited substitutability with other goods; that is, the substitution effect would need to be small, and therefore the indifference curves would have to be highly curved. Second, the income effect needs to be large; this is more likely if, before the price change, a large fraction of the consumer's budget is spent on the good. This way, if the price of the good falls because the consumer is already spending most of her income on it, she's likely to feel a larger bump in effective buying power than if the good were only a small share of her budget.

 **application**

In Search of Giffen Goods

While Giffen goods are a theoretical possibility, they are extremely rare in practice. An often cited example of a Giffen good is the potato in Ireland during the Irish famine of the mid-1800s. The story is that the famine-driven increase in potato prices drastically reduced the purchasing power of Irish families' incomes, shrinking the bundles of goods that they could afford because potatoes already consumed a very large fraction of a typical Irish family's meager cash income. The resulting income effect led to a decrease in the demand for other foods such as meat that were normal goods for Irish families and an increase in the demand for potatoes, an inferior good, that swamped any substitution effect. However, more recent reexaminations of the data by economists Gerald Dwyer and Cotton Lindsay, and later Sherwin Rosen in a separate study, found that even this canonical example proved not to be a Giffen good.[6]

These reexaminations differ in their explanations, but one common element between them is that the purported Giffen demand of Irish households just doesn't add up when confronted with what is known about the potato famine. Specifically, if potatoes were a Giffen good for individual households, then the total market demand curve for potatoes in Ireland should have also sloped up (quantity demanded would have increased as price increased). (We learn about how individuals' demand curves add up to total market demand later in this chapter.) But that would mean that the huge drop in supply due to the blight—about which there is no historical argument—should have led to lower potato prices. This is inconsistent with historical accounts reporting cases where no potatoes were available at any price, and when potatoes were available, they were sold at historically unprecedentedly high prices.

However, a recent policy experiment with extremely poor households in rural areas of China's Hunan province by Robert Jensen and Nolan Miller has produced what might be the most convincing documentation of a Giffen good to date.[7] Jensen and Miller subsidized the purchases of rice to a randomly selected set of such households, effectively lowering the price of rice that they faced. They then compared the change in rice consumption in the subsidized households to rice consumption in unsubsidized households of similar incomes and sizes.

Jensen and Miller found that the subsidy, even though it made rice cheaper, actually caused the households' rice consumption to fall. Rice was a Giffen good for these households. (Jensen and Miller conducted a similar experiment subsidizing wheat purchases in Gansu province and also found evidence that wheat was a Giffen good for some families, though the effect was weaker in this case.) The apparent mechanism behind this result is in accordance with our discussion above. Rice purchases took up so much of these households' incomes that the subsidy greatly increased the households' effective buying power. The resulting income effect made them want to consume less rice in place of other foods for the sake of dietary variety. This income effect was large enough to outweigh the substitution effect. To oversimplify things a little, the households were buying enough rice to meet their caloric needs and spending their leftover income on foods that added variety. When they could meet their caloric needs more cheaply, they used the now freed-up income to buy variety foods—enough to replace some of the calories formerly supplied by rice.

Interestingly, Jensen and Miller also found that while rice was a Giffen good for very poor households, it was not a Giffen good for the very poorest of the poor. Those extremely impoverished households basically ate only rice before the subsidy, and not really

[6] Gerald P. Dwyer, Jr. and Cotton M. Lindsay, "Robert Giffen and the Irish Potato," *American Economic Review* 74, no. 1 (1984): 188–192. Sherwin Rosen, "Potato Paradoxes." *Journal of Political Economy* 107, no. 6 (1999): S294–S313.

[7] Robert T. Jensen and Nolan H. Miller, "Giffen Behavior and Subsistence Consumption," *American Economic Review* 98, no. 4 (2008): 1553–1577.

enough to meet their basic caloric needs at that. When rice became cheaper, they bought more in order to meet some basic level of healthy subsistence. Essentially, even the subsidy didn't raise their income enough to allow them to buy any other foods besides rice. ■

make the grade

Simple rules to remember about income and substitution effects

It is easy to get tripped up when you're asked to identify income and substitution effects. First, remember to always start your analysis on the indifference curve associated with the consumption bundle *before* the price change. If you want to know why consumption changed going from one bundle to the other, you must start with the initial bundle. Next, keep in mind the key distinctions between the two effects listed in the table below.

SUBSTITUTION EFFECTS	INCOME EFFECTS
Involve comparisons of bundles that lie on the same indifference curve.	Involve comparisons of bundles that lie on two different indifference curves.
The direction of the effect on quantity consumed for a given change in the relative price of the good is unambiguous.	The direction of the effect on quantity consumed for a given change in the relative price of the good is ambiguous and depends on whether the good is normal or inferior.
If the good's relative price falls, the substitution effect causes the consumer to want more of it.	If the good is normal, then a fall in either its price or the price of the other good will cause the consumer to want more of it. (A drop in any price, even of another good, increases the effective income of the consumer.) If the good is inferior, then a price drop will cause the consumer to want less of it.
If the good's relative price rises, the substitution effect causes the consumer to want less of it.	If the good is normal, then a rise in either its price or the price of the other good will cause the consumer to want less of it. If the good is inferior, then a rise in either price will cause the consumer to want more of it.

Finally, remember that the total effect of a price change (for either good) on quantity consumed depends on the relative size of the substitution and income effects. If the price of one good falls, the quantities of both goods consumed may rise, or consumption of one good may rise and consumption of the other good may decline. But the quantities consumed of both goods cannot both decline, because this would mean the consumer would not be on her budget constraint.

5.4 The Impact of Changes in Another Good's Price: Substitutes and Complements

The two preceding sections showed how a change in the price of a good leads to a change in the quantity demanded of that same good. In this section, we look at the effects of a change in a good's price on the quantity demanded of *other* goods.

The approach to examining what happens when the price of another good changes is similar to that in the previous sections. We start with a fixed level of income, a set of indifference curves representing the consumer's preferences, and initial prices for the two goods. We compute the optimal consumption bundle under those conditions. Then, we vary one of the prices, holding everything else constant. The only difference is that as we vary that price, we focus on how the quantity demanded of the other good changes.

A Change in the Price of a Substitute Good

Figure 5.17 shows an example of the effects of a change in the price of a substitute good. Initially, the consumer's utility-maximizing bundle is 15 quarts of Pepsi and 5 quarts of Coke—the point labeled A. When the price of Pepsi doubles, the consumer can only afford a maximum of 10 quarts instead of 20. The maximum quantity of Coke the consumer can buy stays at 20 because the price of Coke has not changed. As a result, the budget constraint rotates inward to BC_2. In the new optimal consumption bundle B, the consumer demands more Coke (10 quarts) and less Pepsi (5 quarts).

substitute
A good that can be used in place of another good.

As we learned in Chapter 2, when the quantity demanded of one good (Coke) rises when the price of another good (Pepsi) rises, the goods are **substitutes.** More generally, the quantity a consumer demands of a good moves in the same direction as the prices of its substitutes. The more alike two goods are, the more one can be substituted for the other, and the more responsive the increase in quantity demanded of one will be to price increases in the other. Pepsi and Coke are closer substitutes than milk and Coke, for instance.

Changes in the prices of a good's substitutes lead to shifts in the good's demand curve. When a substitute for a good becomes more expensive, this raises the quantity demanded of that good at any given price level. As a result, the demand curve for the good shifts out (the demand for that good increases). When a good's substitutes become cheaper, the quantity demanded at any given price falls, and the good's demand curve shifts in.

complement
A good that is purchased and used in combination with another good.

When the quantity consumed of a good moves in the opposite direction of another good's price, they are **complements.** Complements are often goods that the consumer would use in tandem, like golf clubs and golf balls, pencils and paper, or home theater systems and installation services. Vanilla ice cream and hot fudge, for example, are complementary goods. Figure 5.18 shows how an increase in ice cream's price leads to a decrease in the quantity demanded of hot fudge. The higher ice cream price causes the budget constraint to rotate in, shifting the utility-maximizing bundle from A (30 quarts

---

Figure 5.17   :   **When the Price of a Substitute Rises, Demand Rises**

At the original prices, the consumer consumes 15 quarts of Pepsi and 5 quarts of Coke at the utility-maximizing bundle A. When the price of Pepsi doubles, the consumer's budget constraint rotates inward from BC_1 to BC_2. At the new optimal consumption bundle B, the consumer decreases his consumption of Pepsi from 15 to 5 quarts and increases his consumption of Coke from 5 to 10 quarts. Since the quantity of Coke demanded rose while the price of Pepsi rose, Coke and Pepsi are considered substitutes.

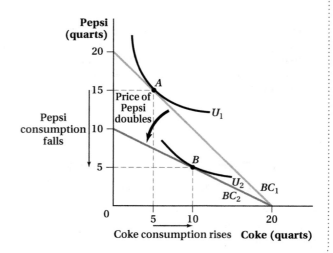

Figure 5.18 | When the Price of a Complement Rises, Demand Falls

At the original prices, the consumer consumes 20 gallons of ice cream and 30 quarts of hot fudge at the utility-maximizing bundle A. When the price of ice cream increases, the consumer's budget constraint rotates inward from BC_1 to BC_2. At the new optimal consumption bundle B, the consumer decreases his consumption of ice cream from 20 to 15 gallons and likewise decreases his consumption of hot fudge from 30 to 20 quarts. Since the quantities demanded of both ice cream and hot fudge decreased with an increase in price of only one of those goods, ice cream and hot fudge are considered complements.

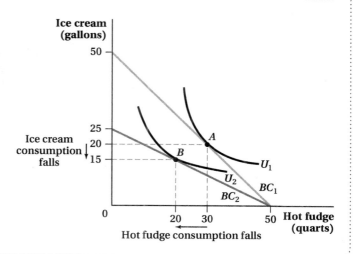

of hot fudge and 20 gallons of vanilla ice cream) to B (20 quarts of hot fudge and 15 gallons of vanilla ice cream). The quantity demanded of both goods falls; an increase in the price of ice cream not only causes the consumer to demand less ice cream (this is the own-price effect we've studied so far in this chapter), but less hot fudge, the complementary good, as well.

When the price of a complement of a good increases, the quantity demanded of that good at every price decreases and its demand curve shifts in. If the price of a complement of a good falls, the quantity demanded of that good rises at all prices and the demand curve shifts out. Changes in the price of a complementary good *shift* the demand curve for the other good. Changes in a good's own price cause a *move along* the same demand curve.

The effects of price changes in substitute and complementary goods on demand are summarized in Figure 5.19.

Figure 5.19 | Changes in the Prices of Substitutes or Complements Shift the Demand Curve

When the price of a substitute good rises or the price of a complement falls, the demand curve for good X shifts out. When the price of a substitute good falls or the price of a complement rises, the demand curve for good X shifts in.

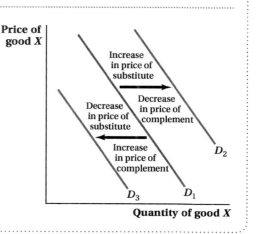

Indifference Curve Shapes, Revisited

As we touched on in Chapter 4, the shape of indifference curves is related to whether two goods are substitutes or complements. The more curved the indifference curve, the less substitutable (or, equivalently, the more complementary) are the goods.

In Section 5.3, we learned that the size of the substitution effect from a change in a good's *own* price was larger for goods with less-curved indifference curves (see Figure 5.11). The logic behind this is that, because the marginal rate of substitution (*MRS*) doesn't change much along straighter indifference curves, a given relative price change will cause the consumer to move a longer distance along his indifference curve to equate his *MRS* to the new price ratio. This logic holds true when it comes to the effects of changes in *other* goods' prices. All that matters to the substitution effect are the *relative* prices; whether it's Good *A*'s or Good *B*'s price that changes doesn't matter. Therefore, an increase (decrease) in a good's price will create a larger movement toward (away from) a substitute good when the indifference curves between the goods are less curved.

 application

Movies in a Theater and at Home—Substitutes or Complements?

If you own a movie theater company, one of the most important issues you face for the long-run viability of your firm is whether watching a movie on a home theater system and seeing a film in your movie-plex are substitutes or complements. Improvements in home electronics like large-screen, high-definition TVs, Blu-ray disc players, downloadable digital movies, and compact surround sound audio systems have greatly reduced the price of having a high-quality movie-watching experience at home. A middle-class family today can buy a home theater system that a multimillionaire could have only dreamed about a few decades ago. If movies at home are a substitute good for movies in a theater, this price reduction will reduce the number of people visiting their local movie-plex. This change will surely lead to some theaters going out of business sooner or later. If movies at home are instead a complement, theater-going will increase and bring newfound growth to the movie exhibition business.

Either case is plausible. On one hand, there is clear scope for substitution. If home electronics can better replicate the theater experience, people could find it less costly (in terms of either direct expenditures, convenience, or both) to watch a movie at home. On the other hand, if people become more interested in films in general because they now watch more at home—perhaps they develop a movie habit, or appreciate the art of film, or get caught up in following their favorite actors or watching their favorite movie again and again—then they might be more likely to see movies in theaters than they were before, particularly if theaters offer some component of the movie-watching experience that you can't get at home (audiences to laugh or be scared with, really big screens, super-greasy popcorn, etc.).

The data are not yet clear about the answer to this question. Figure 5.20 shows the trends in total U.S. box office sales receipts (inflation adjusted to 2010 dollars) and the number of tickets sold per capita since 1980.[8] The overall trend in total box office has been upward over the period, but it topped out in 2002 after a run-up in the 1990s. The decline between 2002 and 2010 was just under 5%, though this is

---

[8] The data in this application are from www.boxofficemojo.com.

Figure 5.20 : U.S. Total Box Office and Tickets Sold per Capita, 1980–2010

The overall trend in total box office was upward over the period, but leveled out after 2002.

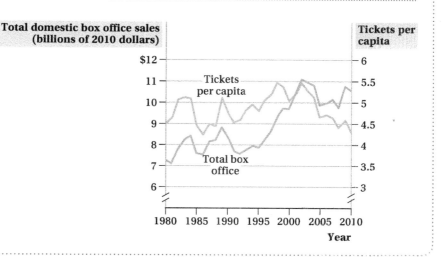

mitigated some by the fact that 2009 and 2010 were good years. The data on the number of tickets sold per capita—you can think of this as the average number of times a person goes to see a movie during the year—are more volatile, but show a similar pattern of a run-up in the 1990s and then a drop after 2002. The drop is larger relative to that for the total box office, though, falling about 20% from 5.5 to 4.3 movies a year by 2010.

The decrease in theater-going after 2002 suggests that watching movies at home is a substitute, because it coincides with the period of the increased availability of big-screen HDTV and disc players. However, the data are fairly noisy: That is, there is a large amount of variation across the years, so it's not completely clear if these are long-run trends or just temporary blips due to the quality of movies or changes in the prices of other entertainment goods such as video game systems. Furthermore, the widespread diffusion of VCRs, DVD players, and early surround-sound systems in the 1980s and 1990s didn't scar the movie exhibition industry because revenues and tickets per capita both rose, indicating that they may have been complements to watching films in a theater.

So perhaps movie-plex owners will be helped by cheap, high-quality home theater systems. Then again, in 1946, before TVs were in most people's homes, over 4 billion tickets were sold in the United States when the population was about 140 million (compared to over 310 million today). That's an average of over 28 movies a year per person! By 1956 attendance was half that. It seems quite likely that movie houses and TVs were substitutes then. Time will tell whether the same holds for movie houses and home theaters. ■

5.5 Combining Individual Demand Curves to Obtain the Market Demand Curve

When studying consumer demand, we're often more interested in the combined demand of all consumers, rather than any one consumer's demand. For instance, if you are a company trying to figure out how many scooters to make and what to charge for them, what ultimately matters is the overall market demand for scooters.[9] Similarly, a government that wants to figure out how much revenue a tax or tariff on tires will raise needs to look at the market demand for tires.

The market demand for a good is the sum of all the individual demand curves for it. That is, the market quantity demanded for a good at a particular price is the sum of every individual consumer's quantity demanded at that price.

Figure 5.21 shows graphically how this adding up works. Suppose you and your cousin are the only two consumers in the market for Razor scooters. The total market demand curve is obtained by summing horizontally each of the individual demand curves. For instance, at a price of $40, you and your cousin each want 3 scooters, so the combined market quantity demanded is 6 scooters. When the price is $20, you want 4 scooters and your cousin wants 8, for a market quantity demanded of 12 scooters. Adding up the individual consumers' quantities demanded at all possible prices gives the market demand curve.

Figure 5.21   The Market Demand Curve

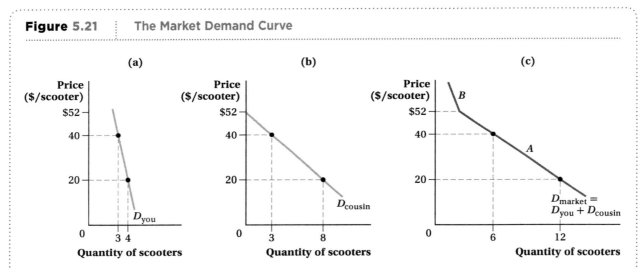

(a) Your market demand curve D_{you} shows the number of scooters you would demand at each price. At a price of $40 per scooter, you demand 3 scooters; at $20 per scooter, you demand 4 scooters.

(b) Your cousin's market demand curve D_{cousin} shows that he is more sensitive to price changes in scooters than you are. At a price of $40 per scooter, he similarly demands 3 scooters, but when the price of a scooter is $20, he demands 8 scooters.

(c) In a market consisting only of you and your cousin, the total market demand curve D_{market} is the sum of your demand curve D_{you} and your cousin's demand curve D_{cousin}. At a price of $40 per scooter, you and your cousin each demand 3 scooters, summing to 6 scooters on D_{market}. When scooters cost $20 each, you demand 4 scooters and your cousin demands 8 scooters, summing to 12 scooters on D_{market}. At prices above $52, your cousin's quantity demanded is zero, so D_{market} overlaps with D_{you}, and therefore D_{market} is kinked at a price of $52. Market demand will always be flatter and to the right of the individual demand curves.

[9] An exception to this rule would be when the firm can charge different prices to different consumers (what economists call *price discrimination*). In that case, which we explore in Chapter 10, the firm can take advantage of individual consumers' demand curves rather than just the overall market demand. By charging different prices to different consumers depending on their individual demand, the firm can make higher profits.

The Market Demand Curve

There are a few things to notice about market demand curves. First, a market demand curve will always be to the right of any individual demand curve, because all consumers combined must consume at least as much of a good at a given price as any single consumer does. For a similar reason, the slope of the market demand curve must also be as flat as or flatter than any of the individual demand curves. That is, for a given change in price, the change in quantity demanded for the market as a whole must be at least as great as the change in quantity demanded by any individual consumer.[10] Finally, if the price is so high that only one consumer wants any of the good, the individual demand curve for that consumer will lie directly on top of the market demand curve at that price. At that point, the consumer *is* the market.

Using Algebra to Move from Individual to Market Demand

We can move from individual to market demand algebraically as well as graphically. The formulas for the two demand curves in Figure 5.21 are

$$Q_{you} = 5 - 0.05P$$
$$Q_{cousin} = 13 - 0.25P$$

To find the market demand for the tickets, we start by adding up the two individual demand curves:

$$Q_{market} = Q_{you} + Q_{cousin} = (5 - 0.05P) + (13 - 0.25P)$$
$$Q_{market} = 18 - 0.3P$$

If we plug in the prices from Figure 5.21, they match the quantities in the figure as long as we are on the part of the curve labeled A in Figure 5.21 where both quantities demanded are above zero. According to the equation, market demand when $P = 40$ is $Q_{market} = 6$, which is what the figure shows, and when $P = 20$, $Q_{market} = 12$, just as on the figure.

We're not quite done yet, though. The prices at which you and your cousin will consume no scooters—the demand choke prices—are different. Yours is $100; your cousin's is $52. (You can check this by plugging these prices into the demand curves and verifying that the quantities demanded equal zero.) That means at prices above $52, the market demand is only *your* demand because your cousin's quantity demanded is zero. There is no negative demand allowed. This isn't accounted for when we add together the two demand curves above, however, because at prices above $52, the part of the market demand curve coming from the formula for Q_{cousin} is less than zero. Therefore, market demand is your demand, $Q = 5 - 0.05P$, for prices between $52 and $100 (quantity demanded is zero at prices higher than $100), and is $Q = 18 - 0.3P$ (yours plus your cousin's) for prices below $52. That is, the market demand has a kink at $P = 52$.

---

[10] Even though the *slope* of the market demand curve is always flatter than that of individual demand curves, it doesn't necessarily imply that the *elasticity* of the market demand curve is higher than that of individual demand curves (though this is often the case). This is because the elasticity doesn't just depend on the slope, but also on the level of demand. The percentage change in prices (the denominator in the elasticity equation) will be the same for both individuals and the market. While the change in quantity will be smaller for individuals, the level of demand will be lower too. If the level is small enough, the percentage change in quantities for the individual can be large enough to make individual demand as or more elastic than market demand.

make the grade

Adding demand curves horizontally, not vertically

Moving from individual demand curves to market demand is conceptually fairly simple. There's just one thing you have to be careful about. Market demand curves are derived by adding *quantities* of individual demand curves, not prices. That is, individual demands are graphically added horizontally, not vertically.

When you add horizontally, you are summing up all the individual quantities demanded, holding price fixed. This is exactly what you want to do because market demand is the total quantity demanded at any given price. If you add individual demand curves vertically, however, you are holding quantities demanded fixed while adding up the prices. That's a very different conceptual exercise and one that, in this case at least, doesn't really make any sense.

Likewise, if you are combining individual demand curves algebraically rather than graphically, make sure you've written out the individual demand curves as quantities demanded as a function of price. When you add those equations, you'll just be adding the quantities, which is again what you want to do. If you instead try to add equations where prices are a function of quantities (economists call these "inverse demand curves"), again you'll be doing the very different exercise of adding up prices across individuals while holding the quantities fixed.

5.4 figure it out

Suppose that at a rural gas station in Toby Acres, there are only two customers, Johnny (who drives a 4X4 pickup) and Olivia (who drives a Prius). Johnny's demand for gasoline is $Q_J = 32 - 8P$, while Olivia's demand is $Q_O = 20 - 4P$, where Q is measured in gallons and P is the price per gallon.

a. Solve for the market demand equation for gasoline at Toby Acres.

b. Draw a diagram showing the market demand curve for gasoline at Toby Acres.

Solution:

a. The market demand curve is the horizontal sum of the buyers' demand curves. Remember that summing horizontally means to add up quantities demanded at each price. This means that we can get the market demand by adding Q_J and Q_O:

$$Q_{\text{market}} = Q_J + Q_O$$
$$= (32 - 8P) + (20 - 4P)$$
$$= 52 - 12P$$

But there is more to the story than solving for the summation of the two demand curves. Johnny is not willing to buy any gas if the price is greater than or equal to $4 per gallon because that is his demand choke price:

$$Q_J = 32 - 8P$$
$$0 = 32 - 8P$$
$$8P = 32$$
$$P = 4$$

So, once the price hits $4, only Olivia will be in the market. Her demand choke price is $5:

$$Q_O = 20 - 4P$$
$$0 = 20 - 4P$$
$$4P = 20$$
$$P = 5$$

Thus, as long as the price is below $4 per gallon, the market demand for gasoline is the horizontal sum of the two buyers' demand curves. Between a price of $4 and $5, the market demand is simply the same as Olivia's demand. At a price greater than or equal to $5, quantity demanded is zero.

b. The figure here shows the market demand for gasoline in Toby Acres. Notice that the market demand curve is kinked as a result of the buyers' different choke prices. Segment A is the section of demand below the price of $4 and is the horizontal summation of Johnny's and Olivia's demand for gasoline. Segment B is the segment of market demand where Olivia is the only buyer (since the price is above Johnny's demand choke price). At a price of $5 or above, quantity demanded is zero.

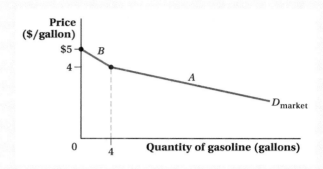

5.6 Conclusion

In this chapter, we used the consumer choice model of Chapter 4 to see where demand curves come from and what factors shift them. We studied how changes in various factors that drive consumer demand for a good—their income, the good's price, and the prices of other goods—affect the consumer's utility-maximizing bundle and, through this, the demand curve.

We decomposed the response of a consumer's choices to a price change in a good into two components: the substitution effect and the income effect. The substitution effect reflects changes in quantities consumed due to the new relative prices of goods after the price change. The income effect reflects the fact that a price change affects a consumer's buying power, and this in turn changes the consumer's optimal consumption bundle.

We also saw how individuals' demand curves for a good are added up to create the market demand curve for that good.

This chapter ends our examination of the factors that determine consumer demand. In the next chapter, we move on to producer behavior and the supply side of markets.

Summary

1. Shifts in income holding prices constant are reflected in parallel shifts in the budget constraint and affect a consumer's demand curve. An **Engel curve** shows the relationship between income and the quantity of a good demanded. Whether an increase in income raises or reduces the quantity demanded of a good depends on the type of good. **Normal goods** are those for which demand increases with income. **Inferior goods** are those for which demand decreases with income. Within normal goods, goods with an **income elasticity** between zero and 1 (those whose share of expenditure rises more slowly than income rises) are called **necessity goods.** Goods with an income elasticity greater than 1 (those whose share of expenditure grows faster than income) are called **luxury goods. [Section 5.1]**

2. The way in which changes in the price of a good affect the quantity demanded of that good is what creates the shape of the demand curve. We construct a consumer's demand curve by examining what happens to a consumer's utility-maximizing bundle as the price of one good changes, holding the price of the other good, income, and preferences fixed. Changes in income, holding preferences and prices constant, can shift the demand curve. Changes in preferences, holding income and prices constant, can shift the demand curve. **[Section 5.2]**

3. The **total effect** on the quantity demanded of a good in response to a change in its own price can be broken down into two components.

   The **substitution effect** causes the consumer to shift toward the good that becomes relatively cheaper and away from the good that becomes relatively more expensive. This shows up as a movement along the consumer's initial indifference curve, driven by the change in relative prices.

   The **income effect** occurs because a change in the price of a good changes the purchasing power of the consumer; a price drop increases purchasing power and expands the set of bundles a consumer may choose from, while a rise in price decreases purchasing power and reduces the consumer's options. The income effect shows up as a move to a new indifference curve, reflecting a change in utility for the consumer. The direction of the income effect on quantity demanded depends on whether the good is normal (where demand rises when income rises) or inferior (demand falls when income rises). If the income effect is large enough for inferior goods,

it is theoretically possible for the quantity demanded of a good to rise when its price rises. However, these types of goods, called **Giffen goods,** are exceedingly rare in the real world. [Section 5.3]

4. Changes in the prices of other goods shift the demand curve for a good. Which ways these cross-price effects shift demand depends on the nature of the relationship between the goods. Goods are **substitutes** if a price increase in one leads to an increase in demand of the other, due to consumers switching away from the now more expensive good and toward the substitute. Goods are **complements** if an increase in one's price causes demand of the other to fall. Complements are goods that are often consumed together. [Section 5.4]

5. Individuals' demand curves are aggregated to get total market demand. Market demand at a given price is the sum of all individual demands at that same price. Another way of saying this is that market demand is the horizontal (i.e., quantity) sum of individual demands. [Section 5.5]

Review Questions

1. Define the income effect. What variables do we hold constant in order to isolate the income effect?
2. What are the differences between normal goods, inferior goods, and luxury goods?
3. Both the income expansion path and the Engel curve show the effect of income on consumption choices. When might you choose to use the income expansion path? When might the Engel curve be more useful?
4. Describe how we can derive a consumer's demand curve from his indifference curves. Why would we expect the demand curve to slope downward?
5. Name at least three factors that can shift an individual's demand curve for pizza. Also describe the effect each factor has on demand (e.g., does it rise or fall?).
6. Define the substitution effect. How does it relate to the income effect?
7. Describe how to decompose the consumer's response to price changes into the substitution and income effects.
8. How do income and substitution effects differ between normal and inferior goods?
9. What is a Giffen good?
10. What are complements and substitutes?
11. When the cross-price elasticity of demand is positive, are the two goods complements or substitutes? What type of goods have a negative cross-price elasticity?
12. What can the shape of the indifference curve tell us about two goods?
13. How does the market demand relate to individual demand curves?
14. Why will a market demand curve always be at least as flat as a given individual demand curve?

Problems

1. A principles of microeconomics instructor regularly asks her class to give an example of an inferior good. "No matter how poor we might be," the students tell her, "ramen noodles are an inferior good." Explain why the students must be wrong in their reasoning.
2. Can you tell whether a good is normal or inferior by looking at the shape of a single indifference curve? Explain your answer.

3. Andrew has an income of $30 he spends on cupcakes and cakes. The price of a cupcake is $5. Suppose that Andrew has the following preferences depicted below:

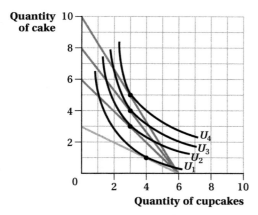

Quantity of cake (vertical axis), **Quantity of cupcakes** (horizontal axis), curves U_1, U_2, U_3, U_4

a. With this in mind, draw Andrew's demand curve for cake.
b. When the price of cake changes, which effect is stronger, the substitution effect or the income effect? Give your answer for every price change depicted in the figure.
c. If Andrew's preferences shifted toward not distinguishing between cake and cupcakes (i.e., if they became closer substitutes), all his indifference curves would become flatter. How would Andrew's demand curve for cake change?

4. Suppose that, holding prices constant, Alice has preferences over the number of books she purchases that look like:

Income (thousands of dollars)	Optimal number of books purchased
5	5
10	6
15	20
20	25
25	26
30	10
35	9
40	8
45	7
50	6

a. Draw a smooth approximation of Alice's Engel curve for books, indicating the ranges over which books are inferior goods and over which they are normal goods.
b. A luxury good is a good that has an income elasticity greater than 1. Give the ranges in which books are luxury goods for Alice.

5. Suppose that Sonya faces an increase in the price of pasta, as depicted below, moving her from an optimum bundle of rice and pasta at A to an optimal bundle at B.
a. Trace a copy of this diagram. Graphically depict the substitution and income effect.
b. Which effect is strongest? How can you tell?

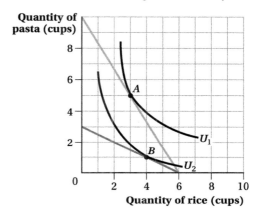

Quantity of pasta (cups) (vertical axis), **Quantity of rice (cups)** (horizontal axis), points A and B, curves U_1 and U_2

6. Kim's utility function is given by $U = 5X + 2Y$, where $MU_X = 5$ and $MU_Y = 2$.
a. Suppose that at the prices P_X and P_Y of good X and good Y, respectively, Kim is consuming (optimally) some positive amount of good X and some positive amount of good Y. What is the price of good X in terms of the price of good Y?
b. How will her consumption change if P_X doubles, while P_Y does not change?

7. You may have noticed that the market demand curve is always flatter than any individual demand curve. Is market price elasticity of demand also always lower than individual price elasticity of demand? Why or why not?

8. Indicate whether the following statements are true, false, or uncertain. If false or uncertain, explain why.
a. The price of a watch increases by 10%, and you spend a larger fraction of your income on it. The watch is a Giffen good.
b. Due to a flood, corn prices and soybean prices increase. If corn and soybeans are substitutes, the quantity of corn demanded falls.
c. Goods 1 and 2 are substitutes, and goods 2 and 3 are substitutes. This must mean that goods 1 and 3 are substitutes.

9. Suppose that Grover consumes two goods, cookies and milk. Grover's income expansion path is shown in the diagram below. Use the information in the diagram to explain whether each of the statements below is true or false. Provide an explanation for each answer.

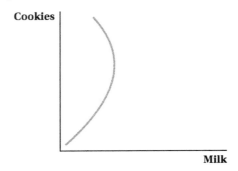

a. At low levels of income, both cookies and milk are normal goods for Grover.
b. As Grover's income grows, eventually cookies become an inferior good.
c. Draw, intuitively, the Engel curve for Grover's consumption of milk at various incomes.
d. Draw, intuitively, the Engel curve for Grover's consumption of cookies at various incomes.

10. Josie gets great pleasure from eating flan. Her preferences for flan and tofu are given in the graph below:

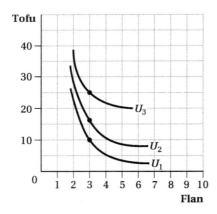

Suppose that Josie's income is $40, and that tofu costs $1.
a. Draw budget constraints for Josie given three different prices for flan: $5, $8, and $10.

b. Find the optimal consumption of flan at each of those prices.
c. What will Josie's demand curve for flan look like? Describe it in terms of the elasticity of demand.
d. What can you say about the size of the income and substitution effects of a change in the price of flan?

11. Consider the following graph, which illustrates Tyler's preferences for DVD rentals and in-theater movie tickets:

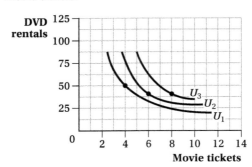

Suppose that DVD rentals always cost $1, and that Tyler's income is $100 per week.
a. If the price of a movie ticket is $10, draw Tyler's budget line. Be very careful to draw to scale. How many movies does he see in the theater?
b. In another graph, plot a point that reflects how many movies Tyler sees in the theater at a price of $10.
c. The movie theater changes the price of tickets to $12.50. Repeat your work in (a) and (b) using this new price.
d. Tyler's mother gives him a discount card that allows him to purchase movie tickets for $7.50. Repeat your work in (a) and (b) using this new price.
e. Connect the dots in your second graph to complete Tyler's demand curve for movie tickets.

12. Consider the following three graphs, which illustrate the preferences of three consumers (Bob, Carol, and Ted) regarding two goods, apples and peaches. Each consumer has an income of $30, and each consumer pays $2 for apples and $3 for peaches.

(a) Bob

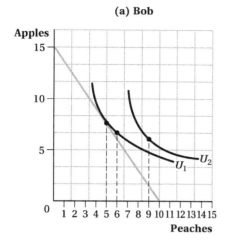

(b) Carol

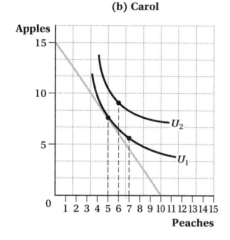

(c) Ted

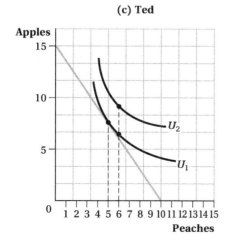

a. Suppose that the price of peaches falls to $2. Draw a new budget line for each consumer and find the new optimal bundle of apples and peaches each would buy. How does the new quantity of peaches compare to the original quantity? Indicate the change in the first column of the table below (an increase of one unit might be denoted as a +1).

b. For each consumer, determine the substitution effect of the price change by drawing a hypothetical budget line with the same slope as your new budget line, but just tangent to the consumer's original indifference curve. How much of a change in peach consumption does the substitution effect account for? Indicate that change in the first column of the table below.

c. Now add in the income effect. Compare each consumer's peach consumption in (b) to his or her final peach consumption in (a). Indicate the difference in column 3 of the table below. Double-check your work to ensure that the last two columns add up to the number in the first column.

d. Do Bob, Carol, and Ted consider peaches normal, inferior, or income-inelastic?

	Total Effect of Price Change	Substitution Effect of Price Change	Income Effect of Price Change
Bob			
Carol			
Ted			

13. Carmen's preferences are such that she is always indifferent between watching two movies or seeing one basketball game.
    a. What must Carmen's indifference curves look like?
    b. Suppose that Carmen has an income of $90. If a movie costs $10 and a basketball game costs $18, what will Carmen's optimal consumption bundle be?

14. Consider the following diagram, which illustrates Gaston's preferences for red beans and rice. Gaston has an income of $20. Rice costs $2 per serving.

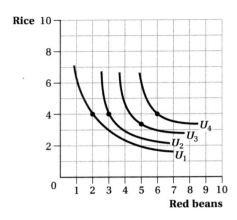

a. Derive Gaston's demand for red beans. Use prices of $2 and $4 in your analysis. Graph your results, and connect the points you plotted to yield Gaston's demand for red beans.

b. Suppose that the price of rice increases to $3. Again, derive Gaston's demand for red beans using the same prices you used in part (a).

c. Does Gaston's demand for red beans increase or decrease as a result of the increase in the price of rice?

d. Does your answer to (c) indicate that red beans and rice are substitutes or complements?

15. Consider Harry's indifference curve indicated in the graph below:

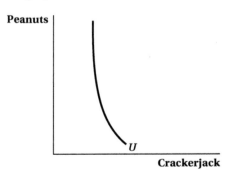

a. True or False (and explain): Peanuts and Crackerjack are clearly complements.

b. True or False (and explain): Peanuts and Crackerjack are clearly both normal goods.

16. True or False: If pizza and calzones are substitutes, then the substitution effect of a price change will be in a different direction than if pizza and calzones are complements. Explain, using a diagram.

17. Armen lives in Washington State, where grapes are grown. Armen's twin Allen lives in New York, where grapes must be trucked in from Washington at a fixed cost of $0.20 per pound of grapes. Armen and Allen have identical tastes, but Armen tends to purchase lower-quality grapes and Allen tends to purchase higher quality grapes. Use indifference curve analysis to explain this oddity.

18. Mitch cares only about how much he can write. Because a pen will write 7 miles of text and a pencil will write 35 miles of text, Mitch considers them perfect 5-to-1 substitutes. If the price of pens is given by P_{pen} and the price of pencils is given by P_{pencil}, and if Mitch's income is given by Y, use indifference curve analysis to *derive* the demand curve for pencils.

19. Brady, who has ordinary-shaped indifference curves, buys 16 ounces of salt each year. Even when the price of salt doubles, Brady continues to purchase exactly 16 ounces.

a. True or False (and explain): Salt is neither inferior nor normal to Brady.

b. What is Brady's price elasticity of demand for salt?

c. What is Brady's income elasticity of demand for salt?

d. What can we say about the substitution and income effects of a change in the price of salt?

20. At a price of $3 per gallon, Yoshi (an average buyer) purchases 200 gallons of gasoline each year. The government proposes imposing a $0.50 tax on each gallon of gas, and then compensating consumers for the price increase by mailing each taxpayer a check for $100.

a. What will happen to Yoshi's consumption of gas? Show, using an indifference curve diagram with gasoline on the horizontal axis and a composite good (price = $1) on the vertical axis.

b. Will Yoshi be better off, worse off, or indifferent to the change? Explain, using your diagram.

c. In terms of revenue, will the government be better off, worse off, or indifferent to the proposal? Explain.

Chapter 5 Appendix:
The Calculus of Income and Substitution Effects

We saw in this chapter that a price change in one good influences a consumer's consumption in two ways. The *substitution effect* is the change in a consumer's optimal consumption bundle due to a change in the relative price of the goods, holding his utility constant. The *income effect* is the change in a consumer's optimal consumption bundle due to the change in his purchasing power. In the chapter, we solved for these two effects using a figure like the one below where good X is shown on the horizontal axis and good Y on the vertical axis. The consumer's original consumption bundle is A. Consumption bundle B is the optimal bundle after a decrease in the price of X. Finally, bundle A' shows what the consumer would buy if the price of X decreased but utility stayed the same as at bundle A (i.e., on indifference curve U_1). Graphically, the substitution effect is the change from bundle A to bundle A', the income effect is the change from A' to B, and the total effect is the sum of these two effects or the change from A to B.

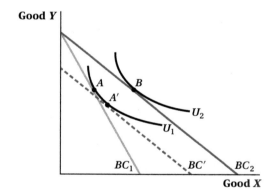

However, the graphical approach to decomposing the income and substitution effects can be a little messy. You have to keep track of multiple budget constraints, indifference curves, and their respective shifts. The calculus links the effects we observed in the graph to the techniques we learned for solving the consumer's problem in the Chapter 4 Appendix. Solving for these effects is a two-step process. We begin by solving for the total effect by finding the new consumption bundle B. Second, we solve for bundle A', which will allow us to identify both the substitution and income effects.

Let's start with a consumer with budget constraint $I = P_X X + P_Y Y$ (BC_1 in the graph) and a standard Cobb–Douglas utility function $U(X,Y) = X^\alpha Y^{1-\alpha}$, where $0 < \alpha < 1$. Point A in the figure is the solution to the constrained optimization problem:

$$\max_{X,Y} U = X^\alpha Y^{1-\alpha} \text{ s.t. } I = P_X X + P_Y Y$$

In the Chapter 4 Appendix, we derived the solution to this particular utility-maximization problem, and found that the optimal bundle A is $\left(X_A = \frac{\alpha I}{P_X}, Y_A = \frac{(1-\alpha)I}{P_Y} \right)$.

Now suppose that the price of good X, P_X, decreases to P_X'. The consumer has the same utility function as before, but because of the price change, his budget constraint rotates outward to $I = P_X'X + P_YY$ (BC_2 on the graph). Once again, we rely on utility maximization to solve for the optimal bundle:

$$\max_{X,Y} U = X^\alpha Y^{1-\alpha} \text{ s.t. } I = P_X'X + P_YY$$

Because we already know the generic solution to this problem, we can plug in the new price of X to find the new optimal bundle $B = \left(X_B = \frac{\alpha I}{P_X'}, Y_B = \frac{(1-\alpha)I}{P_Y}\right)$. This gives us the total effect of the price change on the consumer's consumption bundle—the difference between his new consumption bundle $\left(\frac{\alpha I}{P_X'}, \frac{(1-\alpha)I}{P_Y}\right)$ and his original consumption bundle $\left(\frac{\alpha I}{P_X}, \frac{(1-\alpha)I}{P_Y}\right)$. Note that in this instance the change in the price of X does not affect the quantity of Y the consumer purchases. That the demand for each good is independent of changes in the price of the other good is a quirk of the Cobb–Douglas utility function. This result is not necessarily true of other utility functions.

The solution to the utility-maximization problem gives us the final bundle B. But we want to know more than just the total effect of the price change on the consumption bundle. We want to decompose this total effect into its two components: the substitution and income effects. We can do this by solving for bundle A'.

What is the substitution effect? It is the effect of the change in relative price of two goods on the quantities demanded given the consumer's original level of utility. How can we solve for this effect? It's easy! When we know the consumer's original level of utility and the goods' prices, as we do here, expenditure minimization tells us the answer to the problem. Take the consumer's original level of utility $U_1 = X^\alpha Y^{1-\alpha}$ as the constraint and set up the consumer's expenditure-minimization problem

$$\min_{X,Y} I = P_X'X + P_YY \text{ s.t. } U_1 = X^\alpha Y^{1-\alpha}$$

as a Lagrangian:

$$\min_{X,Y,\lambda} \mathcal{L}(X,Y,\lambda) = P_X'X + P_YY + \lambda(U_1 - X^\alpha Y^{1-\alpha})$$

Write out the first-order conditions:

$$\frac{\partial \mathcal{L}}{\partial X} = P_X' - \lambda\alpha X^{\alpha-1}Y^{1-\alpha} = 0$$

$$\frac{\partial \mathcal{L}}{\partial Y} = P_Y - \lambda(1-\alpha)X^\alpha Y^{-\alpha} = 0$$

$$\frac{\partial \mathcal{L}}{\partial \lambda} = U_1 - X^\alpha Y^{1-\alpha} = 0$$

Solve for Y using the first two conditions:

$$\lambda = \frac{P_X'}{\alpha X^{\alpha-1}Y^{1-\alpha}} = \frac{P_Y}{(1-\alpha)X^\alpha Y^{-\alpha}}$$

$$P_X'(1-\alpha)X^\alpha Y^{-\alpha} = P_Y\alpha X^{\alpha-1}Y^{1-\alpha}$$

$$Y^{1-\alpha}Y^\alpha = \frac{(1-\alpha)}{\alpha}\frac{P_X'}{P_Y}X^\alpha X^{1-\alpha}$$

$$Y = \frac{(1-\alpha)}{\alpha}\frac{P_X'}{P_Y}X$$

Plug this expression for Y as a function of X into the constraint to solve for bundle A':

$$U_1 = X^\alpha Y^{1-\alpha} = X^\alpha \left[\frac{(1-\alpha)}{\alpha}\frac{P_X'}{P_Y}X\right]^{1-\alpha}$$

$$U_1 = X^\alpha X^{1-\alpha}\left[\frac{(1-\alpha)}{\alpha}\frac{P_X'}{P_Y}\right]^{1-\alpha} = X\left[\frac{(1-\alpha)}{\alpha}\frac{P_X'}{P_Y}\right]^{1-\alpha}$$

$$X_{A'} = U_1\left[\frac{\alpha}{(1-\alpha)}\frac{P_Y}{P_X'}\right]^{1-\alpha}$$

Then plug this optimal value of X into the expression for Y as a function of X from above:

$$Y_{A'} = \frac{(1-\alpha)}{\alpha}\frac{P_X'}{P_Y}X_{A'} = \frac{(1-\alpha)}{\alpha}\frac{P_X'}{P_Y}\left[U_1\frac{\alpha}{(1-\alpha)}\frac{P_Y}{P_X'}\right]^{1-\alpha}$$

$$= U_1\frac{(1-\alpha)}{\alpha}\frac{P_X'}{P_Y}\left[\frac{(1-\alpha)}{\alpha}\frac{P_X'}{P_Y}\right]^{\alpha-1}$$

$$= U_1\left[\frac{(1-\alpha)}{\alpha}\frac{P_X'}{P_Y}\right]^{\alpha}$$

Solving the consumer's expenditure-minimization problem at the new prices and original utility level gives us the third piece of the substitution/income effect puzzle: bundle A'.[1] Having these three bundles (A, A', and B) allows us to solve for the substitution and income effects. The substitution effect is the difference between the consumer's original bundle and what he would buy at the new prices but at the old utility level, the difference between A and A'. The income effect is the difference between what he would buy at the new prices and original utility and what he buys with his original income at the new prices, the difference between A' and B. The total effect is the sum of the substitution and income effects or the difference between A and B.

5.A figure it out

A sample problem will make breaking down the total effect of a price change into the substitution and income effects even clearer. Let's return to Figure It Out 4.4, which featured Antonio, a consumer who purchases burgers and fries. Antonio has a utility function $U(B,F) = \sqrt{BF} = B^{0.5}F^{0.5}$ and income of $20. Initially, the prices of burgers and fries are $5 and $2, respectively.

a. What is Antonio's optimal consumption bundle and utility at the original prices?

b. The price of burgers increases to $10 per burger, and the price of fries stays constant at $2. What does Antonio consume at the optimum at these new prices? Decompose this change into the total, substitution, and income effects.

Solution:

a. We solved this question in the Chapter 4 Appendix, but the answer will be crucial to solving for the total, substitution, and income effects in part (b). When a burger costs $5 and fries cost $2, Antonio's original constrained optimization problem is

$$\max_{B,F} U = B^{0.5}F^{0.5} \text{ s.t. } 20 = 5B + 2F$$

We found that Antonio consumes 2 burgers and 5 orders of fries, and his utility for this bundle is $B^{0.5}F^{0.5} = 5^{0.5}2^{0.5} = 10^{0.5}$.

b. When the price of hamburgers doubles to $10 each, Antonio faces a new budget constraint: $20 = 10B + 2F$. Antonio's new utility-maximization problem is

$$\max_{B,F} U = B^{0.5}F^{0.5} \text{ s.t. } 20 = 10B + 2F$$

Therefore, we should write his constrained optimization problem as a Lagrangian and solve for his new optimal bundle at the higher burger price:

$$\max_{B,F,\lambda}\mathcal{L} = B^{0.5}F^{0.5} + \lambda(20 - 10B - 2F)$$

$$\frac{\partial\mathcal{L}}{\partial\mathcal{L}} = 0.5B^{-0.5}F^{0.5} - 10\lambda = 0$$

$$\frac{\partial\mathcal{L}}{\partial F} = 0.5B^{0.5}F^{-0.5} - 2\lambda = 0$$

$$\frac{\partial\mathcal{L}}{\partial\lambda} = 20 - 10B - 2F = 0$$

Then we use the first two conditions to solve for λ and then solve for F as a function of B:

$$\lambda = 0.05B^{-0.5}F^{0.5} = 0.25B^{0.5}F^{-0.5}$$

$$F^{0.5}F^{0.5} = 20(0.25)B^{0.5}B^{0.5}$$

$$F = 5B$$

---

[1] One way to check our answer to bundle A' is to take the new prices, income, and utility function, and solve for the bundle using utility maximization. As we saw in the Chapter 4 Appendix, this approach will yield the same answer.

and substitute this value for F into the budget constraint:

$$20 = 10B + 2F$$
$$20 = 10B + 2(5B)$$
$$20 = 20B$$
$$B^* = 1 \text{ burger}$$
$$F^* = 5B = 5(1) = 5 \text{ orders of fries}$$

In response to the increase in the price of burgers from \$5 to \$10, then, Antonio decreases his consumption of burgers and leaves his consumption of fries unchanged. Therefore, the total effect of the price change is that Antonio's consumption of burgers declines by 1 and his consumption of fries remains the same at 2.

Next, we use expenditure minimization to find the substitution and income effects. Remember that we want to find out how many burgers and fries Antonio will consume if the price of burgers is \$10 but his utility is the same as his utility when burgers cost \$5. His third constrained optimization problem is

$$\min_{B,F} I = 10B + 2F \text{ s.t. } 10^{0.5} = B^{0.5}F^{0.5}$$

We could solve using the Lagrangian as we did above, but instead let's use what we know about the solution to the consumer's optimization problem and set the marginal rate of substitution of burgers for fries equal to the ratio of their prices and solve for F as a function of B:

$$\frac{MU_B}{MU_F} = \frac{P_B}{P_F}$$
$$\frac{0.5B^{-0.5}F^{0.5}}{0.5B^{0.5}F^{-0.5}} = \frac{10}{2}$$
$$\frac{F}{B} = \frac{10}{2}$$
$$F = 5B$$

Now plug this value for F into the consumer's utility constraint:

$$10^{0.5} = B^{0.5}F^{0.5} = B^{0.5}(5B)^{0.5}$$
$$10^{0.5} = B(5^{0.5})$$
$$B' = \frac{10^{0.5}}{5^{0.5}} = 2^{0.5} \approx 1.4 \text{ hamburgers}$$
$$F' = 5B' \approx 5(1.4) \approx 7 \text{ orders of fries}$$

Antonio's expenditure-minimizing bundle for the new prices and the original utility is approximately 1.4 hamburgers and 7 fries compared to his original bundle of 2 hamburgers and 5 fries. As intuition would tell you, the desired consumption of burgers decreases when burgers become relatively more expensive, while the desired consumption of fries increases as fries become relatively less expensive—that's the substitution effect in action. In particular, Antonio's substitution effect is to consume 0.6 fewer burgers (1.4 − 2 burgers = −0.6 burgers) and 2 more orders of fries (7 − 5 orders of fries = 2 orders of fries).

While this bundle gives Antonio the same level of utility as the original bundle, he would have to spend about \$8 more to buy it [his original expenditure was \$20; his new one is \$10(1.4) + \$2(7) = \$28]. Remember, however, that Antonio doesn't actually purchase this \$28 combination of burgers and fries. It's just a step on the way to his final consumption bundle (1 hamburger, 5 orders of fries) that we got from the utility-maximization problem above. We can use this final bundle to find the income effect. Here, the income effect is to consume 0.4 fewer burgers (1 − 1.4 burgers = −0.4 burgers) and 2 fewer orders of fries (5 − 7 orders of fries = −2 orders of fries) because the increase in the price of burgers reduces Antonio's purchasing power. Notice that the quantity of both goods declines as his purchasing power declines. This means that, for Antonio, they are both normal goods.

In the end, the price change only changes Antonio's consumption of hamburgers: The total effect on his consumption bundle is 1 fewer burger (1 − 2 burgers = −1 burger), which is the sum of the substitution effect (−0.6 burgers) and the income effect (−0.4 burgers). On the other hand, the total effect on his consumption of fries is zero because the substitution effect (2 more orders of fries) and the income effect (2 fewer orders of fries) exactly offset one another.

Let's review what we've learned about decomposing the total effect of a price change into the substitution and income effects. To find the original bundle, we solve the utility-maximization problem at the original prices and income. We identify the substitution effect after a price change by solving the expenditure-minimization problem using the new prices with the original level of utility as the constraint. This tells us how a consumer's bundle responds to a price change while leaving the consumer with the same level of utility—the substitution effect. Finally, to find the income effect, we solve the utility-maximization problem using the new prices and the consumer's actual income. Comparing this bundle with the bundle we found using expenditure minimization tells us how consumption responds to the change in purchasing power that is caused by the price change, or the income effect.

Problems

1. Malachi only consumes 2 goods: DVD rentals and coffee. His utility function is

$$U(R,C) = R^{0.75}C^{0.25}$$

where R is the number of rentals and C is cups of coffee. Malachi has $16 in his pocket right now, and he plans to spend all of the $16 on DVD rentals and coffee today.

a. The price of one rental is $4 and the price of coffee is $2 per cup. Solve for Malachi's optimal bundle.

b. Suppose that Malachi signs up for a membership that reduces the price of a rental to $2, while leaving his income unchanged. Find the substitution effect, the income effect, and the total effect of the decrease in the price of video rentals on Malachi's consumption of rentals and coffee.

c. From your answer to part (b), are DVD rentals and coffee normal or inferior goods for Malachi? Explain.

2. Suppose that a consumer has utility given by $U(X, Y) = XY + 10Y$ and income of $100 to spend on goods X and Y.

a. The prices of X and Y are both $1 per unit. Use a Lagrangian to solve for the optimal basket of goods.

b. Suppose that the price of X increases to $5 per unit. Use a Lagrangian to solve for the new optimal basket of goods. Find the total effect of the price change on the consumption of each good.

c. Use a Lagrangian to find the substitution effect of the increase in the price of good X on the consumption of each good. What income would the consumer need to attain the original level of utility when the price of X increases to $5 per unit?

d. Find the income effect of the increase in the price of good X on the consumption of each good. Are the goods normal or inferior? Explain.

e. Show that the total effect of the increase in the price of X is equal to the sum of the substitution effect and the income effect.

Producer Behavior 6

A

t the beginning of Chapter 4, we asked you to imagine you are Jeff Bezos trying to develop the Kindle for introduction to the market. Your task was to decide what features you wanted the Kindle to have so that consumers would find it desirable. Now suppose you've done your market analysis, developed your product concept, and selected the features. Your task at this point is to figure out how to produce the Kindle. How many do you want to make? What mix of inputs are you going to use to do so? What size factory? How many employees? How much plastic? What kind of microprocessor? What will all this cost? Suppose the Kindle is an even bigger hit than you predicted, and you want to ramp up production. If you can't easily adjust the size of your factory, will your factory's size limit your ability to make more units by hiring more employees? And how much will costs rise if you increase production levels?

Any producer of a good or service faces these types of questions and others like them. The economics driving those questions, and their answers, are the focus of our analysis over the next several chapters. Chapters 4 and 5 were about consumer behavior, which determines the demand side of markets. With this chapter, we turn our attention to producer behavior, which drives the supply side of markets.

6.1 The Basics of Production

For a good to be consumed, it must first be produced. **Production** is the process by which a person, company, government, or non-profit agency uses inputs to create a good or service for which others are willing to pay. Production can take many forms. For instance, some producers make **final goods** that are bought by consumers.[1] Others make **intermediate goods** that are inputs into another firm's production, such as electricity, sugar, or advertising services. The range of products is so extensive that formulating a general but still useful model of production presents a formidable challenge—not unlike that involved in building the model of consumer behavior in the previous two chapters.

We begin building our model of production by laying out the assumptions that economists typically adopt to simplify firms' production decisions.[2] Having clarified these assumptions, we introduce the idea of a **production function,** which relates the amount of output a firm can create from different combinations of inputs. We then show how a firm, given its production function, makes its choice about which inputs to use in production—how many workers to hire, how much equipment to buy, and so on. We see how this input mix depends on the inputs' prices and the properties of the production function. Finally, we explore some specific topics about production functions, including how they reflect technological progress and differences in the scale of operations.

Before we begin our detailed analysis, a word of advice: Students often find it more difficult to understand production and supply than consumption and demand because they have more experience consuming than producing. But as you'll see in this chapter, there are a lot of parallels in the economics of consumers' and producers' decisions. For example, a firm's task of minimizing the cost of producing its desired quantity of output is very much like a consumer's desire to minimize her cost of achieving a given utility level.

Simplifying Assumptions about Firms' Production Behavior

In the real world, production is a dizzyingly complicated task. Think about a local restaurant. It sells dozens, maybe hundreds, of items. It has multiple suppliers (of meat, fish, fruit, drinks, glasses, silverware), several employees, and requires decisions about table sizes and placement, décor, dinnerware, advertising, and more. Each of these elements requires hundreds of decisions to be made just to set up for business, and then many more on-the-spot decisions while the restaurant is operating. At large firms like Walmart, Apple, or BMW, with tens of thousands of employees and billions of dollars of annual revenues from sales all over the globe, the production process is incredibly complex.

If we want to draw general conclusions about optimal production behavior in the face of such a complex reality, we need to make some simplifying assumptions. These let us focus on the essentials of a situation, kind of like imagining away all the little ripples and eddies in a river so we can focus on which direction the river is flowing. As always in economics, the goal is to make assumptions that allow us to build a useful model; we do not want to assume away so much reality that the model becomes useless as a tool to understand real-world behavior. In our attempt to model producer behavior in this chapter, we make the following assumptions:

1. **The firm produces a single good.** If a firm sells many products, then the decisions a firm makes about each product can be intertwined in complicated ways. In our basic

production
The process by which a person, company, government, or non-profit agency creates a good or service that others are willing to pay for.

final good
A good that is bought by a consumer.

intermediate good
A good that is used to produce another good.

production function
A mathematical relationship that describes how much output can be made from different combinations of inputs.

---

[1] Throughout this book, we often use the word "good" to mean both tangible goods, such as trucks, computers, jewelry, and so on, as well as services, such as haircuts, dog walking, financial planning, and so on. In this usage, anything a consumer values—tangible or not, concrete or abstract—is a good.

[2] We use the word "firm" as a generic term for any producer. Many producers *are* firms, but the term can also mean persons, governments, or non-profit agencies that create products.

model of the firm, we avoid these complications by assuming that the firm makes just one good.

2. **The firm has already chosen which product to produce.** The firms we study already know what they want to produce; our task is to determine how they can make it most efficiently. Deciding what to produce is an extremely important aspect of a firm's success, but that analysis is a bit beyond the scope of what we analyze here. The branch of economics called *industrial organization* studies many aspects of firm behavior, including product choice.

3. **The firm's goal is to minimize the cost of producing whatever quantity it chooses to make.** There are a couple of reasons why economists assume cost minimization is a goal of the production process. First, *most* firms seem to act this way (do, however, see the Application on Minnesota iron ore producers on the next page). It would certainly seem bizarre for a firm to behave in a way that suggested it knew how to make the very same product it currently makes for a lower cost, but just didn't want to.

   Note that the cost we're talking about here is the firm's total cost of producing *any particular quantity it chooses to make.* The firm can always reduce its total production cost by making less output. In building our model, we want to analyze how a firm will produce a specific quantity of output. (A firm's choice about what specific quantity of output to make depends on the characteristics of the market for its product, including the demand for the product and the number and type of its competitors. We discuss firms' choices of output levels in Chapters 8–11.)

   Second, cost minimization is necessary if a firm is going to maximize its profits. Profit maximization is another standard assumption economists make about firm behavior. We can think of cost minimization as a first step in profit maximization. It's important to remember, however, that we don't need to assume a firm is maximizing profits for it to be minimizing costs. Producers such as non-profits or governments might have priorities other than profits, but they would still want to minimize their costs; they gain nothing from wasting resources to make their products.

4. **The firm uses only two inputs in making its product: capital and labor.** Capital encompasses the buildings, machinery, and raw materials needed to make the product. Labor refers to all of the human resources (such as factory workers, salespeople, and CEOs) that are used to produce the firm's output. In building our model, we lump together all different kinds of capital under one single label, and do the same for labor.[3]

5. **In the short run, a firm can choose to employ as much or as little labor as it wants, but it cannot rapidly change how much capital it uses. In the long run, the firm can freely choose the amounts of both labor and of capital it employs.** This assumption captures the fact that it takes time to put capital into use. For example, between acquiring permits and undertaking construction, it can take many years for an electric company to build a new power plant. In comparison to this, firms can easily adjust worker hours by allowing employees to leave early or asking them to work overtime. In addition, hiring new employees and putting them to work is relatively easy. Even though the company must take time to find and train these workers, such tasks do not usually take as long as building or integrating new capital.

6. **The more inputs the firm uses, the more output it makes.** This assumption is similar to the "more is better" assumption for consumers' utility functions that we discussed in Chapter 4. Here, the analogous implication for production is that if the firm uses more labor or capital, its total output rises.

---

[3] We can lump together different kinds of capital and labor in this way because we measure each input in common units that measure the productive ability of a given input. Economists call these units *efficiency units,* and they allow us to add up all the units across the various types of capital and of labor the firm employs. This simplifies our model by leaving the producer with only two inputs to purchase, labor and capital.

7. **A firm's production exhibits diminishing marginal returns to labor and capital.** If the amount of capital is held constant, each additional worker eventually generates less output than the one before. The same diminishing returns exist for capital when labor is held constant. This assumption captures a basic idea of production: A mix of labor and capital is more productive than labor alone or capital alone. Capital helps workers to be productive, and vice versa. Take, for instance, the case of digging a hole for a building's foundation. Even hundreds of workers will make little progress digging the hole if they have no capital—machinery, or even shovels for that matter—to dig with. Similarly, a large amount of the fanciest digging equipment is of no use without humans to operate it. Only when the two types of inputs are used together and in the right amounts will the task be accomplished most efficiently. This assumption parallels the assumption in consumer theory that consumers derive diminishing marginal utility from additional units of each good.

    Just as diminishing marginal utility is central to understanding consumer behavior, diminishing marginal returns is critical to understanding firm behavior.

8. **The firm can buy as many capital or labor inputs as it wants at fixed prices.** Just as we assumed consumers could buy as much of any good as they wanted at a fixed price, we assume the firm can do the same for its capital and labor purchases. This assumption can be justified in two ways. First, most firms are small relative to the markets for the inputs they use. Even the largest companies employ only a small fraction of an economy's workers. Second, as long as the markets that produce a firm's inputs are reasonably competitive, even the largest firms can likely acquire as much capital and labor as they desire at a fixed price.

9. **If there is a well-functioning capital market (e.g., banks and investors), the firm does not have a budget constraint.** As long as the firm can make profits, it will be able to obtain the resources necessary to acquire the capital and labor it needs to produce. If a firm doesn't have the cash necessary to finance its input expenditures, it can raise funds by issuing stock or by borrowing. Outside investors should be willing to finance a firm's expenditures if they expect it to be profitable. Notice that this assumption about a firm's production does not have a counterpart in consumer choice theory. Consumers always have a budget constraint, and it limits the maximum level of utility they can obtain.

You may have noticed that there are more simplifying assumptions for the production model than for the consumption model. This is because producer behavior is a bit more complicated than consumer behavior. For example, we need to consider producer behavior in two time frames, the short run and the long run. Although much of production theory resembles the consumer theory we covered in Chapter 4, the differences are complex enough that we must be careful to simplify the model as much as possible.

 **application**

Do Firms Really Always Minimize Costs?

One of our assumptions about firms' production behavior is that they seek to minimize the total cost of producing their chosen output level. Sometimes there are limits to firms' abilities to do this, however.

Economist James Schmitz points this out in a study of the iron ore industry in northern Minnesota.[4] During the mid-20th century, this industry had a virtual monopoly on supplying ore to Great Lakes steel mills because of its proximity to them. In the 1980s, however, the steel mills became able to purchase iron ore from new, low-cost mines in Brazil at a much lower price, even after including transportation costs.

---

[4] James A. Schmitz Jr., "What Determines Productivity? Lessons from the Dramatic Recovery of the U.S. and Canadian Iron Ore Industries Following Their Early 1980s Crisis," *Journal of Political Economy* 113, no. 3 (2005): 582–625.

How did the Minnesota iron ore producers respond to this entrance of foreign competition? They experienced a sudden increase in productivity—that is, a sudden reduction in the per-unit costs of producing their output. Schmitz shows that this cost decrease didn't arise from new technologies or higher-cost mines going out of business.

Instead, the lower costs resulted from simple changes in operations practices, such as allowing machine operators to do their own repair work. Previously, if a machine broke down, the mines' employment contracts required that even the simplest fixes be done by specified maintenance workers. Often, these workers would have to travel several miles to the worksite, causing idle machine time. Additionally, maintenance workers were assigned specific types of machines and parts. This meant that if a maintenance worker assigned to, say, shovels, was not available, a broken shovel would have to stay idle, even if a maintenance worker assigned to dump trucks (or any other machine besides shovels) could easily fix the problem.

Does this mean that the Minnesota firms weren't minimizing costs *before* competition from the Brazilian mines? In some sense, they weren't; they could have made these changes and substantially reduced their costs while still mining the same amount of ore. A broader interpretation might be that before competition from Brazil, labor was effectively more expensive for the mines. Workers were being "paid" a substantial amount in on-the-job leisure time ensured by their contracts. Labor was expensive enough that even though the firms' might have been minimizing costs *given the contracts that had already been signed*, there was a lot of potential for costs to go down if the contracts changed. This is exactly what happened: Once their jobs were in jeopardy, the workers agreed to more flexible work rules, reducing both their on-the-job leisure and their effective cost to the mines. As the Nobel Prize–winning economist John Hicks said, "The best of all monopoly profits is a quiet life." Once the iron ore industry became competitive, life wasn't so quiet for Minnesota's miners anymore. ∎

Production Functions

A firm's task is to turn capital and labor inputs into outputs. A production function is a mathematical relationship that describes how much output can be made from different combinations of inputs.

As noted above, we simplify things in our model of production so that we can shrink the many outputs made and inputs used by real-world firms into something that we can get a better handle on. Namely, our firm makes one product as its output and uses two inputs, capital and labor, to do so. Capital includes the equipment and structures that firms use—an enormous range of inputs, from the machinery on assembly lines, to office buildings, to the iPhone that the CEO uses to keep abreast of what's happening at the firm while she's on the road. Labor includes the human inputs a firm uses, ranging from miners to computer programmers to summer interns and executive vice presidents. The production function summarizes how a firm transforms these capital and labor inputs into output. A production function is a formula that describes output (which we label Q for quantity) as a function of our two inputs, capital (K) and labor (L):

$$Q = f(K,L)$$

In this production function, f is a mathematical function that describes how capital and labor are combined to produce the output. Production functions can take a form such as $Q = 10K + 5L$ in which the inputs are separate, or $Q = K^{0.5}L^{0.5}$ in which the inputs are multiplied together. They can also take many other forms depending on the technology a firm uses to produce its output. The type of production function in which capital and labor are each raised to a power and then multiplied together (as in $Q = K^{0.5}L^{0.5}$ above) is known as a *Cobb–Douglas* production function. It is named after mathematician and economist Charles Cobb and economist (and later, U.S. Senator) Paul Douglas. The Cobb–Douglas production function is one of the most common types of production functions used by economists.

6.2 Production in the Short Run

We start by analyzing production in the short run because it is the simplest case. In our earlier discussion of the assumptions of this model, we defined the "short run" as the period during which a firm cannot change the amount of capital. While the capital stock is fixed, the firm can choose how much labor to hire to minimize its cost of making the output quantity. Table 6.1 shows some values of labor inputs and output quantities from a short-run production function. Here, we use the Cobb-Douglas production function of our earlier example and fix capital $(\overline{K})$ at four units, so the numbers in Table 6.1 correspond to the production function $Q = f(\overline{K},L) = \overline{K}^{0.5}L^{0.5} = 4^{0.5}L^{0.5} = 2L^{0.5}$.

Figure 6.1 plots the short-run production function from Table 6.1. The plot contains the numbers in Table 6.1, but also shows output levels for all amounts of labor between 0 and 5 hours per week, as well as amounts of labor greater than 5 hours per week.

Even though capital is fixed, when the firm increases its labor inputs, its output rises. This reflects Assumption 6 above: More inputs mean more output. Notice, however, that the *rate* at which output increases slows as the firm hires more and more labor. This phenomenon of additional units of labor yielding less and less additional output reflects Assumption 7: The production function exhibits diminishing marginal returns to inputs. To see why there are diminishing marginal returns, we need to understand just what happens when one input increases while the other input remains fixed. This is what is meant by an input's *marginal product*.

Marginal Product

marginal product
The additional output that a firm can produce by using an additional unit of an input (holding use of the other input constant).

The incremental output that a firm can produce by using an additional unit of an input (holding use of the other input constant) is called the **marginal product.** In the short run, the marginal product that is most relevant is the marginal product of labor because we are assuming that capital is fixed. The marginal product of labor (MP_L) is the *change* in quantity (ΔQ) resulting from a one-unit *change* in labor inputs (ΔL):

$$MP_L = \Delta Q/\Delta L$$

The marginal product of labor for our short-run production function $Q = 4^{0.5}L^{0.5}$ is shown in the fourth column of Table 6.1. If a firm with this production function (in

Table 6.1   **An Example of a Short-Run Production Function**

Capital, K	Labor, L	Output, Q	Marginal Product of Labor, $MP_L = \frac{\Delta Q}{\Delta L}$	Average Product of Labor, $AP_L = \frac{Q}{L}$
4	0	0.00	—	—
4	1	2.00	2.00	2.00
4	2	2.83	0.83	1.42
4	3	3.46	0.63	1.15
4	4	4.00	0.54	1.00
4	5	4.47	0.47	0.89

which capital is fixed at four units) uses zero units of labor, it produces zero units of output. (Perhaps the firm can't make any output without anyone to run the machines.) If it hires one unit of labor to combine with the four units of capital, it can produce two units of output. Therefore, the marginal product of that first unit of labor is 2.00. With two units of labor (and the same four units of capital), the firm can produce 2.83 units of output, making the marginal product of the second unit of labor the change in output or 2.83 − 2.00 = 0.83. With three units of labor, output rises by 0.63 to 3.46, so the marginal product of labor is 0.63, and so on.

This **diminishing marginal product** of labor—the reduction in the extra output obtained from adding more and more labor—is embodied in our Assumption 7 and is a common feature of production functions. This is why the production function curve in Figure 6.1 flattens at higher quantities of labor. A diminishing marginal product makes intuitive sense, too. If there is a fixed amount of capital, then every time you add a worker, each worker has less capital to use. If a coffee shop has one espresso machine and one worker, she has a machine at her disposal during her entire shift. If the coffee shop hires a second worker to work the same hours as the first, the two workers must share the machine. Because of this sharing, it's unlikely that the second worker will add as much production as the first worker. With three workers per shift and still only one machine, the situation gets worse. Adding a fourth worker will allow the firm to produce a tiny bit more output, but certainly, this fourth worker's marginal product will be smaller than that of the first (or, for that matter, the second and third) worker. The coffee shop's solution to this problem is to buy more espresso machines—that is, add more capital. We've assumed it can't do so in the short run, but it could (and would) do so in the long run. We look at what happens when the firm can change its capital level later in this chapter.

Keep in mind, however, that diminishing marginal returns do not have to occur all the time; they just need to occur eventually. A production function could have increasing marginal returns at low levels of labor before running into the problem of diminishing marginal product.

A Graphical Analysis of Marginal Product   We can plot the marginal product on a graph of the production function. Recall that the marginal product is the change in output quantity that comes from adding one additional unit of input: $MP_L = \Delta Q/\Delta L$. $\Delta Q/\Delta L$ is the slope of the short-run production function in Figure 6.1. Thus, the marginal product of labor at any given level of labor input is the slope of the production

diminishing marginal product
A feature of the production function; as a firm hires additional units of a given input, the marginal product of that input falls.

Figure 6.1   A Short-Run Production Function

This figure graphs the firm's continuous short-run production function using the values from Table 6.1. The production function's positive slope means that an increase in labor increases output. As the firm hires more labor, however, output increases at a decreasing rate and the slope flattens.

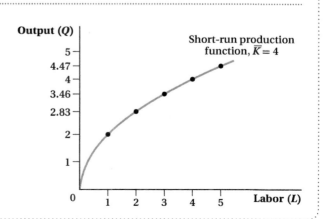

Figure 6.2   Deriving the Marginal Product of Labor

(a)

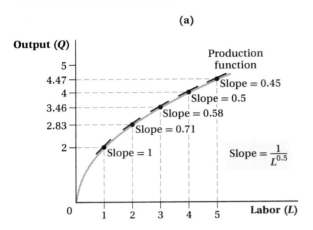

(b)

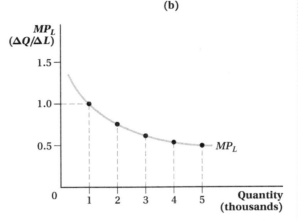

(a) The marginal product of labor is the slope of the production function. As the quantity of labor increases, the marginal product decreases, from $MP_L = 1$ when $L = 1$ to $MP_L = 0.45$ when $L = 5$ and the slope flattens.

(b) Using the production function in panel a, we can derive the marginal product of labor curve. The downward slope of the curve shows the diminishing marginal returns to labor.

function at that point. Panel a of Figure 6.2 shows how the MP_L can be derived from our production function. At $L = 1$, the slope of the production function (i.e., the slope of the line tangent to the production function at $L = 1$) is relatively steep. Adding additional labor at this point will increase output by a substantial amount. At $L = 4$, the slope is considerably flatter, and adding additional labor will boost output by a smaller increment than when $L = 1$. The marginal product of labor falls between $L = 1$ and $L = 4$, as we saw in Table 6.1. Panel b of Figure 6.2 shows the corresponding marginal-product-of-labor curve. Because this production function exhibits diminishing marginal returns at all levels of labor, the marginal product curve is downward-sloping.

A Mathematical Representation of Marginal Product   To find MP_L, we need to calculate the additional output obtained by adding an incremental unit of labor, holding capital constant. So let's compute the firm's increase in output when it uses $L + \Delta L$ units of labor instead of L units (holding capital constant). ΔL is the incremental unit of labor. Mathematically, MP_L is

$$MP_L = \frac{\Delta Q}{\Delta L} = \frac{f(\overline{K}, L + \Delta L) - f(\overline{K}, L)}{\Delta L}$$

Applying this to our short-run production function ($\overline{K}^{0.5} L^{0.5} = 4^{0.5} L^{0.5} = 2L^{0.5}$) gives

$$Q = f(\overline{K}, L)$$

$$MP_L = \frac{2(L + \Delta L)^{0.5} - 2L^{0.5}}{\Delta L}$$

To consider what happens as we let ΔL get really tiny involves some calculus. If you don't know calculus, however, here is the marginal product formula for our Cobb–Douglas production function: $MP_L = \frac{1}{L^{0.5}}$. The MP_L values calculated using this formula are shown in Figure 6.2. (These values are slightly different from those in Table 6.1 because while the table sets $\Delta L = 1$, the formula allows the incremental unit to be much smaller. The economic idea behind both calculations is the same, however.)

Average Product

It's important to see that the *marginal* product is not the same as the *average* product. **Average product** is calculated by dividing the total quantity of output by the number of units of input used to produce that quantity. The average product of labor (AP_L), for example, is the quantity produced Q divided by the amount of labor L used to produce it:

average product
The quantity of output produced per unit of input.

$$AP_L = Q/L$$

The average product of labor for our short-run production function is shown in the last column of Table 6.1. Notice that the average product of labor falls as labor inputs increase.

6.1 figure it out

The short-run production function for a firm that produces pizzas is $Q = f(\overline{K},L) = 15\overline{K}^{0.25}L^{0.75}$, where Q is the number of pizzas produced per hour, $\overline{K}$ is the number of ovens (which is fixed at 3 in the short run), and L is the number of workers employed.

a. Write an equation for the short-run production function for the firm showing output as a function of labor.

b. Calculate the total output produced per hour for $L = 0, 1, 2, 3, 4,$ and 5.

c. Calculate the MP_L for $L = 1$ to $L = 5$. Is MP_L diminishing?

d. Calculate the AP_L for $L = 1$ to $L = 5$.

Solution:

a. To write the production function for the short run, we plug $\overline{K} = 3$ into the production function to create an equation that shows output as a function of labor:

$$Q = f(\overline{K},L) = 15\overline{K}^{0.25}L^{0.75}$$
$$= 15(3^{0.25})L^{0.75} = 15(1.316)L^{0.75} = 19.74L^{0.75}$$

b. To calculate total output, we plug in the different values of L and solve for Q:

$L = 0$	$Q = 19.74(0)^{0.75} = 19.74(0) = 0$
$L = 1$	$Q = 19.74(1)^{0.75} = 19.74(1) = 19.74$
$L = 2$	$Q = 19.74(2)^{0.75} = 19.74(1.682) = 33.20$
$L = 3$	$Q = 19.74(3)^{0.75} = 19.74(2.280) = 45.01$
$L = 4$	$Q = 19.74(4)^{0.75} = 19.74(2.828) = 55.82$
$L = 5$	$Q = 19.74(5)^{0.75} = 19.74(3.344) = 66.01$

c. The marginal product of labor is the additional output generated by an additional unit of labor, holding capital constant. We can use our answer from (b) to calculate the marginal product of labor for each worker:

$L = 1$	$MP_L = 19.74 - 0 = 19.74$
$L = 2$	$MP_L = 33.20 - 19.74 = 13.46$
$L = 3$	$MP_L = 45.01 - 33.20 = 11.81$
$L = 4$	$MP_L = 55.82 - 45.01 = 10.81$
$L = 5$	$MP_L = 66.01 - 55.82 = 10.19$

Note that, because MP_L falls as L rises, there is a diminishing marginal product of labor. This implies that output rises at a decreasing rate when labor is added to the fixed level of capital.

d. The average product of labor is calculated by dividing total output (Q) by the quantity of labor input (L):

$L = 1$	$AP_L = 19.74/1 = 19.74$
$L = 2$	$AP_L = 33.20/2 = 16.60$
$L = 3$	$AP_L = 45.01/3 = 15.00$
$L = 4$	$AP_L = 55.82/4 = 13.96$
$L = 5$	$AP_L = 66.01/5 = 13.20$

This decline occurs because the marginal product of labor is less than the average product at each level of labor in the table, so each unit of labor added on the margin brings down labor's average product. The easiest way to see this is to consider your grades in a course. Suppose that your mid-semester average in a course is 80%. Now, you take an exam and score a 90%. Your average will rise because the score on the last exam taken (the *marginal* exam) is greater than your current average. On the other hand, if your next exam score is only 65%, your course average will fall, because the marginal score is lower than the average score.

 ## application

How Short Is the Short Run?

What sort of time period should we have in mind when thinking about the short-run production function? That is, how long do firms actually need to adjust their capital inputs? How long are they stuck with the capital they currently have? The answer depends on the firm and the industry. It depends on the specifics of the firm's costs of adjusting capital, which in turn are determined by the particular types of capital the firm uses, how large a change in capital inputs the firm wants to make, and the opportunity cost of management's time, among other factors.

Economists Russell Cooper and John Haltiwanger studied the capital adjustment/investment practices of thousands of U.S. manufacturing plants between 1972 and 1988. They found that about 1 of every 10 plants did not change its capital level at all over the course of a year.[5]

Cooper and Haltiwanger also found that when a plant did adjust its capital level, it usually made big changes. Naturally, plants with a larger gap between their actual and ideal capital levels made larger adjustments. (Cooper and Haltiwanger used economic theory to estimate what each factory's ideal capital level should be, based on the demand for the factory's product and on the factory's costs.) And once a big change was made, that plant was less likely to make another big change the next year. This pattern of investment "bursts" implies that once a factory changes its amount of capital, it tends to make the necessary adjustments all at once, rather than stringing out a large change over several years.

So, for Cooper and Haltiwanger's plants at least, the short run seems to range from a few months for factories that have a big desired change in capital to well over a year for those with only small desired changes. ∎

6.3 Production in the Long Run

In the long run, firms can change not only their labor inputs but also their capital. This difference gives them two important benefits. First, in the long run, a firm might be able to lessen the sting of diminishing marginal product. As we saw above, when capital is fixed, diminishing marginal product limits a firm's ability to produce additional output by using more and more labor. If additional capital can make each unit of labor more productive, then a firm could expand its output more by increasing capital and labor inputs *jointly*.

Think back to our example of the coffee shop. If the shop adds a second worker per shift when there is only one espresso machine, the firm will not gain much additional output because of the diminishing marginal product of labor. Hiring still another worker per shift will barely budge output at all. But if the firm bought another machine for each additional worker, output could increase with little drop in productivity. In this way, using more capital and labor at the same time allows the firm to avoid (at least in part) the effects of diminishing marginal products.

---

[5] Russell W. Cooper and John C. Haltiwanger, "On the Nature of Capital Adjustment Costs," *Review of Economic Studies* 73, no. 3 (2006): 611–633.

The second benefit of being able to adjust capital in the long run is that producers often have some ability to substitute capital for labor or vice versa. Firms can be more flexible in their production methods and in the ways they respond to changes in the relative prices of capital and labor. For example, as airline ticket agents became relatively more expensive and technological progress made automated check-in less so, airlines shifted much of their check-in operations from being labor-intensive (checking in with an agent at the counter) to being capital-intensive (checking in at an automated kiosk or even at home online).

The Long-Run Production Function

In a long-run production function, all inputs can be adjusted. The long-run production is the production function we first introduced in Section 6.2: $Q = f(K,L)$, but rather than having a fixed level of $\overline{K}$ and choosing L (as we did for the short run), now the firm can choose the levels of both inputs.

We can also illustrate the long-run production function in a table. Table 6.2 shows the relationship between output and inputs for our example production function $Q = K^{0.5}L^{0.5}$. The columns correspond to different amounts of labor. The rows denote different amounts of capital. The number in each cell is the quantity of output generated by the corresponding combination of inputs.

In the fourth row of the table, where the firm has four units of capital, the values exactly match the short-run production function values from Table 6.1. Table 6.2 adds to Table 6.1 other possible output quantities the firm could achieve once it can change its level of capital. One way to think about the long-run production function is as a combination of all the firm's possible short-run production functions, where each possible short-run function has a different fixed level of capital. Notice that for any given level of capital—that

Table 6.2	An Example of a Long-Run Production Function

		Units of Labor, L				
		1	**2**	**3**	**4**	**5**
Units of Capital, K	**1**	1.00	1.41	1.73	2.00	2.24
	2	1.41	2.00	2.45	2.83	3.16
	3	1.73	2.45	3.00	3.46	3.87
	4	2.00	2.83	3.46	4.00	4.47
	5	2.24	3.16	3.87	4.47	5.00

is, for any particular short-run production function—labor has a diminishing marginal product. For example, when capital is fixed at five units, the marginal product of labor of the first worker is 2.24, the MP_L of the second worker is 0.92 (= 3.16 − 2.24), the MP_L for the third worker is 0.71 (= 3.87 − 3.16), and so on.

6.4 The Firm's Cost-Minimization Problem

At the start of the chapter, we outlined a number of assumptions about a firm's production behavior. The third assumption is that the firm's goal is to minimize the cost of producing whatever quantity it chooses to make. (How a firm determines that quantity is the subject of Chapters 8–11.) The challenge of producing a specific amount of a particular good as inexpensively as possible is the firm's **cost-minimization** problem.

The firm's production decision is another *constrained optimization* problem. Remember from our discussion in Chapter 4 that these types of problems are ones in which an economic actor tries to optimize something while facing a constraint on her choices. Here, the firm's problem is a constrained *minimization* problem. The firm wants to minimize the total costs of its production. However, it must hold to a constraint in doing so: it must produce a particular quantity of output. That is, it can't minimize its costs just by refusing to produce as much as it would like (or refuse to produce anything, for that matter). In this section, we look at how a firm uses two concepts, isoquants (which tell the firm

cost minimization
A firm's goal of producing a specific quantity of output at minimum cost.

the quantity constraint it faces) and isocost lines (which tell the firm the various costs at which the firm can produce its quantity) to solve its constrained minimization problem.

Isoquants

When learning about the consumer's utility function in Chapter 4, we looked at three variables: the quantities of the two goods consumed and the consumer's utility. Each indifference curve showed all the combinations of the two goods consumed that allowed the consumer to achieve a particular utility level.

We can do the same thing with the firm's production function. We can plot as one curve all the possible combinations of capital and labor that can produce a given amount of output. Figure 6.3 does just that for the production function we have been using throughout the chapter; it displays the combinations of inputs that are necessary to produce one, two, and four units of output. These curves are known as **isoquants.** The word "isoquant" is derived from the Greek prefix *iso-*, which means "the same," and *quant*, which is a shortened version of the word "quantity."

Just as with indifference curves, isoquants further from the origin correspond to higher output levels (because more capital and labor lead to higher output), isoquants cannot cross (because if they did, the same quantities of inputs would yield two different quantities of output), and isoquants are convex to the origin (because using a mix of inputs generally lets a firm produce a greater quantity than it could by using an extreme amount of one input and a tiny amount of the other).

The Marginal Rate of Technical Substitution   The slope of the isoquant plays a key role in the analysis of production decisions because it captures the tradeoff in the productive abilities of capital and labor. Look at the isoquant in Figure 6.4. At point A, the isoquant is steeply sloped, meaning that the firm can reduce the amount of capital it uses by a lot while increasing labor only a small amount, and still maintain the same level of output. In contrast, at point B, if the firm wants to reduce capital just a bit, it will have to increase labor a lot to keep output at the same level. Isoquants' curvature and convexity to the origin reflect the fact that the capital–labor tradeoff varies as the mix of the inputs changes.

The negative of the slope of the isoquant is called the **marginal rate of technical substitution** of one input (on the x-axis) for another (on the y-axis), or $MRTS_{XY}$. It is the quantity change in input X necessary to keep output constant if the quantity of input Y changes. For the most part in this chapter, we will be interested in the $MRTS$ of labor for capital or $MRTS_{LK}$, which is the amount of labor needed to hold output constant if the quantity of capital used by the firm changes.

isoquant
A curve representing all the combinations of inputs that allow a firm to make a particular quantity of output.

marginal rate of technical substitution ($MRTS_{XY}$)
The rate at which the firm can trade input X for input Y, holding output constant.

Figure 6.3   Isoquants

Each isoquant shows the possible combinations of labor (L) and capital (K) that produce the output (Q) levels 1, 2, and 4 units.

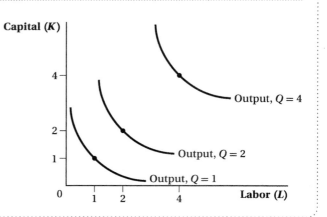

Figure 6.4 : The Marginal Rate of Technical Substitution

The negative slope of the isoquant is the marginal rate of technical substitution of labor L for capital K. At point A, the marginal product of labor is high relative to the marginal product of capital, and a relatively small decrease in labor would require a large quantity of capital to hold output constant. At point B, the marginal product of labor is low relative to the marginal product of capital, and a relatively small decrease in capital would require a large quantity of labor to hold output constant.

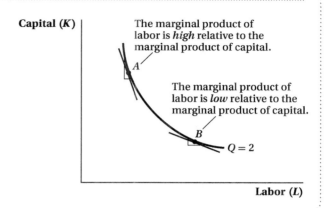

If we imagine moving just a little bit down and to the right along an isoquant, the change in output equals the marginal product of labor times the change in the units of labor due to the move, plus the marginal product of capital times the change in the amount of capital. (This change in capital is negative because we're taking away capital when we move down along the isoquant.) Because we're moving along an isoquant (for which output is held constant), though, this total change in output is zero. So we can write the total change as

$$\Delta Q = MP_L \times \Delta L + MP_K \times \Delta K = 0$$

If we rearrange this to find the slope of the isoquant, $\Delta K/\Delta L$, we have

$$MP_K \times \Delta K = -MP_L \times \Delta L$$

$$MP_K \times \frac{\Delta K}{\Delta L} = -MP_L$$

$$\frac{\Delta K}{\Delta L} = -\frac{MP_L}{MP_K}$$

$$MRTS_{LK} = -\frac{\Delta K}{\Delta L} = \frac{MP_L}{MP_K}$$

Therefore, the $MRTS_{LK}$ at any point on an isoquant tells you the relative marginal products of capital and labor at that point.

The concepts underlying the marginal rate of technical substitution are essentially identical to those of the marginal rate of substitution (MRS) for consumers, which we learned about in Chapter 4. The two are so closely tied together, in fact, that the names are essentially the same—the word "technical" is tacked on to distinguish the producer case. Both the $MRTS$ and MRS are about marginal tradeoffs. The MRS is about a consumer's willingness to trade one good for another while still obtaining the same util-ity level. The $MRTS$ is about a firm's ability to trade one input for another while still producing the same quantity of output. The shape of the curves in both cases tells you about the rate at which one good/input can be substituted for the other.

The nature of the marginal tradeoffs embodied in the MRS and $MRTS$ implies similar things about the shape of the curves from which they are derived. On the con-sumer side, indifference curves are convex to the origin because the MRS varies with the amount of each good the consumer is consuming. On the production side, isoquants are convex to the origin because the $MRTS$ varies with the amount of each input the firm uses to produce output. When the firm uses a lot of capital and just a little labor (point A in Figure 6.4), it can replace a lot of capital with a little more labor and still produce the same quantity of output. At this point, labor has a high marginal product relative to capital, and the firm's isoquant is steep. At point B, the firm uses a lot of labor and only a little capital, so capital has a relatively high marginal product and $MRTS_{LK}$ is small. A smaller $MRTS_{LK}$ means a flatter isoquant at that input mix.

Substitutability   How curved an isoquant is shows how easily firms can substitute one input for another in production. For isoquants that are almost straight, as in panel a of Figure 6.5, a firm can replace a unit of one input (capital, e.g.) with a particular amount of the second input (labor) without changing its output level, regardless of whether it is already using a lot or a little of capital. Stated in terms of the marginal rate of technical substitution, $MRTS_{LK}$ doesn't change much as the firm moves along the isoquant. In this case, the two inputs are close substitutes in the firm's production function, and the relative usefulness of either input for production won't vary much with how much of each input the firm is using.

Highly curved isoquants, such as those shown in panel b of Figure 6.5, mean that the $MRTS_{LK}$ changes a lot along the isoquant. In this case, the two inputs are poor substitutes. The relative usefulness of substituting one input for another in production depends a great deal on the amount of the input the firm is already using.

Perfect Substitutes and Perfect Complements in Production   In Chapter 4, we discussed the extreme cases of perfect substitutes and perfect complements in consumption. For perfect substitutes, indifference curves are straight lines; for perfect complements, the curves are "L"-shaped right angles. The same holds for inputs: It is possible for them to be perfect substitutes or perfect complements in production. Isoquants for these two cases are shown in Figure 6.6.

If inputs are perfect substitutes as in panel a, the $MRTS$ doesn't change at all with the amounts of the inputs used, and the isoquants are perfectly straight lines. This characteristic means the firm can freely substitute between inputs without suffering diminishing marginal returns. An example of a production function where labor and capital are perfect substitutes is $Q = f(K, L) = 10K + 5L$; two units of labor can always be substituted for one unit of capital without changing output, no matter how many units of either input the firm is already using. In this case, imagine that capital took

---

Figure 6.5   The Shape of Isoquants Indicates the Substitutability of Inputs

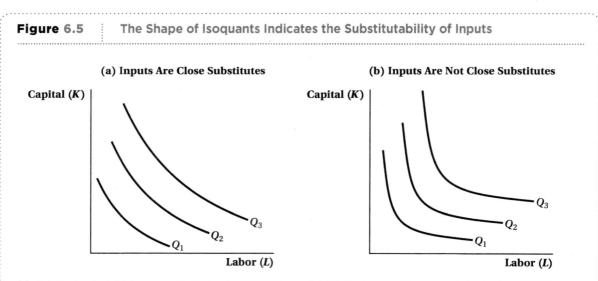

(a) Relatively straight isoquants indicate that $MRTS_{LK}$ does not vary much along the curve. Therefore, labor and capital are close substitutes for each other.

(b) Relatively curved isoquants indicate that $MRTS_{LK}$ varies greatly along the curve. Therefore, labor and capital are not close substitutes for each other.

Figure 6.6 | **Perfect Substitutes and Perfect Complements in Production**

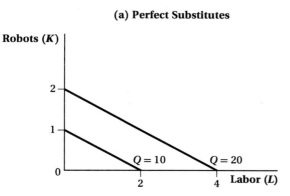

(a) Robots K and labor L are perfect substitutes. The isoquants are straight lines, and the $MRTS_{LK}$ does not change along the isoquant. In this case, two humans can substitute for one robot.

(b) Cabs K and drivers L are perfect complements. The isoquants are L-shaped, and the optimal quantity (K, L) for each output Q is the corner of the isoquant. In this case, 1 cab with 1 driver produces $Q = 1$, while 2 cabs with 2 drivers produce $Q = 2$.

the form of a robot that behaved exactly like a human when doing a task, but did the work twice as quickly as a human. Here, the firm can always substitute one robot for two workers or vice versa, regardless of its current number of robots or workers. This is true because the marginal product of labor is 5 (holding K constant, a one-unit increase in L causes output to grow by 5). At the same time, holding L constant, a one-unit rise in K will increase output by 10 units, making the MP_K equal to 10. No matter what levels of L and K the firm chooses, $MRTS_{LK} = MP_L/MP_K = \frac{5}{10} = \frac{1}{2}$.

If inputs are perfect complements, isoquants have an "L" shape. This implies that using inputs in any ratio outside of a particular fixed proportion—that at the isoquants' corners—yields no additional output. Cabs and drivers on a given shift are fairly close to perfect complements in the production of cab rides. Anything other than a 1 to 1 ratio of cabs to drivers is unlikely to produce any additional cab rides. If a cab company has, say, 30 drivers and 1 cab, it will not be able to offer any more rides than if it had 1 driver and 1 cab. Nor could it offer more rides if it had 1 driver and 30 cabs. Therefore, the production function would be $Q = \min(L, K)$, where "min" indicates that output (Q) is determined by the minimum level of either labor (L) or capital (K). Of course, the cab company could offer more rides if it had 30 drivers *and* 30 cabs, because this would preserve the 1 to 1 driver-to-cab ratio.[6]

Isocost Lines

Up until this point in the chapter, we have focused on various aspects of the production function and how quantities of inputs are related to the quantity of output. These aspects play a crucial part in determining a firm's optimal production behavior, but the production function is only half of the story. As we discussed earlier, the firm's objective is to minimize its costs of producing a given quantity of output. While we've said a lot about how the firm's choices of inputs affect its output, we haven't talked about the costs of those choices. That's what we do in this section.

---

[6] There is nothing special about a 1 to 1 ratio. Inputs can be perfect complements at other ratios as well.

isocost line
A curve that shows all of the input combinations that yield the same cost.

The key concept that brings costs into the firm's decision is the **isocost line**. An isocost line connects all the combinations of capital and labor that the firm can purchase for a given total expenditure on inputs. As we saw earlier, *iso-* is a prefix meaning "the same," so "isocost" is a line that shows all of the input combinations that yield the same cost. Mathematically, the isocost line corresponding to a total expenditure level of C is given by

$$C = RK + WL,$$

where R is the price (the *rental rate*) per unit of capital, W is the price (the Wage) per unit of labor, and K and L are the number of units of capital and labor that the firm hires. It's best to think of the cost of capital as a rental rate in the same type of units as the wage (e.g., per hour, week, or year). Because capital is used over a long period of time, we can consider R to be not just the purchase price of the equipment but also the user cost of capital. The user cost takes into account capital's purchase price, as well as its rate of depreciation and the opportunity cost of the funds tied up in its purchase (foregone interest).

Figure 6.7 shows isocost lines corresponding to total cost levels of $50, $80, and $100, when the price of capital is $20 per unit and labor's price is $10 per unit. There are a few things to notice about the figure. First, isocost lines for higher total expenditure levels are further from the origin. This reflects the fact that, as a firm uses more inputs, its total expenditure on those inputs increases. Second, the isocost lines are parallel. They all have the same slope, regardless of what total cost level they represent. To see why they all have the same slope, let's first see what that slope represents.

We can rewrite the equation for the isocost line in slope-intercept form, so that the value on the vertical axis (capital) is expressed as a function of the value on the horizontal axis (labor):

$$C = RK + WL$$

$$RK = C - WL$$

$$K = \frac{C}{R} - \frac{W}{R}L$$

This means that the y-intercept of the isocost line is C/R, while the slope is the (negative of the) inputs' price ratio, $-W/R$.

Figure 6.7   Isocost Lines

Each isocost line shows all bundles of inputs that have the same cost to the firm. As you move farther from the origin, the isocost lines represent higher total expenditures, from cost $C = \$50$ to $C = \$80$ to $C = \$100$. For wage $W = \$10$ and rental $R = \$20$, the slope of the isocost lines is $-W/R$, or $-\frac{1}{2}$. Therefore, for every one-unit increase in K, the firm has to give up two units of L, in order to keep cost constant.

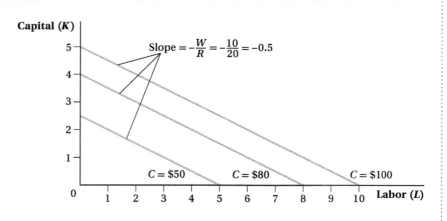

As is so often the case in economics, the slope tells us about tradeoffs at the margin. Here, the slope reflects the cost consequences of trading off or substituting one input for another. It indicates how much more of one input a firm could hire, without increasing overall expenditure on inputs, if it used less of the other input. If the isocost line's slope is steep, labor is relatively expensive compared to capital. If the firm wants to hire more labor without increasing its overall expenditure on inputs, it is going to have to use a lot less capital. (Or if you'd rather, if it chose to use less labor, it could hire a lot more capital without spending more on inputs overall.) If the price of labor is relatively cheap compared to capital, the isocost line will be relatively flat. This means the firm could hire a lot more labor and not have to give up much capital to do so without changing expenditures.

Because of our assumption (Assumption 8) that the firm can buy as much capital or labor as it wants at a fixed price per unit, the slopes of isocost lines are constant. That's why they are straight, parallel lines: Regardless of the overall cost level or the amount of each input the firm chooses, the relative tradeoff between the inputs in terms of total costs is always the same.

If these ideas seem familiar to you, it's because the isocost line is yet another concept that has an analogy in the consumer behavior that we studied in Chapter 4. There, we saw that a consumer's budget line expressed the relationship between the quantities of each good consumed and the consumer's total expenditure on those goods. Isocost lines capture the same idea, except with regard to firms and their input purchases. We saw that the negative of the slope of the consumer's budget constraint was equal to the price ratio of the two goods, just as the negative of the slope of the isocost line equals the price ratio of the firm's two inputs.

Isocost Lines and Input Price Changes   Just like budget lines for consumers, when relative prices change, the isocost line rotates. In our example, say labor's price (W) rose from \$10 to \$20. Now if the firm only hired labor, it would only be able to hire half as much. The line becomes steeper as in Figure 6.8. The isocost line rotates because its slope is $-W/R$. When W increases from \$10 to \$20, the slope changes from $-\frac{1}{2}$ to -1, and the isocost line rotates clockwise and becomes steeper.

Changes in the price of capital also rotate the isocost line. Figure 6.9 shows what happens to the \$100 isocost line when the price of capital increases from \$20 to \$40 per unit, and the wage stays at \$10 per unit of labor. If the firm hired only capital, it could afford half as much, so the slope flattens. A drop in the capital price would rotate the isocosts the other way.

Figure 6.8   When Labor Becomes More Expensive, the Isocost Line Becomes Steeper

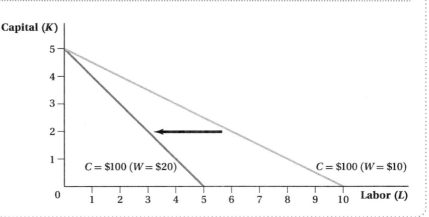

When the price of labor increases from $W = \$10$ to $W = \$20$ and the price of capital stays constant at $R = \$20$, the slope of the isocost changes from $-\frac{1}{2}$ to $-\frac{2}{2}$, or -1. The isocost line, therefore, becomes steeper, and the quantity of inputs the firm can buy for \$100 decreases.

$C = \$100\ (W = \$20)$

$C = \$100\ (W = \$10)$

Figure 6.9   **When Capital Becomes More Expensive, the Isocost Line Becomes Flatter**

When the price of capital increases from $R = \$20$ to $R = \$40$ and the price of labor stays constant at $W = \$10$, the slope of the isocost changes from $-\frac{1}{2}$ to $-\frac{1}{4}$. The quantity of inputs the firm can buy for $100 decreases and the isocost line becomes flatter.

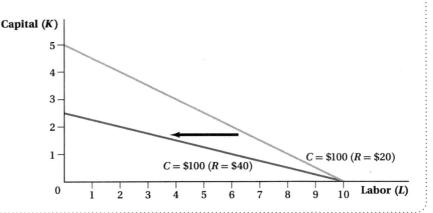

6.2 figure it out

Suppose that the wage rate is $10 per hour and the rental rate of capital is $25 per hour.

   a. Write an equation for the isocost line for a firm.

   b. Draw a graph (with labor on the horizontal axis and capital on the vertical axis) showing the isocost line for $C = \$800$. Indicate the horizontal and vertical intercepts along with the slope.

   c. Suppose the price of capital falls to $20 per hour. Show what happens to the $C = \$800$ isocost line including any changes in intercepts and the slope.

Solution:

   a. An isocost line always shows the total costs for the firm's two inputs in the form of $C = RK + WL$. Here, the wage rate (W) is $10 and the rental rate of capital (R) is $25, so the isocost line is $C = 10L + 25K$.

   b. We can plot the isocost line for $C = \$800 = 10L + 25K$. One easy way to do this is to compute the horizontal and vertical intercepts. The horizontal intercept tells us the amount of labor the firm could hire for $800 if it only hired labor. Therefore, the horizontal intercept is $\$800/W = \$800/\$10 = 80$. The vertical intercept tells us how much capital the firm could hire for $800 if it were to use only capital. Thus, it is $\$800/R = \$800/\$25 = 32$. We can plot these points on the following graph and then draw a line connecting them. This is the $C = \$800$ isocost line labeled C_1.

We can calculate slope in several different ways. First, we can simply calculate the slope of the isocost line as drawn. Remember that the slope of a line is $\Delta Y/\Delta X$ (i.e., rise over run). Therefore, the slope is $\Delta Y/\Delta X = -\frac{32}{80} = -0.4$. We can also rearrange our isocost line into slope-intercept form by isolating K:

$$800 = 10L + 25K$$
$$25K = 800 - 10L$$
$$K = (800/25) - (10/25)L = 32 - 0.4L$$

This equation tells us that the vertical intercept is 32 (which we calculated earlier) and -0.4 is the slope.

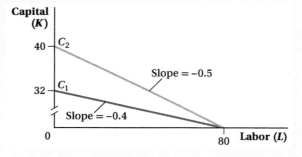

   c. If R falls to $20, the horizontal intercept is unaffected. If the firm is only using labor, a change in the price of capital will have no impact. However, the vertical intercept rises to $\$800/R = \$800/\$20 = 40$ and the isocost line becomes steeper (C_2). The new slope is $-W/R = -\$10/\$20 = -0.5$.

Identifying Minimum Cost: Combining Isoquants and Isocost Lines

As we have discussed, a firm's goal is to produce its desired quantity of output at the minimum possible cost. In deciding how to achieve this goal, a firm must solve a cost-minimization problem: It must achieve an objective given a constraint. The objective is the firm's total cost of inputs, $RK + WL$. The firm chooses capital and labor inputs K and L to minimize these expenditures. What constrains the firm's cost-minimizing decision? The quantity of output the firm has chosen to produce. The firm must hire enough capital and labor inputs to produce a certain level of output. The production function relates input choices to the quantity of output, so we can sum up a firm's cost-minimization problem as follows: Choose K and L to minimize total costs, subject to the constraint that enough K and L must be chosen to produce a given quantity of output. (Remember that at this point in our analysis quantity has already been chosen. Now it's the firm's task to figure out how to optimally produce that quantity.)

Cost Minimization—A Graphical Approach

A graphical solution boils down to determining the right way to combine information about the firm's costs and the firm's production function. We have represented a firm's costs graphically using isocost lines. Isocost lines, however, don't convey any information about how much the firm can produce with a set of inputs. They only indicate how much each set of inputs costs. To represent the production function, we use isoquants. These tell us, for a given production function, how much capital and labor it takes to produce a fixed amount of output.

Before we work through a specific example, let's think about the logic of the firm's cost-minimization problem. The firm's objective is to minimize costs subject to the constraint that it has to produce a particular quantity of output, $\overline{Q}$. The cost-minimization part means the firm wants to be on an isocost line that is as close to the origin as possible, because isocost lines closer to the origin correspond to lower levels of expenditure. The output constraint means that the firm has to somehow end up on the isoquant that corresponds to $\overline{Q}$. Therefore, the firm's best choice is to be on the isocost line that is as close to the origin as possible but still provides enough capital and labor to allow the firm to produce $\overline{Q}$.

Figure 6.10 shows the isoquant for the firm's desired output quantity $\overline{Q}$. The firm wants to produce this quantity at minimum cost. How much capital and labor should it hire to do so? Suppose the firm is considering the level inputs shown at point A, which

---

Figure 6.10   Cost Minimization

The firm wants to minimize the cost to produce the quantity $Q = \overline{Q}$. Because A is on the isoquant, the firm can choose to use input combination A to produce $\overline{Q}$. However, A is not cost-minimizing because the firm can produce $\overline{Q}$ at a lower cost at any point below and to the left of the isocost C_A. Point B, located at the tangency between isocost C_B and the isoquant, is the firm's cost-minimizing capital and labor combination. Input combinations on C_C cost less than those on C_B but are too small to allow the firm to produce $\overline{Q}$.

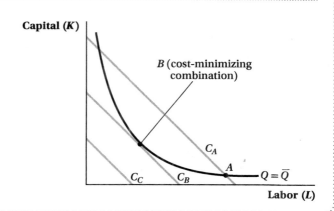

is on isocost line C_A. That point is on the $Q = \overline{Q}$ isoquant, so the firm will produce the desired level of output. However, there are many other input combinations on the $\overline{Q}$ isoquant that are below and to the left of C_A. These all would allow the firm to produce $\overline{Q}$ but at lower cost than input mix A. Only one input combination exists that is on the $\overline{Q}$ isoquant but for which there are no other input combinations that would allow the firm to produce the same quantity at lower cost. That combination is at point B, on isocost C_B. There are input combinations that involve lower costs than B—for example, any combination on isocost line C_C—but these input levels are all too small to allow the firm to produce $\overline{Q}$.

Point B has a special property. It is the point of tangency of the isocost line C_B to the $\overline{Q}$ isoquant. In other words, when the total costs of producing a given quantity are minimized, the isocost line is tangent to the isoquant.

With this tangency property, we once again see a similarity to optimal consumer behavior, which was also identified by a point of tangency. The parallels are particularly strong if we think about the expenditure-minimization interpretation of consumer behavior, where the consumer wants to choose a bundle of goods that minimizes the total expenditure required to achieve a given level of utility. Here, the firm wants to choose a set of inputs that minimizes the total cost of producing a given quantity of output.

Another important feature of the tangency result is that by definition, the isocost line and isoquant have the same slope at a tangency point. We know what these slopes are from our earlier discussion. The slope of the isocost line is the negative of the relative price of the inputs, $-W/R$. For the isoquant, the slope is the negative of the marginal rate of technical substitution ($MRTS_{LK}$), which is equal to the ratio of MP_L to MP_K. The tangency therefore implies that at the combination of inputs that minimizes the cost of producing a given quantity of output (like point B), the ratio of input prices equals the $MRTS$:

$$-\frac{W}{R} = -\frac{MP_L}{MP_K} \text{ or }$$

$$\frac{W}{R} = \frac{MP_L}{MP_K}$$

This condition has an important economic interpretation that might be easier to see if we rearrange the condition as follows:

$$\frac{W}{R} = \frac{MP_L}{MP_K}$$

$$MP_K \times W = MP_L \times R$$

$$\frac{MP_K}{R} = \frac{MP_L}{W}$$

The way we've written it, each side of this equation is the ratio of an input's marginal product to its price (capital on the left, labor on the right). One way to interpret these ratios is that they measure the marginal product per dollar spent on each input, or the input's "bang for the buck." Alternatively, we can think of each of these ratios as the firm's marginal benefit-to-cost ratio of hiring an input.

Why does cost minimization imply that each input's benefit-to-cost ratio is equal? Suppose the firm was producing an input bundle where this wasn't true. For example, if $\frac{MP_K}{R} > \frac{MP_L}{W}$, the firm's benefit-to-cost ratio for capital is higher than for labor. This would mean that the firm could replace some of its labor with capital while keeping its output quantity the same but reducing its total costs. Or if it wanted to, the firm could substitute capital for labor in a way that kept its total *costs* constant but raised its *output*. These options are possible because capital's marginal product per dollar is higher than labor's. If the sign of the inequality were reversed so $\frac{MP_K}{R} < \frac{MP_L}{W}$, the firm could reduce the costs of producing its current quantity (or raise its production without increasing costs) by substituting labor for capital. That's because, in this case, the marginal product per dollar spent is higher for labor. Only when the benefit-to-cost ratios of all the firm's inputs are the same is the firm unable to reduce the cost of producing its current quantity by changing its input levels.

Again, this logic parallels that from the consumer's optimal consumption choice in Chapter 4. The optimality condition for the consumer's expenditure-minimization problem was that the marginal rate of substitution between goods equals the goods' price ratio. Here, the analog to the MRS is the $MRTS$ (the former being a ratio of marginal utilities, the latter a ratio of marginal products), and the price ratio is now the input price ratio. There is one place where the parallel between consumers and firms does *not* hold. The budget constraint, which plays a big role in the consumer's utility-maximization problem, doesn't really have a parallel in the firm's production problem. As we discuss in later chapters, firms' desires to maximize their profits lead to a particular quantity of output they want to produce. If for some reason they don't have enough resources to pay for the inputs necessary to produce this quantity, then someone should always be willing to lend them the difference, because the lender and the firm can split the extra profits that result from producing the profit-maximizing output, making both parties better off. This outcome means that with well-functioning capital markets, firms should never be limited to a fixed amount of total expenditure on inputs in the same way a consumer is constrained to spend no more than her income. That's the idea embodied in our Assumption 9.

Input Price Changes

We've established that the cost-minimizing input combination is at the point of tangency between an isocost line and the isoquant that corresponds to the output quantity the firm wants to produce. In other words, a firm is producing that level of output at the lowest cost when the marginal product per dollar spent is equal across all inputs. Given this result, a very useful question to ask is how changes in input prices affect the firm's optimal input mix. We analyze this question in the next sections.

6.3 figure it out

A firm is employing 100 workers ($W = \$15/$hour) and 50 units of capital ($R = \$30/$hour). At the firm's current input use, the marginal product of labor is 45 and the marginal product of capital is 60. Is the firm producing its current level of output at the minimum cost or is there a way for the firm to do better? Explain.

Solution:

The cost-minimizing input choice occurs when $MP_L/W = MP_K/R$. We need to determine if this is the case for this firm:

$$MP_L = 45 \text{ and } W = 15 \text{ so } MP_L/W = 45/15 = 3$$
$$MP_K = 60 \text{ and } R = 30 \text{ so } MP_K/R = 60/30 = 2$$

Therefore, $MP_L/W > MP_K/R$. The firm is not currently minimizing its cost.

Because $MP_L/W > MP_K/R$, \$1 spent on labor yields a greater marginal product (i.e., more output) than \$1 spent on capital. The firm would do better by reducing its use of capital and increasing its use of labor. Note that as the firm reduces capital, the marginal product of capital will rise. Likewise, as the firm hires additional labor, the marginal product of labor will fall. Ultimately, the firm will reach its cost-minimizing input choice where $MP_L/W = MP_K/R$.

A Graphical Representation of the Effects of an Input Price Change   We know that differences in input costs show up as differences in the slopes of the isocost lines. A higher relative cost of labor (from an increase in W, decrease in R, or both) makes isocost lines steeper. Decreases in labor's relative cost flatten them. A cost-minimizing firm wants to produce using the input combination where the slope of the isocost line equals the slope of the isoquant. This requirement means that when the inputs' relative price changes, the point of tangency between the isocost line (now with a new slope) and the isoquant must also change. Input prices cause the firm to move along the isoquant corresponding to the firm's desired output level to the input combination where an isocost line is tangent to the isoquant.

Figure 6.11 shows an example of this. The initial input price ratio gives the slope of isocost line C_1. The firm wants to produce the quantity $\overline{Q}$, so initially the cost-minimizing combination of inputs occurs at point A. Now suppose that labor becomes relatively more expensive (or equivalently, capital becomes less expensive). This change causes the isocost lines to become steeper. With the steeper isocost lines, the point of tangency shifts to point B. Therefore, the increase in the relative cost of labor causes the firm to shift to an input mix that has more capital and less labor than before.

The implication of this outcome makes sense: If a firm wants to minimize its production costs and a particular input becomes relatively more expensive, the firm will substitute away from the now relatively more expensive input and toward the relatively less expensive one.

This is why we sometimes observe very different production methods used to make the same or at least very similar products. For example, if you spend a growing season observing a typical rice-farming operation in Vietnam, you will see days where dozens of workers tend to a small paddy. Depending on the time of season, they might be planting, transplanting, or harvesting plants one-by-one. Whatever their particular task, they use only the most basic of tools. If you visit a rice farm in Texas, on the other hand, a typical day at work will involve a single farmer (and maybe a hired hand or two) driving large machines of various types. The farmer uses these machines to do the same tasks as the Vietnamese workers. A key reason for the differences in production methods is that the relative prices of capital and labor are very different in Vietnam and Texas. In Vietnam, labor is relatively cheap compared to capital. Therefore, the tangency of Vietnamese rice farms' isoquants and isocost lines is at a point such as point A in Figure 6.11. At point A, a lot of labor and only a little capital are used to grow rice. In Texas, on the other hand, labor is relatively expensive. This implies steeper isocost lines for Texas farms, making their cost-minimizing input mix much more capital-intensive, as at point B.

Figure 6.11 | A Change in the Price of Labor Leads to a New Cost-Minimizing Input Choice

When labor becomes relatively more expensive, the isocost line shifts from C_1 to C_2. With the steeper isocost line, the cost-minimizing input choice shifts from point A, with a high ratio of labor to capital, to point B, with a low ratio of labor to capital.

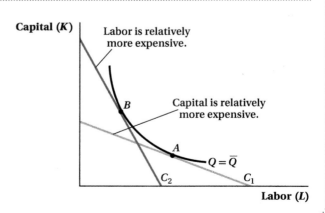

theory and data

Hospitals' Input Choices and Medicare Reimbursement Rules

Medicare is the government-paid medical insurance system for the elderly and disabled in the United States. It involves massive expenditures: $550 billion in 2011 (which works out to roughly $12,000 per beneficiary), accounting for about one-fifth of all health-related spending in the United States. Not surprisingly, then, Medicare is a huge source of revenues for producers of medical care like hospitals, physicians, and (due to the addition of the Medicare Part D drug benefit in 2006) pharmaceutical companies. This also means that when Medicare changes its rules about how it pays providers, such a change affects the way health care is produced.

In a 2008 study, economists Daron Acemoglu and Amy Finkelstein looked at how changes in Medicare payment structures affect health-care providers' input choices.[*] Medicare introduced what is called the Prospective Payment System (PPS) in 1983. The PPS changed how Medicare reimbursed hospitals for services they provided to Medicare patients. Before PPS, Medicare would simply reimburse a portion of a hospital's total costs (including both capital and labor costs), where the portion equaled the share of Medicare patient-days out of a hospital's total patient-days. That is, Medicare payments subsidized a hospital's expenditures on both capital and labor inputs.

The shift to PPS changed this reimbursement approach. Capital expenditures — building additions, renovations, and purchases of medical technologies — were rebated as before. But for everything else, PPS paid a flat rate based on the patient's diagnosis, regardless of the hospital's actual labor expenditures. So, for example, a cataract surgery would entitle the hospital to a pre-specified payment regardless of whether the hospital spent more or less on the labor inputs necessary to complete the patient's treatment. What PPS did, in effect, was change hospitals' relative prices of capital and labor inputs. Capital was priced as before, because PPS treated capital expenditures the same way as it always had. But now the hospital was completely responsible on the margin for any additional labor inputs. Rather than being reimbursed for any extra labor expenses as before, the hospital bore the full cost of any additional staffing time. Therefore, PPS raised the relative price of labor to hospitals, shifting the hospitals' isocost lines in the same way the lines shifted from C_1 to C_2 in Figure 6.11.

The prediction of our cost-minimization analysis is that hospitals would switch to more capital-intensive production because they now faced a higher relative price for labor (leading to steeper isocost lines). So, for example, whereas in the past a hospital might have admitted a patient with a minor head injury overnight for observation (hospital stays are labor-intensive), they would now take a CT scan of the patient's brain (using their newly purchased scanner) to verify that there is no significant damage, and send the patient home rather than admit her.

How can this prediction of our model be tested in the data? A straightforward way might be to look at hospitals' capital-to-labor ratios before and after PPS, and see if they increased. Acemoglu and Finkelstein did this and found that capital intensity, in fact, increased. The authors estimate that the average hospital saw a 10% increase in its capital-to-labor ratio within the first three years after the introduction of PPS. However, one might worry that capital-to-labor mixes change over time for other reasons. Perhaps, for example, wage levels have generally increased over time. It might just be coincidence that the average capital intensity in hospitals rose after PPS began.

To address this possible coincidence, Acemoglu and Finkelstein also conducted another more powerful test of the theory. Hospitals differ substantially in their share of patients who are on Medicare. Because PPS only applies to Medicare-related expenditures, the new payment structure should affect hospitals with a lot of Medicare patients more than it affects those with only a few. Expectedly, then, hospitals with a greater share of Medicare patients should have made larger shifts from labor to capital inputs.

---

[*] Daron Acemoglu and Amy Finkelstein, "Input and Technology Choices in Regulated Industries: Evidence from the Health Care Sector," *Journal of Political Economy* 116, no. 5 (2008): 837–880.

That is what happened. Capital-to-labor ratios went up overall after PPS, but hospitals with 75% Medicare patients moved to a capital-to-labor ratio that was, on average, about 13% higher than those with only 25% of their patients on Medicare.

Acemoglu and Finkelstein identified the specific types of capital inputs that hospitals bought more of. Hospitals with a large fraction of Medicare patients were more likely to adopt a number of advanced medical technologies like CT scanners, cardiac-care devices, and radiation-based cancer treatment equipment. The same hospitals were also more likely to decrease the average length of patient stays, a labor-intensive input into health-care production.

These results speak to the power of our model of firms' production behavior. Despite all the simplifications we made (our nine assumptions), the model seems to be a good predictor of actual firms' choices in the real world.

6.5 Returns to Scale

returns to scale
A change in the amount of output in response to a proportional increase or decrease in all of the inputs.

constant returns to scale
A production function for which changing all inputs by the same proportion changes the quantity of output by the same proportion.

increasing returns to scale
A production function for which changing all inputs by the same proportion changes output *more* than proportionately.

decreasing returns to scale
A production function for which changing all inputs by the same proportion changes output *less* than proportionately.

Economists use the term **returns to scale** to describe what happens to the amount of output in response to a proportional increase or decrease in all of the inputs.

A production function is said to have **constant returns to scale** if changing the amount of capital and labor by some multiple changes the quantity of output by exactly the same multiple. (For example, a doubling of capital and labor results in a doubling of output.) Our Cobb–Douglas production function $Q = K^{0.5}L^{0.5}$ has constant returns to scale. This is apparent in Table 6.2. When $L = K = 1$, $Q = 1$; when labor and capital are doubled to $L = K = 2$, then output doubles, too: $Q = 2$. If labor and capital are doubled again to $L = K = 4$, then $Q = 4$.

A production function has **increasing returns to scale** instead if changing all inputs by some multiple changes output *more* than proportionately. (Doubling capital and labor more than doubles output.) Finally, **decreasing returns to scale** exist if adjusting all inputs by the same multiple changes output by *less* than that multiple. (Output does not fully double when inputs are doubled.)

We assumed earlier in the chapter that inputs have diminishing returns—their marginal products fall as firms use more of them. So, how can returns to scale be constant or increasing when there are diminishing returns to inputs? The key difference between the two concepts is that marginal products refer to changes in *only one input while holding the other input constant*, but returns to scale is about changes in *all inputs at the same time*. In other words, diminishing marginal returns refers to short-run changes, while returns to scale is a long-run phenomenon because we are changing all inputs simultaneously.

Figure 6.12 on the next page demonstrates these returns to scale cases using isoquants. In the first panel, a doubling of inputs leads to the doubling of outputs, so the technology exhibits constant returns to scale. Similarly, the isoquants in panel b indicate increasing returns to scale, while decreasing returns to scale are shown in panel c.

Factors Affecting Returns to Scale

A number of aspects of a production technology determine a production function's returns to scale.

In some ways, it is natural for a production function to have constant returns to scale. If a production process can easily be replicated lock, stock, and barrel, output should expectedly grow proportionately with inputs. For example, if a firm has a factory that makes 1,000 cars a day using 3,000 units of labor and 4,000 units of capital, it seems reasonable that the firm could build an identical factory somewhere else (maybe even next door) and, having doubled all of its inputs, double its output. Adding a third identical factory and set of workers should again increase output commensurately, and so on.

Figure 6.12   Returns to Scale

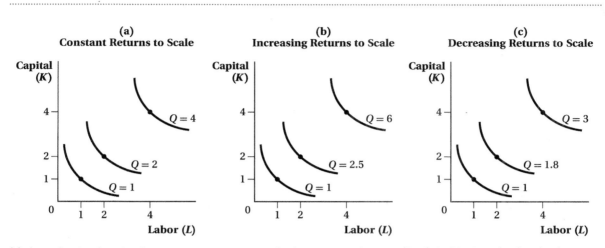

(a)
Constant Returns to Scale

(b)
Increasing Returns to Scale

(c)
Decreasing Returns to Scale

(a) A production function has constant returns to scale if changing the amount of capital and labor by some multiple changes the output by exactly the same multiple. When the input combination (L, K) doubles from $(1, 1)$ to $(2, 2)$, output doubles from $Q = 1$ to $Q = 2$.

(b) A production function has increasing returns to scale if changing the amount of capital and labor by some multiple changes the output by more than that multiple. When the input combination (L, K) doubles from $(1, 1)$ to $(2, 2)$, output more than doubles from $Q = 1$ to $Q > 2.5$.

(c) A production function has decreasing returns to scale if changing the amount of capital and labor by some multiple changes the output by less than that multiple. When the input combination (L, K) doubles from $(1, 1)$ to $(2, 2)$, output less than doubles from $Q = 1$ to $Q = 1.8$.

But there are other influences than can push production functions toward increasing or decreasing returns to scale as well. For example, a common source of increasing returns to scale is **fixed costs.** These are payments to inputs that must be used no matter what the output quantity is, even if it is zero. (We talk more about fixed costs in Chapter 7.) If a certain quantity of inputs must be used before the firm can produce its first unit of output, increasing inputs after these fixed costs are paid will increase output more than proportionately. Consider the example of a firm that uses three inputs to earn its revenues: capital, labor, and a Web page. We assume the Web page input is a fixed cost, because the cost of its upkeep is basically the same whether the firm makes a lot of product or just a little. If the firm doubles its capital and labor inputs while keeping the same Web page, it will probably double its output. Therefore, the firm was able to double its output without having to double all its inputs. This is just another way of stating the definition of increasing returns to scale.

fixed cost
An input cost that does not vary with the amount of output.

A firm can also experience increasing returns to scale if there is **learning by doing.** As a company makes more of a good, it tends to become more and more efficient at production. This sort of learning takes place with virtually any task that is repeated over and over (as you've probably learned from your own personal experience). If a firm gets better at producing the more output it makes, then it may be able to produce the second batch of output using fewer resources than it required for the first batch. That is, it will be able to double its output without having to double its inputs.

learning by doing
The process by which a firm becomes more efficient at production as it produces more output.

Decreasing returns to scale are possible but should be unlikely for the same reason that constant returns to scale are natural. If inputs are measured properly, and the firm has ample time to adjust all its inputs, the firm should be able to replicate its current production operation, allowing it to increase output by the same factor as inputs. Nevertheless, economists sometimes measure firms' production functions and find that

make the grade

How to determine a production function's returns to scale

A common question you will see on an intermediate micro exam is one that asks if a production function exhibits constant, increasing, or decreasing returns to scale. If you approach this question the right way, it is one of the easiest questions on which you will ever be tested.

Given a formula, first solve for the quantity when both capital and labor equal 1. Next, multiply the inputs by 2, and work out the quantity. If the total quantity doubles, the production function exhibits constant returns to scale. If it less than doubles, then the production function has diminishing returns to scale. More than doubles? You guessed it: increasing returns to scale.

Here is one last trick. If the production function is a Cobb–Douglas function, then all you need to do is add up all of the exponents on the inputs. If these add up to 1, then the production function exhibits constant returns to scale. If they sum to more than 1, it indicates increasing returns to scale, and if they add up to less than 1, it shows decreasing returns to scale.

Say you're given the production function $Q = K^{0.3}L^{0.8}$. Solving using the first method gives you $Q = 1$ when $K = 1$ and $L = 1$, and $Q = 2^{0.3}2^{0.8} = 2^{1.1}$ when $K = 2$ and $L = 2$. Since $2^{1.1}$ is greater than 2, this production function has increasing returns to scale. But this is a Cobb–Douglas function, so you could instead simply add the exponents $(0.3 + 0.8 = 1.1 > 1)$ and find the same result.

they exhibit decreasing returns to scale. Most often, such a finding indicates that not all inputs are being fully measured. For instance, suppose a company builds a seemingly identical second factory with the same number of workers and capital as its first one, yet the second is less efficient. This might be because the second factory's manager is not as talented as the manager at the first, or because the company's productive corporate culture isn't as well established as at the original factory. Managerial talent and corporate culture are inputs to the firm's production, but are often too difficult to measure to include in standard labor and capital inputs measures. To have true decreasing returns to scale, the second factory would have to be less efficient even if the managerial talent and corporate culture were at the same level as at the first factory.

One reason a firm might have true decreasing returns to scale is regulatory burden. Many business regulations exempt small companies. As a result, as a company grows, it often has to comply with additional rules and regulations. Because the cost of complying with these regulations can be substantial, small firms that expand the scale of their operations above the threshold find themselves having to deal with a new set of costs now that they are no longer exempt.

6.4 figure it out

For each of the following production functions, determine if they exhibit constant, decreasing, or increasing returns to scale.

a. $Q = 2K + 15L$

b. $Q = \min(3K, 4L)$

c. $Q = 15K^{0.5}L^{0.4}$

Solution:

The easiest way to determine the returns to scale for a production function is to simply plug in values for L and K, calculate Q, and then double the input levels to see what happens to output. If output exactly doubles, the production function exhibits constant returns to scale. If output rises by less than double, there are decreasing returns to scale. If output more than doubles, the production function has increasing returns to scale.

So, for each of these production functions, we will start with $K = L = 1$ and calculate Q and then perform the same exercise for $K = L = 2$. Note that K and L do not have to be equal for this method to work, but it does simplify the solution a bit.

a. If $L = 1$ and $K = 1$: $Q = 2K + 15L = 2(1) + 15(1) = 2 + 15 = 17$.
If $L = 2$ and $K = 2$: $Q = 2K + 15L = 2(2) + 15(2) = 4 + 30 = 34$.

Since output exactly doubles when inputs are doubled, the production function exhibits constant returns to scale.

b. If $L = 1$ and $K = 1$: $Q = \min(3K, 4L) = Q = \min(3(1), 4(1)) = \min(3, 4) = 3$.
If $L = 2$ and $K = 2$: $Q = \min(3K, 4L) = Q = \min(3(2), 4(2)) = \min(6, 8) = 6$.

Because output exactly doubles when inputs are doubled, the production function exhibits constant returns to scale.

c. If $L = 1$ and $K = 1$: $Q = 15K^{0.5}L^{0.4} = Q = 15(1)^{0.5}(1)^{0.4} = 15(1)(1) = 15$.

If $L = 2$ and $K = 2$: $Q = 15K^{0.5}L^{0.4} = Q = 15(2)^{0.5}(2)^{0.4} = 15(1.41)(1.31) = 27.71$.

Because output less than doubles when inputs are doubled, the production function exhibits decreasing returns to scale.

6.6 Technological Change

When economists try to measure production functions using data from firms' operations over time, they will often find that output rises in later periods even though the firms might still be using the same amount of inputs. The only way to explain this is that the production function must somehow be changing over time in a way that allows extra output to be obtained from a given amount of inputs. This shift in the production function is referred to as **total factor productivity growth** (or sometimes **technological change**).

We can adjust a production function to allow for technological change. There are many possible ways to do this, but a common and straightforward method is to suppose that the level of technology is a constant that multiplies the production function:

$$Q = Af(K, L)$$

where A is the level of total factor productivity, a parameter that affects how much output can be produced from a given set of inputs. Usually, we think of this as reflecting technological change. Increases in A mean that the amount of output obtainable from any given set of labor and capital inputs will increase as well.

How does this kind of technological change affect a firm's cost-minimization decisions? Consider the impact of a change in A on the components of the firm's cost-minimization problem above. First, the firm's isocost lines won't change. A is a feature of the production function, not the prices of inputs. Because A is part of the production function, though, it will affect the isoquants. An increase in A means that the same number of inputs will produce more output, so it also implies that the *same* output can be made with *fewer* inputs. Because an isoquant reflects the combinations of inputs that produce a given amount of output, higher values of A shift isoquants in (toward the origin).

total factor productivity growth (or technological change)
An improvement in technology that changes the firm's production function such that more output is obtained from the same amount of inputs.

Figure 6.13 : The Impact of Technological Change

An improvement in technology shifts the isoquant $Q_1 = \overline{Q}$ inward to $Q_2 = \overline{Q}$. The new cost-minimizing input combination (L_2, K_2) is located at the tangency between Q_2 and the isocost C_2. (L_2, K_2) uses fewer inputs and is, therefore, cheaper than the original cost-minimizing input combination (L_1, K_1) located at the tangency between Q_1 and the isocost C_1.

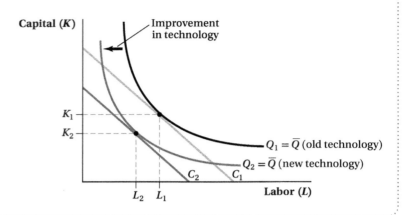

This is shown in Figure 6.13. Before, to produce $\overline{Q}$, the firm needed some combination of inputs on isoquant $Q_1 = \overline{Q}$. After technological change leads to an increase in A, the firm doesn't need to use as many inputs to produce $\overline{Q}$. Therefore, the isoquant for $\overline{Q}$ shifts in, to $Q_2 = \overline{Q}$.

If the firm's desired output remains $\overline{Q}$ after the technological change, then the firm's choice of inputs will be determined by the tangency of $Q_2 = \overline{Q}$ and its isocost lines, as in Figure 6.13. The initial cost-minimizing input combination (before the technological change) is where $Q_1 = \overline{Q}$ is tangent to isocost line C_1, that is, K_1 units of capital and L_1 units of labor. After the technological change, the optimal input combination becomes K_2 and L_2, where $Q_2 = \overline{Q}$ is tangent to isocost line C_2. Because the firm needs to use fewer inputs, technological change has reduced its costs of producing $\overline{Q}$.

For a vivid description of the power of technological change, see the Freakonomics study on pages 6-30 and 6-31.

 **application**

Technological Change in U.S. Manufacturing

You might have noticed there's no shortage of talk about the shrinking (and in some more strident commentators' minds, impending disappearance) of the U.S. manufacturing sector. It's true that manufacturing employment has fallen—a lot. In 1994 there were 17 million manufacturing workers in the United States, about 18% of the total private sector workforce. Of these, 10 million workers were employed by companies manufacturing **durable goods**—goods that have long service lives, such as appliances, airplanes, cars, metal and wood products, and electrical equipment. By the end of 2011 there were only 11.8 million manufacturing workers, less than 11% of the private workforce, 7.4 million of whom were making durable goods. (This wasn't just due to the 2008–2009 recession, either. Manufacturing's share of employment had dropped steadily before 2008 as well.)

Given this, it might surprise you to find out that the total value of manufactured products made in the United States *increased* over the same period. Not by just a little, either. While the total inflation-adjusted output of private businesses grew by 53% between 1994 and 2010, the manufacturing sector's total output grew 49%, just about as fast. Furthermore, the total inflation-adjusted output of U.S. durable goods *more than doubled* over the period.

durable good
A good that has a long service life.

Figure 6.14 : U.S. Total Factor Productivity, 1994–2009

Data from the U.S. Bureau of Labor Statistics show that total factor productivity increased much more in the manufacturing industries than in the overall private business sector over the period 1994–2009. In particular, durable goods manufacturers saw a 37% increase in total factor productivity, enabling these firms to increase production while decreasing the number of laborers. As a result, unemployment rose even as output increased.

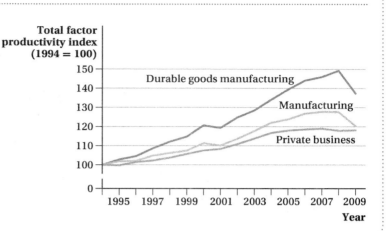

How is it possible for manufacturing employment to fall for an extended time while the sector's output grows just as fast as, or even considerably faster than, the rest of the economy? A partial answer to this question is that manufacturing firms shifted from using labor to using more capital inputs. But that's not the whole story. Much of the explanation lies in the fact that technological change was faster in manufacturing than in the rest of the economy, particularly in durable goods manufacturing.

Figure 6.14 shows the growth of technology (total factor productivity) for three segments of the U.S. economy. (These technology data were compiled by the U.S. Bureau of Labor Statistics.) The largest segment is the private business sector, which includes just about every producer in the economy outside of government bodies, including manufacturers. The second is the manufacturing sector, and the third isolates durable goods manufacturers specifically. The level of technology in each segment is given by an index, where the value of the index expresses the segment's total factor productivity level as a fraction of its value in 1994. So, for instance, an index value of 120 in a particular year means that the segment's total factor productivity is 20% higher than it was in 1994. This means that, given any fixed set of inputs, the segment's producers can make 20% more output than they could in 1994.

A comparison of the rates of technological change helps explain why manufacturing output could have gone up even as employment fell. Total factor productivity for the entire private business segment grew by about 18% during the period, meaning producers were able to make 18% more output from the same set of inputs in 2009 as they could in 1994. Manufacturers saw a somewhat greater 20% increase in total factor productivity during the period, and that includes a big slide during the recent recession that wasn't experienced by the economy as a whole. Before that slide, manufacturing total factor productivity had grown by over 25% since 1994. Durable goods manufacturers, in particular, saw a much stronger rate of technological change during the period. They were able to produce 37% more output in 2009 with the same inputs they used in 1994. This meant that they could use even fewer inputs than producers in other segments of the economy and still experience the same total output growth. This relative productivity growth, combined with the fact that they substituted more capital-intensive production, explains how they were able to double output over the period even while using less labor. ■

freakonomics

Why Do Indian Fishermen Love Their Cell Phones So Much?

There are few products more cherished by American consumers than the cell phone. The modern smart phone is truly a technological wonder—used not just for phone calls and text, but also as a browser, calendar, GPS device, MP3 player, and video streamer. It's hard to imagine, as you lovingly caress your iPhone, that it was only a little over 25 years ago that the first cell phone, the Motorola DynaTAC 8000x, hit the consumer marketplace.[*] Weighing in at a hefty 1.75 pounds (almost six times the weight of the iPhone), it had a battery life of 60 minutes of use. All it did was make phone calls, and the sound quality was horrible. The price tag, adjusting for inflation: over $9,000. In the history of humankind, there are few examples of technological progress occurring as rapidly as has been the case with cell phones.

A local fisherman uses a mobile phone as he works Nariman Point in Mumbai, a commercial hub of India.

Prashanth Vishwanathan/Bloomberg via Getty Images

When economists talk about technological progress, they are referring to changes in the production function. Compared to thirty years ago, we've gotten much better at taking a set of inputs (e.g., plastic, silicon, metal, the time of engineers and factory workers, etc.) and turning them into cell phones.

Although it is natural to think of technological progress in terms of innovations in manufacturing, there are many other sources of such progress. Indeed, the cell phone is not just the beneficiary of technological progress—in some parts of the world, it is an important *source* of technological progress. Economist Robert Jensen has studied fishing villages in Kerala, a state on India's southern coast.[†] In the area observed, he looked at 15 markets where fishermen and consumers met to buy and sell the day's catch. If there were not enough buyers, the excess fish would go to waste because of the absence of refrigeration. If there were not enough sellers, some of the consumers went away empty-handed. Prices varied wildly in response to daily fluctuations in supply and demand, and up to 8% of fishermen had to let their fish go to waste because there was no demand.

Traditionally, fishermen would take their boats out to sea, make their catch, and face a guessing game as to which market to choose on a given day. Then cell phone coverage came to the area. Very quickly, fishermen adopted cell phones, which allowed them to call ahead to determine which market would offer them the best prices on their fish. Better information led to better matching of buyers and sellers. There were rarely wasted fish; in fact, Jensen found that after the complete adoption of cell phones, it became extremely rare for sellers not to find buyers for their fish. The figure presents evidence of just how profoundly cell phones affected this market. It shows the fluctuation in fish prices over time in three areas in Kerala. Each colored line in the graph represents prices at one particular market. The introduction of cell phones was staggered across regions, and the points at which cell phones became available are denoted by the vertical lines near week 20 for Region I, week 100 for Region II, and week 200 for Region III.

Before cell phones, prices in each region were extremely volatile. Sometimes prices were almost as high as 12 rupees per kilogram on one beach, whereas at another beach on the same day, the fish were basically given away for free. From day to day, it was difficult if

---

[*] The DynaTAC 8000x was the first cell phone available to the general public, but it was not the first cell phone produced or even to make a successful phone call. That distinction goes to an even heavier prototype in 1973.

[†] Robert Jensen, "The Digital Provide: Information (Technology), Market Performance, and Welfare in the South Indian Fisheries Sector," *The Quarterly Journal of Economics* 122, no. 3 (2007): 879–924.

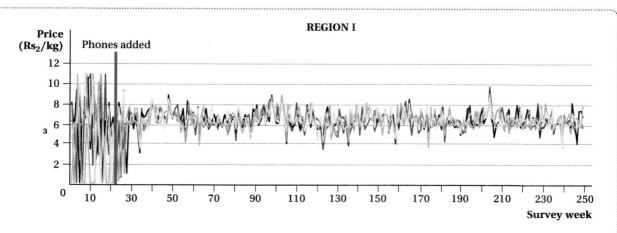

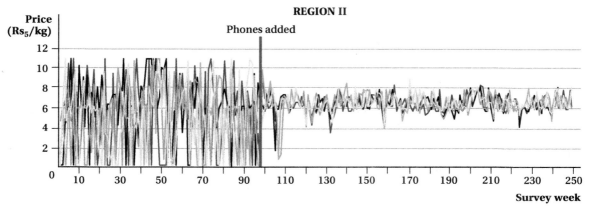

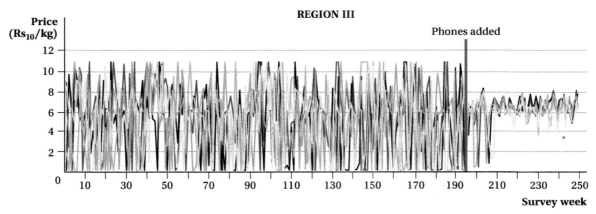

Each colored line shows the price of fish at a particular beach in each region. Before cell phones became available, prices were extremely volatile. After cell phones became available, as denoted by the vertical red lines, prices showed less variation.

---

not impossible to predict which market would have the best price. The impact of cell phone use on the market was seen as soon as cell phone service became available in each area, although as you might expect, it took a few weeks for people to learn how to adjust and figure out how best to use this new technology. Roughly 10 weeks after the introduction of cell phones into this industry, though, the variation in prices across beaches in each of the three regions on a given day had shrunk dramatically.

6.7 The Firm's Expansion Path and Total Cost Curve

We've seen so far how a firm minimizes its costs at the optimal production quantity. We can now use this information to illustrate how the firm's production choices and its total costs change as the optimal production quantity changes.

Panel a of Figure 6.15 shows sets of isoquants and isocost lines for a hypothetical firm, Ivor's Engines. The figure illustrates three isoquants and isocost lines, but remember that there are isoquants for every possible quantity level and isocost lines for every cost level. Recall that the combination of labor and capital that minimizes the cost of producing a given quantity of output is at the tangency of an isocost line and the isoquant corresponding to that output level. The figure shows three such tangencies. On the lower left, $Q = 10$ is the isoquant that corresponds to input combinations that allow Ivor's Engines to make 10 engines. This isoquant is tangent at point X to the $C = \$100$ isocost line, so $100 is the lowest cost at which Ivor can build 10 engines. The isoquant representing input combinations that produce 20 engines, $Q = 20$, is tangent to the $C = \$180$ isocost line at point Y, indicating that Ivor's minimum cost for producing 20 engines is $180. At point Z, the $Q = 30$ isoquant is tangent to the $C = \$300$ isocost line, so $300 is the minimum cost of making 30 engines.

The line connecting the three cost-minimizing input combinations in Figure 6.15a (as well as all the other cost-minimizing isoquant-isocost line tangencies for output levels that are not shown) is the firm's **expansion path.** It illustrates how the optimal mix of labor and capital varies with total output.

The expansion path shows the optimal input combinations at each output quantity. If we plot the total cost from the isocost line and the output quantity from the isoquants located along the expansion path, we have a **total cost curve** that shows the cost of producing particular quantities. Panel b of Figure 6.15 gives these cost and quantity combinations for the expansion path in Figure 6.15a, including the three cost-

expansion path
A curve that illustrates how the optimal mix of inputs varies with total output.

total cost curve
A curve that shows a firm's cost of producing particular quantities.

Figure 6.15 : The Expansion Path and the Total Cost Curve

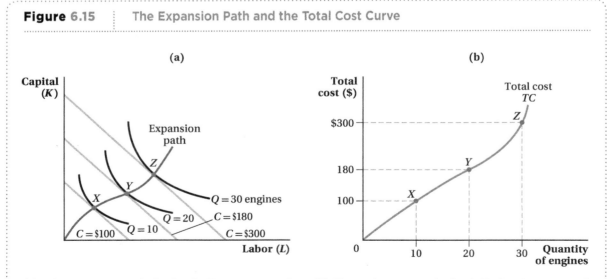

(a)

(b)

(a) The expansion path for Ivor's Engines maps the optimal input combinations for each quantity Q. Here, points X, Y, and Z are the cost-minimizing input combinations given output levels $Q = 10$, $Q = 20$, and $Q = 30$, respectively.

(b) The total cost curve for Ivor's Engines is constructed using the isocost lines from the expansion path in panel a. The cost-minimizing input combinations cost $100, $180, and $300 at output levels $Q = 10$, $Q = 20$, and $Q = 30$, respectively.

minimizing points at 10, 20, and 30 units of output. The total cost curve is another representation of the information revealed by the expansion path. Both the total cost curve and the expansion path show how, when the firm is minimizing its costs of producing any given quantity, the firm's minimized costs change when its output changes.

Note that the expansion path and the total cost curve that corresponds to it are for a given set of input prices (as reflected in the isocost lines) and a given production function (as reflected in the isoquants). As we saw earlier, if input prices or the production function changes, so will the cost-minimizing input combinations. Therefore, the expansion path and the total cost curve will change, too. In Chapter 7, we use the total cost curve—as derived from the expansion path—in our discussion of a firm's cost functions.

6.8 Conclusion

Much like the consumer from Chapter 4 minimizes her expenditures of achieving a given utility level, a firm minimizes its costs of producing a given quantity of a good. These optimal production decisions that a firm makes trace out its total cost curve, which shows the costs of producing a given quantity. In Chapter 7, we deepen our understanding of a firm's cost structure and delve into a discussion of the specific costs a firm faces. We'll see that a firm uses its knowledge of its cost structure to inform its cost-minimizing behavior.

Summary

1. In looking at a firm's **production** practices, we made several simplifying assumptions. Most importantly, we assume that **cost minimization**—minimizing the total cost of producing the firm's desired output quantity—is a key objective of any producer. [**Section 6.1**]

2. A **production function** relates the quantities of inputs that a producer uses to the quantity of output it obtains from them. Production functions typically have a mathematical representation in the form $Q = f(K,L)$. A commonly used production function is the Cobb–Douglas production function, which has the form $Q = K^{\alpha}L^{\beta}$, where α and β are constants. [**Section 6.1**]

3. In the short run, a firm's level of capital is fixed. Differences in output must be achieved by adjusting labor inputs alone. We looked at properties of the production function including an input's **marginal** and **average product** (we focused on labor in this case, because capital is fixed). We saw examples of **diminishing marginal products** for labor, where the incremental output obtained from using another unit of labor in production decreases. [**Section 6.2**]

4. The ability to adjust capital inputs, which firms enjoy in the long run, has two important implications. One is that the firm can alleviate diminishing marginal products of labor by increasing the amount of capital it uses at the same time. Second, it has an ability to substitute between capital and labor. [**Section 6.3**]

5. An isoquant curve shows all combinations of inputs that allow a firm to make a particular quantity of output. The curvature and slope of the isoquant represent the substitutability of the inputs in the production of the good. In particular, the negative slope of the isoquant is equal to the **marginal rate of technical substitution** of labor for capital. [**Section 6.4**]

6. An isocost line connects all the combinations of capital and labor that the firm can purchase for a given total expenditure on inputs. The relative costs of capital and labor determine the slope of the isocost line. [**Section 6.4**]

7. A firm aims to minimize its costs at any given level of output. The firm's cost-minimizing output occurs where the isocost line is tangent to the isoquant, or where the marginal rate of technical substitution is equal to the relative price of labor to capital. [**Section 6.4**]

8. **Returns to scale** is a property of production functions that describes how the level of output changes when all inputs are simultaneously changed by the same amount. Production functions can have returns to scale that are constant (if all inputs increase by a factor, output changes by the same factor), increasing (if all inputs increase by a factor, output changes by more than that factor), or decreasing (if all inputs increase by a factor, output changes by less than that factor). [**Section 6.5**]

9. When there is **technological change,** a production function changes over time so that a fixed

amount of inputs can produce more output. This is reflected by a shift of a production function's isoquants toward the origin. [Section 6.6]

10. A firm's cost curves are derived from its **expansion path,** which uses isoquants and isocost curves to show how its input choices change with output. The total cost curve relates the costs tied to the isocost lines and the quantities tied to the isoquants that intersect the expansion path. Productivity growth shifts total cost downward. [Section 6.7]

Review Questions

1. What are the differences between a firm's production in the short run and the long run?
2. What does a production function tell us?
3. Why is a firm's marginal product of labor more relevant than the marginal product of capital in the short run?
4. What does the diminishing marginal product of labor tell us about the relationship between labor inputs and marginal product?
5. How does the amount of output change as the isoquants are farther from the graph's origin? Why can't two isoquants cross?
6. What is the marginal rate of technical substitution? What does it imply about an isoquant's shape?
7. What does the curvature of an isoquant imply about the two inputs, capital and labor?
8. What is an isocost line? What does its slope tell us about the relative cost of labor and capital?
9. How will a firm react to an increase in the price of one input relative to another?
10. When is a production function said to have constant returns to scale, increasing returns to scale, or decreasing returns to scale?
11. How does technological change affect a firm's output?
12. What is an expansion path and how does it relate to a firm's total cost curve?

Problems

1. Consider the production function presented in the table below:

		Labor (L)					
		0	**1**	**2**	**3**	**4**	**5**	**6**
	1	100	200	300	400	500	600
Capital	**2**	200	400	600	800	1,000	1,200
(K)	**3**	300	600	900	1,200	1,500	1,800
	4	400	800	1,200	1,600	2,000	2,400
	5	500	1,000	1,500	2,000	2,500	3,000
	6	600	1,200	1,800	2,400	3,000	3,600

a. If the firm decides to employ 6 units of capital and 1 worker, what is its output?
b. What other combinations of capital and labor could be used to produce the same level of output you found in (a)?
c. Plot the combinations you determined in (a) and (b) on a graph, with labor on the horizontal axis and capital on the vertical axis. Connect the dots to form the production isoquant corresponding to 600 units of output.

2. The table below represents the production function for Hawg Wild, a small catering company specializing in barbecued pork. The numbers in the cells represent the number of customers that can be served with various combinations of labor and capital.

		Labor (L)					
	1	100	132	155	174	190	205
	2	152	200	235	264	289	310
Capital	**3**	193	255	300	337	368	396
(K)	**4**	230	303	357	400	437	470
	5	263	347	408	457	500	538
	6	293	387	455	510	558	600

a. Is this production function a short-run or long-run production function. How can you tell?
b. Suppose that Hawg Wild employs 5 units of capital and 2 workers. How many diners will be served?
c. Suppose that Hawg Wild employs 5 units of capital and 2 workers, but that the owner,

Billy Porcine, is considering adding his nephew to the payroll. What will the marginal product of Billy's nephew be?

d. Notice that when Hawg Wild uses 1 unit of capital, the marginal product of the fifth unit of labor is 16. But when Hawg Wild uses 5 units of capital, the marginal product of the fifth unit of labor is 43. Does this production function violate the law of diminishing marginal product of labor? Why or why not?

e. Suppose that Hawg Wild employs 5 units of capital and 2 workers, but that the owner, Billy Porcine, is considering adding another meat smoker to the kitchen (which will raise the amount of capital input to 6 units). What will the marginal product of the smoker be?

f. Hawg Wild employs 5 units of capital and 2 workers. Billy is considering the choice between hiring another worker or buying another smoker. If smokers cost $8 and workers $12, then at the margin, what is the most cost-effective choice for Billy to make?

3. Complete the table below:

Labor Input	Total Product	Marginal Product	Average Product
0	0	—	—
1		70	
2	135		
3			63
4		51	
5			60
6	366		

4. Suppose that a firm's production function is given by $Q = K^{0.33}L^{0.67}$, where $MP_K = 0.33K^{-0.67}L^{0.67}$ and $MP_L = 0.67K^{0.33}L^{-0.33}$.

a. As L increases, what happens to the marginal product of labor?

b. As K increases, what happens to the marginal product of labor?

c. Why would the MP_L change as K changes?

d. What happens to the marginal product of capital as K increases? As L increases?

5. Fetzer valves can be made in either China or the United States, but because labor in the United States is more skilled, on average, than labor in China, the production technologies differ. Consider the two production isoquants in the figure. Each represents either the production technol-

ogy for the United States or for China. Based on the $MRTS$, which production isoquant is more likely to represent the United States and which represents China? Explain.

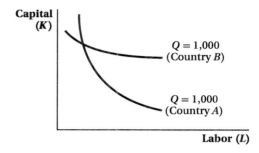

6. Contrast the production functions given below:

a. Suppose that the production function faced by a 30-weight ball bearing producer is given by $Q = 4K^{0.5}L^{0.5}$, where $MP_K = 2K^{-0.5}L^{0.5}$ and $MP_L = 2K^{0.5}L^{-0.5}$. Do both labor and capital display diminishing marginal products? Does the production function display a diminishing marginal rate of technical substitution?

b. Suppose that the production function faced by a 40-weight ball bearing producer is given by $Q = 4KL$, where $MP_K = 4L$ and $MP_L = 4K$. Do both labor and capital display diminishing marginal products? Does the isoquant you drew in (a) display a diminishing marginal rate of technical substitution?

c. Compare your results. Must labor and capital display diminishing marginal products in order for the $MRTS$ to diminish?

7. Suppose that Manny, Jack, and Moe can hire workers for $12 per hour, or can rent capital for $7 per hour.

a. Write an expression for Manny, Jack, and Moe's total cost as a function of how many workers they hire and how much capital they employ.

b. Assume that Manny, Jack, and Moe wish to hold their total costs to exactly $100. Use your answer from (a) to find the equation for an isocost line corresponding to exactly $100 of costs. Rearrange your equation to isolate capital.

c. Graph the equation for the isocost line, putting labor on the horizontal axis and capital on the vertical axis.

d. What is the vertical intercept of the line you drew? The horizontal intercept? What does each represent?

e. What is the slope of the line you drew? What does it represent?

f. Suppose that bargaining with the local labor union raises wages. Manny, Jack, and Moe must now pay $14 per hour. What happens to the isocost line corresponding to $100 of expenditure? Explain. Show the new isocost line on your graph.

8. A jeweler can potentially use two inputs in her handcrafted jewelry: copper or bronze. She finds that when she minimizes her costs, she uses either copper or bronze, but never both. What must her isoquants look like?

9. Consider the production and cost information depicted below:

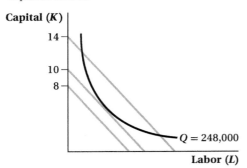

a. Suppose that capital can be hired for $24 per hour. Label each of the isocost lines with the appropriate total expenditure for the firm.
b. Suppose that labor can be hired for $36 per hour. Label the horizontal intercept of each isocost line, and determine the slope of each line.
c. Can the firm produce 248,000 units of output for exactly $336?
d. What is the minimum cost for which 248,000 units of output can be produced?
e. Suppose the firm is spending exactly $240 to make 248,000 units of output. If the marginal product of labor is 400 units of output, what must the marginal product of capital be?

10. Jake and Paul run a paper company. Each week they need to produce 1,000 reams of paper to ship to their customers. The paper plant's long-run production function is $Q = 4K^{0.75}L^{0.25}$, where Q is the number of reams produced, K is the quantity of capital rented, and L is the quantity of labor hired. For this production function, the $MP_L = K^{0.75}/L^{0.75}$ and the $MP_K = 3L^{0.25}/K^{0.25}$. The weekly cost function for the paper plant is $C = 10K + 2L$, where C is the total weekly cost.
a. What ratio of capital to labor minimizes Jake and Paul's total costs?
b. How much capital and labor will Jake and Paul need to rent and hire in order to produce 1,000 reams of paper each week?
c. How much will hiring these inputs cost them?

11. Use a diagram to explain the following: In the case of perfect substitutes, if the ratio of input prices equals the $MRTS$, will a unique solution to the firm's cost-minimization problem exist? In the case of perfect substitutes, if the ratio of input prices does not equal the $MRTS$, where will we find the solution to the firm's cost-minimization problem graphically?

12. Suppose that Gloucester Old Bank's customers can complete their transactions at a teller's window (involving labor) or at an ATM (involving capital). The production function for the bank's services is given as follows: $Q = 4K + 6L$, where Q is the number of customers served, K is the number of ATMs the bank has installed in town, and L is the number of tellers the bank has hired.
a. Suppose that Gloucester currently has 20 ATMs and 20 tellers. If 3 ATMs suddenly fail, how many additional tellers must the bank hire to maintain their original level of service?
b. Does your answer to (a) change if Gloucester originally only uses 17 ATMs? 30 ATMs?
c. What do production isoquants look like for Gloucester Old Bank? (*Hint*: Graph different combinations of tellers and ATMs that can serve an arbitrary number of customers, such as 200.)
d. How would you verbally describe the relationship between tellers and ATMs?
e. Suppose that installing and maintaining an ATM costs $20, and hiring a teller costs $32. What will happen to Gloucester's total number of customers served if it lays off 2 workers and installs 3 ATMs? What will happen to the bank's costs?
f. Using the idea developed in (e), if Gloucester Old Bank is interested in minimizing its costs, what strategy should it employ regarding its input mix?

13. Baldor, Inc. measures the marginal rate of technical substitution ($MRTS$) at $MP_L/MP_K = 3$. The prices of labor and capital faced by Baldor are such that currently $W/R = 4$.
a. Is Baldor minimizing its costs?
b. What can Baldor do to improve its situation?

14. Suppose that the production function for iPods is $Q = 20K^{0.5}L^{0.5}$. The marginal product of labor is $10(K/L)^{0.5}$, and the marginal product of capital is $10(L/K)^{0.5}$.
a. Suppose that labor can be hired for $6, and capital can be hired for $9. When the firm is producing 49 units at lowest cost, what will the firm's marginal rate of technical substitution be?

b. Solve for the lowest-cost combination of labor and capital that will allow the firm to produce 49 iPods. Fractional units of labor and capital are certainly permissible.

c. What is the minimum cost of producing 49 iPods?

d. Suppose that the firm has exactly $300 to spend on producing iPods. What is the maximum number of iPods it can produce?

15. You are the CEO of large-scale corporate farms, and your managers run two farms in neighboring counties. Your chief financial officer reports that in both Rice and Reno counties, farm labor can be hired for $7.36 per hour, farm equipment can be rented for $433 per hour, and land can be rented for $50 per acre. She also reports that the $MRTS_{LK}$ in Rice county is higher than the $MRTS_{LK}$ in neighboring Reno county. Are you minimizing your costs? Explain.

16. With the production function $Q = 2 \min(K, L)$ and the cost function $C = 2K + 3L$, what combination of inputs minimizes costs for $Q = 10$? Show this solution graphically.

17. A young college student on a tight budget is campaigning for an open city council seat. A friend in her economics class estimates that voters are influenced by TV and newspaper ads according to the following function: Votes = $300TV^{0.6}NP^{0.2}$, where TV represents the number of television ads and NP represents the number of newspaper ads. Thus, the marginal product of a newspaper ad is $60TV^{0.6}NP^{-0.8}$ and the marginal product of a TV ad is $180TV^{-0.4}NP^{0.2}$. A local television ad costs $400, and a local newspaper ad costs $250. If the candidate needs 1,800 votes to win, what is the lowest-cost combination of newspaper and TV ads that will bring her victory?

18. Mad Max's Road Warriors fix potholes in interstate highways. Max's road crews fill potholes using workers and shovels in 1 to 1 correspondence. A worker with 1 shovel can fill 10 potholes in a day. A worker with 2 shovels can still only fill 10 potholes, as can 2 workers with 1 shovel.

a. Draw the production isoquant corresponding to filling 30 potholes.

b. Assume that production displays constant returns to scale, and draw a few more isoquants.

c. If shovels rent for $5, and workers must be paid $25, draw several isocost lines.

d. If Mad Max has received a state contract to fill 30 potholes, what is the minimum cost at which it can fulfill the contract?

e. If the cost of renting a shovel suddenly rises from $5 to $6, what will happen to the composition of inputs that Mad Max uses to fill potholes? Why?

19. Determine whether each of the production functions below displays constant, increasing, or decreasing returns to scale:

a. $Q = 10K^{0.75}L^{0.25}$

b. $Q = (K^{0.75}L^{0.25})^2$

c. $Q = K^{0.75}L^{0.75}$

d. $Q = K^{0.25}L^{0.25}$

e. $Q = K + L + KL$

f. $Q = 2K^2 + 3L^2$

g. $Q = KL$

h. $Q = \min(3K, 2L)$

20. Suppose that the production function for Alfred Barbuda, a producer of fine violins, is given by the following: $Q = 10K^{0.5}L^{0.5}$.

a. Suppose that Alfred is currently using 1 unit of capital. If he hires 4 workers, how many violins will they produce?

b. Suppose that Alfred is currently using not 1, but 2 units of capital. How many workers must he hire to match the level of production you found in (a)?

c. Rework your answer to (b), assuming that Alfred is currently using 4 units of capital.

d. Plot the combinations of labor and capital you found in (a–c) as a production isoquant.

e. (A test of your math skills) A change in capital technology alters Alfred's production function. Now Alfred's output is given by $Q = 10K^{0.7}L^{0.3}$. If Alfred employs 3 workers, how many machines will he have to use to achieve the production level you found in (a)? What happens to the isoquant you drew?

Chapter 6 Appendix:
The Calculus of Cost Minimization

In the appendix to Chapter 4, we saw that calculus makes solving the consumer's optimization problem easier. The benefits of using calculus also extend to the firm's constrained optimization problem, cost minimization. Cost minimization is analogous to expenditure minimization for the consumer, and the exercise of solving the producer's optimization problem will serve as a refresher in constrained optimization problems.

Marginal Product of Labor and Marginal Rate of Technical Substitution

To begin solving the firm's cost-minimization problem, we start with the Cobb–Douglas functional form (as we did in the Chapter 4 appendix). In this case, we use the production function that relates output Q to the amount of inputs capital K and labor L: $Q = AK^{\alpha}L^{1-\alpha}$, where $0 < \alpha < 1$, and where the parameter for total factor productivity, A, is greater than zero. We have been relying almost exclusively on the Cobb–Douglas functional form throughout our calculus discussions because this functional form corresponds closely with the assumptions we make about the consumer and the producer. In the context of the producer, the Cobb–Douglas production function satisfies all the assumptions we've made about capital, labor, and firm output, while still yielding simple formulas. In addition, we have chosen a Cobb–Douglas function with another unique property: Because the exponents on K and L $(\alpha, 1 - \alpha)$ sum to 1, the production function exhibits constant returns to scale.

Before we jump into the producer's cost-minimization problem, let's confirm that the Cobb–Douglas production function satisfies the assumptions about the marginal products of labor and capital and the marginal rate of technical substitution. Specifically, we need to show first that the marginal products of labor and capital are positive, and that they exhibit diminishing marginal returns. Next, we will confirm that the $MRTS$ is the ratio of the two marginal products.

Consider first the concept of the marginal product of capital, or how much extra output is produced by an additional unit of capital. Mathematically, the marginal product of capital is the partial derivative of the production function with respect to capital. It's a partial derivative because we are holding the amount of labor constant. The marginal product of capital is

$$MP_K = \frac{\partial Q(K,L)}{\partial K} = \frac{\partial AK^{\alpha}L^{1-\alpha}}{\partial K} = \alpha AK^{\alpha-1}L^{1-\alpha}$$

Similarly, the marginal product of labor is

$$MP_L = \frac{\partial Q(K,L)}{\partial L} = \frac{\partial AK^{\alpha}L^{1-\alpha}}{\partial L} = (1 - \alpha)AK^{\alpha}L^{-\alpha}$$

Note that the marginal products above are positive whenever both capital and labor are greater than zero (any time output is greater than zero). In other words, the MP_L and MP_K of the Cobb–Douglas production function satisfy an important condition of production—that output increases as the firm uses more inputs.

We also need to show that the assumptions about the diminishing marginal returns of capital and labor hold true; that is, the marginal products of capital and labor decrease as the amount of that input increases, all else equal. To see this, take the second partial derivative of the production function with respect to each input. In other words, we are taking a partial derivative of each of the marginal products with respect to its input:

$$\frac{\partial^2 Q(K,L)}{\partial K^2} = \frac{\partial MP_K}{\partial K} = \frac{\partial \alpha AK^{\alpha-1}L^{1-\alpha}}{\partial K} = \alpha(\alpha-1)AK^{\alpha-2}L^{1-\alpha} = -\alpha(1-\alpha)AK^{\alpha-2}L^{1-\alpha}$$

$$\frac{\partial^2 Q(K,L)}{\partial L^2} = \frac{\partial MP_L}{\partial L} = \frac{\partial (1-\alpha)AK^{\alpha}L^{-\alpha}}{\partial L} = -\alpha(1-\alpha)AK^{\alpha}L^{-\alpha-1}$$

As long as K and L are both greater than zero (i.e., as long as the firm is producing output), both of these second derivatives are negative so the marginal product of each input decreases as the firm uses more of the input. Thus, we're guaranteed diminishing marginal returns to both labor and capital.

We also know from the chapter that the marginal rate of technical substitution and the marginal products of capital and labor are interrelated. In particular, the *MRTS* shows the change in labor necessary to keep output constant if the quantity of capital changes (or the change in capital necessary to keep output constant if the quantity of labor changes). The *MRTS* equals the ratio of the two marginal products. To show this is true using calculus, first recognize that each isoquant represents some fixed level of output, say $\overline{Q}$, so that $Q = Q(K,L) = \overline{Q}$. Begin by totally differentiating the production function:

$$dQ = \frac{\partial Q(K,L)}{\partial K} dK + \frac{\partial Q(K,L)}{\partial L} dL$$

We know that dQ equals zero because the quantity is fixed at $\overline{Q}$:

$$dQ = \frac{\partial Q(K,L)}{\partial K} dK + \frac{\partial Q(K,L)}{\partial L} dL = 0$$

so that

$$\frac{\partial Q(K,L)}{\partial K} dK = -\frac{\partial Q(K,L)}{\partial L} dL$$

Now rearrange to get $-\frac{dK}{dL}$ on one side of the equation:

$$-\frac{dK}{dL} = \frac{\frac{\partial Q(K,L)}{\partial L}}{\frac{\partial Q(K,L)}{\partial K}} = \frac{MP_L}{MP_K}$$

The left-hand side of this equation is the negative of the slope of the isoquant, or the marginal rate of technical substitution.[1] Therefore,

$$MRTS_{LK} = \frac{MP_L}{MP_K}$$

In particular, we differentiate the Cobb–Douglas production function, $Q = AK^{\alpha}L^{1-\alpha}$, and set dQ equal to zero:

$$dQ = \frac{\partial Q(K,L)}{\partial K} dK + \frac{\partial Q(K,L)}{\partial L} dL = \alpha AK^{\alpha-1}L^{1-\alpha}dK + (1-\alpha)AK^{\alpha}L^{-\alpha}dL = 0$$

Again, rearrange to get $-\frac{dK}{dL}$ on one side of the equation:

$$MRTS_{LK} = -\frac{dK}{dL} = \frac{(1-\alpha)AK^{\alpha}L^{-\alpha}}{\alpha AK^{\alpha-1}L^{1-\alpha}} = \frac{MP_L}{MP_K}$$

which simplifies to

$$MRTS_{LK} = \frac{(1-\alpha)}{\alpha} \frac{K}{L}$$

Thus, we can see that the marginal rate of technical substitution equals the ratios of the marginal products for the Cobb–Douglas production function. We can also see that the

---

[1] Recall that isoquants have negative slopes; therefore, the negative of the slope of the isoquant, the *MRTS*, is positive.

$MRTS_{LK}$ decreases as the firm uses more labor and less capital, holding output constant, as we learned in the chapter. Using calculus also makes it clear, however, that the rate at which labor and capital can be substituted is determined by α, the relative productivity of capital.

Cost Minimization Using Calculus

Now that we have verified the usefulness of the Cobb–Douglas function for modeling production, let's turn to the firm's cost-minimization problem. Once again, we are faced with a constrained optimization problem: The objective function is the cost of production, and the constraint is the level of output. The firm's goal is to spend the least amount of money to produce a specific amount of output. This is the producer's version of the consumer's expenditure-minimization problem.

As we saw with the consumer's problem, there are two approaches to solving the cost-minimization problem. The first is to apply the cost-minimization condition that we derived in the chapter. At the optimum, the marginal rate of technical substitution equals the ratio of the input prices, wages W and capital rental rate R. We just showed that the marginal rate of technical substitution is the ratio of the marginal products, so the cost-minimization condition is

$$MRTS_{LK} = \frac{MP_L}{MP_K} = \frac{W}{R}$$

For our Cobb–Douglas production function above, finding the optimum solution is easy using this relationship between the marginal rate of technical substitution and the input prices. We start by solving for K as a function of L using the equation for the marginal rate of technical substitution above:

$$\frac{MP_L}{MP_K} = \frac{(1-\alpha)}{\alpha}\frac{K}{L} = \frac{W}{R}$$

$$K = \frac{\alpha}{(1-\alpha)}\frac{W}{R}L$$

Next, plug K into the production constraint to solve for the optimum quantity of labor L^*:

$$\overline{Q} = AK^\alpha L^{1-\alpha} = A\left[\frac{\alpha}{(1-\alpha)}\frac{W}{R}\right]^\alpha L^\alpha L^{1-\alpha}$$

$$\overline{Q} = A\left[\frac{\alpha}{(1-\alpha)}\frac{W}{R}\right]^\alpha L$$

$$L^* = \left[\frac{(1-\alpha)}{\alpha}\frac{R}{W}\right]^\alpha \frac{\overline{Q}}{A}$$

Now solve for K^* by plugging L^* into the earlier expression for K as a function of L:

$$K^* = \left[\frac{\alpha}{(1-\alpha)}\frac{W}{R}\right]L^*$$

$$= \left[\frac{\alpha}{(1-\alpha)}\frac{W}{R}\right]\left[\frac{(1-\alpha)}{\alpha}\frac{R}{W}\right]^\alpha \frac{\overline{Q}}{A}$$

We can simplify this expression by inverting the term in the second set of brackets:

$$K^* = \left[\frac{\alpha}{(1-\alpha)}\frac{W}{R}\right]\left[\frac{\alpha}{(1-\alpha)}\frac{W}{R}\right]^{-\alpha}\frac{\overline{Q}}{A}$$

and combining the first and second terms:

$$K^* = \left[\frac{\alpha}{(1-\alpha)}\frac{W}{R}\right]^{1-\alpha}\frac{\overline{Q}}{A}$$

Thus, we have found that the cheapest way of producing $\overline{Q}$ units of output is to use $\left[\frac{\alpha}{(1-\alpha)}\frac{W}{R}\right]^{1-\alpha}\frac{\overline{Q}}{A}$ units of capital and $\left[\frac{(1-\alpha)}{\alpha}\frac{R}{W}\right]^\alpha\frac{\overline{Q}}{A}$ units of labor.

Now let's use a second approach to solve for the cost-minimizing bundle of capital and labor: the constrained optimization problem. In particular, the firm's objective, as before, is to minimize costs subject to its production function:

$$\min_{K,L} TC = RK + WL \text{ s.t. } \overline{Q} = AK^{\alpha}L^{1-\alpha}$$

Next, write this constrained optimization problem as a Lagrangian so that we can solve for the first-order conditions:

$$\min_{X,Y,\lambda} \mathcal{L}(K,L,\lambda) = RK + WL + \lambda(\overline{Q} - AK^{\alpha}L^{1-\alpha})$$

Now take the first-order conditions of the Lagrangian:

$$\frac{\partial \mathcal{L}}{\partial K} = R - \lambda(\alpha AK^{\alpha-1}L^{1-\alpha}) = 0$$

$$\frac{\partial \mathcal{L}}{\partial L} = W - \lambda[(1-\alpha)AK^{\alpha}L^{-\alpha}] = 0$$

$$\frac{\partial \mathcal{L}}{\partial \lambda} = \overline{Q} - AK^{\alpha}L^{1-\alpha} = 0$$

Notice that λ is in both of the first two conditions. Let's rearrange to solve for λ:

$$R = \lambda(\alpha AK^{\alpha-1}L^{1-\alpha})$$

$$\lambda = \frac{R}{\alpha AK^{\alpha-1}L^{1-\alpha}}$$

$$W = \lambda[(1-\alpha)AK^{\alpha}L^{-\alpha}]$$

$$\lambda = \frac{W}{(1-\alpha)AK^{\alpha}L^{-\alpha}}$$

Now set these two expressions for λ equal to one another:

$$\lambda = \frac{W}{(1-\alpha)AK^{\alpha}L^{-\alpha}} = \frac{R}{\alpha AK^{\alpha-1}L^{1-\alpha}}$$

How can we interpret λ in the context of the firm's cost-minimization problem? In general, the Lagrange multiplier is the value of relaxing the constraint by one unit. Here, the constraint is the quantity of output produced; if you increase the given output quantity by one unit, the total cost of production at the optimum increases by λ dollars. In other words, λ has a very particular economic interpretation: It is the marginal cost of production, or the extra cost of producing an additional unit of output when the firm is minimizing its costs. We can see that in our λs above: the cost of an additional unit of capital (or labor) divided by the additional output produced by that unit. In Chapter 7, we develop other ways to find marginal costs, but it's good to keep in mind that marginal cost *always* reflects the firm's cost-minimizing behavior.

We can get another perspective on cost minimization by inverting the expressions for λ:

$$\frac{(1-\alpha)AK^{\alpha}L^{-\alpha}}{W} = \frac{\alpha AK^{\alpha-1}L^{1-\alpha}}{R}$$

This relationship shows us precisely what we know is true at the optimum, that $\frac{MP_K}{R} = \frac{MP_L}{W}$, which we can rearrange to get the cost-minimization condition:

$$\frac{W}{R} = \frac{MP_L}{MP_K} = MRTS_{LK}$$

To solve for the optimal bundle of inputs that minimizes cost, we can first solve for K as a function of L:

$$\frac{K^{\alpha}}{K^{\alpha-1}} = \frac{W(\alpha L^{1-\alpha})}{(1-\alpha)RL^{-\alpha}}$$

$$K = \left[\frac{\alpha}{(1-\alpha)}\frac{W}{R}\right]L$$

Plug K as a function of L into the third first-order condition, the constraint:

$$\overline{Q} - AK^{\alpha}L^{1-\alpha} = \overline{Q} - A\left[\frac{\alpha}{(1-\alpha)}\frac{W}{R}\right]^{\alpha}L^{\alpha}L^{1-\alpha} = 0$$

Now solve for the cost-minimizing quantity of labor, L^*:

$$A\left[\frac{\alpha}{(1-\alpha)}\frac{W}{R}\right]^{\alpha}L^{\alpha}L^{1-\alpha} = A\left[\frac{\alpha}{(1-\alpha)}\frac{W}{R}\right]^{\alpha}L = \overline{Q}$$

$$L^* = \frac{\overline{Q}}{A}\left[\frac{\alpha}{(1-\alpha)}\frac{W}{R}\right]^{-\alpha} = \frac{\overline{Q}}{A}\left[\frac{(1-\alpha)}{\alpha}\frac{R}{W}\right]^{\alpha}$$

Substitute L^* into our expression for K as a function of L:

$$K^* = \left[\frac{\alpha}{(1-\alpha)}\frac{W}{R}\right]L^* = \left[\frac{\alpha}{(1-\alpha)}\frac{W}{R}\right]\frac{\overline{Q}}{A}\left[\frac{(1-\alpha)}{\alpha}\frac{R}{W}\right]^{\alpha}$$

To simplify, invert the third term and combine:

$$K^* = \frac{\overline{Q}}{A}\left[\frac{\alpha}{(1-\alpha)}\frac{W}{R}\right]\left[\frac{(1-\alpha)}{\alpha}\frac{R}{W}\right]^{-\alpha} = \frac{\overline{Q}}{A}\left[\frac{\alpha}{(1-\alpha)}\frac{W}{R}\right]^{1-\alpha}$$

So using the Lagrangian, we arrive at the same optimal levels of labor and capital that we found using the cost-minimization condition:

$$L^* = \left[\frac{(1-\alpha)}{\alpha}\frac{R}{W}\right]^{\alpha}\frac{\overline{Q}}{A}$$

$$K^* = \left[\frac{\alpha}{(1-\alpha)}\frac{W}{R}\right]^{1-\alpha}\frac{\overline{Q}}{A}$$

6A.1 figure it out

A firm has the production function $Q = 20K^{0.2}L^{0.8}$, where Q measures output, K represents machine hours, and L measures labor hours. If the rental rate of capital is $R = \$15$, the wage rate is $W = \$10$, and the firm wants to produce 40,000 units of output, what is the cost-minimizing bundle of capital and labor?

Solution:

We could solve this problem using the cost-minimization condition. But let's solve it using the Lagrangian, so we can get more familiar with that process. First, we set up the firm's cost-minimization problem as

$$\min_{K,L} TC = 15K + 10L \text{ s.t. } 40{,}000 = 20K^{0.2}L^{0.8} \text{ or}$$

$$\min_{K,L,\lambda} \mathcal{L}(K,L,\lambda) = 15K + 10L + \lambda(40{,}000 - 20K^{0.2}L^{0.8})$$

Find the first-order conditions for the Lagrangian:

$$\frac{\partial \mathcal{L}}{\partial K} = 15 - \lambda(4K^{-0.8}L^{0.8}) = 0$$

$$\frac{\partial \mathcal{L}}{\partial L} = 10 - \lambda(16K^{0.2}L^{-0.2}) = 0$$

$$\frac{\partial \mathcal{L}}{\partial \lambda} = 40{,}000 - 20K^{0.2}L^{0.8} = 0$$

Solve for L as a function of K using the first two conditions:

$$\lambda = \frac{15}{4K^{-0.8}L^{0.8}} = \frac{10}{16K^{0.2}L^{-0.2}}$$

$$15(16K^{0.2}L^{-0.2}) = 10(4K^{-0.8}L^{0.8})$$

$$240(K^{0.2}K^{0.8}) = 40(L^{0.2}L^{0.8})$$

$$L = 6K$$

Now plug L into the third first-order condition and solve for the optimal number of labor and machine hours, L^* and K^*:

$$40{,}000 - 20K^{0.2}L^{0.8} = 0$$

$$20K^{0.2}(6K)^{0.8} = 40{,}000$$

$$20(6)^{0.8}K = 40{,}000$$

$$K^* \approx 477 \text{ machine hours}$$

$$L^* \approx 6(477) \approx 2{,}862 \text{ labor hours}$$

At the optimum, then, the firm will use approximately 477 machine hours and 2,862 labor hours to produce 40,000 units. But once again, the Lagrangian provides us with one additional piece of information: the value of λ, or marginal cost:

$$\lambda = \frac{15}{4K^{-0.8}L^{0.8}} = \frac{15}{4(477^{-0.8})(2862^{0.8})} \approx \$0.89$$

Therefore, if the firm wants to produce just one more unit of output—its 40,001st unit of output, to be precise—it would have to spend an additional $0.89.

The Firm's Expansion Path

So far, we have only solved the firm's cost-minimization problem for a specific quantity. In other words, we've assumed that the firm knows how much output it wants to produce and then decides how best to produce that quantity at the lowest cost. But it might make sense to expand our thinking about how the firm makes its production decisions. In particular, what if a firm wants to know how its optimal input mix varies with its output quantity? This is the firm's expansion path, and it's something we found graphically in the chapter. Recall that an expansion path shows the cost-minimizing relationship between K and L for all possible levels of output. Let's now find the expansion path using calculus.

Consider again the firm with the familiar Cobb–Douglas production function, $Q = AK^{\alpha}L^{1-\alpha}$, and rental cost of capital and wage equal to R and W, respectively. First, write out the constrained optimization problem and the Lagrangian. Note that, unlike before, we are not going to assume that Q is a fixed level of output. In the expansion path, quantity is a variable, and that is reflected in the way we set up the constrained optimization problem below:

$$\min_{K,L} TC = RK + WL \text{ s.t. } Q = AK^{\alpha}L^{1-\alpha}$$

$$\min_{K,L,\lambda} \mathcal{L}(K,L,\lambda) = RK + WL + \lambda(Q - AK^{\alpha}L^{1-\alpha})$$

Take the first-order conditions for the Lagrangian:

$$\frac{\partial \mathcal{L}}{\partial K} = R - \lambda(\alpha AK^{\alpha-1}L^{1-\alpha}) = 0$$

$$\frac{\partial \mathcal{L}}{\partial L} = W - \lambda[(1-\alpha)AK^{\alpha}L^{-\alpha}] = 0$$

$$\frac{\partial \mathcal{L}}{\partial \lambda} = Q - AK^{\alpha}L^{1-\alpha} = 0$$

As we saw earlier, solving the first two conditions gives us the optimal value of capital K^* as a function of L^*:

$$K^* = \left[\frac{\alpha}{(1-\alpha)}\frac{W}{R}\right]L^*$$

What does this tell us? Given a set of input prices, we now know the cost-minimizing amount of capital at every quantity of labor. The combination of labor and capital then determines the quantity of output. So, what have we found? The expansion path! We could also solve for the optimal amount of labor for every quantity of capital, but it's easier to graph the expansion path with K^* as a function of L^*. Notice that any Cobb–Douglas production function with exponents α and $(1-\alpha)$ generates a linear expansion path with slope

$$\frac{\alpha}{(1-\alpha)}\frac{W}{R}$$

This linear expansion path is yet *another* useful property of the Cobb–Douglas functional form.

6A.2 figure it out

Using the information from Figure It Out 6A.1, derive the firm's expansion path.

Solution:

Because we've already solved the expansion path for the generalized Cobb–Douglas production function, we can plug in the parameters from the firm's cost-minimization problem ($\alpha = 0.2$, $W = \$10$, $R = \$15$)

into the equation for the expansion path we found above:

$$K^* = \left[\frac{\alpha}{(1-\alpha)}\frac{W}{R}\right]L^* = \frac{0.2(10)}{0.8(15)}L^* = 0.167L^*$$

Therefore, when minimizing costs, this firm will always choose a combination of inputs in which there is 6 times as much labor as capital, no matter what its desired output is.

Problems

1. For the following production functions,
   - Find the marginal product of each input.
   - Determine whether the production function exhibits diminishing marginal returns to each input.
   - Find the marginal rate of technical substitution and discuss how $MRTS_{LK}$ changes as the firm uses more L, holding output constant.
   a. $Q(K,L) = 3K + 2L$
   b. $Q(K,L) = 10K^{0.5}L^{0.5}$
   c. $Q(K,L) = K^{0.25}L^{0.5}$

2. A more general form of the Cobb–Douglas production function is given by

$$Q = AK^\alpha L^\beta$$

   where A, α, and β are positive constants.
   a. Solve for the marginal products of capital and labor.
   b. For what values of α and β will the production function exhibit diminishing marginal returns to capital and labor?
   c. Solve for the marginal rate of technical substitution.

3. Catalina Films produces video shorts using digital editing equipment (K) and editors (L). The firm has the production function $Q = 30K^{0.67}L^{0.33}$, where Q is the hours of edited footage. The wage is $25, and the rental rate of capital is $50. The firm wants to produce 3,000 units of output at the lowest possible cost.
   a. Write out the firm's constrained optimization problem.
   b. Write the cost-minimization problem as a Lagrangian.
   c. Use the Lagrangian to find the cost-minimizing quantities of capital and labor used to produce 3,000 units of output.
   d. What is the total cost of producing 3,000 units?
   e. How will total costs change if the firm produces an additional unit of output?

4. A firm has the production function $Q = K^{0.4}L^{0.6}$. The wage is $60, and the rental rate of capital is $20. Find the firm's long-run expansion path.

Costs

7

Ryanair is one of the largest and fastest-growing airlines in the world. It started flying in 1985 and, after an initial brush with financial problems in 1990, found its key to success: building a cost structure so low that its European customers, who were accustomed to dowdy and expensive national carriers, started flying Ryanair all over the continent. Ryanair's total passenger traffic increased almost 20-fold between 1997, when it launched its first routes outside Ireland and the United Kingdom, and 2011. In the five years from 2005 to 2010 alone, the number of passengers Ryanair carried grew by almost 38 million. To put that in perspective, this additional number of passengers equals about 7 months' worth of traffic for *all* airlines at London's busy Heathrow Airport.

Ryanair's cost-conscientiousness is famous. To save landing fees, it rarely flies to a city's main airport. Instead, it flies to secondary airports often located far away from the main city. (For example, its flights to Frankfurt, Germany, arrive at Frankfurt Hahn Airport, 78 miles [126 km] from Frankfurt's city center.) Its pilots are only allowed to load the legally mandated minimum requirement of fuel for each trip. The seats on its planes don't recline; the way Ryanair sees it, that's just a source of unnecessary maintenance costs. Nor do the seats have tray tables or seatback pockets—too much extra weight means extra fuel. Ryanair has discussed squeezing in 6 more seats on each plane—by getting rid of all but one of the plane's bathrooms. You better check yourself in for your flight online; it costs €40 (about $55 in 2011) to do it at the airport. (Ryanair doesn't like to employ a lot of desk agents.) To keep it simple, Ryanair only handles point-to-point itineraries. If you want to make a connection, you have to book two separate tickets. And if you miss your connection, even if you missed it because it was Ryanair's fault your first flight was late, you have to pay for a new ticket. This last rule might seem harsh until you realize that some of the airline's flights cost as little as €9 (a little more than $12) each way.

Flying Ryanair isn't for everyone; comfort and customer service aren't its specialties. But the Ryanair example raises an important point: Costs are key to firms' operations, and a firm's cost structure is a hugely important factor in its production decisions and in determining whether it makes a profit. Costs play a crucial part in determining a firm's optimal output level, how much the firm should grow or shrink in response to changing market conditions, and how easily it can start producing another product if it wants to.

We started to look at a firm's production cost at the end of Chapter 6 when we introduced the expansion path (which shows how a firm's optimal mix of inputs varies with total output) and the total cost curve (which shows a firm's cost of producing particular quantities of output). These two concepts provide the foundation for understanding a firm's cost structure. It is vital for a firm's management to have a thorough understanding of what a firm's costs are and how they change as output changes. This understanding is also important for economists and other outside observers who want to comprehend why producers act the way they do, and it is the key force explaining where supply curves come from (a topic we explore in Chapter 8). In this chapter, we examine the nature of a firm's costs by considering how a firm's production function and level of output determine its costs, given the prices of its inputs. We also consider how a firm's costs vary between the short run and the long run.

7.1 Costs That Matter for Decision Making: Opportunity Costs

accounting cost
The direct cost of operating a business, including costs for raw materials.

economic cost
The sum of a producer's accounting and opportunity costs.

opportunity cost
The value of what a producer gives up by using an input.

Economists think about cost differently than many others do. Most people are familiar with **accounting cost,** the direct cost of operating a business, including costs for raw materials, wages paid to workers, rent paid for office or retail space, and the like. **Economic cost**—the cost that economists pay attention to—includes accounting cost and something else: the producer's opportunity cost. **Opportunity cost** is what the producer gives up by using an input, whether that use is associated with an accounting cost or not. What the producer gives up is the return the input would earn in its next-best use: If a firm is using an input to do one thing, it is giving up the ability to use the input for something else. The lost value of this "something else" is the input's opportunity cost.

To operate its flight schedule, for example, Ryanair keeps on hand an inventory of fuel. You might think that because Ryanair has already paid for the fuel, there is no longer any cost associated with it. But that statement is based on the notion of accounting cost, not economic cost. If we think about the fuel's economic cost, then we quickly realize that it has an opportunity cost: Ryanair could sell the jet fuel to other companies instead of using the fuel itself. When might the airline choose to do this? Let's say the demand for its no-frills flights decreases (maybe a new, even lower cost airline enters the market). Now Ryanair makes fewer flights and is left with excess fuel. Savvy, cost-cutting company that it is, Ryanair isn't going to just sit on the excess fuel; it's going to sell the fuel, because Ryanair executives recognize opportunity cost.

It is important to understand the distinction between economic cost and accounting cost because production decisions are made, or at least *should* be made, based on economic cost, not accounting cost. Ryanair should use its jet fuel for flights only if that is the most profitable use for it. That is, the firm should consider its **economic profit** (total revenue minus economic cost) rather than its **accounting profit** (total revenue minus accounting cost).

When thinking about the most cost-effective use of its inputs, it doesn't matter if Ryanair's accounting profit is positive. If its *economic* cost is large enough, its economic profit may be negative. In this case, it may make more sense for the firm to have fewer flights and sell its excess fuel to another company. Making decisions about the use of inputs using only accounting cost can lead to profit-losing practices.

The recognition that a firm's decisions about production must be based on economic cost (which takes into account a firm's opportunity costs) underlies *everything* we discuss about costs in the rest of this chapter and throughout the remaining chapters of this book. Unless otherwise stated, when we talk about a firm's costs, we are talking about its economic costs.

economic profit
A firm's total revenue minus its economic cost.

accounting profit
A firm's total revenue minus its accounting cost.

application

Making Big Money by *Not* Operating Your Business—a Lesson about Opportunity Cost

When electricity prices spiked in California in the summer of 2000, many businesses and homeowners winced as they saw their power bills rise to several multiples of their normal levels. However, one set of producers (besides the power generators) made out very well that summer: aluminum companies. Why was that? Because they decided to *not* make aluminum. This wasn't because their customers didn't want aluminum anymore. Instead, it was all about opportunity costs.

Aluminum smelting—the process through which metallic aluminum is extracted from ore—is done through electrolysis, which consumes massive amounts of electricity. Because of their need for a reliable supply of so much power, aluminum companies typically sign multiyear contracts with power generators that guarantee delivery of electricity at a price agreed upon in the contract.

The key to understanding why aluminum companies benefited so much from sky-high electricity prices, and why they acted as they did, is to recognize that the pre-specified prices in the aluminum companies' electricity supply contracts did *not* reflect the companies' true economic cost for electricity. By using that power to refine aluminum as they usually would, the firms would be giving up the ability to use that electricity for its next-best use. The value of this next-best use was the aluminum companies' opportunity cost of its electricity, which in this case was the price at which the aluminum smelters could sell that power back to the electrical grid.

During the price spike of 2000, this sell-back price was very high compared to the delivery price in the smelters' contracts. This meant that even though the contractual rate for the aluminum companies' electricity purchases hadn't changed, their economic costs of smelting aluminum, which included the opportunity cost of their electricity use, were extremely high.

How did they respond to these high economic costs? They stopped being aluminum companies and started being electricity companies. The firm Kaiser Aluminum, for example, shut down its plant and took the power that it had earlier contracted to obtain for $22.50 per megawatt-hour (MWh) and sold it back for $555 per MWh—or about 25 times what they paid! Kaiser made millions that year by *not* operating its plant. Kaiser's employees benefited from this recognition of opportunity costs, too: Under pressure from unions and local and federal politicians, the company continued to pay its employees full wages while the plant was shut down—and it still made a profit. ■

7.1 figure it out

Cooke's Catering is owned by Daniel Cooke. For the past year, Cooke's Catering had the following statement of revenues and costs:

Revenues	$500,000
Supplies	$150,000
Electricity and water	$15,000
Employee salaries	$50,000
Dan's salary	$60,000

Dan has always had the option of closing his catering business and renting out his building for $100,000 per year. In addition, Dan currently has job offers from another catering company (offering a salary of $45,000 per year) and a high-end restaurant (at a salary of $75,000 per year). Dan can only work one job at any time.

    a. What is Cooke's Catering's accounting cost?

    b. What is Cooke's Catering's economic cost?

    c. What is Cooke's Catering's economic profit?

Solution:

    a. Accounting cost is the direct cost of operating a business. This includes supplies, utilities, and salaries:

$$\text{Accounting cost} = \$150,000 + \$15,000 + \$50,000 + \$60,000 = \$275,000$$

    b. Economic cost includes both accounting cost and the opportunity costs of owner-supplied resources. Dan's opportunity costs include the rent he could earn on his building ($100,000) and the opportunity cost of his time. Because Dan could give up the store and earn a higher salary at the restaurant, we need to take into account the difference in the salary he could earn ($75,000) and the salary he currently earns ($60,000). Note that his offer with the caterer is not relevant because opportunity cost measures the value of the next best alternative, which is working at the restaurant. Therefore, economic cost is Accounting cost + Opportunity costs:

$$\text{Economic cost} = \$275,000 + \$100,000 + \$15,000 = \$390,000$$

    c. Economic profit is equal to Total revenue − Economic cost = $500,000 − $390,000 = $110,000. Dan should continue to operate his catering business.

freakonomics

Paying for Papers: The Economics of Cheating

There's an old joke about an economics professor who got hauled into the dean's office after it was discovered that the professor had given the same exam to his students for four years in a row, not changing a single question. The dean admonished the professor, "If you never change the questions, the students can just memorize last year's solutions and get a perfect score!" Offended, the professor responded, "That's not true! The questions stay the same, but the answers change every year!" (Just to be clear, the professor had to have been a macroeconomist. In microeconomics, the answers rarely, if ever, change.)

Cheating by college students, like almost any human choice, can be understood using the tools of economics. The concept of opportunity cost is clearly central to the decision to cheat. Studying for exams, working through problem sets, and writing essays are all time-intensive activities. To carry out these tasks requires foregoing other activities, like going to parties, earning money at a part-time job, or even studying for another class. Of course, hiring *someone else* to write your essay or complete your problem set also has costs, including financial costs. The person who writes your essay also has opportunity costs, so in order to be willing to do your work, he or she will usually need to be paid. In addition there are other costs, such as the possibly life-changing punishment you will receive if caught, the guilt you will feel over cheating, and your continuing ignorance because you have not actually learned the material.

As with so many other goods and services produced in the modern economy, technological progress has radically changed the economics of cheating. Before the Internet, the supply of people who could help cheaters was local—typically, classmates who also had high opportunity costs—meaning that the price of forged essays was likely to be high. The covert nature of the market also made it difficult for buyers and sellers to coordinate.

The Internet changed all that. The first generation of Internet-based cheating took the form of pre-written essays that with few or no tweaks would fit a college assignment. Need a paper on Adam Smith's economic theories in *The Wealth of Nations*? How about the symbolism of Big Brother in George Orwell's *1984*? A simple Google search yields a host of pre-written options, ranging in cost from free to $50. Following this path, however, runs a high chance of getting caught. It didn't take long for services such as Turnitin.com, which scours Internet web pages for evidence of plagiarism, to become popular destinations for faculty members.

More sophisticated cheaters turn to essay-writing mills that resist automatic detection. In the modern essay mill, writers from around the world pound out papers for American college students for a per-page fee. These services cater to a wide swath of students, from community college freshmen to Ph.D. candidates, and each paper is written to the buyer's specifications. Just as many U.S. companies have found it profitable to outsource manufacturing to developing countries, U.S. students have discovered there is no shortage of offshore workers willing to write essays.

As for the quality of the essays-for-hire, that may be another story. After all, whoever is writing that essay is willing to do the work for less money than you are. For example, if you offer someone $100 to write a paper for you, it must be worth at least that amount to not have to write it yourself. That implies, from an economic standpoint, the opportunity cost of the writer's time is lower than yours. This could possibly mean that the writer has lower-paying job opportunities as a result of having relatively low human capital.

Thinking like an economist may actually help you get a better paper delivered. Remember that people, including illicit-paper writers, respond to incentives. So be sure to make it clear that if you get an A on the essay, a sizable bonus will be forthcoming . . . unless you are kicked out of school.

7.2 Costs That Do Not Matter for Decision Making: Sunk Costs

Unlike opportunity costs, which a firm must always consider when making production decisions, there are some costs that should never be taken into account when making such decisions.

In Chapter 6, we learned that some of a firm's costs are **fixed costs,** payments to inputs that must be used no matter what the output quantity is, even if it is zero. Suppose you own a restaurant. Some of your fixed costs would be rent (if you have

fixed cost
The cost of the firm's fixed inputs, independent of the quantity of the firm's output.

signed a lease), insurance, license fees, cookware, advertising expenses, and kitchen appliances such as the stovetop or a refrigerator. Now suppose your restaurant goes out of business. Even though you are no longer producing any output, you still must pay your fixed costs. However, you might be able to recover some of these. For example, you might sell the kitchen cookware and appliances, or you might also be able to sublet the building to another firm. Suppose that, instead of renting, you own the building and equipment. You can still probably recover some of your fixed cost by selling or renting these items to other firms. These types of fixed costs are sometimes said to be *avoidable* because the firm can take action so that it does not have to pay them if it stops operating.

sunk cost
A cost that, once paid, the firm cannot recover.

Some fixed costs, however, are not avoidable. This type of cost is called a **sunk cost**. Once such a cost is paid by a firm, it can never be recovered. For your restaurant, for example, license fees and advertising costs are sunk. And if you've signed long-term rental agreements and are not allowed to sublet the building or equipment, you are on the hook for all the remaining rental payments even if you close the restaurant before the agreements expire. These remaining payments are sunk—you cannot recover them even by shutting down.

To sum up: If a fixed cost is avoidable, then it is not a sunk cost. If a firm cannot recover an expense even when shut down, then it is a sunk cost. The difference between sunk cost and avoidable fixed cost is crucial to the decisions a firm makes about how it will react if things begin to go south and the firm suffers a downturn in its business.

One part of a firm's cost that is sunk is the difference between what the firm still owes on its fixed capital inputs (such as the equipment and cookware at your restaurant) and what the firm can resell this capital for. This difference should be relatively small for restaurant equipment, for example, because most of it can be easily used by other restaurants—a grill is handy for almost any foodservice business—and there are active used equipment and rental markets that make it easy to find possible buyers.

Now suppose that your restaurant has a space theme, so every booth is shaped and painted as if it were the inside of a spaceship, and the tables look like control panels. Such booths, tables, and other items (menus, staff uniforms/spacesuits, etc.) tied specifically to your space-themed restaurant are not of much use to other restaurants, unless you happen to get lucky and find a similarly themed restaurant looking to expand. The cost of these booths and other space-themed equipment is likely to be sunk because you cannot recover it even if you shut down.

specific capital
Capital that cannot be used outside of its original application.

As you can see from this last example, whether capital can be used by another firm is an important determinant of sunk costs. Capital that is not very useful outside of its original application is called **specific capital**. Expenditures on buildings or machines that are very specific to a firm's operations are likely to be sunk, because the capital will have little value in another use.

Sunk Costs and Decisions

An important lesson about sunk costs is that once they are paid, *they should not affect current and future production decisions*. The reason for this is simple: Because they are lost no matter what action is chosen next, they cannot affect the relative costs and benefits of current and future production decisions.

For example, you've no doubt attended an event like a concert, sporting event, or show where you became bored well before the event ended. Should you have felt compelled to stay because you paid so much for the ticket? No. Once you are at the event, the ticket price is sunk—it's gone whether or not you decide to stay at the event. So, if you are asking yourself, "Should I stay or should I go?" (was it a Clash concert?), the ticket price shouldn't affect your answer. Whether the ticket price was $1 or $1,000, that cost is sunk and cannot be recovered whether you stay or leave. The only thing that you should consider in deciding to stay or go is whether you will have more fun doing something else (going for a walk, taking a nap, or calling a friend). If the alternative would be more entertaining, then you should go.

To put this in a production context, let's go back to our restaurant example. You, as the owner, are deciding between staying open for business or shutting down operations. Some of the restaurant's costs are sunk costs, including nonavoidable fixed costs and the possible losses you would incur if you had to resell capital for less than it is worth. These costs are not recoverable and must be paid whether the restaurant remains open or is shut down. In thinking about staying open for business, you know there will be some potential benefits (the money brought in from selling meals and drinks—your output), but there will also be definite costs (paying the waitstaff, purchasing ingredients, or turning on the heat or air conditioning). These benefits can be defined as the firm's **operating revenue,** while these costs are called **operating costs.** If you decide to shut down, you don't have to pay operating costs, but you also won't reap any benefit (operating revenue) either.

If business falls off, then, how should you decide whether to stay open for business or close the doors? Generally, the restaurant should stay open if the value of staying open is greater than the value of shutting down. But here's the important part: *Sunk costs should not enter into this decision.* You are going to lose your sunk costs whether you keep the restaurant open or not, so they are irrelevant to your decision about your restaurant's future. Therefore, the choice between staying open and shutting down depends *only* on whether the firm's expected revenues are greater than its expected operating costs. If it's going to cost you more to stay open than you'll bring in, you should close the restaurant. It doesn't matter if you are facing one dollar or one million dollars of sunk costs.

The Sunk Cost Fallacy This stay-open or shut-down decision might sound simple enough. When faced with actual choices that involve sunk costs, however, people and firms sometimes have a difficult time making such decisions because they do not think properly about sunk costs. If they make the mistake of allowing sunk costs to affect their decisions, they commit what economists call the **sunk cost fallacy.** In making economic, finance, and life decisions, you want to avoid falling victim to this fallacy, but it's not hard to imagine scenarios where you might be tempted to do so.

Suppose, for example, that you are responsible for overseeing the construction of a new manufacturing facility for your firm. Construction has gone on for 3 years and has cost $300 million thus far (we'll assume this entire expenditure is sunk—the factory is specialized enough so that you can't sell it to another firm), and will need another 6 months and $50 million to complete. You then find out that a new and equally good production technology has just become available. Implementing this new technology would require an entirely different factory that will take only 6 months and $40 million to build. If you build this new factory, you can't use any part of the factory you are currently building. What should you do?

The correct answer is that you should stop the original building project and begin constructing the new factory. That's because the $300 million (and the prior 3 years) are sunk costs. They are lost whether you finish the first project or abandon it. The only comparison that should affect your decision, then, is between the relative benefits of finishing the first project and building an entirely new factory. Both will result in equally good production facilities in the same timeframe, but the new factory will cost only $40 million rather than the $50 million you would spend to complete the original factory. Thus, you should build the new factory. (This analysis assumes that the original building can be abandoned without incurring large costs—no more than $10 million.) Despite this logic, many people would be reluctant to let go of $300 million and 3 years of effort. The important point to realize is that the mere presence of this type of reluctance does not make it a good idea to give in to the temptation of the sunk cost fallacy.

operating revenue
The money a firm earns from selling its output.

operating cost
The cost a firm incurs in producing its output.

sunk cost fallacy
The mistake of letting sunk costs affect forward-looking decisions.

theory and data

Gym Memberships

"Should I stay or should I go?" applies to more than just a Clash concert, as economists Stefano DellaVigna and Ulrike Malmendier can attest to.* They studied consumers' actual behavior in buying—and using—gym memberships.

What they found probably won't surprise you: People are overly optimistic about how many times they'll go to the gym. Members who bought a membership that allowed unlimited visits ended up going to the gym just over four times per month on average, making their average cost per visit about $17. They did this even though the gym offered 10-visit passes for $100 (i.e., $10 per visit). This added up to an average overpayment for each member of about $600 over the course of their membership.

People often buy these memberships with the hope that such behavior will induce them to go to the gym more often. The fact that people then don't take full advantage of their memberships might, at first glance, seem like an irrational action. But the key point is that a gym membership is a sunk cost. In other words, when you're sitting on the couch watching TV and debating whether you should go work out, you're not going to consider how much you paid for your membership. It's sunk, after all. You will, on the other hand, consider the opportunity cost of going to the gym—maybe you'd rather spend more time studying economics, or more likely, watching your favorite show. Whatever the reason, the fact that your decision is based on opportunity cost, not sunk cost, makes it sound economics, even if it's not what your doctor would recommend.

*Stefano DellaVigna and Ulrike Malmendier, "Paying Not to Go to the Gym," *American Economic Review* 96, no. 3 (2006): 694–719.

application

Why Do Film Studios Make Movies That They Know Will Lose Money?

Its losses on *Waterworld* made Universal Studios want to scream.

The feature film industry is a multibillion dollar enterprise. Blockbuster movies like *Avatar* or franchises like *Star Wars* and *Harry Potter* drive the industry. A single major blockbuster movie can cost hundreds of millions of dollars, but there are no guarantees that people will like it enough to make back the costs. It is a risky business.

Sometimes while filming a movie, things go so wrong that the studio making the movie knows that it will almost certainly lose money. Yet, filmmakers often finish these movies and release them. Why they do this can be explained by the existence of sunk costs and their irrelevance to decision making.

One of the most infamous movie productions ever was *Waterworld*. You have probably never seen it—not many people did. It was nominated for four "Razzies" ("saluting the worst that Hollywood has to offer that year"), including worst picture, worst actor, worst director, and worst supporting actor.

Waterworld is set in a future in which the ice caps have melted and water covers the earth. Kevin Costner stars as the Mariner, a mutant who can breathe under water. His job is to protect (from the evil Smokers) a young girl who has what may be a map of land tattooed on her back. The movie was filmed almost entirely on and under water.

Waterworld was released by Universal Studios in 1995, and at the time it was the most expensive movie ever made: It cost almost $175 million to produce even before the marketing and distribution expenses, basically ensuring a loss no matter how well it was received. It ended up grossing only $88 million in the United States and about twice that abroad. Because studios get to keep only a portion of the total ticket sales, experts presume it flopped terribly.

Let's think through Universal's decision to complete the movie and release it. At the outset, the studio expected the movie to bring in $150 million of revenue (a 50% cut of $300 million of global ticket sales), and the movie's budget was $100 million with 96 days of filming.[1] As filming began, about $16 million of the $100 million expected costs were sunk—including Kevin Costner's minimum guaranteed salary of $14 million.

Waterworld Economics as of June (in millions of dollars)

Expected Profit	Expected Revenue	Expected Additional Cost	Sunk Cost
+50	+150	–84	–16

Things started to go wrong quickly. The filming location in Kawaihae Harbor on the Big Island of Hawaii was so windy that scores of the crew became seasick each day. The medicines to alleviate the symptoms made them drowsy and impaired their ability to use cameras and other equipment. Several divers suffered decompression sickness and embolisms from being underwater for too long. There were rumors of contractual meal penalties exceeding $2.5 million because of so many overtime shoots, and a one-minute action scene in the movie ended up taking more than five weeks to film. Every additional day of filming added something like $350,000 to the film's cost. A few months into filming, the movie was expected to take 120 days and cost $140 million. Of the $140 million, about $100 million was sunk. But, the movie remained on path to turn a small profit.

Waterworld Economics as of September (in millions of dollars)

Expected Profit	Expected Revenue	Expected Additional Cost	Sunk Cost
+10	+150	–40	–100

Then the biggest accident struck. The "slave colony," a multi-ton part of a metal set located out in the harbor, sank 160 feet, and had to be hauled up at great expense. It took 21 days. At this late point in the filming, the expected total costs had now risen to $175 million, with fully $140 million of them already sunk (in some cases, quite literally) and $35 million still needed to complete the project.

Waterworld Economics as of December (in millions of dollars)

Expected Profit	Expected Revenue	Expected Additional Cost	Sunk Cost
–25	+150	–35	–140

By now, the studio had to know the movie would lose money. If the studio considered sunk costs in making its decision to keep going or close down the production, it would have definitely stopped production. However, that would have been a mistake. To see why, compare the tradeoffs the studio faced when weighing whether to stop filming or to finish the movie. If the studio went ahead and paid the additional $35 million of expected costs to complete the movie, it would earn an expected $150 million of revenue. Of course, it would lose the $140 million of sunk costs, but that would also be true if the studio canceled production instead. Canceling would allow the studio to avoid the

[1] Movie accounting is both secretive and notoriously "flexible," so we present a stylized version of the movie's economics. For more information on movie economics and to see some gory details about what went wrong in the filming and the various cost overruns, plus a fair amount of movie gossip, see Charles Fleming, "That Sinking Feeling," *Vanity Fair*, August 1, 1995; and "Fishtar? Why 'Waterworld,' with Costner in Fins, Is Costliest Film Ever," *Wall Street Journal*, January 31, 1996.

incremental $35 million cost, but it would forgo the $150 million in expected revenue. Looking forward and ignoring sunk costs as it should have, then, the studio faced a choice between an expected incremental gain of $115 million ($150 million in revenue – $35 million in costs) from finishing the movie and an expected incremental loss of $115 million ($35 million in saved costs – $150 in lost revenue) from halting production.

To be sure, if Kevin Costner and the makers of the movie had had a crystal ball in June to see what terrible events would transpire and the massive costs that were to come, the decision would have been different. But, that was before the costs were sunk. In June they could have halted production at a loss of only $16 million. Discovering the problems only after having sunk $140 million, on the other hand, meant that it made sense for the movie's producers to hold their noses, take the plunge, and hope that the expected gain would materialize. That's why copies of *Waterworld* still grace literally dozens of home movie collections today. ∎

7.3 Costs and Cost Curves

We've seen that a firm considers its economic costs when making decisions about how much output to produce. Remember that the firm's economic costs include both accounting and opportunity costs so that the costs of all inputs are considered.

Economic analysis of costs divides costs into two basic types: fixed costs and variable costs. As we learned in Chapter 6, fixed costs (FC) are the costs of the firm that do not depend on how much output the firm produces. They must be paid even if the firm produces no output. **Variable costs** (VC) are costs that change as the firm changes its quantity of output. Every cost is either a fixed or variable cost, so a firm's **total cost** (TC) is the sum of its fixed and variable costs: $TC = FC + VC$.

variable cost
The cost of inputs that vary with the quantity of the firm's output.

total cost
The sum of a firm's fixed and variable costs.

Fixed Cost

BMW has an assembly plant in Spartanburg, South Carolina, where the company manufactures what it calls its Sport Activity series of SUVs. BMW has to pay for the building and its basic operating costs—electricity, heating fuel, security, and so on—whether it makes 0 cars per day, 1 car per day, or 1,000 cars per day. These basic costs, sometimes called *overhead*, are types of fixed costs.

We often think of fixed costs as being related primarily to capital inputs, but labor input costs can sometimes be fixed, too. For example, if BMW hires security guards to ensure that the plant is not broken into or vandalized, they work and have to be paid regardless of the factory's output. Thus, the security guards' wages are part of fixed cost. Furthermore, if the assembly line workers' contracts specify that they must be paid for a certain number of hours of work regardless of whether the plant is building cars or not, those workers' salaries would also be part of fixed cost because those costs don't vary by output level.

If fixed costs aren't sunk, they *can* be avoided, but only if the firm closes its business and exits the market completely. Exiting the market is different from producing zero output. If BMW stops production at the plant but keeps possession of the plant and its capital, it still has to pay fixed costs for its capital inputs. Even if it owns the capital, those inputs still have an opportunity cost that will be borne by the firm. To close its business completely, BMW would have to sell off its plant and all the capital within it. Only by selling off its capital can BMW avoid paying its fixed costs.

Variable Cost

Variable cost is the cost of all the inputs that change with a firm's level of output. When a firm needs more of an input to make more output, the payment for that input counts as a variable cost.

For every hamburger McDonald's makes, for example, it has to buy the ingredients. Payments for buns, ketchup, and beef are included in variable cost. Most labor costs are part of variable cost as well. When more workers are needed to make more hamburgers, when more doctors are needed to treat more patients, or when more programmers are needed to write more computer code, these additional workers' wages and salaries are added to variable cost. Some capital costs can also be variable. Suppose a construction firm occasionally rents a crane to build houses. If it has to rent more cranes when it builds more houses, the extra rental payments are included in variable cost. If it owns the cranes, and they wear out faster when they are used more often, this depreciation (the crane's loss in value through use) is part of variable cost as well, because the amount of depreciation depends on the firm's output.

Flexibility and Fixed versus Variable Costs

There is an important relationship between how easy it is for a firm to change how much of an input it uses and whether the cost of that input is considered part of fixed or variable cost. When a firm can easily adjust the levels of inputs it uses as output changes, the costs of these inputs are variable. When a firm cannot adjust how much of an input it buys as output varies, the input costs are fixed.

Time Horizon   The chief factor in determining the flexibility of input levels, and therefore whether the costs of the input are considered fixed or variable, is the time span over which the cost analysis is relevant.

Over very short time periods, many costs are fixed because a firm cannot adjust these input levels over short spans of time even if the firm's output level changes. As the time horizon lengthens, however, firms have greater abilities to change the levels of all inputs to accommodate output fluctuations. Given a long enough time span, all inputs are variable costs: There are no long-run fixed costs. This concept is very closely related to the distinction between short- and long-run production functions in Chapter 6, in which capital inputs are fixed in the short run and flexible in the long run.

Let's again suppose you run a small restaurant. On a given day, many of your costs are fixed: Regardless of how many customers come to eat, you are paying for the building, the kitchen equipment, and the dining tables. You've scheduled the cooks and waitstaff, so unless you can dismiss them early, you must pay them whether or not you are busy that day. About the only costs that are variable on an hour-to-hour basis are the food ingredients (if you make no omelets, you don't have to pay for more eggs) and the natural gas that heats the grill (if you don't have to turn the grill on to cook as much, you won't use as much gas).

Over a month, more of the restaurant's input costs become variable. You can schedule more workers on days that tend to be busy and fewer on slow days, for example. You can also choose hours of operation that exclude times which are sluggish, so that you only pay for full light and air conditioning when you are open and expect to be busy. All of those are variable costs now. But, you still have a one-year lease no matter what you produce, so that's a fixed cost.

Over longer horizons, even the building becomes a variable cost. If business isn't what you thought it would be when you first opened, you can terminate the lease (or sell the building if you own it). If business is great, you can build an addition. In the long run, all inputs are variable and so are the firm's costs.

Other Factors   Other features of input markets can sometimes also affect how easily firms may adjust their input levels, and thus determine their relative levels of fixed and variable costs.

One such factor is *the presence of active capital rental and resale markets*. These markets allow firms that need certain pieces of machinery or types of buildings only occasionally (like the construction firm above that sometimes needs a crane to build houses) to pay for the input just when it's needed to make more output. Without rental markets, firms would have to buy such inputs outright and make payments whether they use the inputs or not. By making capital inputs more flexible, rental markets shift capital costs from fixed to variable costs.

A great example of how rental markets have changed what costs are considered fixed and variable comes from the airline industry. In the past, airlines owned virtually all their planes. Today, however, about one-half of commercial jet aircraft worldwide are leased. Sometimes airlines lease planes directly from Airbus or Boeing, but more often they use specialized aircraft-leasing companies such as GE Capital Aviation Services or International Lease Finance Corporation. These leasing companies buy planes from manufacturers (over 30% of new aircraft are sold directly to specialized leasing companies) and then lease them out under contract to airlines needing extra capacity. If the capacity is no longer needed, the airline returns the plane to the leasing company, which typically then leases the plane to another airline that needs more capacity. These big leasing companies make the market for passenger airplanes very flexible, making it less likely that airlines will be stuck paying for planes when they have low demand. An active resale market for capital can function the same way as a rental. If you buy a textbook for $150, but there are students who will buy a used book from you at any time for $100, then it's as if you are renting the book for $50.

Labor contracts are another factor that affects the fixed versus variable nature of labor costs. Some contracts require that workers be paid a specified amount regardless of how much time they spend producing output. These payments are fixed costs. For example, U.S. automakers began running what were called "jobs banks" for their laid-off workers during the mid-1980s. These programs required that laid-off workers receive 95% of their regular salary, retain their health benefits, and continue to accrue pension benefits until they reach retirement age. (Jobs banks were a negotiated incentive for the United Auto Workers union—the UAW—to accept increased automation in factories.) Because of these contractual conditions, automakers' labor costs changed very little with their output. Jobs banks made autoworkers' pay a fixed cost; it was roughly the same whether or not the workers were building cars. In the face of declining sales, this high-fixed-cost structure was deadly for the automakers, and became one of many contributing factors to the Detroit Three's financial troubles from 2007 to 2009. The UAW, perhaps recognizing this, agreed to suspend the jobs bank program in late 2008. It wasn't enough, however: Chrysler and GM filed for bankruptcy in early 2009. In 2009 the federal government provided Chrysler and GM with $28.4 billion in loans. Part of the bailout agreement was a requirement for these firms to dramatically cut their fixed costs and restructure their businesses. In 2011 both firms were profitable for the first time in years.

Deriving Cost Curves

When producing output, firms face varying levels of the types of costs discussed above. The nature and size of a firm's costs are critically important in determining its profit-maximizing production behavior. To understand why firms act as they do, we have to recognize how their costs change with their production choices, and in particular with their choice of how much output to produce. The relationship between different types of costs and output is summarized in **cost curves.**

cost curve
The mathematical relationship between a firm's production costs and its output.

There are different types of cost curves depending on what kind of costs are being related to the firm's output. An example might be the most useful way to understand the different types of curves. Before we work through the example, however, it's important to note that both the costs and output quantities summarized by cost curves are measured over a particular time period. There can be hourly, daily, or yearly cost curves, for example. The specific period depends on the context, and as we discussed, what cost is fixed and what cost is variable depend on the time frame.

Consider the example of Fleet Foot (FF), a running shoe company. In the short run, FF uses fixed inputs (such as machinery) and variable inputs (such as labor and materials) to produce shoes. Table 7.1 shows the weekly costs for FF. These cost data are also shown graphically in Figure 7.1.

Table 7.1   Fixed, Variable, and Total Cost for Fleet Foot

Output Quantity Q (Pairs of Shoes per Week)	Fixed Cost FC ($ per Week)	Variable Cost VC ($ per Week)	Total Cost TC ($ per Week)
0	50	0	50
1	50	10	60
2	50	17.5	67.5
3	50	22.5	72.5
4	50	25	75
5	50	30	80
6	50	37.5	87.5
7	50	47.5	97.5
8	50	60	110
9	50	75	125
10	50	100	150
11	50	150	200
12	50	225	275

Figure 7.1   Fixed, Variable, and Total Costs

Plotting the values from Table 7.1 generates the total, fixed, and variable cost curves for Fleet Foot (FF). Because fixed cost is constant at $50 per week, the fixed cost curve is horizontal. The variable cost curve rises with output: At lower outputs, it increases with output at a diminishing rate, while at higher outputs, it begins to rise at an increasing rate. The total cost curve is the sum of the fixed and variable cost curves. It runs parallel to the variable cost curve and is greater than the variable cost curve by the amount of the fixed cost.

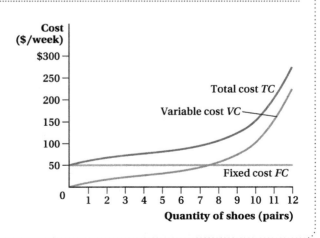

Fixed Cost Curve

Fixed cost does not vary with output, so it is constant and the fixed cost curve is horizontal. And because fixed cost must be paid in the short run even if the firm chooses to not produce anything, fixed cost is the same at $Q = 0$ as it is at every other level of output. As shown in Table 7.1, FF's fixed cost is $50 per week, so the fixed cost curve FC in Figure 7.1 is a horizontal line at $50.

Variable Cost Curve

Variable cost changes with the output level. Fleet Foot's variable cost rises as output increases because FF must buy a greater number of variable inputs. The relationship between the amount of variable inputs a firm must buy and its output means the slope of the VC curve is always positive. The shape of FF's particular VC curve in Figure 7.1 indicates that the *rate* at which FF's variable cost increases first falls and then rises with output. Specifically, the curve becomes flatter as weekly output quantities rise from 0 to 4 pairs of shoes, indicating that the additional cost of producing another pair of shoes is falling as FF makes more shoes. However, at quantities above 4 pairs per week, the VC curve's slope becomes steeper. This indicates that at these output levels, the additional cost of producing another pair of shoes is rising. We talk more about why this is the case later in the chapter.

Total Cost Curve

The total cost curve shows how a firm's total production cost changes with its level of output. Because all costs can be classified as either fixed or variable, the sum of these two components always equals total cost. In fact, as is clear in Figure 7.1, the total and variable cost curves have the same shapes and are parallel to one another, separated at every point by the amount of fixed cost. Note also that when output is zero, total cost isn't zero; it is $50. This is Fleet Foot's fixed cost, which must be paid in the short run even when the firm produces no output.

7.4 Average and Marginal Costs

Understanding the total cost curve (and its fixed and variable cost components) is an important part of analyzing firms' production behavior. To see why, we introduce two other cost concepts that play a key role in production decisions: average cost and marginal cost. In our Chapter 6 analysis of a firm's production decisions, we took the firm's desired output level as given. In the next few chapters, we will see that average and marginal costs are important in determining a firm's desired output level.

Average Cost Measures

Average cost is fairly straightforward. It's just cost divided by quantity. Since there are three costs (total, fixed, and variable), there are three kinds of average cost. Each of these measures examines the *per-unit* cost at that level of output. We compute these measures in Table 7.2 and illustrate them in Figure 7.2.

average fixed cost
A firm's fixed cost per unit of output.

   Average fixed cost (AFC) is measured as fixed cost per unit of output, or

$$AFC = FC/Q$$

Column (6) of Table 7.2 shows average fixed cost AFC for Fleet Foot (FF). AFC falls as output rises. Since fixed cost doesn't change with the quantity of output, the fixed cost is spread over more and more units of output. The numerator (fixed cost) is constant while the denominator (quantity) rises, so average fixed cost becomes smaller and smaller as quantity goes up. Thus, as FF manufactures more running shoes, the average fixed cost it pays per pair of shoes declines.

Table 7.2 : **Costs for Fleet Foot**

(1) Output Quantity Q	(2) Fixed Cost FC	(3) Variable Cost VC	(4) Total Cost TC	(5) Marginal Cost MC ($= \Delta TC/\Delta Q$) ($= \Delta VC/\Delta Q$)	(6) Average Fixed Cost AFC ($= FC/Q$)	(7) Average Variable Cost AVC ($= VC/Q$)	(8) Average Total Cost ATC ($= TC/Q$)
0	50	0	50	—	—	—	—
1	50	10	60	10	50	10	60
2	50	17.5	67.5	7.5	25	8.75	33.75
3	50	22.5	72.5	5	16.67	7.5	24.17
4	50	25	75	2.5	12.5	6.25	18.75
5	50	30	80	5	10	6	16
6	50	37.5	87.5	7.5	8.33	6.25	14.58
7	50	47.5	97.5	10	7.14	6.79	13.93
8	50	60	110	12.5	6.25	7.5	13.75
9	50	75	125	15	5.56	8.33	13.89
10	50	100	150	25	5	10	15
11	50	150	200	50	4.55	13.64	18.18
12	50	225	275	75	4.17	18.75	22.92

Figure 7.2 : **Average Cost Curves**

We can construct the average fixed, average variable, and average total cost curves for Fleet Foot using the values from Table 7.2. As FF makes more pairs of shoes, the average fixed cost per pair decreases. The average variable cost initially decreases slightly and then increases after five pairs. Average total cost, the sum of average fixed and average variable costs, is U-shaped, and is separated from the average variable cost curve by the value of average fixed cost.

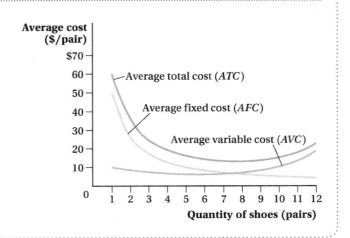

average variable cost
A firm's variable cost per unit of output.

Average variable cost measures the per-unit variable cost of production. It is calculated by dividing variable cost by the quantity of output:

$$AVC = VC/Q$$

Unlike average fixed cost, average variable cost can go up or down as quantity changes. In this case, it declines until five units are produced, after which it rises, leading to a U-shaped average variable cost curve.

average total cost
A firm's total cost per unit of output.

Average total cost is total cost TC per unit of output Q:

$$ATC = TC/Q$$

Average total cost for Fleet Foot is shown in the last column of Table 7.2. For FF, average total cost at first falls and then rises as output rises. Firms' average total costs often exhibit this sort of U-shaped pattern. To see why, first note that average total cost (ATC) is the sum of average fixed cost (AFC) and average variable cost (AVC):

$$ATC = TC/Q = (FC + VC)/Q$$
$$= FC/Q + VC/Q$$
$$= AFC + AVC$$

(This equation also implies that average fixed cost can be measured as the vertical distance between the average total cost curve and the average variable cost curve at any quantity.) Average total cost first falls as output rises because the dominant influence on average total cost is the rapidly declining average fixed cost. But as output continues to rise, average variable cost keeps increasing, first slowing the rate at which average total cost is falling and eventually causing average total cost to increase with output. These changes create a U-shaped average total cost curve.

Marginal Cost

marginal cost
The additional cost of producing an additional unit of output.

The other key cost concept is **marginal cost,** a measure of how much it costs a firm to produce one more unit of output:

$$MC = \Delta TC/\Delta Q$$

where ΔTC is the change in total cost and ΔQ is a one-unit change in output.

Fleet Foot's marginal cost is shown in the fifth column of Table 7.2. It is the difference in total cost when output increases by one pair of shoes. But notice something else: Marginal cost also equals the difference in variable cost when one additional unit is produced. That's because, by definition, fixed cost does not change when output changes. Therefore, *fixed cost does not affect marginal cost*; only variable cost changes when the firm produces one more unit. This means marginal cost can also be defined as the change in variable cost from producing another unit of output:

$$MC = \Delta VC/\Delta Q \ (= \Delta TC/\Delta Q)$$

For this reason, there is no decomposition of marginal cost into fixed and variable cost components, as there was with average costs. Marginal cost is marginal variable cost.

Fleet Foot's marginal cost initially declines as output increases. After a certain output is reached (four units in Table 7.2), marginal cost begins to rise, and at higher output levels, it rises steeply. Why does marginal cost follow this pattern as quantity rises? Marginal cost may initially fall at low quantities because complications may arise in producing the first few units that can be remedied fairly quickly. Thus, declining marginal cost at lower output quantities could come from *learning by doing*, the process by which firms learn better, more efficient cost-lowering methods of production as they produce more output. As output continues to increase, however, these marginal cost reductions stop and marginal cost begins to increase with the quantity produced, as seen in Figure 7.3. There are many reasons why it becomes more and more expensive

---

Figure 7.3 ⋮ Marginal Cost

Fleet Foot's marginal cost curve MC shows the additional cost of producing one more pair of shoes. It is U-shaped because average total cost decreases initially and then increases at higher output levels.

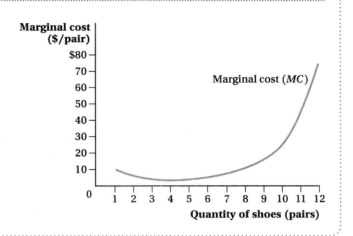

---

to make another unit as output rises: Decreasing returns to scale could kick in, capacity constraints may occur, inputs may become more expensive as the firm uses more of them, and so on.

Understanding the concept of marginal cost is critically important to firms' managers (and to your understanding of the next several chapters!). Marginal cost is one of the most central concepts in all of economics, and *it is the cost that matters for most of the key decisions a firm makes*.

7.2 figure it out

Fields Forever is a small farm that grows strawberries to sell at the local farmers' market. It produces strawberries using 5 acres of land that it rents for $200 per week. Fields Forever also hires labor at a price of $250 per week per worker. The table below shows how the output of strawberries (measured in truckloads) varies with the number of workers hired:

LABOR (WORKERS PER WEEK)	QUANTITY OF STRAWBERRIES (TRUCKLOADS PER WEEK)
0	0
1	1
3	2
7	3
12	4
18	5

Calculate the marginal cost of 1 to 5 truckloads of strawberries for Fields Forever.

Solution:

The easiest way to solve this problem is to add several columns to the table on the previous page. We should add fixed cost, variable cost, and total cost. Fixed cost is the cost of land that does not vary as output varies. Therefore, fixed cost is $200. Variable cost is the cost of labor. It can be found by multiplying the quantity of labor by the wage rate ($250). Total cost is the sum of fixed cost and variable cost.

LABOR PER WEEK	QUANTITY OF STRAWBERRIES (TRUCKLOADS)	FIXED COST, FC	VARIABLE COST, $VC = W \times L$	TOTAL COST, $TC = FC + VC$	MARGINAL COST, MC
0	0	$200	$250 \times 0 = $0	$200	—
1	1	200	$250 \times 1 = 250	450	$250
3	2	200	$250 \times 3 = 750	950	$500
7	3	200	$250 \times 7 = 1,750	1,950	$1,000
12	4	200	$250 \times 12 = 3,000	3,200	$1,250
18	5	200	$250 \times 18 = 4,500	4,700	$1,500

Marginal cost is the change in total cost per unit increase in output, or $\Delta TC/\Delta Q$. When output rises from 0 units to 1 truckload of strawberries, total cost rises from $200 to $450. Therefore, the marginal cost of the first truckload of strawberries is $450 − $200 = $250. As output rises from 1 to 2 truckloads, total cost rises from $450 to $950, so the marginal cost is $950 − $450 = $500. When the third truckload is produced, total cost rises from $950 to $1,950 so marginal cost is $1,950 − $950 = $1,000. Production of the fourth truckload pushes total cost to $3,200, so the marginal cost of the fourth truckload is $3,200 − $1,950 = $1,250. When production rises from 4 to 5 truckloads, total cost rises from $3,200 to $4,700, so the marginal cost of the fifth truckload is $1,500.

We could have also calculated the marginal cost of each truckload by looking at only the change in variable cost (rather than the change in total cost). Because the amount of land is fixed, Fields Forever can only get more strawberries by hiring more labor and increasing its variable cost.

Relationships between Average and Marginal Costs

Because average cost and marginal cost are both derived from total cost, the two are directly related. If the marginal cost of output is less than the average cost at a particular quantity, producing an additional unit will reduce the average cost because the extra unit's cost is less than the average cost of making all the units before it. (This relationship is the same as that between the average and marginal products of labor we learned about in Chapter 6.) Suppose, for example, that a firm had produced nine units of output at an average cost of $100 per unit. If the marginal cost of the next unit is $90, the average cost will fall to $(\$900 + \$90)/10 = \$99$, because the marginal cost of that extra unit is less than the average cost of the previous units.

This means that if the marginal cost curve is below an average cost curve for a particular quantity, average cost must be falling—that is, the average cost curve is downward-sloping. This is true whether we're talking about average total cost or average variable cost, because the marginal cost of producing another unit of output creates the same increment to both total and variable cost. This is also true even if, as is often the case, marginal costs are rising while they are below average costs. Producing another unit of output at a cost below the firm's current average will still bring down the average even if that marginal cost is rising with output. Just remember that the marginal cost curve is the cost at a specific output level—how much it costs to produce that specific unit—while average costs are averaging over all the previous units' costs, too.

This relationship is demonstrated in Figure 7.4, which shows an average total cost curve, an average variable cost curve, and a marginal cost curve all derived from a single total cost curve. At lower quantities, when the marginal cost curve is below the average cost curves, the average cost curves are downward-sloping.

When the marginal cost of the additional unit is above average cost, then producing it increases the average cost. Therefore, if the marginal cost curve is above an average cost curve at a quantity level, average cost is rising, and the average cost curve slopes up at that quantity. Again, this is true for both average total cost and average variable cost. This property explains why average variable cost curves and average total cost curves often have a U-shape. If marginal cost continues to increase as quantity increases, it eventually rises above average cost, and begins pulling up the average variable and average total cost curves.

The only point at which there is no change in average cost from producing one more unit occurs at the minimum point of the average variable and average total cost curves, where marginal and average cost are equal. These minimum points are indicated on Figure 7.4. (In the next chapter, we see that the point at which average and marginal costs are equal and average total cost is minimized has a special significance in competitive markets.)

Figure 7.4   The Relationship between Average and Marginal Costs

When the marginal cost curve is below an average cost curve, the average cost curve is downward-sloping. At higher quantities, the marginal cost curve is above the average cost curve, and the average cost curve slopes upward. Therefore, the marginal cost curve intersects the average total and average variable cost curves at their minimums.

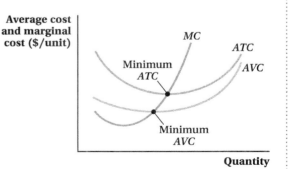

7.3 figure it out

Suppose a firm's total cost curve is $TC = 15Q^2 + 8Q + 45$, and $MC = 30Q + 8$.

    a. Find the firm's fixed cost, variable cost, average total cost, and average variable cost.

    b. Find the output level that minimizes average total cost.

    c. Find the output level at which average variable cost is minimized.

Solution:

    a. Fixed cost is a cost that does not vary as output changes. We can find FC by calculating total cost at zero units of output:

$$TC = 15(0)^2 + 8(0) + 45 = 45$$

Variable cost can be found by subtracting fixed cost from total cost:

$$VC = TC - FC = (15Q^2 + 8Q + 45) - 45 = 15Q^2 + 8Q$$

Notice that, as we have learned in the chapter, VC depends on output; as Q rises, VC rises.

Average total cost is total cost per unit or TC/Q:

$$ATC = \frac{TC}{Q} = \frac{15Q^2 + 8Q + 45}{Q}$$
$$= 15Q + 8 + \frac{45}{Q}$$

Average variable cost is variable cost per unit or VC/Q:

$$ATC = \frac{VC}{Q} = \frac{15Q^2 + 8Q}{Q}$$
$$= 15Q + 8$$

    b. Minimum average total cost occurs when $ATC = MC$:

$$15Q + 8 + \frac{45}{Q} = 30Q + 8$$

$$15Q + \frac{45}{Q} = 30Q$$

$$\frac{45}{Q} = 15Q$$

$$15Q^2 = 45$$

$$Q^2 = 3$$

$$Q = \sqrt{3} = 1.732$$

    c. Minimum average variable cost occurs where $AVC = MC$:

$$15Q + 8 = 30Q + 8$$

$$15Q = 0$$

$$Q = 0$$

7.5 Short-Run and Long-Run Cost Curves

Earlier in this chapter, we discussed how time horizons affect fixed and variable costs. Over longer periods of time, a firm has more ability to shift input levels in response to changes in desired output, making even "heavy-duty" capital inputs such as factories more flexible. In turn, this flexibility renders the firms' costs more variable and less fixed.

Recall from Chapter 6 that we defined the short-run production function as having a fixed level of capital, $\overline{K}$; that is, $Q = F(\overline{K}, L)$. In the long-run production function, $Q = F(K, L)$, capital can adjust. There is a related short-run versus long-run distinction in cost curves. Short-run cost curves relate a firm's production cost to its quantity of output when its level of capital is fixed. Long-run cost curves assume a firm's capital inputs can change just as its labor inputs can.

Short-Run Production and Total Cost Curves

A firm's **short-run total cost curve** shows the firm's total cost of producing different quantities of output when it is stuck at a particular level of capital $\overline{K}$. Just as there is a different short-run production function for every possible level of capital, so too is there a different short-run total cost curve for each capital level.

In Chapter 6, we saw that a firm's total cost curve (which relates cost and quantity of output) is related to its expansion path (which relates cost-minimizing input combinations to output). This relationship holds true in both the long run and the short run. However, in the short run, we must remember that a firm has only a fixed level of capital. Therefore, to examine how the firm minimizes its cost in the short run, we must examine the firm's expansion path given its fixed capital. Let's return to Ivor's Engines, the firm we looked at in Section 6.7. Figure 7.5 shows the same isoquants and

short-run total cost curve
The mathematical representation of a firm's total cost of producing different quantities of output at a fixed level of capital.

Figure 7.5 | **The Long-Run and Short-Run Expansion Path for Ivor's Engines**

Along Ivor's Engines long-run expansion path, the firm can change its level of capital. Along Ivor's short-run expansion path, capital is fixed at 6, and the expansion path is horizontal at $\overline{K} = 6$. Ivor's Engines can change its output quantity only by changing the quantity of labor used. At points X', Y, and Z', Ivor's Engines minimizes cost in the short run by using 5, 9, and 14 laborers to produce 10, 20, and 30 engines at a cost of $120, $180, and $360, respectively. At $Q = 20$, the cost-minimizing capital and labor combination, Y, is the same in the long run and short run, and production cost is the same ($180). At $Q = 10$ and $Q = 30$, production is more expensive in the short run than in the long run.

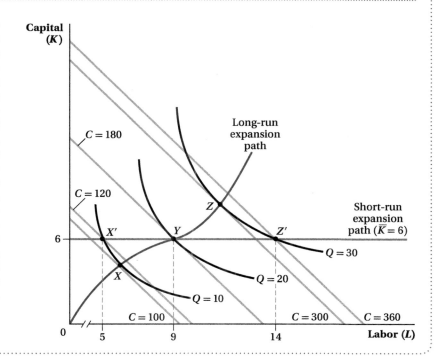

isocost lines we used to construct the long-run expansion path in Chapter 6. In the short run, Ivor's has a fixed capital level, and the expansion path is a horizontal line at that capital level. In the figure, we've assumed $\overline{K} = 6$. If the firm wants to adjust how much output it produces in the short run, it has to move along this line. It does so by changing its labor inputs, the only input it *can* change in the short run.

Suppose Ivor's Engines initially produces 20 units as shown by the isoquant $Q = 20$. Suppose also that the cost of producing 20 engines is minimized when 6 units of capital are employed. That is, the $Q = 20$ isoquant is tangent to the $C = \$180$ isocost line at point Y, when Ivor's capital inputs are 6. (We can justify this assumption by imagining that in the past, when it had the ability to change its capital input levels, Ivor's was making 20 engines and chose its optimal capital level accordingly.) The labor input level that minimizes the cost of producing 20 engines is $L = 9$ units.

To see the difference between short-run and long-run cost curves, compare the points on the isoquants on the short-run (fixed-capital) expansion path to those on the long-run (flexible-capital) expansion path. For an output level of 20 engines, these are the same (point Y) because we have assumed that a capital level of $K = 6$ was cost-minimizing for this quantity.

For the $Q = 30$ isoquant, however, the short-run and long-run input combinations are different. In the short run when capital is fixed at 6 units, if the firm wants to produce 30 units, it has to use the input combination at point Z', with 14 units of labor. But notice that Z' is outside (i.e., further from the origin than) the $C = \$300$ isocost line that is tangent to the long-run cost-minimizing input combination at point Z (which uses 11 units of labor). Instead, Z' is on the $C = \$360$ isocost line. In other words, it is more expensive for Ivor's Engines to produce 30 engines in the short run, when it cannot adjust its capital inputs. This is because it is forced to use more labor and less capital than it would if it could change all of its inputs freely.

The same property holds true if Ivor's wants to make 10 engines. When capital is fixed in the short run, the firm must use the input combination at point X' (with 5 units of labor). This point is on the $C = \$120$ isocost line, while the flexible-capital cost-minimizing input combination X is on the $C = \$100$ isocost line. So again, the firm's short-run total costs are higher than its long-run total costs. Here, it is because Ivor's is forced to use more capital than it would if it could adjust its capital inputs.

While we only looked at two quantities other than 20 engines, this general pattern holds at all other quantities. Whether Ivor's Engines wants to make more or fewer than 20 engines (the output level at which short- and long-run costs are the same), its total costs are higher in the short run than in the long run. Restricting the firm's ability to freely choose its capital input *necessarily* increases its costs, except when $Q = 20$ and the current level of capital and labor happens to be optimal.

Figure 7.6   Short-Run and Long-Run Total Cost Curves for Ivor's Engines

The short-run total cost curve (TC_{SR}) for Ivor's Engines is constructed using the isocost lines from the expansion path in Figure 7.5. At Y, when $Q = 20$, TC_{SR} and the long-run total cost curve (TC_{LR}) overlap. At all other values of Q, including $Q = 10$ and $Q = 30$, TC_{SR} is above TC_{LR}, and short-run total cost is higher than long-run total cost. This is also true when $Q = 0$ since some input costs are fixed in the short run, while in the long run all inputs are flexible.

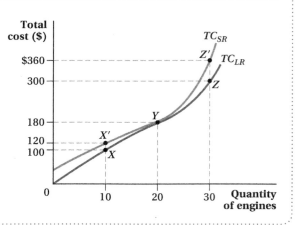

If we plot the total cost curves that correspond to these short- and long-run expansion paths, we arrive at Figure 7.6. The long-run total cost curve TC_{LR} is the same as when we assumed the firm was free to adjust all inputs to minimize costs. At $Q = 20$ engines, this curve and the short-run total cost curve TC_{SR} overlap because we assumed that capital was at the cost-minimizing capital level at this quantity. (We've labeled this point Y because it corresponds to the quantity and total cost combination at point Y in Figure 7.5.) For every other quantity, however, the short-run (fixed-capital) total cost curve is higher than the long-run (flexible-capital) total cost curve. Note that short-run total costs are positive when $Q = 0$ but zero in the long run. In other words, there are fixed costs in the short run but not in the long run when all inputs are flexible.

Short-Run versus Long-Run Average Total Cost Curves

From the total cost curves in Figure 7.6, we can construct Ivor's Engines long-run and short-run average total cost curves. These are shown in Figure 7.7. The long-run average total cost curve is ATC_{LR} and the short-run average total cost curve $ATC_{SR,20}$. (We add the "20" subscript to denote that the curve shows the firm's average total cost when its capital is fixed at a level that minimizes the costs of producing 20 units of output.)

As with the total cost curves, the short- and long-run average total cost curves overlap at $Q = 20$ engines, because that's where the firm's fixed capital level of 6 units is also cost-minimizing. Here, long-run and short-run average total costs are $180/20 = \$9$.

For all other output quantities, short-run average total cost is higher than long-run average total cost. Short-run total cost is higher than long-run total cost at every quantity level. Because average total cost divides these different total costs by the same quantity, average total cost must be higher in the short run, too. When Ivor's is making 30 engines with capital fixed at 6 units, its total costs are $360, and its short-run average total cost is $12 per unit. When it makes 10 engines, short-run average total cost is $120/10 = \$12$ per unit as well. These points on the short-run average total cost curve $ATC_{SR,20}$ are labeled Z' and X' to correspond to the analogous points on the short-run total cost curve in Figure 7.6. The long-run average total costs at 10 and 30 units are labeled Z and X, and these correspond to the similarly labeled points in Figure 7.6.

Up to this point, we've analyzed the distinction between long-run and short-run total and average total costs assuming that the short-run level of capital was fixed at 6 units, the level that minimized the cost of producing 20 engines. But suppose capital had been fixed at some other level instead. To be concrete, let's say it was fixed at 9 units of capital, the level that minimizes the cost of producing 30 engines. (This is the capital level at point Z in Figure 7.6.)

Figure 7.7   Short-Run and Long-Run Average Total Cost Curves for Ivor's Engines

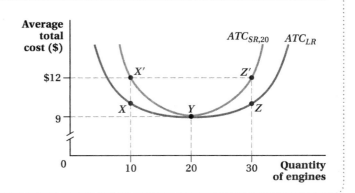

The short-run average total cost curve ($ATC_{SR,20}$) and the long-run average total cost curve (ATC_{LR}) are constructed using TC_{SR} and TC_{LR} from Figure 7.6. At Y, when $Q = 20$ and the cost-minimizing amount of capital is 6 units, the ATC_{SR} and ATC_{LR} both equal $9. At all other values of Q, including $Q = 10$ and $Q = 30$, ATC_{SR} is above ATC_{LR}, and short-run average total cost is higher than long-run average total cost.

The analysis is exactly the same as above. The long-run total and average total cost curves don't change, because the firm will still choose the same capital inputs (resulting in the same costs) given its flexibility in the long run. However, the short-run cost curves change because the fixed level of capital has changed. By the same logic as above, the short-run total and average total cost curves will be above the corresponding long-run curves at every quantity except one. In this case, though, rather than overlapping at 20 units of output, it overlaps at $Q = 30$, because capital is now fixed at the cost-minimizing level for 30 engines. The logic behind why short-run total and average total costs are higher at every other quantity than 30 is the same: Not allowing the firm to change its capital with output raises the cost of producing any quantity except when the firm would have chosen that capital level anyway.

We can make the same comparisons with capital held fixed at 4 units, which minimizes the costs of producing 10 engines (corresponding to point X in Figure 7.6). Again, the same patterns hold. The short-run total and average total cost curves are higher at every quantity except $Q = 10$.

These other short-run average total cost curves are shown in Figure 7.8 along with $ATC_{SR,20}$ and the long-run average total cost curve ATC_{LR} from Figure 7.7. $ATC_{SR,10}$ and $ATC_{SR,30}$ show short-run average costs when the firm has a fixed capital level that minimizes the total costs of making 10 and 30 engines, respectively. As can be seen in Figure 7.8, the long-run average total cost curve connects the locations (only one per fixed capital level) at which the short-run average total cost curves touch the long-run curve. We could repeat our short-run analysis with capital held fixed at any level, and the short-run average total cost curve will always be higher than the long-run curve, except in one point. If we drew out every such short-run average total cost curve, they would trace the long-run average total cost curve just like the three we have shown in the figure. As economists say, the long-run average total cost curve is an "envelope" of short-run average total cost curves, because the long-run average total cost curve forms a boundary that envelops the entire set of possible short-run average total cost curves, as seen in Figure 7.8.

One interesting thing to notice about Figure 7.8 is that $ATC_{SR,10}$ and $ATC_{SR,30}$ do not touch ATC_{LR} at their lowest points. That's because even the output levels that minimize average total costs in the short run when capital is fixed (the low points on $ATC_{SR,10}$ and $ATC_{SR,30}$) can be produced more cheaply if capital inputs were flexible. In the one case where the short-run level of capital is fixed at the fully cost-minimizing level even if capital were flexible (the $ATC_{SR,20}$ curve), the two points are the same. For Ivor's Engines, this occurs at point Y, where output is 20 units.

Figure 7.8 | **The Long-Run Average Total Cost Curve Envelops the Short-Run Average Total Cost Curves**

$ATC_{SR,10}$ and $ATC_{SR,30}$ show short-run average costs when the firm has a fixed capital level that minimizes the total costs of making 10 and 30 engines, respectively. With, respectively, $\overline{K} = 4$ and $\overline{K} = 9$, $ATC_{SR,10}$ and $ATC_{SR,30}$ overlap ATC_{LR} at the cost-minimizing points X and Z, respectively. However, X and Z are not at the lowest points on $ATC_{SR,10}$ and $ATC_{SR,30}$ because the output levels that minimize $ATC_{SR,10}$ and $ATC_{SR,30}$ can be produced more cheaply if capital inputs are flexible.

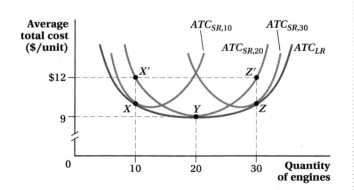

7.4 figure it out

Steve and Sons Solar Panels has a production function represented by $Q = 4KL$, where the $MP_L = 4K$ and the $MP_K = 4L$. The current wage rate (W) is \$8 per hour, and the rental rate on capital (R) is \$10 per hour.

a. In the short run, the plant's capital stock is fixed at $K = 10$. What is the cost the firm faces if it wants to produce $Q = 200$ solar panels?

b. What will the firm wish to do in the long run to minimize the cost of producing $Q = 200$ solar panels? How much will the firm save? (*Hint*: You may have to review Chapter 6, to remember how a firm optimizes when both labor and capital are flexible.)

Solution:

a. If capital is fixed at $K = 10$ units, then the amount of labor needed to produce $Q = 200$ units of output is

$$Q = 4KL$$
$$200 = 4(10)L = 40L$$
$$L = 5$$

Steve and Sons would have to hire 5 units of labor. Total cost would be

$$TC = WL + RK = \$8(5) + \$10(10) = \$40 + \$100 = \$140$$

b. In Chapter 6, we learned that in the long run, a firm minimizes costs when it produces a quantity at which the marginal rate of technical substitution of labor for capital equals the ratio of the costs of labor (wage) and capital (rental rate): $MRTS_{LK} = W/R$. We know that

$$MRTS_{LK} = \frac{MP_L}{MP_K} = \frac{4K}{4L} = \frac{K}{L}$$
$$\frac{W}{R} = \frac{8}{10}$$

To minimize costs, the firm will set $MRTS_{LK} = W/R$:

$$10K = 8L$$
$$K = 0.8L$$

To produce $Q = 200$ units, we can substitute for K in the production function and solve for L:

$$Q = 200 = 4KL = 4(0.8L)(L)$$
$$200 = 3.2L^2$$
$$L^2 = 62.5$$
$$L = 7.91$$
$$K = 0.8L = (0.8)(7.91) = 6.33$$

To minimize cost, the firm will want to increase labor from 5 to 7.91 units and reduce capital from 10 to 6.33 units. Total cost will fall to

$$TC = WL + RK = \$8(7.91) + \$10(6.33) = \$63.28 + \$63.30 = \$126.58$$

Therefore, the firm will save \$140 − \$126.58 = \$13.42.

Short-Run versus Long-Run Marginal Cost Curves

Just as the short- and long-run average total cost curves are related to the total cost curve, so are marginal costs over the two time horizons. Long-run marginal cost is the additional cost of producing another unit when inputs are fully flexible.

Every short-run average total cost curve has a corresponding short-run marginal cost curve that shows how costly it is to build another unit of output when capital is fixed at some particular level. A short-run marginal cost curve always crosses its corresponding short-run average total cost curve at the minimum of the average total cost curve.

While a long-run average total cost curve is the envelope of all the short-run average total cost curves, this isn't true for short- and long-run marginal cost curves. Let's look at the relationship between the two step-by-step.

Figure 7.9 shows again the short- and long-run average total cost curves from Figure 7.8, and adds the short-run marginal cost curves corresponding to each short-run average total cost curve. ($MC_{SR,10}$ is the short-run marginal cost for $ATC_{SR,10}$, etc.)

How do we figure out what long-run marginal costs are? We know that in the short run with capital fixed, there is only one output level at which a firm would choose that same level of capital: the output at which the short-run average total cost curve touches the long-run average total cost curve. So, for example, if $Q = 10$, Ivor's Engines would choose a level of capital in the long run ($K = 4$) that is the same as that corresponding to short-run average total cost curve $ATC_{SR,10}$. Because the short- and long-run average total cost curves coincide at this quantity (but only at this quantity), so too do the short- and long-run marginal cost curves. In other words, because the firm would choose the same level of capital even if it were totally flexible, the long-run marginal cost *at this quantity* is the same as the short-run marginal cost on $MC_{SR,10}$. Therefore, to find the long-run marginal cost of producing 10 units, we can go up to the short-run marginal cost curve at $Q = 10$. This is point A in Figure 7.9 and represents the long-run marginal cost at an output level of 10 engines.

Likewise, the long-run marginal cost at $Q = 20$ is the value of $MC_{SR,20}$ when Ivor's Engines is making 20 engines. Therefore, long-run marginal cost at $Q = 20$ can be found at point Y in Figure 7.9 (this is the same point Y as in Figures 7.7 and 7.8). Repeating the logic, Ivor's long-run marginal cost for producing 30 engines equals the value of $MC_{SR,30}$ when output $Q = 30$, which is point B in the figure.

When we connect these long-run marginal cost points A, Y, and B, along with the similar points corresponding to every other output quantity, we trace out the long-run

Figure 7.9   Long-Run and Short-Run Marginal Costs

$MC_{SR,10}$, $MC_{SR,20}$, and $MC_{SR,30}$ are derived from $ATC_{SR,10}$, $ATC_{SR,20}$, and $ATC_{SR,30}$, respectively. The long-run marginal cost curve must intersect $MC_{SR,10}$, $MC_{SR,20}$, and $MC_{SR,30}$ at A, Y, and B, respectively, the points at which labor is cost-minimizing for $Q = 10$, $Q = 20$, and $Q = 30$ given, respectively, $\overline{K} = 4$, $\overline{K} = 6$ and $\overline{K} = 9$. Therefore, A, Y, and B are the long-run marginal costs for $Q = 10$, $Q = 20$, and $Q = 30$, respectively, and the long-run marginal cost curve MC_{LR} connects A, Y, and B.

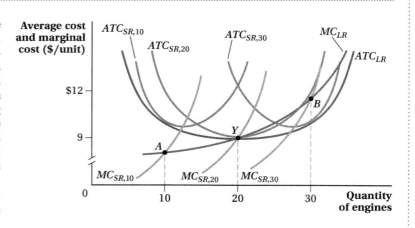

marginal cost curve MC_{LR}. Notice that, just as we have discussed, long-run marginal cost is below long-run average total cost when average total cost is falling (such as at point A), above long-run average total cost when average total cost is rising (such as at point B), and equal to long-run average total cost when average total cost is at its minimum (point Y).

7.6 Economies in the Production Process

Now that we have categorized the long-run average total cost, we want to examine how these average costs change as the firm size grows. Because all inputs are variable in the long run, we can consider how per-unit costs are affected as the firm alters its scale of operation. In other words, what happens to the firm's long-run average total cost as the firm increases all of its inputs by the same proportion?

Economies of Scale

We talked about returns to scale in Chapter 6. Remember that a production technology has increasing returns to scale if doubling all inputs leads to more than a doubling of output. If doubling all inputs exactly doubles output, returns to scale are constant, and if output less than doubles, there are decreasing returns to scale.

Economies of scale are the cost-based flip-side of returns to scale. Instead of looking at the way output changes in proportion to inputs, economies of scale look at the way cost changes in proportion to output. If doubling output causes cost to less than double, a firm has **economies of scale.** If doubling output causes cost to more than double, a firm has **diseconomies of scale.** If doubling output causes cost to double, a firm has **constant economies of scale.**

Because economies of scale imply that total cost increases less than proportionately with output, they also imply that long-run average total cost falls as output grows. That is, the long-run average total cost curve is downward-sloping when there are economies of scale because average total cost is total cost divided by output ($ATC = TC/Q$), and economies of scale imply the total cost rises at a slower rate than quantity. Similarly, diseconomies of scale imply an upward-sloping long-run average total cost curve because total cost rises more quickly than output. Constant economies of scale make the long-run average total cost curve flat.

Putting together these relationships, we can see what the typical U-shaped long-run average total cost curve implies about economies of scale. At low output levels (the left, downward-sloping part of the ATC curve where ATC is declining), total cost rises more slowly than output does. As a result, average total cost falls, and the firm has economies of scale.

At the very bottom of the average total cost curve where it is flat, average cost does not change, total cost rises proportionally with output, and marginal cost equals ATC. Here, therefore, average total cost increases at the same rate that output increases, and there are constant economies of scale.

At higher output levels (the right upward-sloping part of the ATC curve where ATC is rising), marginal cost is above average total cost, causing total cost to rise more quickly than output does. As a result, there are diseconomies of scale.

Economies of Scale versus Returns to Scale

Economies of scale and returns to scale are not the same thing. They are related—cost and the level of inputs move closely together—but there is a difference. Returns to scale describe how output changes when all inputs are increased by a common factor. But nothing says cost-minimizing firms must keep input ratios constant when they increase

economies of scale
Total cost rises at a slower rate than output rises.

diseconomies of scale
Total cost rises at a faster rate than output rises.

constant economies of scale
Total cost rises at the same rate as output rises.

7.5 figure it out

Suppose that the long-run total cost function for a firm is $LTC = 22{,}600Q - 300Q^2 + Q^3$ and its long-run marginal cost function is $LMC = 22{,}600 - 600Q + 3Q^2$. At what levels of output will the firm face economies of scale? Diseconomies of scale? (*Hint*: These cost functions yield a typical U-shaped long-run average cost curve.)

Solution:

If we can find the output that minimizes long-run average total cost, we can determine the output levels for which the firm faces economies and diseconomies of scale. We know that when $LMC < LATC$, long-run average total cost is falling and the firm experiences economies of scale. Likewise, when $LMC > LATC$, the long-run average total cost curve slopes up and the firm faces diseconomies of scale. So, if we can figure out where the minimum $LATC$ occurs, we can see where economies of scale end and diseconomies begin.

Minimum average cost occurs when $LMC = LATC$. But, we need to determine $LATC$ before we

begin. Long-run average total cost is long-run total cost divided by output:

$$LATC = \frac{LTC}{Q} = \frac{22{,}600Q - 300Q^2 + Q^3}{Q}$$

$$= 22{,}600 - 300Q + Q^2$$

Now, we need to set $LATC = LMC$ to find the quantity that minimizes $LATC$:

$$LATC = LMC$$
$$22{,}600 - 300Q + Q^2 = 22{,}600 - 600Q + 3Q^2$$
$$300Q = 2Q^2$$
$$300 = 2Q$$
$$Q = 150$$

Long-run average total cost is minimized and economies of scale are constant when the firm produces 150 units of output. Thus, at $Q < 150$, the firm faces economies of scale. At $Q > 150$, the firm faces diseconomies of scale. (You can prove this to yourself by substituting different quantities into the long-run average total cost equation and seeing if $LATC$ rises or falls as Q changes.)

output. So, the measure of economies of scale, which is about how total costs change with output, does not impose constant input ratios the way returns to scale does.

Because a firm can only reduce its cost more if it is able to change its input ratios when output changes, it can have economies of scale if it has constant or even decreasing returns to scale. That is, even though the firm might have a production function in which doubling inputs would exactly double output, it might be able to double output without doubling its total cost by changing the proportion in which it uses inputs. Therefore, increasing returns to scale imply economies of scale, but not necessarily the reverse.[2]

 application

Economies of Scale and Makin' Bacon

Examining the sizes of firms in an industry can often tell us about economies of scale. For example, U.S. Department of Agriculture economists James MacDonald and Michael Ollinger studied why meat-packing plants, and those that process pork in particular, have become so much larger in recent decades.[3] Plants that processed more

---

[2] The only case in which the two concepts are the same is when it happens to be optimal for the firm to hold input ratios constant as output increases. (This would show up as an expansion path that is a straight line extending out from the origin.) In this case, the firm gets no extra cost reduction from changing the proportions in which it uses its inputs as its output changes.

[3] James M. MacDonald and Michael E. Ollinger, "Scale Economies and Consolidation in Hog Slaughter," *American Journal of Agricultural Economics* 82, no. 2 (2000): 334–346.

than 1 million hogs per year accounted for 38% of the industry's output in 1977, but a whopping 87% of output only 15 years later. During the same period, one-third of the country's plants processing fewer than 50,000 hogs a year had shut down.

MacDonald and Ollinger hypothesized that the nature of scale economies in the industry had changed over that period. New technologies had reduced costs, especially at higher output levels. These new technologies could widen the output ranges over which processing plants experience economies of scale, allowing plants to become larger without increasing their average costs and, in fact, possibly decreasing average costs even further. We will see in later chapters that technologies that expand the downward-sloping portion of the average total cost curve can lead to higher optimal output levels.

To test their hypothesis, MacDonald and Ollinger needed to estimate the cost curves of pork-processing plants. Their task would have been easier if they had cost data from the same plant at different output levels, but they didn't. They only had annual data on plants' costs, and not many years of data for each plant. So, they used variation in output and cost levels *across* plants to measure the cost curves and assumed that every plant in the industry had the same cost curve—a bit of a stretch, perhaps, but probably a reasonable one given the standardized production methods.[4]

Figure 7.10 shows the long-run average total cost curves that MacDonald and Ollinger estimated from their data. Two long-run average total cost curves are shown: one for plants operating in 1977 and the other for plants operating in 1992. The figure also indicates the sizes at which the average-sized and 95th percentile plants operated in each year. (If the industry had 100 plants, the 95th percentile would be the fifth largest plant in the industry.) The curves show average total costs as an index, where costs are expressed as a percentage of average total costs for the average-sized plant in 1977.

The first thing to notice is that the industry definitely experienced total factor productivity growth; average total cost at all quantities fell over the 15 years. A plant in 1992 that was the same size as the average plant in 1977 had 4% lower average total cost than it had in 1977. Second, the cost decreases were larger for bigger plants. In 1977 the industry's largest plants (those around the 95th percentile) were operating at roughly the output quantity where economies of scale ended. This can be seen by the

Figure 7.10   Average Total Cost Curves for Pork Processing Plants, 1977 and 1992

ATC_{1977} and ATC_{1992} are the long-run average total cost curves for pork processing plants in 1977 and 1992, respectively. Average total costs for both the average-sized plant and the 95th percentile plant were significantly lower in 1992 than in 1977. At the same time, the average-sized and 95th percentile plants grew in size. These findings support the idea that the cost structure and scale economies of the pork industry changed from 1977 to 1992.

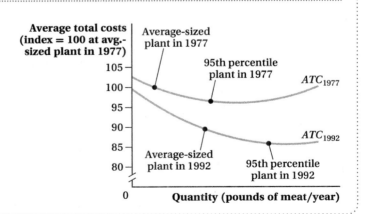

[4] The approach also raised the complication that input prices, which as we know from Chapter 6 affect plants' costs but are held constant when drawing a cost curve, likely varied across plants. MacDonald and Ollinger used statistical techniques to control for these differences and remove their influence from the estimated cost curves.

fact that they are located very near the bottom of the 1977 average total cost curve. But looking at the average total cost curve for 1992, we see that the *average-sized* plant in that year was just about as large as the 95th percentile plant in 1977, and its costs were still about 7% lower. Third, the average-sized plant in 1992 was still operating where there were substantial economies of scale. This is because new technologies had increased the range over which industry plants experienced scale economies. Industry plants became larger between 1977 and 1992 as a result. Fourth, not just the average, but the largest plants grew, too. The 95th percentile plant in 1992 was again operating near the output level where scale economies were exhausted, but this output level was much higher in 1992 than 1977. Had plants grown that large in 1977, they would have been operating on the upward-sloping part of the long-run average total cost curve, where there are diseconomies of scale.

Therefore, the results showed significant changes in the cost structure of these firms and the nature of scale economies. This may explain why so much production shifted to large plants in a relatively short period. ∎

Economies of Scope

economies of scope
The simultaneous production of multiple products at a lower cost than if a firm made each product separately.

Many firms make more than one product. Just as economies of scale indicate how firms' costs vary with the quantity they produce, **economies of scope** indicate how firms' costs change when they make more than one product. Economies of scope exist when a producer can simultaneously make multiple products at a lower cost than if it made each product separately and then added up the costs.

To be more explicit, let's call a firm's cost of simultaneously producing Q_1 units of Good 1 and Q_2 units of Good 2 $TC(Q_1, Q_2)$. If the firm produces Q_1 units of Good 1 and nothing of Good 2, its cost is $TC(Q_1, 0)$. Similarly, if the firm produces Q_2 units of Good 2 and none of Good 1, its cost is $TC(0, Q_2)$. Under these definitions, the firm is considered to have economies of scope if $TC(Q_1, Q_2) < TC(Q_1, 0) + TC(0, Q_2)$. In other words, producing Q_1 and Q_2 together is cheaper than making each separately.

We can go beyond just knowing whether or not economies of scope exist, and actually quantify them in a way that allows us to compare scope economies across companies. We call this measure $SCOPE$, and it's the difference between the total costs of single-good production $[TC(Q_1, 0) + TC(0, Q_2)]$ and joint production $[TC(Q_1, Q_2)]$ as a fraction of the total costs of joint production. That is,

$$SCOPE = \frac{[TC(Q_1, 0) + TC(0, Q_2)] - TC(Q_1, Q_2)}{TC(Q_1, Q_2)}$$

If $SCOPE > 0$, the total cost of producing Goods 1 and 2 jointly is less than making the goods separately, so there are economies of scope. The greater $SCOPE$ is, the larger are the firm's cost savings from making multiple products. If $SCOPE = 0$, the costs are equivalent, and economies of scope are zero. And if $SCOPE < 0$, then it's actually cheaper to produce Q_1 and Q_2 separately. In other words, there are **diseconomies of scope.**

diseconomies of scope
The simultaneous production of multiple products at a higher cost than if a firm made each product separately.

There are two important things to remember about economies of scope. First, they are defined for a *particular* level of output of each good. Economies of scope might exist at one set of output levels—for example, 100 units of Good 1 and 150 units of Good 2—but not at a different pair, like 200 units of each, for instance. (The specificity of economies of scope to particular output levels is shared with economies of scale. As we discussed earlier in this section, for example, a U-shaped average total cost curve embodies changing scale economies over different output levels—positive economies at low output levels, negative ones at higher output.) Second, economies of scope do not have to be related to economies of scale. A firm can have one without the other or both at the same time. In fact, it gets a bit difficult to even define economies of scale once there are multiple outputs. We don't need to go into why this is so; it's enough to recognize that scale and scope economies are different things.

Why Economies of Scope Arise

There are many possible sources of scope economies. They depend on the flexibility of inputs and the inherent nature of the products.

A common source of economies of scope is when different parts of a common input can be applied to the production of the firm's different products. Take a cereal company that makes two cereals, bran bricks and wheat flakes. The firm needs wheat to produce either cereal. For bran bricks, it needs mostly the bran, the fibrous outer covering of the wheat kernel, but for wheat flakes, the firm needs the rest of the kernel. Therefore, there are natural cost savings from producing both cereals together. The wheat the firm buys can be split between the production of the two cereals. For example, if the firm makes only wheat flakes, the outer covering of the kernel of wheat might go to waste.

In oil refining, the inherent chemical properties of crude oil guarantee economies of scope. Crude oil is a collection of a number of very different hydrocarbon molecules; refining is the process of separating these molecules into useful products. It is physically impossible for a refining company to produce only gasoline (or kerosene, diesel, lubricants, or whatever petroleum product might be fetching the highest price at the time). While refiners have some limited ability to change the mix of products they can pull out of each barrel of crude oil, this comes at a loss of scope economies. That's why refineries always produce a number of petroleum compounds simultaneously.

The common input that creates scope economies does not have to be raw materials. For example, Google employees might be more productive using their knowledge about information collection and dissemination to produce multiple products (e.g., Google Earth, Google Docs, and Google+) than to produce just the main search engine.

7.7 Conclusion

We've covered all sorts of concepts about firms' costs in this chapter: opportunity costs, fixed costs, variable costs, sunk costs, marginal costs, average costs, long-run and short-run costs, economies of scale and scope, and more. That's a lot to keep straight, but the information we have covered here is important for understanding the constraints firms face when making production decisions. This information also allows us to connect what we learned in Chapter 6, which is how a firm optimally produces a *given* output quantity, to many of the analyses we do in Chapters 8–11, when we look at how firms decide what output quantity to produce in the first place, or even whether to produce at all.

Summary

1. Economic cost includes **accounting cost** plus the **opportunity cost** of inputs. Opportunity cost is the value of the input's next-best use. Decisions should be made taking opportunity costs into account—that is, on the basis of **economic cost,** not accounting cost. [**Section 7.1**]

2. **Sunk costs** are costs that can never be recovered even if the firm shuts down completely. Costs that are already sunk should not affect decisions going forward, because they have already been paid regardless of what choice is made in the present. [**Section 7.2**]

3. A firm's **total cost** can be split into fixed and variable components. **Fixed cost** does not change

when the firm's output does and must be paid even if output is zero. It can only be avoided by the firm completely shutting down and disposing of the inputs (an action that can be undertaken only in the long run). **Variable costs** are costs that change with the output level. [**Section 7.3**]

4. Cost curves relate a firm's cost to its output quantity. Because fixed cost doesn't change as output changes, fixed cost curves are horizontal, and **total cost curves** are parallel to **variable cost curves** (separated by the amount of fixed cost). [**Section 7.3**]

5. Two additional important cost concepts are **average** and **marginal costs.** Average cost at a

given output quantity equals the ratio of cost to output. **Average fixed cost** falls continuously as output increases. **Average variable cost** and **average total cost** tend to be U-shaped, falling initially, but then rising as output increases. Marginal cost is the additional cost of making one more unit of output. [**Section 7.4**]

6. In the short run, the firm's capital inputs are held constant along its expansion path, and all changes in output come from changing labor inputs. This means that, for all quantities except that quantity at which the fixed capital level is cost-minimizing, short-run total and average total costs must be higher than their long-run values. Every fixed capital level has its own short-run cost curves. The long-run average total cost curve is an "envelope" of all the short-run average total cost curves. Long-run marginal cost equals the short-run marginal costs at the quantities at which the fixed capital level is cost-minimizing. [**Section 7.5**]

7. **Economies of scale** describe the relative rate at which a firm's cost changes when its output changes. When cost increases at a slower rate than output, the firm has economies of scale. Average cost is falling and the long-run average total cost curve is downward-sloping when there are economies of scale. If cost increases at a faster rate than output, **diseconomies of scale** occur. Average total cost is rising and the long-run average total cost curve is upward-sloping in this case. If cost increases at the same rate as output, there are neither scale economies nor diseconomies, and long-run average total cost is constant. [**Section 7.6**]

8. **Economies of scope** describe how a firm's total cost changes with its product specialization. If producing two outputs jointly is cheaper than producing the same amount of the two outputs separately, then there are economies of scope. [**Section 7.6**]

Review Questions

1. What is the difference between a firm's accounting and economic costs? How do these costs relate to a firm's accounting and economic profits?
2. Define opportunity cost. How does a firm's opportunity cost relate to its economic cost?
3. What is the sunk cost fallacy?
4. Provide some examples of unavoidable fixed costs. How are these related to sunk costs? Describe why a firm should not consider sunk costs when making decisions.
5. Describe the relationship between fixed, variable, and total costs.
6. Why is a fixed cost curve horizontal? Why does a variable cost curve have a positive slope?

7. Name the three measures that examine a firm's per-unit cost at a given level of output.
8. Why does a firm's fixed cost not affect its marginal cost of producing an additional unit of a product?
9. Why is a firm's short-run total cost greater than its long-run total cost? Explain why this is also true for a firm's short-run and long-run *average* costs.
10. Describe the conditions under which a firm has economies of scale, diseconomies of scale, and constant economies of scale.
11. When does a producer face economies of scope? When does a producer face diseconomies of scope?

Problems

1. Jenny is considering starting a new business selling organic groceries. It would cost her $350,000 a year to rent store space and buy the groceries from a wholesaler, and she would have to quit her current job and give up a $70,000 annual salary.
   a. What is Jenny's opportunity cost of starting the business?
   b. If Jenny can make an accounting profit of $50,000 a year selling the organic groceries, should she start the business?

2. Casey is an expert poker player and can make $35 an hour playing poker online. On Saturday Casey goes to a local tournament with a $15 entry fee. He plays for four hours and wins first place, taking home the $150 prize. Did Casey make an economic profit at the tournament?
3. Indicate whether the following statements are true or false, and then briefly explain your reasoning.
   a. It is possible for accounting and economic costs to be equal, but it is never possible for economic costs to be less than accounting costs.

b. It is possible for a firm to show an economic profit without showing an accounting profit.

4. Kyle recently opened a bar & grill. The costs associated with his new business are as follows:
   a. $300,000 to build the restaurant
   b. $30,000 for a liquor license
   c. $50,000 on furniture and kitchenware
   d. 2 cooks who will each be paid $5,000 per month
   e. 5 waiters who will each be paid $3 per hour plus tips
   Which of Kyle's costs are fixed, and which are variable? Explain.

5. Amanda owns a toy manufacturing plant with the production function $Q = 100L - 3,000$, where L is hired labor hours. If the wage rate that Amanda pays her laborers is $7 per hour, what is her cost function?

6. A Toyota Camry costs $19,600 and has an average gas mileage of 27 mpg. A Toyota Prius costs $23,000 and has an average gas mileage of 50 mpg. Assuming gas costs $4 per gallon, generate total cost equations as a function of miles driven for each of these cars and identify the fixed and variable costs. How many miles do you have to drive before the two cars have the same total cost?

7. Philo T. Farmsworth is a corn farmer with a 40-acre tract of land. Each acre can produce 100 bushels of corn. The cost of planting the tract in corn is $20,000, and the cost of harvesting the corn is $10,000. In May, when corn is selling for $10 per bushel, Philo plants his crop. In September the price of corn has fallen to $2 per bushel. What should Philo do? Explain, assuming that there are no costs involved with bringing the corn to market to sell.

8. Complete the cost table below:

Quantity	Total Cost ($)	Average Total Cost ($)	Marginal Cost ($)
0	0	—	—
1	35		
2			25
3		28	
4	115		
5			40

9. Consider the costs for Catherine's cupcake business:

Quantity (batches)	Fixed Cost ($)	Total Cost ($)
1	50	75
2	50	85
3	50	102
4	50	127
5	50	165
6	50	210

Re-create the above table with columns showing Catherine's variable cost, average total cost, average fixed cost, and average variable cost.

10. Daniel's Midland Archers (DMA) makes children's wooden practice arrows. Draw a set of representative short-run cost curves for DMA. Include average variable cost, average fixed cost, average total cost, and marginal cost.
    a. Suppose that Congress imposes a 39-cent excise tax on each children's wooden practice arrow DMA sells. Illustrate the effects of this tax on the cost curves of DMA. Which curves shift and which do not?
    b. Suppose that the city where DMA produces arrows increases the annual property tax on DMA's factory from $80,000 to $150,000. Illustrate the effects of this tax on the cost curves of DMA. Which curves shift and which do not?

11. Derive formulas for average fixed cost, average variable cost, average total cost, and marginal cost for the following cost function:

$$TC = 100 + 10Q$$

12. Suppose a firm has the following production function: $Q = 2KL$. The marginal product of capital for this production function is $2L$, and the marginal product of labor is $2K$. If capital rents for $100 per unit per day, labor can be hired for $200 per unit per day, and the firm is minimizing costs,
    a. What is the total cost of producing q units of output?
    b. What is the average cost of producing q units of output?
    c. What is the marginal cost of producing q units of output?

13. You are the CEO of a major producer of funnel cakes. Your cost accountant has provided you with a table describing your cost structure, but you have inadvertently dripped cooking grease on it and most of the table is illegible. Reconstruct the table below, given the remaining legible numbers.

Q	TC	FC	VC	MC	AVC	AFC	ATC
0				—	—	—	—
1			17				
2				15			
3	101						
4					14.5		
5	122		67			11	
6							21

14. How does a firm's short-run ATC curve differ from its long-run ATC curve? Explain your answer.

15. Suppose an increase in the minimum wage alters the cost of producing fast-food hamburgers. Show what happens to McDonald's long-run expansion path as a result of this wage increase.

16. Digging trenches requires two types of labor: unskilled labor (aka workers) and skilled labor (aka supervisors). Unskilled labor can be hired for $50 per day, and skilled labor can be hired for $100 per day. If, by hiring another unskilled laborer, K&B Construction Company can dig another 20 feet of trenches per day, and if by hiring another skilled laborer, it can dig another 30 feet of trenches per day, is K&B Construction Company minimizing its costs?

17. A builder of custom motorcycles has a choice of operating out of one garage or two. When it operates out of one garage, its average total cost of production is given by $ATC_1 = Q^2 - 6Q + 14$. If it operates out of two garages, its average total cost of production is given by $ATC_2 = Q^2 - 10Q + 30$. What does this firm's $LATC$ look like? Can you describe it as a function?

18. Mike's Bicycle Factory builds specialty bicycles with the following long-run cost function: $TC = 2.5(Q^3)$. Plot Mike's ATC and MC curves for quantities 1 through 5.
   a. For which quantities does Mike's Bicycle Factory exhibit economies of scale?
   b. For which quantities does it exhibit diseconomies of scale?

19. Suppose that a firm has the following Cobb–Douglas production function: $Q = 12K^{0.75}L^{0.25}$.
   a. What must its long-run total cost curve look like? Its long-run average total cost curve?
   b. How do your answers to part (a) change if the firm's production function is $Q = KL$?

20. In the short run, your firm can vary only the amount of labor it employs. Labor can be hired for $5 per unit, and your firm's fixed costs are $25. Your firm's short-run production function is given in the table below:

Labor Input	Output	Marginal Product of Labor	Average Product of Labor	Total Cost	Average Total Cost	Average Variable Cost	Marginal Cost
1	5						
2	12						
3	20						
4	28						
5	34						
6	39						
7	43						
8	46						
9	48						

a. Compute the marginal and average product of each worker. What shape does each take? When does the marginal product begin to fall? Average product?
b. Compute the total cost of producing each output level indicated in the table.
c. Compute the average total, average variable, and marginal cost at each level of output. When does marginal cost begin to rise? Average variable cost?
d. Is there a link between your answers to (a) and (c)?

Chapter 7 Appendix:
The Calculus of a Firm's Cost Structure

We saw in this chapter that firms face a multitude of costs—from opportunity costs and sunk costs to fixed and variable costs to marginal costs and more. These costs can be obtained directly from the firm's production function and its wage and rental rate for particular levels of output. But it is often helpful to have a more generalized form of a firm's costs that allows us to know its cost structure at any optimal input bundle. In this appendix, we use calculus to come up with total and marginal cost curves starting from the firm's production function.

Let's return to the firm with the Cobb–Douglas production function $Q = AK^{\alpha}L^{1-\alpha}$ with wages equal to W, the rental rate of capital equal to R, and the technology parameter A. Assume $0 < \alpha < 1$, and $A > 0$. The firm's total costs are

$$TC = RK + WL$$

This formula specifies the firm's total costs when the firm produces a specific quantity and, thus, knows its cost-minimizing bundle of capital and labor for that particular quantity. If the firm hasn't yet decided how much to produce, however, the firm would want to know its entire total cost curve—that is, what its total costs are at *any* quantity it chooses to produce. How can a firm find these costs? The firm wants to find its total costs as a function of its demands for capital and labor. To do this, the firm first has to consider whether it is operating in the short or the long run. In the short run, capital is fixed at some level $\overline{K}$, and the firm's production function is $Q = A\overline{K}^{\alpha}L^{1-\alpha}$. Its demand for labor in the short run is then determined by how much capital the firm has. Finding the short-run demand for labor is as simple as solving for L in the production function:

$$L^{1-\alpha} = \frac{Q}{A\overline{K}^{\alpha}}$$

$$L = \left(\frac{Q}{A\overline{K}^{\alpha}}\right)^{\frac{1}{(1-\alpha)}}$$

Plugging this short-run demand for labor and the fixed amount of capital ($\overline{K}$) into the total cost equation, the firm faces short-run total cost:

$$TC_{SR} = R\overline{K} + WL$$

$$TC_{SR} = R\overline{K} + W\left(\frac{Q}{A\overline{K}^{\alpha}}\right)^{\frac{1}{(1-\alpha)}}$$

In the long run, the firm chooses the optimal amount of capital *and* labor, so its long-run demands for capital and labor look different. We know from the firm's cost-minimization problem in the Chapter 6 Appendix that at a fixed quantity $\overline{Q}$, the firm demands $L^* = \left[\frac{(1-\alpha)}{\alpha}\frac{R}{W}\right]^{\alpha}\frac{\overline{Q}}{A}$ and $K^* = \left[\frac{\alpha}{(1-\alpha)}\frac{W}{R}\right]^{1-\alpha}\frac{\overline{Q}}{A}$. At any level of Q, then, the firm demands $L^* = \left[\frac{(1-\alpha)}{\alpha}\frac{R}{W}\right]^{\alpha}\frac{Q}{A}$ and $K^* = \left[\frac{\alpha}{(1-\alpha)}\frac{W}{R}\right]^{1-\alpha}\frac{Q}{A}$, where Q is variable and not a fixed quantity.

These are the firm's long-run capital and labor demand curves. As with all demand curves, these are downward-sloping: As the wage (or rental rate) increases, the firm will want to purchase less labor (or capital), all else equal. Now that we have the firm's demands for both of its inputs, we can substitute them into the expression for total cost as a function of inputs to get the long-run total cost curve as a function of output:

$$TC_{LR} = RK + WL$$

$$TC(Q)_{LR} = R\left[\frac{\alpha}{(1-\alpha)}\frac{W}{R}\right]^{1-\alpha}\frac{Q}{A} + W\left[\frac{(1-\alpha)}{\alpha}\frac{R}{W}\right]^{\alpha}\frac{Q}{A}$$

Notice that total cost increases as output and the prices of inputs increase, but that total cost decreases as total factor productivity A increases.

We can now also find the firm's generalized marginal cost curve by taking the derivative of the total cost curve with respect to quantity Q. But be careful before you do this! We have to again consider whether the firm is operating in the short run or the long run. In the short run, the cost of capital is a fixed cost and will not show up in the firm's marginal cost curve. Short-run marginal cost is only a function of the change in labor costs:

$$MC(Q)_{SR} = \frac{dTC(Q)_{SR}}{dQ} = \frac{d}{dQ}\left[R\overline{K} + W\left(\frac{Q}{A\overline{K}^{\alpha}}\right)^{\frac{1}{(1-\alpha)}}\right]$$

$$= \frac{1}{(1-\alpha)}W\left(\frac{1}{A\overline{K}^{\alpha}}\right)^{\frac{1}{(1-\alpha)}}\left[Q^{\frac{1}{(1-\alpha)}-1}\right] = \frac{W}{(1-\alpha)}\left(\frac{1}{A\overline{K}^{\alpha}}\right)^{\frac{1}{(1-\alpha)}}\left[Q^{\frac{\alpha}{(1-\alpha)}}\right]$$

$$= \frac{W}{(1-\alpha)}\left(\frac{Q^{\alpha}}{A\overline{K}^{\alpha}}\right)^{\frac{1}{(1-\alpha)}}$$

As we would expect, marginal costs increase with output in the short run. Why? Because in the short run capital is fixed. The firm can only increase output by using more and more labor. However, the diminishing marginal product of labor means that each additional unit of labor is less productive and that the firm has to use increasingly more labor to produce an additional unit of output. As a result, the marginal cost of producing this extra unit of output increases as short-run production increases, all else equal.

In the long run, the firm can change both inputs, and its marginal cost curve reflects the firm's capital and labor demands. To get long-run marginal cost, take the derivative of long-run total cost with respect to Q:

$$MC(Q)_{LR} = \frac{dTC(Q)_{LR}}{dQ} = \frac{d}{dQ}\left[R\left[\frac{\alpha}{(1-\alpha)}\frac{W}{R}\right]^{1-\alpha}\frac{Q}{A} + W\left[\frac{(1-\alpha)}{\alpha}\frac{R}{W}\right]^{\alpha}\frac{Q}{A}\right]$$

$$= \frac{1}{A}\left[R\left[\frac{\alpha}{(1-\alpha)}\frac{W}{R}\right]^{1-\alpha} + W\left[\frac{(1-\alpha)}{\alpha}\frac{R}{W}\right]^{\alpha}\right]$$

Notice that this expression for marginal cost consists only of constants (A, α, W, and R). So, long-run marginal cost is constant for this production function. What is more, average total cost for this production function is exactly the same as marginal cost—you should be able to show this by dividing TC by Q. Both of these results (constant marginal cost and $MC = ATC$) are unique to firms with constant returns to scale. If these firms want to double output, they have to double labor and capital. This, in turn, doubles the firms' costs, leaving *average* total cost—total cost divided by total inputs—unchanged. If the firm does not face constant returns to scale, these results will not hold true. In particular, a firm with decreasing returns to scale would see increasing long-run marginal costs, while a firm with increasing returns to scale faces decreasing long-run marginal costs.

7A.1 figure it out

Let's revisit Figure It Out 7.4. Steve and Sons Solar Panels has a production function of $Q = 4KL$ and faces a wage rate of \$8 per hour and a rental rate of capital of \$10 per hour. Assume that, in the short run, capital is fixed at $\overline{K} = 10$.

a. Derive the short-run total cost curve for the firm. What is the short-run total cost of producing $Q = 200$ units?

b. Derive expressions for the firm's short-run average total cost, average fixed cost, average variable cost, and marginal cost.

c. Derive the long-run total cost curve for the firm. What is the long-run total cost of producing $Q = 200$ units?

d. Derive expressions for the firm's long-run average total cost and marginal cost.

Solution:

a. To get the short-run total cost function, we need to first find L as a function of Q. The short-run production function can be found by substituting $\overline{K} = 10$ into the production function:

$$Q = 4\overline{K}L = 4(10)(L) = 40L$$

Therefore, the firm's short run demand for labor is

$$L = 0.025Q$$

Now plug $\overline{K}$ and L into the total cost function:

$$TC_{SR} = R\overline{K} + WL = 10(10) + 8(0.025Q)$$
$$TC_{SR} = 100 + 0.2Q$$

This is the equation for the short-run total cost curve with fixed cost FC equal to 100 and variable cost VC equal to $0.2Q$. Notice that the fixed cost is just the total cost of capital, $R\overline{K} = 10(10) = \$100$. The short-run total cost of producing 200 units of output is

$$TC_{SR} = 100 + 0.2(200) = \$140$$

b. Average costs are a firm's costs divided by the quantity produced. Hence, the average total cost, average fixed cost, and average variable cost measures for this total cost function are

$$ATC_{SR} = \frac{TC}{Q} = \frac{100 + 0.2Q}{Q} = \frac{100}{Q} + 0.2$$

$$AFC_{SR} = \frac{FC}{Q} = \frac{100}{Q}$$

$$AVC_{SR} = \frac{VC}{Q} = \frac{0.2Q}{Q} = 0.2$$

Marginal cost is the derivative of total cost with respect to quantity, or

$$MC_{SR} = \frac{dTC}{dQ} = 0.2$$

Marginal cost for Steve and Sons is constant and equal to average variable cost in the short run because the marginal product of labor is constant when capital is fixed.

c. In the long run, Steve and Sons solves its cost-minimization problem:

$$\min_{K,L} TC = 10K + 8L \text{ s.t. } Q = 4KL \quad \text{or} \quad \min_{K,L,\lambda} \mathcal{L}(K,L,\lambda) = 10K + 8L + \lambda(Q - 4KL)$$

The first-order conditions are

$$\frac{\partial \mathcal{L}}{\partial K} = 10 - \lambda(4L) = 0$$

$$\frac{\partial \mathcal{L}}{\partial L} = 8 - \lambda(4K) = 0$$

$$\frac{\partial \mathcal{L}}{\partial \lambda} = Q - 4KL = 0$$

To find the optimal levels of labor and capital, we need to set the first two conditions equal to solve for K as a function of L:

$$\lambda = \frac{10}{4L} = \frac{8}{4K}$$

$$40K = 32L$$

$$K = 0.8L$$

To find the firm's long-run labor demand, we plug this expression for K as a function of L into the production function and solve for L:

$$Q = 4KL = 4(0.8L)L = 3.2L^2$$
$$L^2 = 0.31Q$$
$$L = 0.56Q^{0.5}$$

To find the firm's long-run demand for capital, we simply plug the labor demand into our expression for K as a function of L:

$$K = 0.8L = 0.8(0.56Q^{0.5})$$
$$= 0.45Q^{0.5}$$

The firm's long-run total cost function can be derived by plugging the firm's long-run input demands L and K into the long-run total cost function:

$$TC_{LR} = RK + WL = 10(0.45Q^{0.5}) + 8(0.56Q^{0.5})$$
$$= 8.98Q^{0.5}$$

Therefore, the cost for producing 200 units of output in the long run is

$$TC_{LR} = 8.98(200)^{0.5} \approx \$127$$

d. We can also find the long-run marginal and average total costs for this firm:

$$MC_{LR} = \frac{dTC}{dQ} = 4.99Q^{-0.5}$$

$$ATC_{LR} = \frac{TC}{Q} = \frac{8.98Q^{0.5}}{Q} = 8.98Q^{-0.5}$$

Notice that marginal cost in this case decreases as output increases. Furthermore, $MC < ATC$ for all levels of output. This is because Steve and Sons' production function, $Q = 4KL$, exhibits increasing returns to scale at all levels of output.

Problems

1. A firm has a production function of $Q = 0.25KL^{0.5}$, the rental rate of capital is $100, and the wage rate is $25. In the short run, $\overline{K}$ is fixed at 100 units.
   a. What is the short-run production function?
   b. What is the short-run demand for labor?
   c. What are the firm's short-run total cost and short-run marginal cost?

2. Margarita Robotics has a daily production function given by $Q = K^{0.5}L^{0.5}$, where K is the monthly number of hours of use for a precision lathe (capital) and L is the monthly number of machinist hours (labor). Suppose that each unit of capital costs $40, and each unit of labor costs $10.
   a. In the short run, $\overline{K}$ is fixed at 16,000 hours. What is the short-run demand for labor?
   b. Given that $\overline{K}$ is fixed at 16,000 hours, what are total cost, average total cost, average variable cost, and marginal cost in the short run?
   c. What are the long-run demands for capital and labor?
   d. Derive total cost, average cost, and marginal cost in the long run.
   e. How do Margarita Robotics' marginal and average costs change with increases in output? Explain.

3. A firm has a production function given by $Q = 10K^{0.25}L^{0.25}$. Suppose that each unit of capital costs R and each unit of labor costs W.
   a. Derive the long-run demands for capital and labor.
   b. Derive the total cost curve for this firm.
   c. Derive the long-run average and marginal cost curves.
   d. How do marginal and average costs change with increases in output? Explain.
   e. Confirm that the value of the Lagrange multiplier you get from the cost-minimization problem in part (a) is equal to the marginal cost curve you found in part (c).

Supply in a Competitive Market

8

Raising chickens in urban areas is a new trend among fans of locally produced food. Suppose Ty is an aspiring urban farmer and has to decide on how many chickens to raise in his backyard. He might eat a few of the eggs and an occasional chicken himself, but he plans to sell most of his production at local markets. In essence, Ty is starting a firm, and he is facing the same production decisions any firm faces. How many chickens Ty raises isn't going to noticeably affect the total supply of eggs or chicken in the market. Not only do tens of thousands of people now raise chickens in their backyards, but there are also large farms that supply chickens to the market. How many chickens Ty raises *is* going to affect his profits, however. So, how does Ty—or any firm—make production decisions?

In Chapters 6 and 7, we learned how a firm chooses an input mix to minimize the cost of producing a particular amount of output and how this cost changes with the output level. In this chapter, we start exploring how a firm chooses how much output to make in the first place. In doing this, we move from talking about a firm's cost-minimizing behavior to a discussion of how a firm chooses an output level to maximize its profits. You will see that it gives us the supply curves we learned about in Chapters 2 and 3.

Although all firms use knowledge of marginal revenue, marginal costs, and prices to guide their actions, profit-maximizing behavior is different for different types of firms. We begin the chapter by explaining the different types of market structures within which firms operate and what competition truly means. Most of this chapter focuses on **perfect competition,** a market (or industry) with many firms producing an identical product with no barriers to entry, and explores how firms behave in a perfectly competitive industry to maximize their profits.

8.1 Market Structures and Perfect Competition in the Short Run

To say more about how a firm makes its production decisions, it is useful to think about the competitive environment, or **market structure,** in which it operates. There are four different types of markets that we will explore in the next several chapters: perfect competition, monopolistic competition, oligopoly, and monopoly.

We categorize a market or industry using three primary characteristics:

- **Number of firms.** Generally, the more companies in the market, the more competitive it is.

- **Whether the consumer cares which company made the good.** Can a consumer distinguish one firm's product from another, or are all of the goods identical? In general, the more indistinguishable the products are, the more competitive the market is.

- **Barriers to entry**. If new firms can enter a market easily, the market is more competitive.

Table 8.1 describes each market structure using these characteristics.

These three characteristics tell us a lot about the production decisions of firms in a given industry. For example, firms that can differentiate their products may be able to convince some consumers to pay a higher price for their products than for products made by their competitors. The ability to influence the price of their products has important implications for these firms' profit-maximizing decisions. Only firms in a perfectly competitive market have no influence on the price of their products; they take as given whatever price is determined by the forces of supply and demand at work in the wider market. A truly perfectly competitive market is rare, but it offers many useful lessons about how a market works, just as the supply and demand framework does. In this chapter, we focus on perfectly competitive markets. In Chapters 9 and 10, we look at monopoly and how monopolies can use different strategies to gain more profit, and in Chapter 11, we examine market structures that fall in between perfect competition and monopoly.

perfect competition A market with many firms producing identical products and no barriers to entry.

market structure The competitive environment in which firms operate.

Table 8.1   **The Four Basic Market Structures**

	Perfect Competition	Monopolistic Competition	Oligopoly	Monopoly
Number of Firms	Many	Many	Few	One
Type of Products Sold	Identical	Differentiated	Identical or Differentiated	Unique
Barriers to Entry	None	None	Some	Many

Perfect Competition

What makes a market perfectly competitive? In Table 8.1, we saw that to be perfectly competitive, three conditions have to be satisfied. First, there need to be a large number of firms. If there are, then the impact that any one firm has on the market equilibrium price and output is small. Indeed, we assume that any one firm can change its behavior without the overall market equilibrium being affected at all.

The second requirement for perfect competition is that all firms produce an identical product. By identical, we don't just mean that all the firms make televisions or all the firms make smoothies. We mean the consumers view the output of the different producers as perfect substitutes; they do not care who made it. This might be more accurate for nails or gasoline or bananas, but is probably far from true for smart phones or automobiles.

Finally, for an industry to be perfectly competitive, there cannot be any barriers to entry. In other words, if someone decides she wants to start selling nails tomorrow, there is nothing that prevents her from doing so.

The key economic implication of these three assumptions (small firms, identical products, free entry) is that firms don't have a choice about what price to charge. If the firm charges a price above the market price, it will not sell any of its goods. (We'll show you the math behind this result later in this section.) And because we assume that the firm is small enough relative to the industry that it can sell as much output as it wants at the market price, it will never choose to charge a price below the market price. For that reason, economists call perfectly competitive firms *price takers*. The market price is determined solely by the forces of supply and demand, and the individual firm takes that price as a fact of its decision-making life.

The classic example of a firm operating in a perfectly competitive market is a farmer who produces a commodity crop, such as corn or soybeans. Because an individual farmer's output is tiny relative to total production for the entire market, the choice of how much to produce (or whether to produce at all) isn't going to create movements along the industry's demand curve. One farmer's decision to sell part or all of her soybean crop will not affect the price of soybeans. The *combined* effect of many soybean farmers' decisions *will* affect the market price, however, just as everyone in a city simultaneously turning on their faucets will cause water pressure throughout the city to drop. The key is that the city's water pressure won't fluctuate simply because one person decides to take a shower.

Note one important thing: Having a large number of firms in an industry does not automatically mean the industry is perfectly competitive. In the United States, for example, there are over 2,000 firms that sell ready-mixed concrete (the fluid form of concrete delivered to construction sites in the familiar barrel-backed mixer trucks). The output of any one of these firms is small relative to all the concrete sold in a year. Still, these firms are probably not price takers; they choose the prices they charge for their products.

How do these firms differ from soybean farmers? Why are they not price takers, too? Ready-mixed concrete firms have the ability to set their own prices for their output because, despite their small size relative to the overall market, their products are not homogeneous; perhaps most importantly, you can't ship concrete very far because it's heavy and perishable. So, the concrete of a firm in one town can't be substituted easily for that of a firm in another town (or even in some cases, a firm on the other end of the same town). This product differentiation makes the markets for these products noncompetitive and allows the concrete firms to have some market power—that is, to have some ability to set the price at which their product sells. On the other hand, the outputs of perfectly competitive firms are perceived by consumers to be exactly the same and perfect substitutes: a soybean is a soybean is a soybean. The identity of the soybean's producer doesn't matter.

If firms have to meet such strict criteria to be considered perfectly competitive, you might wonder why we devote so much time to understanding their production decisions. After all, if they're so rare in the real world, what's the point? There are several reasons why it's useful to start our study of market behavior with the perfectly competitive market.

First, it is the most straightforward. Because a perfectly competitive firm takes the market price as given, the only decision a firm must worry about to maximize profit is choosing the correct level of output. It doesn't need to think about what price to charge because the market takes care of that.

Second, there are a few perfectly competitive markets, and it's useful to know how they work (maybe you've dreamed of farming soybeans).

Third, there are many markets that are *close* to perfectly competitive. Perfect competition provides a fairly good idea about how these markets work.

Last, perfect competition is an important benchmark against which economists like to measure how efficient other markets are. Perfectly competitive markets are, in a specific sense, the most efficient markets there are (as we see later in this chapter). In competitive markets, goods sell at their marginal costs, firms produce at the minimum cost possible, and the combined producer and consumer surplus can't get any larger. Comparing a market to the outcome under perfect competition is a useful way to measure how efficient a market is.

The Demand Curve as Seen by a Price Taker

A perfectly competitive firm is a price taker. It must sell its output at whatever price is dictated by supply and demand forces in the market as a whole. The small size of each firm relative to the size of the total market also ensures that the perfectly competitive firm can sell as much output as it wants to at the market price.

Let's again think about our egg farmer Ty. The price for a dozen Grade-A large eggs is determined by the market forces of supply and demand. Panel a of Figure 8.1 shows the perfectly competitive market for Grade-A large eggs. Quantity demanded is equal to quantity supplied at the equilibrium market price of $1.25 per dozen.

As a producer in this market, Farmer Ty can sell all the eggs his hens can produce as long as he is willing to sell them at $1.25 per dozen. He can't sell them for more than that price because from a consumer's standpoint, a Grade-A large egg is a Grade-A large egg. If he insisted on charging $1.30 per dozen, consumers will just buy other producers' identical eggs at the market price of $1.25 per dozen, and Ty will end up selling nothing. At the same time, Ty has no incentive to lower his price below $1.25. He can already sell all the eggs he wants to at that price because his hens' output is such a tiny fraction of what is available on the market (you can see this by looking at the quantity axis for Ty's firm: he supplies dozens of eggs, while the market has *millions* of dozens of eggs)—he's not going to drive down the market price by selling a few more (or a few hundred more) dozen eggs.

This means the demand curve Ty (or any other egg farmer like him) faces personally is horizontal—that is, perfectly elastic—at a price of $1.25 (panel b of Figure 8.1). This logic holds for any firm in any perfectly competitive market: *The demand curve facing a firm in a perfectly competitive market is perfectly elastic at the market equilibrium price.*

8.2 Profit Maximization in a Perfectly Competitive Market

profit
The difference between a firm's revenue and its total cost.

We just saw that Ty—and, by extension, any perfectly competitive firm—sells at the price set by the market. Although perfectly competitive firms are price takers, they do have one decision to make: the quantity to supply. Economists usually assume firms choose their actions—like how much output to produce—to maximize profits. **Profit**

Figure 8.1 : Market and Firm Demand in Perfect Competition

(a) In the perfectly competitive market for Grade-A large eggs, farmers supply millions of dozens of eggs at a market price of $1.25 per dozen.

(b) Ty, an individual supplier of dozens of eggs in the market, must sell at the price set by the market. Hence, he faces a perfectly elastic demand curve at the market price of $1.25 per dozen.

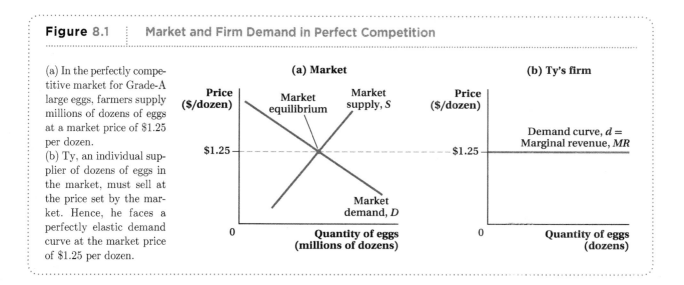

is the difference between a firm's revenue and its total cost. What does it mean to maximize profit? A firm does so by choosing the output level at which the gap between its total revenue and its total cost is largest. In this section, we will see that a perfectly competitive firm maximizes its profit when it produces the quantity of output at which the marginal cost of production equals the market price.

Total Revenue, Total Cost, and Profit Maximization

There are two basic elements to profit: revenue and cost. In general, these are both affected by a firm's decisions about how much output to produce and the price it will charge for its product. Because perfectly competitive firms cannot choose the market price, we only need to focus on the choice of output.

Mathematically, let's denote the profit a firm makes as π. The profit function is total revenue TR minus total cost TC (each of which is determined by the firm's output quantity):

$$\pi = TR - TC$$

To figure out the level of output that maximizes profit, we need to think about what happens to total cost and total revenue if the firm decides to produce one additional unit of output. Or, saying the same thing differently, we need to determine a firm's marginal cost and marginal revenue.

We know from Chapter 7 that marginal cost is the addition to total cost of producing one more unit of output:

$$MC = \Delta TC / \Delta Q$$

Marginal cost is always greater than zero—it takes more inputs to make more output.

Revenues are the other component of profits, and they are equal to a good's price times the quantity produced of the good. A firm's **marginal revenue** is the additional revenue it gets from selling one additional unit of output:

$$MR = \Delta TR / \Delta Q$$

marginal revenue
The additional revenue from selling one additional unit of output.

A perfectly competitive firm's marginal revenue is the market price for the good. To see why, remember that these firms can only sell their goods at the market price P. Therefore, the extra revenue they obtain from selling each additional unit of output is P. This is really important, and so we'll repeat it here: *In a perfectly competitive market, marginal revenue equals the market price; that is, $MR = P$*:

$$MR_{\text{Perfectly competitive}} = \frac{\Delta TR}{\Delta Q} = \frac{\Delta(P \times Q)}{\Delta Q} = P\frac{\Delta Q}{\Delta Q} = P$$

Think about what this outcome implies. Total revenue is $P \times Q$. When a firm is a price taker, P does not change no matter what happens to Q. For a price taker, P is a constant, not a function of Q.

This fact means that a perfectly competitive firm's total revenue is proportional to its output. If output increases by one unit, total revenue increases by the price of the product. For this reason, a perfectly competitive firm's total revenue curve is a straight line from the origin as shown in Figure 8.2. For example, if Ty sells another dozen eggs, his total revenue rises by the market price of $1.25. And if he keeps selling more, each additional dozen increases total revenue by another $1.25.

As we'll see in Chapter 9, in market structures other than perfect competition, price decreases as the quantity produced by a firm increases. This introduces an additional factor into our marginal revenue calculation for firms in those other types of markets. The price reduction doesn't happen in perfectly competitive markets because a firm does not affect the market price with its output choice. *Therefore, this case of marginal revenue equaling the market price is special: It only applies to firms in perfectly competitive markets.*

How a Perfectly Competitive Firm Maximizes Profit

Now that we're clear about marginal cost and marginal revenue, how does our firm maximize profit in a perfectly competitive market? We know that total cost is always going to rise when output increases (as shown in Figure 8.2)—that is, marginal cost is always positive. Similarly, we know that the firm's marginal revenue is constant at all quantities and equal to the good's market price. The key impact of changing output on the firm's profit depends on which of these marginal values is larger. If the market price (marginal revenue) is greater than the marginal cost of making another unit of output, then the firm can increase its profit by making and selling another unit, because revenues will go up more than costs. If the market price is less than the marginal cost,

---

Figure 8.2   Profit Maximization for a Perfectly Competitive Firm

Because a perfectly competitive firm faces a constant market price, its total revenue curve is a straight line from the origin with a slope equal to the marginal revenue, or the price. At the quantity Q^*, the slope of the total revenue curve (price) equals the slope of the total cost curve (marginal cost), and the firm is maximizing profit.

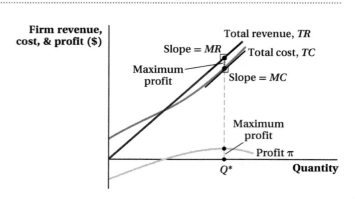

the firm should not make the extra unit. The firm will reduce its profit by doing so because while its revenues will rise, they won't rise as much as its costs. The quantity at which the opposing effects of marginal revenue and cost are balanced—that is, where the marginal revenue (price) from selling one more unit of output just equals the marginal cost of making another unit of output—is the point at which a firm maximizes its profit. This point occurs at Q^* in Figure 8.2. There, the slope of the total revenue curve (the marginal revenue—here, the market price) equals the slope of the total cost curve (the marginal cost at Q^*). In mathematical terms, the profit-maximizing level of output occurs where marginal revenue (here: price) equals marginal cost:

$$\frac{\Delta TR}{\Delta Q} = \frac{\Delta TC}{\Delta Q}$$

$$MR = P = MC$$

A firm should increase production as long as revenue increases by more than cost (i.e., when $MR = P > MC$). Conversely, a firm should decrease production if cost increases by more than revenue (i.e., when $MR = P < MC$).[1]

It should be clear from this discussion why cost plays such an important role in determining a firm's output (and this is true for a firm in any type of market structure): It is half of the firm's profit-maximization story. As cost changes, so does the firm's profit-maximizing output. In the next several chapters (which examine firms that are not perfectly competitive), we will learn how the firm's profit maximization is affected by the relationship between price and marginal revenue.

The analysis we've just completed shows that the output decision is fairly easy for the firm in a perfectly competitive market: It increases output until marginal cost is equal to the market price. If marginal cost rises with output—and we talked in Chapter 7 about the reasons why we might expect this—there will be a certain output level at which marginal cost rises to the market price. This is the profit-maximizing output level of a firm in perfect competition.

The $P = MC$ result is extremely useful because, by linking the market price to the firm's cost curve (or, more precisely, its marginal cost curve), we can determine how a competitive firm's output changes when the market price changes. Consider a firm with the marginal cost curve shown in Figure 8.3. If the market price is initially P_1,

---

Figure 8.3   Profit Maximization for a Perfectly Competitive Firm Occurs Where $MR = P = MC$

At the initial market price P_1, the perfectly competitive firm is maximizing profit at Q_1^*, where $P = MC$. If price increases to P_2, the firm should increase output to Q_2^*. If, instead, price decreases to P_3, the firm is maximizing profit at Q_3^*.

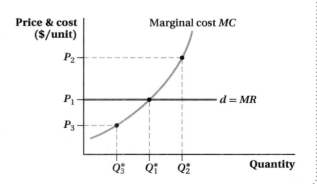

---

[1] Technically, we have to be a bit careful and say that $MR = P = MC$ implies profit maximization as long as marginal cost is rising at the quantity where that condition holds. If there were big economies of scale so that MC falls as output rises, the firm could make more profit by expanding output further.

then the firm's demand and marginal revenue curve is horizontal at that price. The firm will maximize profit by setting $MR = P_1 = MC$ and producing an output of Q_1^*. If the market price increases to P_2, the firm should increase its production to output Q_2^*. Why? Because the firm now faces a horizontal demand and marginal revenue curve at P_2, it should produce up to the point where marginal cost equals the market price. If price rises to P_2 and the firm continues to produce only Q_1, it could be selling those units between Q_1 and Q_2^* at a marginal revenue level (the new market price P_2) that is higher than its marginal costs. These extra sales would raise the firm's profit.

If the market price instead decreases from P_1 to P_3, the firm should reduce its quantity to Q_3^*, which has a lower marginal cost equal to P_3. If the firm does not make this change, it will be producing those units between Q_3^* and Q_1 at a loss because marginal revenue for those units would be lower than marginal cost.

 application

Do Firms Always Maximize Profits?

You've probably heard numerous stories of CEOs who spend firm money on lavish offices, parties, or other perks. Former Tyco CEO Dennis Kozlowski, for example, became famous for his extravagant profit-draining actions. He used $2 million of Tyco's money to throw his wife a birthday party in Italy and allegedly purchased a $6,000 shower curtain for his home. Kozlowski may have enjoyed his spending spree, but it certainly didn't benefit Tyco or its owners.

Given such stories, can we really assume that firms maximize profits? It is easiest to see why a small firm would want to maximize profits: Because the manager is usually the owner of the firm, maximizing the firm's profits directly affects her personally. But larger firms are typically run by people other than the owners. As a result, their managers may be tempted to engage in behavior that does not maximize profits. These profit-killing actions don't have to be as blatant as Kozlowski's. They can be subtle. A manager might want to raise short-run profit if her compensation package is based on it, at the expense of reductions in future profit. These missed profits could be recognized only after the manager has left the company—or never missed at all, because it can be difficult to tell what profits *should be*. Or, managers might undertake mergers and acquisitions that grow management's power but that cost the acquiring firm (and its shareholders) more than the acquisition is worth.

Although managers may sometimes take actions that aren't profit-maximizing, there are mechanisms in place to minimize the impact of such actions. These include boards of directors strong enough to confront management on the behalf of the shareholders, activist shareholders, a nosy financial press, and even the occasional academic economist, who takes it upon herself to look over the shoulders of firms' managers and scrutinize their behavior. These forces tend to push wayward managers back toward maximizing profits, as shareholders (the owners of the capital) would desire.

Perhaps more importantly, the competitive market itself pushes firms to maximize profit. Firms that maximize profits (or get as close to that as possible) will succeed where firms with profit-killing managers do not. Firms that maximize profits will attract additional capital more easily, have more money to invest, and take market share away from firms that fail to maximize profits. Firms that consistently fail to maximize profits will eventually be driven out of business by more profitable competitors.

If you're still unsure about the assumption of profit maximization, consider visiting Kozlowski at the Mid-State Correctional Facility in New York. As soon as Tyco's owners realized he wasn't maximizing profits, they took quick action. In 2005, Kozlowski was tried and convicted of grand larceny and conspiracy, falsifying business records, and violating business law. He'd probably be the first to tell you that owners go to great lengths to ensure that firms are profit-maximizing. ■

Measuring a Firm's Profit

We've seen that a profit-maximizing firm in a perfectly competitive industry maximizes its profit by producing the quantity at which $P = MC$. But this doesn't tell us anything about the level of profit the firm is earning (or even if it is positive) at this point. To measure profit π, we subtract total cost (TC) from total revenue (TR):

$$\pi = TR - TC$$

Panel a of Figure 8.4 shows the firm's average total cost curve, its marginal cost curve, and its demand (marginal revenue) curve. The firm's total revenue equals the area of the rectangle with height P and base Q^*. Its total cost is the area of the rectangle with height ATC^* (ATC at the profit-maximizing level of output Q^*) and base Q^*. Because total revenue is greater than total cost at Q^*, the firm is earning a positive level of profit. Substituting the equations for TR and TC into the equation for profit, we see that

$$\pi = TR - TC$$
$$= (P \times Q) - (ATC \times Q)$$
$$= (P - ATC) \times Q$$

Therefore, the firm's profit can be seen in Figure 8.4 as the rectangle with height $(P - ATC^*)$ and base equal to the profit-maximizing quantity Q^*.

The profit equation tells us that profit $\pi = (P - ATC) \times Q$, and profit is positive only when $P > ATC^*$. If $P = ATC^*$, profit is zero, and when $P < ATC^*$, profit is negative. These scenarios are shown in panels b and c of Figure 8.4. Panel b shows that a firm earns zero profit when $P = ATC^* = MC$. In Chapter 7, we learned that $MC = ATC$ only when ATC is at its minimum. (Remember this fact! It will become very important to us toward the end of this chapter.) Panel c of Figure 8.4 shows a firm earning a negative profit because $P < ATC^*$. The obvious question is, why would a firm produce anything at a loss? We answer that question in the next section.

Figure 8.4   Measuring Profit

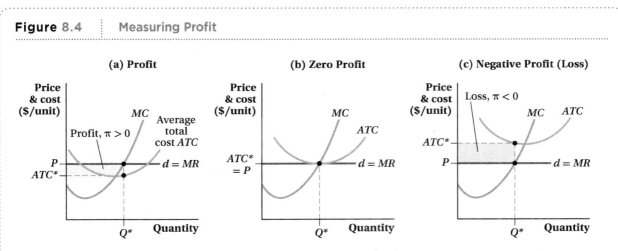

Given a firm's marginal cost curve MC, average total cost curve ATC, and market price P, the firm's profit can be measured by the area of the rectangle with length Q^* and height $(P - ATC^*)$.
(a) A firm facing a market price above its average total cost curve at Q^* will earn a positive economic profit, $\pi > 0$.
(b) A firm facing a market price equal to its average total cost at Q^* earns zero economic profit.
(c) A firm with average total cost above the market price, at Q^*, will earn negative economic profit (loss), $\pi < 0$.

8.1 figure it out

Suppose that consumers see haircuts as an undifferentiated good and that there are hundreds of barbershops in the market. The current market equilibrium price of a haircut is $15. Bob's Barbershop has a daily short-run total cost given by $TC = 0.5Q^2$. The associated marginal cost curve is $MC = Q$.

a. How many haircuts should Bob give each day if he wants to maximize profit?

b. If the firm maximizes profit, how much profit will it earn each day?

Solution:

a. Firms in perfect competition maximize profit by producing the quantity for which $P = MC$:

$$P = MC$$
$$15 = Q$$

b. If Bob gives 15 haircuts and charges $15 for each, the total revenue will be

$$TR = P \times Q$$
$$= \$15 \times 15 = \$225$$

We can use the firm's total cost function to find the total cost of producing 15 haircuts:

$$TC = 0.5Q^2 = 0.5(15)^2 = \$112.50$$

Since profit is $TR - TC$,

$$\pi = \$225 - \$112.50 = \$112.50 \text{ per day}$$

If Profit Is Negative, Should a Firm Shut Down? How does a perfectly competitive firm know if it is better off operating at a loss or shutting down and producing zero output? (Remember that shutting down in the short run is not the same thing as exiting the industry, because firms have some fixed costs they still must pay if they shut down in the short run.) The answer depends on the firm's costs and revenues under each scenario (continue to operate at a loss or shut down). Table 8.2 shows the information the firm needs to make its decision.

If the firm decides to shut down in the short run and produce nothing, it will have no revenue. Because it still must pay its fixed cost, we know that the firm's loss will exactly equal its fixed cost:

$$\pi_{\text{shut down}} = TR - TC = TR - (FC + VC)$$
$$= 0 - (FC + 0) = -FC$$

If the firm continues to operate at a loss in the short run, it will accumulate some revenue, but will have to pay both fixed and variable costs. The profit from operating is the difference between total revenue and fixed and variable costs:

$$\pi_{\text{operate}} = TR - TC = TR - FC - VC$$

What is the difference between these two scenarios? If you said, "revenue and variable cost," you are correct:

$$\pi_{\text{operate}} - \pi_{\text{shut down}} = TR - FC - VC - (-FC)$$
$$= TR - VC$$

Therefore, in the short-run a firm should operate as long as its revenue is greater than or equal to its *variable* cost, not its total cost ($TR \geq VC$). That's because fixed cost needs to be paid whether the plant operates or not, so it doesn't enter into the operate/shut-down decision. Making enough revenue to cover the firm's variable cost is sufficient to justify operating in the short run, even if

Table 8.2	Deciding Whether to Operate at a Loss or Shut Down in the Short Run	
	Shut Down	**Operate**
Revenue	None	Some (*TR*)
Cost	Fixed (*FC*)	Fixed (*FC*) + Variable (*VC*)
Loss	−*FC*	*TR* − *FC* − *VC*

Figure 8.5 | **Deciding Whether to Operate or Shut Down in the Short Run**

At market price P, the firm earns a negative economic profit equal to the area of the rectangle with length Q^* and height $(P - ATC^*)$. Because price is above the firm's average variable cost AVC^* at the profit-maximizing quantity Q^*, however, the firm will continue to operate in the short run. That is because in doing so the firm can at least cover its variable cost.

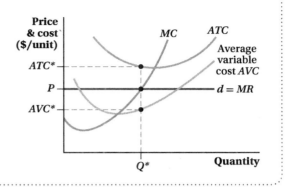

---

the firm can't cover all of its fixed cost. However, if the firm has total revenue that is lower than its variable cost $(TR < VC)$, the firm should shut down. It can't cover its variable cost at this point and loses money on every unit it sells. The operate-or-shut-down decision can be summed up as follows:

$$\text{Operate if } TR \geq VC.$$

$$\text{Shut down if } TR < VC.$$

Figure 8.5 illustrates these rules. It shows a perfectly competitive firm's average total cost, average variable cost, marginal cost, and marginal revenue (market price) curves. In the case shown in the figure, the firm is losing money because $TR < TC$, but it continues to operate because $TR > VC$. How can we tell this from the figure? We know that TR is the area of a rectangle where P is the height and Q^* is the base $(TR = P \times Q)$, and VC is the rectangle with height AVC^* (AVC at Q^*) and base Q^* $(VC = AVC \times Q)$. Both TR and AVC contain Q^*, so this quantity cancels out and plays no role in the operate/shut-down decision. We can now rewrite our rules from above in terms of the market price P facing the firm and its average variable cost AVC^* at the profit-maximizing (or in this case loss-minimizing) quantity:

$$\text{Operate if } P \geq AVC^*.$$

$$\text{Shut down if } P < AVC^*.$$

Therefore, the firm should keep operating as long as the market price is at least as large as its average variable cost at the quantity where price equals its marginal cost. Keep in mind that these rules apply to all firms in all industries in any type of market structure.

8.2 figure it out

Cardboard boxes are produced in a perfectly competitive market. Each identical firm has a short-run total cost curve of $TC = 3Q^3 - 18Q^2 + 30Q + 50$, where Q is measured in thousands of boxes per week. The firm's associated marginal cost curve is $MC = 9Q^2 - 36Q + 30$. Calculate the price below which a firm in the market will not produce any output in the short run (the shut-down price).

Solution:

A firm will not produce any output in the short run at any price below its minimum AVC. How do we find the minimum AVC? We learned in Chapter 7 that AVC is minimized when $AVC = MC$. So, we need to start by figuring out the equation for the average variable cost curve and then solving it for the output that minimizes AVC.

AVC is equal to VC/Q. Remember that total cost is the sum of fixed cost and variable cost:

$$TC = FC + VC$$

Fixed cost is that part of total cost that does not vary with output (changes in Q have no effect on FC). Therefore, if $TC = 3Q^3 - 18Q^2 + 30Q + 50$, then FC must be 50. This means that $VC = 3Q^3 - 18Q^2 + 30Q$. Because $AVC = VC/Q$,

$$AVC = VC/Q = \frac{3Q^3 - 18Q^2 + 30Q}{Q} = 3Q^2 - 18Q + 30$$

Next, we find the output for which AVC is at its minimum by equating AVC and MC:

$$AVC = MC$$
$$3Q^2 - 18Q + 30 = 9Q^2 - 36Q + 30$$
$$18Q = 6Q^2$$
$$18 = 6Q$$
$$Q = 3$$

This means that AVC is at its minimum at an output of 3,000 cardboard boxes per week. To find the level of AVC at this output, we plug $Q = 3$ into the formula for AVC:

$$AVC = 3Q^2 - 18Q + 30$$
$$= 3(3)^2 - 18(3) + 30 = 27 - 54 + 30 = \$3$$

Therefore, the minimum price at which the firm should operate is \$3. If the price falls below \$3, the firm should shut down in the short run and only pay its fixed cost.

make the grade

A tale of three curves

One of the easiest ways to examine the diagrams of cost curves for a perfectly competitive firm is to remember that each of these cost curves tells only a part of the story.

What is the profit-maximizing output? The marginal cost curve: If you want to know the level of output that maximizes profit for any firm, you need to use the firm's marginal cost curve and equate marginal revenue and marginal cost. For a perfectly competitive firm *only,* you equate price and marginal cost because in perfect competition, marginal revenue is equal to price.

Is the firm earning a positive profit? The average total cost curve: Once you know the optimal level of output, you can use the average total cost curve to compare price and average total cost to determine whether a firm is earning a positive profit. Profit is measured as the rectangle with a base equal to output and a height equal to the difference between *P* and *ATC* at that quan-tity of output. If a perfectly competitive firm is earning a positive profit, the story ends there. You don't even need to consider the firm's average variable cost curve.

Operate or shut down? The average variable cost curve: If a firm is earning a loss (negative profit) because its price is less than its average total cost, the decision of whether or not the firm should continue to operate in the short run depends entirely on the relationship between price and average variable cost. Look at the average variable cost curve to determine how these two variables compare at the profit-maximizing/loss-minimizing level of output. If price is greater, the firm should continue to operate; if average variable cost is greater, the firm should shut down.

Knowing which curve is used to answer these questions makes it easier to analyze complicated diagrams and answer questions for homework, quizzes, and exams. Remember that each curve has its own role and focus on that curve to simplify your analysis.

8.3 Perfect Competition in the Short Run

We've just learned that a perfectly competitive firm maximizes its profit where $MR = P = MC$, and that the firm will operate in the short run (even at an economic loss) as long as price is greater than or equal to average variable cost. We can now take our analysis one step further and derive the short-run supply curve for a perfectly competitive firm.

A Firm's Short-Run Supply Curve in a Perfectly Competitive Market

Because the supply curve shows the quantity supplied at any price, and the firm chooses to produce where $P = MC$, the short-run marginal cost curve must be the firm's short-run supply curve. There is one caveat: Only the portion of the marginal cost curve above the minimum average variable cost will be on the firm's supply curve. Why? Because at any price below the minimum average variable cost, the firm would shut down and its quantity supplied would be zero.

Figure 8.6 shows that the firm's short-run supply curve is the portion of its marginal cost curve MC that is at or above its average variable cost AVC, including the portion that is below its average total cost ATC. For prices below AVC, supply is zero, as shown in the figure. Keep in mind that we hold everything else constant except price and output when deriving the firm's supply curve.

Because of this relationship between marginal cost and the firm's short-run supply curve, anything that changes marginal cost will shift supply. As you may recall from Chapter 7, factors that shift the marginal cost curve include changes in input prices and technology. Fixed cost, on the other hand, does not affect a firm's marginal cost, and therefore changes in fixed cost do not shift the short-run supply curve. In the long run, as we know, no costs are fixed. Later in the chapter, we talk about how firms' long-run behavior in perfectly competitive markets differs from their short-run behavior.

Figure 8.6   The Perfectly Competitive Firm's Short-Run Supply Curve

Because a firm will only operate in the short run when the market price is above its average variable cost curve AVC, the perfectly competitive firm's short-run supply curve is the portion of the marginal cost curve MC above AVC. At prices below AVC, the firm shuts down, its quantity supplied is 0, and its supply curve is represented by the y-axis.

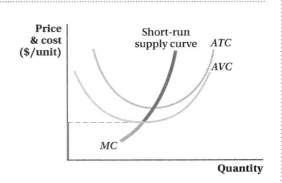

🧩 application

The Supply Curve of a Power Plant

In 2008 economists Ali Hortaçsu and Steven Puller published a detailed study of the Texas electricity industry.[2] Using data from this study, we can construct the supply curve for a single firm (Figure 8.7). This, along with the supply curves of the other firms in the industry, is a building block in the industry supply curve that we construct later in the chapter.

The first and most important step in deriving the firm's supply curve is to determine its marginal cost curve. In the electric power generation industry, marginal cost reflects the firm's cost of producing one more megawatt of electricity for another hour (this amount of energy, called a *megawatt-hour* [MWh], would power about 1,000 homes for an hour). This marginal cost comes from the firm's variable cost of running its generators at its various power plants—this includes the labor cost of operating and maintaining generators, the cost of environmental permits, and, most importantly, the cost of fuel.

Our firm has three power plants. Plant A uses coal to power its generator and has a capacity of 200 megawatts (MW); Plants B and C use natural gas and each has a capacity of 25 MW. Coal generators are generally cheaper to run than natural gas generators.

The marginal cost of running Plant A's coal generator is $18 per MWh and it is constant across the plant's production quantity up to 200 MW. The plant cannot produce quantities above this level, so the *plant's* marginal cost is, in effect, infinite at quantities greater than 200 MW. Plant B's natural-gas-fired generator has a constant marginal cost of $37 per MWh (up to its 25-MW capacity), and Plant C's natural gas generator has the highest constant marginal cost of $39 per MWh (up to its 25-MW capacity).

If the firm is generating 200 MW or less, only Plant A (its coal plant) will be on line (i.e., producing electricity), because that's the lowest-cost way of generating that quantity. Thus, the firm's marginal cost curve is flat at $18 per MWh for quantities from 0 to 200 MWh, as shown in Figure 8.7.

To generate quantities above 200 MWh, the firm has to use at least one of its other generators. If it wants to produce a quantity between 200 and 225 MWh, it only needs to run one of its natural gas plants, and it will put Plant B on line, the one with the smaller marginal cost of the two, $37 per MWh. Therefore at a quantity of 200 MWh, the firm's marginal cost curve jumps up to $37 per MWh. It stays at this level up to the quantity

Figure 8.7   The Marginal Cost Curve for an Electricity Firm (Firm 1)

A firm in the Texas electricity industry faces a stepwise marginal cost curve. When this firm supplies 200 MW or less, only its coal plant, Plant A, is on line, and its marginal cost is horizontal at $18 per MWh. At output quantities greater than 200 MW, the firm will also run its natural gas plants, Plants B and C, at marginal costs of $37 per MWh and $39 per MWh, respectively.

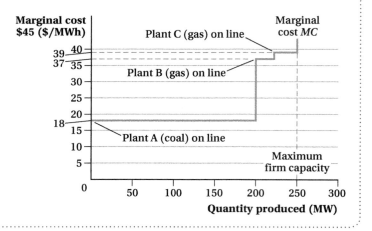

[2] Ali Hortaçsu and Steven Puller, "Understanding Strategic Bidding in Multi-Unit Auctions: A Case Study of the Texas Electricity Spot Market," *RAND Journal of Economics* 39, no. 1 (2008): 86–114.

of 225 MWh. To produce a quantity above 225 MWh, it needs to put Plant C on line, its natural gas generator with the $39 marginal cost, so the marginal cost curve jumps up to $39 per MWh. The firm's marginal cost remains at $39 per MWh up to the quantity of 250 MWh. At this point, the firm has exhausted its generating capacity and cannot produce any more electricity. Above 250 MWh, the firm's marginal costs effectively become infinite. Figure 8.7 reflects this as a vertical line extending off the graph at 250 MWh.

The portion of this marginal cost curve at or above the firm's average variable cost is its supply curve. We saw in Chapter 7 that a firm's total variable cost at any quantity is the sum of its marginal cost of producing each unit up to and including that quantity. Therefore, the firm's total variable cost of producing its first megawatt-hour is $18, and its average variable cost of producing that quantity is $18 per MWh. Its total variable cost of producing 2 megawatt-hours is $36, so its average variable cost is $36/2 = $18 per MWh. It's clear, therefore, that the average variable cost will be $18 per MWh at quantities up to 200 MWh. In other words, the marginal cost curve *is* the average variable cost curve up to that quantity. When marginal cost rises to $37 per MWh for the 201st megawatt-hour the firm produces, the *total* variable cost rises by $37 for 201 MWh, but the average variable cost only rises to ($18 × 200 MWh + $37)/201 MWh = $18.09 per MWh. By this logic, the firm's marginal cost curve will always be above its average variable cost curve at all quantities above 200 MWh. So, for this firm at least, its entire marginal cost curve is its supply curve. ∎

The Short-Run Supply Curve for a Perfectly Competitive Industry

We know that an individual firm in a perfectly competitive market cannot affect the price it receives for its output by changing the level of its output. What *does* determine the price in a perfectly competitive market? The *combined* output decisions of all the firms in the market: the industry supply curve. In this section, we look at how this combined output response is determined.

Before we begin, we must clarify what we mean by firms' "combined" decisions. What we do *not* mean is "coordinated." Firms in a perfectly competitive market do not gather at an annual convention to determine their output levels for the year, or have an industry newsletter or website that serves the same function. (Such a practice would typically get a firm's executives indicted for price fixing, in fact.) "Combined" here instead means aggregated—the total of all the individual firms' independent output decisions added together. An industry supply curve, then, indicates how much total output an industry supplies at any particular price.

It's easy to see how you can add up firms' short-run supply curves in an example. We assume that firms' combined output responses do not have any notable impact on *input* prices, so the industry short-run supply curve is the sum of firm-level short-run supply curves. Let's suppose that there are 100 firms in a perfectly competitive industry, each with the same short-run supply curve. Below a market price of $1 per unit, the firms do not operate because this is less than their average variable costs. For prices greater than or equal to $1 and less than $2, each firm supplies one unit of output. At any price equal to or above $2, each firm produces two units of output, but no more because of capacity limitations. (This is a ridiculously contrived example, but it keeps things simple enough so that we can concentrate on the concepts rather than the arithmetic.)

To derive the industry short-run supply curve from these firm supply curves, we add up the individual firm outputs at each possible market price. At prices below $1, the industry supplies no output, again because none of its firms can cover its average variable cost at those prices. When the price is between $1 and $2, the industry produces 100 units of output—1 unit from each of the 100 firms. When the price is at $2 or above, the industry quantity supplied is 200 units because each firm now makes 2 units. Therefore, the short-run supply curve for this industry is 0 units for prices below $1, 100 units for prices at or above $1 but below $2, and 200 units for prices $2 and higher.

The Short-Run Supply Curve: A Graphical Approach If we use a graphical approach to the short-run industry supply curve, the firms' supply curves would look as they do on the left-hand side of Figure 8.8. There, we've drawn the short-run supply curve that each of the industry's 100 firms share. To build the industry short-run supply curve, we horizontally add the firm's short-run supply curves: At any given price, we find the individual firms' outputs, add them up, and plot their sum to get the industry quantity supplied. These values yield the industry short-run supply curve on the right-hand side of the figure. Note how individual firms' supply curves are added up horizontally, not vertically, to obtain the industry supply curve, just as individual consumers' demand curves were horizontally added to obtain the market demand curve in Chapter 5.

In Figure 8.8, all industry firms have the same short-run supply curves (this is equivalent to saying they have the same cost curves). The analysis gets more complicated if firms in a perfectly competitive industry have different costs. In this case, the process for determining the industry supply curve is the same (we add up the supply curves of the individual firms), but there are additional ways in which the supply curves of individual firms can affect the shape of the industry supply curve.

To illustrate this point, let's now suppose that the industry (which still has 100 firms) has 50 firms with supply curves like those in Figure 8.8 and another 50 that have different supply curves. Let's say these other firms have higher costs and therefore will not produce any output at a market price less than \$2. For prices greater than or equal to \$2 and less than \$3, they produce 1 unit of output, and at prices at or above \$3, they produce 2 units. Now the industry supply curve is 0 units for prices under \$1, because no firms can profitably produce below that price. For prices from \$1 to just under \$2, industry supply is 50 units; only the 50 low-cost firms can operate at these prices, and they produce 1 unit each. At prices at or above \$2 and less than \$3, the industry supplies 150 units: 100 units (50 firms times 2 units each) for the low-cost firms, and 1 unit for each of the 50 high-cost firms. At prices greater than or equal to \$3, supply is 200 units, because all firms now produce 2 units of output.

In general, the industry supply curve is the horizontal sum of the supply curves of the individual firms within it. The examples above use very simple "step-type" firm-level supply curves, but conceptually there is little difference if the supply curves are

---

Figure 8.8 | Deriving the Short-Run Industry Supply Curve When Firms Have the Same Costs

Supply$_{\text{Firm}}$ is the short-run supply curve of each firm in an industry with 100 firms. The short-run industry supply curve, Supply$_{\text{Industry}}$, is the horizontal sum of the individual firms' supply curves.

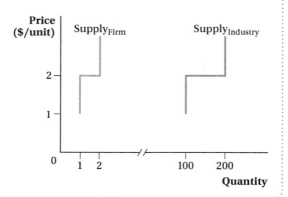

Figure 8.9 : Short-Run Industry Supply Curve When Firms Have Different Costs

In a four-firm industry, in which each firm faces different costs, these cost differences are reflected in their individual supply curves ($S_{\text{Firm A}}$, $S_{\text{Firm B}}$, $S_{\text{Firm C}}$, and $S_{\text{Firm D}}$). The industry supply curve, S_{Industry}, is the horizontal sum of the four individual firms' supply curves. At prices between P_1 and P_2, only Firms A and B produce; at price P_2, Firm C also supplies its product on the market; and at price P_3, all four firms supply positive quantities.

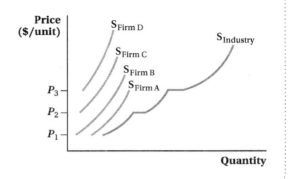

the more standard type that we're accustomed to. The firms' supply curves would look something like what we've drawn on the left-hand side of Figure 8.9. We're assuming there are four firms in the industry, with Firm A having the lowest costs, Firm B the next lowest, and so on. Again, the industry supply curve is the horizontal sum of the firms' supply curves. Only at prices above P_1 does any firm produce, so the industry supplies positive quantities only at price P_1 or higher. For prices between P_1 and P_2, the industry supply curve is the sum of Firm A and Firm B's supply curves. At P_2, Firm C starts producing. The industry supply curve shifts right by the quantity that C produces at P_2 when this happens, and Firm C's supply is also added to the industry supply curve above this price. Finally, Firm D starts producing at P_3, and again the industry supply curve shifts horizontally as this output is added.

These examples make an interesting point: Industry output increases as price increases for two reasons. One is that individual firms' supply curves are often upward-sloping—an individual firm will tend to produce more as the market price rises. The other comes from the fact that some firms might have higher costs than others, so they only begin operating at higher price levels.

 application

The Short-Run Supply of Crude Oil

U.S. politicians are constantly calling for the country to reduce its dependence on oil from the Middle East. About 25% of the oil the United States consumes comes from OPEC (the Organization of Petroleum Exporting Countries), and just under half of that (10% of U.S. consumption) is supplied by Middle Eastern countries who are members of OPEC. Many politicians take this to mean that reducing the country's dependence on Middle Eastern oil is simple: Cut consumption by 10%, and that will effectively eliminate imports from the Middle East. This will also increase the share of imported oil that comes from "friendlier" nations, such as Canada.

This type of logic ignores what we know about how perfectly competitive firms make production decisions. We've seen that a competitive firm's short-run supply curve is the portion of its marginal cost curve above its minimum average variable cost curve. If the market price dips below the price at the intersection between the marginal cost and average variable cost curves, then the firm will shut down in the short run.

While the crude oil market is not perfectly competitive, the same relationship between price and average variable cost holds for all firms. If we reduce our consumption of oil, the countries that will be hurt by a decrease in demand and the price drop that accompanies it will be those with the highest costs—those countries for which the market price falls below their average variable costs first. Where are oil production costs higher, the Middle East or Canada? You guessed it: Canada. Saudi Arabia can extract and process oil at an average variable cost of only a couple of dollars per barrel, but producers tapping the Canadian oil sands face much higher average variable costs, greater than $30 per barrel. If the United States reduces its oil consumption, we will reduce the oil we consume from Canada before we reduce oil consumed from Saudi Arabia.[3]

This outcome has been borne out historically. Today with oil prices at relatively high levels, the United States actually imports more oil from Canada than it does from the Middle East. In the late 1990s, on the other hand, when crude oil prices were at historic lows, only about 7% of U.S. oil consumption came from Canadian imports, while about 15% of consumption was imported from the Middle East. Thus, if we want to reduce our dependence on the Middle East, cutting back consumption a bit isn't the answer. ■

Producer Surplus for a Competitive Firm

The intersection of the short-run industry supply curve and the market demand curve determines the market equilibrium price. Each perfectly competitive firm then takes this price as given and chooses the quantity of output at which it maximizes profit (and chooses whether to operate at all). We showed how we can measure a firm's short-run profit earlier. Equally important is producer surplus, which we first learned about in Chapter 3. Remember that producer surplus is the vertical difference between the market price and the supply curve, which we now know reflects firms' marginal costs.

At all but the lowest market price levels, firms will sell some units of output at a price above their marginal cost of production. In the Application on Texas electricity generation, for example, if the market price is at or above $37 per MWh, the firm would be able to sell the electricity generated by its coal plant at a marginal cost of $18 per MWh at a considerably higher price.

We can see this in a more general case in Figure 8.10, which shows the production decision of a particular firm. Profit maximization implies the firm will produce Q^*, the quantity where the firm's marginal cost equals the market price P. Notice that for all units the firm produces before Q^*, the firm's marginal cost of producing them is lower than the market price. The firm earns a markup for each of these units.

If we add up all these price-marginal cost markups across every unit of output the firm makes, we get the firm's producer surplus. This is equal to the shaded area in panel a of Figure 8.10. (If this isn't obvious to you, imagine slicing the shaded area into many tiny vertical slices, one for each unit of output. Each slice equals the difference between price and marginal cost for that unit of output. If we add up all the slices—i.e., sum the price-cost gaps for all the units of output—we get the firm's producer surplus.)

There's another way to compute producer surplus. First, remember from Chapter 7 that marginal cost involves only variable cost, not fixed cost. If we add up the firm's

---

[3] Austan Goolsbee, "Refined Thought: Dependency Paradox," *Fortune*, August 22, 2005. http://money.cnn.com/magazines/fortune/fortune_archive/2005/08/22/8270013/index.htm.

Figure 8.10   Producer Surplus for a Firm in Perfect Competition

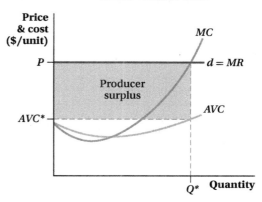

(a) Producer Surplus: Adding All of the Price-Marginal Cost Markups

(b) Producer Surplus: Total Revenue Minus Variable Costs

(a) At market price, a perfectly competitive firm produces Q^*. For each unit the firm produces below Q^*, the marginal cost MC is less than the market price, and the firm earns a producer surplus on that unit. As a result, total producer surplus is equal to the area below the demand curve and above MC.

(b) Producer surplus can also be calculated by a firm's total revenue minus its variable cost. A firm's total revenue is the entire rectangle with height P and length Q^*, and its variable cost is the rectangle with height AVC^* and length Q^*. Its producer surplus, therefore, is the area of the rectangle with height $(P - AVC^*)$ and length Q^*.

marginal cost for all the units of output it produces, we have its variable cost. And if we add up the firm's revenue for every unit of output it produces, we have its total revenue. That means the firm's total revenue minus its variable cost equals the sum of the price-marginal cost markups it earns on every unit it sells—that is, its producer surplus:

$$PS = TR - VC$$

In panel b of Figure 8.10, the firm's total revenue is the area of the rectangle with a height of P and a base of Q^*. Variable cost is output multiplied by average variable cost, so the firm's variable cost is the area of the rectangle with a base of Q^* and a height of AVC^* (AVC at the profit-maximizing level of output). The difference between these two areas is the shaded rectangle with base Q^* and height $(P - AVC^*)$. The area of this rectangle also equals the firm's producer surplus.

Producer Surplus and Profit

You're probably not going to be surprised when we tell you that producer surplus is closely related to profit. But it's really important to recognize that producer surplus is *not* the same thing as profit. The difference is that producer surplus includes no fixed costs, while profit does. In mathematical terms, $PS = TR - VC$ and $\pi = TR - VC - FC$.

A new firm may operate with profit less than zero. It will never operate with producer surplus less than zero because that means each unit is costing more to produce than it sells for, even without fixed costs.

Producer Surplus for a Competitive Industry

Producer surplus for an entire industry is the same idea as producer surplus for a firm. It is the area below the market price but above the short-run supply curve—now, however, it is the industry supply curve rather than the firm's (Figure 8.11). This surplus reflects the industry's gain from producing units at a lower cost than the price at which they are sold.

Figure 8.11 | **Industry Producer Surplus**

An industry's producer surplus is the entire industry's surplus from producing units at a lower cost than the market price. This is represented by the shaded triangle above the industry supply curve and below the market price P.

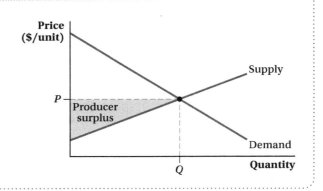

8.3 figure it out

Assume that the pickle industry is perfectly competitive and has 150 producers. One hundred of these producers are "high-cost" producers, each with a short-run supply curve given by $Q_{hc} = 4P$. Fifty of these producers are "low-cost" producers, with a short-run supply curve given by $Q_{lc} = 6P$. Quantities are measured in jars and prices are dollars per jar.

a. Derive the short-run industry supply curve for pickles.

b. If the market demand curve for jars of pickles is given by $Q^d = 6,000 - 300P$, what are the market equilibrium price and quantity of pickles?

c. At the price you found in part (b), how many pickles does each high-cost firm produce? Each low-cost firm?

d. At the price you found in part (b), determine the industry producer surplus.

Solution:

a. To derive the industry short-run supply curve, we need to sum each of the firm short-run supply curves horizontally. In other words, we need to add each firm's quantity supplied at each price. Since there are 100 high-cost firms with identical supply curves, we can sum them simply by multiplying the firm supply curve by 100:

$$Q_{HC} = 100Q_{hc} = 100(4P) = 400P$$

Similarly, we can get the supply of the 50 low-cost firms by summing their individual supply curves or by multiplying the curve of one firm by 50 (since these 50 firms are assumed to have identical supply curves):

$$Q_{LC} = 50Q_{lc} = 50(6P) = 300P$$

The short-run industry supply curve is the sum of the supply by high-cost producers and the supply of low-cost producers:

$$Q^S = Q_{HC} + Q_{LC} = 400P + 300P = 700P$$

b. Market equilibrium occurs where quantity demanded is equal to quantity supplied:

$$Q^D = Q^S$$
$$6,000 - 300P = 700P$$
$$1,000P = 6,000$$
$$P = \$6$$

The equilibrium quantity can be found by substituting $P = \$6$ into either the market demand or supply equation:

$$Q^D = 6{,}000 - 300P \qquad\qquad Q^S = 700P$$
$$ = 6{,}000 - 300(6) \qquad\qquad = 700(6)$$
$$ = 4{,}200 \text{ jars} \qquad\qquad = 4{,}200 \text{ jars}$$

c. At a price of $6, each high-cost producer will produce $Q_{hc} = 4P = 4(6) = 24$, while each low-cost producer will produce $Q_{lc} = 6P = 6(6) = 36$ jars.

d. The easiest way to calculate industry producer surplus is to graph the industry supply curve. Producer surplus is the area below the market price but above the short-run industry supply curve. In the figure to the right, this is the triangle with a base of 4,200 (the equilibrium quantity at a price of $6) and a height of $6:

$$PS = \frac{1}{2} \times \text{base} \times \text{height} = (0.5)(4{,}200)(\$6) = \$12{,}600$$

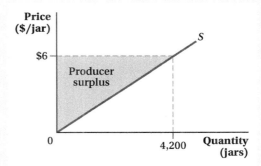

 ## application

Short-Run Industry Supply and Producer Surplus in Electricity Generation

Let's suppose that Firm 1 from the Application on the Texas electricity industry earlier in this section is in an industry with two other firms. (In reality, the Texas electricity industry comprises many firms, but we have chosen three to make it less complicated.) Like Firm 1, Firm 2 has both coal and natural gas plants, and it relies on its relatively low-cost coal plant up to its production capacity of 675 MW. To produce quantities above that, Firm 2 needs to also operate its natural gas generators. Firm 3, on the other hand, has only natural gas generators, though each has a different marginal cost. The three panels of Figure 8.12 show each firm's marginal cost curve.

We can construct the industry marginal cost curve by finding the horizontal sum of the three firms' individual marginal cost curves. This is demonstrated in Figure 8.13. As was true for Firm 1's marginal cost curve, the industry will rely first on generators with relatively cheaper marginal costs. In other words, the industry will first use all available coal generators. For the first 675 MW, only Firm 2's coal plant operates, because it has the lowest marginal cost of all the industry's plants ($15 per MWh). If a higher quantity is produced, Firm 1 brings its 200-MW coal plant on line, raising the industry's marginal cost to $18 per MWh. At quantities above 875 MW (the combined capacity of the industry's coal-fired plants), Firm 3, which has the lowest-marginal-cost natural gas plant, at $23 per MWh, also starts generating power. Once that plant's 1500-MW capacity is used up—that is, when the industry is producing more than 2,375 MW—the industry marginal cost curve shifts up again as more plants are brought on line. Notice that this next step up in the industry marginal cost curve (to $24 per MWh) actually reflects the total production capacity of two plants, one each from Firms 2 and 3, because both these firms have generators that operate at this same marginal cost. The horizontal summation of the three firms' supply curves continues as the industry must bring additional plants on line to produce higher and higher quantities, and the industry marginal cost curve shifts up to reflect the higher marginal costs of operating these plants. Once the industry has exhausted its production capacity, just above 7,000 MWh, its

Figure 8.12 : Differing Marginal Cost Curves across Electricity Producers

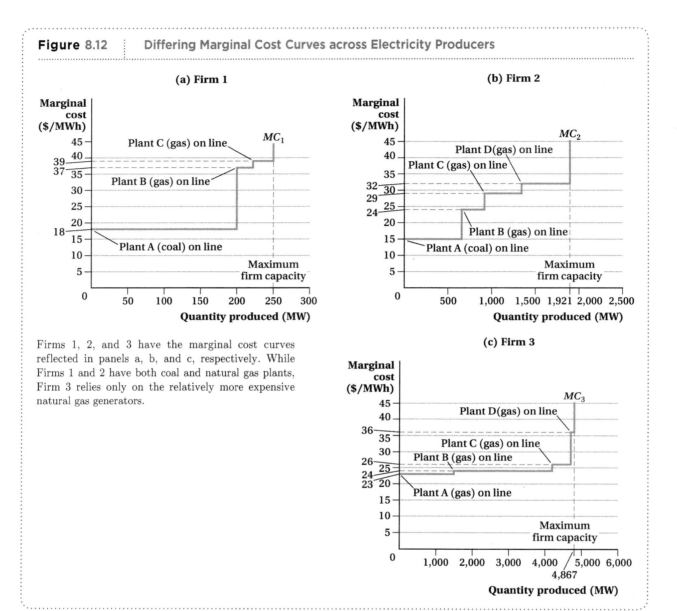

Firms 1, 2, and 3 have the marginal cost curves reflected in panels a, b, and c, respectively. While Firms 1 and 2 have both coal and natural gas plants, Firm 3 relies only on the relatively more expensive natural gas generators.

marginal costs become infinite. This is reflected in the figure by the vertical marginal cost curve at that total capacity.

For all market prices at or above $18 per MWh, the industry is going to have at least one plant operating at a marginal cost that is below the market price. For example, if the market price were $23 per MWh, Firm 1 and 2's coal plants would both be operating at marginal costs that are smaller than the market price. In other words, price equals marginal cost only for the *marginal* plant—the last plant that needs to be brought on line to produce the industry quantity at that price. At a market price of $23 per MWh, the marginal plant is Firm 3's lowest-cost natural gas plant. The two coal plants therefore earn a markup above their marginal costs; they are able to sell their output at a price above their marginal cost of production. This markup is producer's surplus. ∎

Figure 8.13   :   **The Short-Run Supply of Electricity in Texas**

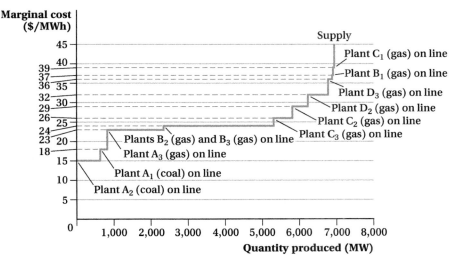

The short-run supply of electricity in Texas is the horizontal sum of the firms' marginal cost curves in Figure 8.12. When the market price is at least $15 per MWh, Firm 2 supplies electricity on the market. At prices at or above $18 per MWh, Firms 1 and 2 both supply on the market. At a market price of $23 per MWh, Firm 3 generates electricity using natural gas, and all three firms are suppliers on the electricity market.

8.4 Perfectly Competitive Industries in the Long Run

We already noted that there are differences between firms' short- and long-run supply curves. In the short run, a firm supplies output at the point where its short-run marginal cost equals the market price. This price can be below the firm's average total cost, but it must be at least as high as its short-run average variable cost. In other words, the firm must earn producer surplus, or else it shuts down. The short-run supply curve is therefore that portion of a firm's short-run marginal cost curve above its short-run average variable cost curve and zero otherwise.

In the long run, however, a firm produces where its *long-run* marginal cost equals the market price. Moreover, because all inputs and costs are variable in the long run, the firm's long-run supply curve is the part of its long-run marginal cost curve above its long-run average total cost curve ($LATC = LAVC$, because there are no fixed costs in the long run).

At the industry level, there are other distinctions between the short run and long run. The primary difference is that, in the long run, firms can enter and exit the industry. In the short run, the number of firms in the industry is assumed fixed, so only firms already in the market make production choices. This assumption makes sense; some inputs are fixed in the short run, making it difficult for new firms to start producing on a whim or for existing firms to avoid paying a fixed cost. In the long run, though, firms can enter or leave the industry in response to changes in profitability. In this section, we learn how this process works and what it implies about how competitive industries look in the long run.

Entry

Firms decide to enter or exit a market depending on whether they expect their action will be profitable.

Think about a firm that is considering entering a perfectly competitive market. We assume for now that all firms in the market, including this and any other potential entrants, have the same cost curves. (We look at what happens when firms have different costs later.)

Figure 8.14 shows the current market price and long-run cost curves for a typical firm in this industry. A profit-maximizing firm would produce the quantity where its long-run marginal cost curve equals the market price. We know that this quantity must be at a point where the firm's (long-run) marginal cost curve is at or above its (long-run) average total cost curve. If the market price is P_1, the firm's profit-maximizing quantity is Q^*, where LMC equals P_1. Notice that because P_1 is greater than the firm's minimum average total cost, the firm is making a profit of $(P_1 - LATC^*)$ on each unit of output.

Because firms in this industry are earning positive profits, new firms will want to take advantage of this opportunity by entering the industry. What would happen? If there is **free entry** into the industry—which doesn't have to mean "free" in the monetary sense (there can be startup costs), but rather, indicates that entry is not blocked by any special legal or technical barriers—the market price will fall until it equals the minimum average total cost. Let's consider why this is the case. First, think about what entry of new firms would do to the *industry's* short-run supply curve. Since this supply curve is derived from the sum of all industry firms' marginal cost curves, adding new firms would cause the industry to provide more output at any given price, as the supply from the new entrants is added to the industry total. In other words, entry shifts the short-run industry supply curve out from S_1 to S_2 (Figure 8.15). This outward shift lowers the market price from P_1 to P_2.

If P_2 is still above the minimum average total cost, an incentive remains for more firms to enter because they would be making profits by doing so. They would be making less profit than earlier entrants, but they're still better off entering the market than staying out. New entrants will shift the industry supply curve further out, lowering the market price even further.

This process continues until the last set of entrants drives down the market price to the minimum average total cost and there are no profits to be made by entering the industry. At this point, any potential entrant would be indifferent between entering

free entry
The ability of a firm to enter an industry without encountering legal or technical barriers.

Figure 8.14   Positive Long-Run Profit

In the long run, a perfectly competitive firm produces only when the market price is equal to or greater than its long-run average total cost $LATC^*$. Here, the firm produces Q^*, market price P_1 equals its long run marginal cost LMC, and its long-run economic profit equals $(P_1 - LATC^*)$ per unit.

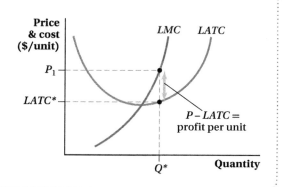

Figure 8.15 : Entry of New Firms Increases Supply and Lowers Equilibrium Price

When firms in an industry are earning positive economic profits, new firms will enter, shifting the short-run industry supply curve out from S_1 to S_2 and lowering the market price from P_1 to P_2.

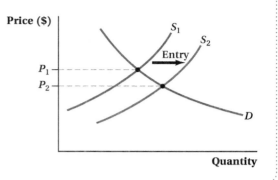

the industry and staying out, entry ceases, and the market is in **long-run competitive equilibrium.** The bottom line is that if there is free entry, the price in a perfectly competitive industry will be driven down toward the minimum average total cost of the industry's firms, and no firms will be making a profit.

This is an important idea and seems odd. How could they make no profit? And, if they make no profit, why bother? The answer is that in perfect competition, it's a tough world. You may have a good idea, but the profit you make only lasts until everyone else enters and copies it. One thing to remember about this no-profit condition is that it refers to *economic* profit, not accounting profit. It includes covering the opportunity cost of their time. It means business owners make only enough to stay in business—that is, to be no worse off than their outside option—and no more.

Exit

Now suppose the market price is *below* the minimum average total cost instead. No firms will enter the industry, because they would earn negative profits if they did. Further, firms already in the industry are making negative profits, so this market situation isn't sustainable. If there is **free exit** from the market, some of these firms will close up shop and leave the industry. Since we've assumed all firms in the market are the same, all firms are equally unprofitable and would prefer to exit. Which firms exit first? There are two ways to look at how firms make this decision. One is that there are a lucky few who figure out that they're losing money before the others, and they leave first. The other, probably more realistic possibility is that cost differences actually exist across firms, and the highest-cost firms exit first. (We'll talk more about this case below.)

This exit from the industry shifts its supply curve in, raising the market price. Just as entry continues until higher prices are driven down to the minimum average total cost, exit continues until the market price rises to minimum average total cost. At this point, exiting would not make any firms better off.

Free entry and exit are forces that push the market price in a perfectly competitive industry toward the long-run minimum average total cost. This outcome leads to two important characteristics of the long-run equilibrium in a perfectly competitive market. First, even though the industry's short-run supply curve is upward-sloping, the industry's *long-run* supply curve is horizontal at the long-run minimum average cost. Remember that a supply curve indicates the quantity supplied at every price. Long-run competitive equilibrium implies that firms produce where price is equal to minimum average total cost.

long-run competitive equilibrium
The point at which the market price is equal to the minimum average total cost and firms would gain no profits by entering the industry.

free exit
The ability of a firm to exit an industry without encountering legal or technical barriers.

Graphing the Industry Long-Run Supply Curve

Figure 8.16 shows how we can derive the industry long-run supply curve graphically. Suppose the industry (panel a) is currently in equilibrium at a price of P_1. Each firm takes the price as given and maximizes profit by producing where $P_1 = LMC$. Because price is also equal to long-run average total cost, the firm is earning zero profit. This means that firms have no incentive to enter or exit the market, so the industry is in long-run competitive equilibrium at P_1.

Now, suppose that the demand for the product rises as a result of a change in consumer tastes. This change increases the quantity demanded at each price and the demand curve shifts to D_2. Prices would rise temporarily to P_2. As a result, each firm would move upward along its supply curve and produce a higher quantity where $P_2 = LMC$. This increase in output would be reflected at the industry level as an increase in quantity to the level at the intersection of D_2 and S_1 in panel a. But even after this increase in output among existing industry firms, the market price is still above the firms' minimum $LATC$. As a result, new firms enter the market to take advantage of these economic profits. This shifts the industry quantity supplied at any given price, thereby shifting the short-run industry supply curve to the right. Eventually, the industry returns to long-run equilibrium when short-run supply shifts to S_2 and the market price falls back to long-run minimum average total cost (P_1). If we connect the two long-run equilibria, we have the industry's long-run supply curve S_{LR}, which is horizontal at P_1.

Figure 8.16   Deriving the Long-Run Industry Supply Curve

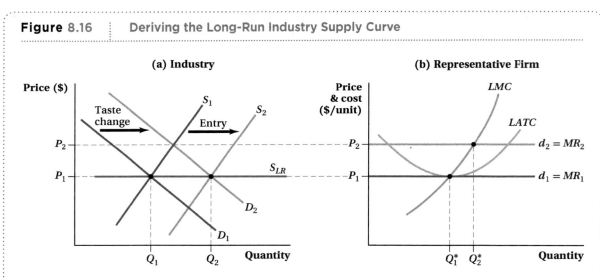

(a) The original long-run equilibrium for an industry is (P_1, Q_1) at the intersection between the long-run supply curve S_{LR} and the original demand curve D_1. After a change in tastes, demand increases to D_2, price increases to P_2, and firms earn positive economic profits in the short run. In the long run, new firms enter the industry, shifting the short-run supply curve to S_2 until it reaches the long-run equilibrium price P_1 at the new equilibrium quantity Q_2.

(b) At the long-run market price P_1, the representative firm earns zero economic profit and produces quantity Q_1^*. When market demand rises, the market price increases to P_2 and the firm's output increases to Q_2^*. At this combination, the firm earns positive economic profit. As entry into the industry occurs, the price falls back to P_1, and the firm reduces its output to Q_1^*. At this point, the firm earns zero economic profit.

theory and data

Entry and Exit at Work in Markets—Residential Real Estate

Residential real estate brokerage in the United States is a peculiar industry. For one thing, real estate agents' commissions are essentially the same everywhere, consistently hovering around 6% of the selling price, even though every city is a different market. Many have wondered whether that's from collusion among agents, but regardless of the reason, agents selling houses in, say, Boston, Massachusetts, charge essentially the same commission rate as those in Fargo, North Dakota.

Given that agents across the country get paid the same percentage of the sales price, it seems like it would be better to be an agent in a place with higher house prices, such as Boston or Los Angeles. With an average house selling for a little over $400,000 in Boston, real estate agents get around $24,000 per house. Compare this to the $12,000 they would make on a typical home in Fargo (average price $200,000). But it turns out that Boston agents pull in approximately the same average yearly salary as those in Fargo, despite the higher house prices. The same pattern holds across the United States: Regardless of house prices, agents' average salaries are roughly equal across cities.

Why do real estate agents everywhere end up making around the same yearly salary? Free entry. In a 2003 study, Chang-Tai Hsieh and Enrico Moretti look into just this phenomenon.[4] They find the key to explaining this pattern is that the typical Boston agent sells fewer homes over the course of the year than does the typical agent in Fargo. In other words, as housing prices increase, agents' productivity decreases, and the reduction in houses sold per year in high-house-price cities just about exactly counteracts the higher commission per house. So while average commissions *per house* might be twice as high in Boston as in Fargo, the typical Boston agent sells half the number of houses per year as the typical agent in Fargo. They end up making the same income.

Are the agents in Boston and other high-price real estate markets just being lazy? Hardly. This decrease in productivity is the result of free entry into the real estate market. It's not hard to become a real estate agent—spend maybe 30 to 90 hours in the classroom and pass a test, and you'll have your license. Therefore in cities with high housing costs (and high commissions per house sold), more people choose to become real estate agents. Having more agents means each agent sells fewer houses, on average. This drives down agents' average yearly salaries until they are on par with those for agents in other lower-cost cities.

Not only did Hsieh and Moretti find this pattern across cities with different average house prices, they found it *within* cities over time as well. When housing prices increased in a city, so did the number of agents seeking to sell those houses, keeping average agent salaries from rising along with house prices. If prices fell, the opposite happened: Agents left the market until the average productivity of those remaining rose to keep salaries at their original level. In this way, entry and exit into the market kept the long-run average price for agents (i.e., their salaries) more or less constant. So while the constant commission rate still marks residential real estate brokerage as a peculiar business, free entry into the business explains why average salaries are the same.

---

[4] Chang-Tai Hsieh and Enrico Moretti, "Can Free Entry Be Inefficient? Fixed Commissions and Social Waste in the Real Estate Industry," *Journal of Political Economy* 111, no. 5 (2003): 1076–1122.

freakonomics

The Not-So-Simple Economics of Blackmail

In 2006, a suspicious envelope arrived at Pepsi headquarters. The envelope wasn't laced with anthrax and didn't contain an explosive booby trap, but the contents *were* potentially deadly to Pepsi's main competitor, the Coca-Cola Corporation. The letter, sent by three Coke employees, offered to sell Coke's closely guarded secret recipe. No doubt, the value of the information to Pepsi would be massive. The letter writers would be rich beyond imagination. Or, at least that is what they must have thought. Instead, they found themselves behind bars, serving up to eight years on conspiracy charges after being caught in an FBI sting operation.

These three sketchy industrial spies (Edmund Duhaney, Joya Williams, and Ibrahim Dimson) appeared in an Atlanta court in 2006 for trying to sell confidential Coca-Cola Co. information to PepsiCo Inc.

While their fate must have come as a surprise to the formula stealers, if they had paid better attention in intermediate microeconomics, they might have ended up far better off.

The PepsiCo and Coca-Cola Corporations have been entrenched in the Cola Wars since at least the 1970s when Pepsi introduced the Pepsi Challenge in America's grocery stores and argued that soda drinkers prefer the taste of Pepsi in blind taste tests. Pepsi has won some victories (for instance, Coke's introduction of New Coke in 1985 is widely viewed as one of the worst marketing missteps in history), but mostly Coca-Cola has maintained the upper hand. Coke's U.S. market share today is around 40% compared to Pepsi's 30%.

In light of that fact, wouldn't Pepsi be desperate to weaken Coke by, say, buying Coke's secret formula and making it public? Most likely, the availability of the formula would cause dozens of new cola manufacturers to enter the market, making perfect substitutes for Coke, much like generic drug manufacturers enter the market when a prescription drug goes off patent. If all the Coke knockoffs tasted exactly like real Coke, and there were free entry, one might imagine that the market for the Coke version of cola would start to look a whole lot like perfect competition. The price of Coke would plunge. (In practice, it is unlikely that an exactly perfect-competition-like outcome would actually happen because so much of what buyers get when they purchase Coke is the mystique that comes from the advertising, but let's just ignore that for a second for the sake of argument.)

What would such a scenario do to Pepsi's profits? Coke and Pepsi are close substitutes. If the price of Coke falls, the demand for Pepsi falls, and along with it Pepsi's profits. A (near) perfectly competitive market for Coke would likely be disastrous for Pepsi, not the boon that the formula stealers imagined.

Thus, it is no surprise that the executives at Pepsi quickly delivered the letter offering to sell the secret formula to Coca-Cola, which then turned it over to the FBI. Unlike the criminals, the Pepsi execs must have been paying attention in their economics classes.

If the three renegade Coke employees had been better economists, what would they have done differently? For starters, they would have sent the letter not to Pepsi, but to a firm that was thinking of entering the cola market. A company like that might very well have put a great value on knowing Coke's formula and paid handsomely for it. So if you really want to begin a career of dastardly criminal enterprise, be sure to know your microeconomics or you may end up behind bars (where you belong!).

Adjustments between Long-Run Equilibria

In theory, the long-run implications of perfect competition are clear: a stable price, just high enough to cover firms' average total costs, with total industry quantity supplied adjusted by the free flow of firms in and out of the market. In reality, getting to the long run can take a long time. When changes in an industry's underlying demand or costs occur, some interesting things can happen while the industry transitions from the old long-run equilibrium to the new one.

A Demand Increase   Suppose an industry is in long-run equilibrium when the demand for its product unexpectedly rises. As before, let's say this change in demand comes from a change in consumer tastes. That is, at any price, consumers now want to consume more of the product. This change shifts out the industry demand curve as we saw in Figure 8.16, which is replicated in panels a and b in Figure 8.17. In the short run, when entry is limited, the relevant industry supply curve is the short-run curve S_1. The initial short-term response to the demand increase is an increase in both equilibrium output and the market price as the industry moves up its short-run supply curve.

During this short-run response, firms earn positive economic profits and producer surplus. The market price, which was originally at the minimum long-run average total cost and therefore only just high enough for firms to earn zero economic profit, is now above this level.

Because price is above average cost, profit is positive and so new firms will enter the market. As firms enter, industry output increases at every price and the industry's short-run supply curve shifts out, from S_1 to S_2. With the demand curve now stable and fixed at its new level D_2, the supply shift raises industry output and lowers the market price, and consumers move along their demand curve. Entry continues until the price falls back to the minimum average cost level P_1. Total industry output Q_2 is higher in this new long-run equilibrium because the demand for the industry's product is higher than before, but the price is the same as that in the old long-run equilibrium. The horizontal line connecting the two long-run equilibria is the industry's long-run supply curve because it reflects the industry's supply response once free entry and exit are accounted for.

Figure 8.17 | Long-Run Adjustments to an Increase in Demand in a Perfectly Competitive Industry

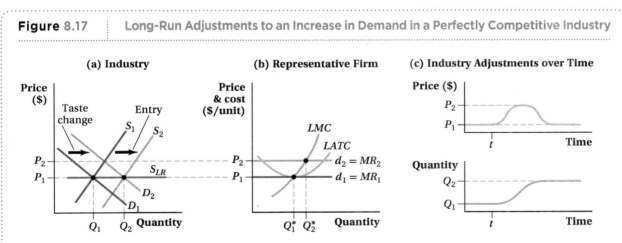

(a) As in Figure 8.16, an increase in demand will temporarily increase the market price from P_1 to P_2 and induce new firms to enter the market to capture the positive profits.

(b) An increase in demand leads to short-run economic profit for a perfectly competitive firm.

(c) An increase in demand leads to a short-run increase in price. Over time, new firms will enter the market, increasing equilibrium quantity to Q_2 and returning the market price to its long-run equilibrium P_1.

If we were to plot the industry's output and market prices over time during this adjustment between two long-run equilibria, we would see something like panel c of Figure 8.17. The industry is initially in equilibrium at quantity Q_1 and price P_1 (where P_1 equals the minimum long-run average total cost of industry firms). When demand shifts at time t, both quantity and price start to rise as the industry moves along its short-run supply curve. As entry begins, the industry's short-run supply curve shifts out, quantity continues to rise, and price falls. Eventually, price falls back to its original level P_1, while quantity rises to Q_2, the new equilibrium quantity.

The response to a decrease in demand for the industry's product would basically look the same, but with the direction of all the effects reversed: Demand falls, price and quantity fall along the initial supply curve, firms make negative profits, some firms leave the industry, supply decreases, Q falls, and prices rebound. When demand falls, exit from the industry is the force that brings price back (up) to the minimum long-run average total cost level.

A Cost Decrease   Now let's think about what happens if the costs faced by industry firms fell. This might occur because of a technological innovation or a permanent decrease in the cost of one of the industry's inputs. In either case, we assume that the cost reduction shifts down both the marginal and average total cost curves of industry firms.

Because of the decrease in marginal cost, every firm will want to supply more output at every given price, and each firm's short-run supply curve shifts out. The industry short-run supply curve also shifts out as a result.

These changes can be seen in Figure 8.18. Panel b shows what happens at the firm level. The firm initially has marginal and average total cost curves LMC_1 and $LATC_1$. In the initial long-run equilibrium, the market price P_1 equals the firm's minimum average total cost. Given these market conditions, the firm produces an output of Q_1^*. When costs fall, the firm's marginal and average total cost curves shift to LMC_2 and $LATC_2$. The original market price P_1 is now above the firm's average total cost.

Figure 8.18   Long-Run Adjustments to a Reduction in Costs in a Perfectly Competitive Industry

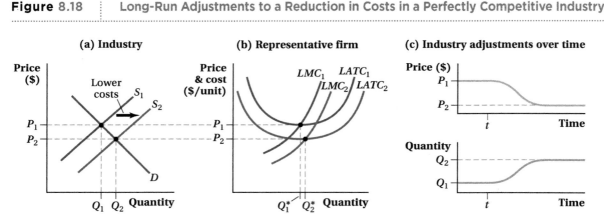

(a) A decrease in industrywide marginal costs leads to an increase in supply from S_1 to S_2. Industry quantity increases from Q_1 to Q_2, and the market price decreases from P_1 to P_2 in the long run.
(b) The decrease in industrywide marginal costs shifts the firm's long-run marginal cost from LMC_1 to LMC_2 and long-

run average total cost from $LATC_1$ to $LATC_2$. In the long run, the firm increases output from Q_1^* to Q_2^*.
(c) An increase in supply leads to a long-run decrease in price from P_1 to P_2, and quantity increases from Q_1 to Q_2.

At the industry level (panel a), supply shifts out both because the lower costs mean existing firms in the industry have a higher optimal quantity, Q_2^*, and because the high price P_1 attracts new firms to enter the industry. This outward shift in supply raises the industry quantity supplied and lowers the market price. It continues until supply reaches S_2, at which point the market price has fallen to the new minimum average total cost level P_2.

If we plot the quantity and price changes over time in this case, as in panel c of Figure 8.18, we see that quantity rises and prices fall throughout the transition from the high-cost to the low-cost long-run equilibrium. Here, unlike the response to the demand shift, there is a permanent drop in the long-run price. This is because long-run costs have declined.

application

The Increased Demand for Corn

The recent increase in the demand for corn driven by the U.S. ethanol boom provides a good opportunity to explore the predictions of our analysis. Small corn farmers operate in an essentially perfectly competitive market, so we can look at total corn output and its market price as reflecting perfectly competitive industry outcomes.

The ethanol boom arguably started with the passage of the Energy Policy Act of 2005, which both mandated increased biofuels (which include ethanol) consumption and raised ethanol subsidies. The number of ethanol plants in the United States grew from 81 in January 2005 to 204 by January 2011, and many existing plants expanded.[5] We can think of the Act as creating an outward shift in the demand for corn, which is the major input into ethanol production in the United States. Our

Prices as high as an elephant's eye induce entry into corn production.

analysis from above predicts that this would increase both corn output and prices in the short run.

The data reflect this prediction. Estimated U.S. corn production in 2010 was 313 million metric tons, up about 10% from 2005. While quantities increased, prices rose even more steeply. At the Chicago Board of Trade, corn prices, which had hovered around a long-run average of between $2.50–3.00 per bushel for the decade prior to 2005, were over $6 per bushel in 2011.[6]

Our analysis also predicts that in the long run, prices that high should induce entry into corn production and eventually bring corn prices back down even as output continues to rise. Farms that once grew other crops will switch to corn production to take advantage of the new profit opportunities from growing corn. This shift in industry supply, if demand remains fixed (at its higher post-ethanol level), will increase quantity further and decrease price.

Time will tell if our prediction holds. There are a couple of reasons why it might not. First, further expansion of the ethanol industry (more plants have been planned but not yet built) will create further shifts in the demand curve. This could lead to still more short-run price increases and would delay the return of prices to their earlier levels. A

[5] Renewable Fuels Association, "Ethanol Industry Overview," Accessed March 28, 2012. http://www.ethanolrfa.org/pages/statistics#EIO.

[6] The production data here and the price data below are from the Feed Grains Database, U.S. Department of Agriculture.

second possibility is that growing corn has increasing costs in the long run. It might be, for example, that the growth in corn acreage drives up the demand and prices of the special equipment farmers use to plant, tend, and harvest corn or drives corn onto more and more marginal land.

Still, history offers a guide to the power of entry (plus some productivity improvement) to hold down prices. For example, there was a very substantial increase in grain prices in the 1970s. Corn prices rose to more than $3 per bushel in 1974 (this is almost $14 per bushel in 2011 dollars). Within three years, they had fallen back to $2 per bushel—still high compared to today, but a third lower than 1974—and over a longer period of time remained around the $2.50–3.00 per bushel mark (in 2011 dollars) all the way through 2005. Similar things happen in the oil market when prices rise—oil drillers scour the world for new reserves trying to enter the market. ■

8.4 figure it out

Suppose that the market for cantaloupes is currently in long-run competitive equilibrium at a price of $3 per melon. A listeria outbreak in cantaloupe crops leads to a sharp decline in the demand for cantaloupes.

a. In the short run, what will happen to the price of a cantaloupe? Explain and use a graph to illustrate your answer.

b. In the short run, how will firms respond to the change in price described in part (a)? What will happen to each producer's profit in the short run? Explain, using a diagram to illustrate your answer.

c. Given the situation described in (b), what can we expect to happen to the number of producers in the cantaloupe industry in the long run? Why?

d. What will the long-run price of a cantaloupe be?

Solution:

a. As we can see in panel a of the diagram below, a decline in the demand for cantaloupes will lead to a fall in the equilibrium market price of cantaloupes (from $3 to P_2).

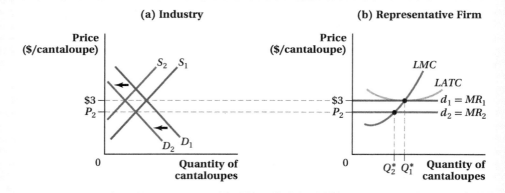

b. As shown in panel b, when price declines to P_2, each firm moves along its long-run marginal cost curve to determine its output, which falls from Q_1^* to Q_2^*. Remember that, before the decrease in demand, the industry was in long-run competitive equilibrium so that, at a price of $3 per cantaloupe, each firm was earning zero economic profit. Therefore, when price falls to P_2, it must be below the firm's average total cost. The drop in demand has led to an economic loss (or negative economic profit) for the firm.

c. If firms are incurring losses, we can expect some to exit the industry. Thus, the number of producers in the industry will fall, the quantity of cantaloupes will fall, and the price will rise.

d. The price of cantaloupes will continue to rise until it is once again at the minimum average total cost of $3. At this point, the industry is in long-run competitive equilibrium and firms have no incentive to enter or exit the industry.

Long-Run Supply in Constant-, Increasing-, and Decreasing-Cost Industries

We saw above that the long-run supply curve of a perfectly competitive industry is horizontal, at a price equal to the minimum average total cost of its producers. However, that analysis made an implicit assumption that firms' total cost curves didn't change when total industry output did. That is, we assumed that the industry is a **constant-cost industry.**

This might not always be the case. Firms in **increasing-cost industries** see their cost curves shift up when industry output increases. This might occur because the price of an input rises in response to the industry's higher demand for that input. Suppose an industry requires special capital equipment that is in limited supply. When there is an increase in the industry's output, firms compete for this scarce capital, pushing up its price. This means that, the higher industry output, the greater firms' average total costs, even in the long run. For this reason, the long-run supply curves of increasing-cost industries are upward-sloping. They're not as steeply sloped as the short-run supply curve for the industry, because they account for entry and exit, but they're not horizontal either.

Shifts from one long-run equilibrium to another in response to a demand shift are similar to the case above for a constant-cost industry. The only difference is that entry only brings price back down to the new, higher long-run average total cost level.

In **decreasing-cost industries,** firms' cost levels decline with increases in industry output. This might be because there are some increasing returns to scale at the industry level, or in the production of one or more of the industry's inputs. The long-run supply curves for these industries are downward-sloping. Again, the short-run transition between long-run equilibria when demand for the industry's product increases looks like the constant-industry case, but now entry continues past the point where the market price is driven down to the old long-run average cost level. Instead, entry continues until the price falls all the way to the new, lower minimum average total cost.

constant-cost industry
An industry whose firms' total costs do not change with total industry output.

increasing-cost industry
An industry whose firms' total costs increase with increases in industry output.

decreasing-cost industry
An industry whose firms' total costs decrease with increases in industry output.

8.5 Producer Surplus, Economic Rents, and Economic Profits

Our analysis of perfect competition has shown that in the long run, perfectly competitive firms earn no economic profit.

Cost Differences and Economic Rent in Perfect Competition

In looking at long-run outcomes in perfectly competitive markets, however, we've assumed that all firms in an industry had the same cost curves. This isn't very realistic, however. Firms differ in their production costs for many reasons: They might face different prices for their inputs; they might have various degrees of special know-how or other production abilities that make them more efficient; or they might be lucky through an accident of history to be blessed with a superior location or access to superior resources. When there are cost differences between firms in a perfectly competitive industry, the more efficient producers earn a special type of return called **economic rent.**

economic rent
Returns to specialized inputs above what firms paid for them.

We saw in Section 8.3 that cost differences among firms is one of the reasons why industry marginal cost curves (and therefore their short-run supply curves) slope up. Higher-cost firms produce only when the market price is high.

To see what happens in the long run when firms have different cost curves, let's first think about how output quantities vary when firms' costs do. If all firms have the same cost, their marginal cost curves are the same. Therefore, their profit-maximizing outputs are the same, too: the quantity at which the market price equals (their common) marginal cost. But if firms have different marginal cost curves, their profit-maximizing outputs will differ as well.

Consider an example in which the factors that cause these firms' costs to differ are specific fixtures of the firm; that is, these costs can't be influenced by the firm's actions or sold to other firms. For instance, the factors might involve access to special technologies or a premium location. In any case, these factors affect only the cost structure of that particular firm. Figure 8.19 shows the long-run marginal cost curves for three firms. Firm 1 has a high marginal cost shown by curve LMC_1, Firm 2 has a moderate marginal cost LMC_2, and Firm 3 has a low marginal cost LMC_3. Each firm's marginal cost curve intersects the market price at a different quantity of output. Firm 1's profit-maximizing output is the smallest, Q_1^*. The next largest is Firm 2, which produces Q_2^*. Finally, Firm 3 produces the highest output Q_3^*. Therefore, higher-cost firms produce less, and lower-cost firms produce more, when firms have different costs. This negative

---

Figure 8.19   Firms with Different Long-Run Marginal Costs

Firms in the same industry with differing long-run marginal costs will produce different quantities of output at the market price. Because each firm maximizes profit where $P = LMC$, low-cost producers will produce a greater quantity of output (Q_3^*) than high-cost producers (Q_1^*).

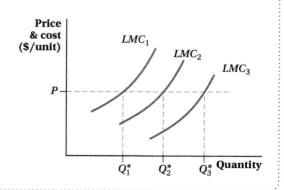

relationship between a firm's size (measured by its output) and its cost has been observed in many industries and countries.

Let's think for a minute about the industry's highest-cost firm. Suppose Firm 1 is this firm, and that the market price is above Firm 1's minimum average total cost. As we discussed above, if all producers have the same cost curve, a perfectly competitive market in which price is above the minimum average total cost will attract new entrants. These entrants shift the industry supply curve out and reduce the price until it equals the minimum average total cost. That's exactly what would happen here, too: If the market price is above Firm 1's minimum average total cost, the price is above all producers' minimum average total costs. Therefore, new firms will enter the market. If all these firms have lower costs than Firm 1, the industry supply curve will shift out until the price falls to the minimum average total cost of Firm 1.

If, on the other hand, some entrants have costs *above* Firm 1's cost, entry will occur until the supply curve shifts out only enough to lower the price to the minimum average total cost of the highest cost entrant.

In either case, the important thing to realize is that in a perfectly competitive market where firms have different costs, *the long-run market price equals the minimum average total cost of the highest-cost firm remaining in the industry*. That highest-cost firm makes zero profit and zero producer surplus. What about the other firms in the market? They have minimum average total costs that are lower than the minimum average total cost of the highest-cost firm, and therefore lower than the market price. They make a positive profit on every sale, and this profit is larger the lower their costs. It's just like what we saw in the earlier Application on electricity in Texas: the market price was determined by the marginal cost of the marginal producer, and the lower-cost generating plants could make extra producer surplus at that price. You might wonder why more firms with costs less than those of the highest-cost firm in the market don't enter. Well, they would, if they existed. By entering, they could make a positive margin over their average total cost on every sale. Furthermore, their entry could shift the industry supply curve out and drive down price enough so that the formerly highest-cost firm in the industry would no longer want to operate, because the long-run price would be below its minimum average total cost. Entry would occur, in fact, until there are no more firms left to enter that have costs below those of the industry's highest-cost firm. Note that if an existing low-cost firm can expand capacity at the existing low-cost level, that's a different form of entry but is entry nonetheless.

The long-run outcome in an industry in which firms have different costs occurs once all entry has stopped. All firms except the one with the highest cost sell their output at a price above their long-run average total costs, so they all earn producer surplus and economic rent. This surplus is tied to their special attributes that allow them to produce at a lower cost. As we said earlier, their lower cost could be the result of access to a special technology, better know-how of some sort or another, a better location, or a number of other possibilities. The greater this cost advantage is, the larger the producer surplus or economic rent.

Economic rents measure returns to specialized inputs above what the firms paid for them. Suppose a firm is a lower-cost firm because it was lucky enough to have hired a manager like Steve Jobs who was particularly smart and adept at efficiently running its production process. If the firm only needed to pay this manager the same salary as every other firm was paying its manager (or, at least not so much more as to wipe out the cost advantage of the manager's ability), *and* if there is a limited supply of similarly exceptional managers, the manager's human capital earns economic rent for the firm. If the firm is instead lower-cost because it has a favorable location that makes servicing customers easier, the location is the source of economic rent to the firm because not all firms can use that same location. What's important to recognize is that economic rents are determined by cost differences *relative* to other firms in the industry. That's because the profit earned by the scarce input depends on how much lower the firm's costs are than its competitors' costs. The larger the cost difference, the larger the rent.

Economic Profit ≠ Economic Rent At this point, you might be a little confused: Earlier we said that perfectly competitive markets had zero economic profit in the long run, yet now we're saying that firms earn economic rents if they have different costs. Does the zero economic profit outcome only occur if all producers' costs are the same?

Firms in perfectly competitive industries make zero economic profit even if they have different costs. There is a distinction between economic profit and economic rent. Economic profit counts inputs' opportunity costs, and economic rent is included in the opportunity cost for inputs that earn them. This is because inputs that earn rents would still earn them if they were given to another firm. If we gave another firm the brilliant manager or better location discussed above, it would lower that firm's costs. That other firm would therefore be willing to pay more for that rent-earning input. This willingness to pay for the economic rent inherent to the input raises the opportunity cost of the input to the firm that currently owns it—by using the input, they're giving up the ability to sell it to another firm. Once this opportunity cost is subtracted from the firm's revenue, its economic profit is no higher than if the input earned no rent at all.

In practice, this is often hugely important. If one firm has lower costs because it has better programmers and engineers than a different firm, the wages paid to the scarce talent may very well end up absorbing the advantage. The rent in such a case goes to the owner of the scarce resource itself (the workers) rather than to the firm.

8.6 Conclusion

In this chapter, we learned about a firm's profit-maximizing behavior in a perfectly competitive industry. Perfectly competitive industries are characterized by having few barriers to entry, a large number of firms with identical products, and firms that are price takers. A perfectly competitive firm maximizes its profits by producing where the market price (the same as marginal revenue in a perfectly competitive market) is equal to its marginal costs. We saw that a firm's supply curve is the portion of its marginal cost curve at or above its average cost curve and that individual firms' supply curves combine to form the market supply curve.

In the real world, most firms have some influence over the market price, and although many industries approach perfect competition, truly perfectly competitive industries are rare. Even so, the profit-maximization framework we developed here will prove useful as a simple foundation on which to build analyses of more complicated market structures. We will start in Chapters 9 and 10 by looking at the type of firm that is most unlike the perfectly competitive firm—the monopoly that sells a unique product on the market. Firms in monopolistic competition and oligopolies share some characteristics with both monopolies and perfectly competitive firms. We examine those in Chapter 11.

Summary

1. An industry's **market structure** is characterized by the number of firms in the industry, the type of product sold, and the degree of barriers to entry. Given these criteria, there are four different types of market structures in an economy: perfect competition, monopolistic competition, oligopoly, and monopoly. **Perfectly competitive** industries have no barriers to entry and feature a large number of firms selling identical products. As a result of such character-

istics, these firms are price takers, facing horizontal demand curves equal to their marginal revenue curves. [**Section 8.1**]

2. A firm aims to maximize its **profits,** or the difference between its total revenue and its total costs. A perfectly competitive firm produces its profit-maximizing output when its **marginal revenue** equals the market price. [**Section 8.2**]

3. Because firms will operate in the short run only when price is greater than or equal to the firm's

average variable costs, a firm's short-run supply curve is the portion of its marginal cost curve at or above the average variable cost curve. For all prices below that, the firm's supply curve is vertical at the y-axis because quantity produced equals zero. [**Section 8.3**]

4. The industry supply curve is the horizontal sum of individual firms' supply curves; that is, the industry quantity supplied at any given price equals the sum of firms' quantities supplied at that price. Like a firm's supply curve, the industry supply curve generally slopes upward, but this may result from two factors. First, individual firms produce more as market prices rise; second, the quantity supplied by the industry will increase as firms operating with higher costs begin supplying at higher prices. [**Section 8.3**]

5. A firm's producer surplus is equal to its total revenue minus its variable cost, while a firm's profit is equal to its total revenue minus its *total* cost. Graphically, we can see both the firm's and industry's producer surpluses as the area below the market price but above the firm's or industry's short-run supply curve. [**Section 8.4**]

6. When a perfectly competitive industry is in **long-run competitive equilibrium,** firms earn zero economic profits. This is because perfectly competitive industries have no barriers to entry: Firms have **free entry** and **free exit** into and out of the industry, and will choose to enter or exit an industry when it is profitable to do so. Over time, changes in demand or in costs will change the long-run equilibrium quantity supplied. For **constant-cost industries,** the long-run supply curve is horizontal, while **increasing-cost industries** and **decreasing-cost industries** result in upward- and downward-sloping supply curves, respectively. [**Section 8.4**]

7. While a perfectly competitive firm earns zero economic profits in the long run, it can earn positive **economic rents.** A firm earns positive rents when its costs are lower relative to those of other firms in the industry. [**Section 8.5**]

Review Questions

1. Economists categorize an industry by three criteria: the number of firms in the industry, the type of product sold, and barriers to entry. Using these three criteria, describe a perfectly competitive industry.

2. Why does a perfectly competitive firm face a horizontal demand curve?

3. Define a firm's profit.

4. What is the relationship between the market price and marginal cost when a perfectly competitive firm is maximizing its profit?

5. A firm operating at a loss will decide whether to shut down based on the relationship between the market price and the firm's average variable cost. When will a firm choose to operate? Why does a firm ignore its fixed cost when making this decision?

6. What is a perfectly competitive firm's short-run supply curve?

7. How do we use firms' short-run supply curves to create the industry short-run supply curve?

8. What happens to short-run industry supply when firms' fixed costs change?

9. Define producer surplus. What is the relationship between profit, producer surplus, and fixed costs?

10. Perfectly competitive industries have free entry and exit in the long run. When will firms decide to enter an industry? When will a firm exit an industry?

11. When do economists say that a market is in a long-run competitive equilibrium?

12. Economic rents are returns to scarce inputs above what firms paid for them. When will a firm earn economic rents?

13. Perfectly competitive firms earn zero economic profits in the long run. How can a firm earn zero economic profits and still yield positive economic rents?

Problems

1. Nancy sells beeswax in a perfectly competitive market for $50 per pound. Nancy's fixed costs are $15, and Nancy is capable of producing up to 6 pounds of beeswax each year. Use that information to fill in the table below. (*Hint*: Total variable cost is simply the sum of the marginal costs up to any particular quantity of output!)

Quantity	Total Revenue	Fixed Cost	Variable Cost	Total Cost	Profit	Marginal Revenue	Marginal Cost
0	0	15				—	—
1							30
2							35
3							42
4							50
5							60
6							72

a. If Nancy is interested in maximizing her total revenue, how many pounds of beeswax should she produce?

b. What quantity of beeswax should Nancy produce in order to maximize her profit?

c. At the profit-maximizing level of output, how do marginal revenue and marginal cost compare?

d. Suppose that Nancy's fixed cost suddenly rises to $30. How should Nancy alter her production to account for this sudden increase in cost?

e. Suppose that the bee's union bargains for higher wages, making the marginal cost of producing beeswax rise by $8 at every level of output. How should Nancy alter her production to account for this sudden increase in cost?

2. The graph below depicts the long-run equilibrium condition in the market for aloe vera gel. The left-hand panel depicts market demand and industry supply; the right-hand panel depicts the cost curves for a representative firm in the industry.

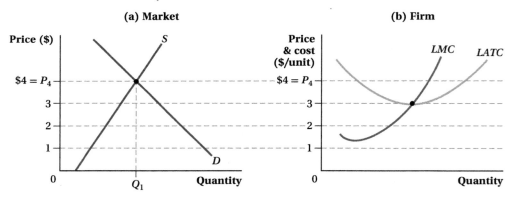

a. Are the firms in the industry earning economic profits or losses? How can you tell?

b. The condition you indicated in (a) will result in entry or exit from the aloe vera gel industry. Indicate whether we will see entry or exit, and depict the effects of that movement in the diagram for the industry.

c. As a result of this change in the market, the price will change. Depict the effects of the price change on the representative firm in the right-hand panel.

d. At what price will entry/exit stop? Briefly explain why.

3. The egg industry is comprised of thousands of firms producing an identical product. Demand and supply conditions are indicated in the left-hand panel of the figure below; the long-run cost curves of a representative egg producer are shown in the right-hand panel. Currently, the market price of eggs is $2 per dozen, and at that price consumers are purchasing 800,000 dozen eggs per day.

(a) Market   **(b) Firm**

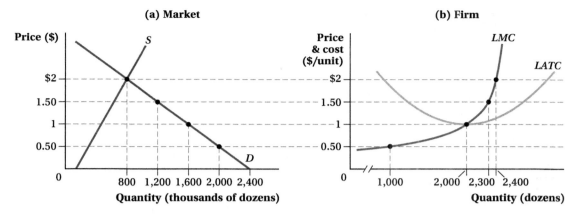

a. Determine how many eggs each firm in the industry will produce if it wants to maximize profit.
b. How many firms are currently serving the industry?
c. In the long run, what will the equilibrium price of eggs be? Explain.
d. In the long run, how many eggs will the typical firm produce?
e. In the long run, how many firms will comprise the industry?

---

4. The diagram below depicts the revenues and costs of a firm producing vodka.

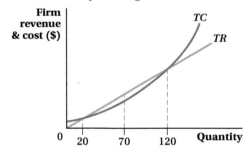

a. What will the firm's profit be if it decides to produce 20 units of output? 120 units?
b. Suppose the firm is producing 70 units of output and decides to cut output to 60. What will happen to the firm's profit as a result?
c. Suppose the firm is producing 70 units of output and decides to increase output to 80. What will happen to the firm's profit as a result?
d. At an output level of 70, draw a line tangent to the total cost curve. Does your line look similar to the total revenue curve? What does the slope of the total revenue curve indicate? What does the slope of the total cost curve indicate?

5. Josie's Pussycats sells ceramic kittens. The marginal cost of producing a particular kitten depends on how many kittens Josie produces, and is given by the formula $MC = 0.8Q$. Thus, the first kitten Josie produces has a marginal cost of $0.80, the second has a marginal cost of $1.60,

and so on. Assume that the ceramic kitten industry is perfectly competitive, and Josie can sell as many kittens as she likes at the market price of $16.
a. What is Josie's marginal revenue from selling another kitten? (Express your answer as an equation.)
b. Determine how many kittens Josie should produce if she wants to maximize profit. How much profit will she make at this output level? (Assume fixed costs are zero. It may help to draw a graph of Josie's marginal revenue and marginal cost.)
c. Suppose Josie is producing the quantity you found in (b). If she decides to produce one extra kitten, what will her profit be?
d. How does your answer to part (c) help explain why "bigger is not always better"?

6. Heloise and Abelard produce letters in a perfectly competitive industry. Heloise is much better at it than Abelard: On average, she can produce letters for half the cost of Abelard's. True or False: If Heloise and Abelard are both maximizing profit, the last letter that Heloise produces will cost half as much as the last letter written by Abelard. Explain your answer.

7. Hack's Berries faces a short-run total cost of production given by $TC = Q^3 - 12Q^2 + 100Q + 1{,}000$.
a. What is the level of Hack's fixed cost?
b. What is Hack's short-run average variable cost of producing berries? (Express AVC as a function of Q.)

c. If the price of berries is $60, how many berries should Hack produce? How do you know? [*Hint*: You may want to carefully graph the *AVC* function you derived in part (b).]

d. If the price of berries is $73, should Hack be producing berries? Explain.

8. Minnie is one producer in the perfectly competitive pearl industry. Minnie's cost curves are shown below. Pearls sell for $100, and in maximizing profits, Minnie produces 1,000 pearls per month.

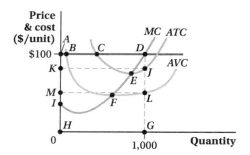

a. Find the area on the graph that illustrates the total revenue from selling 1,000 units at $100 each.

b. Find the area on the graph that indicates the variable cost of producing those 1,000 units.

c. Find the area on the graph that indicates the fixed cost of producing those 1,000 units.

d. Add together the two areas you found in (b) and (c) to show the total cost of producing those 1,000 units.

e. Subtract the total cost of producing those 1,000 units from the total revenue from selling those units to determine the firm's profit. Show the profit as an area on the graph.

9. True or False: "In the short run, if a firm is not earning a profit, it should shut down." Explain your answer.

10. Consider the diagram below that depicts the cost curves for a perfectly competitive firm. The market price (and marginal revenue) faced by this firm is $7.

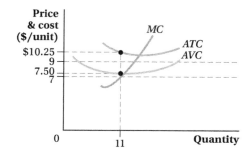

a. The owner of the firm finds that marginal cost and marginal revenue are equal at 11 units of output. If the owner produces 11 units, what will his profit or loss be?

b. Suppose instead that the owner decides to produce nothing—he idles the production line and cuts his variable costs to zero. What will his profit or loss be?

c. If the price is $7, is it better for the firm to produce 11 units, or nothing at all? What if the price is $9?

11. Marty sells flux capacitors in a perfectly competitive market. His marginal cost is given by $MC = Q$. Thus, the first capacitor Marty produces has a marginal cost of $1, the second has a marginal cost of $2, and so on.

a. Draw a diagram showing the marginal cost of each unit that Marty produces.

b. If flux capacitors sell for $2, determine the profit-maximizing quantity for Marty to produce.

c. Repeat part (b) for $3, $4, and $5.

d. The supply curve for a firm traces out the quantity that firm will produce and offer for sale at various prices. Assuming that the firm chooses the quantity that maximizes its profits [you solved for these in (b) and (c)], draw another diagram showing the supply curve for Marty's flux capacitors.

e. Compare the two diagrams you have drawn. What can you say about the supply curve for a competitive firm?

12. Consider the following graph, which depicts the cost curves of a perfectly competitive seller of potatoes. Potatoes currently sell for $3 per pound.

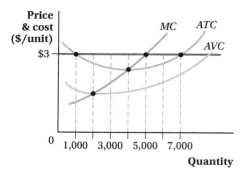

a. To maximize profit, how many pounds of potatoes should this seller produce?

Suppose that the potato grower's bank ratchets up the interest rate applicable to the grower's adjustable-rate mortgage loan. This increases the size of the potato grower's monthly mortgage payment.

b. Illustrate the change in the mortgage payment by shifting the appropriate cost curves.

c. Which curves shift? Which do not? Why?

d. How does the change in interest rates affect the grower's decision on how many potatoes to produce?

e. What happens to the potato grower's profit as a result of the increased interest rate?

f. How does the change in interest rates affect the shape and/or position of the grower's short-run supply curve?

13. The graphs below depict supply curves for John, Paul, and George, who are three producers in the perfectly competitive songwriting industry.

(a) John

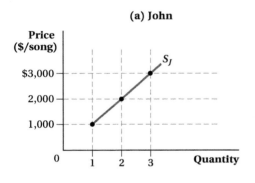

(b) Paul

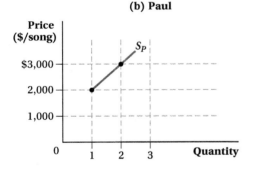

(c) George

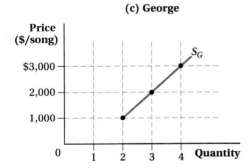

a. If the price of songs is $1,000, how many songs will John write? Paul? George? The three combined?

b. If the price of songs is $2,000, how many songs will John write? Paul? George? The three combined?

c. If the price of songs is $3,000, how many songs will John write? Paul? George? The three combined?

d. Assume that John, Paul, and George are the only three producers in the industry. Using your answers to (a–c), graph the short-run industry supply curve.

14. Consider Minnie the pearl producer with cost curves as shown below. Minnie produces 1,000 pearls when the price of pearls is $100.

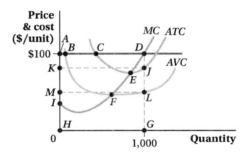

a. What is the area of producer surplus earned by Minnie if the price of pearls is $100?

b. Explain why areas *ADI* and *ADLM* must be equal.

15. For the past nine months, Iliana has been producing artisanal ice creams from her small shop in Chicago. She's been just breaking even (earning zero economic profit) that entire time. This morning, the state Board of Health informed her that they are doubling the annual fee for the dairy license she operates under, retroactive to the beginning of her operations.

a. In the short run, how will this fee increase affect Iliana's output level? Her profit?

b. In the long run, how will this fee increase affect Iliana's output level?

c. Suppose that instead of doubling the annual fee for a license, the state Board of Health required Iliana to treat every pint of ice cream to prevent the growth of bacteria. How would this stipulation affect Iliana's production decision and profit in both the short and long run?

16. Martha is one producer in the perfectly competitive jelly industry. Last year, Martha and all of her competitors found themselves earning economic profits.

a. If entry and exit from the jelly industry are free, what do you expect to happen to the number of suppliers in the industry in the long run?

b. Because of the entry/exit you described in part (a), what do you expect to happen to the industry supply of jelly? Explain.

c. As a result of the supply change you described in part (b), what do you expect to happen to the price of jelly? Why?

d. As a result of the price change you indicated in part (c), how will Martha adjust her output?

17. The canola oil industry is perfectly competitive. Every producer has the following long-run total cost function: $LTC = 2Q^3 - 15Q^2 + 40Q$, where Q is measured in tons of canola oil. The corresponding marginal cost function is given by $LMC = 6Q^2 - 30Q + 40$.

a. Calculate and graph the long-run average total cost of producing canola oil that each firm faces for values of Q from 1 to 10.

b. What will the long-run equilibrium price of canola oil be?

c. How many units of canola oil will each firm produce in the long run?

d. Suppose that the market demand for canola oil is given by $Q = 999 - 0.25P$. At the long-run equilibrium price, how many tons of canola oil will consumers demand?

e. Given your answer to (d), how many firms will exist when the industry is in long-run equilibrium?

18. Suppose that the restaurant industry is perfectly competitive. All producers have identical cost curves, and the industry is currently in long-run equilibrium, with each producer producing at its minimum long-run average total cost of $8.

a. If there is a sudden increase in demand for restaurant meals, what will happen to the price of restaurant meals? How will individual firms respond to the change in price? Will there be entry into or exit from the industry? Explain.

b. In the market as a whole, will the change in the equilibrium quantity be greater in the short run or the long run? Explain.

c. Will the change in output on the part of individual firms be greater in the short run or the long run? Explain and reconcile your answer with your answer to part (b).

19. Suppose that the market for eggs is initially in long-run equilibrium. One day, enterprising and profit-hungry egg farmer Atkins has the inspiration to fit his laying hens with rose-colored contact lenses. His inspiration is true genius—overnight his egg production rises and his costs fall.

a. Will farmer Atkins be able to leverage his inspiration into greater profit in the short run? Why?

b. Farmer Atkin's right-hand man, Abner, accidentally leaks news of the boss' inspiration at the local bar and grill. The next thing Farmer Atkins knows, he's being interviewed by Brian Williams for the NBC evening news. What short-run adjustments do you expect competing egg farmers to make as a result of this broadcast? What will happen to the profits of egg farms?

c. In the long run, what will happen to the price of eggs? What will happen to the profits of egg producers (including those of Farmer Atkins)?

d. Explain how, in the long run, competition coupled with the quest for profits ends up making producers better off only for a little while, but consumers better off forever.

20. Assume that the ice cream industry is perfectly competitive. Each firm producing ice cream must hire an operations manager. There are only 50 operations managers that display extraordinary talent for producing ice cream; there is a potentially unlimited supply of operations managers with average talent. Operations managers are all paid $200,000 per year.

- The long-run total cost (in thousands of dollars) faced by firms that hire operations managers with exceptional talent is given by $LTC_E = 200 + Q^2$, where Q is measured in thousands of gallon tubs of ice cream. The corresponding marginal cost function is given by $LMC_E = 2Q$, and the corresponding long-run average total cost is $LATC_E = 200/Q + Q$.

- The long-run total cost faced by firms that hire operations managers with average talent is given by $LTC_A = 200 + 2Q^2$. The associated marginal cost function is given by $LMC_A = 4Q$, and the corresponding long-run average total cost is $LATC_A = 200/Q + 2Q$.

a. Derive the firm supply curve for ice cream producers with extraordinary operations managers.

b. Derive the firm supply curve for ice cream producers with average operations managers.

c. The minimum $LATC_A$ (for firms with average operations managers) is $40, achieved when those firms produce 10 units of output. The minimum $LATC_E$ (for firms with exceptional operations managers) is $28.28, achieved when those firms produce 14 units of output. Explain why, given only that information, it is not possible to determine the long-run equilibrium price of gallon tubs of ice cream.

d. Referring to part (c), suppose that you know that the market demand for ice cream is given by $Q^d = 8,000 - 100P$. Explain why, in the long run, that demand will not be filled solely by firms with extraordinary managers. (*Hint*: Derive the industry supply of extraordinary producers and then use the demand curve to determine the equilibrium price. Can that price persist in the long run?)

e. In part (d), you explained why the supply side of the market will consist of both firms with extraordinary managers and firms with average managers. What will the long-run equilibrium price of ice cream be?

f. At the price you determined in part (e), all 50 firms with extraordinary managers will find remaining in the industry worthwhile. How many firms with average managers will also remain in the industry?

g. At the price you determined in part (e), how much profit will a firm with an average manager earn?

h. At the price you determined in part (e), how much profit will a firm with an extraordinary manager earn? How much economic rent will that talented manager generate for her firm?

Market Power and Monopoly

9

f you were in the market for a tablet computer in the spring of 2010, you had exactly one option: You could go for the iPad or, well, the iPad. It didn't even come in a choice of colors.

Apple couldn't have been happier. They had introduced a fantastically popular product, people were literally lined up ready to buy it, and the company was more or less the only game in town. Other technology companies were rushing their own tablets into production and distribution, but it would take time. It would probably also take considerable persuading to convince many wannabe iPad owners to give up their plans and buy a different product even if it were available.

This sort of situation doesn't fit the perfectly competitive model of a firm's supply behavior we covered in Chapter 8. In a perfectly competitive market, a firm's output is so small relative to the total market that its choice of whether or how much to produce does not have a noticeable impact on the total supply in the market. For this reason, a perfectly competitive firm takes the market price of its products as given when making its

market power
A firm's ability to influence the market price of its product.

monopoly
A market served by only one firm.

monopolist
The sole supplier and price setter of a good on the market.

barriers to entry
Factors that prevent entry into markets with large producer surpluses.

natural monopoly
A market in which it is efficient for a single firm to produce the entire industry output.

profit-maximizing production choices. But that was not at all the case for Apple and the iPad in mid-2010. After all, Apple more or less *was* the market supply. By adjusting the number of iPads it produced for the market, it could cause movements along the market demand curve. If Apple produced only a few iPads, for example, the low quantity supplied would meet the demand curve at a high price, and quantity demanded would also be low. If it produced more, the quantity supplied would equal quantity demanded further down the demand curve, at a lower price. Therefore, Apple's choice of the quantity of iPads it supplied to the market gave it effective control over the price at which the iPad sold.

In this chapter, we start to look at firms' production choices when they have some ability to control the price at which their product sells. A firm that can influence the price its product sells for is said to have **market power**. The most extreme version of market power is a **monopoly**, a market that is served by only one firm. In the spring of 2010, Apple basically had a monopoly in the tablet computer market. A firm that has a monopoly (a **monopolist**) has the most market power; for a given market demand curve, its decision about how much to supply completely determines the market price (it's a price setter). On the other end of the spectrum, firms in perfectly competitive markets are price takers. Because they have no influence over the market price, they have no market power.

As we see in this chapter, firms with market power do not behave in the same way as perfectly competitive firms do. They recognize that their supply decisions will influence the price at which they can sell their output, so they take this into account when choosing how much to produce and sell. Perfectly competitive firms don't have this concern, so they make different output choices. One interesting outcome that we'll learn about is that market power can be measured, and that as firms' market power falls, their supply behaviors become more and more like those of perfectly competitive firms. In fact, perfect competition is really just a special case of our more general model of supply behavior: When market power falls all the way to zero, a firm with market power behaves exactly like a perfectly competitive firm.

9.1 Sources of Market Power

Some industries, like computer operating systems, airlines, and car manufacturers, for example, invariably end up with only a few companies having substantial market power. What differentiates these industries from perfectly competitive ones? How do firms in these industries gain the ability to influence the price at which they sell their goods? Where does their market power come from?

A key element of sustainable market power is that there must be something about the market that prevents competitors from entering it until the price is as low as it would be if the market were perfectly competitive. A firm with market power can generate a substantial amount of producer surplus and profit in a way that a competitive firm cannot. (Remember that producer surplus is the same thing as a firm's profit plus its fixed cost. In the long run, when fixed cost is zero, profit and producer surplus are equal.) As we saw in Chapter 8, however, that producer surplus should be an irresistible draw for other firms to enter the market and try to capture some of it. **Barriers to entry** are the factors that keep entrants out of a market despite the existence of a large producer surplus that comes from market power. The next few sections discuss the most important barriers to entry.

Extreme Scale Economies: Natural Monopoly

The existence of a **natural monopoly** is one barrier to entry. A natural monopoly refers to a situation in which the cost curve of a firm in an industry exhibits economies of scale at any output level. In other words, the firm's long-run average total cost curve is always downward-sloping—the bigger the firm gets, the lower is its average total cost, even if it sells the entire market quantity itself.

In this type of situation, it is efficient (from a production standpoint) for society if a single firm produces the entire industry output; splitting output across more firms would raise the average total cost of production. Suppose a company could produce as large a quantity as it wants at a constant marginal cost of $10 per unit and has a fixed cost of $100. In this case, average total cost (total costs divided by output) declines across all quantities of output. In equation form,

$$TC = FC + VC = 100 + 10Q$$

so

$$ATC = \frac{TC}{Q} = \frac{100 + 10Q}{Q} = \frac{100}{Q} + 10$$

The larger the firm's quantity produced, Q, the lower is its average total cost. If all the firms in an industry have this same cost structure, the lowest-total-cost way to serve industry demand would be for one firm to produce everything. If more than one firm produces, the industry's average total cost of producing output rises because each firm that operates has to pay the fixed cost of $100 to produce anything at all. Having only one firm in the industry saves the replication of those fixed costs. That's why it is more cost-effective from society's perspective to have only one producer in the industry. Further, at a more practical level, it's difficult in these types of markets for new firms to enter and compete with the incumbent, because the incumbent's size usually gives it a cost advantage. Therefore, in markets with cost curves like this (high fixed cost and constant or slowly rising marginal cost), one firm will tend to become very large and dominate the industry with its low cost.

Many economists believe electricity transmission is a natural monopoly. The fixed cost of building a network of transmission lines, substations, meters, and so on, to supply homes and businesses is very large. Once the network is built, however, the marginal cost of delivering another kilowatt-hour of electricity is fairly close to constant. Therefore, we might expect a single firm to handle electrical transmission in a given market, and that is exactly what we often observe. If even just two competing firms operated in the transmission market in an area, there would be two sets of power lines running everywhere, and the fixed costs of the two firms would be huge. The additional cost of this second distribution network would be reflected in higher electricity prices.

Because electricity transmission companies are often natural monopolies, they are regulated by the government. Later in the chapter, we discuss why the government often regulates the behaviors of firms with market power whether their market power is the result of a natural monopoly or not. All that said, it is important to realize that even natural monopolies can disappear if demand changes sufficiently over time. Demand can rise so much that average total cost eventually rises enough to enable new firms to enter the market. This has been argued to have happened in a number of markets formerly believed to be natural monopolies, such as the markets for telephone and cable television service.

 **application**

Natural Monopoly in Satellite Radio

A real-life example of an industry that was probably a natural monopoly but consisted of two firms is satellite radio. Two companies, XM Radio and Sirius, launched satellites at a tremendous fixed cost and broadcast their own radio stations across the country. The advantage of satellite radio is that the quality of the audio is high, you can get the same stations in different markets if you are traveling, and you can access much more specialized channels (like the Bluegrass channel or the NASCAR channel) than you can from regular, over-the-air FM broadcasts. Customers pay a monthly subscription fee of about $20 per month.

The two services were quite similar technologically, so they tried to distinguish themselves from one another in customers' minds. XM signed an exclusive deal to carry all NFL football games on the radio, for example. Sirius signed deals to carry all MLB baseball games and to carry shock-jock Howard Stern (thus giving him wider latitude to be offensive than he had on regular radio).

It didn't work. Because the cost structure of a satellite radio company comprises a whopping fixed cost (building and launching the satellite) and a very low marginal cost, splitting the market meant that both companies operated at high levels of average total cost. They each incurred large losses as a result. The economics of the market said that two firms shouldn't exist, and the market finally realized this: In 2008 XM and Sirius merged to become one firm. ■

Switching Costs

A second common type of barrier to entry is the presence of consumer switching costs. If customers must give something up to switch to a competing product, this will tend to generate market power for the incumbent and make entry difficult. Think of a consumer who flies one airline regularly and has built up a preferred status level in the airline's frequent flyer program. Even if a competing airline comes into the market with lower prices, it may have a hard time getting that person to fly with it, because the customer might lose his privileged status (shorter lines, upgrades, no checked-bag fees, etc.) on his current carrier. This lost status is a switching cost that inhibits the consumer's ability to switch to a competitor, raising the incumbent airline's market power.

For some products, the switching cost comes from technology. For example, once you buy a DirecTV satellite dish and install it on your roof, the only way to switch to the DISH Network is to get a new satellite dish and converter box installed. Similarly, once you have typed in all your shipping information at Amazon or built up your reputation at eBay, you can't just transfer that information to a competitor. This also serves as a barrier to entry in the market for online retailers or auction sites.

For other products, switching costs arise from the costs of finding an alternative. If you have your car insurance with one company, it can be very time consuming to call around to different competitors to find out whether you could save money, and then fill out the paperwork required to actually switch.

Switching costs are not insurmountable barriers to entry. For example, some companies invest in trying to make comparing new options as easy as possible to convince people to swallow the switching costs and go with their (often) cheaper product. Progressive Insurance, for example, has a feature on its website that lets customers compare what their auto insurance premiums would be not just with Progressive, but with several of their competitors as well. But switching costs don't need to be insurmountable to be effective. To reduce the threat of competition and give the incumbent firm some market power, switching costs only need to be high enough to make entry costly, not impossible.

network good
A good whose value to each consumer increases with the number of other consumers of the product.

Perhaps the most extreme version of switching costs exists with a **network good:** a good whose value to each customer rises with the number of other consumers who use the product. With network goods, each new consumer creates a benefit for every other consumer of the good. Facebook is one example of a network good. If you are the only person in the world on Facebook, your account is not going to be much fun or very useful. If you're one of millions with accounts, however, now you're talking (. . . to each other).

The combination of large economies of scale (at or approaching natural monopoly levels) and network goods' attributes creates powerful entry barriers. Computer operating systems like Microsoft Windows are prone to become monopolies because they both have major economies of scale in production (software is a high-fixed-cost, low-marginal-cost business) and are network goods (people want to use a common operating system so that they can share software and file structure platforms).

Product Differentiation

Even if firms sell products that compete in the same market, all consumers might not see each firm's product as a perfect substitute for other firms' versions. For example, all bicycle makers operate in what could be thought of as the same market, but not every potential bike buyer will see a $500 Trek as exactly the same thing as a $500 Cannondale (or a $500 Giant, or...). That means firms can price slightly above their competition without losing all of their sales to their competitors. There is a segment of consumers who have a particular preference for one firm's product and will be willing to pay a premium (a limited premium, but a premium nonetheless) for it. This imperfect substitutability across varieties of a product is called **product differentiation,** and it is another source of market power. Product differentiation, which exists in one form or the other in most industries, prevents new firms from coming into the market and stealing most of the market demand just by pricing their product version a bit below the incumbents' prices. We discuss product differentiation in greater detail in Chapter 11.

product differentiation
Imperfect substitutability across varieties of a product.

Absolute Cost Advantages or Control of Key Inputs

Another common barrier to entry is a firm's absolute cost advantage over other firms in obtaining a key input. If a firm has control of a key input, that means it has some special asset that other firms do not have. For example, a key input might be a secret formula or a scarce resource. Controlling this input allows a firm to have costs lower than those of any competitor. To give an extreme example, suppose one firm owns the only oil well in existence and can prevent anyone else from drilling one. That would be a major advantage, because everyone else's cost of producing oil is infinite. The control of the input does not need to be that extreme, though. If a firm has one oil well whose production cost is substantially below that of everyone else's wells, that would be a cost advantage, too. These other firms would find it difficult to take business away from the low-production-cost firm, thus preserving its market power.

 application

Controlling a Key Input—The Troubled History of Fordlandia, Brazil

In the 1800s, there was no synthetic rubber. All rubber came from trees, and Brazil's rubber trees (*Hevea brasiliensis*) were the world's leading source. Rubber was one of Brazil's great exports.

In their natural state, the trees were often miles apart and hard to reach. In addition, because South American leaf-blight fungus (which attacked the trees in Brazil) could spread so easily from one tree to another, people could not plant the trees closer together. In 1876 an Englishman named Henry Wickham stole 70,000 rubber seeds for the British, who then planted them in concentrated plantations of many trees in what is now Malaysia. The innovation of planting the trees close together in a place without disease dramatically reduced the cost of harvesting rubber, gave

Rubber trees planted close together on a plantation in Malaysia.

Gavin Hellier/Alamy

the British an absolute cost advantage over everyone else in the rubber industry, and conferred market power on British rubber producers. By the early 1900s, Britain's plantations in Asia were meeting 95% of the world's demand for rubber. It was "the first worldwide monopoly of a strategic resource in human history."[1]

[1] Joe Jackson, *The Thief at the End of the World*: *Rubber, Power and the Seeds of Empire*. New York: Viking, 2008.

Fordlandia ruins in Brazil.

In 1927 Henry Ford needed rubber for car tires and tried to copy the British. He set up a rubber plantation city in the Amazon called Fordlandia. Unfortunately, because Ford never consulted any experts on rubber trees, the Fordlandia plantation rapidly fell prey to the leaf-blight fungus, culture clash, social unrest, and other ills. Repeated efforts to start new plantations all failed. As a result, Ford was unable to imitate the success of the British, and no rubber from Fordlandia was ever used in a Ford car.

Britain's market power from the absolute cost advantage by controlling this key input (rubber plants not threatened by the fungus) survived until the development of cheap synthetic rubber after World War II. It's still true, though, that if you travel from Brazil to Malaysia, the Malaysian government requires you to walk through a fungicide treatment at the airport and irradiates your luggage with ultraviolet radiation to kill any South American leaf blight you might be harboring. ■

Government Regulation

A final important form of entry barrier is government regulation. If you want to drive a cab in New York, you need to have a medallion (a chunk of metal that is actually riveted to a car's hood to show that the New York Taxi & Limousine Commission has granted the cab a license to operate). The number of medallions is fixed; currently, there are just over 13,000 available. If you want to enter this industry, you need to buy a medallion from its current owner, and you better start saving: Lately, medallion prices have been more than $700,000. That's a considerable entry barrier for a taxi driver. There are numerous other rules that prevent entry, such as licensing requirements in many occupations and industries.

Note, however, that some regulatory barriers are intentional and probably good, as we discuss later in the chapter when we consider government responses to monopoly. Examples include things like patents and copyrights, which explicitly give companies protection from entry by forbidding direct competitors.

Where There's a Will (and Producer Surplus), There's a Way

One important aspect to remember about barriers to entry is that they seldom last forever. If the producer surplus protected by entry barriers is large, competitors can often eventually find their way around even the most formidable barriers to entry. DuPont invented Nylon, the synthetic material, and patented it. In theory, this should have prevented entry. In reality, other companies figured out ways to develop competing, though not identical, synthetic fabrics that ultimately undermined the Nylon monopoly. Because there is no limit to the inventive capacity of the human mind, in the long run entrepreneurs and entrepreneurial firms will often find ingenious ways to encroach on other firms' protected positions.

9.2 Market Power and Marginal Revenue

Most firms have some sort of market power, even if they are not monopolists. We recognized this reality in Chapter 8 when we noted that truly perfectly competitive firms are rare—farmers who grow commodity crops and maybe a few other firms take prices as completely given, but they're the exception. The competitive market model is more of a useful starting point for studying market structures than it is a description of most product markets.

freakonomics

Why Drug Dealers Want Peace, Not War

When it comes to gaining market power, monopolists have been extremely creative in the strategies they employ: lobbying governments for privileged access to markets, temporarily pricing below marginal cost to keep out rivals, and artificially creating entry barriers, just to name a few.

But murder?

Can you imagine the CEO of Anheuser Busch InBev ordering a hit man to take out the board of directors of MillerCoors? No chance. Yet, not too long ago, when Prohibition laws made it illegal to produce and consume alcohol, such actions were commonplace among the "firms" that produced alcohol. For gangsters like Al Capone, violence was key to establishing and maintaining market power.

The crack cocaine trade offers a modern example of the same phenomenon. Because crack is illegal, crack markets function without legal property rights or binding contracts. Violence becomes a means of enforcing contracts and establishing market power. And because these gangsters are already working illegally, the costs of murder aren't nearly as high as in legal ventures. Researchers estimate that roughly one-third of *all* the homicides that occur in the United States—nearly 5,000 per year—are carried out by drug dealers fighting over property rights. But in a study based on the actual financial records of a Chicago gang over a three-year period, Steven Levitt and Sudhir Venkatesh showed that gang leaders try to avoid excessive use of violence. Why? Because it's bad for business! The shootings associated with a gang war scare away customers, reducing revenues by nearly 30%. During gang wars, the drug gang actually generated negative profits, on average.

Violence is one of the biggest costs of the illegal drug trade. Reducing this violence is one of the benefits touted by advocates of drug legalization. Simple economics suggests an alternative way to reduce the illegal drug trade and its effects. It is the high demand for drugs that makes drug sellers willing to take such extreme actions to establish market power. If the demand for illegal drugs were reduced, the ills associated with these markets would shrink, too. Several approaches along these lines have been tried—harsher punishments for users, education campaigns about drugs' health effects, and telling people to "Just Say No." These policies have met with mixed success, at best. Still, it's worth thinking about how to design better ways to reduce illegal drug demand, given the enormous benefits a sustained demand reduction would create.

What does it mean, practically speaking, for a firm to have market power? Suppose BMW quintupled production of all its vehicle models. We would expect the greater quantity of BMWs supplied to cause a movement down and along the demand curve to a new quantity at a lower price. Conversely, if BMW cut its production to one-fifth of its current level, we would expect BMW prices to rise. These outcomes mean that BMW should not act as if its production decisions don't affect its prices. That is, BMW is not a price taker because the price of its product depends on the quantity of cars it produces. It faces a downward-sloping demand curve: If BMW produces more cars, it will drive down the market price. If it produces fewer cars, it will increase price.

In fact, because BMW doesn't take its price as given, we could express the equivalent concept in terms of BMW choosing its price and letting the market determine the quantity it sells. That is, having market power means that if BMW sets a lower price for its cars, it will sell more of them, while if it raises prices, it will sell fewer. If a price-taking firm charges more than the market price, it will lose all its demand. But BMW won't. This is exactly the idea introduced in our earlier discussion of

Apple and the iPad. We can describe the firm's decision in terms of either choosing its profit-maximizing price or choosing its profit-maximizing level of output; either way, we (and the firm) get the same result.

Market Power and Monopoly

We made the argument that Apple was, effectively, a monopolist in the tablet computer market in the spring of 2010, but clearly we couldn't say the same about BMW. It competes against several other automakers in every market in which it operates. Why, then, do we talk about its price-setting ability the same way we talk about Apple in the tablet computer market? We do so because the basic lessons of this chapter apply whenever a firm has any market power, even if it isn't a monopolist. The key element of our analysis in this chapter is that a firm with market power faces a downward-sloping demand curve. In other words, its output level and price are interrelated. The firm cannot just sell whatever quantity it produces at a fixed market price that it takes as given, as a perfectly competitive firm can.

For a true monopolist, the firm's demand curve is exactly the market demand curve. But even if a firm is not a true monopolist, its demand curve still can slope downward. This condition exists in many market structures in which firms face competitors. As we will see in Chapter 11, two common types of these other market structures are **oligopoly,** in which a few competitors operate in a market, and **monopolistic competition,** in which there are many firms in the market but each firm's product is different enough that it faces a downward-sloping demand curve for the product it produces. The difference between monopoly and these other two cases is that in oligopoly and monopolistic competition, the particular shape of the demand curve faced by any given firm (even though it still slopes down) depends on the supply decisions of the *other* firms in the market. In a monopoly, there are no such interactions between firms. The monopoly's demand curve is the market demand, and that's that.

While we'll deal more extensively with the nature of interactions between firms in oligopoly and monopolistically competitive markets in Chapter 11, in this chapter we analyze how a firm in those kinds of markets chooses its production (or price) level *if it assumes that other firms will not change their behaviors in response to its choices.* Having made this assumption, as long as the firm's demand curve slopes downward, our analysis is the same whether this demand curve can be moved around by a competitor's actions (as in an oligopoly or monopolistically competitive market) or not (as in a monopoly). As a result, we sometimes interchange the terms "market power" and "monopoly power" even if the firm we are analyzing is not literally a monopolist. The point is that once the firm's demand curve is determined, its decision-making process is the same whether it is a monopoly, an oligopolistic firm, or a monopolistically competitive firm.[2]

oligopoly
Market structure in which a few competitors operate.

monopolistic competition
Market structure with a large number of firms selling differentiated products.

---

[2] This similarity between the supply behavior of a monopolist and nonmonopoly firms that face downward-sloping demand curves is very handy, because it is often difficult to say definitively whether a firm is a monopolist or not. A key element of defining monopoly is in deciding what the relevant market is. Your favorite hamburger place on the corner might be the only firm selling *those kinds of hamburgers* in *that location.* But you'd be hard pressed to call it a monopolist, even if you defined the market as narrowly as just "hamburger restaurants," and certainly not if you defined the market as including "places to eat." That's because you recognize that many of the restaurant's customers would be willing to substitute to other eateries, hamburger or otherwise, if the corner place significantly raised its prices. Even Apple, with iPads in 2010, wouldn't be a monopolist if we defined the market as "computing devices." Where to draw the boundaries of a market depends a lot on expected substitution patterns and can be tricky, but the nice thing is the gray area between monopoly and not-monopoly isn't that important to our analysis in this chapter. Again, what matters is that the firm faces a downward-sloping demand curve for any reason.

Marginal Revenue

The key to understanding how a firm with market power acts is to realize that, because it faces a downward-sloping demand curve, it can only sell more of its good by reducing its price. This one fact enters into every decision such firms make. As we learn later in the chapter, because firms with market power recognize the relationship between output and price, they will restrict output in a way that perfectly competitive firms won't. They do so to keep prices higher (and thereby make more money).

To see why these firms restrict output to keep their prices high, we need to remember the concept of a company's marginal revenue, the additional revenue a firm earns from selling one more unit. At first, that just sounds like the price of the product. And as we saw in Chapter 8, for a firm with no market power, this is exactly the case; the price is the marginal revenue. If a hotdog vendor walking the stands at a football game (a "firm" that can reasonably be thought of as a price taker) sells another hotdog, his total revenue goes up by whatever price he sells the hotdog for. The price doesn't depend on how many hot dogs he sells; he is a price taker. He could sell hundreds of hot dogs and it wouldn't change the market price, so his marginal revenue is just market price P.

But for a seller with market power, the concept of marginal revenue is more subtle. The extra revenue from selling another unit is no longer just the price. Yes, the firm can get the revenue from selling one more unit, but because the firm faces a downward-sloping demand curve, the more it chooses to sell, the lower the price will be for *all* units it sells, not just that one extra unit. (*Important note*: The firm is not allowed to charge different prices to different customers here. We deal with that scenario in Chapter 10.) This reduces the revenue the firm receives for the other units it sells. When computing the marginal revenue from selling that last unit, then, the firm must also subtract the loss it suffers on every other unit.

An example will clarify the firm's situation. Let's suppose that the firm in this case is Durkee-Mower, Inc., a Massachusetts firm that makes Marshmallow Fluff. Fluff has been around since 1920 and has a dominant position in the marshmallow creme market in the northeastern United States (you may have had some in a Fluffernutter sandwich, a s'more, or a Rice Krispies bar). This prominence in the market means that Durkee-Mower faces a downward-sloping demand curve for Fluff. If it makes more Fluff, its market price will fall, because the only way to get consumers to buy up the extra Fluff is to lower its price.

Table 9.1 shows how the quantity of Fluff produced this year varies with its price. As the quantity produced rises, the price falls because of the downward-sloping demand

---

Table 9.1   Marginal Revenue for Marshmallow Fluff

Quantity (millions of pounds) (Q)	Price ($ per pound) (P)	Total Revenue ($ millions) (TR = P × Q)	Marginal Revenue ($ millions) (MR = $\frac{\Delta TR}{\Delta Q}$)
0	6	0	—
1	5	5	5
2	4	8	3
3	3	9	1
4	2	8	−1
5	1	5	−3

curve. The third column in Table 9.1 shows the total revenue for the year for each level of output. The marginal revenue of an additional unit of output (in this example, a unit is a million pounds) is shown in the last column. It equals the difference between total revenue at that level of output minus the total revenue had Durkee-Mower made one fewer unit.

If Durkee-Mower makes only 1 million pounds of Fluff, its price is $5 per pound, and its revenue is $5 million. Because total revenue would be zero if the firm didn't produce anything, the marginal revenue of the first million pounds is $5 million. If Durkee-Mower makes 2 million pounds of Fluff instead, the market price falls to $4 per pound—the lower price makes consumers willing to buy another million pounds of Fluff. Total revenue in this case is $8 million. Therefore, the marginal revenue of increasing output from 1 to 2 million pounds is $3 million, $3 per pound. Note that this is less than the $5 per pound price at a quantity of 1 million pounds. As we discussed earlier, the lower marginal revenue reflects the fact that a firm with market power must reduce the price of its product when it produces more. Therefore, the marginal revenue isn't just the price multiplied by one more unit of quantity (which would be $5 million in this case, or $5 per pound). It also includes the loss of revenue due to the fact that the firm now sells all units at a lower price. Because producing the extra million pounds drops price by $1 per pound, this portion of marginal revenue is equal to the quantity the firm now sells, 2 million pounds, times the drop in price, $1 per pound, or a loss of $2 million. The $3 million marginal revenue is therefore the gain from selling another unit at the old price, $5 million, minus the $2 million loss from the price reduction the extra output creates.

If Durkee-Mower produces 3 million pounds, the market price drops to $3 per pound. Total revenue at this quantity is therefore $9 million. The marginal revenue is now only $1 million. Again, this marginal revenue is less than the product of the market price and the extra quantity because producing more Fluff drives down the price that Durkee-Mower can charge for every unit it sells.

If the firm chooses to make still more Fluff, say, 4 million pounds, the market price drops further, to $2 per pound. Total revenue is now $8 million. That means in this case, Durkee-Mower has actually *reduced* its revenue (from $9 million to $8 million) by producing *more* Fluff. That is, the marginal revenue is now negative (−$1 million). In this case, the price-drop revenue loss due to the extra production outweighs the revenue gains from selling more units. If Durkee-Mower insists on making 5 million pounds, the price drops to $1 per pound and total revenue falls to $5 million. Again, the marginal revenue of this million-pound unit is negative, −$3 million, because the revenue loss due to price reductions outweighs the extra units sold.

Why Does the Price Have to Fall for Every Unit the Firm Sells?   One thing about marginal revenue that can be confusing for students at first glance is why the seller loses money on all of its sales if it decides to produce one more unit. For instance, in the Marshmallow Fluff example, why can't Durkee-Mower sell the first million pounds for $5 per pound, and then the second million pounds for $4 a pound, the third million for $3 a pound, and so on? That way the marginal revenue will always equal the price.

There are two reasons why the price drop applies to all units sold. The first is that we are not thinking of the firm's decision as being sequential. Durkee-Mower isn't deciding whether to sell a second million pounds after it has already sold its first million at $5 per pound. Instead, the firm is deciding whether to produce 1 million *or* 2 million pounds in this period. If it makes 1 million pounds, the price will be $5 per pound and revenue will be $5 million. If it instead produces 2 million pounds, each will be sold at a price of $4 per pound, and revenue will be $8 million. We are making the same assumption about the demand curve here that we have done throughout the book: The demand curve reflects demand during a given time period. All other issues of timing are ignored. Therefore, the demand curve reflects the quantity demanded *in this period* (a year in the Fluff example) at every price; whatever number of units the firm produces, they all sell at the same price.

The second reason why a price drop applies to all units sold is that we are assuming that, even within a particular time period, the market price has to be the same for *all* the units the firm sells. The firm can't sell the first unit to a consumer who has a high willingness to pay and the second unit to a consumer with a slightly lower willingness to pay. This is probably a realistic assumption in many markets, including the market for marshmallow creme. Grocery stores don't put multiple price tags on a given product. Imagine for a moment a scenario in which the price tag reads, "$5 if you really like Marshmallow Fluff, $4 if you like it, but not quite as much, and $1 if you don't really like Fluff but will buy it if it's cheap."

Marginal Revenue: A Graphical Approach   The idea that marginal revenue is different from the price is easy to see in a graph like Figure 9.1. On the downward-sloping demand curve, we can measure the total revenue TR (price × quantity) at two different points, x and y. At point x, the quantity sold is Q_1 and the price at which each unit is sold is P_1. The total revenue is price times quantity, seen in the figure as the rectangle $A + B$.

If the firm decides to produce more, say, by increasing output from Q_1 to Q_2, it will move to point y on the demand curve. The firm sells more units, but in doing so, the price falls to P_2. The new total revenue is $P_2 \times Q_2$ or the rectangle $B + C$. Therefore, the marginal revenue of this output increase is the new revenue minus the old revenue:

$$TR_2 = P_2 \times Q_2 = B + C$$

$$TR_1 = P_1 \times Q_1 = A + B$$

$$MR = TR_2 - TR_1$$

$$MR = (B + C) - (A + B) = C - A$$

The area C contains the extra revenue that comes from selling more goods at price P_2, but this alone is not the marginal revenue of the extra output. We must also subtract area A, the revenue the firm loses because it now sells all units (not just the marginal unit) for the lower price P_2 instead of P_1. In fact, if the price-lowering effect of increasing output is large enough, it is possible that marginal revenue could be less than zero. In other words, selling more product could actually end up reducing a firm's revenue.

Firms would like to sell different units at different prices if they could, charging high willingness-to-pay consumers a high price and low willingness-to-pay consumers a low price, because they could avoid the loss in marginal revenue caused by price falling for all their sales. This practice, called **price discrimination**, is possible in certain circumstances. We discuss them in Chapter 10.

price discrimination
Pricing strategy in which firms with market power charge different prices to customers based on their willingness to pay.

Figure 9.1   Understanding Marginal Revenue

For a firm with market power, the marginal revenue from producing an additional unit of a good is not equal to the good's price. When the firm decides to increase production from point x on the demand curve (quantity Q_1) to point y (Q_2), the price of the good decreases from P_1 to P_2. The firm's initial total revenue ($P_1 \times Q_1$) is equal to the area $A + B$. At the new production point, total revenue ($P_2 \times Q_2$) is equal to the area $B + C$. The firm's marginal revenue is the difference between the initial total revenue and the new total revenue, equal to $C - A$.

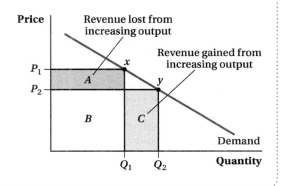

Marginal Revenue: A Mathematical Approach   We can compute a formula for a firm's marginal revenue using the logic we just discussed. As we saw, there are two effects of the firm selling an additional unit of output. Each of these will account for a component of the marginal revenue formula.

The first effect comes from the additional unit being sold at the market price P. In Figure 9.1, if we define $Q_2 - Q_1$ to be one unit, then this effect would be area C.

The second effect occurs because the additional unit drives down the market price for all the units the firm makes. To figure out how to express this component of marginal revenue, let's first label the change in price ΔP (so that, had the additional unit not been sold, the price would have been $P + \Delta P$). Let's also label the quantity before adding the incremental unit of output as Q and the incremental output as ΔQ. The second component of marginal revenue is therefore $\left(\frac{\Delta P}{\Delta Q}\right) \times Q$, the change in price caused by selling the additional unit of revenue times the quantity sold before adding the incremental unit. In Figure 9.1, this is area A. Note that because price falls as quantity rises—remember, the firm faces a downward-sloping demand curve—the term $\Delta P/\Delta Q$ is negative. This conforms to our logic above that this second component of marginal revenue is negative. It is the loss in revenue resulting from having to sell the non-incremental units at a lower price.

Putting together these components, we have the formula for marginal revenue (MR) from producing an additional quantity (ΔQ) of output (notice that we add the two components together even though the second represents a loss in revenue because $\Delta P/\Delta Q$ is already negative):

$$MR = P + \left(\frac{\Delta P}{\Delta Q}\right) \times Q$$

This negative second component means that marginal revenue will always be less than the market price. If we map this equation into Figure 9.1, the first term is the additional revenue from selling an additional unit at price P (area C) and the second is area A.

Looking more closely at this formula reveals how the shape of the demand curve facing a firm affects its marginal revenue. The change in price corresponding to a change in quantity, $\Delta P/\Delta Q$, is a measure of how steep the demand curve is. When the demand curve is really steep, price falls a lot in response to an increase in output. $\Delta P/\Delta Q$ is a large negative number in this case. This will drive down MR and can even make it negative. On the other hand, when the demand curve is flatter, price is not very sensitive to quantity increases. In this case, because $\Delta P/\Delta Q$ is fairly small in magnitude, the first (positive) component P of marginal revenue plays a larger relative role, keeping marginal revenue from falling too much as output rises. In the special case of perfectly flat demand curves, $\Delta P/\Delta Q$ is zero, and therefore marginal revenue equals the market price of the good. We know from Chapter 8 that when a firm's marginal revenue equals price, the firm is a price taker: Whatever quantity it sells will be sold at the market price P. This is an important insight that we return to below: Perfect competition is just the special case in which the firm's demand curve is perfectly elastic, so $MR = P$.

This connection between the slope of the demand curve and the level of a firm's marginal revenue is important in understanding how firms with market power choose the output levels that maximize their profits. We study this profit-maximization problem in detail in the next section, but it's useful to reflect a bit now on what the marginal revenue formula implies about it. Firms that face steep demand curves obtain small revenue gains (or even revenue losses, if MR is negative) when they increase output. This makes high output levels less profitable. Firms facing flatter demand curves obtain relatively large marginal revenues when raising output. This contrast suggests that (holding all else equal) the steeper the demand curve facing a firm, the lower its profit-maximizing output level. In the next section, we see that this is exactly the case.

We can apply the marginal revenue formula to any demand curve. For nonlinear demand curves, the slope $\Delta P/\Delta Q$ is the slope of a line tangent to the demand curve at quantity Q. But the formula is especially easy for linear demand curves, because $\Delta P/\Delta Q$ is constant. For any linear (inverse) demand curve of the form $P = a - bQ$, where a (the vertical intercept of the demand curve) and b are constants, $\Delta P/\Delta Q = -b$. The inverse demand curve itself relates P (the other component of marginal revenue) to Q, so if we also plug $P = a - bQ$ and $\Delta P/\Delta Q = -b$ into the MR formula above, we arrive at an expression for the marginal revenue of any linear demand curve:

$$MR = P + \left(\frac{\Delta P}{\Delta Q}\right)Q$$

$$= (a - bQ) + (-b)Q = a - 2bQ$$

This formula shows that marginal revenue varies with the firm's output. This is true in this specific case of a linear demand curve, but it's important to recognize that it holds more generally. (The only exception to this outcome is for a perfectly competitive firm, for which marginal revenue is constant and equal to the market price for any production quantity.) Here, the marginal revenue curve looks a lot like the inverse demand curve. It has the same vertical intercept as the inverse demand curve, which is equal to a. (To see this, just plug $Q = 0$ into the demand and marginal revenue curves.) It also slopes down: A higher Q leads to lower marginal revenue. The only difference between the marginal revenue and demand curves is that the former is twice as steep: bQ in the inverse demand curve has been replaced with $2bQ$.[3]

The formula for MR doesn't just look a lot like an inverse demand curve, it is conceptually similar, too. Just as the inverse demand curve shows how the price changes with production levels, the marginal revenue formula shows how marginal revenue changes with production levels. Further connecting the two curves is the fact that both the market price and marginal revenue are measured in the same units—dollars per unit of the good, for example.

9.1 figure it out

Suppose the demand curve is $Q = 12.5 - 0.25P$.

    a. What is the marginal revenue curve that corresponds to this demand curve?

    b. Calculate marginal revenue when $Q = 6$. Calculate marginal revenue when $Q = 7$.

Solution:

    a. First, we need to solve for the inverse demand curve by rearranging the demand function so that price is on the left side by itself:

$$Q = 12.5 - 0.25P$$
$$0.25P = 12.5 - Q$$
$$P = 50 - 4Q$$

So, we know that the inverse demand curve is $P = 50 - 4Q$, with $a = 50$ and $b = 4$. Because $MR = a - 2bQ$, we know that $MR = 50 - 8Q$.

    b. We can plug these values into our MR equation to solve for marginal revenue:

    When $Q = 6$, $MR = 50 - 8(6) = 50 - 48 = 2$.

    When $Q = 7$, $MR = 50 - 8(7) = 50 - 56 = -6$.

Note that, as we discussed above, MR falls as Q rises and can even become negative.

---

[3] If you know calculus, you can see that the multiplier of 2 comes from the derivative of the total revenue function. For a linear inverse demand curve $P = a - bQ$, the total revenue curve (the firm's revenue as a function of its quantity produced) that corresponds to it is $P \times Q$, or $aQ - bQ^2$. To find marginal revenue, which is the additional revenue from an incremental increase in quantity, we take the derivative of this total revenue function with respect to Q. Doing so gives $MR = a - 2bQ$.

9.3 Profit Maximization for a Firm with Market Power

Now that we know how to compute marginal revenue, we can figure out the profit-maximizing output level for any firm with market power.

Many students' first instinct is to suppose that a firm with market power seeking to maximize its profit should sell until the marginal revenue falls to zero and then stop. After all, any more production after that would reduce revenues, and couldn't be profitable. That sort of production rule would, in fact, be correct if there was no cost of production. With production costs, however, it's not quite accurate. A firm with market power should pay attention to its marginal revenue, but one more piece of the puzzle is necessary to figure out the profit-maximizing output level.

How to Maximize Profit

In Chapter 8, we discussed the two basic elements of firm profit—revenue and cost—and how each of these is determined by the firm's choice of how much output to produce. We saw there that the profit-maximizing output was the one that set marginal revenue equal to marginal cost. We went on to show that marginal revenue for a perfectly competitive firm equals the market price, so maximizing profit meant producing the quantity at which price equals marginal cost. The logic behind this condition is that if price is above marginal cost, the perfectly competitive firm should produce more because the additional revenue it would earn exceeds the additional cost. If price is below marginal cost, it should cut back on production because it's losing money on those extra units.

The same underlying logic works for firms with market power except that *marginal revenue no longer equals price*. To maximize its profit, a firm should choose its quantity where its marginal revenue equals its marginal cost:

$$MR = MC$$

If marginal revenue is above marginal cost, a firm can produce more and earn more revenue than the extra cost of production, and increase its profit. If marginal revenue is below marginal cost, a firm can reduce its output, lose less revenue than it saves in cost, and again raise its profit. Only when these two marginal values are equal does changing output not increase profit.

Thus, we see that the monopolist and the perfectly competitive firm do exactly the same thing. They both produce at the level where $MR = MC$. It's just that marginal revenue no longer equals price for a firm with market power, and that explains why it behaves differently than a perfectly competitive firm.

The $MR = MC$ condition gives us the quantity that maximizes the firm's profit, but it also allows us to figure out the profit-maximizing price. The height of the demand curve at the profit-maximizing quantity Q^* tells us what market price will prevail for the firm's product if it produces that quantity.

For a firm with market power, we can think of the firm choosing a profit-maximizing quantity as equivalent to choosing a profit-maximizing price. The demand curve ties together price and quantity, so picking one implies the other. The monopolist can either produce the profit-maximizing quantity of output and let the market determine the price (which will be the profit-maximizing price), or it can set the profit-maximizing price and let the market determine the quantity (which will be the profit-maximizing quantity).

An important factor to remember is that even though firms with market power have an ability to set the price for their output, they (even monopolists) cannot profitably charge whatever price they want to. A firm with market power could *try* to keep raising its price (or equivalently, keep cutting its output), but if the firm raises the price by too much, its customers will stop buying—even if there are no other competitors.

For example, in 2010 the iPad dominated the market and Apple clearly had market power as a result. Does this mean Apple could have charged whatever price it wanted? Suppose Apple had charged $20,000 for each iPad. Just about everyone would have stopped buying it, even if it was the only tablet computer on earth. The vast majority of people would simply not find it worth having the iPad at that price. By raising the price for its product, even a monopolist can lose business, not to competitors, but by driving consumers out of the market altogether. The firm is limited by the demand for its product. Because the demand curve is downward-sloping, any rise in price is accompanied by a decline in quantity demanded. This sensitivity to price means that monopolists can't (or more precisely, wouldn't want to if they cared about profit) set sky-high prices. They'll charge a higher price than a more competitive firm, but the price won't be infinitely higher.

Profit Maximization with Market Power: A Graphical Approach

We can apply the exact logic of the previous analysis to graphically derive the profit-maximizing output and price of a firm with market power, given the firm's demand and marginal cost curves. Let's assume we are again looking at the market for iPads and that marginal cost is constant at $200. Specifically, we will follow these steps:

Step 1: Derive the marginal revenue curve from the demand curve. For a linear demand curve, this will be another straight line with the same vertical intercept that is twice as steep. In Figure 9.2, the marginal revenue curve is shown as MR.

Step 2: Find the output quantity at which marginal revenue equals marginal cost. This is the firm's profit-maximizing quantity of output. In Figure 9.2, Apple's profit-maximizing level of output is Q^*, or 80 million iPads.

Step 3: Determine the profit-maximizing price by locating the point on the demand curve at the optimal quantity level. To determine the price Apple should charge consumers to maximize its profit, we follow Q^* up to the demand curve and then read the price off the vertical axis. If Apple produces the profit-maximizing output level of 80 million, the market price will be $600. (Or equivalently, if Apple charges a price of $600, it will sell 80 million iPads.)

That's all there is to it. Once we have the firm's MR curve, we can use the profit-maximization rule $MR = MC$ to find the firm's optimal level of output and price.

Figure 9.2 : How a Firm with Market Power Maximizes Profit

Apple will maximize its profit from the iPad by producing where $MR = MC$. Therefore, Apple will sell 80 million iPads at a price of $600 each, well above Apple's marginal cost of $200 per iPad.

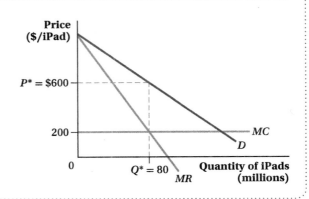

Profit Maximization with Market Power: A Mathematical Approach

We can also solve for the profit-maximizing quantity and price mathematically, given equations for the firm's demand and marginal cost curves. Again, we'll use the Apple iPad example.

Suppose Apple's marginal cost of producing iPads is constant at $200, and the demand curve for iPads (where Q is in millions and P in dollars) is $Q = 200 - 0.2P$. How much should Apple charge for iPads, and how many will it sell at that price? (Again, because of the equivalence of choosing price and choosing output level for firms with market power, we could ask how many iPads Apple should produce and at what price the iPads would sell, and the answer would be the same.)

We can figure this out using the same three-step process described above: Derive the marginal revenue curve, find the quantity at which the marginal revenue equals marginal cost, and then determine the profit-maximizing price by computing the price at that quantity on the demand curve.

Step 1: Derive the marginal revenue curve from the demand curve. Let's start by obtaining the inverse demand curve by rearranging the demand curve so that price is a function of quantity rather than the other way around:

$$Q = 200 - 0.2P$$
$$0.2P = 200 - Q$$
$$P = 1,000 - 5Q$$

This is a linear inverse demand curve of the form $P = a - bQ$, where $a = 1,000$ and $b = 5$. Earlier we learned that the marginal revenue curve for this type of demand curve is $MR = a - 2bQ$.[4] So for this demand curve, Apple's marginal revenue curve is

$$MR = 1,000 - 2(5Q) = 1,000 - 10Q$$

Step 2: Find the output quantity at which marginal revenue equals marginal cost. Apple's marginal cost is constant at $200, so we just set the marginal revenue curve equal to this value and solve for Q:

$$MR = MC$$
$$1,000 - 10Q = 200$$
$$800 = 10Q$$
$$Q^* = 80$$

So, Apple's profit-maximizing quantity of iPads is 80 million.

Step 3: Determine the profit-maximizing price by locating the point on the demand curve at the optimal quantity level. Find the profit-maximizing price by plugging the optimal quantity into the demand curve. This tells us at what price the optimal quantity (80 million iPads) will be sold:

$$P^* = 1,000 - 5Q^*$$
$$= 1,000 - 5(80)$$
$$= 1,000 - 400 = 600$$

---

[4] If we had a more complicated demand curve, we could compute the marginal revenue curve by using calculus. We would start with calculating total revenue by multiplying the inverse demand curve by Q. Then we would take the derivative with respect to Q to get the marginal revenue.

Given this demand curve and a constant marginal cost of $200 per iPad, then, Apple can maximize its profits by charging $600 per unit. It will sell 80 million iPads at this price. Notice that this price is well above Apple's marginal cost of $200, the price Apple would be charging in a perfectly competitive market. That's why firms like to have market power. The idea is simple: Reduce output. Raise prices. Make money.

9.2 figure it out

Babe's Bats (BB) sells baseball bats for children around the world. The firm faces a demand curve of $Q = 10 - 0.4P$, where Q is measured in thousands of bats and P is dollars per bat. BB has a marginal cost curve that is equal to $MC = 5Q$.

 a. Solve for BB's profit-maximizing level of output. Show the firm's profit-maximization decision graphically.

 b. What price will BB charge to maximize its profit?

Solution:

 a. To solve this problem, we should follow the three-step procedure outlined in the text. First, we need to derive the marginal revenue curve for BB bats. Because the firm faces a linear demand curve, the easiest way to obtain the marginal revenue curve is to start by solving for the firm's inverse demand curve:

$$Q = 10 - 0.4P$$
$$0.4P = 10 - Q$$
$$P = 25 - 2.5Q$$

For this inverse demand curve, $a = 25$ and $b = 2.5$. Therefore, since $MR = a - 2bQ$, we know that BB's MR curve will be

$$MR = 25 - 2(2.5Q) = 25 - 5Q$$

To solve for the profit-maximizing level of output, we can follow the profit-maximization rule $MR = MC$:

$$MR = MC$$
$$25 - 5Q = 5Q$$
$$10Q = 25$$
$$Q^* = 2.5$$

Therefore, BB should produce 2,500 bats. This profit-maximization decision is shown in the figure below. Profit is maximized at the output level at which the marginal revenue and marginal cost curves intersect.

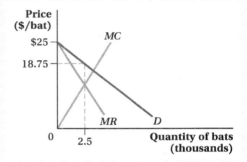

 b. To find BB's optimal price, we plug its profit-maximizing level of output ($Q^* = 2.5$) into its inverse demand curve:

$$P^* = 25 - 2.5Q^*$$
$$= 25 - 2.5(2.5)$$
$$= 25 - 6.25 = 18.75$$

BB should charge a price of $18.75 per bat. This is also demonstrated on the figure by following $Q^* = 2.5$ up to the demand curve and over to the vertical axis.

A Markup Formula for Companies with Market Power: The Lerner Index

We can take the logic we've just learned even further to come up with a rule-of-thumb for pricing that firms can use to determine profit-maximizing prices and output levels.

Start with the definition of MR from above:

$$MR = P + \left(\frac{\Delta P}{\Delta Q}\right) \times Q$$

We know that the firm maximizes its profits by setting $MR = MC$, so plug that in:

$$MR = P + \left(\frac{\Delta P}{\Delta Q}\right) \times Q = MC$$

Now we'll use a math trick of multiplying the second term on the left side of the equation by P/P. This doesn't change the value of the equation, because multiplying by P/P is just another way of multiplying by 1. This changes our expression to

$$P + \left(\frac{\Delta P}{\Delta Q}\right) \times \left(\frac{P}{P}\right) \times Q = MC$$

or $$P + \left(\frac{\Delta P}{\Delta Q} \times \frac{Q}{P}\right) \times P = MC$$

If the section in parentheses looks familiar to you, it's because it is the inverse of the elasticity of demand. Remember in Chapter 2 that we defined the price elasticity of demand E^D as $\frac{\Delta Q/Q}{\Delta P/P}$ or $\frac{\Delta Q}{\Delta P} \times \frac{P}{Q}$. The inverse of this value is $\frac{1}{E^d} = \frac{\Delta P}{\Delta Q} \times \frac{Q}{P}$. Substituting the inverse elasticity into the profit-maximization condition gives us

$$P + \left(\frac{\Delta P}{\Delta Q} \times \frac{Q}{P}\right) \times P = MC$$

$$P + \frac{1}{E^d} \times P = MC$$

A final bit of algebraic rearranging gives

$$P - MC = -\left(\frac{1}{E^d}\right) \times P$$

or $$\frac{P - MC}{P} = -\frac{1}{E^d}$$

markup
The percentage of the firm's price that is greater than its marginal cost.

Lerner index
A measure of a firm's markup, or its level of market power.

The left-hand side of this equation equals the firm's profit-maximizing **markup,** the percentage of the firm's price that is greater than (or "marked up" from) its marginal cost. What this equation indicates is that this markup should depend on the price elasticity of demand that the firm faces. Specifically, as demand becomes more elastic—that is, as E^D becomes more negative, or equivalently, larger in absolute value—the optimal markup as a fraction of price falls. (If you can't quite see this in the equation, notice that elastic demand means a large negative number for E^D is in the denominator, making the right-hand side of the equation small.) On the other hand, as demand becomes less elastic, E^D becomes smaller in absolute value, indicating that the markup should be a larger fraction of price.

If we stop to think about these implications for a minute, they make perfect sense. If demand is quite inelastic, consumers' purchases of the firm's product are not sensitive to changes in price. This makes it easier for the firm to increase its profit by raising its price—it will sell fewer units, but not too many fewer, and it will make a higher margin on every unit it does sell. This is exactly what the equation implies; the firm should mark up its price by a considerable amount over its marginal cost. A firm facing relatively elastic demand, on the other hand, will suffer a greater loss in quantity sold when it raises its price, making it less beneficial to charge a high markup over cost.

The measure of the markup given by the equation above has a special name: the **Lerner index** (after Abba Lerner, the economist who proposed it in 1934). As we just discussed, assuming the firm is trying to maximize its profit, the Lerner index tells us something about the nature of the demand curve facing the firm. When the index is high (i.e., when the markup accounts for a large fraction of the price), the demand for the firm's product is relatively inelastic. When the index is low, the firm faces relatively elastic demand. Because the ability to price above marginal cost is the definition of market power, the Lerner index is a measure of market power. The higher it is, the greater the firm's ability to price above its marginal cost.

The extreme case of perfectly elastic demand is interesting to study in terms of its implications for the Lerner index. When demand is perfectly elastic—the firm faces a horizontal demand curve and any effort to charge a price higher than the demand curve will result in a loss of all sales—then $E^d = -\infty$. As we see in the equation above, the Lerner index is equal to zero in this case. That means the markup is also zero; the firm sells at a price equal to marginal cost.

At the other end of the spectrum is the case when demand is perfectly inelastic—that is, when the demand curve is vertical and consumers are completely unresponsive to prices. In this case, $E^d = 0$, and the Lerner index equals 1. In this case, the product's price is all markup; the profit-maximizing price is, essentially, infinitely high.[5]

Another interesting case occurs when E^d is between 0 and −1—that is, when the firm faces a demand curve that is inelastic or unit elastic. In this case, the Lerner Index is greater than 1. But this would imply that $P - MC > P$, or $MC < 0$, and marginal cost can't be negative. Why does the optimal markup equation imply this nonsensical result? There is a mathematical answer that involves calculus, but there is an economic explanation as well. A firm should never operate at a point on its demand curve where demand is inelastic or unit elastic. (In the linear demand case, demand becomes less elastic as price falls.) To see why, let's think about what would happen if a firm was setting a price (or a quantity) that put it on an inelastic or unit elastic portion of its demand curve, and then decided to increase its price (or equivalently sell a smaller quantity). By definition, because demand is inelastic, whatever the percentage increase in price, the percentage drop in quantity will be smaller (or will exactly equal the percentage increase in price if demand is unit elastic). That means that the price increase will raise the firm's revenue (or not change it if demand is unit elastic). At the same time, because the firm is producing a smaller quantity, its total cost must fall, because cost curves always increase in quantity. So, the net effect of the price increase is to raise the firm's revenue (or keep it constant) while lowering its cost. In other words, the firm is guaranteed to raise profit by increasing prices as long as demand is inelastic. Therefore, it can't be profit maximizing to set a price where demand is inelastic.

The Lerner index can range anywhere from 0 (perfect competition) to 1 (perfectly inelastic demand). It is a summary of the amount of market power a firm has. In comparing degrees of market power across firms, the firm with the highest Lerner index has the most market power; the firm with the second-highest Lerner index has the second-most market power, and so on.

Measuring the Lerner Index   Firms with market power are keenly aware that their profit-maximizing markups are tied to the price elasticities they face. The difficulty from a practical standpoint, however, is that firms don't have a gauge from which they can simply read off a Lerner index to see what markup they should be charging. So, they can spend considerable effort trying to learn about the shape of the demand and marginal revenue curves they face, because that tells them about the price elasticity of demand of their customers.

Technologies that allow firms to change prices more frequently, and even offer different prices simultaneously to different consumers, have made firms' processes of feeling out their demand curves easier. This can lead to negative publicity, however. For example, Amazon

---

[5] We don't see firms charging infinite prices in practice, of course. That's because no firm faces perfectly inelastic demand. At some point, even if consumers' purchases don't depend on price up to that level, the price becomes high enough so that the consumers stop buying. In that case, the profit-maximizing price would be equal to the highest price at which consumers still buy.

got into a bit of trouble early in its history for conducting what it called a "pricing experiment" on its customers. Amazon was experimentally offering different prices to different customers for the same products, in an effort to measure the elasticity of demand by seeing how consumers' purchases responded to price changes. A customer sued when he discovered that when he removed the Amazon cookie from his computer, the price of the product he was shopping for dropped significantly. In the uproar that followed, people assumed that Amazon was price-discriminating, a practice we discuss in the next chapter. Amazon CEO Jeffrey Bezos apologized for the episode and indicated that there was no systematic price discrimination ongoing. He insisted that Amazon was simply randomizing prices to develop a better sense of demand in its market. This chapter shows exactly why Amazon might bother to do this. If a company has a good sense of the shape of its own demand curve, it can figure out the most profitable price to charge using the markup formula or the full monopoly pricing system.

 application

Market Power versus Market Share

Market power involves more than the size of a particular firm. For example, consider Dr. Brown's, a manufacturer of specialty sodas in the United States that produces a celery-flavored soda called Cel-Ray. Even though the sales of Coca-Cola are thousands of times larger than the sales of Cel-Ray, it turns out that Dr. Brown's has more market power than Coca-Cola by the economist's definition.

How can that be? The key factor to consider is the price elasticity of demand for the two products. Coca-Cola drinkers are, on average, fairly price-sensitive in the short run. The price elasticity of demand for a six-pack of Coke in a grocery store is around -4.1.[6] On the other hand, people who drink Cel-Ray must have a unique preference for the celery flavor. Whereas there are many substitutes for Coca-Cola, there really aren't many substitutes for Cel-Ray. Thus, Cel-Ray drinkers will likely be less price-sensitive than Coke drinkers. A reasonable guess at the price elasticity of demand for a six-pack of Cel-Ray is about -2.

If we use these two elasticities to measure the Lerner index for each product, we indeed see that Cel-Ray has more market power than Coke:

$$\text{Lerner index for Coke} = -\frac{1}{E^d} = -\frac{1}{-4.1} = 0.244$$

$$\text{Lerner index for Cel-Ray} = -\frac{1}{E^d} = -\frac{1}{-2} = 0.5$$

Therefore, Cel-Ray's profit-maximizing price is a higher markup over its marginal costs than Coke's profit-maximizing price. In other words, Coca-Cola's pricing behavior is actually closer to the pricing behavior of a competitive firm than Cel-Ray's. It is not the size of the market or the firm's market share that determines or measures market power, it is the firm's ability to price above its marginal cost. ■

The Supply Relationship for a Firm with Market Power

We now know how to figure out the profit-maximizing quantity and price for a firm with market power, and we can do so for any given marginal cost and demand curves the firm might face. As you might imagine, we could sketch out all the combinations of the firm's profit-maximizing quantities and prices implied by any possible set of marginal cost and demand curves.

Guzzle & Nosh

Dr. Brown's Cel-Ray soda, a lock on its market since 1869.

[6] Jean-Pierre Dube, "Product Differentiation and Mergers in the Carbonated Soft Drink Industry," *Journal of Economics and Management Strategy* 14, no. 4 (2005): 879–904.

This might sound a lot like a supply curve—it is, after all, a set of prices and the quantities produced. But it's not a supply curve. Firms with market power don't have supply curves, strictly speaking. Their profit-maximizing price and quantity combinations are not supply curves because those combinations depend on the demand curve the firm faces. As we saw in Chapter 8, supply curves exist completely independently of demand. They depend only on firms' marginal costs, because a perfectly competitive firm produces the quantity at which the market price (which the firm takes as given) equals its marginal cost. That's why a perfectly competitive firm's supply curve is a portion of its marginal cost curve, and a perfectly competitive industry's supply curve is the industry marginal cost curve. Neither of these supply curves is determined by anything having to do with demand; they are only about costs.

This strict relationship between costs and price isn't true for a firm with market power. Its optimal output level depends not only on the marginal cost curve, but also on the firm's marginal revenue curve (which is related to the demand curve). Put another way, a supply curve gives a one-to-one mapping between the price and a firm's output. But for a firm with market power, even holding constant its marginal cost curve, the firm could charge a high price at a given quantity if it faces a steeper demand curve or a lower price at the same quantity if it faced a flatter demand curve. Therefore, a simple mapping of price and quantity supplied is not possible for a firm with market power and there would be no supply curve.

9.4 How a Firm with Market Power Reacts to Market Changes

Now that we know how to figure out exactly how firms with market power should make production and pricing decisions to maximize profit, we can think through the market effects of various market changes, much as we did with supply and demand in the competitive setting. Even though firms with market power do not have a supply curve, we will see that in some ways they react similarly to competitive firms. There are some ways they can react, however, that are quite different.

Response to a Change in Marginal Cost

Let's first think about the effect of an increase in marginal cost. In the iPad example, marginal cost was constant at \$200 and the inverse demand curve was $P = 1{,}000 - 5Q$ (where Q is in millions). Suppose there's a fire in the plant that manufactures the screen on the iPad, raising the marginal cost of the screen, and as a result, the marginal cost of the iPad increases from \$200 to \$250. What will happen in the market for iPads?

To determine the market impact of this increase in marginal cost, we follow the three-step method but with the new marginal cost curve:

Step 1: **Derive the marginal revenue curve.** The demand curve hasn't changed, so this is the same as before: $MR = 1{,}000 - 10Q$.

Step 2: **Find the quantity at which $MR = MC$.** The MC is now \$250, so

$$1{,}000 - 10Q = 250$$

$$750 = 10Q$$

$$Q^* = 75$$

The new profit-maximizing quantity is 75 million units, down from 80 million.

Step 3: **Determine the profit-maximizing price using the optimal quantity and the demand curve.** The (inverse) demand curve is $P = 1{,}000 - 5Q$. Plugging in the new quantity, we have $P^* = 1{,}000 - 5(75) = \$625$. The new price will be \$625, up from \$600 before the fire.

Figure 9.3   How a Firm with Market Power Reacts to an Increase in Marginal Cost

If the marginal cost of producing an iPad rises from $200 to $250, Apple will decrease its output from 80 million to 75 million and the price of an iPad will rise from $600 to $625.

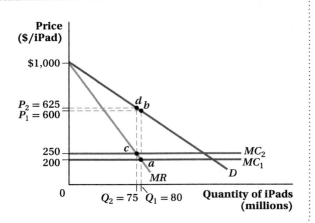

We illustrate the change from the initial equilibrium to the new one in Figure 9.3. The initial quantity of 80 million is set by $MR = MC_1$ ($200) at point a. This quantity corresponds to a price of $600, as indicated at point b. After the fire, the marginal cost curve shifts up to $250 ($MC_2$). Because the fire only affects the supply side of the market, the consumer's willingness to pay does not change, and the demand and marginal revenue curves do not shift. Now marginal revenue equals marginal cost at point c, at a quantity of 75 million. Following that quantity up to the demand curve (at point d), we can see that the price of an iPad will rise to $625.

A firm with market power responds to a cost shock in a way that is similar to a competitive firm's response. When marginal cost rises, price rises, and output falls. When marginal cost falls, price falls, and output rises.

But in competition, a change in marginal cost is fully reflected in the market price, because $P = MC$. That's not the case when the seller has market power. In the iPad example, the market price rose only $25 in response to a $50 increase in marginal cost. To maximize its profit, Apple does not want to pass along the full increase in its cost to its customers. The drop in quantity that results from the increase in cost is also smaller than the drop that would occur in a perfectly competitive market. Note, however, that the equilibrium quantity is still higher in a competitive market than one with market power, even after the cost increase. It's the *change* in Q that is smaller.

Response to a Change in Demand

Now suppose that instead of a cost shift, there is a parallel shift in the demand curve. Perhaps iPads become even more fashionable, increasing demand and shifting out the demand curve. Specifically, let's say the new inverse demand curve is $P = 1,400 - 5Q$. How would the market react to this change?

Again, we follow the three-step method. Because the demand curve has shifted in this case, the marginal revenue curve changes as well. The new demand curve is linear, so we know how to derive the marginal revenue curve; we double the number in front of the quantity in the inverse demand curve. So,

$$MR = 1,400 - 10Q$$

Setting this equal to the marginal cost (which we'll assume is back at its original level of $200) implies:

$$1{,}400 - 10Q = 200$$

$$10Q = 1{,}200$$

$$Q = 120$$

The quantity produced after the demand shift is now 120 million units, up from 80 million. Finally, we find the new price by plugging this quantity into the inverse demand curve:

$$P = 1{,}400 - 5Q$$

$$= 1{,}400 - 5(120)$$

$$= 800$$

The new price is $800, up from $600 before the demand shift.

An outward demand shift leads to an increase in both quantity and price in a market where the seller has market power, the same direction as in perfect competition. But again, the size of the changes differs.

The Big Difference: Changing the Price Sensitivity of Customers

One type of market change to which firms with market power react very differently from competitive firms is a change in the price sensitivity of demand—in other words, making the demand curve steeper or flatter. Say a new competing tablet comes along so that consumers' demand for iPads becomes more price-sensitive but doesn't change the quantity demanded at the current price. With perfect competition, as in panel a of Figure 9.4, the

Figure 9.4   Responses to a Rotation in the Demand Curve

(a) Perfect competition

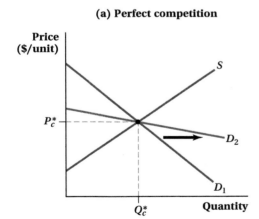

(b) Market power

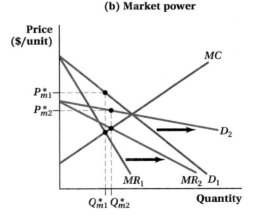

(a) For a perfectly competitive market, a rotation in the demand curve from D_1 to D_2 does not change the equilibrium quantity Q_c^* and price P_c^*.

(b) For a firm with market power, a rotation in the demand curve from D_1 to D_2 rotates the marginal revenue curve from MR_1 to MR_2. Prior to the rotation, the profit-maximizing quantity and price (Q_{m1}^*, P_{m1}^*) occurred where $MR_1 = MC$. After the rotation, the firm is profit-maximizing at a higher quantity and lower price (Q_{m2}^*, P_{m2}^*) where $MR_2 = MC$.

9.3 figure it out

The Power Tires Company has market power and faces the demand curve shown in the figure below. The firm's marginal cost curve is $MC = 30 + 3Q$.

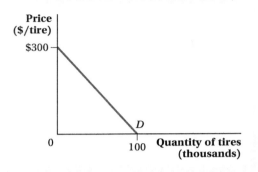

a. What is the firm's profit-maximizing output and price?

b. If the firm's demand declines to $P = 240 - 2Q$ while its marginal cost curve remains the same, what is the firm's profit-maximizing level of output and price? How does this compare to your answer for (a)?

c. Draw a diagram showing these two outcomes. Holding marginal cost equal, how does the shape of the demand curve affect the firm's ability to charge a high price?

Solution:

a. To solve for the firm's profit-maximizing level of output, we need to find the firm's marginal revenue curve. But, we only have a diagram of the demand curve. So, we will start by solving for the inverse demand function. The inverse demand function will typically have the form

$$P = a - bQ$$

where a is the vertical intercept and b is the absolute value of the slope $\left(= \left| \frac{\Delta P}{\Delta Q} \right| \right)$. We can see from the figure of the demand curve that $a = 300$. In addition, we can calculate the absolute value of the slope of the demand curve as $\left| \frac{\Delta P}{\Delta Q} \right| = \left| \frac{-300}{100} \right| = 3$. Therefore, $b = 3$. This means that the demand for Power Tires is

$$P = 300 - 3Q$$

We know that the equation for marginal revenue (when demand is linear) is $P = a - 2bQ$. Therefore,

$$MR = 300 - 6Q$$

Setting marginal revenue equal to marginal cost, we find

$$MR = MC$$
$$300 - 6Q = 30 + 3Q$$
$$270 = 9Q$$
$$Q = 30$$

To find price, we substitute $Q = 30$ into the firm's demand equation:

$$P = 300 - 3Q$$
$$= 300 - 3(30) = 210$$

The firm should produce 30,000 tires and sell them at a price of $210.

b. If demand falls to $P = 240 - 2Q$, marginal revenue becomes $MR = 240 - 4Q$ because now $a = 240$ and $b = 2$. Setting $MR = MC$, we find

$$240 - 4Q = 30 + 3Q$$
$$210 = 7Q$$
$$Q = 30$$

Even with reduced demand, the firm should still produce 30 units if it wants to maximize profit. Substituting into the new demand curve, we can see that the price will be

$$P = 240 - 2Q$$
$$= 240 - 2(30) = 180$$

Here, the equilibrium price is lower even though the profit-maximizing output is the same.

c. The new diagram appears below. Because D_2 is flatter than D_1, the firm must charge a lower price. Consumers are more responsive to price.

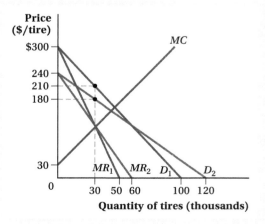

flattening of the demand curve does not change the point at which $P = MC$ (as embodied in the supply curve), so neither price nor quantity moves. The price sensitivity of consumers does not impact the sellers' output decisions as long as price is still equal to marginal cost.

Things are different, though, if the same demand curve rotation happens in a market in which there is a seller with market power. That's because with market power, the rotation in demand also moves the marginal revenue curve as shown in panel b of Figure 9.4. Even though the new demand curve D_2 crosses the marginal cost curve at the same quantity as the old demand curve, MR_2 intersects the marginal cost curve at a higher quantity than did MR_1 (Q^*_{m2} instead of Q^*_{m1}). Therefore, the firm's output rises as a result of the demand curve rotation and the price falls.

The opposite pattern holds when consumers become less price-sensitive and firms have market power: Output falls and price rises. Again, these changes wouldn't happen in perfect competition because suppliers' choices don't depend on the price sensitivity of demand.

9.5 The Winners and Losers from Market Power

Given that a firm with market power charges a price that is above its marginal cost, you might suspect that having market power is beneficial for firms, and it is. We see just exactly how beneficial it is in this section. We also see how market power affects consumers (*Hint*: badly). To do all this, we use the same tools we used to analyze competitive markets in Chapter 3—consumer and producer surplus. This approach allows us to directly compare markets in which firms have market power to those that are competitive.

Consumer and Producer Surplus under Market Power

Let's return to the Apple iPad example. Recall that Apple has a marginal cost of $200 and an inverse demand curve of $P = 1,000 - 5Q$ (where Q is in millions). This demand curve implied a marginal revenue curve $MR = 1,000 - 10Q$. We set that equal to marginal cost to solve for Q and found that to maximize profit, Apple should produce 80 million iPads and set its price at $600 per iPad.

We can compute the consumer and producer surplus when a firm has market power in the same way we computed these surpluses in a competitive market. The consumer surplus is the area under the demand curve and above the price. The producer surplus is the area below the price and above the marginal cost curve. At first glance, you might think this is different from producer surplus in a competitive market, which is the area below the price and above the supply curve. But remember that the supply curve in a perfectly competitive market is actually part of its marginal cost curve, so there is no difference in the case of market power.

We illustrate these surplus values in Figure 9.5. Apple's profit-maximizing price and quantity occur at point m. The consumer surplus is the triangle above the price $600 and below the demand curve. This area is labeled A. The producer surplus is the rectangle below $600 and above the marginal cost curve. It is labeled B.

We can compute these surplus values easily. The consumer surplus triangle has a base equal to the quantity sold and a height equal to the difference between the demand choke price and the market price. The demand choke price is especially easy to calculate from an inverse demand curve; you just plug in $Q = 0$ and solve for the price. In this case, it's $P_{DChoke} = 1,000 - 5(0) = 1,000$. So, the consumer surplus is

$$CS = \text{Triangle } A = \frac{1}{2} \times 80 \text{ million} \times (\$1,000 - \$600) = \$16 \text{ billion}$$

Figure 9.5 | **Surplus from the Apple iPad**

We can compute Apple's producer surplus, consumer surplus, and deadweight loss using the marginal cost curve, the demand curve, and the profit-maximizing output and price levels. Consumer surplus is the area of triangle A, equal to $\frac{1}{2}$ × 80 million × ($1,000 − $600) or $16 billion. The producer surplus, rectangle B, is (80 million) × ($600 − $200) or $32 billion. The deadweight loss is triangle C and can be calculated as $\frac{1}{2}$ × (160 million − 80 million) × ($600 − $200) or $16 billion.

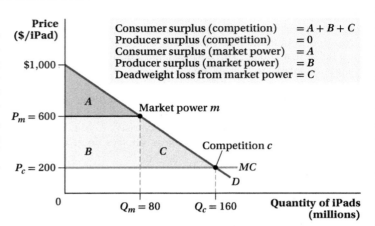

The producer surplus is a rectangle with a base equal to the quantity sold and a height equal to the difference between the monopoly price and marginal cost. Therefore,

$$PS = \text{Rectangle } B = (80 \text{ million}) \times (\$600 - \$200) = \$32 \text{ billion}$$

So far, so good. Consumers earn $16 billion of consumer surplus from buying iPads, a fairly sizeable sum, and Apple does great, making $32 billion of surplus.

Consumer and Producer Surplus under Perfect Competition

Now let's think about how the market would look if Apple behaved like a competitive firm and priced at marginal cost. The price would be $200 because marginal cost is constant at $200. Plugging $200 into the demand curve equation yields a quantity of 160 million. Therefore, in the competitive equilibrium Apple would sell 160 million iPads at a price of $200 (point c in Figure 9.5). Note that because $P = MC$, Apple would earn zero producer surplus in a competitive market.

With competition, then, iPad prices would be lower, the quantity sold would be higher, and Apple would make a lot less money—producer surplus would fall by $32 billion. This competitive market outcome provides a way to see the standard result for markets in which firms have pricing power: A firm with market power reduces output and raises price relative to the perfectly competitive equilibrium, and by doing so, it raises producer surplus (and profit).

How does *consumer* surplus compare under market power and perfect competition? In Figure 9.5, consumer surplus under perfect competition is the entire triangular area $A + B + C$ below the demand curve and above the competitive price of $200. The triangle's base is the competitive quantity of 160 million and its height is the difference between the demand choke price of $1,000 and the competitive price. This means consumer surplus under perfect competition is

$$CS = \frac{1}{2} \times \text{Base} \times \text{Height} = \frac{1}{2} \times 160 \text{ million} \times (\$1,000 - 200) = \$64 \text{ billion}$$

Recall that when Apple exercises its market power, consumer surplus is $16 billion. So, consumers are much better off when there is competition. In this example, they have four times the consumer surplus under competition than with Apple having market power. On the other hand, by exploiting its market power, Apple would move from having no producer surplus to $32 billion of producer surplus. That's why firms want to use their market power whenever they can, even if it costs their customers a large amount of consumer surplus.

 **application**

Southwest Airlines

Southwest Airlines, the spunky low-cost carrier, has made a habit of entering the stronghold airports of incumbent carriers and driving down fares. One way to think about how this happens is that Southwest's arrival moves the airport from a situation in which incumbents have considerable market power to a situation that is closer to perfect competition.

The impact can be dramatic. Prices fall 25 to 50% on routes that Southwest starts to fly, and the number of passengers flying the route goes up substantially. It's probably no coincidence that among the 20 busiest airports in the United States, the four that saw the biggest drops in average fares from 2001 to 2011 were all airports at which Southwest began operating during that period. The lucky passengers were flying into and out of Denver (an average fare drop of 30% during the period), San Francisco (average drop of 17%), Philadelphia (average drop of 16%), and Boston (average drop of 15%). By the way, the fifth-largest fare drop occurred at New York's JFK airport, where Jet Blue, another low-cost airline patterned partially on the Southwest model, began operating in 2000.[7]

Passengers across the country have become familiar with these sorts of changes, which have become known as the "Southwest effect." As a result, many local governments and airport authorities have actively tried to recruit Southwest to come to or expand service in their city. We suspect you could hear a collective cheer coming from students at local schools in the cities where Southwest came to town. Thanks to competition from Southwest, their consumer surplus was going to rise—and their spring breaks in Florida were going to be more affordable. ∎

The Deadweight Loss of Market Power

We've just seen how exercising market power can be great for firms and bad for consumers. Firms can earn considerably more producer surplus by restricting output and raising price, but this costs consumers a sizable chunk of their consumer surplus. That's not the only consequence of market power, though. Notice that, in the example above, the total surplus under market power is $48 billion ($16 billion consumer surplus + $32 billion producer surplus), which is smaller than the total surplus under competition of $64 billion. That missing $16 billion of surplus has been destroyed by the firm's exercise of market power. It's important to recognize that this loss is not surplus that is transferred from consumers to producers when producers restrict output and raise prices. No one gets it. It just disappears. In other words, it is the deadweight loss from market power.

The deadweight loss of market power can be seen in Figure 9.5. It is the area of triangle C whose base is the difference between the firm's output with market power and its output under perfect competition and whose height is the difference between the prices under market power (P_m) and competition (P_c). We know from our comparison of the total surplus of the market power and competitive cases above that this area is $16 billion. We can confirm that value by calculating the area of triangle C:

$$\text{DWL} = \frac{1}{2} \times (160 \text{ million} - 80 \text{ million}) \times (\$600 - \$200) = \$16 \text{ billion}$$

---

[7] These numbers were taken from data compiled by the Bureau of Transportation Statistics of the U.S. Department of Transportation.

The deadweight loss (DWL) is the inefficiency of market power. Note that this cost is exactly like the DWL from a tax or regulation we discussed in Chapter 3—a triangular area below the demand curve and above the marginal cost curve (supply curve, in Chapter 3). A firm with pricing power essentially puts a market power "tax" on consumers and keeps the revenue for itself. The DWL comes about because there are consumers in the market who are willing to buy the product (an iPad in this example) at a price above its cost of production, but can't because the firm has hiked up prices to increase its profit. Just as with the DWL from taxes and regulations, the size of the DWL from market power is related to the size of the difference between the monopoly and competitive output levels. The more the firm withholds output to maximize profits, the bigger is the efficiency loss.

Differences in Producer Surplus for Different Firms

One more important point about the surplus implications of market power is how the slope of the demand curve influences the relative size of consumer and producer surplus in the market.

Consider two different markets, one with a relatively steep (inelastic) demand curve and one with a flatter (elastic) one. Each is served by a monopolist. To keep things easy to follow, imagine that both firms have the same constant marginal cost curves, and that it just so happens that each firm's profit-maximizing output is the same. We plot this case in Figure 9.6.

In the market in panel a of Figure 9.6, buyers aren't very price-sensitive, so the demand curve is steep. In the market in panel b, consumers are quite sensitive to prices, as reflected in the flatter demand curve. The marginal revenue curves in both markets are also shown in the figure. To maximize their profits, both firms choose quantity and price to set $MR = MC$. It is clear from looking at the figure that for the same-sized market (measured by the total quantity of the good that is produced, which we've set to be the same here), producer surplus is higher when the demand curve is steeper.

Figure 9.6   :   Gains from Market Power under Different Demand Curves

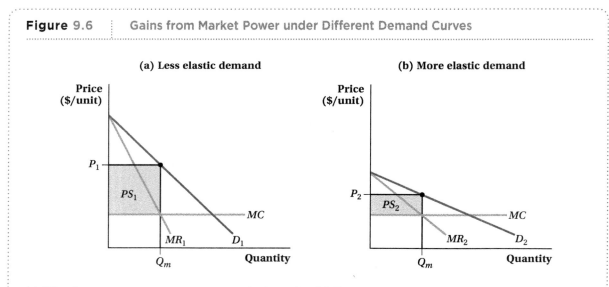

(a) Less elastic demand

(b) More elastic demand

(a) When buyers are not very price-sensitive, the demand curve is steep. At $MR_1 = MC$ the producer supplies quantity Q_m at the relatively high price P_1, and generates the relatively large producer surplus PS_1.

(b) When buyers are price-sensitive, the demand curve is flat. At $MR_2 = MC$, the producer supplies quantity Q_m at the relatively low price P_2, and generates the relatively small producer surplus PS_2.

Let's return to our earlier problem regarding Babe's Bats (BB). Remember that BB faces an inverse demand curve of $P = 25 - 2.5Q$ and a marginal cost curve $MC = 5Q$. Calculate the deadweight loss from market power at the firm's profit-maximizing level of output.

Solution:

The easiest way to find deadweight loss is to use a diagram. Therefore, we should start by drawing a graph with demand, marginal revenue, and marginal cost:

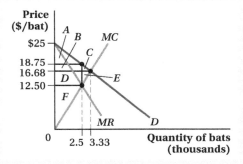

We know from our earlier problem that the profit-maximizing level of output is 2,500 bats sold at a price of $18.75.

To find the deadweight loss from market power, we need to consider the consumer and producer surplus and compare it with the competitive outcome. If BB participated in a competitive market, it would set price equal to marginal cost to determine its output:

$$P = MC$$
$$25 - 2.5Q = 5Q$$
$$25 = 7.5Q$$
$$Q = 3.33$$

Therefore, BB would sell 3,333 bats. Of course, the price will be lower at this level of output:

$$P = 25 - 2.5Q$$
$$= 25 - 2.5(3.33)$$
$$= 16.68$$

If the market were competitive, the bats would sell for $16.68 each. Consumer surplus would be areas $A + B + C$ (the area below the demand curve and above the competitive price), and producer surplus would be areas $D + E + F$ (the area below the competitive price but above the marginal cost curve). Total surplus would be areas $A + B + C + D + E + F$.

When BB exercises its market power, it reduces its output to 2,500 bats and increases its price to $18.75. In this situation, consumer surplus is only area A (the area below demand but above the monopoly price). Producer surplus is areas $B + D + F$ (the area below the monopoly price but above marginal cost). Total surplus under market power is $A + B + D + F$.

So, what happens to areas C and E? Area C was consumer surplus but no longer exists. Area E was producer surplus but also has disappeared. These areas are the deadweight loss from market power. We can calculate this area by measuring the area of the triangle that encompasses areas $C + E$. To do so, we have one more important calculation to make. We need to be able to calculate the height of the triangle, so we need to determine the marginal cost of producing 2,500 units:

$$MC = 5Q$$
$$= 5(2.5)$$
$$= 12.5$$

Now, we can calculate the area of the deadweight loss triangle:

$$DWL = \text{Areas } C + E = \frac{1}{2} \times \text{Base} \times \text{Height}$$
$$= \frac{1}{2} \times (3.33 - 2.5) \times (\$18.75 - \$12.50)$$
$$= \frac{1}{2} \times 0.83 \times \$6.25$$
$$= \$2.59375$$

Remember that the quantity is measured in thousands, so the deadweight loss is equal to $2,593.75.

That's because, as we pointed out earlier, a steeper demand curve raises the firm's profit-maximizing markup of price over marginal cost.

Firms with market power find it very lucrative to operate in markets in which consumers are relatively price-insensitive. If you're a consumer in that market, though, look out: Prices are going to be high.

9.6 Governments and Market Power: Regulation, Antitrust, and Innovation

We've seen the impact that market power can have on an industry—higher prices, smaller output, lower consumer surplus, and deadweight loss. The deadweight loss created by market power can justify government intervention in markets if such regulation can move the market toward a more competitive outcome and reduce deadweight loss. And, indeed, governments attempt to do this in several ways. Given this, it might be surprising that in certain markets the government actually encourages and protects market power, and that this too can be justified as a policy that benefits society as a whole. In this section, we explore several of the ways governments intervene in markets to either restrain or encourage market power.

Direct Price Regulation

When there is a concern that firms in an industry have too much market power, governments sometimes directly regulate prices. This often occurs in markets considered to be natural monopolies. If it appears that there is no way to prevent the existence of a natural monopoly because of the nature of the industry's cost structure, the government will often allow only a single firm to operate but will limit its pricing behavior to prevent it from fully exploiting its market power. Governments have used this argument to justify regulating, at various times, the prices of electricity, natural gas, gasoline, cable television, local telephone service, long-distance telephone service, airfares, trucking rates, and all sorts of other products.

To understand the logic behind these actions, consider a typical natural monopoly case as shown in Figure 9.7. Let's suppose it is the market for electricity distribution, which we argued earlier may, in fact, be a natural monopoly. With a demand curve of D, an unregulated electric company would produce at the point where marginal revenue equals marginal cost. This would lead to a price of P_m, substantially higher than the firm's marginal cost. The consumer surplus in this situation will be only the area A,

---

Figure 9.7   Government Regulation of a Natural Monopoly

Before government regulation, the electric company produces at point m, where quantity is Q_m and price P_m is well above the firm's marginal cost curve. If the government sets a price cap at the level equal to the firm's marginal cost, the firm will produce at the perfectly competitive price (P_c) and quantity (Q_c). Consumer surplus under the regulation will expand from triangle A to the triangle $A + B + C$. However, since P_c falls below the firm's average total cost curve, the firm will be operating with negative profit, and the price cap is not a sustainable regulation.

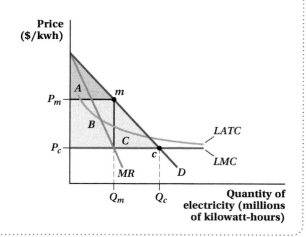

rather than the area $A + B + C$, as would be the case if prices were instead set at P_c, a level equal to the firm's marginal cost.

If the government imposes a price cap regulation such that the electric company cannot charge prices above P_c, output could equal its perfectly competitive level, and consumer surplus will equal area $A + B + C$. But there's a problem. P_c is below the firm's average total cost; if it sells every unit it produces at the regulated price, the firm will earn a negative profit, as it won't be able to cover its fixed cost. Therefore, a simple price regulation requiring competitive pricing is not a sustainable solution in regulating a natural monopoly. However, any regulation that would allow a price above marginal cost in order to allow the natural monopolist to recoup its fixed cost would also lead to a deadweight loss and less consumer surplus than the competitive case (though the deadweight loss may be smaller and the reduction in consumer surplus smaller than in the unregulated monopoly case).[8]

Aside from this problem, there are several other serious difficulties involved in using direct price regulations. First and foremost, only the company knows its true cost structure. Government regulators don't actually know what the firm's marginal cost is nor, for that matter, does the government actually know what the demand curve is. It's difficult to set the regulated price at the perfectly competitive level without knowing these two pieces of information. So, the regulator is left to estimate them. Further, the firm has an incentive to misrepresent the truth and make people believe its costs are higher than they really are, because this would justify a higher regulated price. In addition, companies that are regulated based on their cost often have no incentive to reduce their costs because the regulator would then reduce the regulated price, destroying any profit gained from the increase in efficiency.

Antitrust

Another approach governments use to address the effects of market power is **antitrust law** (sometimes called *competition law*, particularly outside the United States). Antitrust laws are meant to promote competition in a market by restricting firms from certain behaviors that may limit competition, especially if the firm is an established and substantial current player in the industry. In some cases, antitrust laws are used to prevent firms from merging with or acquiring other firms in order to stop them from becoming too dominant. Occasionally, these laws are even used to force the break-up of an established firm that is determined to have too much market power. Antitrust law tends to be strong and well enforced in wealthier countries, but is often much weaker elsewhere in the world.

One of the strongest and most common prohibitions in antitrust law is the ban on collusion among competitors with regard to pricing and market allocation (agreements to divide up a market among firms). In the United States, for example, even discussing prices or market entry strategies with your competitors is a criminal act.

The antitrust authorities are also allowed to investigate whether a firm is monopolizing an industry unfairly and, if so, they can sue to change the behavior. There have been many such investigations in recent years—for example, those investigating Intel for its pricing of its CPUs to computer makers, American Express, Visa, and MasterCard for the rules they require merchants to follow when customers want to use credit cards to make purchases, and Realtors for the rules they set about who is allowed to list houses for sale.

The drawbacks of antitrust enforcement as a way of preventing market power have to do with the large potential costs and uncertainties involved. The government should not fight concentration that would increase efficiency and make consumers better off, but that's hard to measure directly.

antitrust law
Laws designed to promote competitive markets by restricting firms from behaviors that limit competition.

---

[8] There is a way, at least theoretically, that regulation could achieve both the perfectly competitive outcome and allow the firm to pay its fixed costs. This would involve not just a per-unit price P_c, but also a lump-sum payment to the monopolist either from consumers or the government. Many regulated utilities have payment structures that try to replicate this in part, with a fixed monthly fee for service regardless of the quantity used plus an additional fee tied to the quantity the consumer purchases. However, these fee schedules are often only approximations to the true cost structure of the monopolist and can also be constrained by political considerations, so it is difficult to achieve perfectly competitive outcomes exactly.

Promoting Monopoly: Patents, Licenses, and Copyrights

Even as the government tries to limit market power through regulation and antitrust policy, it sometimes *encourages* monopolies and helps them legally enforce their market power by conferring patents, licenses, copyrights, trademarks, and other assorted legal rights to exercise market power.

Why would the government do this if it cares about consumers and competitive markets? Why give inventors a 20-year monopoly for their innovations in the form of a patent? Pharmaceutical companies, for example, receive patent-based monopolies on all sorts of medicines, which raise the prices people pay. Why license spectrum to radio stations and mobile phone companies, which prohibits others from broadcasting? Why give copyright owners of a book or movie 125 years of protection from anyone copying their works without getting approval and paying royalties? Michael Buffer, a professional boxing and wrestling ring announcer, has a trademark on his exhortation "Let's get ready to rumble!" The Transformers are similarly protected. You might like to pump up the crowd at a sales event or have a great idea for using the Transformers in your own movie, but the government has given Buffer and Hasbro the rights to determine how "Let's get ready to rumble!" and the Transformers will be used commercially.

Collectively, all of the monopolies created by the government add up to immense amounts of market power that inevitably lead to higher prices and lower quantities than would exist in a competitive market. The reason why it still might make sense for the government to do this is for the sake of encouraging innovation. Giving someone the exclusive right, at least temporarily, to the profits from innovation can provide a powerful incentive to create new things. Governments have decided that the consumer surplus created by these new goods can outweigh the deadweight loss from their producers having market power for a period of time. In some cases, innovation can be the upside of market power.

To see why, think about the market for a medical drug to cure the common cold, which affects hundreds of millions of people every year. There would certainly be demand for the product. We label that demand curve D in Figure 9.8.

Let's assume that the marginal cost of producing a dose of this medicine once it is discovered is constant at \$5. (Once a drug is in production, the marginal cost of manufacturing it is very low. It doesn't cost much to make another pill or another dose of vaccine using a formula that's been developed and a production line that's already built.) The rest of the world would like the drug company that discovers the cure to act like a perfectly competitive firm and sell it at the marginal cost of \$5 per dose, as at point c. This would create the largest possible consumer surplus of $A + B + C$.

Figure 9.8   Monopoly Power and Innovation

The government encourages innovation by giving companies monopolies on products. D represents the demand curve for the cure for the common cold. In a perfectly competitive market, the drug would be sold at a price equal to its marginal cost, \$5, and consumer surplus would be $A + B + C$. However, at this price, the firm would be unable to recover the fixed cost of developing the drug and would choose not to invest in the cure for the common cold. By giving the firm a patent, the government allows it to recover the costs of innovation, and the firm produces at the monopoly price P_m and quantity Q_m. The consumer surplus is now the triangle A.

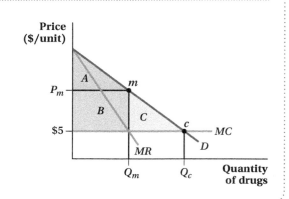

The problem is that selling the drug for $5 would leave the drug company with no producer surplus. Because the firm would need to expend massive amounts of fixed cost on discovering and developing the drug, it will not bother to do so if it immediately has to sell the drug at marginal cost. In other words, having to act like a perfectly competitive firm as soon as it develops this new drug would mean the firm won't want to actually develop the drug in the first place.

In theory, the government could try to subsidize the development cost (and it does subsidize many types of research and development), but all sorts of problems arise such as trying to figure out what will work, avoiding corruption, and so on.[9] Instead, the government makes a compromise. It promises the firm a monopoly on the drug if it develops it. The company realizes this means it can produce the quantity level Q_m (where $MR = MC$) and charge a price of P_m, giving it a producer surplus equal to area B from selling the drug. Therefore, as long as the firm expects the fixed cost of discovering the drug to be smaller than the producer surplus B, it will set out to discover the cure for the common cold. Ultimately, this benefits consumers by giving them a consumer surplus equal to area A. This is lower than the consumer surplus consumers would get in a competitive market $(A + B + C)$, but given that the firm would not have developed the drug in the first place if it had to charge a competitive price, consumers are better off with the more limited consumer surplus of A than none at all.

Overall, the economics of intellectual property protection suggest that it will tend to lead to innovations in just the types of goods that people like most. If a market for an innovation is large because there are a lot of consumers who would want to purchase it, that will tend to also make the monopoly profits in that market big. In addition, recall that in Chapter 3, we saw that goods with steeper demand curves tend to be those with the highest consumer surplus. Earlier in this chapter, we observed that the steeper demand curves are exactly the ones where monopoly profits are largest. So, a patent, license, or copyright that gives innovators a monopoly will tend to encourage innovation in exactly the types of goods that people value. The downside, of course, is that this will tend to lead to especially high prices as well.

 **application**

Internet File-Sharing and the Music Industry

Bands and record labels earn money from selling music. This is a risky business. Most of the costs associated with making a CD are development costs that must be paid up-front, before anyone knows how well the CD will sell. (The marginal cost of burning another disc is virtually zero.) And, in fact, most CDs aren't successful; by some reports, more than 90% of CDs released lose money. The few success stories have to cover the fixed costs for the losers.

Copyright law in the music industry is designed to encourage this risky creative activity by giving artists and record labels the exclusive right to sell their music. The market power generated is meant to allow them to cover their costs of development. But this system has been facing challenges. File-sharing sites that allow people to download music for free—violating the copyrights on the music in the process—started in 1999 and grew rapidly. By 2004 there were about 10 million simultaneous users of file-sharing systems. During the same time period, CD sales fell by about 20%. The argument made by the record industry was that if people stopped paying for music, essentially driving down price to the marginal cost of zero,

---

[9] Because drug development costs are fixed costs for pharmaceutical firms, such an approach is related to the fixed-cost transfer scheme we discussed for a natural monopoly. Again, these can theoretically reach an efficient market outcome, but there are many practical roadblocks to their successful implementation.

Table 9.2	Number of New Artists Releasing Albums by Genre, 1999 and 2004	
	1999	**2004**
Urban/Rap	1493	1297
Rock	1984	1919
Jazz	1453	1627
Country	644	904

music producers would no longer be able to cover the costs of developing new bands and new CDs. The implication was that, ultimately, consumers would be worse off. They would miss the consumer surplus they would have obtained from new music produced in a market where consumers actually paid for music.

Economists Julie Mortimer and Alan Sorensen explored whether this might be the case in a study of the music industry during the period when Internet file-sharing became prevalent.[10] They found that the number of new artists in rock and urban/rap, two music formats for which listeners are especially heavy users of the Internet, fell between 1999 and 2004. However, the number of new artists in jazz and in country, two genres with a smaller share of listeners who used file-sharing programs online, rose over this period. You can see the results from Mortimer's and Sorensen's study in Table 9.2.

These changes might be mere coincidence, but they are at least consistent with the idea that Internet file-sharing has reduced the amount of investment music producers put into new artists, because it reduces artists' and record labels' market power by undermining their copyright protection. Mortimer and Sorensen argue that the decrease in the demand for paid-for CDs has raised the incentive for bands to seek alternative ways to earn income from their art. Specifically, they document that artists are more likely to go on tour than they were before the rise of the file-sharing sites. ■

Patent Protection in Practice

A cure for the common cold is an example of a situation in which allowing monopoly power can make consumers better off. Intellectual property law raises many deeper issues, however. One issue is the optimal length of patents. A longer monopoly period will lead to a longer period during which consumer surplus is lower than it would be in a competitive market. On the other hand, it creates more producer surplus for innovators and could therefore induce more invention. But it's important to realize that to spur innovation, all the patent system needs to do is to protect enough producer surplus to pay for the innovation costs. Any additional market power beyond that will lead to a transfer of surplus from consumers to the firm without more innovation, and will involve deadweight loss, too. In the common cold example above, if the drug development costs are equal to B, then the amount B is all the producer surplus a patent would need to protect to convince the firm to develop the drug. If patents were lengthened and the amount of protected producer surplus were larger, the drug would still be invented, but consumers would pay higher prices (and consume lower quantities) for a longer period of time.

Another difficult question regards how substantial an innovation must be beyond existing goods in order to get a patent. If the government gives out patents for things that have already been invented, the only effect will be to create deadweight loss and transfer surplus from consumers to producers due to market power. Many people believe that the government has granted intellectual property rights too leniently, objecting to decisions like giving a patent to Amazon for any transaction involving one-click shopping (this happened in 1999 and the decision was reconfirmed in 2010); allowing MasterCard to trademark the term "priceless"; extending copyright to 125 years, much longer than the lifetime of any author; or letting biologist Craig Venter actually patent the human genes that his firm Celera Genomics

---

[10] Julie Holland Mortimer and Alan Sorensen, "Supply Responses to Digital Distribution: Recorded Music and Live Performances," Preliminary, December 29, 2005, cited by permission of the authors. http://www.aeaweb.org/assa/2006/0107_0800_0702.pdf.

mapped in its research. Someone was even granted a patent for a crustless peanut butter sandwich.

A further downside of patents, licenses, and other government-granted monopolies is that they can induce battles among firms to obtain market power that actually result in firms' squandering the producer surplus that the monopoly right would protect. Companies sometimes lobby to acquire a monopoly through expenditures on public relations, lawyers, advertising, and in situations with less scrupulous participants, even outright bribes. Much of that spending is just waste. All this useless spending is called **rent-seeking.** If this spending doesn't lead to more of the good being produced (someone is going to get the patent or license in any case) or to higher-quality output, it is just pure deadweight loss.

rent-seeking
A firm's attempts to gain government-granted monopoly power and, therefore, additional producer surplus.

theory and data

Determining a New Drug's Potential Market

Pfizer, the American pharmaceutical company, spent over $9 billion on research and development in 2010. To put that in perspective, that's nearly one-third of the federal government's budget for health research and development (R&D). The company's history of sizable investments like these in developing new drugs has certainly paid off, though—that same year, Pfizer pulled in nearly $68 billion in revenues. So how does a company like Pfizer know how to allocate its $9 billion dollar budget? Was it just good luck that led past research teams to pursue products as varied and popular as Chapstick and Xanax? Not really; you shouldn't be surprised to hear that firms do, in fact, use some basic market analysis to decide where to look for potential cash cows.

Pharmaceutical companies are willing to spend a lot on R&D in large part because the government grants them patents, thereby guaranteeing the companies' monopoly profits on new products. But while the promise of a patent certainly has spurred on Pfizer's R&D team, simply giving the firm a monopoly on a product isn't enough. The firm has to believe that when developing a new drug, the R&D costs will be offset by the good's potential revenues.

What do these companies look at to determine what products will sell? Economists Daron Acemoglu and Joshua Linn proposed that companies consider a drug's potential market size—in other words, what the future demand for a drug will likely be.[11] The age profile of the populations can be used as a rough estimate of market size for a given drug, since most drugs taken by the middle-aged are not prescribed to the elderly and vice versa. But Pfizer and its competitors don't just care about the *number* of people in a market; they also want to know how much money those people can fork over for pharmaceuticals. For this reason, Acemoglu and Linn looked at the share of income by age groups. As can be seen in Figure 9.9, the income share of people between the ages of 30 and 60 has steadily increased since 1970, and in 2000 it accounted for approximately 50% of income. Theoretically, then, Big Pharma should have diverted more of its funds to the development of drugs demanded by people aged 30 to 60 years old over the development of new pharmaceuticals for, say, glaucoma or vertigo, which are primarily consumed by older patients.

This is exactly what pharmaceutical companies have done. Acemoglu and Linn found that for every 1% increase in potential market size for a given drug type, development of new nongeneric drugs in that category increased around 4%. In other words, Big Pharma firms target their development toward products that offer the largest potential monopoly profits.

---

[11] Daron Acemoglu and Joshua Linn, "Market Size in Innovation: Theory and Evidence from the Pharmaceutical Industry," *The Quarterly Journal of Economics* 119, no. 3 (2004): 1049–1090.

Figure 9.9 ┊ Income Shares of People in Various Age Groups

The income share of people between the ages of 30 and 60 has steadily increased since 1970, and in 2000 it accounted for approximately 50% of income. Pharmaceutical companies devoted more of their drug development funds to drugs demanded by people of this age group.

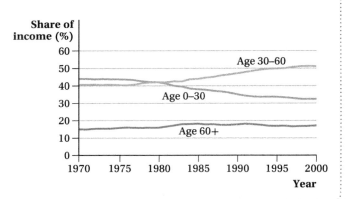

The pharmaceutical companies' actions make economic sense, but unfortunately leave a lot of drugs underfunded. Conditions such as Tourette syndrome or muscular dystrophy afflict a relatively small population and therefore have a small potential market size. For this reason, Congress passed the Orphan Drug Act, which offers tax credits and other economic incentives to companies that develop drugs for these "orphaned" diseases. Congress believed that to influence Big Pharma's R&D, you have to promise greater profits, and sometimes patents aren't enough.

9.7 Conclusion

Unlike the perfectly competitive firms of Chapter 8, firms with market power don't just choose the quantity they supply at some fixed price determined by the market. Monopolies and other types of firms with market power have the ability to influence the prices of their goods. As a result, they produce at the profit-maximizing quantity where $MR = MC$. This production level is lower than the quantity a perfectly competitive market would produce, leading to a higher market price, more producer surplus, less consumer surplus, and deadweight loss. To raise consumer surplus and reduce deadweight loss, governments often intervene through direct price regulation and antitrust laws to reduce firms' market power. On the other hand, governments also sometimes encourage market power to promote product innovation, such as through the issuance of patents, trademarks, and copyrights.

Even though the firms we've studied in this chapter have the ability to set the price of their products, they are still limited in one important aspect of pricing. In particular, we assumed that if a firm increased the quantity it produces, this would lead to a decrease in the price on *every* unit of the good sold. But what if a firm could sell its product at different prices to different types of consumers? We discuss this use of a firm's market power, a strategy broadly categorized as *price discrimination*, in Chapter 10.

Summary

1. Most firms have some **market power,** meaning that the firm's production decisions affect the market price of the good it sells. Firms maintain market power through **barriers to entry** into the market. These barriers include **natural monopolies,** switching costs, **product differentiation,** and absolute cost advantages of key inputs. [**Section 9.1**]

2. A **monopoly** is the sole supplier of a good in a market and represents the extreme case of a firm with complete market power. Monopolies and other firms with market power base their production decisions in part on their **marginal revenue,** the revenue from selling an additional unit of a good. Unlike perfectly competitive firms, these firms' marginal revenue falls as output rises. As a result, when a firm increases its production of a good, its marginal revenues fall, because it must sell all units of the good (not just the additional unit) at a lower price. [**Section 9.2**]

3. The profit-maximizing output level for a monopolist is found where marginal revenue equals marginal cost, $MR = MC$. A monopoly will charge a price above its marginal cost, meaning that the market price for a monopoly is higher than that for a perfectly competitive firm.

The **Lerner index** computes how much a firm should mark up its price; the more inelastic the demand for a product, the higher the firm's Lerner index and markup. [**Section 9.3**]

4. The changes in quantity supplied and price created by cost and demand shocks have the same direction, but different magnitudes, for firms with market power as for perfectly competitive firms. However, firms with market power respond differently to changes in consumers' price sensitivities—that is, rotations in the demand curve—than do perfectly competitive firms. [**Section 9.4**]

5. When a firm exercises its market power, it increases its producer surplus, decreases consumer surplus, and creates a deadweight loss. Producer surplus is greater when consumers are relatively price-insensitive and the demand curve is steep. [**Section 9.5**]

6. Governments often intervene to reduce the deadweight loss created by firms with market power. Direct price regulation and **antitrust laws** are aimed at reducing firms' market power. Conversely, governments also grant market power to firms through patents, copyrights, and other laws as a way of promoting innovation. [**Section 9.6**]

Review Questions

1. When does a firm have market power?
2. Name and describe three barriers to entry to a market.
3. What are the characteristics of a natural monopoly? Why is it efficient for society for a natural monopoly to produce all the output of an entire industry?
4. Describe the connection between the slope of the demand curve for a good and a firm's marginal revenue.
5. What is the profit-maximizing output level for a firm with market power?
6. Compare the consumer and producer surplus of perfectly competitive firms with that of firms with market power.
7. Why does the profit-maximizing strategy of a firm with market power create a deadweight loss?
8. Why do firms with market power have only demand—and not supply—curves?
9. Firms with market power respond differently to changes in consumers' price sensitivity than do perfectly competitive firms. Explain why this is true.
10. Name some regulations the government imposes on firms with market power.

Problems

1. People are always complaining about Facebook: It changed the way its news feed works, the privacy settings are awful, there are too many game notifications, and so on. Recognizing dissatisfaction with Facebook, Google tried three times to enter the social networking market, first with Buzz, then with Wave, and now with Google Plus. Users say that the Google Plus platform

is far superior to Facebook's, yet Google Plus appears to be failing. Explain why consumers might reject a superior product for an inferior one in a market like this.

2. Sally sells seashells by the seashore. When Sally prices her shells at $7 each, she sells 5 shells every day. When she prices her shells at $6, she sells 6.

   a. What is Sally's total revenue when she chooses to sell 5 shells (by pricing at $7)?

   b. What is Sally's total revenue when she chooses to sell 6 shells (by pricing at $6)?

   c. What is the marginal revenue Sally receives from deciding to sell a 6th shell?

   d. The 6th shell sells for a price of $6. Why is the marginal revenue from selling a 6th shell so much lower than $6?

3. Indicate whether the following statements are true or false, and then explain your answers:

   a. The marginal revenue from selling another unit of eggs can never be higher than the price of eggs.

   b. Because the price a seller charges is always greater than $0, the marginal revenue from selling another unit must also be greater than $0.

4. Consider the demand curve for otter food shown below:

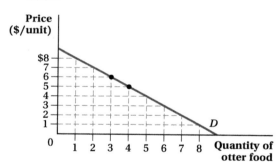

   a. Indicate the area representing the total revenue Oscar the otter food seller would receive if he chose a price of $6.

   b. On the same graph, indicate the area representing the total revenue Oscar the seller would receive if he chose a price of $5.

   c. You should now have added two rectangles to your graph; however, because of some overlap, it actually appears that you've added three. One of the three is common to both scenarios above. The other two (smaller) rectangles are specific to scenario (a) or scenario (b). Label each rectangle with "A," "B," or "both" to indicate which scenario each rectangle belongs to.

   d. Indicate what happens (gain or loss) to rectangle A as Oscar reduces his price from $6 to $5. Why?

   e. Indicate what happens (gain or loss) to rectangle B as Oscar reduces his price from $6 to $5. Why?

   f. Calculate the area of rectangle A and the area of rectangle B. Then, subtract the area of A from the area of B.

   g. Calculate the marginal revenue Oscar receives when he sells a 4th unit. Does your answer agree with the number you calculated in (f)? Explain.

5. In Cleveland, Clive sells 15 cloves at a price of $5 each. If Clive lowers his price by 10%, to $4.50 per clove, he will sell 16, or 6.66% more. In Dallas, Della sells 15 cloves for $5 each. If Della lowers her price by 2%, to $4.90, she will sell 16 cloves, or 6.66% more.

   a. Classify the demand curves that Clive and Della face as elastic or inelastic.

   b. Determine the marginal revenue of the 16th unit for Clive. Then, compute the marginal revenue of the 16th unit for Della.

   c. How does the marginal revenue received by a seller depend on the price elasticity of demand? Explain your answer.

6. The demand for saffron is highly elastic. The demand for cigarettes is highly inelastic. The demand for peanut butter is unit-elastic.

   a. If saffron producers reduce the price of saffron, what will happen to total revenue as a result? Will marginal revenue be positive, zero, or negative?

   b. If cigarette makers reduce the price of cigarettes, what will happen to total revenue as a result? Will marginal revenue be positive, zero, or negative?

   c. If peanut butter producers reduce the price of peanut butter, what will happen to total revenue as a result? Will marginal revenue be positive, zero, or negative?

7. In the chapter, we noted that the marginal revenue a seller receives can be expressed as $MR = P + (\Delta P/\Delta Q) \times Q$.

   a. Using this formula as a starting point, show that marginal revenue can be expressed as $MR = P(1 + 1/E^D)$, where E^D is the price elasticity of demand.

   b. Using your knowledge about the price elasticity of demand, explain why the marginal revenue a firm with market power receives must always be less than the price.

   c. Using your knowledge of the price elasticity of demand, explain why the marginal revenue a perfectly competitive firm receives must be equal to the price.

8. Consider the graph below, which illustrates the demand for Fluff. Fluff can be produced at a constant marginal and average total cost of $4 per case.

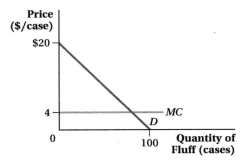

a. Draw in a carefully constructed marginal revenue curve.
b. Apply the $MR = MC$ rule to determine the profit-maximizing level of output. What price must the monopolist charge to maximize profit?
c. Calculate the profit earned by the monopolist.
d. The slope of the demand curve indicates that in order to sell one more unit, the price must fall by 20 cents. Verify that the seller cannot increase profit by reducing price and selling slightly more.
e. The slope of the demand curve indicates that if the price of Fluff increases by 20 cents, consumers will buy one less unit. Verify that the seller cannot increase profit by increasing price and selling slightly less.

9. Irwin is a monopoly seller of specialty bearings. Consider the graph below, which illustrates the demand and marginal revenue curves for Irwin's 30-weight ball bearings, along with the marginal and average total costs of producing bearings:

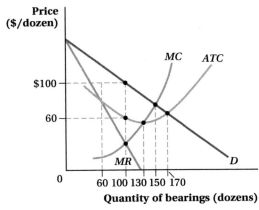

a. Find the monopolist's profit-maximizing level of output.

b. Determine the price the monopolist should charge to maximize profit.
c. Draw an appropriate rectangle on your graph to represent the total revenue the seller receives from selling the profit-maximizing quantity of bearings at the profit-maximizing price.
d. Draw an appropriate rectangle on your graph to represent the total cost of producing ball bearings.
e. The difference in the areas you drew in (c) and (d) represents profit. Calculate the profit Irwin earns from selling 30-weight ball bearings.

10. Suppose that the demand for bentonite is given by $Q = 40 - 0.5P$, where Q is in tons of bentonite per day and P is the price per ton. Bentonite is produced by a monopolist at a constant marginal and average total cost of $10 per ton.
a. Derive the inverse demand and marginal revenue curves faced by the monopolist.
b. Equate marginal cost and marginal revenue to determine the profit-maximizing level of output.
c. Find the profit-maximizing price by plugging the ideal quantity back into the demand curve.
d. How would your answer change if marginal cost were instead given by $MC = 20 + Q$?

11. Suppose that econometricians at Hallmark Cards determine that the price elasticity of demand for greeting cards is −2.
a. If Hallmark's marginal cost of producing cards is constant and equal to $1.00, use the Lerner index to determine what price Hallmark should charge to maximize profit.
b. Suppose that Hallmark Cards wishes to know the price elasticity of demand faced by its archrival, American Greetings. Hallmark hires you to estimate it. Hallmark provides you with an educated guess concerning the marginal cost of producing a greeting card, which they estimate to be constant and equal to $1.22. A quick trip to the store tells you that American Greetings is selling its cards for an average of $3.25. Using these numbers and assuming that American Greetings is maximizing its profit, calculate the price elasticity of demand faced by American Greetings.

12. Many industrywide studies of the elasticity of demand for cigarettes (an industry dominated by a few firms with tremendous market power) indicate a price elasticity near −0.5. Yet, our study of market power tells us that a firm with

any market power at all should never operate at a point on its demand curve where demand is inelastic. How can you reconcile these apparently contradictory statements?

13. A monopolistic seller of fairy dust faces the following inverse demand curve: $P = 100 - Q$, where Q is smidgens of fairy dust per week. Fairy dust can be produced at a constant marginal cost of $20 per smidgen.
    a. Graph this demand curve. Then, calculate the profit-maximizing price and quantity of fairy dust. Finally, calculate the seller's profit.
    b. A midsummer's druid festival greatly increases the demand for fairy dust, so that the price any particular consumer is willing to pay doubles. The inverse demand curve is now given by $P = 200 - 2Q$. Verify graphically that demand has increased and calculate the new profit-maximizing price and quantity.
    c. A tour bus full of druids took a wrong left turn at Albuquerque and showed up in town by accident. Now there are twice as many buyers at any price as there were before, and the inverse demand the seller faces is given by $P = 100 - 0.5Q$. Verify graphically that demand has increased and calculate the new profit-maximizing price and quantity.
    d. Suppose that the demand shift the seller faces is a parallel shift of the inverse demand curve such as $P = 150 - Q$. Verify graphically that demand has increased and calculate the new profit-maximizing price and quantity.
    e. What do your answers to (b), (c), and (d) indicate about how monopolistic suppliers respond to increases in demand?

14. Suppose that a monopolistic seller of designer handbags faces the following inverse demand curve: $P = 50 - 0.4Q$. The seller can produce handbags for a constant marginal and average total cost of $10.
    a. Calculate the profit-maximizing price for this seller.
    b. Suppose the government levies a $4 tax per unit on sellers of handbags. Calculate how this tax will affect the price the monopolist charges its customers.
    c. Who bears the burden of this tax?

15. Consider the market for Pop Rocks depicted in the diagram below:

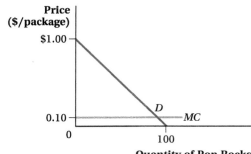

    a. If the Pop Rock industry were competitive, what would the competitive price and quantity be?
    b. If the Pop Rock industry were competitive, what would be the consumer and producer surpluses, respectively?
    c. Suppose that gangland figure Tommy Vercetti monopolizes the Pop Rock market. What price and quantity will he choose to maximize profit?
    d. Calculate the consumer and producer surplus of this Pop Rock monopoly.
    e. Compare your answers to (d) and (b). How big is the deadweight loss of monopoly?

16. Suppose that a monopolistic seller of flux capacitors faces the inverse demand curve $P = 40 - 0.5Q$, and that the monopolist can produce flux capacitors at a constant marginal cost of $5.
    a. How many units will an unregulated monopolist sell?
    b. Suppose that the government imposes a price ceiling of $6. What does this price ceiling do to the monopolist's marginal revenue curve? Specifically, what is the marginal revenue of the 10th unit? The 68th? How about the 69th?
    c. How many units will a profit-maximizing monopolist sell when the price ceiling is in place? At what price?
    d. Compare the deadweight loss of unregulated monopoly to the deadweight losses with the price ceiling. Does the price ceiling improve social welfare?

17. Consider a small, isolated town in which a brewery faces the following inverse demand: $P = 15 - 0.33Q$. The brewery can produce beer at a constant marginal and average total cost of $1 per bottle.
    a. Calculate the profit-maximizing price and quantity, as well as producer and consumer surplus and the deadweight loss from market power.
    b. If it were possible to organize the townsfolk, how much would they be willing to pay the brewery to sell beer at a price equal to its marginal cost?
    c. What is the minimum payment the brewery would be willing to accept to sell beer at a price equal to marginal cost?
    d. Is there potentially a bargain that can be struck between the townsfolk and brewery? What would the deadweight loss be if such a bargain were struck?

18. Consider the firm depicted in the diagram below.

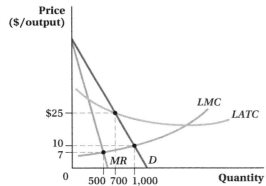

    a. Is the firm a natural monopoly? How do you know?
    b. Will this firm earn a profit if it is not subject to regulation? How do you know?
    c. If the government requires the firm to charge no more than its marginal cost of production, how many units will be sold? At what price? What is the problem with the government capping prices at marginal cost?

    d. Suppose the government allows firms to charge no more than their average total costs of production. How many units will this firm sell? At what price? What is the problem with capping prices at average total cost?
    e. Evaluate the deadweight loss under each of the three pricing regimes above. Show each regime's deadweight loss as an area on the graph.

19. Five networks are vying to receive the pay-per-view broadcast rights to the World Series of Yahtzee. Each estimates that the inverse demand for watching this nail-biter of an event is given by $P = 100 - 0.01Q$. Each can provide the broadcast at a constant marginal cost of $1 per viewer.
    a. Calculate the deadweight loss of monopoly in the market for the televised Yahtzee tournament.
    b. Suppose that tournament Yahtzee's governing body plans to select one network at its discretion to air the tournament. How much will each network be willing to spend lobbying for the broadcast rights?
    c. Explain why, in this situation, the losses to society are much greater than just the deadweight losses of monopoly.

20. In the early days of navigation, sailors had a tough time figuring out exactly where they were. Pinpointing latitude was easy enough with a sextant, but because the earth was constantly spinning, pinpointing longitude by using celestial bodies was impossible. Anxious for a solution to this problem, the British government sponsored a contest with a prize of £20,000 (about $5 million in today's dollars) to the inventor who could devise a reliable method of calculating longitude. Once invented, the method would be made available to anybody who wanted to use it. Explain the advantages of such a system in maximizing social well-being relative to the traditional system of awarding patents.

Chapter 9 Appendix:
The Calculus of Profit Maximization

In Chapters 8 and 9, we saw that all firms—regardless of their degrees of market power—maximize their profits. In particular, the firm faces the optimization problem:

$$\max_Q \pi(Q) = TR(Q) - TC(Q)$$

This problem is relatively straightforward compared to the cost-minimization and utility-maximization problems we've focused on in the past. Why? Look closely at the problem we wrote above, and you'll notice that there aren't any constraints on it. In fact, profit maximization is an *unconstrained* optimization problem and, as such, is much simpler to solve than the constrained optimization problems we've been dealing with so far.

What is more, the profit-maximization problem only has one choice variable, its output Q. Every other variable that factors into a firm's decisions—the quantities and prices of productive inputs, as well as the market price of the good—has already been accounted for in the equations for total revenue and total cost. How? First, total cost is determined only after a firm minimizes its costs, meaning it incorporates information about a firm's productive inputs. Next, consider total revenue, which is the product of price and quantity. For the perfectly competitive firm, price is constant, so given the market price, total revenue only varies with quantity. Firms with market power face variable prices, but we saw that those prices are a function of quantity sold. Therefore, total cost, total revenue, and—by extension—profit are all functions of quantity, holding all else constant.[1]

The Profit-Maximizing Condition

Let's begin by solving for the profit-maximizing condition. We take the first derivative of the profit-maximization problem above with respect to quantity Q to solve for the first-order condition:

$$\frac{d\pi}{dQ} = \frac{dTR}{dQ} - \frac{dTC}{dQ} = 0$$

$$\frac{dTR}{dQ} = \frac{dTC}{dQ}$$

$$MR = MC$$

What does this first-order condition tell us? As we saw in the chapter, *all* firms—firms with some market power, monopolists, and perfectly competitive firms inclusive—produce the profit-maximizing level of output when marginal revenue equals marginal cost.

We do need to check one more condition before considering this result conclusive. Producing where $MR = MC$ doesn't guarantee that the firm is maximizing its profit. It only guarantees that the profit function is at one extreme or another—the firm

---

[1] We could be very explicit about these functions and always write profit, total cost, and total revenue as $\pi(Q)$, $TR(Q)$, and $TC(Q)$; however, this becomes a little cumbersome. So in this appendix, we'll just write π, TR, and TC and remind you now and then that each is a function of Q.

could actually be minimizing its profit instead of maximizing it! To make sure we avoid this pitfall, we need to confirm that the second derivative of the profit function is negative:

$$\frac{d^2\pi}{dQ^2} = \frac{d^2(TR - TC)}{dQ^2} = \frac{d^2 TR}{dQ^2} - \frac{d^2 TC}{dQ^2} = \frac{dMR}{dQ} - \frac{dMC}{dQ} < 0$$

When will $\frac{dMR}{dQ} - \frac{dMC}{dQ} < 0$? This condition holds when

$$\frac{dMR}{dQ} < \frac{dMC}{dQ}$$

or when the *change* in marginal cost exceeds the *change* in marginal revenue. We have seen that marginal cost generally increases with output, while marginal revenue either is constant (for a price taker like the firms we saw in Chapter 8) or decreases as the quantity produced rises (for firms with market power, as we observed in Chapter 9). Therefore, this second-order condition generally is met because

$$\frac{dMR}{dQ} \leq 0 < \frac{dMC}{dQ}$$

The firm has to be careful about assuming this, however. If marginal cost is declining (which can be true of a firm with increasing returns to scale over the range that it is producing), we need to see if marginal revenue is decreasing at a faster rate than marginal cost:

$$\left| \frac{dMR}{dQ} \right| > \left| \frac{dMC}{dQ} \right|$$

If this condition does not hold for a firm experiencing increasing returns to scale, the firm is not maximizing its profit. In this context, the firm could increase its profit by producing more output because the decrease in total cost from the additional output would be greater than the decrease in total revenue.

Marginal Revenue

We know that all firms maximize profits when marginal revenue equals marginal cost. But what exactly is the marginal revenue of a firm? As we did in the past two chapters, we want to derive the relationship between marginal revenue and price. We'll do this first for firms in general and then look specifically at the case of a perfectly competitive firm.

We will start with the expression for total revenue:

$$TR = PQ$$

Note that, in general, price P is not fixed, but is instead a function of the quantity the firm produces.[2] To find marginal revenue, we take the derivative of the total revenue function with respect to Q:

$$\frac{dTR}{dQ} = \frac{dPQ}{dQ} = P\frac{dQ}{dQ} + Q\frac{dP}{dQ}$$

Equivalently,

$$MR = P + Q\frac{dP}{dQ}$$

What does this tell us about the relationship between marginal revenue and price? Because a firm with market power faces a downward-sloping demand curve, the good's price *decreases* as the quantity produced increases. Mathematically, $\frac{dP}{dQ} < 0$.

---

[2] The one exception to the general rule that price is a function of output that we've seen so far is for firms in a perfectly competitive market—price takers. We'll come back to this special case shortly.

Therefore, for a firm with market power,

$$MR < P$$

We can also see this result logically. P is the gain from selling an additional unit of the good at the new price. $Q\frac{dP}{dQ}$ is the loss from lowering the price on all previous units in order to sell the increased quantity. Therefore, the revenue from selling an additional unit of the good is less than the good's market price, because for every gain in revenue (P), there is a corresponding loss ($Q\frac{dP}{dQ}$).

Let's work through a generic example to clarify this. Suppose a firm has the inverse demand curve $P = a - bQ$. (We discussed this particular inverse demand curve in footnote 3 in Chapter 9, but we'll go into more detail here.) To find marginal revenue, we first determine total revenue by multiplying P by Q:

$$TR = PQ = (a - bQ)Q = aQ - bQ^2$$

Now, we can take the derivative of total revenue to get marginal revenue:

$$MR = \frac{dTR}{dQ} = \frac{d(aQ - bQ^2)}{dQ} = a - 2bQ$$

As you can see, the marginal revenue curve derived from a linear demand curve is itself linear. It also has the same price intercept (in this case, a) and is twice as steep as the demand curve. As a result, it's clear that

$$a - bQ > a - 2bQ \quad \text{or} \quad P > MR$$

But what about the special case of the perfectly competitive firm? Unlike firms with market power, perfectly competitive firms are price takers that face horizontal demand curves. We know from above that the marginal revenue for any firm is

$$MR = P + Q\frac{dP}{dQ}$$

For a perfectly competitive firm, price remains fixed with changes in quantity, meaning $\frac{dP}{dQ} = 0$. Thus, $MR = P$ for all quantities of output.

Therefore, the profit-maximizing condition for the perfectly competitive firm is

$$MR = P = MC$$

This unique relationship is precisely what we showed in Chapter 8.[3]

9A.1 figure it out

Let's reconsider the solution to Figure It Out 9.2 and use the calculus approach we learned above. Babe's Bats (BB) faces a demand curve of $Q = 10 - 0.4P$ and a total cost curve of $TC = 2.5Q^2$. BB's output, Q, is measured in thousands of baseball bats, and P in dollars per bat.

a. Solve for BB's profit-maximizing level of output using calculus.

b. What price will BB charge to maximize its profit?

---

[3] We can also show the relationship between price, marginal revenue, and marginal cost for the perfectly competitive firm by starting from profit maximization. For the perfectly competitive firm, $\pi = PQ - TC$. Taking the first-order condition with respect to Q gives us $P - MC = 0$ or $P = MC$ because price is independent of the quantity produced.

Solution:

a. First, we need to set up Babe's profit-maximization problem:

$$\max_{Q} \pi = TR - TC = PQ - TC$$

Because Babe's Bats has some market power, its choice of Q affects the price. So, we need to use the demand curve for BB's bats to solve for price as a function of quantity, or the firm's inverse demand curve:

$$Q = 10 - 0.4P$$
$$0.4P = 10 - Q$$
$$P = 25 - 2.5Q$$

Substituting this expression for P and the total cost curve into the profit function, we find

$$\pi = TR - TC = PQ - TC$$
$$= (25 - 2.5Q)Q - 2.5Q^2$$
$$= 25Q - 2.5Q^2 - 2.5Q^2 = 25Q - 5Q^2$$

So, the firm's profit-maximization problem is

$$\max_{Q} \pi = 25Q - 5Q^2$$

The first-order condition for this problem is

$$\frac{d\pi}{dQ} = \frac{d(25Q - 5Q^2)}{dQ} = 0$$
$$25 - 10Q = 0$$
$$10Q = 25$$
$$Q^* = 2.5 \text{ or } 2,500 \text{ bats}$$

b. Now we need to plug Q^* from (a) into the inverse demand curve to obtain the profit-maximizing price:

$$P^* = 25 - 2.5Q = 25 - 2.5(2.5) = \$18.75 \text{ per bat}$$

Babe's Bats is maximizing its profit when it sells 2,500 baseball bats at a price of \$18.75 per bat. A shortcut to solving is to begin with the profit-maximizing condition $MR = MC$, as we did in the chapter. In general, beginning with the profit-maximizing condition is easiest for firms with linear demand curves and simple cost functions. However, some firms have more complicated demand curves and total cost functions. For these firms, solving the profit-maximization problem directly using calculus may save you some work.

Now that we've worked through the calculus of profit maximization for a firm with market power, let's look at an example for a perfectly competitive firm.

9A.2 figure it out

Let's return to Figure It Out 8.1 and to Bob's Barbershop, the perfectly competitive firm with a daily total cost of $TC = 0.5Q^2$. Assume that the market price of a haircut is \$15.

a. How many haircuts should Bob give each day if he wants to maximize his profit?

b. If the firm maximizes profit, how much profit will it earn each day?

Solution:

a. Bob's problem is to choose the quantity of haircuts that will maximize his profit or

$$\max_{Q} \pi = TR - TC = PQ - TC = 15Q - 0.5Q^2$$

Solving for the first-order condition gives

$$\frac{d\pi}{dQ} = \frac{d(15Q - 0.5Q^2)}{dQ} = 0$$
$$15 - Q = 0$$
$$Q^* = 15 \text{ haircuts}$$

Let's confirm that this is the same result that we get from choosing the quantity where $P = MC$. In the chapter, the question provided you with the marginal cost, but now we can solve for it by taking the first derivative of the total cost curve with respect to quantity, the firm's choice variable:

$$MC = \frac{dTC}{dQ} = \frac{d0.5Q^2}{dQ}$$
$$= (2)0.5Q = Q$$

Now finding Bob's optimal quantity of haircuts per day is easy:

$$P = MC$$
$$P = Q$$
$$Q^* = 15 \text{ haircuts}$$

b. At 15 haircuts per day, Bob will earn

$$\pi = TR - TC = PQ - 0.5Q^2$$
$$= 15(15) - 0.5(15)^2 = \$225 - \$112.50 = \$112.50 \text{ per day}$$

Problems

1. Find marginal revenue for the firms that face the following demand curves:
   a. $Q = 1,000 - 5P$
   b. $Q = 100P^{-2}$

2. Suppose a firm faces demand of $Q = 300 - 2P$ and has a total cost curve of $TC = 75Q + Q^2$.
   a. What is the firm's marginal revenue?
   b. What is the firm's marginal cost?
   c. Find the firm's profit-maximizing quantity where $MR = MC$.
   d. Find the firm's profit-maximizing price and profit.

3. Suppose that American Borax is a monopolist and that the worldwide demand for borax is $Q = 100 - P$ where Q is tons of borax and P is the price per ton. The total cost function for American Borax is $TC = 10Q + 0.5Q^2$.
   a. Write out the firm's total revenue as a function of Q.
   b. What is the profit function for American Borax?
   c. Find the firm's profit-maximizing quantity by applying calculus to the profit function.
   d. Find American Borax's profit-maximizing price and profit.

4. Suppose a firm faces the inverse demand curve $P = 600Q^{-0.5}$. The firm has the total cost curve $TC = 1,000 + 0.5Q^{1.5}$. Find the firm's profit-maximizing output, price, and profit.

5. Consider a firm in a perfectly competitive market with total costs given by

$$TC = Q^3 - 15Q^2 + 100Q + 30$$

   a. What is this firm's marginal cost function? Over what range of output are the firm's marginal costs decreasing? Increasing?
   b. Suppose that the market price is $52. What is this firm's profit-maximizing level of output? How do you know this is the profit-maximizing output? How much profit does this firm earn by producing the profit-maximizing output?

Market Power and Pricing Strategies

You've no doubt noticed many places where you can receive price discounts if you show your student ID. Commonly discounted goods include movie admissions, clothing at the campus bookstore, gym memberships, train fare, and even computer equipment.

It's nice of these sellers to give you a price break while you're getting your education. School isn't cheap, and every little bit helps. The sellers' generosity must say something about the value that they put on everyone receiving a good education. Right?

Not really. The main motivation behind such student discounts isn't altruism. Instead, it is almost surely the sellers' attempt to extract more producer surplus from the market than they would otherwise. That's not to say you're worse off because they've offered these discounts; in fact, they make it more likely you will be able to consume goods that would otherwise be too expensive for you. But there's something in it for the sellers, too—these discounts increase their producer surplus and improve their bottom lines.

pricing strategy
A firm's method of pricing its product based on market characteristics.

price discrimination
The practice of charging different prices to different customers for the same product.

How, exactly, does offering student discounts raise a seller's producer surplus? From our study of market power in Chapter 9, we know that when a firm can influence its own price, it makes a higher profit than a perfectly competitive (i.e., price-taking) company. The market power pricing rule we came up with, however, required the firm to charge the same price to all customers. In this chapter, we see that if a firm can charge different prices to different groups of customers (e.g., students and nonstudents), it can raise surplus and profit above those earned by a standard monopolist charging every customer the same price. There are many ways in which firms with market power can charge different prices for the same good. This chapter explores the most common of these strategies and looks at how they affect producers and consumers in the market.

10.1 The Basics of Pricing Strategy

A **pricing strategy** is a firm's plan for setting the price of its product given the market conditions it faces and its desire to maximize profit. The pricing strategy for a perfectly competitive firm is that it charges the equilibrium market price for its product and earns no economic profit. The pricing strategy for firms with market power is more complex. A firm with market power that charges one price to all its customers sets the market price according to the quantity of output it chooses to produce to maximize its profit. (Remember that firms operating in markets with barriers to entry are able to earn economic profits even in the long run.) Some firms with market power, however, can charge different prices to different customers for the same product using a pricing strategy called **price discrimination.** If a firm with market power can price discriminate, it can earn greater economic profit than a single-price monopoly.

It is important to understand that price discrimination is not the same phenomenon as the existence of different prices for different goods. Price differences can occur across similar products even in a competitive market if the marginal costs of producing the products are different. For example, if the marginal cost of washing SUVs at the car wash is higher than that of washing Mini Coopers because SUVs are bigger, car washes might charge more to wash SUVs. Price discrimination is something different. It implies the use of market power to charge higher prices for the same product to those consumers who are willing to pay more for it. Price variations due to price discrimination do not reflect differences in marginal costs; they exist simply because the firm with market power has the ability to charge different prices for the same product.

There are several pricing strategies a company can use depending on its circumstances. These range from *direct price discrimination* to *indirect price discrimination* to *bundling* to *two-part tariffs* and beyond. The motivation for these strategies is straightforward: A company with market power charges a higher price for the units of output that provide consumers with greater consumer surplus. By adjusting the price, a firm extracts more producer surplus from each transaction.

When Can a Firm Pursue a Pricing Strategy?

All the pricing strategies we discuss in this chapter start from two key requirements:

Requirement 1: The firm must have market power. A company must have market power to price discriminate. It's that simple. If the firm you have in mind does not have market power, you are in the wrong chapter of the book. You should be in Chapter 8 on perfect competition. Without market power, a firm can't choose its price at all, much less choose to charge different prices to different consumers or use more advanced pricing strategies.

Requirement 2: The firm must prevent resale and arbitrage. To take advantage of advanced pricing strategies, a firm must be able to prevent its customers from reselling its product among themselves. Otherwise, the customers able to buy units at a low price could purchase a large number of units and resell them to other customers who would otherwise have had to buy the product from the firm at a higher price. The practice of taking advantage of price differences for a product by buying at a lower price and reselling at a higher price is called **arbitrage.**

The ability to engage in arbitrage makes all customers better off. The low-price customers make a profit on resale, and the high-price consumers can buy the product at a lower price than the firm would charge. The firm isn't better off, though. It is effectively shut out from directly selling to any consumers except those who want to buy at the lowest price. Because it would then be selling at only one price, however, the firm would be back in the traditional situation for a firm with market power described in Chapter 9: It should produce the quantity at which marginal revenue equals marginal cost and charge the price at which buyers would consume that quantity (and therefore not worry about resellers).

If a firm meets these two requirements, it can attempt to implement more profitable pricing strategies. Figure 10.1 provides an overview of these strategies.

arbitrage
The practice of reselling a product at a price higher than its original selling price.

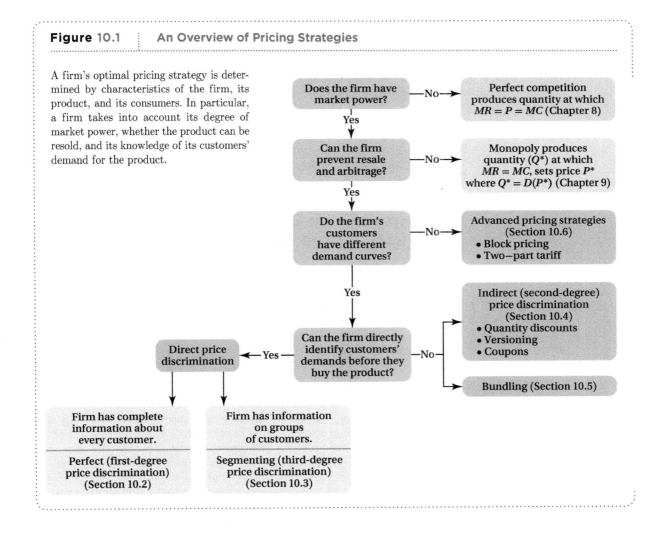

Figure 10.1   An Overview of Pricing Strategies

A firm's optimal pricing strategy is determined by characteristics of the firm, its product, and its consumers. In particular, a firm takes into account its degree of market power, whether the product can be resold, and its knowledge of its customers' demand for the product.

Does the firm have market power? —No→ Perfect competition produces quantity at which $MR = P = MC$ (Chapter 8)

Yes ↓

Can the firm prevent resale and arbitrage? —No→ Monopoly produces quantity (Q^*) at which $MR = MC$, sets price P^* where $Q^* = D(P^*)$ (Chapter 9)

Yes ↓

Do the firm's customers have different demand curves? —No→ Advanced pricing strategies (Section 10.6)
• Block pricing
• Two–part tariff

Yes ↓

Can the firm directly identify customers' demands before they buy the product? —No→ Indirect (second-degree) price discrimination (Section 10.4)
• Quantity discounts
• Versioning
• Coupons

→ Bundling (Section 10.5)

←Yes— Direct price discrimination

Firm has complete information about every customer.

Perfect (first-degree price discrimination) (Section 10.2)

Firm has information on groups of customers.

Segmenting (third-degree price discrimination) (Section 10.3)

Strategies for Customers with Different Demands The first pricing strategies we look at involve price discrimination. For price discrimination to be an option, a firm needs to have different types of customers with different price sensitivities of demand. The exact kind of price discrimination the firm should use depends on the kind of information the firm has.

1. **Can a firm identify its customers' demands before they buy?** If the firm has complete, detailed information about each customer's own demand curve before she buys the product, it can practice *perfect price discrimination* and charge every customer a different price. If information about its customers is less detailed, a firm may be able to discriminate by customer group, as in third-degree price discrimination. The key to these kinds of price discrimination is that a firm must be able to directly identify different customers or groups of customers (as can a store that requires students to show IDs when making purchases) and charge different prices to each customer or group of customers.

2. **Can a firm identify its customers' differing demands only after they make a purchase?** If a firm cannot identify different types of consumers *before* they make their purchases, it can try more indirect price discrimination, which involves offering different pricing packages and then identifying the customer's type from the pricing package she chooses. These pricing packages can take the form of quantity discounts, different versions of the product at different prices, or (under the right conditions) bundling together different products.

Do a Firm's Customers Have the Same Demand Curves? There is still another set of pricing strategies that a firm can use even if its consumers have the same demand curves. These strategies involve offering different unit prices to the same customer for different quantities purchased or charging lump-sum fees on top of per-unit prices.

We explore all these strategies in the remainder of this chapter. To help clarify a firm's decision, each pricing strategy section has a When to Use It feature that explains what a firm needs to know about its market and customers to use a given pricing strategy most effectively. By using the best strategy, the firm can extract the most producer surplus from the market.

10.2 Direct Price Discrimination I: Perfect/ First-Degree Price Discrimination

When to Use It Perfect/First-Degree Price Discrimination
1. The firm has market power and can prevent resale.
2. The firm's customers have different demand curves.
3. The firm has complete information about *every* customer and can identify each one's demand before purchase.

Let's start our study of pricing strategies by looking at a firm that has market power, can prevent resale, and knows that its consumers differ in their willingness to pay and therefore have different demand curves. To choose a price discrimination strategy that will allow the firm to reap the greatest benefits of these three characteristics, the firm must first ask itself whether it can directly identify what type of demand its customers have *before* they purchase the product, or whether it can determine this only *after* they buy the product. That is, do the buyers have some identifiable characteristic that allows the firm to observe their sensitivity to price and willingness to pay for the firm's product? If they do, the company can directly identify its customers' demands beforehand

and increase its producer surplus by using **direct price discrimination,** that is, by charging different prices to different customers based on something that a firm can observe directly about its customers' identities. If it can know its consumers' demands only *after* they buy the product, then the firm has to use *indirect price discrimination,* which we discuss later in the chapter.

Let's first consider the possibilities for a firm that has so much information about its customers before they buy that it knows each individual buyer's demand curve and can literally charge each buyer a different price equal to the buyer's willingness to pay. This type of direct price discrimination is known as **perfect price discrimination** or **first-degree price discrimination.**

Suppose a firm faces a market demand curve like the one labeled D in Figure 10.2. Panel a shows the outcomes for a perfectly competitive firm and a monopolistic firm. We know from Chapter 8 that in a perfectly competitive market, the equilibrium price (which is the same as MR in that case) equals marginal cost MC and the firm produces quantity Q_c. Consumer surplus is the area under the demand curve and above the price, $A + B + C$. Because we assume that marginal cost is constant, there is no producer surplus.

In Chapter 9, we saw that a firm with market power facing demand curve D and with no ability to prevent resale produces the quantity where its marginal cost equals its

direct price discrimination
A pricing strategy in which firms charge different prices to different customers based on observable characteristics of the customers.

perfect price discrimination (first-degree price discrimination)
A type of direct price discrimination in which a firm charges each customer exactly his willingness to pay.

Figure 10.2   Perfect (First-Degree) Price Discrimination

(a) Perfect competition and monopoly

Consumer surplus (competition) $= A + B + C$
Producer surplus (competition) $= 0$
Consumer surplus (market power) $= A$
Producer surplus (market power) $= B$
Deadweight loss from market power $= C$

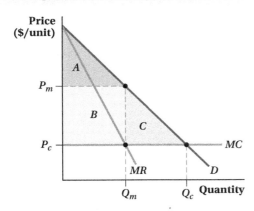

(b) Perfect price discrimination

Consumer surplus $= 0$
Producer surplus $= A + B + C$
Deadweight loss from market power $= 0$

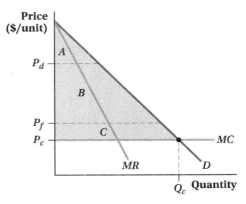

(a) A competitive market will set price equal to marginal cost, producing Q_c and selling at a price of P_c. Consumers will receive a consumer surplus equal to $A + B + C$ and the firm will earn zero producer surplus. A single-price monopoly will sell quantity Q_m at a price of P_m and receive a producer surplus equal to B. Consumers will receive consumer surplus equal to A and the deadweight loss from market power will be area C.

(b) If a firm with market power can identify each customer's demand curve, then it will charge each customer her willingness to pay and capture the entire surplus, $A + B + C$. For example, the firm will charge a customer willing to pay P_d exactly the price P_d and a customer willing to pay P_f the price P_f. The firm will sell up to the quantity Q_c, the perfectly competitive quantity where $P_c = MC$. There is no deadweight loss when a firm practices perfect price discrimination.

marginal revenue, Q_m, and sets the price P_m for that quantity from its demand curve. It charges this single price to everyone in the market. This market power pricing has three outcomes relative to the competitive pricing: (1) There is now a producer surplus equal to the rectangle B (far better from the firm's perspective than the competitive outcome, no producer surplus); (2) there is now a deadweight loss equal to the triangle C, because quantity is below its competitive level; and (3) consumer surplus falls to area A.

If, however, the firm with market power can prevent resale and directly identify each and every customer's demand curve (panel b), the outcome is very different. In this case, the firm can charge every customer her willingness to pay for every unit (or, to guarantee she'd take the deal, just a bit below this level). This is perfect price discrimination, and the benefit to the firm is tremendous. For any unit of output where a customer's willingness to pay is greater than the firm's marginal cost of producing it, the firm captures the whole amount of available surplus. So, for example, a customer accounting for the portion of the demand curve at P_d pays that relatively high price, while another at P_f pays that relatively low price. In these and all other cases, even though the prices are different, customers pay the most they are willing to pay, and the firm gets the entire surplus (the area below demand and above marginal cost).

After all such transactions, the firm will have sold a quantity of Q_c to various consumers at different prices depending on each buyer's willingness to pay. (Because the firm can prevent resale, customers aren't able to buy the product from another customer for a lower price than the firm offers.) The producer surplus the firm earns as a result equals the entire surplus in the market $(A + B + C)$. This is the maximum amount of surplus that can be made from the market because no consumer will pay more than his or her willingness to pay (that rules out the area above the demand curve), and the firm must pay its costs (that eliminates the area below the marginal cost curve). It's good to be a firm that can perfectly price discriminate.

Another interesting feature of perfect price discrimination is that, unlike the single-price market power outcome, there is no deadweight loss! It is efficient: No potential surplus is lost from a reduction in the equilibrium quantity. The quantity sold (Q_c) is the same quantity that would be sold if the market were perfectly competitive. Who *keeps* the market surplus is very different in the two cases, however: Under perfect competition, the entire surplus goes to the consumers, while under perfect price discrimination, the entire surplus goes to the producer. Efficiency is not the same thing as fairness. (We will further discuss issues of market efficiency and distribution in Chapter 14.)

10.1 figure it out

A firm with market power faces an inverse demand curve for its product of $P = 100 - 10Q$. Assume that the firm faces a marginal cost curve of $MC = 10 + 10Q$.

a. If the firm cannot price discriminate, what is the profit-maximizing level of output and price?

b. If the firm cannot price discriminate, what are the levels of consumer and producer surplus in the market, assuming the firm maximizes its profit? Calculate the deadweight loss from market power.

c. If the firm has the ability to practice perfect price discrimination, what is the firm's output?

d. If the firm practices perfect price discrimination, what are the levels of consumer and producer surplus? What is the deadweight loss from market power?

Solution:

a. If the firm cannot price discriminate, it maximizes profit by producing where $MR = MC$. If the inverse demand function is $P = 100 - 10Q$, then the marginal revenue must be $MR = 100 - 20Q$. (Remember that, for any linear inverse demand function $P = a - bQ$, marginal revenue is $MR = a - 2bQ$.)

Setting $MR = MC$, we obtain

$$100 - 20Q = 10 + 10Q$$
$$90 = 30Q$$
$$Q = 3$$

To find the optimal price, we plug $Q = 3$ into the inverse demand equation:

$$P = 100 - 10Q$$
$$= 100 - 10(3)$$
$$= 100 - 30$$
$$= 70$$

The firm sells 3 units at a price of $70 each.

b. To find consumer and producer surplus, we need to start with a diagram showing the demand, marginal revenue, and marginal cost curves:

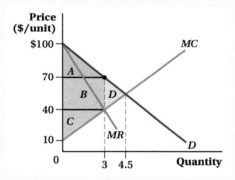

Consumer surplus is the area above price and below demand (area A). Producer surplus is the area above marginal cost but below the price (area $B + C$). (Note that we could just label these two areas as a large trapezoid, but it is easier to remember the formulas for the area of a rectangle and a triangle!) We can calculate the areas:

$$\text{Area } A = \frac{1}{2} \text{ base} \times \text{height}$$
$$= \frac{1}{2} \times 3 \times (\$100 - \$70)$$
$$= 0.5(3)(\$30)$$
$$= \$45$$

Consumer surplus is $45.

$$\text{Area } B = \text{base} \times \text{height}$$

To get the height of areas B and C, we need the MC of producing a quantity of 3:
$MC = 10 + 10Q = 10 + 10(3) = \$40$. So,

$$\text{Area } B = 3 \times (\$70 - \$40)$$
$$= 3(\$30)$$
$$= \$90$$

$$\text{Area } C = \frac{1}{2} \times \text{base} \times \text{height}$$
$$= \frac{1}{2} \times 3 \times (\$40 - \$10)$$
$$= 0.5(3)(\$30)$$
$$= \$45$$

So, Producer surplus = Area B + Area C = $90 + $45 = $135.

The deadweight loss from market power is the loss in surplus that occurs because the market is not producing the competitive quantity. To calculate the competitive quantity, we set $P = MC$:

$$100 - 10Q = 10 + 10Q$$
$$90 = 20Q$$
$$Q = 4.5$$

The deadweight loss can be seen on the diagram as area D:

$$\text{Area } D = \frac{1}{2} \times \text{base} \times \text{height}$$
$$= \frac{1}{2} \times (4.5 - 3) \times (\$70 - \$40)$$
$$= 0.5(1.5)(\$30)$$
$$= \$22.50$$

The deadweight loss from market power is $22.50.

c. If the firm practices perfect price discrimination, it will produce where $P = MC$. As we saw in part (b) above, this means that the firm will produce 4.5 units.

d. If the firm practices perfect price discrimination, consumer surplus will be zero because every consumer will be charged a price equal to his willingness to pay. Producer surplus will be the full area between the demand curve and the marginal cost curve (area $A + B + C + D$):

$$\text{Producer surplus} = \text{area } A + \text{area } B + \text{area } C + \text{area } D$$
$$= \$45 + \$90 + \$45 + \$22.50$$
$$= \$202.50$$

There is no deadweight loss when the firm perfectly price discriminates. The competitive output level is achieved ($Q = 4.5$). Producers end up with the entire surplus available in the market.

Examples of Perfect Price Discrimination

Actual cases of died-in-the-wool perfect price discrimination are rare. What firm really knows every single customer's willingness to pay for its product? There are instances, though, where sellers charge many, many different prices for the same product. Two classic examples are cars and college education.

When people walk into a car dealership, the salesperson sizes them up and eventually begins negotiating over price. While the dealer doesn't have *complete* information about each customer's willingness to pay, haggling differently with every customer is a lot like perfect price discrimination—the auto dealer is trying to simultaneously learn about the customer's valuation of the car and arrive at a price as close as possible to that level. That's why you should think twice when you go to buy a car and the salesman asks you, "How much are you looking to spend on a car?" That's an invitation for you to give up your consumer surplus.

Likewise, families applying for college financial aid are required to submit complete information about their assets and income along with the student's assets and income. From this information, the school has an almost perfect understanding of each student's willingness to pay. This allows schools to produce an individually tailored financial aid plan. But that is another way of saying that they charge a different tuition price to each student, depending on how much they think the student can afford.

 application

How Priceline Learned That You Can't Price Discriminate without Market Power

Priceline is the online travel service known in part for originating the "name your own price" model of online sales. The initial idea was that people would go to Priceline's site and enter what they were willing to pay for an airplane ticket—for example, $300 for a round-trip from Los Angeles to Boston on April 10th. Priceline would then see if there were any airlines willing to supply the ticket to Priceline for less than that. If so, Priceline would charge the customer's credit card $300 and issue the ticket, earning the difference as profit.

The idea was that by asking each person what she was willing to pay, Priceline could engage in something like perfect price discrimination and therefore make a lot of money. We can think of its original business model in terms of Figure 10.3. Priceline figured that, with a marginal cost of tickets of MC and travelers' willingness to pay (demand curve) at D, it stood to earn producer surplus approximately equal to the area $A + B$. The stock market liked this model, too: Within three years of starting up its Web site, the company was valued at $13 billion, more than several of the major airlines combined.

There was a serious problem in Priceline's approach, however. Priceline wanted to price discriminate, but it didn't really have market power in the travel agency industry. There are thousands of offline travel agencies; several other major online travel firms like Orbitz, Travelocity, and Expedia; and airlines sell a lot of tickets directly from their own Web sites. We know from what we've just learned that a company can't price-discriminate if it doesn't have market power. Priceline learned this lesson the hard way.

Priceline's problem was that, because travelers could also get fares at low prices directly from other travel sites, they wouldn't offer their true willingness to pay from their demand curves. Instead, customers would only offer to buy tickets at a lower price than they could buy them elsewhere.

Priceline's market demand curve was therefore not the consumer's demand curve D, but rather a curve strictly below the market price of tickets at other sites. In the figure, the outside price occurs at P_{out}. So, the actual demand curve facing Priceline was not

Figure 10.3   **Perfect Price Discrimination without Market Power: What Went Wrong with Naming Your Own Price**

With market power, Priceline could use perfect price discrimination to capture the entire surplus above MC but below D, the area $A + B$. However, because it does not have market power, Priceline's demand curve D_{act} is below demand curve D. Using perfect price discrimination, Priceline can only capture B, the area above MC but below D_{act}.

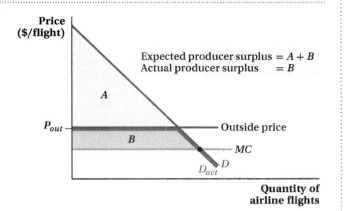

D but D_{act} instead. This kind of price discrimination doesn't make large profits. It left Priceline with a surplus of only B, the small area below the actual demand curve and above marginal cost. Indeed, this demand curve left Priceline with less producer surplus than that earned by other travel sites (which were charging prices at or above P_{out}).

Realizing this, Priceline eventually deemphasized the "name your own price" business model and expanded into the conventionally priced online travel business. It has so far succeeded—its stock market valuation was back up to over $20 billion in 2011 after falling all the way to $225 million in 2000. It had a tough road back. The moral of the story is, as always: Remember your economics. ■

10.3 Direct Price Discrimination II: Segmenting/ Third-Degree Price Discrimination

When to Use It Segmenting/Third-Degree Price Discrimination

1. The firm has market power and can prevent resale.
2. The firm's customers have different demand curves.
3. The firm can directly identify specific *groups* of customers with different price sensitivities (but not the demand of every individual customer) before purchase.

Because it's rare for a firm to have the kind of comprehensive information about customers that it needs to practice perfect price discrimination, a firm can't generally capture *all* of the market surplus using price discrimination. But it can still earn more profit than a regular monopoly by using a pricing strategy called **segmenting** (or **third-degree price discrimination**), charging different prices to different groups (segments) of customers based on the identifiable attributes of those groups.[1]

segmenting (third-degree price discrimination)
A type of direct price discrimination in which a firm charges different prices to different groups of customers.

---

[1] While third-degree discrimination sounds like a variant of first-degree discrimination, the truth is that these names were somewhat arbitrarily coined by economist E. H. Chamberlin back in the 1930s.

For this kind of pricing strategy to work, the company must be able to directly identify *groups* of customers—students, for example—who have systematically different demands than other buyers. This group-level demand identification is typically much easier to determine than figuring out every individual customer's willingness to pay.

Think about a company that sells a clothing line emblazoned with the logo of a local university. If the company knows that students typically don't have a lot of money and tend to be bargain hunters while their parents or the faculty are less price-sensitive, the firm will want to charge students a lower price for clothing and parents or faculty a higher price. To do this, the company needs to be able to identify the groups directly. It must be able to tell before the sale which customers are students and which are parents or faculty, as well as prevent parents and faculty from pretending to be students to get the discount. One way the company can do this is to make showing a student ID a condition of the lower price.

As with all forms of price discrimination, however, the company must be able to prevent resale. They can't sell school sweatshirts at a student discount just to have the students then turn around and sell them to visiting parents or faculty for less than the higher price these groups would be charged. As a practical matter, if such resales became a problem, the company could institute a quota that would limit the number of sweatshirts a student could buy. Limiting resale is critical to price discrimination.

How many of these triathletes had to travel to Cozumel to compete?

Hugo Ortuño Suárez/Demotix/Corbis

The Benefits of Segmenting: A Graphical Approach

If a firm is able to engage in segmenting, how different should the prices be across the groups, and how much does the company stand to gain by price discriminating compared to the standard one-price monopoly strategy?

To answer these questions, let's consider an example with two consumer groups, the market for entry into the prestigious Ironman Cozumel 70.3 Triathlon. This triathlon is a race that comprises a 1.2-mile swim, a 56-mile bike ride, and a 13.1-mile run. It may seem like a masochistic pursuit, but people pay serious money to enter this race.

There are two kinds of people who want to enter the Ironman Cozumel: people who live in and around Cozumel, and people who fly in from somewhere else. The two groups' demand curves for entering the race are shown in Figure 10.4. Panel a shows the demand (D_T) for the participants traveling to Cozumel for the competition. The travelers mostly come from the United States; have high incomes and expensive triathlon equipment; and will have to pay for a plane ticket, a hotel room, food, and a rental car. They don't care if the price of their registration for the race is a bit higher, because it's a small share of the total cost to them. In other words, the demand curve for the traveling participants is fairly inelastic.

Panel b of the figure shows the local group's demand curve, D_L. The local residents' demand is more price-sensitive because they have many other activities they can pursue if the price of entering the race is too high. Thus, their demand curve is flatter and more elastic.

Preventing resale won't be a problem for the firm organizing the race as long as it can tell which athletes are from out of town and which are not. This is easy because out-of-town athletes have to pay their entrance fees with some form of identification

Figure 10.4 | Segmenting Entry Fees at the Ironman Cozumel 70.3 Triathlon

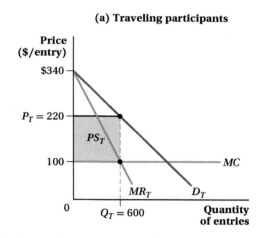

(a) Traveling participants

(b) Local participants

(a) The Cozumel Ironman 70.3 Triathlon segments its participants into two groups, traveling and local participants. Traveling participants are relatively insensitive to price and have an inelastic demand curve D_T. The number of traveling participants will be $Q_T = 600$, and each will pay a registration fee of $P_T = \$220/\text{entry}$. Producer surplus, PS_T, will be relatively large.

(b) Local participants have an elastic demand curve D_L. A greater number of locals will register for the triathlon ($Q_L = 700$) at a lower price ($P_L = \$170/\text{entry}$). Producer surplus for locals, PS_L, is relatively small.

that gives their address, and they have to prove who they are when claiming their bib numbers on race day.

The fundamental economic idea of segmenting is simple. If a firm can directly identify groups that have different demands and charge different prices to each, it can essentially treat each group as a separate market. The firm then sets its profit-maximizing quantity for each one of these "markets" where $MR = MC$ and sets the corresponding single-price profit-maximizing price according to each market's demand curve.

Let's see how the organizers of the Ironman Cozumel competition follow the segmenting strategy. The organizers have identified these two different demand curves and treat each as a separate market. From the demand curve of out-of-town entrants (travelers) D_T, the organizers compute marginal revenue, labeled MR_T in panel a of Figure 10.4. Then from the point at which MR_T equals marginal cost MC, the organizers determine the optimal quantity of entries to sell to out-of-towners ($Q_T = 600$). At that quantity, the entry fee is $P_T = \$220$.

The organizers go through the same process for the local entrants. These entrants' demand curve D_L in panel b implies a marginal revenue curve MR_L. The optimal number of entries for the organizer to offer locals is $Q_L = 700$, the quantity at which marginal revenue from locals equals marginal cost. (The marginal cost is the same for either type of racer. It amounts, basically, to the cost of a bib, some extra Gatorade, some water, a finisher's medal, and a race T-shirt.) The price, determined from the locals' demand curve, is $P_L = \$170$, significantly lower than the $220 price for traveling entrants.

Figure 10.5   Single-Price Monopolist at the Ironman Cozumel Triathlon

A single-price monopolist faces the kinked demand curve D, equal to the horizontal sum of the demand curves for travelers and local participants. The race organizer will sell 1,300 entries at a price of $186.67, between the two prices ($170 and $225) charged when the market is segmented. The resulting producer surplus, rectangle A, is smaller than the producer surplus under market segmentation.

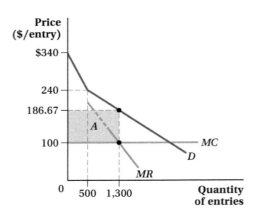

That's all there is to the strategy. As long as a seller can keep people from sneaking into the lower-price group or keep those in the lower-price group from reselling to the higher-price group, it can use segmenting to treat each group like a separate market and set the monopoly price for each market.

A firm following this pricing strategy will not earn as much producer surplus as one using perfect price discrimination (which would allow it to take the entire surplus from the market). However, it will earn more surplus than if it acted like a regular monopoly and charged the same price to everyone, because the strategy gives the firm some ability to charge a higher price to consumers with relatively inelastic demand and lower prices to consumers with relatively elastic demand.

Figure 10.5 shows the total Ironman Cozumel demand and marginal revenue that would face a monopolist forced to set only a single price. As in Chapter 5, we calculate the market demand as the horizontal sum of the participants' demand curves—in this case, the sum of the traveling and local participants' demands. This results in a kink in the market demand curve at $240, the demand choke price for local participants. At prices above $240, no locals purchase tickets, so the market demand curve is just the traveling racers' demand curve.

A single-price monopolist race organizer sets the quantity of entries where its marginal cost equals marginal revenue, and charges the price corresponding to the total market demand curve. This quantity, 1,300 racers, is shown in Figure 10.5, and the corresponding price is $186.67 per entry. Notice how this price falls between the two prices ($170 and $225) that the organizers charge the segments when price-discriminating. Although it might not be obvious from looking at the figure, the producer surplus for the single-price monopolist is considerably smaller than the surplus the monopolist would earn by segmenting the market. (We see that this is indeed the case when we calculate the benefits from segmenting in the next section.)

The Benefits of Segmenting: A Mathematical Approach

To do the same analysis of segmenting using mathematics, we start with the two distinct demand curves for the Ironman Cozumel. The demand curve of the traveling participants is given by $Q_T = 1,700 - 5P_T$, and the locals' demand curve is $Q_L = 2,400 - 10P_L$.

Note that, in accordance with our story, the locals' quantity demanded is more sensitive to price than the travelers' quantity demanded: A $1 increase in the entry fee reduces the number of local entrants by 10, while it only decreases the number of traveling entrants by 5. We assume the marginal cost to the organizer of adding another triathlete to the race is a constant $100, no matter how many entrants there are.

The mathematical analysis of segmenting is done using the same steps as in the graphical analysis above. If the race organizers can identify the separate groups and prevent resale, they can compute the marginal revenue curves for each segment and solve for the monopoly prices separately for each group.

We can follow the methods discussed in Chapter 9 to find the marginal revenue curves from linear demand curves. First, we determine the inverse demand curves by rearranging the demand function to express price in terms of quantity demanded. Doing so gives us the following equations:

$$
\begin{array}{ll}
\textbf{For travelers:} & \textbf{For locals:} \\
Q_T = 1{,}700 - 5P_T & Q_L = 2{,}400 - 10P_L \\
5P_T = 1{,}700 - Q_T & 10P_L = 2{,}400 - Q_L \\
P_T = 340 - 0.2Q_T & P_L = 240 - 0.1Q_L
\end{array}
$$

Next, we know that the marginal revenue curve will look like the inverse demand curve, but the coefficient on quantity will be twice as large. The marginal revenue curves for the two segments are

$$
\textbf{For travelers:} \qquad\qquad \textbf{For locals:}
$$
$$
MR_T = 340 - 0.4Q_T \qquad \text{and} \qquad MR_L = 240 - 0.2Q_L
$$

The organizers want to sell the quantities at which marginal cost ($100, the same for both groups of triathletes) equals its marginal revenue. Setting each marginal revenue equation above equal to marginal costs tells us the optimal number of entrants from each group:

$$
\begin{array}{ll}
\textbf{For travelers:} & \textbf{For locals:} \\
MR_T = MC & MR_L = MC \\
340 - 0.4Q_T = 100 & 240 - 0.2Q_L = 100 \\
240 = 0.4Q_T & 140 = 0.2Q_L \\
Q_T = 600 & Q_L = 700
\end{array}
$$

The last step is to find the entry fees that correspond to these quantities by plugging the quantities back into the inverse demand curve:

$$
\begin{array}{ll}
\textbf{For travelers:} & \textbf{For locals:} \\
P_T = 340 - 0.2Q_T & P_L = 240 - 0.1Q_L \\
= 340 - 0.2(600) & = 240 - 0.1(700) \\
= 340 - 120 & = 240 - 70 \\
= \$220 & = \$170
\end{array}
$$

Therefore, in a segmentation strategy, the race organizers sell 600 entries to out-of-towners for $220 each and 700 entries to locals at $170 each.

The total producer surplus the organizers earn is the difference between the price and the marginal cost for each segment times the number of entries sold to that segment. In Figure 10.4, those surpluses are rectangles PS_T for the segment of nonlocal triathletes and PS_L for the local triathletes. Using the results we computed above, we have

$$
\begin{array}{ll}
\textbf{For travelers:} & \textbf{For locals:} \\
PS_T = (220 - 100) \times 600 & PS_L = (170 - 100) \times 700 \\
= 120(600) & = 70(700) \\
= \$72{,}000 & = \$49{,}000
\end{array}
$$

for a combined producer surplus of $121,000 to the race organizer.

In our graphical analysis, we contended that the price-discriminating monopolist earns more producer surplus than the single-price monopolist. This makes intuitive sense, because a firm that segments the market can charge higher prices to more price-inelastic customers and capture more of their consumer surplus. But how can we show this algebraically?

First, we can see that the marginal cost curve intersects demand at the part of the demand curve below the kink—the portion of the demand curve that is the sum of the local and nonlocal demand:

$$Q = 1{,}700 - 5P + 2{,}400 - 10P = 4{,}100 - 15P$$

The inverse demand curve at this intersection is then $P = \frac{4{,}100}{15} - \frac{Q}{15}$, and the marginal revenue curve has twice the slope, or $MR = \frac{4{,}100}{15} - \frac{2Q}{15}$. We set MR equal to the marginal cost to solve for the optimal number of participants under the single-pricing strategy:

$$\frac{4{,}100}{15} - \frac{2Q}{15} = 100$$

$$4{,}100 + 2Q = 1{,}500$$

$$Q = 1{,}300$$

Note that 1,300 is exactly the sum of the local and traveling participants under the previous pricing system. Single-price monopolists and those who segment differ in the prices they set, but not always in the quantity they provide. That doesn't mean the firm would be selling to the same group of individuals, however. The new price will be lower than the segmented price for travelers (inducing more to buy than in the segmented case) and higher than the segmented price for locals (excluding some locals from buying). Just what is the price in this instance? Plug the quantity into the inverse demand curve:

$$P = \frac{4{,}100}{15} - \frac{1{,}300}{15} = \$186.67$$

Thus, although locals face a slightly higher price, the travelers get a bargain relative to the segmented outcome.

To calculate the producer surplus, we find the area of the rectangle A in Figure 10.5:

$$PS = (186.67 - 100) \times 1{,}300$$

$$= 86.67(1{,}300) = \$112{,}671$$

If the monopolist organizers segment the market for triathlon entries, they earn $121,000 in producer surplus; if they must charge a single price, they earn $112,671. Just by segmenting the market, the monopolist organizers can increase their producer surplus by $8,329, or about 7%.

How Much Should Each Segment Be Charged?

Because the standard market power pricing rule applies in each segment, it also means that the Lerner index, the basic markup formula we derived in Chapter 9, applies in each market. Recall that this formula relates the price elasticity of demand to the markup of price over marginal cost:

$$\frac{(P - MC)}{P} = \frac{1}{-E^D}$$

If the firm sells the same good to both segments of the market, the marginal cost of producing for each segment is the same. In this case, the only reason to charge different prices to customers in different segments is because they have different demand elasticities. To see what the Lerner index implies for the ratio of the prices in the two segments (label them 1 and 2), first solve the Lerner index for price in each segment:

$$\frac{(P_1 - MC)}{P_1} = \frac{1}{-E_1^D}$$

$$P_1 - MC = \frac{1}{-E_1^D} \times P_1$$

$$P_1 + \left(\frac{1}{E_1^D} \times P_1\right) = MC$$

$$P_1\left(1 + \frac{1}{E_1^D}\right) = MC$$

$$P_1\left(\frac{E_1^D}{E_1^D} + \frac{1}{E_1^D}\right) = MC$$

$$P_1 = \left(\frac{E_1^D}{1 + E_1^D}\right) \times MC$$

Likewise,

$$P_2 = \left(\frac{E_2^D}{1 + E_2^D}\right) \times MC$$

Now, we can compute the ratio of these prices:

$$\frac{P_1}{P_2} = \frac{[E_1^D/(1 + E_1^D)] \times MC}{[E_2^D/(1 + E_2^D)] \times MC}$$

$$= \frac{[E_1^D/(1 + E_1^D)]}{[E_2^D/(1 + E_2^D)]}$$

As the demand in Segment 1 becomes less elastic relative to Segment 2 (i.e., E_1^D becomes smaller than E_2^D in absolute value), the ratio P_1/P_2 will rise. That is, the greater the difference in price sensitivities between the segments, the greater should be the ratio in their prices.

Returning to our Ironman Cozumel example, suppose we know that the elasticity of demand for travelers is −1.83 and the elasticity for locals is −2.43.[2] We can immediately determine what the ratio of prices should be by plugging these elasticities into the formula:

$$\frac{P_1}{P_2} = \frac{\dfrac{-1.83}{-1.83 + 1}}{\dfrac{-2.43}{-2.43 + 1}} = \frac{\dfrac{-1.83}{-0.83}}{\dfrac{-2.43}{-1.43}} = \frac{2.2}{1.7} = 1.29$$

In other words, the race organizer should set the price travelers face to be almost 1.3 times (i.e., 30% higher than) the price for locals.

---

[2] If you remember the calculation of elasticity from Chapter 2, you can verify these values.

make the grade

Is it really price discrimination?

We mentioned this before, but it bears repeating: Always be careful about the distinction between *price discrimination,* when firms charge different prices for the same product, and *price differences.* It's often surprisingly hard to tell them apart. Prices can differ across different customer groups if a firm with market power price discriminates, but prices can also differ across the groups if the marginal cost of supplying the groups differs, even in a perfectly competitive market.

For example, a bottle of Coca-Cola, which is basically just carbonated water plus syrup, is often less expensive than a bottle of carbonated water alone. Perhaps this price difference reflects price discrimination because the kinds of people who buy bottled water are less price-sensitive than the people who buy soda. But maybe the cost of bottling fancy carbonated water is greater than the cost of bottling soft drinks (a lot more people buy soda than carbonated water and there might be some economies of scale, e.g.). You can't tell just from the prices.

The only way to tell the difference between price discrimination and price differences due to costs in competitive markets (without actually being able to observe the firm's marginal cost) is to find something that changes the price elasticity of demand without changing the cost. Price discrimination implies that a firm with market power sets its price based on the elasticity of demand and the marginal cost of producing. Price in a competitive market depends only on marginal cost. (This is related to the distinction we discussed in Chapter 9 about how firms with market power react differently than competitive firms to rotations in demand.)

10.2 figure it out

You manage a hair salon that has two locations: one in a large city in Ohio with several competing salons, and another in a small city in Pennsylvania with less competition. In Ohio, your customer's price elasticity of demand is –3, while for your Pennsylvania customers it is –2. Assume that the marginal cost of producing a haircut is $30 regardless of location.

a. What are your salon's optimal markups and prices in each location?

b. Why do they differ?

Solution:

a. The Lerner index provides us with a formula for seeing the relationship between pricing and the price elasticity of demand:

$$\frac{(P - MC)}{P} = \frac{1}{-E^D}$$

Substituting for marginal cost (= $30) and the price elasticity of demand for Ohio customers (= –3), we get

$$\frac{(P - \$30)}{P} = \frac{1}{-(-3)}$$

$$P = 3(P - \$30)$$

$$2P = \$90$$

$$P = \$45$$

Repeating the same steps for Pennsylvania gives

$$\frac{(P - \$30)}{P} = \frac{1}{-(-2)}$$

$$P = 2(P - \$30)$$

$$P = \$60$$

Customers in Ohio will be charged a price of $45 per haircut, while those in Pennsylvania will be charged a price of $60 per haircut.

b. Because demand is relatively more elastic in Ohio than in Pennsylvania (the absolute value of the price elasticity of demand is greater), customers in Ohio are more price-sensitive. Therefore, they will be charged a lower price.

Ways to Directly Segment Customers

There are many ways firms directly identify customer segments for the purposes of price discrimination. Here are some of the most common ones.

By Customer Characteristics Firms sometimes price according to customer characteristics such as age (e.g., senior citizen discounts at the movies or child discounts at a hotel), gender, or whether the customer is a student or local resident. The basic idea remains to identify the more price-sensitive customers and charge them less. Firms need to be careful when pricing based on consumer characteristics in certain countries because in some cases this may be prohibited by laws against discrimination based on age, gender, race, physical disabilities, and so on.

Segmenting can even be based on the user's species. Doctors and veterinarians sometimes use the same medicines. Drug makers recognize that Grandma's willingness to pay for the arthritis medication Lodine probably well exceeds someone's willingness to purchase Lodine for her arthritic dog Rover (and not only because Grandma's savings are larger than Rover's collection of buried rawhides). This difference in willingness to pay probably explains why a congressional investigation found that the price of Lodine for humans was almost three times higher than for dogs. Indeed, it determined that manufacturers priced almost every comparable medication significantly higher for people than for animals.[3]

freakonomics

Victoria's Not-So-Secret Price Discrimination

Sometimes price discrimination can end up being costly not just to consumers, but also to producers. In 1996 Denise Katzman of New York City sued Victoria's Secret for gender discrimination and asked for millions of dollars in damages. In alleging gender discrimination, Katzman didn't object to the catalog's pages of scantily clad women. Rather, she pointed to the promotional coupon on the catalog's back page.

The problem? While Ms. Katzman's catalog offered her $10 off an order of $75, an almost identical catalog for a male friend offered $25 off the same amount. Was her catalog out of date? Nope. The folks at Victoria's Secret were just engaging in a little "naked" price discrimination.

Although the company kept its reasons for the different promotions a secret, we can speculate on why it might employ such price discrimination using our economics reasoning. We know that price discrimination occurs when a company uses its market power to charge higher prices to people who are willing to pay more. In this case, Victoria's Secret recognized that its practice of sending out catalogs gave it the opportunity to segment its customers and advertise different prices to different types of customers. Women might be willing to purchase $75 of fancy underwear for a price of $65, but men are probably not as willing to shell out that kind of money for underwear for their wives or girlfriends. They might only pay $50 for the same order. Because most people don't end up reading through their friends' catalogs, this form of price discrimination could easily go undetected.

Ms. Katzman never did collect her millions in damages, however. Neither did fellow New Yorker Roy Den Hollander who in 2007 brought suit against bars that sponsor Ladies' Nights, which Hollander termed "invidious." He lost his suit, and bars everywhere continue to advertise gender-based price discrimination with weekly Ladies' Nights.

[3] http://www.house.gov/cummings/pdf/animals.pdf

Customer characteristics can also apply to firms or other corporate organizations in business-to-business transactions. Academic journals, for example, know that individuals are much more price sensitive to subscription prices than libraries, so the publishers charge significantly more for institutional subscriptions than for individual ones. Elsevier, for example, one of the largest publishers of academic journals, charges individuals $112 for a year's subscription to the *International Journal of Industrial Organization* (don't all rush to order it at once!), but the publisher charges libraries $1,720 for the same subscription.

By Past Purchase Behavior   Consumers reveal a lot about their willingness to pay when they buy other products, and many sellers use that information to segment customers. In industries like auto insurance or direct-broadcast satellite TV, where people don't like switching companies once they decide on a provider, existing customers tend to be less price-sensitive than potential new customers. As a result, it is common for firms in these industries to give special discounts to new customers, such as reduced premiums during the first policy period or the first three months of a subscription free. These are ways to price discriminate based on whether the customer has bought the product before.

For some other products, the price sensitivity of new customers is *lower* than that of past purchasers. For example, it is notoriously difficult to convince people to upgrade their software to a new version. When Microsoft releases a new version of Windows, the price of upgrading an older version is typically much lower than buying the new version outright. With this low price, Microsoft is trying to entice the more price-sensitive customers to purchase the new version.

By Location   Customers living in one area may have a hard time getting to another to take advantage of a lower price, or they might not even have knowledge of the prices in other locations. This often allows sellers to charge different prices in different locations, depending on the price sensitivity of local demand.

Over Time   One way to price discriminate in certain markets is to take advantage of the different kinds of people who buy a product at different times. When a new generation of computer CPUs first hits the market, for example, the new CPUs usually sell at a substantial premium, sometimes hundreds of dollars more than the last generation's chips. Yet only a few months later, they are available for a fraction of their original price. Maybe marginal cost fell that much, you say? Perhaps. But how about movies in first-run theaters that cost $10 but then cost only $4 when the same movie runs at a discount movie house several weeks later? Or hardcover books that cost $26.95 while their paperback versions cost only $10.95, when the actual difference in production cost is only about a dollar? These are all cases in which the kinds of people who want the latest, greatest, most current version of a product—computer gamers, big movie fans, and active readers—tend to be less sensitive to price than the folks who enter the market later.

In other cases, demand can become less price-sensitive (more inelastic) over time, and price discrimination will lead to price increases over time. Many goods and services that have initially uncertain quality have this feature. For example, tickets to a new play or musical that hasn't been reviewed are often relatively inexpensive. But once local reviewers have given the play a "thumbs up," demand can become much more inelastic and the producers raise the price accordingly.

In either situation, a firm that prices the same good differently in two different time periods applies the basic segmentation rules and uses the standard monopoly pricing rule as it applies to the state of demand in each period.

However, there is one complication in pricing across time that is worth keeping in mind. Technically, pricing across time is only segmenting if the seller *directly* assigns customers to a given time period. That is, in segmentation strategies, the seller is effectively saying, "You buyers over here, this is your price. You buyers over there, you have a different price." Buyers are stuck paying the price designated for their group (assuming again as we have throughout this chapter that the seller can prevent resale). With time-based segmentation, however, if customers are forward-looking, meaning that they consider what the seller might do in the future even as they decide whether to buy today, then the seller is *not* actually directly segmenting its customers. The seller cannot prevent its customers from changing groups; the buyers choose when to buy. So, for example, if buyers believe that the seller is charging a high price today but will reduce the price in the future, they might consider waiting to purchase, even if they had the type of relatively inelastic demand that the seller was trying to take advantage of with the high current price. In cases like this, the seller needs to consider how the different prices it plans to charge over time will affect the consumer's decision of when to buy.

For instance, Intel might want to initially price its fast new CPU at an extremely high level to take advantage of a segment of high-horsepower computer gamers with really inelastic demand, while making deep discounts thereafter. But if gamers realize Intel is likely to do this, they might be willing to trade off waiting to purchase the new CPU in exchange for enjoying the deep discount. This potential response will limit Intel's ability to segment the market in the first place. It could lead to Intel having to charge a lower initial price than it would have otherwise, and perhaps also reduce the discount applied to that price later.

The more forward-looking consumers are, the more segmenting across time actually becomes something known as indirect price discrimination, the pricing strategy we discuss next.

theory and data

Segmenting by Location in the European Market for Cars

Car manufacturers like Volkswagen and BMW who do a lot of business in Europe sell the same car in many different countries. The customers in these countries have very different incomes and tastes in cars. Because the automakers in this market likely have some market power, this is an excellent opportunity for segmenting *if* the automakers can prevent their customers in one country from selling to those in another. Manufacturers could then segment their customers by country, selling the same car at different prices in each country using the price discrimination methods we've been discussing. This practice would allow these manufacturers to earn higher profit and more producer surplus than they could by selling their cars at the same price everywhere.

It turns out the auto companies have many options for preventing resale across countries. First, they can print all manuals and documents only in the country's language. Swedish drivers don't want manuals in Greek, and vice versa. Second, they can forbid servicing a car in a country other than the one in which it was purchased. No one wants to get towed to Romania when

A VW Golf bought in Hanover, Germany costs more than the same car bought in Portugal or Greece.

their car experiences problems in Spain. Third, they can punish dealers who sell cars to people from a different country.

Economists Pinelopi Goldberg and Frank Verboven gathered evidence on car prices in Europe to investigate this issue.[*] They found that the price of the same car could vary substantially across countries. For example, in 2003, the price of a VW Golf in Germany was 10% higher than in Portugal and almost 25% more expensive than in Greece.

Goldberg and Verboven concluded that some of the price differences across countries in Europe arose from differences in the taxation of autos, but that much of the price

---

[*] Pinelopi K. Goldberg and Frank Verboven, "Cross-Country Price Dispersion in the Euro Era: A Case Study of the European Car Market," *Economic Policy* 19, no. 40 (October 2004): 483–521.

difference was due to basic direct price discrimination by segmenting. The auto firms were varying their markups depending on the conditions of local demand. The VW Golf pricing patterns are consistent with the theory that demand in Germany is less elastic than in Portugal or Greece, so VW charged its German customers more.

Goldberg and Verboven had some good news for European consumers (especially those in high-demand countries), though. They uncovered clear evidence that, as Europe has become more economically integrated, it has been much more difficult for car sellers to prevent resale or arbitrage across boundaries and the price differences have narrowed.

10.4 Indirect/Second-Degree Price Discrimination

When to Use It Indirect/Second-Degree Price Discrimination

1. The firm has market power and can prevent resale.
2. The firm's customers have different demand curves.
3. The firm cannot directly identify which customers have which type of demand before purchase.

We've seen how firms with market power can use direct price discrimination to increase their producer surplus above the amount they could earn by charging only a single price. The key is to charge higher prices to customers with relatively inelastic demand and lower prices to those with more elastic demand. However, being able to directly observe a customer's demand type before purchase (as required with direct price discrimination) is often difficult. A firm might know that its customers have different price sensitivities, but it may not be able to tell to which group any particular customer belongs.

indirect price discrimination (second-degree price discrimination)
A pricing strategy in which customers pick among a variety of pricing options offered by the firm.

Even without this knowledge, a firm can still earn extra producer surplus through price discrimination by using a pricing strategy called **indirect price discrimination,** also known as **second-degree price discrimination.** In this pricing strategy, a firm gives its customers various pricing choices and allows the customers to choose among them.

There are many different kinds of indirect price discrimination techniques a company can use. The principle that underlies all of them, however, is the need to set up the pricing options to convince customers to pick the "right" choice; that is, to purchase the option meant for their group rather than another option for a different group. For example, airlines choose ticket rules and prices so that business travelers with inelastic demand pay more, on average, for their tickets than leisure travelers with relatively more elastic demand. At the same time, however, the airline wants to keep business travelers from deciding that tickets meant for them are too expensive and instead buying up cheaper tickets intended for leisure travelers.

Indirect Price Discrimination through Quantity Discounts

quantity discount
The practice of charging a lower per-unit price to customers who buy larger quantities.

The most basic type of indirect price discrimination is the **quantity discount,** a pricing strategy in which customers who buy larger quantities of a good pay a lower per-unit price. For quantity discounting to work, customers who purchase larger quantities of a product need to have relatively more elastic demands than consumers who buy smaller quantities. If the consumers in the market do not have these elasticity characteristics, the firm would be trying to find a way to raise prices on the people who buy greater quantities, the opposite of a quantity discount.

To illustrate the idea, let's say there are two types of customers of the online broker-age house E*TRADE. One type of customer is not very interested in trading stocks. Because of this, these customers don't have a big incentive to shop across different online trading houses in search of lower commission rates (the fees they pay a broker-age firm to facilitate a trade). Thus, their demands are relatively inelastic with respect to the commission charged. The demand curve for uninterested traders is D_u in panel a of Figure 10.6. The other type of customer is obsessed with trading stocks. Because these individuals trade many times each day, they are very sensitive to the commis-sion rate. Thus, their demands are relatively elastic with respect to the commission. The demand curve for these obsessed traders is shown as D_o in panel b. The marginal revenue curves for each group are MR_u and MR_o, respectively. The marginal cost is the same for both groups.

E*TRADE would like to charge higher commissions to the uninterested traders with an inelastic demand than it charges the obsessed traders with the more elastic demand. This third-degree price discrimination (segmenting) would bring E*TRADE more pro-ducer surplus, but the company cannot pursue this strategy because it cannot tell which type of trader each person is when she signs up for an account. What E*TRADE *does* know, however, is what the demand curves of the two groups look like, even if it can't identify to which group any given trader belongs. Based on the demand curve D_u, for example, E*TRADE would want to set its standard profit-maximizing quantity and price (commission per trade) for uninterested traders where MR_u equals MC: For Q_u trades per month, E*TRADE would charge uninterested traders \$30 per trade. For obsessed traders, E*TRADE would like to follow the same procedure and charge them a price of \$9 per trade; at that commission, the obsessed traders would make Q_o trades per month.

Figure 10.6   Quantity Discounts at E*TRADE

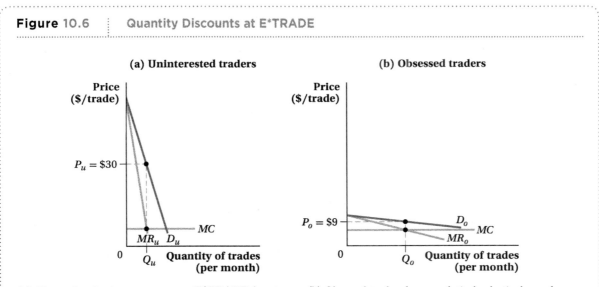

(a) Uninterested traders

(b) Obsessed traders

(a) The online brokerage company E*TRADE has two types of customers: uninterested traders and obsessed traders. Uninterested traders have a relatively inelastic demand curve D_u. E*TRADE would like to charge un-interested traders the profit-maximizing commission rate $P_u = \$30$ per trade and sell quantity Q_u trades per month.

(b) Obsessed traders have a relatively elastic demand curve D_o. E*TRADE would like to charge them the lower com-mission rate $P_o = \$9$ per trade. Although E*TRADE cannot directly identify which group any particular trader belongs to, it can set different prices for the two groups using a quantity discount by requiring traders to make at least Q_o trades per month to get a reduced commission rate.

If E*TRADE could segment the market, it would charge each group P_u and P_o per trade, and at those prices, each group would make Q_u and Q_o trades per month. However, E*TRADE can't directly assign different commission rates to different traders. And it can't just offer new customers a choice of whether to pay $30 or $9 commissions no matter how much or little they trade because every customer would choose the cheaper option. What can E*TRADE do to take as much of each trader's consumer surplus for itself? Rather than offer all customers a $9 per trade commission, E*TRADE can tie that commission rate to a requirement that the customer make at least Q_o trades per month. For customers who do not want to make at least Q_o trades per month, E*TRADE can offer a $30 per trade commission plan that allows them to trade as little or much as they'd like in one month.

The idea behind this strategy is that an obsessed trader, who demands a high quantity of trades and has a more elastic demand, will choose the $9 plan that requires a purchase of at least Q_o trades each month. An uninterested trader, on the other hand, will choose the $30 per trade plan. In other words, traders from both groups will sort themselves into the price and quantity combinations designed for them, even though E*TRADE cannot directly identify either type. This is the essence of any kind of successful indirect price discrimination strategy: The firm must set its prices so that a customer doesn't try to fake her demand type and buy the package meant for another customer type. We discuss this requirement for the successful implementation of all indirect price discrimination (including quantity discounts) next.

Incentive Compatibility The plan to charge uninterested traders a higher commission than obsessed traders is logical, but for such a plan to work well and allow E*TRADE to reap the maximum producer surplus available to it, E*TRADE needs to make sure that the uninterested trader won't want to switch from her $30/$Q_u$ package to the $9/$Q_o$ package designed for the obsessed traders. That is, the $9 commission deal can't be so good that the uninterested trader will make extra trades just to obtain the lower price. E*TRADE has to be sure that the uninterested trader's consumer surplus is bigger with the $30 per trade package than with the $9 package that requires a purchase of at least Q_o trades. The offers need to be internally consistent so that each type of buyer actually chooses the offer designed for it.

Economists have a term for this type of internal consistency: **incentive compatibility.** In this example, the two packages are incentive compatible if:

incentive compatibility
The requirement under an indirect price discrimination strategy that the price offered to each consumer group is chosen by that group.

1. An uninterested trader prefers the $30 package over the $9 package (and she will make this choice if the $30 package gives her greater consumer surplus than the $9 package).

2. An obsessed trader prefers the $9 package because it offers her more consumer surplus than the $30 package.

Let's see whether this set of offers is incentive compatible. First, we need to show that the uninterested trader's consumer surplus from trades at $30 each is greater than her surplus from making Q_o trades at $9 each. Finding the consumer surplus from the first offer is familiar territory. As shown in Figure 10.7, at a price of $30 per trade, an uninterested trader makes quantity Q_u trades, and the consumer surplus is the area under the uninterested trader's demand curve and above the $30 price. This is triangle A in panel a.

Finding the uninterested trader's consumer surplus for the $9 package offer is a bit trickier. The first thing we need to do is put the $9 package's price and quantity combination in the diagram showing the demand for trades of an uninterested trader. Call this point X, as shown in panel a. Notice that point X lies *above* the uninterested trader's demand curve. That means if an uninterested trader were to make trade number Q_o (at a commission of $9), she would actually lose consumer surplus by doing so. At a price of $9, an uninterested trader really only wishes to purchase Q_{max} trades, the quantity demanded at that price.

The fact that Q_{max} is less than Q_o implies that the uninterested trader's willingness to pay for the trades between Q_{max} and Q_o is lower than the $9 she would have to pay

Figure 10.7   Incentive Compatibility

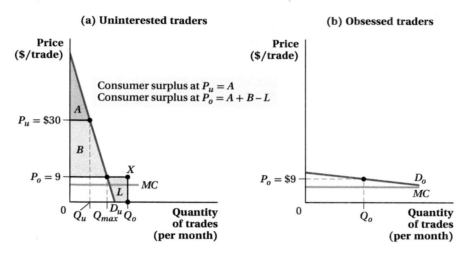

(a) Uninterested traders

(b) Obsessed traders

(a) Before charging a quantity discount to obsessed traders, E*TRADE needs to ensure that its pricing strategy is incentive compatible. At P_u = $30 per trade, uninterested traders make Q_u trades and receive surplus A. At the quantity and price offered to obsessed traders (Q_o, P_o), their surplus is reduced by area L but increases by area B. Uninterested traders will choose to pay $30 per trade if area B is greater than area L.
(b) Under the pricing policy for uninterested traders, obsessed traders would have to pay both a higher price (P_u = $30 > P_u = $9) and make fewer trades per month ($Q_o > Q_u$). Therefore, the quantity discount is incentive-compatible for these traders.

for them. In fact, all trades for which her demand curve (which indicates her willingness to pay) lies below $9 will result in a loss of consumer surplus. In panel a, these surplus-destroying trades are those between Q_{max} and Q_o, and the total consumer surplus lost is the area labeled L. (The demand curve just runs along the horizontal axis once it hits the axis, because willingness to pay for higher quantities is zero.) That area is the downside for an uninterested trader accepting the lower-commission offer. There is an upside, however. The first Q_{max} trades she conducts create consumer surplus, area A + B in the figure. This consumer surplus is quite a bit larger than her surplus under the $30 per trade offer (area A) because the price is so much lower. The net consumer surplus an uninterested trader gets from taking the $9 package offer is therefore area A + area B − area L.

Comparing the uninterested trader's consumer surpluses from the two offers, we can now see that she will choose the $30 per trade offer over the $9 package offer if

$$\text{area } A > \text{area } A + \text{area } B - \text{area } L$$

$$0 > \text{area } B - \text{area } L$$

$$\text{area } B < \text{area } L$$

That is, an uninterested trader will take the offer designed for her ($30 per trade) if the extra consumer surplus she would obtain from the lower commission rate (area B) is smaller than the loss she suffers from having to buy a larger quantity than she would have otherwise at the lower offered price (area L).

For uninterested traders, we have outlined under what conditions the offers are incentive compatible. Will an obsessed trader choose the $9 package meant for her?

We know that at a commission rate of $9 per trade, an obsessed trader earns consumer surplus on every trade up to Q_o; she is happy to trade that much at that price. Taking the $30 offer would require her to make a smaller quantity of trades than Q_o at a higher price per unit. Having to consume a smaller quantity even holding the price fixed at $9 per trade would make an obsessed trader worse off, because it would eliminate surplus-creating trades she would have made otherwise at that price. Even worse, however, would be that the trader would have to pay $30 instead of $9 for each of the trades she did make. Both the quantity restriction and the increase in price reduce the obsessed trader's consumer surplus. Thus, the $9 package offer is better for obsessed traders.

We saw that an uninterested trader also faces a higher price and lower quantity if she takes the $30 per trade offer instead of the $9 package. So, why isn't an uninterested trader automatically worse off by taking the $30 offer as is an obsessed trader? The reason is that if an uninterested trader faced a price of $9 per trade but got to choose how many trades she made, she would never choose to make Q_o trades. She would only choose to make Q_{max}, the quantity of trades demanded at a price of $9 per trade. Any trades between Q_{max} and Q_o destroy consumer surplus for an uninterested trader because the price is higher than her willingness to pay. It is the potential consumer surplus-destroying trades tied to the $9 package that make it likely that an uninterested trader would prefer the $30 offer.

10.3 figure it out

Suppose you are a pricing analyst for MegaDat Corporation, a firm that recently developed a new software program for data analysis. You have two types of clients who use your product. Type A's inverse demand for your software is $P = 120 - 10Q$, where Q represents users and P is in dollars per user. Type B's inverse demand is $P = 60 - 2Q$. Assume that your firm faces a constant marginal cost of $20 per user to install and set up this software.

a. If you can tell which type of buyer is buying the product before a purchase is made, what prices will you charge each type?

b. Suppose instead that you cannot tell which type of buyer the client is until after the purchase. Suggest a possible way to use quantity discounts to have buyers self-select into the pricing scheme set up for them.

c. Determine whether the pricing scheme you determined in part (b) is incentive-compatible.

Solution:

a. To maximize profit, set $MR = MC$ for each type. Therefore, we first need to solve for the marginal revenue curves for each type. Because we have linear inverse demand curves, we know that the MR curves will have the same vertical intercept but twice

the slope. This means that $MR = 120 - 20Q$ for Type A buyers and $MR = 60 - 4Q$ for Type B buyers. Now set $MR = MC$ to find the profit-maximizing quantity for each type:

For Type A:	For Type B:
$120 - 20Q = 20$	$60 - 4Q = 20$
$20Q = 100$	$4Q = 40$
$Q = 5$	$Q = 10$

At these quantities, the prices will be

For Type A:	For Type B:
$P = 120 - 10Q$	$P = 60 - 2Q$
$= 120 - 10(5)$	$= 60 - 2(10)$
$= \$70$	$= \$40$

b. The firm could charge $70 per user for a package where the buyer can purchase any quantity she wishes and a price of $40 for any buyer willing to purchase 10 or more units.

c. This plan is incentive-compatible for Type B users. They are willing to continue to purchase $Q = 10$ at a price of $40 each.

For a Type A consumer, we need to consider the amount of consumer surplus she receives under each scheme. We can do this with the help of a diagram showing the Type A demand curve and the two prices, $70 and $40.

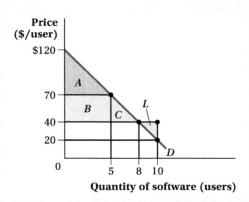

Quantity of software (users)

At a price of $70, a Type A buyer would choose to purchase 5 units. Consumer surplus would equal area A, the area below the demand curve but above price.

If a Type A buyer were to opt to purchase the other package (10 units at a price of $40 each), her consumer surplus would be the area above the price and below demand (areas $A + B + C$), but she would also lose consumer surplus because she would be buying units that she values less than the price of $40. This would be area L in the diagram.

Thus, opting for the quantity discount would change the Type A buyer's consumer surplus by area B + area C – area L. The $40 10-unit package would be incentive-compatible only if Area $L >$ area B + area C. Let's calculate those values:

$$\text{Area } B = \text{base} \times \text{height}$$
$$= (5)(\$70 - \$40)$$
$$= (5)(\$30)$$
$$= \$150$$

To calculate area C, we need to determine the base of the triangle. This means that we need to know the quantity at which the Type A buyer's willingness to pay is exactly $40:

$$P = 120 - 10Q$$
$$40 = 120 - 10Q$$
$$10Q = 80$$
$$Q = 8$$
$$\text{Area } C = \frac{1}{2} \times \text{base} \times \text{height}$$
$$= (0.5)(8 - 5)(\$70 - \$40)$$
$$= (0.5)(3)(\$30)$$
$$= \$45$$

Therefore, Area B + area C = $150 + $45 = $195.

To calculate area L, we need to be able to determine the height of the triangle. To do so, we need the price at which a Type A buyer would be willing to purchase $Q = 10$ units:

$$P = 120 - 10Q$$
$$= 120 - 10(10)$$
$$= 120 - 100$$
$$= \$20$$
$$\text{Area } L = \frac{1}{2} \times \text{base} \times \text{height}$$
$$= (0.5)(10 - 8)(\$40 - \$20)$$
$$= (0.5)(2)(\$20)$$
$$= \$20$$

So, we know that Area B + area C = $50 + $5 = $195 and Area L = $20.

Because Area A + area $B >$ area L, the $40 10-unit pricing scheme is not incentive-compatible for Type A buyers. These buyers will want to receive the quantity discount and will purchase 10 units at a price of $40 each. Thus, this pricing scheme would not be successful at making the buyers self-select into the pricing scheme established for their types.

Indirect Price Discrimination through Versioning

Airline tickets are a classic example of what we call **versioning**—offering a range of products that are all varieties of the same core product. Airlines have a group of business travel customers who are not very sensitive to prices and a group of leisure travelers who are highly sensitive to price. Airlines want to charge different prices to the two passenger groups, but they can't tell who is flying on business when a customer buys a ticket. So, the airlines instead offer different versions of the product (tickets on a given flight) available at different prices. The cheaper version, with many restrictions, is intended for leisure travelers who buy generally well in advance of the travel date, stay over a Saturday night, and book a round-trip flight. The more expensive version has fewer restrictions and is intended

versioning
A pricing strategy in which the firm offers different product options designed to attract different types of consumers.

for business travelers who generally don't like spending a weekend away from home, often need to buy their tickets at the last minute, and may choose to purchase a one-way flight for each segment to provide them with added flexibility. By offering two versions of tickets for a given flight, the airline attempts to make the two types of customers sort themselves (and by doing so, the airline captures more producer surplus).

For this scheme to work, the airlines need to make sure the prices of each version are incentive compatible. If the airline sets the prices for each group based on the markup formula it would use with direct price discrimination, the restricted-travel version might be too cheap relative to the ticket with fewer restrictions. In this case, business travelers might actually bite the bullet and start planning trips earlier or stay at their destination over the weekend. In some cases, business travelers might try to skirt the rules altogether. For example, it's possible to avoid the Saturday stay requirement by buying what is known as "back-to-back" tickets. For example, a business traveler wishing to fly from Philadelphia to Orlando and back for a Wednesday meeting might buy one Philadelphia-Orlando round-trip with a departure on Wednesday morning and a return on Sunday, and an Orlando-Philadelphia round-trip with a Wednesday evening departure and a Sunday return. The traveler would only use the first leg of each trip. As you might expect, this kind of behavior is intensely hated by the airlines, which try to forbid it in every way they can, but, basically, it's just the market's normal response to indirect price discrimination.

Versioning and Price-Cost Margins   With versioning, the different versions' marginal costs do not need to be the same. All that is necessary for versioning to work is for the markup of price over marginal cost to be bigger for the versions bought by customers with less elastic demand.

Consider the example of an automaker like Toyota, which sells a lot of midsize sedans. Some of Toyota's buyers in this segment will not be very price-sensitive. Maybe they are status-conscious, or just have a particular taste for cars with many fancy features. Others will be more price-sensitive. If Toyota could tell which type of customer was which when they walked through the door, Toyota could just use direct price discrimination and charge different prices according to the strategy we discussed in Section 10.3. In reality, however, it's not always easy to tell what type of customer comes through the door at any particular time. So, Toyota uses indirect price discrimination and designs two different versions of the car that it can sell at different markups, hoping to induce buyers to segment themselves based on their sensitivity to price and tastes for features.

For example, Toyota makes the Camry, one of the highest-selling cars in the world. It sells, nicely equipped, for about $25,000 in the United States. But Toyota also makes the Lexus ES 350, which is built on the same platform and in the same plant as the Camry. It is similar in many ways to the Camry but is more luxurious. Think of the ES 350 as being a Camry but with a sun roof, dual-zone climate control, a GPS navigation system, xenon headlights, and a premium stereo system. The ES 350 sells for around $38,000.

While a sunroof, xenon headlights, and all those extra options raise Toyota's marginal cost of producing an ES 350, it's unlikely that this increase in marginal cost would amount to $13,000 per car. Toyota charges more than the cost difference because the different versions split its customers into groups based on their price sensitivities. The Lexus group has less elastic demand, so Toyota's markup over marginal cost can be higher, just like the Saturday-night stay splits an airline's customers into leisure and business travelers.

To be incentive compatible, Toyota can't make the deal for the cheap version so good that it convinces the luxury customers to purchase Camrys instead. Quantitatively, think of it the following way. Suppose there are just two types of customers whose willingness to pay for each car is listed in Table 10.1.

Table 10.1	**Consumer Valuations for Camrys and ES 350s**	
	Toyota Camry	**Lexus ES 350**
Budget consumer	$27,000	$30,000
Luxury consumer	$28,000	$42,000

Notice that both consumers believe the Lexus is worth more than the Camry. It's not that Toyota has made a version that one group likes and the other doesn't. The budget consumers value a Lexus more than a Toyota, but not very much more: $30,000 versus $27,000. The luxury consumers, however, value the ES 350 *a lot* more than the Camry: $42,000 versus $28,000.

If Toyota prices the Camry at $25,000 and the Lexus ES 350 at $38,000, the budget consumers get $2,000 of consumer surplus from buying the Camry and –$8,000 from buying the Lexus (it costs more than they value it), so they will buy the Camry. The luxury consumers get $3,000 of surplus from buying the Camry and $4,000 from the Lexus, so they go with the Lexus. Each group chooses the version designed to take advantage of the nature of their demand curves. That means these prices are incentive compatible.

What would happen if Toyota priced the Lexus at $40,000 rather than $38,000? The budget consumers would still buy the Camry. Now, however, the status consumers would get more consumer surplus from buying the Camry ($3,000) than from buying the Lexus ($2,000), so they would also decide to buy the Camry. That $2,000 price increase for the Lexus would cause Toyota to lose $13,000 (losing a sale of a $38,000 Lexus at the old price for a $25,000 Camry instead) for each luxury consumer. (Or worse: The luxury consumers might go buy another automaker's luxury car.) By charging the group with the less elastic demand too high a price, Toyota would not be setting incentive-compatible prices and its attempt at indirect price discrimination would fail.

One detail that is important to note is that it is not the mere existence of customers with inelastic demand that allows Toyota (or any other firm) to indirectly price-discriminate with versioning. What is required is that *differences* exist in demand elasticities across customer groups. If different consumer groups had the same price elasticities of demand, even if relatively inelastic, then designing versions specifically for each group will not help a firm price discriminate. Automakers offer cars with different paint colors, for example, but there is rarely price discrimination based on paint color because the price sensitivities of people who like blue cars and silver cars are no different.

There is virtually no limit to the kinds of versioning a company can implement to get its customers to self-select into groups based on their price sensitivities. Now that you understand this kind of price discrimination, you will start to see it everywhere you look. Some firms offer "enhanced" features, such as the way Intuit does with its TurboTax software. It has a bare-bones version that is actually free online, versions with special Q&A features, and a small business application package that includes the ability to handle more complex structures like partnerships. The marginal cost difference between editions is trivial, but by offering "bells and whistles" versions, Intuit is able to get the less price-sensitive business customers to pay more.

Indirect Price Discrimination through Coupons

Coupons are also a form of indirect price discrimination. Retailers would like to charge shoppers who have less elastic demands more for products while setting a lower price for consumers who are more sensitive to price. Again, however, they have no way of directly identifying and separating these different groups when they buy, so they have to get the groups to do it themselves. Coupons are the device they use to do so.

The key to the way coupons work is that the trouble of using coupons—searching for the right site or deal online, combing through junk mail, or searching through newspaper inserts—is more likely to be borne by consumers who have more elastic demand. Because both the willingness to do the work clipping the coupons and the willingness to shop around for cheaper groceries are determined by the consumers' perceived value of time, coupon clipping and the price elasticity of demand are likely to be correlated. That way, the people who actually end up getting a price discount from a coupon are those consumers with more elastic demand—exactly the group to whom the retailers would like to offer lower prices. The shoppers who are less sensitive to price end up paying the higher, undiscounted price.

That's why coupons usually aren't right next to (or especially already attached to) the items to which they apply. If they were, it would be easy for even the shoppers with less elastic demand to use them, and everyone would receive the discount. The fact that firms require consumers to expend a little effort to use a coupon is not coincidence; it is exactly the point. Mail-in rebates work on the same principle: Only those consumers willing to go through the trouble of filling out the form and sending it in—presumably the most price-sensitive ones—will receive the discount.[4]

10.5 Bundling

When to Use It Bundling

1. A firm has market power and can prevent resale.
2. A firm sells a second product and consumers' demand for that product is negatively correlated with their demand for the first product.

bundling
A pricing strategy in which the firm sells two or more products together at a single price.

Another indirect price discrimination strategy that firms with market power can use to increase their producer surplus over the standard monopoly pricing surplus is called **bundling.** This strategy involves putting together two or more products that a firm produces and selling them as a single package with its own price.

When you subscribe to cable or satellite television, for example, you are buying a bundled good. You pay a single monthly fee for service, and the cable or satellite company delivers a number of networks together. You don't pick and choose every channel individually. For your $45 per month, you get, say, 90 channels rather than paying $6 per month for ESPN, $4 a month for MTV, and so on.

Sometimes, things can be bundled just because people really prefer buying things together. Think about a pair of basketball shoes. Although shoemakers could sell shoes individually, there really isn't much demand for single shoes or for mixing a Nike basketball shoe for the left foot with an Under Armor shoe for the right. People want to buy both shoes together. This sort of bundling, which occurs because the goods are strong complements to one another (i.e., one good raises the marginal utility of the other), is not a price discrimination strategy. Nike and Under Armor would bundle their left and right shoes together even if they operated in a perfectly competitive market.

In this chapter, we're interested in ways that companies can use bundling as a way to price discriminate. To explain how bundling can be a strategic pricing decision, it is vital that we first clear up an extremely common misconception. Bundling will generally *not* allow a company with market power in one product to leverage its market power into a second product. To illustrate what we mean, let's look at a specific example.

Take a cable company providing TV channels to your home. To make it easy, let's say there are only two cable networks: ESPN and the soap opera network SOAPnet (ESPN is among the most watched cable networks, and SOAPnet is not). Why would the cable company force you to buy both as a bundle for some price rather than just sell them separately?

At first glance, people tend to think it's a way for the cable company to leverage market power/high demand for ESPN to force people to pay more for the lesser product (SOAPnet). But this "forcing it down their throat" argument usually does not make sense. To see why, suppose there are two customers (Jack and Dakota) in the market.

[4] That said, there is occasionally a coupon right next to (or even attached to) an item. In this case, the point of the coupon is not to price discriminate as much as it is to advertise. It's essentially a little sign that says, "Buy me . . . I'm cheaper than usual."

Both like ESPN a lot and SOAPnet less, as reflected in Table 10.2. Jack values ESPN at $9 per month and Dakota values it at $10 per month. Jack values SOAPnet at $1 per month, while Dakota values it at $1.50. For simplicity, let's assume the marginal cost of supplying the networks is zero.

Does the cable company raise its producer surplus by bundling the prized ESPN with SOAPnet? If it sells the channels separately, it would have to price each channel at the lower of the two customers' valuations for each channel ($9.00 for ESPN and $1.00 for SOAPnet). Otherwise, the company would sell to only the one customer and would lose the revenue from the other.[5] Thus, it sells ESPN for $9 per month and SOAPnet for $1 per month, earning a total surplus of $20 per month $(2 \times \$9) + (2 \times \$1)$ from selling the channels separately.

Table 10.2	Positively Correlated Valuations per Subscriber-Month		
	ESPN	**SOAPnet**	**Bundle**
Jack	$9.00	$1.00	$10.00
Dakota	$10.00	$1.50	$11.50

Now suppose the cable company sells the channels as a bundle. The combined value the customers put on the bundle ($10.00 per month for Jack and $11.50 for Dakota) means the company will again set the price at the lower valuation so it won't lose half of the market. It therefore prices the bundle at $10 and sells it to both customers. This yields a surplus of $(2 \times \$10)$, or $20 per month, the same amount it earned selling the networks separately. Bundling has not raised the firm's surplus.

Furthermore, if the company combines ESPN with something customers don't actually want at all (say, e.g., that the valuation on SOAPnet was zero or even negative), then the amount that customers would be willing to pay for that network plus ESPN would be that much lower. As a general matter, then, a company can't make extra money by attaching a highly desired product to an undesired one.

How should a firm bundle products to make more producer surplus? Suppose that, instead of the valuations being what they are in Table 10.2, the two valuations for SOAPnet are switched. Both customers value ESPN far more, but now Jack has a higher valuation for SOAPnet ($1.50 per month) than does Dakota ($1.00). The key thing that has changed, as will become clear in a minute, is that *the willingness to pay for the two goods is now negatively correlated across the consumers*. This means that one of the customers has a higher willingness to pay for one channel than the other customer, but a lower willingness to pay for the other channel. In our example, Jack has lower willingness to pay for ESPN than Dakota but greater demand for SOAPnet, as shown in Table 10.3.

With this change, the firm receives more producer surplus using the bundling strategy. If the cable company sells the channels separately, the calculation is the same as before: ESPN for $9 per month, SOAPnet for $1, and earns a total of $20 of surplus per month. If the firm bundles the channels, however, it can sell the package to both customers for $10.50 per month. This earns the company $(2 \times \$10.50)$ or $21 of producer surplus per month, more than the $20 per month from selling the channels separately.

The reason why bundling works in the second scenario is the negative correlation between the two customers' willingness to pay, which occurs because Dakota values one part of the bundle (ESPN) more than Jack, while Jack values SOAPnet more than Dakota. If the cable company wants to sell to the entire market, it can only set a price equal to the smaller of the two customers' willingness to pay, whether pricing separately or as a bundle. In the first example with positively correlated demand (when Dakota had a higher willingness to pay for both channels), the

Table 10.3	Negatively Correlated Valuations per Subscriber-Month		
	ESPN	**SOAPnet**	**Bundle**
Jack	$9.00	$1.50	$10.50
Dakota	$10.00	$1.00	$11.00

---

[5] In reality, most network owners like Disney, which owns ESPN and SOAPnet, do not own the cable company, so they actually bundle the channels they sell to the cable company that then passes along that bundle to you. The point is the same, however.

lower of the customers' valuations for the bundle ($10 per subscriber for Jack) is smaller by $1.50 than the larger valuation ($11.50 per month for Dakota) because it reflects Jack's lower valuations for both channels. Therefore, if the cable company wants to sell the channels as a bundle, it must offer Dakota a discount that embodies the fact that Jack has a lower willingness to pay for both channels. As a result, the cable company does no better than having sold the channels separately.

With a negative correlation of demands across customers, there is less variation (only $0.50) in each customer's willingness to pay for the bundle: $10.50 per month for Jack and $11.00 per month for Dakota. This reduced variation means the cable company doesn't need to give as large a discount to Dakota to sell to both customers. Bundling has reduced the difference in total willingness to pay across the customers. What's important is that the smaller of the two combined valuations is larger when the channel demands are negatively correlated. Jack will pay $10.50 instead of only $10, which allows the company to raise its price. In this way, bundling allows sellers to "smooth out" variations in customers' demands, raises the prices sellers can charge for their bundled products, and increases the amount of surplus they can extract.

Mixed Bundling

The previous example shows why a firm might choose to sell two products as a bundle instead of separately. Sometimes, however, firms simultaneously offer the products separately *and* as a bundle and then let the consumer choose which to buy. This indirect pricing strategy is called **mixed bundling.** The Extra Value Meals at McDonald's include a sandwich, fries, and a drink at one price. McDonald's also offers these three things individually. This is where mixed bundling acts as a form of indirect price discrimination because the firm offers different choices and lets customers sort themselves in ways that increase producer surplus.

mixed bundling
A type of bundling in which the firm simultaneously offers consumers the choice of buying two or more products separately or as a bundle.

pure bundling
A type of bundling in which the firm offers the products only as a bundle.

Mixed bundling is a lot like the bundling strategy we've just discussed (offering only the bundle is often called **pure bundling**). It is useful in the same type of situations, but is better than pure bundling when the marginal cost of producing some of the components is high enough that it makes sense to let some customers opt out of buying the entire bundle.

Returning to our cable network example, let's suppose there are four customers and that they value the networks according to Table 10.4. The willingness to pay is negatively correlated across the networks, so we know bundling can work as a pricing strategy.

Now suppose instead of marginal costs being zero, the marginal cost of supplying ESPN is $6.00 per month and SOAPnet is $1.00 per month. Therefore, the marginal cost of producing the bundled package is $7.00. If the cable company sells the bundle for $12.15 (the minimum valuation of the bundle across the customers), it will sell the bundle to all four customers. Subtracting costs, this will net a per-customer producer surplus of $5.15 per month for a total of (4 × $5.15), or $20.60.

But look more closely at Penny and Sheldon. Their relative values for the two channels are extreme. Penny really values ESPN and barely values SOAPnet, while the opposite is true for Sheldon. And crucially, the value they put on one of these channels is *below* the marginal cost of supplying it: SOAPnet for Penny and ESPN for Sheldon. As we will see, in these cases it makes sense for the cable company to try to split these customers off from the bundle, because it does not want to supply channels to customers who value them at less than the cost of providing them.

Table 10.4	Negatively Correlated Valuations When the Marginal Cost Exceeds the Valuation for Some Customers		
	ESPN (*MC* = $6)	**SOAPnet** (*MC* = $1)	**Bundle** (*MC* = $7)
Penny	$12.00	$0.50	$12.50
Leonard	$11.00	$1.15	$12.15
Raj	$9.00	$3.15	$12.15
Sheldon	$5.00	$7.75	$12.75

Figuring out the right mixed bundling strategy is slightly complicated because of incentive compatibility, so we'll take it one step at a time. Given the issues we just discussed, the cable company would like to end up selling the bundle to Leonard and Raj, only ESPN to Penny, and only SOAPnet to Sheldon. Because both Leonard and Raj value the bundle at $12.15 per month, that's a reasonable starting point for thinking about the price of the bundle. If this is the price of the bundle, however, the company can't charge Sheldon his full $7.75 valuation for SOAPnet. If it tried to, Sheldon would choose the bundle instead because it would give him 60 cents more consumer surplus ($12.75 − $12.15) than if he bought only SOAPnet (consumer surplus of zero if priced at $7.75). A price of $7.75 for SOAPnet is therefore not incentive compatible. To set an incentive-compatible price for SOAPnet, the cable company has to leave Sheldon with at least 60 cents of consumer surplus per month. Thus, the incentive-compatible price for the purchase of SOAPnet alone would be $7.75 − $0.60, or $7.15 per month. And because Leonard and Raj value SOAPnet at less than $7.15, both will buy the bundle rather than take the SOAPnet-only option, so incentive compatibility holds in the other direction, too.

We can do the same type of calculations with ESPN and Penny. The cable company can't charge $12.00 for ESPN alone, because Penny would opt for the bundle to get 35 cents ($12.50 − $12.15) of consumer surplus rather than zero from buying ESPN at $12.00. So, the company has to leave Penny with at least 35 cents of surplus from buying just ESPN. The highest price that will achieve this is $12.00 − $0.35, or $11.65. Again, offering this option won't move Leonard and Raj away from the bundle, because both value ESPN at less than $11.65.

So with those three prices—ESPN alone for $11.65, SOAPnet alone for $7.15, and the bundle for $12.15—the cable company will sell two bundles (to Leonard and Raj) to earn a producer surplus (subtracting out the marginal costs) of $5.15 per month for each bundle. Additionally, it will sell ESPN alone to Penny to earn a surplus of $11.65 − $6.00 = $5.65 and SOAPnet alone to Sheldon for a surplus of $7.15 − $1.00 = $6.15. The total monthly producer surplus from using mixed bundling is therefore (2 × $5.15) + $5.65 + $6.15 = $22.10. That is more than the $20.60 per month the cable company would make by using pure bundling.

Producer surplus has increased because the cable company has saved itself the trouble of delivering a product to a customer who values it at less than it costs to produce.

10.4 figure it out

Fit Club Inc. is a health club that offers two types of equipment: weight machines and a swimming pool. There are currently three customers (Abe, Betty, and Chris), whose willingness to pay for using each type of equipment per month is listed in the table below:

	Willingness to Pay (per month)	
	WEIGHT MACHINES	**INDOOR POOL**
Abe	$60	$50
Betty	50	125
Chris	25	140

The weight room and the swimming pool each have a constant marginal cost of $20 per month. In the case of the pool, the marginal cost is the price of the water and chemicals used, while the marginal cost of the weight machines is the cost of cleaning and maintaining them. Each customer is considering monthly access to each type of equipment, and the firm has to decide what type of membership package to offer the customers.

a What price will the firm charge for each product if it wishes to sell a health club membership to all three customers? What is the firm's producer surplus if it sells separate access to the weight room and the pool room at these prices?

b. What price will the firm charge for a bundle of access to both the weight room and the swimming pool if it wishes to sell the bundle to all three customers? How much producer surplus will Fit Club, Inc. earn in this case?

c. Suppose the firm is considering offering its customers a choice to either purchase access to the weight room and the swimming pool separately at a price of $60 for the weight machine and $140 for the pool, or to purchase a bundle at a price of $175. Which option will each customer choose? How much producer surplus will Fit Club, Inc. earn in this situation?

Solution:

a. To sell access to the weight machines to all three customers, the health club must charge a price no greater than $25, the lowest willingness to pay of the customers (Chris). For the same reason, the price for the pool will be $50.

At these prices, the firm's producer surplus for its sales of access to the weight machines will be

$$\text{Producer surplus for weight machine} = (\text{Price} - \text{marginal cost}) \times \text{quantity}$$
$$= (\$25 - \$20) \times 3$$
$$= (\$5)(3) = \$15$$

For access to the pool, producer surplus will be

$$\text{Producer surplus for the pool} = (\$50 - \$20) \times 3$$
$$= (\$30)(3) = \$90$$

Total producer surplus will be $15 + $90 = $105.

b. To determine the price of the bundle, we need to calculate each buyer's willingness to pay for the bundle. This is done simply by summing the customers' willingness to pay for each product as shown in the table below:

	Willingness to Pay (per month)		
	WEIGHT MACHINES	INDOOR POOL	BUNDLE
Abe	$60	$50	= $60 + $50 = $110
Betty	50	125	= $50 + $125 = $175
Chris	25	140	= $25 + $140 = $165

So, the maximum price the health club can charge for its bundle (and still sell to all three buyers) is $110. It will sell 3 bundles at this price. Therefore, its producer surplus will be

$$\text{Producer surplus for bundle} = (\text{Price} - \text{marginal cost}) \times \text{quantity}$$
$$= (\$110 - \$20) \times 3$$
$$= (\$90)(3) = \$270$$

c. We need to compare each buyer's willingness to pay to the prices set for purchasing access to each room separately and the price of the bundle.

Abe will only purchase a weight machine membership. His willingness to pay for the pool is below the price of $140. The same is true for the bundle, which he values only at $110. Therefore, the health club will only sell Abe access to the weight machines.

Betty will not be willing to buy either membership separately, because her willingness to pay for each is below the set price. However, Betty's willingness to pay for the bundle ($175) is exactly equal to the price, so she will purchase the bundle.

Chris will only purchase access to the indoor pool. His willingness to pay for weight machines is only $25, far below the price of $60. Likewise, Chris is willing to pay only $165 for the bundle. Thus, the health club will only be able to sell pool access to Chris.

Total producer surplus will therefore be:

$$\text{Producer surplus for weight machines} = (\text{price} - \text{marginal cost}) \times \text{quantity}$$
$$= (\$60 - \$20) \times 1$$
$$= \$40$$
$$\text{Producer surplus for the pool} = (\$140 - \$20) \times 1$$
$$= \$120$$
$$\text{Producer surplus for bundle} = (\$175 - \$40) \times 1$$
$$= \$135$$

Total producer surplus when the health club offers customers a choice of bundling or separate prices is $40 + $120 + $135 = $295.

10.6 Advanced Pricing Strategies

When to Use It Block Pricing and Two-Part Tariffs

1. The firm has market power and can prevent resale.
2. The firm's customers may have either identical or different demand curves.

In the previous sections, we analyzed pricing strategies based on price discrimination, the ability of a firm to charge more for units of output sold to those willing to pay more and, as a result, extract producer surplus by departing from the single-price monopoly pricing discussed in Chapter 9. In this section, we look at how firms with market power can achieve that goal not by charging a given price per unit, but by varying unit prices offered to the same customer or charging lump-sum fees on top of per-unit prices. We start with a return to our discussion of quantity discounts.

Block Pricing

We call the strategy in which a firm reduces the price of a good if the customer buys more of it **block pricing.** You see this sort of thing all the time. Buying a single 12-oz can of Pepsi might cost $1, but a six-pack of 12-oz cans costs only $2.99. However, unlike indirect price discrimination (such as quantity discounts), block pricing does not require that buyers' have different demand curves and price sensitivities. All buyers of Pepsi may, in fact, have the same demand curve, but Pepsi could still gain producer surplus from providing buyers with an option to buy a larger quantity of soda at a lower price.

Consider Figure 10.8, which shows a demand curve for Walmart's photo holiday cards. Here, we assume this is the demand curve of just one customer (or we could suppose all customers have this same demand curve), so the firm is not trying to price-discriminate across customers with different types of demand, as would be the case if Walmart offers quantity discounts. If Walmart follows the pricing rule for firms with market power in Chapter 9, it will pick the quantity at which marginal revenue equals marginal cost and charge a price equal to the height of the demand curve at that quantity. In the figure, the monopoly quantity is 100 cards and the price is 25 cents per card. Walmart's producer surplus from pricing at that point equals the area of rectangle A.

If Walmart can prevent resale, however, it doesn't have to charge a single price. Suppose it offers the first 100 holiday cards for sale at 25 cents each, but then allows a consumer to buy as many as 25 more cards (numbers 101–125) at a lower per-unit price of 20 cents each. The customer will take advantage of this offer because the incremental purchase at the lower price yields an additional consumer surplus equal to the area of triangle B. Walmart is better off, too, because it adds an additional amount of producer surplus equal to the area of rectangle C.

Walmart could keep offering discounted prices on larger quantities. For example, it could offer the next 50 cards, up to the 175th photo card, for 10 cents each. Again, the consumer will take the deal because the consumer surplus from that block of cards (area D in the figure) is positive. Walmart also comes out ahead because it earns producer surplus E. Note that the price strategy we just described could also be expressed in the following way: 100 units are $25, 125 units are $30, and 175 units are $35. Even if all customers have this same demand, all will opt to purchase 175 cards at a price of $35 and Walmart still increases its producer surplus. (This is why block pricing is different

---

Figure 10.8   :   Block Pricing

D is the demand curve of an individual consumer of Walmart's photo cards. Under monopoly pricing, Walmart sells at the point on the demand curve corresponding to the quantity where $MR = MC$ ($Q = 100$ photo cards, $P = \$0.25$ per card). When Walmart can prevent resale, it can use a block pricing strategy instead. It could still sell the first 100 at a price of $0.25 per card, while charging a lower price of $0.20 each for the next 25 photos purchased (for a total quantity of 125 cards) and $0.10 each for the next 50 cards (for a total of 175 cards). Producer surplus increases from area A to $A + C$ to $A + C + E$, respectively, and consumer surplus increases by area B and areas $B + D$, respectively.

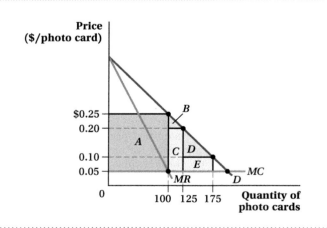

from the quantity discounts we saw when discussing indirect price discrimination. Here, no customer sorting needs to occur for Walmart to gain producer surplus.)

A block-pricing strategy like this raises more producer surplus for a firm than does the conventional single-price monopoly strategy because it allows a firm to better match the prices of different quantities of its output to consumers' valuations of those quantities. For the first set of units that customers buy—the units for which customers have a high willingness to pay—the firm charges a relatively high price. With block pricing, the firm doesn't have to completely give up selling a large number of units by charging that initial high price. Block pricing lets it sell additional units of its product, those for which consumers have lower willingness to pay, at lower prices.

This example shows how block pricing can work for even a single customer type, though if there were lots of identical customers, the firm would need to be able to prevent resale to avoid being undercut by its own customers.

Two-Part Tariffs

Another pricing strategy available to firms with market power and identical consumers is the **two-part tariff,** a pricing strategy in which a firm breaks the payments for a product into two parts. One component is a standard per-unit price. The second is a fixed fee that must be paid to buy any amount of the product at all, no matter how large or how small.

For example, a lot of mobile phone "unlimited service" calling plans have this structure. You might pay, say, $50 a month for service and then be able to make as many calls as you would like at no additional cost. Here, the fixed fee portion of the two-part tariff is $50 and the per-unit price is zero (though for other markets and products, the per-unit price is often positive). A video game system such as Microsoft's XBox is like a two-part tariff, too. Here, the cost of the console itself is the fixed fee and the cost of the individual games represents the per-unit price.

To see why using a two-part tariff can be advantageous for a firm with market power, consider the market in Figure 10.9. It shows the demand for mobile phone service offered by the firm, the marginal revenue curve corresponding to demand, and the firm's constant marginal cost.

The firm's conventional single-price monopoly profit-maximizing price is 10 cents per minute, the price at which marginal revenue equals marginal cost. The quantity at which this condition holds is 300 minutes per month, and the price at which consumers

two-part tariff
A pricing strategy in which the payment has two components, a per-unit price and a fixed fee.

Figure 10.9   Two-Part Tariff

As a single-price monopoly, a mobile phone service will sell 300 minutes of mobile service per month at a price of $0.10 per minute. Using a two-part tariff, however, the firm can increase its producer surplus from rectangle B to the triangle $A + B + C$. To do this, it will charge the per-unit price of $0.05 per minute, where $D = MC$, and set a fixed fee equal to the consumer's surplus at this quantity, the area $A + B + C$. Under this pricing scheme, the firm will sell 600 minutes of mobile service per month.

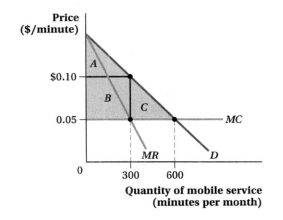

are willing to purchase that quantity is 10 cents per minute. At the price of 10 cents per minute, the consumer surplus is area A and the firm's producer surplus is rectangle B.

Now suppose instead that the firm uses the following two-part tariff pricing structure. First, it reduces the per-unit price all the way to marginal cost, 5 cents. This change increases the number of units it sells from 300 minutes to 600, but drives per-unit profit to zero. However, the firm knows that each customer will buy a quantity of 600 minutes per month of air time at this price and have a consumer surplus equal to area $A + B + C$ as a result. Knowing that this consumer surplus represents the willingness of the consumers to pay above the market price, the firm will set a fixed fee to try to capture that consumer surplus. Therefore, the firm decides to set the fixed-fee portion of the two-part tariff equal to $A + B + C$. This fee is not per minute; it's a one time per month fee for any consumer who wants to buy *any* number of units at 5 cents per minute.

What happens under this two-part tariff pricing structure? At a unit price of 5 cents per minute, the consumer buys 600 minutes of air time. This part of the price structure doesn't make the phone company any money, because its marginal cost of delivering service is also 5 cents per minute. However, the company is also charging the fixed fee $A + B + C$. And importantly, the consumer is willing to pay that, because if she uses 600 minutes of air time, she will enjoy consumer surplus equal to the same area. The company has set the size of the fixed fee so that the consumer is no worse off (and actually it could make her strictly better off if it charged just a touch less than $A + B + C$) than if she bought nothing. By using a two-part tariff, the firm captures the *entire* surplus in the market for itself, as opposed to only area B under standard market power pricing.

Again, if you spread this insight to a market with many identical customers, the ability to prevent resale would be crucial for making the pricing strategy work. If the phone company couldn't prevent resale, one customer could pay the fixed fee, buy up a huge amount of minutes at marginal cost, sell off these extra minutes at a small markup to other consumers who did not pay the fixed fee, and make lots of money. For example, if the consumer could rig her phone so other people would pay her 6 cents per minute to make calls on it when she wasn't using the phone, this would defeat the company's strategy.

10.5 figure it out

You have been hired as an intern at the Golden Eagle Country Club Golf Course. You have been assigned the task of creating the pricing scheme for the golf course, which typically charges an annual membership fee and a per-use cost to its customers. Each of your customers is estimated to have the following demand curve for rounds of golf per year:

$$Q = 300 - 5P$$

If Golden Eagle can provide rounds of golf at a constant marginal cost of $50 and charges that amount per round of golf, what is the most that members would be willing to pay for the annual membership fee?

Solution:

This pricing scheme, with an annual membership fee and a per-unit price, is a two-part tariff. If the

price per round of golf is set at $P = \$50$, then each member will want to play

$$Q = 300 - 5P$$
$$= 300 - 5(50)$$
$$= 300 - 250$$
$$= 50 \text{ rounds per year}$$

With this knowledge, we can determine the maximum annual membership each customer is willing to pay. This will be equal to the amount of consumer surplus the customer will get from playing 50 rounds of golf each year at a price of $50 per round.

To calculate consumer surplus, it is easiest to draw a diagram, plot the demand curve, and find the area of consumer surplus. To simplify matters, let's rearrange the demand function into an inverse demand function:

$$Q = 300 - 5P$$
$$5P = 300 - Q$$
$$P = 60 - 0.2Q$$

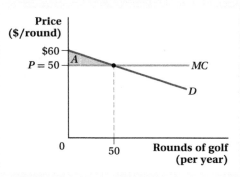

The vertical intercept is 60 and the consumer surplus is the area below the demand curve and above the price of $50, area A. We can calculate the area of triangle A:

$$\text{Area of } A = \frac{1}{2} \times \text{base} \times \text{height}$$

$$= \frac{1}{2} \times 50 \times (\$60 - \$50) = 0.5(50)(\$10)$$

$$= \$250$$

If the golf course set the price of a round of golf at $50, the consumer would purchase 50 rounds per year. This gives the golfer a consumer surplus equal to $250. Therefore, customers would be willing to pay up to $250 for an annual membership.

Being able to capture the entire surplus in the market is great if you're running a firm, but it's important to realize that a firm can attain this extreme result only if its customers have the same demand curve. The problem is much more complicated when there are customers with different demand curves.

For this more advanced two-part tariff pricing case, think about a firm that faces two kinds of customers whose demand curves for the firm's product are shown in Figure 10.10. Panel a shows the demand curve of the firm's relatively low-demand

---

Figure 10.10   Two-Part Tariff with Different Customer Demands

(a) Low-demand customer

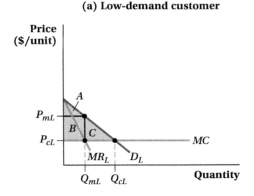

(b) High-demand customer

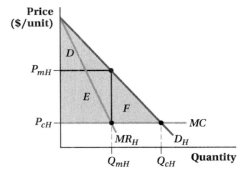

(a) In a market with low-demand customers, the firm will sell a quantity of Q_{cL}, charge a per-unit price of P_{cL} and a fixed fee equal to the consumer surplus $A + B + C$. Since this is much lower than the consumer surplus for high-demand customers ($D + E + F$ in panel b), such a pricing strategy will leave a lot of surplus to the high-demand customers in the market.

(b) In a market with high-demand customers, the firm will sell a quantity of Q_{cH}, and charge a per-unit price of P_{cH} and a fixed fee equal to $D + E + F$. Since this fixed fee is higher than the consumer surplus for low-demand customers, low-demand customers won't buy anything.

customers, while panel b shows the demand of the firm's relatively high-demand customers. If the firm tries to use a two-part tariff where it sets the unit price at marginal cost MC and the fixed fee at $A + B + C$, it will capture all of the surplus from the relatively low-demand customers in panel a but leave a lot of surplus to the relatively high-demand customers in panel b, because area $A + B + C$ is much smaller than area $D + E + F$. If the firm instead sets the fee at $D + E + F$ to capture the surplus of the high-demand customers, low-demand customers won't buy at all. This is not necessarily better than the first strategy. If the firm has a lot of low-demand customers, this could be a big loss for the firm, even if the reduction in profit from losing any given low-demand customer might be small. So, neither approach is perfect. Computing the profit-maximizing two-part tariff when consumers have different demands is a mathematical challenge beyond the scope of this book, but it usually entails a unit price above the firm's marginal cost.

10.7 Conclusion

We explored a number of different ways in which firms with market power, under the right conditions, can increase the producer surplus they earn above and beyond the surplus they can earn by following the standard, one-price market power pricing rule we focused on in Chapter 9. These pricing strategies are all around us; after learning about them in this chapter, you will start to recognize them in practice. You may also find yourself wondering why a particular firm isn't using one of these strategies. Just remember that certain conditions must be met for the price discrimination to work.

These various pricing strategies work in different ways, but there are some common threads. First, none will work unless the firm has market power. Therefore, any firm operating in a perfectly competitive market cannot use these strategies because it is a price taker. Second, the firm must prevent resale. Without the ability to prevent resale, doing anything besides the single-price monopoly pricing in Chapter 9 is futile. Third, while price discrimination strategies differ in the specifics of their mechanisms and the types of markets in which they are applicable, all of these methods work on the basic principle that the firm can make more producer surplus if it can adjust the price it charges so that consumers end up paying higher prices for those units of its output that provide them with greater consumer surplus. Price discrimination also works by charging higher prices to consumers with less elastic demand and lower prices to consumers with more elastic demand.

Other pricing strategies, such as block pricing and two-part tariffs, can be used even in markets where all consumers have the same demand. These strategies work by allowing consumers to buy relatively large quantities at a low price on the margin, but then grab back producer surplus for the firm through higher up-front payments.

In the next chapter, we examine firms with degrees of market power that fall between perfect competition and monopoly. We will find that these firms' decisions are not made in a vacuum (where they only consider their own costs and their customers' demands), but are also based on the decisions made by other firms in the same market. Although many may choose to follow the pricing strategies discussed in this chapter, each firm has to take into account how its competitors may react to such a move before determining if the strategy increases its producer surplus.

Summary

1. By using **pricing strategies,** a firm with market power can extract more producer surplus from a market than it can from following the monopoly pricing rule of Chapter 9 (the firm produces the quantity at which marginal revenue equals marginal cost, and then charges the price at which buyers would consume that quantity). It can only do so, however, if the situation satisfies certain criteria. A crucial factor is that in addition to market power, the firm has to be able to prevent resale among customers. If the firm can prevent resale, the amount of information it has on its customers determines what kind of pricing strategy it can follow. [**Section 10.1**]

2. When customers differ and the firm has sufficient information about its customers' demands to charge every person a different price, **perfect** or **first-degree price discrimination** is possible. This **direct price discrimination** strategy allows the firm to capture the entire surplus in the market for itself. It is very rare to have this kind of information, however. [**Section 10.2**]

3. If the firm has different types of customers and can directly identify at least two groups whose price elasticities of demand differ, it can charge different prices to the two groups and earn more producer surplus. The profit-maximizing direct price discrimination strategy in this case is to follow the single-price monopoly pricing rule separately for each group. There are many ways to directly separate customers, including customer characteristics, geography, past purchase behavior, the timing of the purchase, and so on, a practice known as **segmenting.** [**Section 10.3**]

4. If the company knows that there are different types of customers but cannot directly identify which group a customer belongs to before the purchase, it must rely on **indirect (second-degree) price discrimination.** This involves designing choices that induce customers to sort themselves into groups. **Quantity discounts** can be used if customers who demand a higher quantity also have a more elastic demand. **Versioning** a product can also work. The key additional requirement for indirect price discrimination is that the pricing structure has to be **incentive compatible,** meaning that each consumer group wants to take the offer designed specifically for them. [**Section 10.4**]

5. Sometimes, particularly if a company sells multiple products and consumers' demands for the products are negatively correlated, it can sell the products together as a bundle and increase producer surplus beyond what it could earn by selling the products separately. If the marginal cost of producing one of the products exceeds the value that a customer places on that product, the company may be better off using **mixed bundling,** which gives customers the choice of buying individual products at high prices or a bundle of products at a discount. [**Section 10.5**]

6. Even when there are not different types of customers, a firm can use advanced pricing strategies like **block pricing** (a discount for buying extra quantity) or a **two-part tariff** (a fixed fee paid up-front in addition to a price per unit of the good) as a way to capture more producer surplus than it could earn with standard monopoly pricing. However, each of these strategies is much more complicated to implement when there are many consumers with different demand curves. [**Section 10.6**]

Review Questions

1. What are the two requirements of price discrimination?
2. Why is producer surplus maximized under perfect price discrimination?
3. What are the two types of direct price discrimination?
4. What are some ways that a firm can segment its customers?
5. Contrast direct price discrimination and indirect price discrimination.
6. What is incentive compatibility? Why is it necessary for an indirect price discrimination strategy to be incentive compatible?
7. Provide an example of product versioning.
8. What are the differences between the following three pricing strategies: block pricing, segmenting, and quantity discounts?
9. What is the difference between mixed bundling and pure bundling?
10. What are the two component prices of a two-part tariff?

Problems

1. Consider the demand for schnitzel in the diagram below. Suppose that there is a single seller of schnitzel, who acts as a single-price monopolist.

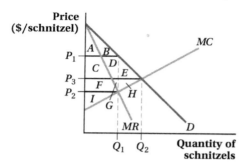

a. Indicate the profit-maximizing price and quantity.
b. List the areas of consumer and producer surplus.
c. Suppose the seller begins perfectly price discriminating. How many schnitzels will she sell?
d. What happens to areas A and B when the seller begins perfectly price discriminating?
e. What happens to areas E and H when the seller begins perfectly price discriminating?

2. Indicate whether the following statement is true or false, and explain your answer: Because the potential profit from perfect price discrimination is always higher than the potential profit from third-degree price discrimination (segmenting), firms that practice third-degree price discrimination must not be maximizing profit.

3. There are seven consumers, each of whom is hungry for exactly one Butterfinger. The consumers' maximum willingness to pay is given in the table below:

Consumer (age, gender)	Maximum Willingness to Pay
Marge (34, female)	$2
Homer (38, male)	4
Lisa (6, female)	5
Maggie (2, female)	6
Ned (46, male)	1
Krusty (55, male)	3
Bart (9, male)	7

a. Given that each consumer wants one and only one Butterfinger, draw the demand curve for Butterfingers.
b. If Butterfingers are priced at $7, only one will be sold. Who buys that Butterfinger? Label the point at $7 on the demand curve with the name of that buyer.
c. If Butterfingers are priced at $6, a second buyer will be priced into the market. Who is that buyer? Label the point at $6 on the demand curve with the name of that buyer.
d. Continue to label each point on the demand curve with the name of the buyer represented by that point.
e. Suppose that you are a monopoly seller of Butterfingers, which you can produce at a constant marginal and average total cost of $2. Suppose you charge every customer the same price for Butterfingers. What price should you set to maximize your profit? How many Butterfingers will you sell? Calculate your profit. Calculate the consumer surplus received by the buyers. Calculate the deadweight loss.
f. Suppose that every customer that comes into your Butterfinger store has their maximum willingness to pay displayed in neon on their foreheads. You decide to use this information to increase your profit by practicing first-degree price discrimination. How many Butterfingers will you sell? Calculate your profit. Calculate the consumer surplus received by the buyers. Calculate the deadweight loss.
g. Where does the consumer surplus go when you begin price discriminating?
h. What happens to the deadweight loss?

4. Consider the problem faced by the Butterfinger seller in Problem 3.
a. Assume that the seller is able to prevent resale between customers. In the real world, why is the seller *still* unlikely to be able to perfectly price discriminate?
b. Because of the reason you just indicated, the Butterfinger seller decides to segment her customers into two groups, each of which will be charged a different price. In order to maximize profit, should the seller sort by gender or by age?
c. Based on your answer to (b), determine who is in each group, and indicate (1) the price the seller should set for each group, (2) the total profit received by the seller, (3) total consumer surplus, and (4) the deadweight loss.

d. Is this pricing strategy (segmenting) more profitable to the seller than perfectly price discriminating? Is this pricing strategy more profitable than charging every consumer the same price?

e. What happens to consumer surplus and deadweight loss when a single-price monopolist begins segmenting in this way?

5. Promoters of a major college basketball tournament estimate that the demand for tickets on the part of adults is given by $Q_{ad} = 5{,}000 - 10P$, and that the demand for tickets on the part of students is given by $Q_{st} = 10{,}000 - 100P$. The promoters wish to segment the market and charge adults and students different prices. They estimate that the marginal and average total cost of seating an additional spectator is constant at $10.

   a. For each segment (adults and students), find the inverse demand and marginal revenue functions.

   b. Equate marginal revenue and marginal cost. Determine the profit-maximizing quantity for each segment.

   c. Plug the quantities you found in (b) into the respective inverse demand curves to find the profit-maximizing price for each segment. Who pays more, adults or students?

   d. Determine the profit generated by each segment, and add them together to find the promoter's total profit.

   e. How would your answers change if the arena where the event was to take place had only 5,000 seats?

6. In Problem 5, you found the profit that a promoter of a major college basketball tournament would earn if he were to segment the market into adults and students. Suppose that the promoter's CEO decides that price discrimination presents a poor public image, and announces that everybody will be charged the same price. His resident economist (you) is tasked with figuring out what that price should be.

   a. Find the total demand for tickets by adding the demand curves of adults and students.

   b. Derive the inverse demand curve for tickets, as well as the associated marginal revenue curve associated with that demand.

   c. Find the profit-maximizing quantity of tickets and the corresponding price.

   d. Determine the promoter's profit.

   e. Compare the promoter's profit when he tries to price for the entire market, to his profit when he simply charges the adult price from the previous problem. Is it better for the

promoter to price for the entire market and almost fill the arena, or to price for adults only and have a lot of empty seats?

7. You are the owner of a nail salon. Your female customer's price elasticity of demand for manicures is –2.5; your male customer's price elasticity of demand for manicures is –1.2. The marginal cost of manicuring a customer's nails is $12.

   a. If you segment the market by gender, what price should you charge women? What price should you charge men?

   b. Explain intuitively why you should charge each group a different price.

8. Movie theaters often charge substantially less for afternoon showings than for evening showings. Explain how theaters use time of day to segment their customers into low-elasticity and high-elasticity groups.

9. Owners of a movie theater have determined that the elasticity of demand for movie tickets equals –2.0 for students and –1.5 for adults.

   a. If the owners of the theater decide to segment the market, who should be charged a higher price, students or adults? Use your knowledge of microeconomic theory to explain why.

   b. Use the Lerner index as described in the text to determine the ratio of prices. In percentage terms, how big a price premium should be charged to the group that pays the higher price?

10. Owners of a Florida restaurant estimate that the elasticity of demand for meals is –1.5 for senior citizens and –1.33 for everyone else.

   a. Given this information, how big (in percentage terms) should the senior citizen discount be?

   b. Suppose that the restaurant owners discover that seniors tend to demand more attention from their waiters and send back more food as unsatisfactory, to the extent that the marginal cost of serving a senior is twice as high as serving an adult. Accounting for these costs, how large should the senior citizen discount be? (*Hint*: Refer back to the example in the text, but don't cancel out marginal costs!)

   c. Were your results in part (b) surprising? Explain them, intuitively.

11. A local golf course's hired-gun econometrician has determined that there are two types of golfers, frequent and infrequent. Frequent golfers' annual demand for rounds of golf is given by $Q_f = 24 - 0.3P$, where P is the price of a round of golf. In contrast, infrequent golfers' annual demand for rounds of golf is given by $Q_i = 10 - 0.1P$. The marginal and average total cost of providing a round of golf is $20.

a. If the golf course could tell a frequent golfer from an infrequent golfer, what price would it charge each type? How many times would each type golf? How much profit would the golf course generate?

The greens manager has difficulty telling frequent from infrequent golfers, so she decides to use second-degree price discrimination (quantity discounts) to make different types of golfers self-select into the most profitable pricing scheme. The course sets a price for individual rounds of golf, but also offers a quantity discount for members willing to buy a rather large quantity of rounds in advance. The course's owners hope that frequent golfers will self-select into the discounted plan, and that infrequent golfers will choose to buy individual rounds.

b. What price should the golf course set for individual rounds of golf? Why?

c. If the course wishes to maximize profit, what price and minimum quantity should it establish for the discounted plan?

d. Which plan will generate the greatest consumer surplus for frequent golfers, the individual-round plan or the discount plan? Illustrate your answer by showing and measuring the areas of surplus on frequent golfers' inverse demand curves.

e. Which plan will generate the greatest consumer surplus for infrequent golfers, the individual-round plan or the discount plan? Illustrate your answer by showing the areas of surplus on infrequent golfers' inverse demand curves.

f. Based on your answers to (c), (d) and (e), will the plan be successful in making golfers self-select into the most profitable plan for the golf course?

g. Suppose that each type of golfer came to the course with the word "frequent" or "infrequent" tattooed on his or her forehead. Is this information of any value to the golf course owner? (In other words, can the owner earn any more profits by segmenting than it did with its quantity discount plan?)

12. Many textbooks are now available in two versions, a high-priced "domestic" version and a low-priced "international" version. Each version generally contains exactly the same text, but slightly altered homework problems.

a. Why would a textbook publisher go to the trouble to produce two versions of the same text?

b. Discuss whether the publisher's strategy would be more effective if it made the alterations secret, or if it announced them boldly.

c. The production of international versions of textbooks was concurrent with the explosion of the Internet. Explain why this is likely to be more than just a coincidence.

13. Rockway & Daughters Piano Co. wishes to sell a piano to everyone. But some consumers are budget-conscious, and others are not, and unfortunately, Rockway cannot tell which is which. So, Rockway produces a premium line of pianos that it markets under the Rockway name, and a similar line of pianos that it markets under the Dundee name. While the cost of producing these pianos is quite similar, all consumers agree that Rockway pianos are of higher quality than Dundee pianos, and would be willing to pay more for a Rockway. Budget-conscious consumers feel that Dundee pianos are worth $6,000, and Rockway are worth $8,000. Performance artists believe that Dundee pianos are worth $7,000 and Rockways are worth $12,000.

a. Suppose Rockway & Daughters prices its Dundee pianos at $5,000 and its Rockway pianos at $10,500. Are these prices incentive compatible—that is, will more price-conscious consumers purchase the Dundee line, while more performance-oriented players choose the Rockway? Explain.

b. How much must Rockway & Daughters reduce the price of its Rockway line in order to achieve incentive compatibility?

c. Suppose instead that Rockway & Daughters tries to achieve incentive compatibility by raising the price of its Dundee line. Can it do so? And if so, how?

14. London's Market Bar has a unique pricing system where a computer sets the price based on demand. When demand picks up, the computer begins to gradually reduce prices. This pricing strategy is puzzling to those who have studied supply and demand. Celene Berman, the assistant manager, says a group of "young city-boy types" recently kept asking why prices "were going the wrong way around." Explain, using your knowledge of block pricing, why the owner's strategy of reducing prices as sales increase might actually lead to increased profit for the bar.

15. Microsoft sells two types of office software, a word processor it calls Word, and a spreadsheet it calls Excel. Both can be produced at zero marginal cost. There are two types of consumers for these products, who exist in roughly equal proportions in the population: authors, who are willing to pay $120 for Word and $40 for Excel, and economists, who are willing to pay $50 for Word and $150 for Excel.

a. Ideally, Microsoft would like to charge authors more for Word and economists more for Excel. Why would it be difficult for Microsoft to do this?

b. Suppose that Microsoft execs decide to sell Word and Excel separately. What price should Microsoft set for Word? (*Hint*: Is it better to sell only to authors, or to try to sell to both authors and economists?) What price should Microsoft set for Excel? What will Microsoft's profit be from a representative group of one author and one economist?

c. Suppose that Microsoft decides to bundle together Word and Excel in a package called Office, and not offer them individually. What price should Microsoft set for the package? Why? How much profit will Microsoft generate from a representative group of one author and one economist?

d. Does bundling allow Microsoft to generate higher profit than selling Word and Excel separately?

16. Three consumers, John, Kate, and Lester, are in the market for two goods, dates and eggs. Their willingness to pay for dates and eggs is given in the table below:

	Dates (1 package)	Eggs (1 dozen)
John	$0.60	$2.00
Kate	$1.30	$1.30
Lester	$2.00	$0.60

a. If you are a local farmer who can produce dates and eggs for free, what is the optimal price for dates and eggs if you price them individually? How much profit will you generate?

b. If you bundle dates and eggs together, what price should you set for a bundle containing one package of dates and a dozen eggs? How much profit will you generate?

c. Is there any advantage to mixed bundling in this case? Why or why not?

d. Suppose that the cost of producing dates and eggs rises to $1.00 per package and $1.00 per dozen, respectively. Now is there any advantage to mixed bundling? Why or why not? Explain your answer with a numerical illustration.

e. What accounts for the change in optimal strategy when costs change?

17. Elaine makes delicious cupcakes that she mails to customers across the country. Her cupcakes are so delicious that she has a great degree of pricing power. Elaine's customers have identical demands for cupcakes. A representative customer's demand is shown in the diagram below. Elaine can make a cupcake for a constant marginal and average total cost of $0.50.

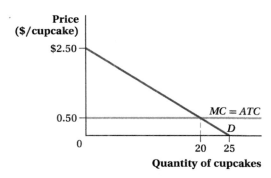

a. If Elaine is an ordinary monopolist, what price should she charge for cupcakes? How many will each customer order? How much profit will Elaine earn? How much consumer surplus will the buyer get?

b. Suppose that Elaine decides to offer a quantity discount according to the following terms: The first 10 cupcakes can be bought for $1.50 each; any cupcake over 10 will be offered at a discounted price. What discount price will maximize Elaine's profit from this pricing scheme? (*Hint*: Draw a new demand curve for Elaine's customers' demand, but since her customers have already purchased 10, begin your demand curve at the 11th unit. Alternatively, shift the vertical axis to the right by 10 units.)

c. How many cupcakes will customers order at full price? How many at the discounted price?

d. What will Elaine's profit be? How does this scheme compare to the profit she earned as an ordinary monopolist?

e. Suppose that Elaine gets super-greedy and decides to implement a three-tiered pricing system. What three prices should she choose to maximize her profit? At what quantities will the price points change? What will her profit be?

f. Suppose Elaine decides to charge $1.90 for the first cupcake, $1.80 for the second, and so on. How many cupcakes will she sell, and what will her profit be?

g. What happens to consumer surplus as Elaine adds more price points? Where does it go?

18. Consider the demand for cupcakes in Problem 17. Suppose Elaine decides to sell cupcakes only in packages of 20.

a. How much would customers be willing to pay to obtain a 20-pack of Elaine's cupcakes? (*Hint*: Remember that the value of each cupcake is given by the corresponding point on the demand curve. Add up those values for cupcakes 1–20.)

b. How much profit will Elaine earn from each customer?

c. How does the profit from this scheme compare to the profit Elaine earned in part (f) of Problem 17?

19. Many gyms offer a mixed two-part tariff pricing scheme. One can join the gym and then have daily access at a very low cost (often, free); alternatively, one can choose not to join and pay a higher daily fee (perhaps $10 or $15). Explain the rationale for this dual pricing scheme. What must be true of the gym's customers' demands?

20. SmacFone is a major provider of pay-by-the-minute, no contract cellphones that are very popular with ordinary consumers. They are also quite popular with drug dealers, who appreciate the anonymity that such phones provide. The demand curves for talking minutes that SmacFone faces from each type of customer are given in the diagrams below. SmacFone's marginal and average total cost of service is 5 cents per minute.

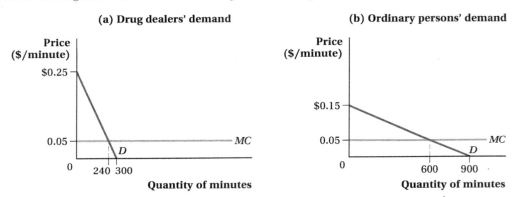

(a) Drug dealers' demand   **(b) Ordinary persons' demand**

a. Determine the profit-maximizing price and quantity that SmacFone would like to charge each type of consumer, and show it on the appropriate graph. Then, determine the potential profit that SmacFone could generate from each segment.

Because SmacFone cannot tell whether a new customer is an ordinary person or a drug dealer, it decides to use second-degree price discrimination to separate consumers. SmacFone sets a Plan A price of 15 cents per minute, but offers a special Plan B price of 10 cents per minute if a customer purchases 300 or more minutes.

b. Determine how much consumer surplus ordinary consumers would receive under Plans A and B. Which plan should ordinary consumers choose if they are trying to maximize their utility?

c. Determine how much consumer surplus drug dealers would receive under Plans A and B. Which plan should drug dealers choose if they are trying to maximize their utility?

d. Is the plan SmacFone derived incentive compatible? (In other words, will the plan successfully direct drug dealers to Plan A and ordinary consumers to Plan B?) How much profit will SmacFone generate with this set of plans?

e. SmacFone is considering making some adjustments to their plans. One option is to change Plan B to 11 cents per minute with a 240-minute minimum. Determine whether the new plan selection is incentive-compatible. Why doesn't SmacFone simply raise the price to 11 cents without altering the 300-minute minimum? How much profit will the new set of plans generate for SmacFone?

f. Another option that SmacFone is considering is dropping the price of its ordinary service to 14 cents per minute. Determine whether the new plan selection is incentive compatible. How much profit will the new set of plans generate for SmacFone?

g. Why does lowering the price of ordinary service work better at creating an incentive-compatible set of calling plans than raising the price of the large-quantity plan?

Imperfect
Competition

11

n previous chapters, we studied the two ends of the market power spectrum: perfect competition and monopoly. In perfect competition, a firm has no market power because it is only one of many producers in the market, the price is driven down to marginal cost, and output is relatively high. In a monopoly, one firm has complete market power because it is the only producer of a good in the market, price is greater than marginal cost, and output is lower. We also learned about the many pricing strategies that firms with market power can use to earn greater economic profit.

Between these two ends of the spectrum are lots of industries, most of them perhaps, that are neither perfectly competitive nor monopolistic. Coke and Pepsi dominate the cola market. Nintendo, Sony, and Microsoft dominate video games. These companies compete but are hardly the personification of perfect competition. Yet they aren't stand-alone monopolies either. The industry structure between perfect competition and monopoly is known as **imperfect competition.**

This chapter introduces that important but sometimes complicated market structure. We begin by looking at several types of **oligopoly,** a market structure characterized by competition among a small number of firms. Because there are many possible ways in which oligopolistic firms compete, there is no single model of oligopoly that is applicable to every situation. One theme of this chapter is that having a few competitors in an industry—rather than many or only one—can lead to multiple possible price and output outcomes. Several kinds of price and quantity outcomes *could* occur in an oligopoly, depending on the market circumstances. This isn't the case with perfect competition or monopoly. With perfect competition, price equals marginal cost and the market's output equals the point on the market demand curve at that price/cost level. With a monopoly (ignoring price discrimination), the firm equates marginal revenue and marginal cost to determine its output, and the price corresponds to the level of the demand curve at that quantity.

With oligopolies, firms have some market power but not necessarily monopoly power, and there is some competition but not perfect competition. This means that we need to be a little more specific about aspects of the particular market we're studying before we can figure out what prices they will charge, how much each company will produce, and how much profit each firm will earn. Just knowing how many companies are in the market is not enough information to analyze behavior in an oligopolistic market, however. Other factors that have an effect on price and quantity decisions in an oligopoly include whether the companies make identical products (as in an oil oligopoly) or products that are slightly different from one another (like Coke and Pepsi), how intensely the companies compete, and whether they compete with one another by choosing the prices they charge or the quantities they produce.

In this chapter, we present five of the most common models of how oligopolies behave, plus one additional model of a type of imperfect competition called **monopolistic competition,** a market in which a large number of firms have some market power but each makes zero economic profit in the long run. Whenever you have this many models as possible explanations for market behavior, it's important to figure out which one is appropriate for a specific case. This decision isn't always obvious in practice, so we discuss some ideas for determining which model is most appropriate for various real-world situations.

11.1 What Does Equilibrium Mean in an Oligopoly?

Before we introduce the many oligopoly models, we need to lay some groundwork. Specifically, we have to expand on our idea of what equilibrium is. The concept of equilibrium in perfect competition and in monopoly is easy. It means a price at which the quantity of the good demanded by consumers equals the quantity of the good supplied by producers. That is, the market "clears." The market is stable at such a point: There are no shortages or surpluses, and consumers and producers do not want to change their decisions.

The problem with applying that idea of equilibrium to an oligopolistic industry is that each company's action influences what the other companies want to do. To achieve an outcome in which no firm wants to change its decision requires determining more than just a price and quantity for the industry as a whole.

An equilibrium in an oligopoly starts with the same idea as in perfect competition or monopoly: The market clears. But it adds the requirement that no company wants to change its behavior (its own price or quantity) once it knows what other companies are doing. In other words, each company must be doing as well as it can *conditional* on what the other companies are doing. Oligopoly equilibrium has to be stable not only in equating the total quantities supplied and demanded, but also in remaining stable among the individual producers in the market.

imperfect competition
Market structures with characteristics between those of perfect competition and monopoly.

oligopoly
Competition between a small number of firms.

monopolistic competition
A type of imperfect competition with a large number of firms in which each firm has some market power but makes zero economic profit in the long run.

This idea of equilibrium—that each firm is doing its best conditional on the actions taken by other firms—is called a **Nash equilibrium.** It is named after Nobel Laureate John Nash who was the subject of the award-winning book and movie titled *A Beautiful Mind.* The Nash equilibrium concept is even more central in the next chapter when we study game theory that further explores strategic interaction among firms. For our purposes in this chapter, however, the following example will help clarify what is and what is not a Nash equilibrium in an oligopoly.

Nash equilibrium
An equilibrium in which each firm is doing the best it can conditional on the actions taken by its competitors.

 application

An Example of Nash Equilibrium: Marketing Movies

Major computer-animated movies like Disney's *Cars 2* or DreamWorks's *Kung Fu Panda 2* are amazingly expensive to make. Paying for the computer rendering, the animators, the actors—these things add up. *Cars 2* and *Kung Fu Panda 2* each cost almost $175 million to produce. But on top of these production costs, Disney and DreamWorks each then had to pay another $75 million or so for advertising. In other words, they spent the equivalent of almost half the production cost trying to get people to watch their movie.

Let's suppose Disney and DreamWorks are the only two movie companies that make animated feature films, and that their advertising influences people's choices of what movie to see. However, advertising doesn't increase the overall number of movies people see, just which movie they watch. From Disney's or DreamWorks' point of view, then, advertising can convince a moviegoer to see its movie instead of the competition's, but advertising is not going to bring people into theaters who wouldn't have gone otherwise.

Now suppose both studios plan to make the next installments in these series, *Kung Fu Panda 3* and *Cars 3*, and release them on the same summer weekend. Further, we assume that the cost of production is still $175 million and the cost of advertising is $75 million. If both studios advertise and compete with one another, their marketing efforts will cancel out. As a result, the two will split the market, and each will bring in, let's say, $400 million of revenue. Subtracting the $175 million production cost and the $75 million advertising cost, that leaves $150 million of profit to each studio.

If, on the other hand, the studios could somehow agree not to advertise at all, they would again split the market, but this time each would save the $75 million in advertising costs. The studio profits in this case would be greater at $225 million each.

Disney and DreamWorks would prefer the second, higher-profit outcome. The problem is that, due to the nature of advertising's influence on moviegoers, if only one studio advertises and the other doesn't, then the studio that advertises will get a larger share of the audience and the other one will be left with less. Suppose, for example, that the studio engaged in advertising would earn $700 million of revenue, and the other would earn only $100 million. The firm advertising its film therefore earns a profit of $450 million ($700 million of revenue minus the $175 million production cost and the $75 million in advertising). The other studio, the one that doesn't advertise, *loses* $75 million ($100 million of revenue minus the $175 million production cost).

Table 11.1 lays out these scenarios. The table's four cells correspond to the four possible profit outcomes if each firm pursues the strategy described at the top of each column and the start of each row: Both firms advertise (upper left), neither firm advertises (lower right), DreamWorks advertises and Disney doesn't (upper right), or vice versa (lower left). Profit is measured in millions of dollars.

Table 11.1	**An Advertising Game***		
		Disney	
		Advertise	**Don't Advertise**
DreamWorks	**Advertise**	150 , 150	450 , −75
	Don't Advertise	−75 , 450	225 , 225

*Outcomes are measured in millions of dollars of profit.

The number before the comma in each cell is DreamWorks' profit if both studios take the actions that correspond to that cell. The number after the comma is Disney's profit.

Look at the table and think about where equilibrium might occur in this industry. At first glance, you might expect that, because they could maximize their joint profits by agreeing not to advertise, the studios should just collaborate and earn $225 million each. This is not a Nash equilibrium, however. Here's why: Suppose a studio used this reasoning and actually held off from advertising because it believed its profit would be higher. Once the first studio decides not to advertise, however, the other studio has a strong incentive to advertise. The other studio can now earn far more profit by advertising than by going along with the don't-advertise plan. Recall that Nash equilibrium means that both companies are doing the best they can, *given what the other is doing*. Because one studio can earn a higher profit by advertising when the other doesn't, agreeing not to advertise is not a Nash equilibrium.

To make this concrete, let's say Disney has decided not to advertise. Looking at the profits in Table 11.1, you can see that if DreamWorks goes along, it will earn $225 million in profit. If it instead abandons the agreement and chooses to advertise, however, it will earn $450 million. Clearly, DreamWorks will do the latter. You can also see in the table that it works the other way, too: If DreamWorks chooses not to advertise, Disney does better by advertising (also earning $450 million instead of $225 million).

Therefore, any agreement to hold off from advertising is not stable because both parties have an incentive to cheat on it. Even if one of them sticks to the agreement, the other will earn more profit by backing out of it. Because each studio will earn higher profit by advertising when the other does not, an outcome in which neither studio advertises cannot be a Nash equilibrium. Agreeing not to advertise is not a Nash equilibrium.

Our analysis so far has established that if one studio *doesn't* advertise, the other studio wants to advertise. What is a studio's optimal action if the other studio *does* advertise? The answer may be found in Table 11.1. If Disney advertises, DreamWorks earns $150 million by advertising and loses $75 million by not advertising. A similar situation holds for Disney's best response to DreamWorks. Therefore, advertising is each studio's best response to the other's choice to advertise.

We have just shown that choosing to advertise is a studio's best course of action regardless of whether the other studio advertises or not. Because this is true for both Disney *and* DreamWorks, the only Nash equilibrium in this case is for both studios to advertise. It is stable because each company is doing the best it can given what the other is doing.

Notice that this is true even though it means the studios' profits in the Nash equilibrium will be $150 million each—lower than the $225 million each would earn if they could both hold off from advertising. Situations like these, in which the Nash equilibrium is an outcome that is somehow worse for all involved than another (unstable) outcome, are known as **prisoner's dilemmas** in game theory. We will look at such situations in more detail in the next few sections and in the next chapter. ■

prisoner's dilemma
A situation in which the Nash equilibrium outcome is worse for all involved than another (unstable) outcome.

11.2 Oligopoly with Identical Goods: Collusion and Cartels

Model Assumptions Collusion and Cartels

- Firms make identical products.
- Industry firms agree to coordinate their quantity and pricing decisions, and no firm deviates from the agreement even if breaking it is in the firm's best self-interest.

In the next several sections, we examine several models of imperfect competition. They give very different answers about the way in which firms make decisions, so it's important to know which model is the right one to use. Each section will have a box that lists the conditions an industry must meet for that model to apply. In the first model, all the firms in an oligopoly coordinate their production and pricing decisions to collectively act as a monopoly would. They then split the monopoly profit among themselves.

This type of oligopoly behavior is known as **collusion** and the organization formed when firms collude is often called a **cartel.** (Sometimes the term "cartel" is reserved for joint monopoly behavior when the firms involved have a public agreement, while "collusion" is used to refer to this behavior when it is done in secret. Both describe the same economic behavior, however.)

If the companies in an oligopoly can successfully collude, figuring out the oligopoly equilibrium is easy. The firms act collectively as a single monopolist would, and the industry equilibrium is the monopoly equilibrium (output is the level for which $MR = MC$ and the price is determined by the demand curve as we saw in Chapter 9).[1] Don't try this at home, though. Cartels and collusion violate the law in most every country of the world, and in the United States, it is a criminal offense that has landed many executives in prison. We discussed in Chapter 9 that governments pass and aggressively enforce antitrust laws because of monopolies' potential to harm consumers. That doesn't mean collusion doesn't happen, but it explains why it's often done in secret. This secrecy can make the instability problem we discuss next—which would exist even if collusion were legal—worse.

cartel or collusion
Oligopoly behavior in which firms coordinate and collectively act as a monopoly to gain monopoly profits.

The Instability of Collusion and Cartels

The firms in an oligopoly would love to collude because they can earn more profit; Adam Smith, the eighteenth-century philosophy professor and one of the fathers of the discipline of economics, recognized this. He wrote in *The Wealth of Nations*, "People of the same trade seldom meet together, even for merriment and diversion, but the conversation ends in a conspiracy against the public, or in some contrivance to raise prices."

But colluding is not easy. It turns out that each member of a cartel has strong incentives not to go along. Although firms in a market might be able to come to some initial agreement over a bargaining table, collusion turns out to be very unstable.

Think about a situation in which there are two firms, Firm A and Firm B, in an industry trying to collude. To keep things simple, suppose both firms have the same constant marginal cost c. If the two firms can act collectively as a monopolist, we can follow the monopoly method from Chapter 9 to figure out the market equilibrium. We know that each firm will operate where marginal revenue equals marginal cost. The problem is that each will want to increase its output at the other's expense.

Suppose the inverse market demand curve for their product is $P = a - bQ$, where P is the price per unit and Q is the quantity produced. We know from Section 9.2 that the marginal revenue curve corresponding to this linear inverse demand curve is $MR = a - 2bQ$. The firms will produce a quantity that sets this equal to their marginal cost c:

$$MR = MC$$
$$a - 2bQ = c$$

Solving this equation for Q gives $Q = (a - c)/2b$. This is the industry's output when its firms collude to act like a monopolist. If we plug this back into the demand curve equation, we find the market price at this quantity: $P = (a + c)/2$.

This is the industry's *total* production in the collusive monopoly outcome. Any combination of the individual firms' outputs that adds to this total will result in the

[1] While figuring out the market equilibrium price, total quantity, and total profits in a cartel is easy, it's not always easy (either for economists studying cartels or the firms in the cartels themselves) to determine how the cartel's quantity and profits will be divided among its members. We discuss this later in the chapter.

monopoly price and profit. Of course, the firms have to decide how to split this profit. A reasonable assumption is that because they both have the same costs, they'll each produce half of the output, $Q/2 = (a - c)/4b$, and split the monopoly profit equally. That's what we assume here. (Later in this section, we discuss why collusion is even more unstable when firms have different costs.)

Cartel Instability: A Mathematical Analysis   To see why collusion is unstable, let's work though an example with specific numbers. Suppose the inverse demand curve is $P = 20 - Q$ and $MC = \$4$. Setting $MR = MC$, as above, the total industry output in a collusive equilibrium will be $Q = 8$ units, and the monopoly price will be $P = \$12$. Assuming that Firms A and B split production evenly, each makes 4 units under collusion. This outcome is shown in Figure 11.1.

Collusion and cartels fall apart for the same reason that Disney and DreamWorks can't agree to stop advertising in our earlier example. It's in each company's interest to expand its output once it knows the other company is restricting output. Each company has the incentive to cheat on the collusive agreement. In other words, collusion is not a Nash equilibrium.

To see why, think about either company's output choice in our example. Will Firm A want to stick with the output of 4 (half the monopoly output of 8) if Firm B agrees to produce 4? If Firm A decides to increase its output to 5 instead of 4, then the total quantity produced would increase to 9. This higher output level lowers the price from $12 to $11 (the demand curve in Figure 11.1, like most demand curves, shows that a higher quantity lowers price).

Once Firm A cheats and increases its output, the industry is no longer at the monopoly quantity and price level, and total industry profit will fall because of overproduction. Total profit drops from $Q \times (P - C) = 8 \times (12 - 4) = \$64$ at the monopoly/cartel level down to $9 \times (11 - 4) = \$63$ after Firm A increases its output on the sly.

Although the profit of the industry as a whole falls, Firm A, the company that violates the agreement, succeeds by earning more. Its profit under collusion was $32 (half of the monopoly profits of $64). But now its profit is higher: $5 \times (11 - 4) = \$35$. The extra sales from increasing production more than make up for the lower prices caused by the increase in production.

Remember that a Nash equilibrium requires each firm to be doing the best it can given what the other firm is doing. This example clearly shows that one firm *can* do

---

Figure 11.1   Cartel Instability

A cartel would like to operate as a monopoly, restricting output to 8 (where $MR = MC$) and selling each unit at a price of $12 for an industry profit of $(\$12 - \$4) \times 8 = \$64$. If production and profit are shared equally between two firms, each firm earns a profit of $(\$12 - \$4) \times 4 = \$32$. However, Firm A may earn a greater profit by cheating on the agreement and producing another unit, which raises total output in the market and lowers price to $11 per unit. At this price and output, Firm A earns a profit of $(\$11 - \$4) \times 5 = \$35$.

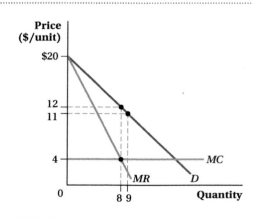

better by violating the collusive agreement if the other firm continues to uphold it, so collusion is not a Nash equilibrium. In fact, the cheating firm can do better still by producing more than 5 units. If one firm sticks to the collusive agreement and makes 4 units, the profit-maximizing output for the other firm is 6 units. At this quantity, the price is $20 - (4 + 6) = \$10$, and the cheating firm's profit is $6 \times (10 - 4) = \$36$. (Test this out for yourself. Notice that the cheating firm's profit only starts to fall if it produces 7 or more units.)

Because both firms face the same incentive—both can do better by cheating if the other one continues to abide by the collusive agreement—collusion is extremely difficult to sustain.

Increasing the Number of Firms in the Cartel   This example was for a two-firm cartel. If there are more firms, the difficulties of holding an agreement together get even worse. When a cartel has many firms, each stands to gain more by cheating on the agreement. Consider the above example again, but now with four firms instead of two. In a collusive agreement, each firm would make 2 units (one-fourth of the total quantity of 8) and earn $16 (one-fourth of the monopoly profit of $64). Suppose three of the firms are abiding by the cartel agreement and making 2 units but the fourth decides to cheat and make 3. Price would again fall to $11. The company that cheated on the agreement would earn a profit of $3 \times (11 - 4) = \$21$. The $5 increase in profit from cheating here is even larger than the $3 increase when there were only two firms. Would the cheater want to increase production beyond 3 units? Yes. In fact, if the other firms remain at the collusive output (2 units per firm), the cheater will increase its profit by producing both a 4th and a 5th unit. However, producing a 6th unit would reduce the cheater's profit. (To see this, consider the prices that would occur when total output is 8, 9, and 10 units and calculate the cheating firm's profits at those prices.) Because profit falls when the cheating firm produces 6 units, its profit-maximizing output will be 5 units.

This outcome implies that the profit-maximizing output level for the cheating firm (5 units) is also larger relative to the collusive quantity (2 units per firm) when there are more firms. With two firms, the cheater's profit-maximizing output (6 units) was only 2 units more than the collusive quantity (4 units per firm). With four firms, the cheater's profit-maximizing output (5 units) is 3 units more than the collusive quantity (2 units). Cheating becomes more pervasive (and more rewarding) as the number of firms in the cartel grows.

Besides raising the value to cheating, having more firms in a cartel also reduces the damages suffered by any firm that continues to abide by the collusive agreement. This is because the profit losses caused by the cheating will be spread across more firms. This factor further contributes to the difficulty of maintaining collusion when more firms are involved.

This cheating problem is familiar to cartels everywhere. Each firm in the cartel wants every *other* firm to collude, thereby raising the market price, while it steals away business from everyone else by producing more output, thus lowering the market price. Because every firm in a cartel has this same incentive to cheat, it's difficult to persuade anyone to collude in the first place.

 **application**

OPEC and the Control of Oil

The Organization of Petroleum Exporting Countries (OPEC) is an example of a cartel that has a lot of difficulty coordinating the actions of all 12 of its members to keep the price of its good, oil, high. First of all, OPEC nations wouldn't be monopolists even if they could coordinate their actions, because they don't control

Figure 11.2   OPEC's Actual Production versus Quota

OPEC's member nations regularly produce higher quantities than their agreed upon quotas, a symptom of the cartel's instability.

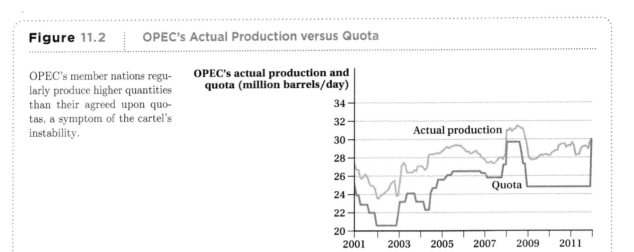

all of the world's supply of oil. About half of the world's current oil production and a substantial portion of its proven reserves are in non-OPEC nations.[2] Oil producers in those non-OPEC counties are happy to let OPEC try to collude, because if OPEC is successful, it raises the price at which these other countries can sell their oil, but the non-OPEC countries don't have to abide by the cartel restrictions and can sell as much oil as they like. So right away, there's a problem: OPEC can't keep all of the gains from its collusion.

On top of that, OPEC has trouble keeping itself together because of a cartel's natural instability. The cartel meets monthly to assign production quotas for each member. Frequently, however, the members choose not to abide by the agreement and overpump oil. And in this case, "frequently" more or less means all the time. Figure 11.2 shows OPEC's production quota agreements compared to its actual production during the 2001–2012 period.[3] Actual production never matches the agreed upon numbers. Member countries always pump more, just as economics tells you will happen. Each member has a great temptation to overproduce given the cartel setup. The exception to this outcome is Saudi Arabia, which often produces *less* than its allocation from the collusive agreement (at a considerable cost to Saudi profit) to keep some semblance of collusive discipline. Otherwise, OPEC might completely disintegrate into a free-for-all production frenzy.

So next time you pay $60 to fill your gas tank, go ahead and get mad! But don't just blame it on OPEC. They don't have their act together often enough to actually make your gas prices high. ■

[2] See http://www.nationmaster.com/graph/ene_oil_res-energy-oil-reserves and http://www.nationmaster.com/graph/ene_oil_pro-energy-oil-production for details.

[3] OPEC's actual production data are from the U.S. Energy Information Administration's *International Petroleum Monthly*. Quota data are taken from the OPEC Statistical Bulletin. Both series have been adjusted to remove Iraq (which OPEC exempted from quotas during the period) as well as the entry of Ecuador and Angola into OPEC in 2008, and Indonesia's departure in 2009.

Suppose that Squeaky Clean and Biobase are the only two producers of chlorine for swimming pools. The inverse market demand for chlorine is $P = 32 - 2Q$, where Q is measured in tons and P is dollars per ton. Assume that chlorine can be produced by either firm at a constant marginal cost of $16 per ton and there are no fixed costs.

a. If the two firms collude and act like a monopoly, agreeing to evenly split the market, how much will each firm produce and what will the price of a ton of chlorine be? How much profit will each firm earn?

b. Does Squeaky Clean have an incentive to cheat on this agreement by producing an additional ton of chlorine? Explain.

c. Does Squeaky Clean's decision to cheat affect Biobase's profit? Explain.

d. Suppose that both firms agree to each produce 1 ton more than they were producing in part (a). How much profit will each firm earn? Does Squeaky Clean now have an incentive to cheat on this agreement by producing another ton of chlorine? Explain.

Solution:

a. If the firms agree to act like a monopoly, they will set $MR = MC$ to solve for the profit-maximizing output:

$$MR = MC$$
$$32 - 4Q = 16$$
$$4Q = 16$$

$Q = 4$ and each firm will produce 2 tons. To find the price, we substitute the market quantity ($Q = 4$) into the inverse demand equation:

$$P = 32 - 2Q = 32 - 2(4) = \$24 \text{ per ton}$$

Each firm will earn a profit of ($24 – $16) × 2 = $16.

b. If Squeaky Clean cheats and produces 3 tons, Q rises to 5 and price falls to $22. Squeaky Clean's profit will be equal to ($22 – $16) × 3 = $18. Therefore, Squeaky Clean does have an incentive to cheat on the agreement because its profit would rise.

c. If Squeaky Clean cheats, the price in the market falls to $22. This reduces Biobase's profit, which is now ($22 – $16) × 2 = $12.

d. If both firms agree to limit production to 3 tons, $Q = 6$ and $P = \$20$. Therefore, each firm earns a profit of ($20 – $16) × 3 = $12. If Squeaky Clean tries to produce 4 tons of chlorine, Q rises to 7 and P falls to $18. Therefore, Squeaky Clean's profit will be ($18 – $16) × 4 = $8. Thus, Squeaky Clean does not have an incentive to cheat on this agreement because its profit would fall.

What Makes Collusion Easier?

Although collusion isn't an especially stable form of oligopoly, there are some conditions that make it more likely to succeed.

The first thing an aspiring cartel needs is a way to detect and punish cheaters. We just saw that companies in a cartel have the private incentive to produce more output (or charge a lower price) than the collusive level. If the other firms in a cartel have no way of knowing when a member cheats—and no form of punishment to inflict when they discover someone is cheating—there is zero chance that any agreement will hold. That's why collusion is more likely to work when firms can closely observe the transaction quantities and prices of other firms. Such transparency limits the ability of potential cheaters to cut secret, lower-price deals with customers. If a firm cheats, the cartel needs to have some way to enforce the agreement or punish the cheater. Because collusion is generally illegal, the cartel can't really take the cheaters to court but it might be able to take other actions that reduce the profits of firms that stray from the agreement, such as shutting them out of a share of future cartel profits.

Second, a cartel may find it easier to succeed if there is little variation in marginal costs across its members. To maximize profit, a monopoly (or a cartel trying to act like a monopoly) wants to use the lowest-cost production method. This desire complicates any scheme to share the monopoly profit among the cartel members and leaves open more opportunities to cheat. Within OPEC, for example, Saudi Arabia can pump its oil out of the ground for about $4 a barrel, while in Nigeria it costs about $20 per barrel to do so. How can OPEC explain to Nigeria that the most efficient production strategy would be to sell only Saudi Arabian oil and none from Nigeria? Third, cartels are more stable when firms take the long view and care more about the future. Think of staying in a cartel (i.e., choosing not to cheat on a collusive agreement) as trading off a short-term opportunity cost to earn a long-term gain. The short-term opportunity cost is giving up the higher profit a firm could obtain by cheating on the agreement. The long-term benefit is that, if the cartel can avoid dissolving into competition, it stands to make monopoly profits. The more the firm values those future monopoly profits relative to the quick hit of additional profit from cheating, the more they will abide by the collusive agreement. Impatient companies, like those in danger of bankruptcy and therefore in desperate need of profit today, are more likely to cheat.

 ## application

The Indianapolis Concrete Cartel

In 2006 and 2007 the U.S. Department of Justice busted up a long-lived ready-mixed concrete cartel in the Indianapolis Metro and Southwest Indiana areas. The case ended up being one of the largest domestic price-fixing prosecutions in the history of the United States. Millions of dollars in fines were levied, and ten executives were given prison sentences.[4]

The Indianapolis cartel struggled with instability issues. Despite the fact that price-fixing conversations had gone on "for as long as anyone could remember," the cartel members were constantly dealing with cheating by members and struggling for ways to punish firms that deviated from agreements. They also had to figure out how to handle a financially struggling firm that was desperate for revenue and perhaps willing to slash prices to get it.

The group held regular meetings at local restaurants or hotels (paying cash for conference rooms to avoid leaving a paper trail) to try to adjust the agreement to current market conditions. Executives monitored agreements by anonymously gathering price quotes from their competitors over the phone. If a violation occurred, the cartel would issue threats, though it's unclear exactly what was threatened and how many threats were actually carried out. If violations were widespread enough, the ringleaders would call an emergency meeting at the local Cracker Barrel restaurant.

These efforts met with mixed success. Sometimes cheating would overwhelm their effort to hold to an agreement. Firms were reluctant to give up the customers they had gained by undercutting the other cartel members. Still, the cartel was on occasion able to maintain enough discipline to inflate prices by an amount estimated to be as much as 17% above their noncollusive level.

Everything began to fall apart when the cartel tried to deal too aggressively with a noncooperative manager from a firm that was not part of the cartel. After repeated attempts to cajole the manager into joining the scheme, the cartel members started

---

[4] Much of the material for this box was taken from: Kevin Corcoran, "The Big Fix," *The Indianapolis Star*, (2007): A1, A22-A23.

complaining about various aspects of his performance to his corporate bosses. Feeling backed into a corner, the manager went to the FBI and informed them of the cartel's operations. By the time criminal proceedings ended a few years later, many careers had been destroyed and several of the cartel companies had been liquidated or bought out. ■

freakonomics

How the Government Lost the Fight against Big Tobacco

Things were looking grim for tobacco companies in 1997. The Big Four—an oligopoly consisting of Philip Morris, Reynolds, Brown and Williamson, and Lorillard—were in serious financial trouble. Smoking had been in decline for decades. Even more worrisome were the many health-based lawsuits that had been brought against the companies. Philip Morris, home of the Marlboro Man, alone faced over 500 litigation cases. All four companies were on thin financial ice.

So you would think that when the government started to threaten further legislation on cigarette sales, the companies would have been frightened. Instead, tobacco executives secretly licked their chops. They were fairly sure they could trick government officials into helping, not hurting, them. Turns out that in some ways the executives were right.

After prolonged negotiations, state governments and the tobacco companies signed what became known as the Tobacco Settlement. The final deal involved a $368.5 billion payment from tobacco companies to the states over twenty-five years, seemingly a huge blow to the tobacco companies.

In reality, however, the tobacco companies didn't pay for the settlement. Smokers did. The revenue from the settlement came in the form of a per-pack cigarette tax. But as we know from our discussion of tax incidence in Chapter 3, when consumer demand is very inelastic (as is likely the case with an addictive good like cigarettes), the consumers bear most of the tax. In addition, the settlement gave companies protection from future litigation.

On top of all these goodies, the settlement included features that helped the tobacco companies solidify their status as a tight-knit oligopoly and, arguably, made it easier for them to collude on prices. For example, the settlement created enormous barriers for new entrants seeking to enter into the market and effectively guaranteed existing non–Big Four tobacco companies a minimum market share over a wide range of possible market prices. Both of these features reduced competition overall in the market, making it easier for the Big Four to raise their prices without fear of losing market share.

So what could the government have done? Jeremy Bulow and Paul Klemperer, two economists who closely documented the tobacco settlement saga, had a novel suggestion for the government: Buy out the companies and run the cigarette industry itself.[5] Their argument was that this would have been cheaper than the settlement proved to be and would have given the government the freedom to run the tobacco industry the way it wanted. But would a buyout lessen the impact of the government's anti-smoking campaigns, causing many to turn again to smoking? Not according to Bulow and Klemperer, who write, "If there is one thing government monopolies are traditionally good at, . . . it is deglamorizing their products and making them as consumer-unfriendly as possible."

[5] Jeremy Bulow and Paul Klemperer, "The Tobacco Deal," *Brookings Papers on Economic Activity* (1998): 323–394.

11.3 Oligopoly with Identical Goods: Bertrand Competition

> **Model Assumptions** Bertrand Competition with Identical Goods
> - Firms sell identical products
> - The firms compete by choosing the price at which they sell their products.
> - The firms set their prices simultaneously.

Bertrand competition
Oligopoly model in which each firm chooses the price of its product.

In the previous section, we learned that the collusion/cartel model of oligopoly in which firms behave like a monopoly is unlikely to hold in reality. If firms don't (or can't) cooperate to act as a single monopolist would, we need a model in which they compete directly against one another. The first such model is as simple as it gets: Firms sell the same product, and consumers compare prices and buy the product with the lowest price. Economists call this structure **Bertrand competition,** after Joseph Bertrand, the nineteenth-century French mathematician and economist who first wrote about it. When firms are selling identical products, as we're assuming here, Bertrand oligopoly has a particularly simple equilibrium and it's just like perfect competition. Later in the chapter, we see how things change if firms sell products that are not identical.

Setting Up the Bertrand Model

To set up this model, let's suppose there is a market with only two companies in it. They sell the same product and have the same marginal cost. For example, suppose there are only two stores in a city, a Walmart and a Target, and these stores are located next to one another. They both sell Sony PlayStations. Each firm's marginal cost is $150 per console. This includes the wholesale price the firm has to pay Sony as well as miscellaneous selling costs such as stocking the consoles on shelves, checking customers out, and so on.

We make one further assumption: Consumers don't view either store differently in terms of service, atmosphere, and the like. This assumption isn't completely realistic, but it preserves our assumption that the firms are selling the same product. If consumers did value these things separately from the video games then, in a way, the products would no longer be identical and we would need to model the firms' behavior using the model of differentiated products discussed later in the chapter.

With only two companies in a market, it might seem as if there would be a lot of market power and high markups over cost. But suppose the customers in this market have a simple demand rule: They buy the PlayStation from the store that sells it at the lowest price. If both stores charge the same price, consumers flip a coin to determine where they buy. This rule means, in effect, that the store charging the lower price will get all the demand for PlayStations in the market. If both stores charge the same price, each store gets half of the demand.

Suppose the total demand in the market is for Q consoles. Let's denote Walmart's price as P_W and Target's price P_T. The two stores then face the following demand curves:

Demand for PlayStations at Walmart:

$$Q, \quad \text{if } P_W < P_T$$

$$\frac{Q}{2}, \quad \text{if } P_W = P_T$$

$$0, \quad \text{if } P_W > P_T.$$

Demand for PlayStations at Target:

$$Q, \quad \text{if } P_T < P_W$$

$$\frac{Q}{2}, \quad \text{if } P_T = P_W$$

$$0, \quad \text{if } P_T > P_W.$$

Each store chooses its price to maximize its profit, realizing that it will sell the number of units according to the demand curves above. We've assumed the total number of consoles sold, Q, doesn't depend on the price charged. The price only affects which store people buy from. (We could alternatively have allowed Q to depend on the lowest price charged; all of the key results discussed below would remain the same.)

Nash Equilibrium of a Bertrand Oligopoly

Remember that in a Nash equilibrium, each firm is doing the best it can given whatever the other firm is doing. So to find the equilibrium of this Bertrand model, let's first think about Target's best response to Walmart's actions. (We could do this in the other order if we wanted.) If Target believes Walmart will charge a price P_W for PlayStations, Target will sell nothing if it sets its price above P_W, so we can probably rule that out as a profit-maximizing strategy. Target is left with two options: Match Walmart's price and sell $Q/2$ units, or undercut Walmart and sell Q. Because all it has to do is undercut Walmart by *any* amount, dropping its price just below P_W will only reduce its per-unit margin by a tiny amount, but the store will double its sales because it will take the whole market.

As an example, suppose $Q = 1{,}000$ and Target thinks Walmart will charge $P_W = \$175$. If Target also charges $P_T = \$175$, it will sell 500 PlayStations at a profit of $25 each (the $175 price minus the $150 marginal cost). That's a total profit of $12,500. But if Target charges $174.99, it will sell 1,000 PlayStations at a profit of $24.99 each. This is a profit of $24,990—almost double what it was at $175. Target has a strong incentive to undercut Walmart's expected price.

Of course, things are the same from Walmart's perspective: It has the same incentive to undercut whatever price it thinks Target will choose. If it believes Target is going to charge $P_T = \$174.99$ for a PlayStation, Walmart could price its consoles at $174.98 and gain back the entire market. But then Target would have the incentive to undercut *this* expected price, and so on.

This incentive for undercutting would only stop once the price each store expects the other to charge falls to the level of the stores' marginal costs ($150). At that point, cutting prices further would let a store gain the entire market, but that store would be selling every PlayStation at a loss (try to make that up on increased volume!).

The equilibrium of this Bertrand oligopoly occurs when each store charges a price equal to its marginal cost—$150 in this example. Each obtains half of the market share, and each store earns zero economic profit. The stores would like to make more, but if either firm raises its price above marginal cost by even the smallest amount, the other firm has a strong incentive to undercut it. And dropping prices below marginal cost would only cause the stores to suffer losses. So the outcome isn't the most preferable outcome for the firms, but neither firm can do better by unilaterally changing its price. This is the definition of a Nash equilibrium.

In the identical-good Bertrand oligopoly, one firm cannot increase its profit by raising its price *if* the other firm still charges a price equal to its marginal cost. If the firms could somehow figure out a way to coordinate changes in their actions so that they both raised prices together, they would raise their profits. However, the problem with this strategy, as we saw earlier, is that collusion is unstable. Once the firms are charging prices above marginal cost, a firm can raise its profits by unilaterally changing its action and lowering its price just slightly.

The Bertrand model of oligopoly shows you that even with a small number of firms, competition can still be extremely intense. *In fact, the market outcome of Bertrand competition with identical goods is the same as that in a perfectly competitive market: Price equals marginal cost.* This super-competitiveness occurs because either firm can steal the whole market away from the other by dropping price only slightly. The strong incentive to undercut the price leads both firms to drop their prices to marginal cost.

This example had only two firms, but the result would be the same if there were more. The intuition is the same: Every firm's price-cutting motive is so strong that the only equilibrium is for them to all charge a price equal to marginal cost, leading them to split the market evenly.[6]

theory and data

Computer Parts I

Bertrand markets with identical goods turn out to have a simple equilibrium solution, but the conditions present in the model are rare in the real world. One actual market that comes fairly close to these conditions is an online market for computer chips, which was the focus of the study by Glenn Ellison and Sara Fisher Ellison that we discussed briefly in Chapter 2.[*] In this market, high-tech customers who like to build their own computers shop for CPUs and memory chips using an online price search engine that tracks down and lists the products of various electronic parts retailers. The photo shows an example of the array of options available to a customer shopping in this market for a particular CPU.

The search engine lists choices by ascending price. A search for this particular CPU at this site yields 20 pages of listings. But as you can see, the chips are all similar. Chances are if you were a buyer, you probably aren't going to bother going through each and every page. These are basically identical products.

In addition, in this market, most consumers seem to simply buy the cheapest product available, just as in the Bertrand model. As we discussed in Chapter 2, Ellison and Ellison measured the price elasticity of demand for chips like these to be around −25, so pricing just 1% above its competitors decreases a company's sales by 25%.

Demand this responsive to changes in prices is fairly close to what we just described for a Bertrand oligopoly with identical products. Even a small price cut below that of a competitor will

Pricewatch.com

An online search engine lists an array of CPUs from various retailers at different prices.

[*] Glenn Ellison and Sara Ellison, "Search, Obfuscation, and Price Elasticities on the Internet," *Econometrica* 77, no. 2, (2009): 427-452.

[6] This again assumes all firms in the market have the same marginal cost. If firms have different marginal costs in an identical-product Bertrand oligopoly, then the equilibrium is for the lowest-cost firm (or firms, if there are more than one with the same, lowest-in-market costs) to charge a price just under the *second-lowest* cost in the market. At any price higher than that, the lowest-cost firm(s) will have to split the demand with other firms without holding any pricing advantage (the other firms can now undercut). But there's no reason to charge any less than that amount, either. It would only reduce profit without resulting in any additional sales. Therefore in equilibrium, the lowest-cost firm(s) sell(s) at a price just below the second-lowest cost level, split demand (if more than one firm has this lowest cost), and earn(s) positive profit because it (they, if more than one) earn(s) a profit margin on every sale.

bring in a large number of extra sales. At the same time, though, pricing higher than another firm will result in the firm losing a lot of sales.

The identical-product Bertrand model predicts that this price inelasticity of demand will lead to an equilibrium where firms charge a price equal to their marginal cost. This outcome is close to what Ellison and Ellison found in the computer parts market they studied. First, prices didn't vary too much across retailers. Second, after collecting a significant amount of information to estimate the CPU retailers' marginal costs, Ellison and Ellison determined that the lowest-priced products were being sold at prices that approximately equaled the retailers' marginal costs.

11.4 Oligopoly with Identical Goods: Cournot Competition

Model Assumptions Cournot Competition with Identical Goods

- Firms sell identical products.
- Firms compete by choosing a quantity to produce.
- All goods sell for the same price—the market price, which is determined by the sum of the quantities produced by all the firms in the market.
- Firms choose quantities simultaneously.

When firms sell identical goods, the Bertrand competition model results in the same equilibrium that we find in a perfectly competitive market, where price equals marginal cost. Since consumers care only about the price of the good (since the product is identical across firms), each firm faces a demand that is perfectly elastic. Any increase in a firm's price results in it losing all of its market share. The demand for the product will go to the firm offering the lowest price.

But what if firms face capacity constraints, and thus a limit on how much demand they can fill in the short run? With this restriction, if a firm undercuts another's price, it can only steal as many customers as it has available capacity and this capacity is probably not the size of the whole market.

In this model, there won't be as much pressure for a firm to respond to price cuts because each firm will not lose all of its customers even if it keeps its price higher than that of a competitor. In fact, if the capacity of the low-price company is small enough, its competitor may not feel the need to cut prices much at all. This avoids the price-cutting spiral we saw in the Bertrand model.

In this situation, the critical issue is for a firm to determine how much capacity it has and thus what quantity it can produce.

Setting Up the Cournot Model

We raise the idea of capacity constraints to motivate another major oligopoly model, **Cournot competition** (named after its first modeler, Augustin Cournot—yet another nineteenth-century French mathematician and economist).

In Cournot competition, firms produce identical goods and choose a quantity to produce rather than a price at which to sell the good. Individual firms do not control the price of their goods as they do in the Bertrand model. First, all firms in the industry decide how much they will produce; then based on the quantity produced by all firms, the market demand curve determines the price at which all firms' output will sell. In Chapter 9, we learned that when dealing with a monopolist, the price-quantity outcome is the same whether a firm sets the price of its product or the number of units of output

Cournot competition
Oligopoly model in which each firm chooses its production quantity.

it produces. In an oligopoly, however, the market outcome differs depending on whether the firm chooses to set its price or its quantity.

To be more specific, let's say there are two firms in a Cournot oligopoly, Firm 1 and Firm 2. (There can be more; we keep it at two to simplify our analysis.) Each has a constant marginal cost of c, and both firms independently and simultaneously choose their production quantities q_1 and q_2. The good's inverse demand curve is

$$P = a - bQ$$

where Q is the *total* quantity produced in the market. Therefore, $Q = q_1 + q_2$.

Firm 1's profit π_1 is the quantity q_1 it produces times the difference between the market price P and its production costs c, or

$$\pi_1 = q_1 \times (P - c)$$

Substituting the inverse demand equation for P, we find that

$$\pi_1 = q_1 \times [a - b(q_1 + q_2) - c]$$

Similarly, Firm 2's profits are given by the equation

$$\pi_2 = q_2 \times [a - b(q_1 + q_2) - c]$$

These two profit equations make clear that the firms in this oligopoly strategically interact. Firm 1's profit is not just a function of its own quantity choice q_1, but also of its competitor's quantity q_2. Likewise, Firm 2's profit is affected by Firm 1's output choice. The logic is that each firm's production choice, through its influence on the market price P, affects the other firm's profit.

An example of an industry that is like the Cournot model is the crude oil industry. Crude oil is a commodity; consumers are indifferent about oil from different sources. The price of oil is set on a worldwide market, and it depends on the total amount of oil supplied at a given time. Therefore, it's realistic to assume that oil producers, even those such as Saudi Arabia or Iran with large oil reserves, do not choose the price of their outputs. They just choose how much to produce. (As we discussed beforehand, OPEC chooses production quantity targets, not prices.) Oil traders observe these production decisions for all oil producers, and they bid oil's market price up or down depending on how the total quantity produced (the market supply) compares to current demand. This price-setting process derives from the demand curve that connects total output to a market price.

Equilibrium in a Cournot Oligopoly

Finding the equilibrium for a Cournot oligopoly will be easier to follow using an example. Suppose for simplicity that only two countries pump oil, Saudi Arabia and Iran. Both have a marginal cost of production of $20 per barrel. Also assume that the inverse demand curve for oil is $P = 200 - 3Q$, where P is in dollars per barrel and Q is in millions of barrels per day.

Finding the equilibrium for the Cournot model is similar to doing so for a monopoly, but with the one change noted above: The market quantity Q is the sum of the quantities produced in Saudi Arabia q_S and Iran q_I, rather than just the monopolist's output: $Q = q_S + q_I$. After recognizing this difference, we follow the same steps we used to solve for a monopoly's profit-maximizing output. That is, we find each country's marginal revenue curve, and then find the quantity at which marginal revenue equals marginal cost.

Let's examine Saudi Arabia's profit maximization first. As we learned in Section 9.2, we can more easily find a firm's marginal revenue curve by starting with its inverse demand curve. Therefore, we start by writing the inverse demand curve equation in terms of the quantity choices of each country:

$$P = 200 - 3Q = 200 - 3(q_S + q_I) = 200 - 3q_S - 3q_I$$

Because the slope of the marginal revenue curve is twice the slope of the inverse demand function, Saudi Arabia's marginal revenue curve is[7]

$$MR = 200 - 6q_S - 3q_I$$

Saudi Arabia maximizes profit when it produces the quantity at which its marginal revenue equals its marginal cost:

$$200 - 6q_S - 3q_I = 20$$

We can solve this equation for Saudi Arabia's profit-maximizing output:

$$q_S = 30 - 0.5q_I$$

This outcome differs from the monopoly outcome: If Saudi Arabia were a monopoly, setting marginal revenue equal to marginal cost would result in a single quantity Q because its quantity supplied q_S would be the market quantity supplied Q. In this example, however, Saudi Arabia's profit-maximizing output depends on the competitor's output q_I. Similarly, Iran's profit-maximizing q_I depends on q_S because it faces the same market demand curve and has the same marginal cost:

$$q_I = 30 - 0.5q_S$$

This result shows that one country's output choice effectively decreases the demand for the other country's output. That is, the demand curve for the other country's output is shifted in by the amount of the other country's output. If the Saudis expect Iran to produce, say, 10 million barrels per day (bpd), then Saudi Arabia would effectively be facing the demand curve

$$P = 200 - 3q_S - 3q_I = 200 - 3q_S - 3(10) = 170 - 3q_S$$

If it expected Iran to pump out 20 million bpd, Saudi Arabia would face the demand curve

$$P = 200 - 3q_S - 3(20) = 140 - 3q_S$$

This demand that is left over to one country (or more generally, firm), taking the other country's output choice as given, is called the **residual demand curve.** We just derived Saudi Arabia's residual demand curves for two of Iran's different production choices, 10 and 20 million bpd.

In effect, a firm in a Cournot oligopoly acts like a monopolist, but one that faces its residual demand curve rather than the market demand curve. The residual demand curve, like any regular demand curve, has a corresponding marginal revenue curve (it's called . . . wait for it . . . the **residual marginal revenue curve** . . . yes!). The firm produces the quantity at which its residual marginal revenue equals its marginal cost. That's why Saudi Arabia's optimal quantity is the one that sets $200 - 6q_S - 3q_I = 20$. The left-hand side of this equation is Saudi Arabia's residual marginal revenue (expressed in terms of any expected Iranian output level q_I). The right-hand side is its marginal cost.

How does the profit-maximizing output of one country change with the other country's expected production? In other words, what role do strategic interactions play in a Cournot oligopoly? This can be seen in Figure 11.3, which shows Saudi Arabia's residual demand, residual marginal revenue, and marginal cost curves. (The Iranian case would be the same, just with the two countries' labels switched.) The residual demand RD_S^1 and residual marginal revenue RMR_S^1 curves correspond to an Iranian output level of 10 million bpd. In other words, if Saudi Arabia expects Iran to produce 10 million bpd, Saudi Arabia's optimal output quantity is 25 million bpd. If it expects Iran to produce 30 million bpd, Saudi Arabia's residual demand and marginal revenue curves shift in

residual demand curve
In Cournot competition, the demand remaining for a firm's output given competitor firms' production quantities.

residual marginal revenue curve
A marginal revenue curve corresponding to a residual demand curve.

---

[7] The inverse demand curve for Saudi Arabia is plotted in a diagram with quantity, q_S, on the horizontal axis and price on the vertical axis. The slope is $\Delta P/\Delta q_S = 3$. This means that only the coefficient on q_S is used to determine the slope of the marginal revenue curve. The slope of the marginal revenue curve is $\Delta MR/\Delta q_S = 6$.

Figure 11.3 : **Cournot Equilibrium**

Saudi Arabia's optimal production quantity is dependent on Iran's production quantity. If the Iranian output level is 10 million bpd, Saudi Arabia's optimal output is 25 million bpd, where its residual marginal revenue curve intersects its marginal cost. If Iranian output increases to 30 million bpd, Saudi Arabia's residual demand and residual marginal revenue curves shift to RD_S^2 and RMR_S^2. As a result, Saudi Arabia's optimum output decreases to 15 million bpd.

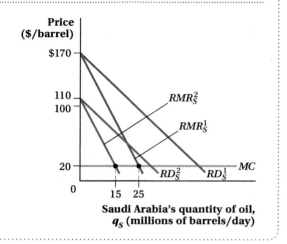

---

to RD_S^2 and RMR_S^2, to $P = 110 - 3q_S$ and $MR = 110 - 6q_S$, respectively. The Saudis' optimal quantity then falls to 15 million bpd. At Iranian output levels higher than 30 million bpd, Saudi Arabia's residual demand and marginal revenue curves would shift in further and its optimal quantity would fall.

It's clear that each competitor's profit-maximizing output depends on the other's, and in an opposite direction: If a firm expects its competitor to produce more, it should reduce its production. Although this kind of interaction seems to create a hopeless chicken-and-egg problem, we can still pin down the specific production quantities for each country if we return to the concept of Nash equilibrium: Each producer does the best it can, taking the other producer's action as given.

To see what that implies for a Cournot oligopoly, note that the equation for each country's profit-maximizing output is described given the particular output choice of the other country. The equation for q_S gives Saudi Arabia's best response to any production level q_I that Iran might choose. Likewise, the q_I equation gives Iran's best response to any Saudi production decision. In other words, when both equations hold simultaneously, each country is doing the best it can given the other country's action. So, the Nash equilibrium is the combination of outputs that make both equations hold.

Cournot Equilibrium: A Graphical Approach   We can show this graphically in Figure 11.4. Saudi Arabia's output is on the vertical axis and Iran's output is on the horizontal axis. The curves illustrated are **reaction curves.** A reaction curve shows the best production response a country (or firm, in a more general oligopoly context) can make given the other country's/firm's action. Because both reaction curves are downward-sloping, a firm's optimal output falls as the other producer's output rises.

Reaction curve SA shows Saudi Arabia's best response to any production choice of Iran—it shows the points at which $q_S = 30 - 0.5q_I$. If it expects Iran to produce no oil ($q_I = 0$), for example, the profit-maximizing Saudi response is to produce $q_S = 30$ million bpd. This combination is at point A. The optimal q_S falls as Iranian production rises. If Iran produces $q_I = 10$, then Saudi Arabia maximizes its profit by producing $q_S = 30 - 0.5(10) = 25$ million bpd (point B). If $q_I = 30$, then the optimal q_S is 15 million bpd (point C). Saudi Arabia's optimal production continues to fall as Iran's production rises until it hits zero at $q_I = 60$ million bpd (point D). At any q_I greater than 60 million bpd, the market price is below $20 per barrel (see the demand curve). Because this price is below the marginal cost of production, it wouldn't be profitable for Saudi Arabia to pump any oil if Iran produced 60 million bpd.

reaction curve
A function that relates a firm's best response to its competitor's possible actions. In Cournot competition, this is the firm's best production response to its competitor's possible quantity choices.

Figure 11.4 | Reaction Curves

A reaction curve represents a firm's optimal production response given its competitor's production quantity. SA and I are the reaction curves for Saudi Arabia and Iran, respectively. At point E, where Iran and Saudi Arabia each produce 20 bpd ($q_I = q_S = 20$), the market has reached a Nash equilibrium. Here, the two countries are simultaneously producing optimally given the other's actions.

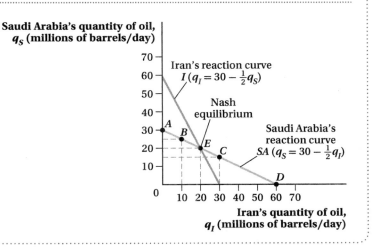

Line I is the corresponding reaction curve for Iran's profit-maximizing quantity $q_I = 30 - 0.5q_S$. It's essentially the same as SA, except with the axes flipped. Just as Saudi Arabia's profit-maximizing output falls with Iran's production choice, Iran's optimal production decreases with expected Saudi production q_S. The optimal q_I is 30 million bpd if $q_S = 0$, and it falls toward 0 as q_S rises toward 60 million bpd.

Each country realizes that its actions affect the desired actions of its competitor, which in turn affect its own optimal action, and so on. This back-and-forth strategic interaction is captured in firms' reaction curves, and is why the equilibrium is found where reaction curves intersect. The intersection of the two reaction curves at point E shows the quantities at which both competitors are simultaneously producing optimally given the other's actions. That is, point E is the Nash equilibrium of the Cournot oligopoly—the mutual best response. If one country is producing at point E, the other country would only reduce its profits by unilaterally producing at some other point. At this equilibrium, each country produces 20 million bpd, and total output is 40 million bpd.

Cournot Equilibrium: A Mathematical Approach In addition to finding the Cournot equilibrium graphically, we can solve for it algebraically by solving for the output levels that equate the two reaction curves. One way to do this is to substitute one equation into the other to get rid of one quantity variable and solve for the remaining one. For example, if we substitute Iran's reaction curve into Saudi Arabia's reaction curve for q_I, we find

$$q_S = 30 - 0.5q_I = 30 - 0.5(30 - 0.5q_S)$$

$$= 30 - 15 + 0.25q_S$$

$$0.75q_S = 15$$

$$q_S = 20$$

Thus, the equilibrium output for Saudi Arabia is 20 million bpd. If we substitute this value back into Iran's reaction curve, we find that $q_I = 30 - 0.5q_S = 30 - 0.5(20) = 20$. Iran's optimal production is also 20 million bpd. Equilibrium point E in Figure 11.4 has the coordinates (20, 20), and total industry output is 40 million bpd.

The equilibrium price of oil at this point can be found by plugging these production decisions into the inverse market demand curve. Doing so gives $P = 200 - 3(q_S + q_I) = 200 - 3(20 + 20) = \$80$ per barrel. Each country's profit is 20 million bpd × ($\$80 - \$20$) = $\$1,200$ million = $\$1.2$ billion per day, so the industry's total profit is $\$2.4$ billion per day.

11.2 figure it out

OilPro and GreaseTech are the only two firms who provide oil changes in a local market in a Cournot duopoly. The oil changes performed by the two firms are identical, and consumers are indifferent about which firm they will purchase an oil change from. The market inverse demand for the oil changes is $P = 100 - 2Q$, where Q is the total number of oil changes (in thousands per year) produced by the two firms, $q_O + q_G$. OilPro has a marginal cost of \$12 per oil change, while GreaseTech has a marginal cost of \$20. Assume that neither firm has any fixed cost.

    a. Determine each firm's reaction curve and graph it.

    b. How many oil changes will each firm produce in Cournot equilibrium?

    c. What will the market price for an oil change be?

    d. How much profit does each firm earn?

Solution:

    a. Start by substituting $Q = q_O + q_G$ into the market inverse demand curve:
$$P = 100 - 2Q = 100 - 2(q_O + q_G) = 100 - 2q_O - 2q_G$$

From this inverse demand cure, we can derive each firm's marginal revenue curve:
$$MR_O = 100 - 4q_O - 2q_G$$
$$MR_G = 100 - 2q_O - 4q_G$$

Each firm will set its marginal revenue equal to its marginal cost to maximize profit. From this, we can obtain each firm's reaction curve:
$$MR_O = 100 - 4q_O - 2q_G = 12$$
$$4q_O = 88 - 2q_G$$
$$q_O = 22 - 0.5q_G$$
$$MR_G = 100 - 2q_O - 4q_G = 20$$
$$4q_G = 80 - 2q_O$$
$$q_G = 20 - 0.5q_O$$

These reaction curves are shown in the figure below.

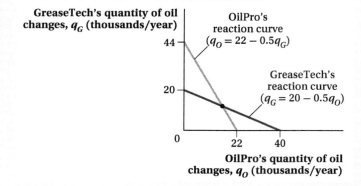

b. To solve for equilibrium, we need to substitute one firm's reaction curve into the reaction curve for the other firm:

$$q_O = 22 - 0.5q_G$$
$$q_O = 22 - 0.5(20 - 0.5q_O) = 22 - 10 + 0.25q_O = 12 + 0.25q_O$$
$$0.75q_O = 12$$
$$q_O = 16$$
$$q_G = 20 - 0.5q_O = 20 - 0.5(16) = 20 - 8 = 12$$

Therefore, OilPro produces 16,000 oil changes per year, while GreaseTech produces 12,000.

c. We can use the market inverse demand curve to determine the market price:

$$P = 100 - 2Q = 100 - 2(q_O + q_G) = 100 - 2(16 + 12) = 100 - 56 = 44$$

The price will be $44 per oil change.

d. OilPro sells 16,000 oil changes at a price of $44 for a total revenue $TR = $ 16,000 × $44 = $704,000. Total cost $TC = $ 16,000 × $12 = $192,000. Therefore, profit for OilPro is $\pi = $704,000 - $192,000 = $512,000$.

GreaseTech sells 12,000 oil changes at a price of $44 for a total revenue of $TR = $ 12,000 × $44 = $528,000. Total cost $TC = $ 12,000 × $20 = $240,000. Thus, GreaseTech's profit is $\pi = $528,000 - $240,000 = $288,000$.

Note that the firm with the lower marginal cost produces more output and earns a greater profit.

Comparing Cournot to Collusion and to Bertrand Oligopoly

Let's compare this equilibrium in a Cournot oligopoly ($Q = 40$ million bpd at P = $80) and profit ($2.4 billion per day) to the outcomes in other oligopoly models we've analyzed. These results are described in Table 11.2.

Collusion   Let's first suppose Saudi Arabia and Iran can actually get their acts together and collude to act like a monopolist. In that case, they would treat their separate production decisions q_I and q_S as a single total output $Q = q_S + q_I$. Following the normal marginal-revenue-equals-marginal-cost procedure, we would find that $Q = 30$ million bpd. Presumably, the two countries would split this output evenly at 15 million bpd because they have the same marginal costs. This is less

Table 11.2   **Comparing Equilibria across Oligopolies**

Oligopoly Structure	Total Output (million bpd)	Price ($ per barrel)	Industry Profit (per day)
Collusion	30	$110	$2.7 billion
Bertrand (identical products)	60	20	0
Cournot	40	80	2.4 billion

than the total Cournot oligopoly production of 40 million bpd that we just derived. Furthermore, because monopoly production is lower, the price is higher, too: Plugging this monopoly quantity into the demand curve, price becomes $P = 200 - 3(30) = $110 per barrel. We also know that total industry profit must be higher in the collusive monopoly outcome. In this case, it's 30 million bpd × ($110 − $20) = $2.7 billion per day (or $1.35 billion for each country). This total is $300 million per day higher than the Cournot competition outcome. At the collusive monopoly equilibrium, output is lower than at the Cournot equilibrium, and price and profit are higher.

Bertrand Oligopoly with Identical Products   Next, let's consider the Nash equilibrium in the Bertrand case with identical products. This is easy: We know that price will equal marginal cost, so $P = \$20$. Total demand at this price is determined by plugging $20 into the demand curve: $P = 20 = 200 − 3Q$, or $Q = 60$ million bpd. The two countries would split this demand equally, with each selling 30 million bpd. Because they both sell at a price equal to their marginal cost, each country earns zero profit. At the Bertrand equilibrium, output quantity is higher than at the Cournot equilibrium, price is lower, and there is no profit.

Summary   To summarize, then, in terms of total industry output, the lowest is the collusive monopoly outcome, then Cournot, then Bertrand:

$$Q_m < Q_c < Q_b$$

The order is the opposite for prices, with Bertrand prices the lowest and the collusive price the highest:

$$P_b < P_c < P_m$$

Similarly, profit is lowest in the Bertrand case (at zero), highest under collusion, with Cournot in the middle:

$$\pi_b = 0 < \pi_c < \pi_m$$

Therefore, the Cournot oligopoly outcome is something between those for monopoly and Bertrand oligopoly (for which the outcome is equivalent to perfect competition). And, unlike the collusive and Bertrand outcomes, the price and output in the Cournot equilibrium depend on the number of firms in the industry.

What Happens If There Are More Than Two Firms in a Cournot Oligopoly?

These intermediate outcomes are for a market with two firms. If there are more than two firms in a Cournot oligopoly, the total quantity, profits, and price remain between the monopoly and perfectly competitive extremes. However, the more firms there are, the closer these outcomes get to the perfectly competitive case with price equaling marginal cost and economic profits being zero. Having more competitors means that any single firm's supply decision becomes a smaller and smaller part of the total market. Its output choice therefore impacts the market price less and less. With a very large number of firms in the market, a producer essentially becomes a price taker. It therefore behaves like a firm in a perfectly competitive industry, producing where the market price equals its marginal cost. Most Cournot markets are not at this limit, so price is usually above marginal cost, but for intermediate cases, more firms in a Cournot oligopoly lead to lower prices, higher total output, and lower average firm profits.

Cournot versus Bertrand: Extensions

The fact that the intensity of competition changes with the number of firms in the market is a nice feature of the Cournot model. This prediction is more in line with many people's intuitive view of oligopoly than the Bertrand model's prediction that anything more than a single firm leads to a perfectly competitive outcome. The downside of the Cournot framework is that it's a bit more of a stretch than usual to assume that companies can only compete in their quantity choices and have no ability to charge different prices. How many oligopolies could that describe? Oil seems a very special case, but is it?

Economists David Kreps and José A. Scheinkman examined this assumption in more detail. They proved an important result (though it's too mathematically advanced to detail here) that helps expand the applicability of the Cournot model.[8] Kreps and Scheinkman showed that under certain conditions, even if firms actually set their prices instead of quantities, the industry equilibrium looks like the Cournot outcome. The key added element in Kreps's and Scheinkman's Cournot story is that firms must first choose their production capacity before they set their prices. The firms are then constrained to produce at or below that capacity level once they make their price decisions.

As an example of a market described by the Cournot model, imagine that a few real estate developers in a college town build student apartments that are identical in quality and size. Once these developers build their apartment buildings, they can charge whatever price the market will bear for the apartments, but their choice of prices will be constrained by the number of apartments they have all built. If, for some reason, the developers want to charge a ridiculously low rent of, say, $50 per month, they would probably not be able to satisfy all of the quantity demanded at that low price because they only have a fixed number of apartments to rent. If the developers first choose the number of apartments in their buildings and then sell their fixed capacity at whatever prices they choose, Kreps and Scheinkman show that the equilibrium price and quantity (which, as it turns out, will equal the developers' capacity choice in this case) will be like a Cournot oligopoly.

This result means that in industries in which there are large costs of investing in capacity so that firms don't change their capacity very often, the Cournot model will probably be a good predictor of market outcomes even if firms choose their prices in the short run. (In the long run, the firms could both change their capacity by building more apartment buildings and change the prices they choose.)

11.5 Oligopoly with Identical Goods: Stackelberg Competition

Model Assumptions Stackelberg Competition with Identical Goods

- Firms sell identical products.
- Firms compete by choosing a quantity to produce.
- All goods sell for the same price (which is determined by the sum total of quantities produced by all the firms combined).
- Firms do *not* choose quantities simultaneously. One firm chooses its quantity first. The next firm observes this and then chooses its quantity.

The Cournot model gave us a way to analyze oligopolistic markets that are somewhere between collusion/monopoly and Bertrand/perfect competition. As in most oligopoly models, equilibrium in the Cournot model came from firms rationally thinking through how other firms in the market are likely to behave in response to their production decisions.

---

[8] David M. Kreps and José A. Scheinkman, "Quantity Precommitment and Bertrand Competition Yield Cournot Outcomes," *The Bell Journal of Economics* 14, no. 2, (1983): 326-337.

Importantly, the Cournot model also relies on another assumption whose implications we didn't think about in much detail, namely, that the firms choose simultaneously. That is, each firm chooses its optimal quantity based on what the firm believes its competitor(s) *might* do. If it expects its competitor(s) to produce some other quantity, its own optimal action changes—that was the logic of the reaction curve.

If you think about it, though, each company has an incentive to try to choose its output level first and force its competitors to be the one who has to react. The first firm to make its decision could increase its output and say "Oops, I have already made more than Cournot says I am supposed to produce. What are you going to do about it?" Because the competitor's reaction curve slopes downward in this case, the competitor, seeing the high quantity the original firm is producing, would want to reduce its output. Therefore, there is a **first-mover advantage** in this market.

An oligopoly model in which firms move sequentially—first one, then another, then (if there are more than two firms) another, and so on, is called **Stackelberg competition.** (Heinrich Freiherr von Stackelberg was an early-twentieth-century German economist who first analyzed this type of oligopoly.) The firm that moves first is sometimes called the Stackelberg leader. To see how sequential competition changes things, let's revisit our oil producers, Saudi Arabia and Iran.

In that example, the market inverse demand for oil was $P = 200 - 3Q$, and both countries had a constant marginal cost of $20 per barrel. Each firm produced where marginal revenue equaled marginal cost:

$$MR_S = 200 - 6q_S - 3q_I = 20$$
$$MR_I = 200 - 6q_I - 3q_S = 20$$

In Cournot competition, we rearranged this equation to solve for each country's reaction curve:

$$q_S = 30 - 0.5q_I$$
$$q_I = 30 - 0.5q_S$$

We know that this formula gives the best output a country can choose, taking as given the other country's output level. Plugging one reaction curve into the other gave us the Nash equilibrium, in which each country produced 20 million bpd at a market price of $80 per barrel.

Stackelberg Competition and the First-Mover Advantage

Now suppose Saudi Arabia is a Stackelberg leader: It chooses its quantity first. What will Saudi Arabia do with this first-mover advantage?

Iran's incentives remain unchanged. It still has the same reaction curve, and the reaction curve continues to show Iran's best response to any choice by Saudi Arabia. In Stackelberg competition, however, Iran will know with certainty what Saudi Arabia's production decision is before it makes its own. Iran reacts optimally to any production choice that Saudi Arabia makes by plugging this value for q_S into its reaction function. Importantly, *Saudi Arabia realizes Iran will do this before it makes its first move.*

Because Saudi Arabia knows that Iran's output is going to be a function of whatever Saudi Arabia chooses first, the Saudis want to take that impact into account when they make their *initial* production decision. In this way, Saudi Arabia can take advantage of being the first-mover. To do so, it plugs Iran's best response (which it knows from previous experience) into its own demand and marginal revenue curve equations. The fact that the Saudi marginal revenue curve changes means that Saudi Arabia will no longer have the same reaction curve it had in the Cournot model. In that model, Saudi Arabia faced the demand curve

$$P = 200 - 3(q_S + q_I)$$

first-mover advantage
In Stackelberg competition, the advantage gained by the initial firm in setting its production quantity.

Stackelberg competition
Oligopoly model in which firms make production decisions sequentially.

Now that it is a first-mover in a Stackelberg oligopoly, Saudi Arabia's demand is

$$P = 200 - 3q_S + 3q_I = 200 - 3q_S - 3(30 - 0.5q_S) = 200 - 3q_S - 90 + 1.5q_S$$

Do you see what happened? We substituted Iran's reaction function ($q_I = 30 - 0.5q_S$) directly into the Saudi demand curve. We did this because Saudi Arabia recognizes that, by going first, its output choice affects its demand (and therefore its marginal revenue) both directly and indirectly through its effect on Iran's production decision. The direct effect is captured by the term $-3q_S$ in the equation; this effect is the same as in the Cournot model. The indirect effect comes from the impact of Saudi Arabia's output choice on Iran's production response. This is embodied in the equation's second q_S term ($1.5q_S$).

We can further simplify this demand curve:

$$P = 110 - 1.5q_S$$

We know from Chapter 9 that Saudi Arabia's marginal revenue curve is then $MR_S = 110 - 3q_S$. Setting this equal to marginal cost ($20 per barrel) and solving for q_S give Saudi Arabia's profit-maximizing output in this Stackelberg oliopoly:

$$MR_S = 110 - 3q_S = 20$$

$$3q_S = 90$$

$$q_S = 30$$

As the first-mover, Saudi Arabia finds it optimal to produce 30 million bpd, 10 million more than the Cournot oligopoly output (20 million bpd).

Next, we have to see how Saudi Arabia's decision affects Iran's optimal production level. To do that, we plug Saudi Arabia's output level into Iran's reaction curve:

$$q_I = 30 - 0.5q_S = 30 - 0.5(30) = 15$$

Iran now produces 15 million bpd, rather than 20 as in the Cournot case. By moving first, Saudi Arabia gets the jump on Iran, leaving Iran no choice but to drop its output level from 20 to 15 million bpd.

Therefore, total production is 45 million bpd in the Stackelberg case. This is more than the output produced in the Cournot oligopoly (40 million). And, because production is higher, the market price must be lower under sequential production decisions than under Cournot's simultaneous-decision framework. Specifically, the price is $200 - 3(30 + 15) = \$65$ per barrel (instead of the Cournot equilibrium price of $80).

What happens to profit? For Saudi Arabia, profit is $30 \times (65 - 20) = \$1,350$ million/day. This is $150 million more than its $1,200 million/day profit in the (simultaneous-move) Cournot oligopoly. Such an outcome shows us the advantage of being the first-mover. Iran, on the other hand, makes a profit of only $15 \times (65 - 20) = \$675$ million per day, well below its Cournot profit level of $1,200 million per day. In the next chapter on game theory, we discuss the role of first-mover advantage in strategic decision making in more detail. For now, we can already see why firms might want to come into a market early, and try to make their production decisions before other firms have a chance.

Although it's somewhat abstract and mathematical, the idea of Stackelberg competition in which one firm moves first and obtains an advantage that leads later firms to adjust their strategy and reduce their output is very true to life. The market for touch-screen smartphones like the iPhone is a good example of this sort of competition. Apple released the iPhone before any other firm had a smartphone to market. Apple signed up a large number of customers before the competitors' phones were released and those competitors then had to choose their production plans with the full knowledge that Apple's quantity was already high.

11.3 figure it out

Consider again the case of the two oil change producers OilPro and GreaseTech from Figure It Out 11.2. Recall that the market inverse demand for the oil changes is $P = 100 - 2Q$, where Q is the total number of oil changes (in thousands per year) produced by the two firms, $q_O + q_G$. OilPro has a marginal cost of \$12 per oil change, while GreaseTech has a marginal cost of \$20.

a. Suppose this market is a Stackelberg oligopoly and OilPro is the first mover. How much does each firm produce? What will the market price of an oil change be? How much profit does each firm earn?

b. Now suppose that GreaseTech is the first-mover in this Stackelberg oligopoly. How much will each firm produce and what will the market price be? How much profit does each firm earn?

Solution:

a. We need to start by reconsidering the demand for OilPro's product. It is going to move first and we assume that it knows from previous experience that GreaseTech's output is a function of OilPro's output. Thus, we need to substitute GreaseTech's reaction curve, from the figure in the prior Figure It Out 11.2, into the market inverse demand curve to solve for the inverse demand for OilPro.

GreaseTech's reaction curve is $q_G = 20 - 0.5q_O$. Substituting this into the inverse market demand curve, we get

$$P = 100 - 2Q = 100 - 2(q_O + q_G) = 100 - 2q_O - 2q_G$$
$$= 100 - 2q_O - 2(20 - 0.5q_O) = 100 - 2q_O - 40 + q_O = 60 - q_O$$

So, the inverse demand curve for OilPro oil changes is $P = 60 - q_O$. This means that the marginal revenue curve for OilPro is

$$MR_O = 60 - 2q_O$$

Setting $MR = MC$ will provide us with OilPro's profit-maximizing output:

$$MR_O = 60 - 2q_O = 12$$
$$2q_O = 48$$
$$q_O = 24$$

Now that we know q_O, we can substitute it into GreaseTech's reaction curve to find q_G:

$$q_G = 20 - 0.5q_O = 20 - 0.5(24) = 20 - 12 = 8$$

OilPro will produce 24,000 oil changes, while GreaseTech will only produce 8,000. Using the inverse market demand, we can determine the market price:

$$P = 100 - 2(q_O + q_G) = 100 - 2(32) = 100 - 64 = \$36$$

OilPro's profit will be $\pi_O = (\$36 - \$12) \times 24,000 = \$576,000$. GreaseTech's profit will be $\pi_G = (\$36 - \$20) \times 8,000 = \$128,000$.

b. If GreaseTech is the first-mover, we can use OilPro's reaction curve (from the figure in the prior Figure It Out 11.2) to find the inverse market demand for GreaseTech.

OilPro's reaction curve is $q_O = 22 - 0.5q_G$. Substituting into the market inverse demand, we get

$$P = 100 - 2q_O - 2q_G = 100 - 2(22 - 0.5q_G) - 2q_G = 100 - 44 + q_G - 2q_G$$
$$= 56 - q_G$$

This is the inverse demand for GreaseTech's oil changes. Its marginal revenue is therefore

$$MR_G = 56 - 2q_G.$$

Setting $MR = MC$, we can see that

$$MR_G = 56 - 2q_G = 20$$
$$2q_G = 36$$
$$q_G = 18$$

To find OilPro's output, we substitute q_G into OilPro's reaction curve:

$$q_O = 22 - 0.5q_G = 22 - 0.5(18) = 22 - 9 = 13$$

So, when GreaseTech is the first-mover, OilPro only produces 13,000 oil changes, while GreaseTech produces 18,000. We can determine the price using the inverse market demand:

$$P = 100 - 2(Q_O + Q_G) = 100 - 2(31) = \$38$$

GreaseTech's profit will be $\pi_G = (\$38 - \$20) \times 18{,}000 = \$324{,}000$. OilPro's profit will be $\pi_O = (\$38 - \$12) \times 13{,}000 = \$182{,}000$.

11.6 Oligopoly with Differentiated Goods: Bertrand Competition

Model Assumptions Bertrand Competition with Differentiated Goods

- Firms do *not* sell identical products. They sell differentiated products, meaning consumers do not view them as perfect substitutes.
- Each firm chooses the prices at which it sells its product.
- Firms set prices simultaneously.

Every model of imperfect competition that we've looked at so far—collusion, Bertrand, Cournot, and Stackelberg—has assumed that the industry's producers all sell the same product. Often, however, a more realistic description of an industry is a set of firms that make similar but not identical products. When consumers buy a car, breakfast cereal, pest-control services, or one of many other products, they must choose between competing versions of the product, each with its own unique features, produced by a small number of companies. A market in which multiple varieties of a common product type are available is called a **differentiated product market.**

How can we analyze a "market" when the products aren't the same? Shouldn't each product be considered to exist in its own separate market? Not always—it is often

differentiated product market
Market with multiple varieties of a common product.

possible to treat the products as interacting in a single market. The key is to explicitly account for the way consumers are willing to substitute among the products.

To see how a Bertrand oligopoly works with differentiated products, think back to the Bertrand model we studied in Section 11.3. There, two companies (Walmart and Target in our example) competed by setting prices for an identical product (the Sony PlayStation). Now, however, instead of thinking of the firms' products as identical as we did in Section 11.3, we assume that consumers view the products as being somewhat distinct. Maybe this is because, even though a PlayStation console is the same regardless of where customers buy it, the stores have different locations and customers care about travel costs. Or, perhaps the stores have different atmospheres or return policies or credit card programs that matter to certain customers. The specific source of the product distinction isn't important. Regardless of its source, this differentiation helps the stores exert more market power and earn more profit. When products were identical, the incentive to undercut price was so intense that firms competed the market price right down to marginal cost and earned zero economic profit as a result. That is not the outcome in the differentiated-product Bertrand model, as we see in the following example.

Equilibrium in a Differentiated-Products Bertrand Market

Suppose there are two main manufacturers of snowboards, Burton and K2. Because many snowboarders view the two companies' products as similar but not identical, if either firm cuts its prices, it will gain market share from the other. But because the firms' products aren't *perfect* substitutes, the price-cutting company won't take all of the business away from the other company just because it sets its price a bit lower. Some people are still going to prefer the competitor's product, even at a higher price.

This product differentiation means that each firm faces its own demand curve, and each product's price has a different effect on each firm's demand curve. So, Burton's demand curve might be

$$q_B = 900 - 2p_B + p_K$$

As you can see, the quantity of boards Burton sells goes down when it raises the price it charges for its own boards, p_B. On the other hand, Burton's quantity demanded goes up when K2 raises its price, p_K. In this example, we've assumed that Burton's demand is more sensitive to changes in its own price than to changes in K2's price. (For every one dollar change in p_B, there is a two-unit change in quantity demanded; this ratio is 1 to 1 for changes in p_K.) This is a realistic assumption in many markets.

K2 has a demand curve that looks similar, but with the roles of the two firms' prices reversed:

$$q_K = 900 - 2p_K + p_B$$

The responses of each company's quantity demanded to price changes reflect consumers' willingness to substitute across varieties of the indus-

There is profit to be made from consumers' perceived differences between the Burton snowboard on the left and the K2 snowboard on the right.

try's product. But this substitution is of limited magnitude; a firm can't take over the entire market with a 1 cent price cut, as it can in the identical-products Bertrand model.

To determine the equilibrium in a Bertrand oligopoly model with differentiated products, we follow the same steps we used for all the other models. We assume each company sets its price to maximize its profit, taking the prices of its competitors as given. That is, we look for a Nash equilibrium. To make things simple, we assume that both firms have a marginal cost of zero.[9]

Burton's total revenue is

$$TR_B = p_B \times q_B = p_B \times (900 - 2p_B + p_K)$$

Notice that we've written total revenue in terms of Burton's price, rather than its quantity. This is because in a Bertrand oligopoly, Burton chooses the price it will charge rather than how much it will produce. Writing total revenue in price terms lets us derive the marginal revenue curve in price terms as well. Namely, marginal revenue is

$$MR_B = 900 - 4p_B + p_K$$

We can solve for Burton's profit-maximizing price through the usual step of setting this marginal revenue equal to the marginal cost, zero in this case. Doing so and rearranging give

$$MR_B = 900 - 4p_B + p_K = 0$$

$$4p_B = 900 + p_K$$

$$p_B = 225 + 0.25p_K$$

Notice how this again gives a firm's (Burton's) optimal action as a function of the other firm's action (K2's). In other words, this equation describes Burton's reaction curve. But here, the actions are price choices rather than quantity choices as in the Cournot model.

K2 has a reaction curve, too. It looks similar, but is a little different than Burton's because K2's demand curve is a little different. Going through the same steps as above, we have

$$MR_K = 900 - 4p_K + p_B = 0$$

$$4p_K = 900 + p_B$$

$$p_K = 225 + 0.25p_B$$

An interesting detail to note about these reaction curves in the Bertrand differentiated-product model is that a firm's optimal price *increases* when its competitor's price increases. If Burton thinks K2 will charge a higher price, for example, Burton wants to raise its price. That is, the reaction curves are upward-sloping. This is the opposite of the quantity reaction curves in the Cournot model (review Figure 11.4). There, a firm's optimal response to a competitor's output change is to do the opposite: If a firm expects its competitor to produce more, then it should produce less.

---

[9] We assume zero marginal cost in this example because the concept of marginal cost is a little different when firms choose prices rather than quantities. Remember that marginal cost is the change in total cost driven by changing output by one unit: $MC = \Delta TC/\Delta q$. As in all other market structures, a firm in a differentiated-product Bertrand oligopoly maximizes profit by setting its marginal revenue equal to its marginal cost. But the expression for marginal revenue in a Bertrand setup is the change in revenue resulting from small *price* changes, or $MR = \Delta TR/\Delta P$, rather than from small *quantity* changes, or $MR = \Delta TR/\Delta q$. Therefore, the profit-maximizing price in a differentiated-product Bertrand oligopoly sets this price-based marginal revenue equal to a price-based marginal cost: $\Delta TR/\Delta P = \Delta TC/\Delta P$. We could go through some extra algebra to tie the two together—there is an equilibrium with nonzero marginal costs in the example—but it's easier for our purposes here to just assume marginal costs are zero.

Differentiated Bertrand Equilibrium: A Graphical Approach   Figure 11.5 plots Burton and K2's reaction curves. The vertical axis shows Burton's optimal profit-maximizing price; the horizontal axis represents K2's optimal profit-maximizing price. The positive slope of Burton's reaction curve indicates that Burton's profit-maximizing price rises when K2 charges more. The positive slope of K2's reaction curve indicates that K2's profit-maximizing price rises when Burton charges more. If Burton expects K2 to charge $100, then Burton should price its boards at $250 (point A). If instead Burton believes K2 will price at $200, then it should price at $275 (point B). A K2 price of $400 will make Burton's optimal response $325 (point C), and so on. K2's reaction curve works the same way.

The point where the two reaction curves cross, E, is the Nash equilibrium. There, both firms are doing as well as they can given the other's actions. If either were to decide on its own to change its price, that firm's profit would decline.

Differentiated Bertrand Equilibrium: A Mathematical Approach   We can algebraically solve for this Nash equilibrium as we did in the Cournot model—by finding the point at which the reaction curve equations equal one another. Mechanically, that means we substitute one reaction curve into the other, solve for one firm's optimal price, and then use that price to solve for the other firm's optimal price.

First, we plug K2's reaction curve into Burton's and solve for Burton's equilibrium price:

$$p_B = 225 + 0.25p_K$$

$$p_B = 225 + 0.25 \times (225 + 0.25p_B)$$

$$p_B = 225 + 56.25 + 0.0625p_B$$

$$0.9375p_B = 281.25$$

$$p_B = 300$$

Substituting this price into K2's reaction curve gives its equilibrium price:

$$p_K = 225 + 0.25p_B = 225 + (0.25 \times 300) = 225 + 75 = 300$$

At equilibrium both firms charge the same price, $300. This isn't too surprising. After all, the two firms face similar-looking demand curves and have the same (zero) marginal costs. Interestingly, *that* particular implication of the identical-products Bertrand oligopoly that we looked at in Section 11.3 (that both firms charge the same price in equilibrium) holds here. The difference is that the price no longer equals

---

Figure 11.5   ┆   Nash Equilibrium in a Bertrand Market

This shows Burton and K2's reaction curves. At point E, when each sells 600 snowboards at a market price of $300 per snowboard, the market is at a Nash equilibrium, and the two companies are producing optimally.

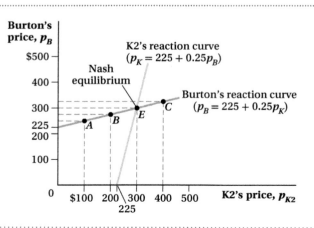

marginal cost. Instead, equilibrium prices are above marginal cost ($300 is certainly more than zero!).

To figure out the quantity each firm sells, we plug each firm's price into its demand curve equation. Burton's quantity demanded is $q_B = 900 - 2(300) + 300 = 600$ boards. K2 sells $q_K = 900 - 2(300) + 300 = 600$ boards also. Again, the fact that both firms sell the same quantity is not surprising because they have similar demand curves and charge the same price. Total industry production is therefore 1,200 boards, which is two-thirds of what it would be if both firms charged their marginal costs (each firm in that case would make 900 boards, meaning total production of 1,800 boards). In the Bertrand model where the firms produce differentiated products, each firm earns a profit of $600 \times (300 - 0) = \$180,000$.

11.4 figure it out

Consider our example of the two snowboard manufacturers, Burton and K2. We just determined that at the Nash equilibrium for these two firms, each firm produced 600 snowboards at a price of $300 per board. Now let's suppose that Burton launches a successful advertising campaign to convince snowboarders that its product is superior to K2's so that the demand for Burton snowboards rises to $q_B = 1,000 - 1.5p_B + 1.5p_K$, while the demand for K2 boards falls to $q_K = 800 - 2p_K + 0.5p_B$. (For simplicity, assume that the marginal cost is still zero for both firms.)

a. Derive each firm's reaction curve.

b. What happens to each firm's optimal price?

c. What happens to each firm's optimal output?

d. Draw the reaction curves in a diagram and indicate the equilibrium.

Solution:

a. To determine the firms' reaction curves, we first need to solve for each firm's marginal revenue curve:

$$MR_B = 1,000 - 3p_B + 1.5p_K$$
$$MR_K = 800 - 4p_K + 0.5p_B$$

By setting each firm's marginal cost equal to marginal revenue, we can find the firm's reaction curve:

$$MR_B = 1,000 - 3p_B + 1.5p_K = 0$$
$$3p_B = 1,000 + 1.5p_K$$
$$p_B = 333.33 + 0.5p_K$$
$$MR_K = 800 - 4p_K + 0.5p_B = 0$$
$$4p_K = 800 + 0.5p_B$$
$$p_K = 200 + 0.125p_B$$

b. We can solve for the equilibrium by substituting one firm's reaction curve into the other's:

$$p_B = 333.33 + 0.5p_K$$
$$p_B = 333.33 + 0.5(200 + 0.125p_B) = 333.33 + 100 + 0.0625p_B$$
$$p_B = 433.33 + 0.0625p_B$$
$$0.9375p_B = 433.33$$
$$p_B = \$462.22$$

We can then substitute p_B back into the reaction function for K2 to get the K2 price:

$$p_K = 200 + 0.125p_B$$
$$= 200 + 0.125(462.22) = 200 + 57.78 = \$257.78$$

So, the successful advertising campaign means that Burton can increase its price from the initial equilibrium price of \$300 (which we determined in our initial analysis of this market) to \$462.22, while K2 will have to lower its own price from \$300 to \$257.78.

c. To find each firm's optimal output, we need to substitute the firms' prices into the inverse demand curves for each firm's product. For Burton,

$$q_B = 1{,}000 - 1.5p_B + 1.5p_K = 1{,}000 - 1.5(462.22) + 1.5(257.78)$$
$$= 1{,}000 - 693.33 + 386.67 = 693.34$$

For K2,

$$q_K = 800 - 2p_K + 0.5p_B = 800 - 2(257.78) + 0.5(462.22) = 800 - 515.56 + 231.11 = 515.55$$

Burton now produces more snowboards (693.34 instead of 600), while K2 produces fewer (515.55 instead of 600).

d. The reaction curves are shown in the diagram below:

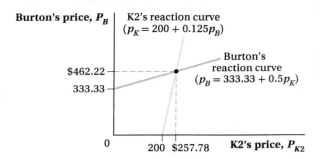

---

theory and data

Computer Parts II—Differentiation Out of Desperation

The computer chip retailers in the Ellison and Ellison study discussed in the Theory and Data application in Section 11.3 operated in what was essentially a Bertrand market with identical goods. As a result, they charged prices equal to their marginal costs. At prices that low, they were making little profit and struggling to cover their fixed costs.

This intense competition made such firms desperate to move away from the strictures of this kind of market. Ellison and Ellison documented how some computer parts retailers used a little economic know-how to get away with setting their prices above marginal cost. Those firms realized that the key to getting more producer surplus was to differentiate their products, thus shifting the structure of competition from a Bertrand oligopoly with identical products to one with differentiated products.

Just how could these firms differentiate what were otherwise identical computer chips? They couldn't do this the way K2 and Burton can with the snowboards they sell, by varying designs, materials, and so on. So they turned to slightly more, well, creative methods — methods that Ellison and Ellison categorized as "obfuscation."

Ellison and Ellison found that online firms rely on two primary means of obfuscation. In the first, the firm lists a cheap but inferior product that the price search engine displays at the beginning of its listings. Customers click on this product and are redirected to the firm's website, where the company then offers a more expensive product upgrade. Once one firm undercuts its competitors with this "loss leader" strategy, all firms will list similarly cheap products or risk having their product listing buried deep in the last pages of the listings. As a result, it becomes more time-consuming for the customer to compare the prices of the product "upgrades," and the firm can charge a price higher than marginal cost without the risk of being priced out.

Another common strategy is the use of product add-ons. As with the first method, firms list artificially cheap products that bait consumers into visiting the firm website. This time, instead of upgraded products, customers are offered product add-ons, such as additional screws to fasten the chip to the circuit board or a snazzy mouse pad. Often, these products are added on automatically; that is, to purchase only the original product, the consumer has to unselect a number of additional products. Although the product the consumer initially selected may be selling at or even below marginal cost, the add-ons often sell at inflated prices—the mouse pad one online firm offered Ellison and Ellison cost nearly $12. This practice allows the firm to sell the entire bundle of products at a price above marginal cost.

Obfuscation methods such as these are part of the reason the Bertrand model with identical products that we first studied is so unusual in the real world. Even products that aren't obviously differentiable can be made to stand out through some clever strategies by the firms. Given that firms selling such products would otherwise expect to earn something close to nothing, they have a massive incentive to figure out differentiation strategies, and thus try to reduce competition.

11.7 Monopolistic Competition

Model Assumptions Monopolistic Competition

- Industry firms sell differentiated products that consumers do not view as perfect substitutes.
- Other firms' choices affect a firm's residual demand curve, but the firm ignores any strategic interactions between its own quantity or price choice and its competitors'.
- There is free entry into the market.

In the models we've studied so far, we haven't considered the possibility that other firms might want to enter markets in which firms are earning positive economic profits. Presumably, there are other firms that would like a piece of that action. If there are no barriers to entering a market such as the snowboard market, an additional firm will cause Burton and K2's profits to decline. We saw in the Cournot model that adding more firms to the industry drove the equilibrium closer to perfect competition. In this section, we look at our last model of imperfect competition, and see what happens when there is entry into a market with differentiated products. **Monopolistic competition** is a market structure characterized by many firms selling a differentiated product with no barriers to entry. This term might sound like an oxymoron—competitive monopoly?—and in a way it is, but the term reflects the basic tension between market power and competitive forces that exists in these types of markets.

Every firm in a monopolistically competitive industry faces a downward-sloping demand curve, so it has some market power and every firm follows the monopoly pricing rule. That's where the "monopolistic" comes from. What is *competitive* about such

monopolistic competition
A market structure characterized by many firms selling a differentiated product with no barriers to entry.

markets is that there are no restrictions on entry as exist in monopoly markets—any number of firms can come into the industry at any time. This means that the firms in a monopolistically competitive industry, despite having market power, earn zero economic profit. (If they were making a profit, more firms would enter to acquire some of this profit. Entry only stops when profit is driven to zero for every firm in the market.)

Many markets are monopolistically competitive. For example, there are hundreds of fast-food restaurants in Chicago and probably a similar number in every other major city in the United States. There are some differences between them, but basically people view such restaurants as largely interchangeable. Because travel is costly, though, each restaurant has a bit of market power in its local neighborhood. So, a restaurant does have some ability to set its own prices. At the same time, however, there's little to stop a new restaurant from opening. If people in a neighborhood become more enthralled with eating out, an existing restaurant might be able to raise its prices and earn economic profit for a brief period, but if the demand increase is expected to be anything more than temporary, we would likely see a new restaurant (or restaurants) opening up to grab some of that profit.

Keep in mind that, while monopolistic competition is categorized as "imperfect competition" along with oligopoly, there are differences between these two market structures. One is that oligopoly markets have barriers to entry, while monopolistically competitive markets do not. However, the key distinction between oligopoly and monopolistic competition is the assumption about strategic interaction. In an oligopoly, firms know that their production decisions affect their competitors' optimal choices, and all oligopolistic firms take this feedback effect into account when making their decisions. On the other hand, in monopolistic competition firms do not worry about the production decisions of their competitors because the impact of any competitor on another is assumed to be too small for these firms to worry about.

Equilibrium in Monopolistically Competitive Markets

To analyze monopolistically competitive markets, let's look at a single company with market power—say for a moment that, for some reason, a city has only one fast-food burger restaurant. In this city, this restaurant has a monopoly on fast-food burgers. The firm faces a downward-sloping demand curve for meals served per day, as in Figure 11.6. We'll label this demand D_{ONE} (for one firm). The figure also shows the

---

Figure 11.6   Demand and Cost Curves for a Monopoly

A monopolist restaurant has demand D_{ONE}, marginal revenue MR_{ONE}, average total cost ATC, and marginal cost MC. The restaurant produces where marginal revenue equals marginal cost, at quantity Q^*_{ONE}. The restaurant's profit, represented by the shaded rectangle, is the difference between the firm's price P^*_{ONE} and average total cost ATC^* multiplied by Q^*_{ONE}.

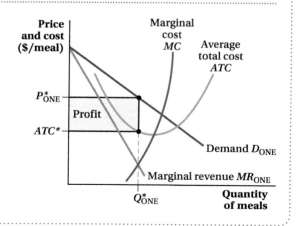

marginal revenue curve that corresponds to this demand and the firm's average total and marginal cost curves.

Because the restaurant in Figure 11.6 is a monopolist, it produces where its marginal revenue equals marginal cost, Q^*_{ONE}. The price it charges is P^*_{ONE}. In addition to the marginal cost of production, however, the restaurant has to pay fixed cost equal to F (this fixed cost is the reason why the firm's average total cost curve is U-shaped). The monopolist restaurant's profit is shown by the shaded rectangle: the difference between the price and the average total cost at the quantity produced, multiplied by that quantity. Because average total cost includes both variable and fixed costs, the average total cost at Q^*_{ONE}—that is, ATC^*—fully reflects all of the firm's production costs.

So far, this market is just like a regular monopoly. But now suppose a restaurateur notices that this firm is making an economic profit and decides to open a second, slightly different fast-food restaurant in the city. The new restaurant may differ in location, type of food served, anything that differentiates it from the existing restaurant.

The key to understanding what happens in monopolistically competitive markets is to recognize what happens to the demand curve(s) of the market's existing firm(s) when another firm enters. We know that when there are more substitutes for a good available, the demand curve for the initial good becomes more elastic (less steep). Having another restaurant open up means that more substitution possibilities now exist for consumers. Instead of there being one firm with a demand curve, as in Figure 11.6, the entry of a second firm means that each restaurant now has a demand curve that is a bit flatter than the monopolist firm's demand curve. And, because the demand is being split across two firms, not only is the monopolist firm's demand curve flatter, but it has shifted in as well. Figure 11.7 shows this change from one to two firms, as the initial (monopolist) firm's demand curve (now it is a residual demand curve) shifts from D_{ONE} to D_{TWO}. Notice how D_{TWO} is both flatter than and to the left of D_{ONE}. The marginal revenue curves also shift accordingly. (The figure illustrates only what's going on for one of the two firms in the market; the picture is exactly the same for the other firm.)

Even after entry, however, both firms are essentially monopolists over their own residual demand curves. Each individual firm's demand curve reflects the fact that (1) it is splitting the market with another firm and (2) the presence of a substitute product makes the firm's demand more elastic. The competitor's presence *is* accounted

---

Figure 11.7   **The Effect of Firm Entry on Demand for a Monopolistically Competitive Firm**

When a second restaurant enters the market, the original restaurant's demand curve shifts left from D_{ONE} to the more elastic residual demand curve D_{TWO}, and the marginal revenue curve MR_{ONE} shifts to MR_{TWO}. The restaurant now sells quantity Q^*_{TWO} at price P^*_{TWO} and earns profit represented by the shaded rectangle.

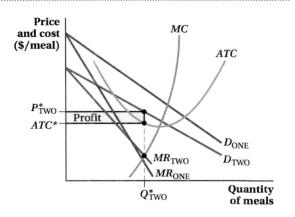

for, but it is incorporated in the firm's residual demand curve. In monopolistic competition, the firm takes this residual demand as given. This is different from the oligopoly models we covered, in which firms realize that their actions affect the desired actions of their competitors, which in turn affect their own optimal action, and so on. This strategic interaction is captured in firms' reaction curves. A monopolistically competitive firm, on the other hand, acts like it is in its own little monopoly world, even though its competitors' actions affect the residual demand it faces. This assumption about monopolistically competitive firms' ignorance of strategic interactions is more likely to hold in industries where there are a large number of firms selling related but differentiated products.

Assuming the two firms have identical residual demand curves, both produce the quantity Q^*_{TWO} at which marginal revenue equals marginal cost and charge the profit-maximizing price P^*_{TWO} at that quantity. Each firm earns the profit given by the shaded rectangle in the figure.

Because two firms in the market make positive economic profit, we should expect still more firms to enter. Each new firm that enters will further shift any individual company's demand curve to the left and make it more elastic (flatter).

Entry will cease only when industry firms are no longer making any economic profit. When that point is reached, the market will be described by Figure 11.8. When there are N firms in the market, each firm's residual demand curve eventually shifts back to D_N. Faced with this demand curve, the firm produces the quantity Q^*_N at which marginal revenue equals marginal cost and charges a price of P^*_N and earns zero economic profit.

Why does economic profit equal zero at this point? Look at where the firm's average total cost curve is relative to its demand curve. The two curves are tangent at Q^*_N and P^*_N. If price equals average total cost, profit is zero. The firm is just covering its costs of operation (variable and fixed) at this point.

Here's an important point about monopolistically competitive markets: Even though entry occurs until profits are zero, the entry process does not ultimately lead to a perfectly competitive outcome in which price equals marginal cost. Firms in a monopolistically competitive market face a downward-sloping demand curve, so marginal revenue is always less than price. At the profit-maximizing output, marginal cost will equal marginal revenue, which means that marginal cost will also be less than price. Free entry ensures that this markup over marginal cost is just enough to cover the firm's fixed cost, and no more.

Figure 11.8   Long-Run Equilibrium for a Monopolistically Competitive Market

In a monopolistically competitive market with N firms, firms face long-run demand D_N, marginal revenue MR_N, marginal costs MC, and average total cost ATC. At the long-run equilibrium, the firm's quantity is Q^*_N, price P^*_N is equal to average cost ATC^*, and each firm earns zero economic profit.

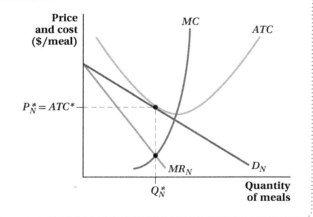

Sticky Stuff produces cases of taffy in a monopolistically competitive market. The inverse demand curve for its product is $P = 50 - Q$, where Q is in thousands of cases per year and P is dollars per case.

Sticky Stuff can produce each case of taffy at a constant marginal cost of \$10 per case and has no fixed cost. Its total cost curve is therefore $TC = 10Q$.

a. To maximize profit, how many cases of taffy should Sticky Stuff produce each month?

b. What price will Sticky Stuff charge for a case of taffy?

c. How much profit will Sticky Stuff earn each year?

d. In reality, firms in monopolistic competition generally face fixed costs in the short run. Given the information above, what would Sticky Stuff's fixed costs have to be in order for this industry to be in long-run equilibrium? Explain.

Solution:

a. Sticky Stuff maximizes its profit by producing where $MR = MC$. Since the demand curve is linear, we know from Chapter 9 that the MR curve will be linear with twice the slope. Therefore, $MR = 50 - 2Q$. Setting $MR = MC$, we get

$$50 - 2Q = 10$$
$$Q = 20$$

Sticky Stuff should produce 20,000 cases of taffy each year.

b. We can find the price Sticky Stuff will charge by substituting the quantity into the demand curve:

$$P = 50 - Q = 50 - 20 = \$30 \text{ per case}$$

c. Total revenue for Sticky Stuff will be $TR = P \times Q = \$30 \times 20,000 = \$600,000$. Total cost will be $TC = 10Q = (10 \times 20,000) = \$200,000$. Therefore, Sticky Stuff will earn an annual profit of $\pi = TR - TC = \$600,000 - \$200,000 = \$400,000$.

d. Long-run equilibrium occurs when firms have no incentive to enter or exit. Therefore, firms must be earning zero economic profit. From (c), we know that Sticky Stuff is earning a profit of \$400,000. In order for its profit to fall to zero, Sticky Stuff must face annual fixed cost equal to \$400,000.

11.8 Conclusion

In this chapter, we've looked at multiple models of imperfect competition—that middle ground between perfect competition (which we studied in Chapter 8) and monopoly (which we studied in Chapter 9). We started with the reminder that the number of firms in a market is only one of many factors that can determine market prices, quantities, and producer profits. So, it's no surprise that there are different models of imperfect competition, each of which has different predictions about market outcomes. Which model is the most applicable to any market situation requires some judgment on the part of the economist. Are the products essentially identical, or slightly or completely differentiated? Are the firms setting prices or quantities? Are firms making their choices simultaneously or in sequence? Are there barriers to entry or is entry into the market free? These and other questions need to be considered when choosing the imperfect competition model most applicable to the industry being analyzed. In the next chapter, we examine how individuals and firms may act strategically to achieve a greater outcome (such as increased utility or higher profits).

Summary

1. In oligopolistic markets, each firm makes production decisions conditional on its competitors' actions. The resulting market equilibrium is known as a **Nash equilibrium,** one of the cornerstones of economic game theory. A Nash equilibrium occurs when each firm is doing its best given the actions of other firms. [**Section 11.1**]

2. Oligopolistic firms may be able to form cartels, in which all participating firms coordinate their production decisions and act collectively as a monopoly. The resulting market quantity and price are equal to those from a monopoly, and industry profit is maximized. While collusive behavior allows firms to capture monopoly profits, **collusion** and **cartels** are rarely stable because every firm has the incentive to increase its own profit by producing more (pricing lower). [**Section 11.2**]

3. In **Bertrand competition,** products are identical and firms compete on price. Each firm simultaneously sets the price of its good, and consumers then choose to purchase all of the quantity demanded from whichever firm has the lowest price, even if the price is only one penny lower. The Bertrand model shows that only two firms need to be in a market to achieve the perfectly competitive market outcome where price equals marginal cost. This result arises because firms in these situations have such a strong incentive to try to undercut the prices of their rivals. Market output is equal to the competitive level of output and firm profits are zero. [**Section 11.3**]

4. In contrast to firms in Bertrand competition, firms in **Cournot competition** simultaneously choose the quantity of a good to produce, and not the price at which the good sells. The Cournot equilibrium price is generally above the price in Bertrand competition, but below the monopoly price. The Cournot output is less than the Bertrand level of output, but greater than the output generated by a cartel. Firms in a Cournot oligopoly earn greater profits than those in the Bertrand model, but less than the monopoly profit. [**Section 11.4**]

5. In **Stackelberg competition,** firms make production decisions sequentially. Because the first firm in an industry can make production decisions independently of other firms and may be able to capture larger profits, a **first-mover advantage** exists for these firms. [**Section 11.5**]

6. In the Bertrand model with differentiated products, consumers in these markets are willing to substitute across goods, but do not consider them identical, or perfect substitutes. As a result, small differences in prices do not lead to all demand being satisfied by the producer with the lowest price (as in the Bertrand oligopoly with identical products). [**Section 11.6**]

7. **Monopolistic competition** is a market structure in which firms sell differentiated products, and firms have some characteristics of both monopolies and perfectly competitive firms. Because there are no barriers to entry in a monopolistically competitive market, economic profit is driven to zero through the entry of firms. [**Section 11.7**]

Review Questions

1. Name some different forms of imperfect competition.
2. Define Nash equilibrium. Why do firms in oligopoly situations reach Nash equilibria?
3. Why are collusions and cartels often unstable?
4. What is the market equilibrium in Bertrand competition with identical goods?
5. Contrast Bertrand and Cournot competition. Why do they reach different market equilibria?
6. What does the residual demand curve tell us about a firm's output in Cournot competition?
7. How can reaction curves be used to find a firm's equilibrium in Cournot competition?
8. What causes the first-mover advantage in Stackelberg competition?
9. Contrast the market equilibria in Betrand competition with identical products and with differentiated products.
10. What are the characteristics of a monopolistically competitive firm?
11. When will firms enter a monopolistically competitive industry? At what point will firms stop entering a monopolistically competitive industry?
12. Why do firms in monopolistic competition not reach the perfectly competitive equilibrium?

Problems

1. Because cooking soufflés is incredibly difficult, the supply of soufflés in a small French town is controlled by two bakers, Gaston and Pierre. The demand for soufflés is given by $P = 30 - 2Q$, and the marginal and average total cost of producing soufflés is $6. Because baking a soufflé requires a great deal of work and preparation, each morning Gaston and Pierre make a binding decision about how many soufflés to bake.
   a. Suppose that Pierre and Gaston agree to collude, evenly splitting the output a monopolist would make and charging the monopoly price.
      i. Derive the equation for the monopolist's marginal revenue curve.
      ii. Determine the profit-maximizing collective output for the cartel.
      iii. Determine the price Pierre and Gaston will be able to charge.
      iv. Determine profits for Pierre and Gaston individually, as well as for the cartel as a whole.
   b. Suppose that Pierre cheats on the cartel agreement by baking one extra soufflé each morning.
      i. What does the extra production do to the price of soufflés in the marketplace?
      ii. Calculate Pierre's profit. How much did he gain by cheating?
      iii. Calculate Gaston's profit. How much did Pierre's cheating cost him?
      iv. How much potential profit does the group lose as a result of Pierre's cheating?
   c. Suppose that Gaston, fed-up with Pierre's behavior, also begins baking one extra soufflé each morning.
      i. How does the extra production affect the price of soufflés in the marketplace?
      ii. Calculate Gaston's profit. How much did he gain by cheating?
      iii. Calculate Pierre's profit. How much did Gaston's cheating cost him?
      iv. How much potential profit does the group lose as a result of Pierre's and Gaston's cheating?
      v. Demonstrate that it is in neither Pierre's nor Gaston's best interest to cheat further on their agreement.

2. Suppose in the previous problem that Gaston can produce soufflés at a constant marginal cost of $5, but Pierre produces soufflés for $7. Together, they collude to produce three units each.
   a. How much profit will each producer earn? What will be the total profit of the cartel?
   b. Gaston observes that he is a more efficient producer than Pierre, and suggests that if they are going to produce six units, the cartel's interests are better served if Gaston produces all of the soufflés.
      i. If Gaston produces and sells all of the soufflés and Pierre produces nothing, what happens to the profit of the cartel?
      ii. Is Pierre likely to agree not to produce any soufflés?
      iii. Suppose Gaston offers to pay Pierre not to produce any soufflés. How much would Gaston potentially be willing to offer? What is the minimum offer that Pierre should accept?
      iv. Suppose that the deal in part (iii) is reached for Pierre's minimum price. What happens to Pierre's profit if he cheats on his agreement with Gaston and increases his output from zero soufflés to one? What happens to Gaston's profit?
      v. Compare Pierre's incentive to cheat under this arrangement with the incentive that exists when they split production equally. Also compare Gaston's vulnerability to Pierre's cheating under both arrangements. Why might this cartel choose to use the less-profitable method of each member producing three units to the potentially more-profitable method of having Gaston produce everything?

3. Suppose that the inverse market demand for pumpkins is given by $P = \$10 - 0.05Q$. Pumpkins can be grown by anybody at a constant marginal cost of $1.
   a. If there are lots of pumpkin growers in town so that the pumpkin industry is competitive, how many pumpkins will be sold, and what price will they sell for?
   b. Suppose that a freak weather event wipes out the pumpkins of all but two producers, Linus and Lucy. Both Linus and Lucy have produced bumper crops, and have more than enough pumpkins available to satisfy the demand at even a zero price. If Linus and Lucy collude to generate monopoly profits, how many pumpkins will they sell, and what price will they sell for?
   c. Suppose that the predominant form of competition in the pumpkin industry is price competition. In other words, suppose that Linus and Lucy are Bertrand competitors.

What will be the final price of pumpkins in this market—in other words, what is the Bertrand equilibrium price?

d. At the Bertrand equilibrium price, what will be the final quantity of pumpkins sold by both Linus and Lucy individually, and for the industry as a whole? How profitable will Linus and Lucy be?

e. Would the results you found in parts (c) and (d) be likely to hold if Linus let it be known that his pumpkins were the most orange in town, and Lucy let it be known that hers were the tastiest? Explain.

4. Suppose that three grocery stores sell Bubba's Gourmet Red Beans and Rice. Bullseye market is able to acquire, stock, and market them for $2.00 per package. OKMart can acquire, stock, and market them for $1.98 per package. SamsMart can acquire, stock, and market them for $1.96 per package.

a. If the three competitors are located in close proximity to one another, so that the cost of going to a different store to purchase red beans and rice is negligible, and if the market for prepackaged gourmet red beans and rice is characterized by Bertrand competition, what will the prevailing market price be?

b. Where will customers buy their red beans and rice? Bullseye, OKMart, or SamsMart? What does your answer suggest about the potential rewards to small improvements in efficiency via cost-cutting?

c. Suppose that each day, equal numbers of customers begin their shopping at each of the three stores. If the cost of going to a different store to purchase red beans and rice is 2 cents, is the Bertrand result likely to hold in this case? Where will customers purchase red beans and rice? Where will they not purchase them?

5. Suppose that two firms are Cournot competitors. Industry demand is given by $P = 200 - q_1 - q_2$, where q_1 is the output of Firm 1 and q_2 is the output of Firm 2. Both Firm 1 and Firm 2 face constant marginal and average total costs of $20.

a. Solve for the Cournot price, quantity, and firm profits.

b. Firm 1 is considering investing in costly technology that will enable it to reduce its costs to $15 per unit. How much should Firm 1 be willing to pay if such an investment can guarantee that Firm 2 will not be able to acquire it?

c. How does your answer to (b) change if Firm 1 knows the technology is available to Firm 2?

6. Jack and Annie are the only sellers of otters in a three-state area. The inverse market demand for otters is given by $P = 100 - 0.5Q$, where Q = the total quantity offered for sale in the marketplace. Specifically, $Q = q_J + q_A$, where q_J is the amount of otters offered for sale by Jack and q_A is the amount offered for sale by Annie. Both Jack and Annie can produce otters at a constant marginal and average total cost of $20.

a. Graph the market demand curve. What would be the prevailing price and quantity if this industry were controlled by a monopolist?

b. Suppose that Jack, an excellent mathematician (but perhaps not quite as brilliant an economist), solves part (a). Being a very egalitarian sort, Jack announces that he will bring half of the monopoly quantity to market each day.

   i. The market inverse demand for otters is given by $P = 100 - 0.05(q_J + q_A)$. Plug in Jack's announced output for q_A to solve for the residual demand curve faced by Annie.

   ii. Solve for, and graph, the residual marginal revenue curve faced by Annie.

   iii. Given Annie's otter production cost of $20, how many units should Annie bring to market to maximize her profit?

c. Given your answers to (b), what will the industry quantity and final price of otters be? How much profit will Annie earn? Jack?

d. Suppose that Jack observes Annie's output from part (b), and decides to change his own.

   i. Solve for, and graph, the residual demand curve faced by Jack.

   ii. Solve for, and graph, the residual marginal revenue curve faced by Jack.

   iii. Given Jack's otter production cost of $20, how many units should he bring to market to maximize his profit?

   iv. What will the industry quantity and final price of otters be? How much profit will Annie earn? Jack?

e. Is the outcome you found in part (d) an equilibrium outcome? How do you know?

7. The platypus is a shy and secretive animal that does not breed well in captivity. But two breeders, Sydney and Adelaide, have discovered the secret to platypus fertility and have effectively cornered the market. Zoos across the globe come to them to purchase their output; the world inverse demand for baby platypuses is given by $P = 1,000 - 2Q$, where Q is the combined output of Sydney (q_S) and Adelaide (q_A).

a. Sydney wishes to produce the profit-maximizing quantity of baby platypus. Given Adelaide's choice of output, q_A, write an equation for the residual demand faced by Sydney.

b. Derive Sydney's residual marginal revenue curve.

c. Assume that the marginal and average total cost of raising a baby platypus to an age at which it can be sold is $200. Derive Sydney's reaction function.

d. Repeat steps (a), (b), and (c) to find Adelaide's reaction function to Sydney's output choice.

e. Solve for Sydney's profit-maximizing level of output and Adelaide's profit-maximizing level of output.

f. Determine industry output, the price of platypus, and the profits of both Sydney and Adelaide.

g. If Adelaide were hit by a bus on her way home from work, and Sydney were to become a monopolist, what would happen to industry quantity, price, and profit?

8. Suppose that there are two producers of prokrypton-B, a rare mineral capable of incapacitating aliens from distant planets. Governments across the globe are interested in purchasing defensive stores of the rare mineral. The market demand for prokrypton-B is given by $P = 200 - 0.2Q$, where Q is the collective output of the industry, in tons; q_A is the output of Firm A; and q_B is the output of Firm B. Assume that each firm produces prokrypton-B at a marginal cost of $10 per ton.

a. Derive each firm's reaction function.

b. Solve for the equilibrium quantity of each firm, as well as industry output.

c. Solve for the market price of prokrypton-B.

d. Solve for the profit earned by each firm.

e. Suppose that a labor dispute drives Firm B's cost to $12 per ton.
   i. What happens to the output of each firm as a result?
   ii. What happens to the market price of prokrypton-B?
   iii. What happens to the profit of each firm?

9. Suppose that the market demand for concrete is given by the equation $P = 300 - \frac{1}{3}Q$, where Q is the total quantity, in yards, supplied by three existing firms. Assume that the three firms are identical, and that the marginal and average cost of producing a cubic yard of concrete is exactly $30.

a. Derive reaction curves for Firm 1, Firm 2, and Firm 3.

b. By repeated substitution, find the output of each firm.

c. Solve for the market price, firm profits, and industry profits.

d. How would the price, quantity, and industry profit change if one of the firms were to exit the industry?

10. Consider the demand for boccie balls shown in the diagram below. Demand is given by $P = 80 - Q$. Boccie balls can be produced at a constant marginal and average total cost of $20.

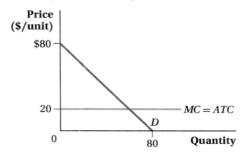

a. If the boccie ball industry were perfectly competitive, what quantity would be sold, and what price would prevail in the market?

b. Suppose that the boccie ball industry were a monopoly. Draw in a marginal revenue curve and determine the profit-maximizing quantity.
   i. Divide the monopoly (one-firm) quantity by the competitive quantity to determine the proportion of competitive output that a monopolist provides. Present your answer in reduced fractional form.
   ii. Determine the price, and draw a dot on the demand curve indicating the monopolist's price and quantity.

c. Suppose the boccie ball industry were a Cournot duopoly (two-firm), with two firms. Use the procedures developed in this chapter to determine the industry output.
   i. Divide the duopoly quantity by the competitive quantity to determine the proportion of competitive output that a duopoly provides. Present your answer in reduced fractional form.
   ii. Determine the price, and draw a dot on the demand curve indicating the duopoly's price and quantity.

d. Hypothesize as to the fraction of competitive output that would be sold if the boccie ball industry had three identical Cournot competitors. Then check your answer.

e. In general, what fraction of the competitive output level will be brought to market if there are N identical firms in the industry?

f. What happens to the quantity sold as more competitors are added to the industry? The price? What happens to consumer surplus and deadweight loss? Does this provide support for the government's desire to ensure competitive industries rather than monopolies or small oligopolies?

11. Two organic emu ranchers, Bill and Ted, serve a small metropolitan market. Bill and Ted are Cournot competitors, making a conscious decision each year regarding how many emus to breed. The price they can charge depends on how many emus they collectively raise, and demand in this market is given by $Q = 150 - P$. Bill raises emus at a constant marginal and average total cost of $10; Ted raises emus at a constant marginal and average total cost of $20.

a. Find the Cournot equilibrium price, quantity, profits, and consumer surplus.

b. Suppose that Bill and Ted merge, and become a monopoly provider of emus. Further, suppose that Ted adopts Bill's production techniques. Find the monopoly price, quantity, profits, and consumer surplus.

c. Suppose that instead of merging, Bill considers buying Ted's operation for cash. How much should Bill be willing to offer Ted to purchase his emu ranch? (Assume that the combined firms are only going to operate for one period.)

d. Has the combination of the two ranches discussed above been good for society or bad for society? Discuss how the forces of monopoly power and increased efficiency tend to push social well-being in opposite directions.

12. Suppose that in a particular market, the inverse demanded for hasenpfeffer is given by $P = 100 - Q$. The market is served by two Cournot competitors, Hansel and Gretel, whose quantities are denoted q_H and q_G, respectively. Both competitors can produce hasenpfeffer at a constant marginal and average total cost of $10.

a. Find the Cournot equilibrium output and price.

b. Suppose that demand doubles so that at each price, twice as many servings are demanded as before. Specifically, $P = 100 - 0.5Q$. What happens to the Cournot price and quantity as a result of the increase in demand?

c. Suppose that the original demand doubles, but in a different way, so that each customer is willing to pay twice as much as before to obtain hasenpfeffer. Specifically, $P = 200 - 2Q$.

What happens to the Cournot price and quantity as a result of the increase in demand?

d. Would your answers to (b) and (c) remain the same if Hansel and Gretel were Bertrand competitors rather than Cournot competitors?

13. The market for nutmeg is controlled by two small island nations, Penang and Grenada. The market demand for bottled nutmeg is given by $P = 100 - q_P - q_G$, where q_P is the quantity Penang produces and q_G is the quantity Grenada produces. Both Grenada and Penang produce nutmeg at a constant marginal and average cost of $20 per bottle.

a. Verify that the reaction function for Grenada is given by $q_G = 40 - 0.5q_P$. Then verify that the reaction function for Penang is given by $q_P = 40 - 0.5q_G$.

b. Find the Cournot equilibrium quantity for each island. Then solve for the market price of nutmeg and for each firm's profit.

c. Suppose that Grenada transforms the nature of competition to Stackelberg competition by announcing its production targets publicly in an attempt to seize a first-mover advantage.

   i. Grenada must first decide how much to produce, and to do this, it needs to know the demand conditions it faces. Substitute Penang's reaction function into the market demand curve to find the demand faced by Grenada.

   ii. Based on your answer to the problem above, find the marginal revenue curve faced by Grenada.

   iii. Equate marginal revenue with marginal cost to find Grenada's output.

   iv. Plug Grenada's output into Penang's reaction function to determine Penang's output.

   v. Plug the combined output of Grenada and Penang into the market demand curve to determine the price. How do the industry quantity and price compare to those under Cournot competition?

   vi. Determine profits in Grenada and Penang. How do the profits of each compare to profits under Cournot competition? Is there an advantage to being the first-mover?

14. Consider the islands of Penang and Grenada discussed in the previous problem. What will happen to Grenada's and Penang's output if:

a. Grenada's cost of production decreases to $16, while Penang's stays at $20. Explain.

b. Penang's cost of production decreases to $16, while Grenada's stays at $20. Explain.

15. The market for cellular service is dominated by two sellers, AT&T and Verizon. AT&T and Verizon are Bertrand competitors, but because the services offered by those two sellers are not identical, customers have some degree of preference that makes them slightly resistant to switching from one to another. The demand for AT&T services is given by $q_A = 1{,}000 - 3p_A + 2p_V$, where q_A is the number of customers in a particular service area, p_A is the price of AT&T service, and p_V is the price of Verizon service. The demand for Verizon services is given by $q_V = 1{,}000 - 3p_V + 2p_A$. Assume that both sellers can produce cellular service at zero marginal cost.

   a. Derive AT&T's reaction curve. Your answer should express p_A as a function of p_V. If Verizon raises its price by $9, how should AT&T respond to that price increase?

   b. Derive Verizon's reaction curve. Your answer should express p_V as a function of p_A.

   c. Solve for the price AT&T should charge to maximize profit.

   d. Solve for the price Verizon should charge to maximize its profit.

   e. Determine the quantity each seller will sell. Then calculate its profits, assuming that its marginal and average total costs are zero.

16. Internet users in a small Colorado town can access the Web in two ways: via their television cable or via a digital subscriber line (DSL) from their telephone company. The cable and telephone companies are Bertrand competitors, but because changing providers is slightly costly (waiting for the cable repairman can eat up at least small amounts of time!), customers have some slight resistance to switching from one to another. The demand for cable Internet services is given by $q_C = 100 - 3p_C + 2p_T$, where q_C is the number of cable Internet subscribers in town, p_C is the monthly price of cable Internet service, and p_T is the price of a DSL line from the telephone company. The demand for DSL Internet service is similarly given by $q_T = 100 - 3p_T + 2p_C$. Assume that both sellers can produce broadband service at zero marginal cost.

   a. Derive reaction functions that show the price each competitor should charge in response to the price charged by the other.

   b. Solve for each competitor's price, quantity, and profit, assuming that average total costs are zero.

   c. Suppose that the cable company begins to offer slightly faster service than the telephone company, which alters demands for the two

products. Now $q_C = 100 - 2p_C + 3p_T$ and $q_T = 100 - 4p_T + p_C$. Show what effect this increase in service has on the prices and profit of each competitor.

17. Consider two Bertrand competitors in the market for brie, François and Babette. The cheeses of François and Babette are differentiated, with the demand for François' cheese given by $q_F = 30 - p_F + p_B$, where q_F is the quantity François sells, p_F is the price François charges, and p_B is the price charged by Babette. The demand for Babette's cheese is similarly given as $q_B = 30 - p_B + p_F$.

   a. Find the Bertrand equilibrium prices and quantities for these two competitors.

   b. Now consider a situation in which François sets his price first, and Babette responds. Follow procedures similar to those you used for Stackelberg quantity competition to solve for François' profit-maximizing price, quantity, and profit.

   c. Solve for Babette's profit-maximizing price, quantity, and profit.

   d. Was François' attempt to seize the first-mover advantage worthwhile?

18. Consider a monopolistically competitive industry. A graph of demand and cost conditions for a typical firm is depicted in the diagram below.

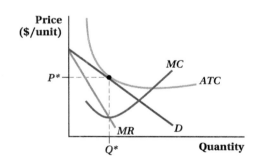

   a. Is this firm generating producer surplus? Is this firm earning a profit? How can you reconcile your answers?

   b. Do you expect any entry into or exit from this industry to occur? Explain.

   c. Suppose that the government reduces annual licensing fees, causing the fixed cost of the typical firm to fall. Make appropriate shifts of all curves that might be affected. What happens to producer surplus? What happens to profit? Do you expect the fall in fixed costs to cause entry into or exit from this industry? Explain.

   d. Shift the demand and marginal revenue curves to reflect the entry/exit you indicated in (c). Find the new equilibrium.

   e. Continue to reduce fixed cost. What happens to the demand curve as fixed cost continues to fall? What happens to producer surplus and profit?

   f. Find the equilibrium as fixed cost falls to zero.

19. When competition between firms is based on quantities (Cournot competition), the reaction functions we derive tell us that when Firm A increases its output, Firm B's best response is to cut its own. However, when competition between firms is based on price (Bertrand competition), reaction functions tell us that Firm B's response to a cut in Firm A's price (which will lead to an increase in the quantity A sells) should be a corresponding cut in B's price (and a corresponding increase in its own output). Reconcile these two results.

20. Suppose that the market demand for rose hips is given by $P = 100 - Q$. There are two firms, A and B, producing rose hips, each at a constant marginal and average total cost of $5. Fill in the table below for each market structure.

	Collusive Monopoly	Cournot Oligopoly	Bertrand Oligopoly	Stackelberg Oligopoly (A is first-mover)
A's Quantity				
B's Quantity				
Industry Quantity				
Price				
A's Profit				
B's Profit				
Industry Profit				

References

Acemoglu, Daron and Amy Finkelstein. "Input and Technology Choices in Regulated Industries: Evidence from the Health Care Sector." *Journal of Political Economy* 116, no. 5 (2008): 837–880.

Acemoglu, Daron and Joshua Linn. "Market Size in Innovation: Theory and Evidence from the Pharmaceutical Industry." *The Quarterly Journal of Economics* 119, no. 3 (2004): 1049–1090.

Bulow, Jeremy and Paul Klemperer. "The Tobacco Deal." *Brookings Papers on Economic Activity* (1998) 323–394.

Cohen, Alma, Rajeev Dehejia, and Dmitri Romanov. "Do Financial Incentives Affect Fertility?" NBER Working Paper, 2007.

Cooper, Russell W. and John C. Haltiwanger. "On the Nature of Capital Adjustment Costs." *Review of Economic Studies* 73, no. 3 (July 2006): 611–633.

Corcoran, Kevin. "The Big Fix." *The Indianapolis Star*, May 6, 2007. A1, A22–A23.

Costa, Dora. "The Wage and the Length of the Work Day: From the 1890s to 1991." *Journal of Labor Economics* 18, no. 1 (2000): 156–181.

Crooker, John R. and Aju J. Fenn. "Estimating Local Welfare Generated by an NFL Team under Credible Threat of Relocation." *Southern Economic Journal* 76, no. 1 (2009): 198–223.

Cutler, David M. and Jonathan Gruber. "Does Public Insurance Crowd Out Private Insurance?" *Quarterly Journal of Economics* 111, no. 2 (1996): 391–430.

de Walque, Damien. "Education, Information, and Smoking Decisions: Evidence from Smoking Histories in the United States, 1940–2000." *Journal of Human Resources* 45, no. 3 (2010): 682–717.

DellaVigna, Stefano and Ulrike Malmendier. "Paying Not to Go to the Gym." *American Economic Review* 96, no. 3 (2006): 694–719.

Dube, Jean-Pierre. "Product Differentiation and Mergers in the Carbonated Soft Drink Industry." *Journal of Economics and Management Strategy* 14, no. 4 (2005): 879–904.

Dwyer, Gerald P. Jr. and Cotton M. Lindsay. "Robert Giffen and the Irish Potato." *American Economic Review* 74, no. 1 (1984): 188–192.

Economides, Nicholas, Katja Seim, and V. Brian Viard. "Quantifying the Benefits of Entry into Local Phone Service." *RAND Journal of Economics* 39, no. 3 (2008): 699–730.

Ellison, Glenn and Sara Ellison. "Search, Obfuscation, and Price Elasticities on the Internet." *Econometrica* 77, no. 2 (2009): 427–452.

Fleming, Charles. "Fishtar? Why 'Waterworld,' with Costner in Fins, Is Costliest Film Ever." *Wall Street Journal*, January 31, 1996.

Fleming, Charles. "That Sinking Feeling." *Vanity Fair*, August 1, 1995.

Gilley, Otis W. and Marc C. Chopin. "Professional Golf: Labor or Leisure." *Managerial Finance* 26, no. 7 (2000): 33–45.

Goldberg, Pinelopi K. and Frank Verboven. "Cross-Country Price Dispersion in the Euro Era: A Case Study of the European Car Market." *Economic Policy* 19, no. 40 (October 2004): 483–521.

Goolsbee, Austan. "Refined Thought: Dependency Paradox." *Fortune*, August 22, 2005. http://money.cnn.com/magazines/fortune/fortune_archive/2005/08/22/8270013/index.htm.

Harford, Tim. *The Logic of Life: The Rational Economics of an Irrational World.* New York: *Random House*, 2008. 18–21.

Hortaçsu, A. and S. Puller. "Understanding Strategic Bidding in Multi-Unit Auctions: A Case Study of the Texas Electricity Spot Market." *RAND Journal of Economics* 39, no. 1 (2008): 86–114.

Hsieh, Chang-Tai and Enrico Moretti. "Can Free Entry Be Inefficient? Fixed Commissions and Social Waste in the Real Estate Industry." *Journal of Political Economy* 111, no. 5 (2003): 1076–1122.

Jackson, Joe. *The Thief at the End of the World: Rubber, Power and the Seeds of Empire.* New York: Viking, 2008.

Jensen, Robert. "The Digital Provide: Information (Technology), Market Performance, and Welfare in the South Indian Fisheries Sector." *The Quarterly Journal of Economics* 122, no. 3 (2007): 879–924.

Jensen, Robert T. and Nolan H. Miller. "Giffen Behavior and Subsistence Consumption." *American Economic Review* 98, no. 4 (2008): 1553–1577.

Kreps, David M. and José A. Scheinkman. "Quantity Precommitment and Bertrand Competition Yield Cournot Outcomes." *The Bell Journal of Economics* 14, no. 2 (Autumn 1983): 326–337.

MacDonald, James M. and Michael E. Ollinger. "Scale Economies and Consolidation in Hog Slaughter." *American Journal of Agricultural Economics* 82, no. 2 (2000): 334–346.

Mortimer, Julie Holland and Alan Sorensen. "Supply Responses to Digital Distribution: Recorded Music and Live Performances." Preliminary, December 29, 2005. http://www.aeaweb.org/assa/2006/0107_0800_0702.pdf.

Nevo, Aviv. "Measuring Market Power in the Ready-to-Eat Cereal Industry." *Econometrica* 69, no. 2 (2001): 307–342.

Renewable Fuels Association. "Ethanol Industry Overview." Accessed March 28, 2012. http://www.ethanolrfa.org/pages/statistics#EIO.

Rosen, Sherwin. "Potato Paradoxes." *Journal of Political Economy* 107, no. 6 (1999): S294–S313.

Schmitz, James A. Jr. "What Determines Productivity? Lessons from the Dramatic Recovery of the U.S. and Canadian Iron Ore Industries Following Their Early 1980s Crisis." *Journal of Political Economy* 113, no. 3 (2005): 582–625.

U.S. House of Representatives. *Prescription Drug Price Discrimination in the 7th Congressional District in Maryland: Drug Manufacturer Prices Are Higher for Humans than for Animals*, February 16, 2000. Accessed May 16, 2012. http://cummings.house.gov/pdf/animals.pdf.

Waldfogel, Joel. "The Deadweight Loss of Christmas." *American Economic Review* 83, no. 5 (1993): 1328–1336.